ROMAN PAPERS

ROMAN PAPERS

RONALD SYME

ROMAN PAPERS

IV

EDITED BY
ANTHONY R. BIRLEY

CLARENDON PRESS · OXFORD

1988

Oxford University Press, Walton Street, Oxford OX2 6DP
Oxford New York Toronto
Delhi Bombay Calcutta Madras Karachi
Petaling Jaya Singapore Hong Kong Tokyo
Nairobi Dar es Salaam Cape Town
Melbourne Auckland
and associated companies in
Beirut Berlin Ibadan Nicosia

Oxford is a trade mark of Oxford University Press

Published in the United States
by Oxford University Press, New York

© *Sir Ronald Syme 1988*

British Library Cataloguing in Publication Data
Syme, Ronald, 1903–
Roman papers.
1. Rome—History—Empire, 30 B.C.–476 A.D.
I. Title   II. Birley, Anthony
937'.06   DG270
ISBN 0–19–814873–9

Library of Congress Cataloging in Publication Data
(Revised for volumes 4 & 5)
Syme, Ronald, Sir, 1903–
Roman papers.
Vol. 3–5 edited by Anthony R. Birley.
Includes bibliographical references and index.
1. Rome—History—Collected works. I. Badian, E.
II. Birley, Anthony Richard. III. Title.
DG209.S95   1979   937'.06   79-40437
ISBN 0–19–814873–9

Set by Hope Services
Printed in Great Britain
at the University Printing House, Oxford
by David Stanford
Printer to the University

EDITOR'S PREFACE

Reviewers of *Roman Papers* iii (1984), who had observed their author's unabated flow of publications, predicted, or called for, a further instalment. These two volumes include forty-two items composed during the years 1981–5. The editors and publishers of the journals or collections for which they were originally written must be thanked for consenting to this rapid appearance in another form (particularly since a handful had not yet received publication). To any 'qui aliquam cupidinem habent notitiae clarorum virorum', this new set of *Roman Papers* will afford considerable delight and instruction. The younger Pliny and Tacitus are to the fore, with a variety of other authors not far behind: Strabo, the Senecas, the elder Pliny, Statius, Martial, Quintilian, Arrian, and Cassius Dio. Emperors, naturally, are prominent: starting with Caesar Augustus and Tiberius, although — in comparison with *RP* i–iii — these two recede, with more attention going to the Flavians and Antonines, above all to Hadrian. But other figures emerge into the light: Italians, such as Bruttius Praesens, the friend of Pliny and of Hadrian, and an assortment of Transpadane notables; a glittering array of eastern magnates, from Julius Quadratus Bassus to Avidius Cassius; and the 'Hispano–Narbonensian nexus' that produced the Antonine dynasty, Sura and Servianus, the heirs of Domitius Afer, the Pedanii, Dasumii, Calvisii. A remarkable galaxy of persons barely mentioned in the ancient literature, or known only from epigraphy, is redeemed for history. Further, the study of names is fully exploited and in places expounded.

Once again, the Editor's main task has been to compile the Index of Ancient Personal Names (printed at the end of vol. V). As with that for *RP* i–iii, some of the 'magna nomina' have proved intractable, especially certain emperors and, of authors, Pliny, Tacitus, Dio: their entries are by no means as full as might be desired. Very few additions or corrections were needed. References have been standardized (and journals cited more or less by the system of *L'Année Philologique*).

Not for the first time, author and editor benefited from vigilant assistance with proof-reading by Sonia Argyle and Eric Birley, and from the benevolent co-operation of John Cordy, Assistant Publisher.

Manchester   A.R.B.
15 July 1987

CONTENTS

VOLUME IV

1. Greeks Invading the Roman Government   I
2. The Career of Arrian   21
3. Hadrianic Governors of Syria   50
4. Rome and the Nations   62
5. Rival Cities, Notably Tarraco and Barcino   74
6. Spaniards at Tivoli   94
7. Partisans of Galba   115
8. Spanish Pomponii. A Study in Nomenclature   140
9. Clues to Testamentary Adoption   159
10. Discours de clôture (Rome, May 1981)   174
11. The Marriage of Rubellius Blandus   177
12. Tacitus: Some Sources of his Information   199
13. The Year 33 in Tacitus and Dio   223
14. Tigranocerta: A Problem Misconceived   245
15. Domitian: The Last Years   252
16. Antistius Rusticus, a Consular from Corduba   278
17. Hadrian and the Senate   295
18. The Proconsuls of Asia under Antoninus Pius   325
19. Problems about Proconsuls of Asia   347
20. Lurius Varus, a Stray Consular Legate   366
21. Eight Consuls from Patavium   371
22. P. Calvisius Ruso, One Person or Two?   397
23. Neglected Children on the *Ara Pacis*   418
    PLATE: *Ara Pacis*, south wall   430

VOLUME V

24. Transpadana Italia   431
25. Correspondents of Pliny   440
26. The Dating of Pliny's Latest Letters   478

27. Superior Suffect Consuls   490

28. Curtailed Tenures of Consular Legates   499

29. Statius on Rutilius Gallicus   514

30. The Testamentum Dasumii. Some Novelties   521

31. Hadrian as Philhellene. Neglected Aspects   546

32. Praesens the Friend of Hadrian   563

33. The Career of Valerius Propinquus   579

34. Prefects of the City, Vespasian to Trajan   608

35. Three Ambivii   622

36. Names and Identities in Quintilian   630

37. The Paternity of Polyonymous Consuls   639

38. The Subjugation of Mountain Zones   648

39. Isauria in Pliny   661

40. Antonine Government and Governing Class   668

41. Avidius Cassius: His Rank, Age, and Quality   689

42. Caesar: Drama, Legend, History   702

    Index   709

I

Greeks Invading the Roman Government

PEACEFUL invasions achieve notable conquests. The Roman acquaintance with Greek civilization went back a long way. It was broadened
and deepened when in the second century B.C. the imperial Republic
defeated and broke the kingdoms founded by the generals of
Alexander. Rome emerged as the dominant power in the world—all
in the space of fifty-three years, as the historian Polybius was
insistent to proclaim. Diverse and fateful perspectives opened.

One of them, not under discussion by Romans at the time, was the
survival of their language. A conquering people is not always able to
preserve it. Think of the helpless Normans who lost their language
in France—and for a second time in England.

Latin, it is clear, was saved by two potent factors. First, that hard,
crude speech had already been shaped and refined, on Greek models,
to produce drama and a national epic (prose among this prosaic
people took much longer to develop). Second, the Roman performance in law and government, achieved under the guidance of an
aristocracy both liberal and cohesive, had nothing to learn from the
republics of old Hellas—and the new kingdoms had been shown
inadequate.

The debt in civilization incurred by the Romans could never be
denied, only qualified. A specimen will afford instruction. Cicero, in
the preface to his *Tusculan Discourses*, conceded the Greek precellence
in arts and science. But Romans hold the first place for law and civic
life, for government and warfare, for religion and the family. And
the national character: what 'gravitas,' what 'constantia'!

That was not all. The native genius could improve on the Greeks
whenever Romans found it worth while to take pains. Cicero (one
assumes) had oratory in mind, with a personal motive. He was
familiar with the unobtrusive technique to which Plutarch devoted a
treatise, namely how to practise self-laudation without arousing
dislike. It shows percipience here and there, but ought to be
superfluous for the educated class in most ages.

Plutarch dedicated the piece to a Spartan nobleman who vaunted

The Seventh Stephen J. Brademas, Sr., Lecture (Hellenic College Press, Brookline, Mass.,
1982).

an ancient (and legendary) pedigree, being the thirty-first in descent
from Castor and Pollux, the brothers of Helen. This person (Julius
Herculanus), so it happens to be known, was a Roman senator.

History had moved a long way. That the language and letters of
Hellas might enjoy a renaissance in the efflux of time was not beyond
hope, | not even beyond a rational forecast. Greeks in the Roman
governing class, however—that notion would evoke horror and
incredulity from Cicero, and from many others in a long sequel.

Under the rule of the imperial Republic, the Greek lands had endured
manifold disasters and tribulation, to mention only the constant
drain of wealth to Italy. The matter can be illustrated by brief
recourse to the balance of trade, to what are called 'invisible exports'.
Italy sent out governors and soldiers, financiers and tax-gatherers,
and Italy drew benefit in return, with enhanced prosperity (though
not for all classes of the population). Those exports, be it added,
were all too visible throughout the Eastern countries: legionaries,
rapacious bankers, and the governor parading in the purple mantle of
war, preceded by lictors who bore axes on their rods. The earliest
Greek term for the mandatory who carries the *imperium* is 'a six-axe
man' (ἑξαπέλεκυς). To the imperial people, by contrast, the
emblems of power convey beauty as well as terror: in the phrase of
the poet Lucretius, 'pulchros fasces saevasque secures'.

Worse followed during the civil wars of the Romans, involving
the whole world. A sequence of great *imperatores* arose, continuous
from Pompeius to Caesar, to Caesar's heir and to Marcus Antonius:
by a suitable term the Greek historian Appian styled them
'monarchic party-leaders'. On historical perspective the epoch
returned of the kingdoms in Alexander's succession—as was
apparent even to an author of modest pretensions such as Cornelius
Nepos. The rivalries of the dynasts led to campaigns and battles east
of the Adriatic; and the Greek cities paid the bill, with enormous
exactions.

In the thirties came a certain respite and new prospects. When the
cause of the Republic went down at Philippi, Marcus Antonius took
for himself the better portion, the eastern lands; and two years later
concord seemed to be established between the rival leaders when
Antonius married the sister of Octavian. That alliance was celebrated
by a poem that many have found enigmatic, the *Fourth Eclogue* of
Virgil. It can be interpreted without effort as an epithalamium, the
Golden Age being inaugurated by a son who will rule the world. |
The child arrived, but it turned out to be a girl. The respite was

brief. In 32 B.C. the young master of the Roman West picked a quarrel with Antonius and enforced a war.

The person and character of Marcus Antonius encouraged defamation, and he came to an unhappy end. His governing of the East has commonly been denied due recognition. Yet his aims were clear enough: to conciliate opinion and offer some compensation for Roman oppression and arrogance. His prime concern lay with the city aristocracies who held power and influence: magistrates and priests and ambassadors, orators and philosophers, artists and doctors. These men could usefully be enlisted in administration. For example, Antonius assigned the island of Cos to a grammarian, the city of Tarsus to the author of an epic poem. Further, as ruler of the vassal kingdom of Pontus he installed Polemo, the son of a famous orator from western Asia.

In fact, the new ordering accorded to the oriental dominions was firm and sagacious. In a wide sweep from the border of Egypt to the Black Sea five princes protected the eastern frontier and occupied much of the interior of Anatolia. In consequence, less territory under direct rule than at any time since the conquests made by Pompeius Magnus. The eastward extension of annexations had been one of the causes for the breakdown of the Republic.

An oriental empire was thus in process of formation. It corresponded with the facts of history, language, and civilization. And notably with geography, or with geopolitics—to use a term questionably popular about fifty years ago, but not to be disdained. The western boundary was the sea that separates Greece from Italy. Indeed, for long ages of history the Adriatic was to delimit empires and civilizations. (I need not name Byzantium and the Ottomans.)

By land the Romans hitherto controlled only a narrow strip along the coast. Then as now, tangled and precipitous mountains forbade easy communication.

To overcome that impediment was an urgent task, perhaps conceived at the end by Caesar the Dictator. Caesar Augustus accomplished it, the principal and lasting achievement of his reign. Wars of conquest in Illyricum and the Balkans advanced the frontier to the Danube and won the land route from Italy to Byzantium, binding West and East together in a compact imperial structure.

If geography spoke for division, human will annulled it. Without the resources of the East, Italy was condemned to impoverishment and dishonour.

Under the name of Italy, now deemed united and in unison ('tota Italia'), | the young Caesar organized a plebiscite, mustering patriotic sentiment for war and for the reconquest of the Roman dominion from a foreign enemy. It is not easy to refrain from quoting the version of Virgil: Antonius, the Roman clad in un-Roman armour ('variis Antonius armis'), with all the resources of the Orient behind him, marching from the lands of morning and the crimson ocean, 'victor ab Aurorae populis et litore rubro', while follows in his train (wicked, wicked), the Queen of Egypt: 'sequiturque, nefas, Aegyptia coniunx.'

The portrayal is moving and magnificent, yet in one point defective. The War of Actium was ambiguous in motive, conduct, and consequences. The poet put emotional emphasis on an Italian nationalism which was now taken to embrace Rome, by a novel definition,

> hinc Augustus agens Italos in proelia Caesar . . .

Virgil omitted the loyal support of the Roman West, the broad frontier extending all the way to furthest Spain. I mean 'frontier' in the American sense. That is, a prosperous and dynamic region, in course of rapid development. It included northern Italy, that is Italia Transpadana, until now part of a Roman province (Cisalpine Gaul), but had a long extension westward to France and Spain. In later terms of European history, the frontier may be defined as Venetia and Lombardy, Provence and Languedoc, Catalonia and Andalusia.

The new Romans of the western lands were mixed in origin: the old Italian emigration, the military colonists, and the natives of the better sort. All responded alike to the Caesarian cause and to an imperial patriotism. As a result, their progress accelerated.

So far the victors in a Roman war. What was to be the fate of the vanquished?

Rancour and emotion abated. There was no thought of penalty or revenge. Normal relations resumed. One sign is a great rush of intellectuals to the capital. In the forefront we observe Strabo, of a good family from Amaseia in Pontus, who went on to produce compilations of history and geography, and Dionysius of Halicarnassus. Dionysius moved on from the study of oratory to compose the annals of the Roman People, from its earliest origins.

Eloquent Greeks are now prominent in the Roman schools of rhetoric; and poets were not slow to eulogize patrons among Roman nobles or women and youths in the imperial family, the 'domus regnatrix' as it might | already have been designated. In short, Rome at once became the capital of the Hellenic literary world.

For the recaptured dominions in the East, few changes save in the matter of Egypt. Caesar Augustus refused to hand over the rich land of the Nile to the mercies of proconsuls or bankers. He segregated Egypt. He ruled there as a monarch, in the line of the Ptolemies, as their dynasty had succeeded the Pharaohs.

For the rest, Augustus was happy to take over the vassal princes chosen by his failed rival. The fact is plain. Augustus inherited the *clientela* of Antonius, just as Caesar had acquired the adherents of Pompeius Magnus. And in like fashion, the city aristocracies. The educated class would find suitable employment in service to the monarch. Philosophers were not only teachers or counsellors in the precincts of power. Augustus put the Stoic Athenodorus in charge of the turbulent city of Tarsus.

As past history indicated and promised, the role of the Greeks in the dual empire seemed clear and compelling.

In the vision vouchsafed to Aeneas in the lower world, government of the nations proclaims the Roman: 'tu regere imperio populos, Romane, memento'. Others, 'alii', may keep the primacy in arts and sciences. They will shape marble or bronze, they will scan and delimit the motions of the stars. They may also have the advantage in eloquence; 'orabunt causas melius'. That verdict, one notes in passing, would have shocked Cicero, and it annoyed those who inherited or exploited his renown.

The dynasty founded by Caesar Augustus went on to exhibit marked favour towards Hellenic civilization. Tiberius Caesar, not generally recognized as a philhellene, had a predilection for the poets of Alexandria. He reflected the taste of an earlier generation; he turned his back on the new classic writers of the Augustan prime. Moreover, the next rulers (Caligula, Claudius, and Nero) had in their veins the blood of Marcus Antonius, being descended from his daughters. With Nero the fashion for all things Greek rose to a notorious culmination.

In the twelfth year of his reign, Nero at last visited Hellas. Towards the end of the tour, before a grand concourse at the Isthmus of Corinth, he proclaimed the liberation of Greece from Roman rule. A text survives. As Nero declared in conclusion, he would have wished to bestow a benefaction on Hellas in her great epoch. But the Hellenes had been enslaved either by foreigners or by members of their own nation. What he now | grants, however, issues not from compassion but from benevolence, and as a thanksgiving to the gods of Hellas, vigilant to protect their worshipper by land and sea. Others in the past had given freedom to cities, only Nero to a whole province.

This document excites due attention and furnishes some entertainment. For present purposes the philhellenism of emperors will introduce a large topic: the relations between authorship and society, between education and government. Greek writers have been already noted in Augustan Rome, but there appears to be a dearth in the sequel, the benefits of peace and prosperity being slow to take effect. The first exponents of note are Dio (from Prusa, in Bithynia) and Plutarch. They were close coevals, born in the early years of Claudius Caesar. Their most productive epoch falls towards the end of the century.

Dio and Plutarch may be regarded as precursors of the Hellenic renaissance that comes to full flowering in the time of Hadrian. The term 'precursor' is normally held suspect in studies of history or literature. It implies a future not known, and seldom to be predicted. The precursor may be only a predecessor, like Plutarch to Suetonius in the art of biography.

Nevertheless, the term has a pertinent application in this context. Both authors indulged in activities which, while congenial to their own natures, could not fail to win approbation from the Roman government. Brief allusion must suffice. Dio, a wealthy man himself, was at pains to alleviate the constant strife between the rich and the poor. He gave benefactions to his own townsfolk, and sermons of earnest exhortation. He told a riotous mob that they had no excuse, that poverty is the parent of good behaviour.

Dio was urgent to extol the advantages of social harmony during his travels elsewhere, notably at Tarsus, where the guild of linen workers was a cause of disturbances. Further, confronted with the rivalry of neighbour cities, he enjoined moderation and concord.

At Rome, Dio delivered orations in praise of monarchy. The King (so he explained) is called by Providence to his exalted estate: like Heracles he passes his life in toil and duty, he loves the citizens and the soldiers, and he selects only the wise and the good for his agents and counsellors.

All of which came as no surprise to the Emperor Trajan and to the audience. Plutarch, not so vocal, confined his advice to the ruling class in the cities. In his *Precepts of Government* he issued sharp admonition. They must cease from strife and ambition, forget the glories of a distant | past and abide in contentment under the superior power. Furthermore, the rule of Rome (he reminded them) was not a product of chance or violence. Virtue and Fortune had collaborated.

The signal contribution that Plutarch made was less obtrusive. He hit upon a genial device, the sequence of parallel biographies, from legendary heroes down to generals and statesmen. The two nations were thereby recognized as standing on parity.

The next testimony follows in the reign of Hadrian, rapid and convincing. A mass of orators emerged in high publicity, giving their name to the 'Age of the Sophists'.

Meanwhile, the literature of the Latins went into decline. The period initiated by Seneca and Lucan terminated with Tacitus and Juvenal. Most of the writers derived from the provinces of the West. Moreover, political success ran parallel with the literary movement. The newcomers won influence, they captured strategic positions in government, and they ended by installing an emperor in the person of Trajan.

Under the dynasty now making its inception, the literary benefit accrued by paradox to the Greeks. At the capital the new Romans from the provinces followed a Greek line of education: hence continuity between Nero and Hadrian. It had been enhanced under the second dynasty, notably by Domitian.

Hadrian, more a Greek than a Roman, paid honour and deference to the exponents of Hellenic eloquence. On short statement, these men were the social and intellectual élite of the Greek world, which they adorned and dominated. Diverse regions contributed, in the forefront the cities of western Asia, with Polemo on early prominence, a descendant of the Polemo whom Antonius appointed ruler of Pontus. Old Hellas was less on show, but Athens, long dormant, was awakening to the role of a university city. Herodes Atticus soon equalled and surpassed the fame of the great Polemo.

Even without support from birth and wealth, the sophists were elevated by professional pride and by the applause of admiring audiences. Other ages may be disposed to less friendly appreciations. Polemo was | ostentatious and arrogant. More is known about Herodes, and much to his discredit—a millionaire, proud, cruel, and revengeful.

In their products the sophists were verbose and often vacuous, yet not without utility to the central government. In the year 143, in the presence of Hadrian's successor, Aelius Aristides delivered an imperial panegyric. It is one world now, he proclaimed, a federation of cities under the presidency of Rome; and the only distinction that obtains is between Hellenes and barbarians.

The oration of Aristides has evoked sympathetic response from enquirers in the modern time. On another estimate it is a farrago of commonplaces, it contributes little to the understanding—and its credit may now be on the wane. Abundant evidence has accumulated about society and government, and a new fabric of history can be elaborated. It depends on facts and names seldom or never disclosed by the written record.

Aristides (it is a disturbing thought) may have conceived an ambition to enter the Roman Senate. The year of his oration was opened by Atticus as *consul ordinarius*. The best that Latin eloquence could put up in this season was the African, Cornelius Fronto (from Cirta, in Numidia). He was only a suffect consul, sharing the honour with half a dozen other senators.

I am now brought at last to confront the central theme: Greeks standing high in the Roman state. It was not a novel and recent phenomenon, and the feature that deserves emphasis is consuls from the Greek lands arriving much earlier than the great resurgence of Hellenic culture. The process will arouse curiosity and provoke comparison with other examples of the convergence between education and government.

Senators from the Greek East. The topic embraces various components and it calls for careful distinctions.

First, the colonists. A *colonia* of Roman citizens is a portion of the *populus Romanus*, wherever it be situated. Caesar, the Triumvirs, and Augustus had planted a number of colonies for veterans from their legions in the lands beyond the Adriatic, to a total of close on twenty; from Macedonia to the shore of Pontus and the Syrian coast. Conspicuous among them may be named Philippi, Alexandria in the Troad, Berytus in Syria. Even the heart of Anatolia had a cluster of colonies, the principal being Pisidian Antioch.

It was no surprise that before long military colonies should provide | officers for the army, financial agents of the Caesars—and then senators and consuls. (The earliest of their consuls come up under the second dynasty, one from Alexandria, the other from Pisidian Antioch.)

Second, products of the great Italian diaspora during the epoch of the imperial Republic. Like Spain, the East offered various sources of enrichment, and, unlike Spain, the appeal of a high culture as well as a life of leisure. Bankers and businessmen settled in western Asia, and, acquiring property, duly improved their condition.

Not all of the immigrants endeared themselves to the natives. One recalls the pogrom that ensued when Mithridates of Pontus invaded the Roman province of Asia. That episode was conveniently covered up in an era of peace and concord. Italians became valued members of society and might intermarry with local families of ancient repute, which would not impair their chances if they aspired to senatorial rank. Several specimens of the returned emigrant can be put on show at quite an early date.

Third, senators of indigenous origin. They fall into two classes, at first sight distinct. First, the descendants of princes whose kingdoms had been mediatized; before that, interlocked in complicated family alliances and producing highly variegated pedigrees. Second, the urban aristocracies. The contrast turns out to be imperfect. For example, the Celtic tetrarchs in Galatia formed close attachments to Pergamum.

For advancement at Rome the stronger claims and the brighter prospects would appertain to the Roman colonists, so it might appear. Not so, the facts refute. The western provinces present a curious and engaging parallel. In the south of France (Narbonensis, the old 'provincia nostra') the colonists could not compete with the descendants of native chieftains who acquired the citizenship from proconsuls of the Republic. Narbonne and Arles are outstripped by Nîmes and Vienne, which had once been tribal capitals.

In the eastern lands, rank, honour, and fame accrue to the descendants of dynastic houses. They make the firmest impact on the governing class. That is a noteworthy phenomenon. How then can it be known and established?

The evidence of contemporary writers tells against. Pliny in his correspondence published an ample survey of life at Rome. Letters are addressed to eminent senators, but none to any of the prominent eastern magnates. Arguments from silence are often a dubious recourse. In this instance, silence | affords various instruction. A whole group may be all but absent. No letter of Pliny notices Hadrian (consul in 108), or certain other persons in the nexus that was to produce the Antonine dynasty, such as Aurelius Fulvus (the future Antoninus Pius), or Annius Verus, the grandfather of Marcus Aurelius. The picture of Roman society is incomplete. It has to be supplemented from other sources.

Next, Juvenal. The wealth and pretensions of the eastern oligarchs was a theme to sharpen satire and embellish declamation. Juvenal kept off it. He reserved easy ridicule for lower specimens of the Greek invasion, denouncing the 'Graeculus esuriens'; by the same token, silence about any prosperous and vulnerable newcomers from Spain and Narbonensis.

Finally, Plutarch. If anybody, Plutarch should have testified, in felicitous profusion. Inspection contradicts.

A passage in one of his treatises (*De tranquillitate animi*) deplores ambition pushed to morbid excess, and refers in passing to the behaviour of certain Greeks. They make a moan because they are not senators—and, if becoming senators, because they do not achieve promotion to the highest rank. That is all. No individual in the voluminous writings of Plutarch is defined as both a Greek and a senator. Into one of his dialogues, set in Athens, enters a character labelled 'the magnificent King Philopappus'. Of whom, more later.

Enough has been said, and more than enough, to undermine faith in the written sources. One turns aside and looks for facts and names. Epigraphy is the guide and master, introducing a long and complex chapter in the annals of society and government.

In the year 1837, W. J. Hamilton (the Secretary of the London Geological Society) was travelling through the interior of Turkey. At Ankara this excellent epigraphist copied two inscriptions on the citadel (one of them by use of a telescope). Those documents disclosed the career of C. Julius Severus, who had been admitted to the Senate by Hadrian. He was styled a descendant of kings and tetrarchs, and further, 'the foremost of the Hellenes'.

For a long time the discovery attracted little attention. Classical scholarship was engaged with other and traditional preoccupations; the eastern provinces were slow to awaken the curiosity of historians; and the careers of senators had not yet come to be properly studied and compared. |

Encouragement emerged from the excavations at Pergamum and Ephesus in the eighties and nineties. They revealed the monuments erected by the magnates, their benefactions to the cities—and the men themselves, not known before, unless as bare names on lists of Roman consuls, such as Julius Celsus and Julius Quadratus (consuls late in the reign of Domitian).

Then Ankara came out with the full and desired information about Julius Severus. By singular felicity it fell to Mommsen to expound the document in 1901, almost the last of his contributions to history and epigraphy.

The lineage of Julius Severus was now declared, the ancestors being King Deiotarus, also two tetrarchs of the Galatians and Attalus the King of Asia. More important, his kinsmen. Severus was cousin to four men of consular rank (namely Julius Quadratus, King Alexander, Julius Aquila, Claudius Severus) and further, cousin to a large number of senators. About the four consulars (consuls under Trajan between 105 and 112), quite a lot could be said. I refrain.

The revelation should have inspired a comprehensive study of the eastern aristocracies. The results would have affected much of what the nineteenth century believed about imperial history. The lesson was there, but it took some time to digest.

Hesitations were abolished by an inscription from Pergamum published in 1932—and, by the way, not well published by the first editor, Wilhelm Weber. It revealed what could never have been suspected. The senator in question was another Julius Quadratus, namely C. Julius Quadratus Bassus of regal ancestry. After his consulship (in 105), he commanded an army corps in Trajan's second war against the Dacians. In the sequel Bassus governed three military provinces in succession, Cappadocia, Syria, Dacia; and in Dacia he died on campaign in the winter of 117/18.

A man of Pergamum leading the armies of the Roman People only four generations after the vaunted victory of the West at Actium, that was beyond hope or fear or forecast. A rapid evolution had taken place. To explain which, it is necessary to revert to Nero.

In the cosmopolitan entourage of the Caesars, Greeks had acquired influence and important functions. At the beginning of Nero's reign the viceroy of Egypt is Claudius Balbillus, whose son married a daughter of the King of Commagene; and at the end, Julius Alexander, a renegade Jew, | the nephew of the learned Philo.

A process was taking shape. Under what kind of rhythm, and how far it might go, remained to be seen. Emperors might modify it, but they could hardly bring it to a stop. An autocrat is not omnipotent. There are facts he cannot fight against, groups and pressures he cannot resist.

Deliberate policy was not much in evidence. On the contrary, chance dominated, with a sequence of accidents that enforced acceleration. The stages may be set forth as follows:

(1) The fall of Nero. His philhellenic tastes and attitudes were premature, provoking annoyance among conservative Romans, and he further alienated influential groups in the upper order. But it was evil counsels and plain folly that subverted a dynasty which had struck deep roots of loyalty in the duration of a century. If Nero, instead of parading at festivals in Greece, had chosen to visit the armies of the Rhine, he might have gone on in iniquity for a long spell.

The catastrophe unloosed civil war throughout the world; pretenders perished in turn; and the power went to a low-born Italian.

(2) The accession of Vespasian. While conducting the war in rebellious Judaea, Vespasian was proclaimed emperor through a military conspiracy managed by his chief allies, the Prefect of Egypt

and the governor of Syria. Partisans got their rewards. Both now and a few years later, a number were promoted to senatorial rank. As the historian Tacitus observes, some excellent men who rose high, others with success as their only virtue.

Of officers in the army, a conspicuous name is Julius Celsus, from Sardis, serving as tribune in an Egyptian legion. Nor were civilian agents neglected, the magnates who influenced public opinion in cities of western Asia. Julius Quadratus of Pergamum became a senator of praetorian rank. Another of these personages was Julius Candidus (his city has not been ascertained or the early stages in his advancement). For two of the three (Celsus and Quadratus) inscriptions supply in full detail the posts they held, at Rome and abroad.

However, caution must intervene. These entrants were not numerous, and the phenomenon might not have been attended with rapid or momentous consequences.

(3) The new dynasty. The East declared an emperor, but the main benefit went to the West. It took a double form. Promotion followed for many adherents, and imperial patriotism or prejudices won reassurance. None the less, there is no warrant for speaking of a period of reaction now to set in.

When the elder son of Vespasian succeeded to the throne, the world was happy. Titus is described as 'amor et deliciae generis humani'. Favourites | of the Roman people tended to die young. Titus passed away after a reign of two years and two months. Radiant prospects of the Greeks were not impaired by his brother, Domitian. As with Titus, education counted heavily in his favour, and accident intervened to accelerate the processes of history.

(4) The return of Nero. In the East the name of Nero kept a potent appeal. His sudden eclipse inspired a widespread belief that he was not dead but had escaped and would come back. A sequence of impostors arose. In the propitious season of the eruption of Vesuvius a false Nero mustered supporters in Asia, marched to the river Euphrates, and found a welcome from the Parthian monarch.

The vivid language of an oracle announced that 'the exiled man of Rome would return, raising a mighty sword and crossing the Euphrates with a myriad host.' In fact a decade later, while Domitian faced grave emergencies on the northern frontiers, Nero came up again. This time he received strong support from Parthia: not an aggressive power, it is true, but alert to exploit Roman embarrassments.

It was expedient for Domitian to overcome the memory of Nero and conciliate opinion in the eastern lands. A counter-measure can be divined. In the year 89 Domitian appointed Julius Celsus and Julius

Quadratus as governors of imperial provinces in Asia Minor (Cilicia and Lycia–Pamphylia). In the routine of promotions, those posts normally led to consulships, and Celsus and Quadratus duly took office (in 92 and 94). Consulates for easterners, that had not been contemplated by Vespasian, or by others, when they entered the Senate twenty years previously.

There is something else for the rubric. The enigmatic Julius Candidus (who had meanwhile become consul in 86) was now put in charge of Cappadocia, the great military command that faced Armenia.

(5) The accession of Trajan. Nero passed into the realm of legend and myth and apocalyptic visions—but he might come back in another incarnation. The Emperor Titus, so some opined at Rome, might turn out to be a second Nero: not for the better reasons, and the satirist Juvenal called Domitian a bald-headed Nero. On one estimate, Nero returns in the person of Hadrian . . .

We are waiting for Hadrian. Trajan is interposed, a more decisive factor in the present theme. After the assassination of Domitian in 96 the government of Nerva soon ran into trouble, and a veiled *coup d'état* imposed one of the army commanders, M. Ulpius Traianus, the governor of Upper Germany. Trajan, by ultimate origin Italian, came from the far edge of the western world (Italica, near Seville). His main support rested upon a nexus of alliances in the new imperial nobility from Spain and Narbonensis. |

Rome now had a ruler, an *imperator*, whose claim and whose façade was military and traditional—of primary import, but not intended to deceive. There was another aspect. Trajan in youth had come to know the eastern provinces under his father, legate of Syria and proconsul of Asia. Results become apparent early in the reign. In the year 100 he consigned the Syrian command to his Pergamene friend, Julius Quadratus, although he had never seen an army hitherto.

The choice declares one of the open secrets of the imperial system. Usurpers themselves, the Caesars had reason to distrust birth or talent. Personal loyalty was paramount, age or mediocrity no bar.

The next manifestation was more startling. On return from Syria, Quadratus opened the year 105 as consul for the second time. His colleague in the *fasces* was Julius Candidus. Second consulates fell to few, save close allies of the Emperor.

The crown of a senator's career was to govern either Asia or Africa (Celsus and Quadratus duly acceded to Asia). There was one post of higher dignity, the city Prefecture, reserved for the most eminent—and indeed for very few, the tenure often being for life. Julius

Candidus became *praefectus urbi*, probably in 105. Inferred by some scholars from the second consulship, the fact has only recently come to knowledge. It is certified by the inscription of one of his descendants found at Ephesus.

In 105 warfare resumed on the Danube. As has already been indicated, the other Pergamene notable, Julius Quadratus Bassus (consul suffect in that year), led an army in the conquest of Dacia and went on to be governor of three military provinces.

Names and facts have been adduced that are absent from the memorials of written history—and some not yet accorded due recognition in modern narrations. Eastern consuls are no longer to be regarded as sudden or sporadic products. All in all, during the two decades of Trajan's reign, a total of about twenty can be identified. In the forefront stand the magnates, with kings and tetrarchs for ancestors, as disclosed by the inscription of Julius Severus at Ancyra. For the rest, a variegated company, with only two from old Greece (one of them the parent of Herodes Atticus). The process that took its inception under the second dynasty has developed into an invasion of the governing class. The newcomers appear firmly ensconced in the new imperial nobility, the oligarchy of the consular families.

As concerns the Imperator himself, ambition was not satisfied by renewing ancient military glory and extending the Empire beyond the Danube. He insisted on settling accounts with the Parthians. The enterprise conveyed a powerful appeal to the Greek world, and a further im|pulsion towards partnership in empire. Rome took up an old quarrel, revenge on the Persian and the Mede—and Trajan was susceptible to the praises of Alexander the Macedonian.

The war failed, and Trajan's successor had to cover up a débâcle. Greeks continued to exploit the blessings of peace under manifold encouragements. Hadrian's policy and predilections were amply advertised at the time, and they do not fail to earn eager approbation.

All that is known and conceded. The present discourse proceeds on a narrower front. It concentrates on the personnel of government.

The reign of Hadrian opened under evil auspices. In the first year four of the marshals of Trajan met their end for treason, on charges of conspiracy that cannot have been easy to render convincing. Hadrian had sore need of friends and allies in the upper order, notably the army commanders with whom the arbitrament resides in a season of crisis.

The record is sadly imperfect. None the less, during the twenty-one years of his reign, only two Greeks were put in charge of consular armies. As one looks to the list of consuls, in sharp contrast to the 'annus mirabilis' under Trajan, at the most one Greek lends his name to the Roman year as *consul ordinarius.*

What consequences should be drawn? That is a question. In the first place, no setback in the general advance of the Greeks. After the influx under Trajan accidents of age and of demography may have caused an apparent abatement, and some of the first consuls left no male issue. Still, one might wonder.

Of set purpose the present enquiry plays down the role of individual emperors, putting emphasis on forces beyond their control; yet personality cannot be excluded. Hadrian was complex and capricious; and a ruler may be inclined to build up a contrast between himself and his predecessor. His character both attracts and repels. The history, such as it is, cannot furnish an adequate answer, nor can fiction help very much, despite the *Mémoires d'Hadrien* of Marguerite Yourcenar (1951). The book receives well-merited acclaim: it is a masterpiece of classical and archaic prose. Yet, as Edward Gibbon said of the poetry of Claudian, it fails to satisfy or to silence our reason. The author has taken over sundry items from a variegated and often doubtful source, the notorious *Historia Augusta.*

A proper and cautious estimate indicates that Hadrian was averse from pomp and national pride, hostile to the claims of birth and wealth and | class. On reliable information, his favourite philosophers were Epictetus and Heliodorus. The former, a severe moral teacher, had been born in slavery, the latter (of lesser fame) belonged to the Epicurean persuasion.

A suspicion arises: Hadrian failed to respond to Trajan's enthusiasm for the descendants of kings and tetrarchs. If so, his preference went to the more modest type, to the cultivated urban aristocracy.

Hadrian selected for his successor a senator endowed with a character contrary to his own, the steady and tranquil man known as Antoninus Pius. The family came from southern France (from Nîmes), but had become, like others, metropolitan in tastes and habits long since. Pius was the third consul in his line.

No changes were to be expected from Pius, and no disadvantages for Greeks. The consulship of Herodes Atticus in 143 is accorded prominence perhaps too much and too often. Another Athenian and a Pergamene were the consuls of the previous year.

The Emperor himself, it is true, was not enamoured of talkers and thinkers. His ironical language, published in an edict, offers a hint of how he might judge the aristocracy of the intellect. The Roman government granted various exemptions and privileges to teachers and doctors and others. But, said the Emperor, a philosopher will not claim financial benefit—that would show him not a genuine philosopher.

Education and money and the name of Herodes Atticus bring up a sharp question. What was the use and value of eastern senators?

At Rome the *novus homo* had to work his way. He rose to public honours through the service of the state. At the same time, social eminence continued to assert its prerogative, alike among survivors of old families and among the recently ennobled. Their function was largely decorative, with no need of enhancement through military or civilian merit. Some of the eastern magnates conformed to this class.

While Trajan was on campaign beyond the Euphrates, the city of Athens witnessed the construction of the huge mausoleum that stands to this day on the Hill of the Muses. It commemorates Philopappus, the grandson of the last ruler of Commagene, with for ancestors the Seleucid mon|archs of Syria. While bearing the title of King, Philopappus was also (as one of the inscriptions states) a Roman senator, by his full style C. Julius Antiochus Philopappus, admitted to the high assembly by Trajan, and a consul (in 109).

The curious will also note (and marvel) that King Philopappus was a member of the Arval Brethren, that primeval fraternity which had been revived (and all but invented) by Caesar Augustus. Apart from lavish banquets, the Brethren convened to reiterate ancient rituals or celebrate dynastic occasions. Which might supply a suitable pastime in a life of dignified leisure—if Philopappus ever attended the meetings. It is not likely that he was often seen in the Senate, although it harboured a mass of mediocrities worthy of most of the business there transacted.

At home in Roman society through the community of education and habits, eastern senators had not been fully integrated, like their counterparts from the western provinces. They tended to go back. In the course of time ex-consuls may be discovered superintending the construction of buildings or in long sojourn at temples and health resorts.

The illustrious Philopappus had no occupations in provinces or armies. When his Athenian monument was erected, the memory of a better man found honour at Ephesus. The heirs of Julius Celsus built a great library at Ephesus (the city he preferred to his native Sardis). When the visitor begins to ascend the steps at the entrance he can contemplate on either side the inscribed record, the Latin version facing the Greek. He there reads the career of Julius Celsus, from military tribune in Egypt to the Asian proconsulate.

The Library of Celsus stands as solid testimony to the alliance between education and government, made manifest towards the end of Trajan's reign. Before long that alliance comes out in fine style, in the career and writings of Arrian. Steady productivity in a long life carried a wide range of interests, including history: not only Alexander and the successors but the Roman wars with the Parthians.

The author is known and valued. Less attention has gone to the senator and consul. Born at Nicomedia in Bithynia, Flavius Arrianus as a young man attended the lectures of the philosopher Epictetus (he wrote up and published his notes many years later). The early stages of his career evade ascertainment. He served as an officer in Trajan's war and entered the Senate soon after, so it might be conjectured. The command of a legion should be assumed; and he was probably proconsul in the far West, governing the province Baetica (the homeland of Trajan and Hadrian), as an inscription found at Corduba renders plausible. Then, consul in 129 or 130, Arrianus went on to hold the military province of Cappadocia for six | years (double the normal tenure). His reports to Hadrian are extant.

Hadrian and Arrian were congenial in many tastes: not only Epictetus but cavalry manœuvres. And both liked horses and dogs.

Cursory reference has been made to the admired masters of eloquence, such as Herodes Atticus and Aelius Aristides, not without allusion to deleterious features in the Hellenic renaissance. A man like Arrian helps to redeem the Age of the Sophists.

In his oration Aristides declared that there are no wars any more, merely trivial unrest among border tribes. Warfare now belongs to myth or memory. Concord and stability prevailed—or, in other words, a firm alliance of the propertied classes east and west. Thus passed the twenty-three years of Antoninus Pius in deep calm, or in a mild torpor that seemed beneficent.

When Pius died in March of the year 161, he transmitted a secure government to Marcus Aurelius, the nephew of his wife, the husband of his daughter. The other adoptive son of Pius was Lucius Verus. Marcus promptly associated him as equal in the power. Moreover, Marcus, deemed by the Romans highly suitable for a ruler, was now, like Titus, completing his fortieth year. And, by an abnormal felicity, five months later Faustina presented him with twin sons—one not long surviving, the other named Commodus.

During long ages the wise and the good had scarcely dared to hope for a philosopher on the throne. He was now vouchsafed by

Providence. But Fortuna holds dominion over the nations, and Fortuna turned against, with no delay or hesitance.

Calamities followed without cessation. The Parthians inflicted defeats on two Roman armies, and when the victorious legions returned four years later they brought with them the plague. Then Germans and Sarmatians came over the Danube, hence long years taken up with continuous campaigns, and Marcus himself at the head of the armies for most of the time.

Epochs of disturbance throw up great generals and may imperil the reigning dynasty. Should Marcus perish, a Greek regent was not out of the question.

In 169 Lucius Verus died. His widow Lucilla was transferred to Claudius Pompeianus, a military man of low birth from Antioch in Syria. Another daughter of Marcus had married Claudius Severus, an eastern aristocrat (grandson of a cousin of Julius Severus). Marcus much admired Severus: | he was expert in the philosophy of Aristotle.

Severus and Pompeianus had the rare distinction of a shared consulate in 173. If in concord, they might have carried on the government and protected the dynasty.

Two years later Avidius Cassius proclaimed himself emperor in Syria. Cassius had won great glory in the Parthian War, and stayed on as governor, soon invested with a superior *imperium* over the eastern provinces. In short, vicegerent for Marcus, and for many years. Like Domitius Corbulo under Nero, Cassius became 'capax imperii'.

Cassius was equipped with other advantages. He was the son of Heliodorus, the Epicurean philosopher, friend and secretary of Hadrian and appointed Prefect of Egypt in the last year of the reign. Heliodorus came from northern Syria and perhaps asserted kinship with the regal house of Commagene. An Avidius Antiochus happens to be on record.

The proclamation of Avidius Cassius caused (and continues to cause) surprise and consternation. Old Herodes Atticus, so it is alleged, sent him a missive in a single Greek word: 'you have gone off your head.'

Other explanations avail: an accident and a mistake. One turns to the historian Cassius Dio, who at that time was a boy aged about twelve and not incapable of recalling what they said about this transaction. Dio supplies two statements. First, the deteriorating health of Marcus alarmed his consort. In fear of his death Faustina wrote to Cassius. She urged him to be in readiness, and she offered him her hand. Second, rumour reported the decease of Marcus, and so Cassius made his abortive proclamation.

Scandal and detraction hangs over the memory of Faustina, perpetuated in classic and eloquent form by Gibbon: 'the grave simplicity of the philosopher was ill calculated to engage her wanton levity', and so on (taken from the *Historia Augusta*).

Dismissing the tradition about Faustina, a sober estimate arises without discomfort from the political situation in the spring of 175. Providing against an emergency, a sagacious and resolute woman took action to preserve the succession for the boy Commodus (now aged thirteen) and safeguard her own position by annexing a powerful ally as regent.

The pair may have been old acquaintances, congenial and even close in age. A piece of papyrus can be adduced. It is identified as Cassius' | announcement to the citizens of Alexandria. He styles Alexandria his native city. That term may yield the date of his birth. In 130 Hadrian visited Egypt. If his parent Heliodorus was imperial secretary at this time (and nothing forbids), he accompanied Hadrian, as had Suetonius on the journey to Britain. On this hypothesis the youthful prime of age would be added to the other advantages of the pretender.

Epilogue

The Greeks in their ascension thus came out with a potential emperor of high capacity. Champions of Hellenism fell by the way, such as Antonius and Nero, but the process had gone on, not to be abated by any form of resistance. It is a story of accidents, of opportunism, and of political success. Above all, the success of higher education: a topic not to be disdained in an exposition presented to a university audience.

What the writers tell us is shown inadequate on so many counts. The other testimony (that is, epigraphy) is likewise sporadic and fragmentary. To become intelligible, history has to aspire to the coherence of fiction, while eschewing most of its methods. There is no choice, no escape.

In the present discourse I have conveyed the reader on a long promenade through the centuries by devious paths and not without digressions; the way led through a dense forest of facts and names, a veritable 'selva selvaggia'.

Voltaire somewhere says that facts are vermin that infest history and prevent understanding. Another feature may be found even more repellent. The perpetual expansion of the governing class at Rome is nothing but the annals of the few and the fortunate.

The concept of élite, like the word itself, enjoys a certain disfavour in the modern time. Historical scholarship takes to embracing the labouring poor with eager solicitude or with doctrinaire affection. Not to much profit or exhilaration, at least as concerns the study of antiquity. Peasants and slaves did not speak or write, their condition denied them freedom of action. By good fortune, the Hellenes, although not always in possession of the liberty which they cherish even to excess, exhibit and avow a strong tendency to be active, visible, and vocal. |

NOTE

For the topics covered in this lecture, the following may be consulted:

Boulanger, A., *Aelius Aristide* (1923).

Bowersock, G. W., *Augustus and the Greek World* (1965).

—— *Greek Sophists in the Roman Empire* (1969).

Bowie, E. L., 'Greeks and their Past in the Second Sophistic', *P&P* xlvi (1970), 3.

Graindor, P., *Un Milliardaire antique. Hérode Atticus et sa famille* (1930).

Habicht. Chr., *Altertümer von Pergamon*, viii. 3. *Die Inschriften des Asklepieions* (1969).

—— 'Zwei neue Inschriften aus Pergamon', *Istanbuler Mitteilungen* ix/x (1959–60), 109.

Halfmann, H., *Die Senatoren aus dem östlichen Teil des Imperium Romanum bis zum Ende des 2 Jh. n. Chr.* (Hypomnemata, lviii, 1979).

Jones, C. P., *Plutarch and Rome* (1971).

—— *The Roman World of Dio Chrysostom* (1978).

Lambrechts, P., 'Trajan et le recrutement du Sénat, *AC* v (1936), 105.

Levick, B., *Roman Colonies in Southern Asia Minor* (1967).

Magie, D., *Roman Rule in Asia Minor* (1950).

Mitchell, S., 'The Plancii in Asia Minor', *JRS* lxiv (1974), 27.

Oliver, J. H., 'The Ruling Power', *TAPhS* xliii.4 (1953), 871.

Stadter, P., *Arrian of Nicomedia* (1980).

Syme, R., 'Tacitus and the Greeks', ch. xxxviii, *Tacitus* (1958).

—— 'The Greeks under Roman Rule', *Proc. Mass. Hist. Soc.* lxxii (1957–60) [1963], 3–20 = *RP* (1979) 566–81.

Walton, C. S., 'Oriental Senators in the Service of Rome', *JRS* xix (1929), 38.

2

The Career of Arrian

WHEN senators compose history they are not always eager to obtrude their occupations or any travels in foreign parts. Erudite enquiry has to seek after hints or traces in the writings, a seductive pastime but often hazardous and liable to deceive.

Arrian excites curiosity on various counts. It is baffled by problems of dating, which extend to the lost works. In his manifold productivity two opuscules belong to the period when under Hadrian he governed the military province of Cappadocia (?131–137). Next, he indited the treatise on hunting and the *Discourses of Epictetus* after he had retired to Athens early in the next reign, becoming an honorary citizen and holding the archonship. For the rest, and notably for his history of Alexander (the *Anabasis*), disputation goes on.

A tradition obtained, and a recurrent phenomenon. The senator turns to history when reaching high office—or rather when employment lapsed, writing for consolation and sometimes for revenge. In consonance therewith the bulk of Arrian's works was consigned to the late season of a long life. Weighty authority commended the notion.[1]

Brief reflection dissuades. In the happy epoch of the Antonines performance in oratory or letters led notoriously to public honour, as witness Herodes Atticus and Cornelius Fronto, consul and consul suffect in 143. Arrian, so he affirmed, had been devoted from early years to the study of warfare and philosophy as well as hunting.[2] Official duties whether at Rome or in a province were never as exacting as the ingenuous fancy. They conveyed the need or the excuse for recreation. A scholar could take a provision of books to far Cappadocia—or find them there.

That region, which bore a sad name for bleak and rural retardation, had cities such as Mazaca (now styled Caesarea) and primeval Tyana. Cappadocia had already anticipated the epoch of the sophists with Apollonius, the magician and charlatan. Perhaps an

---

[1] E. Schwartz, *RE* ii 1231, cf. 1234.   [2] Arrian, *Cyneg.* 7,4.

Harvard Studies in Classical Philology lxxxvi (1982), 181–211.

isolated figure. Yet | Cappadocia was soon to exhibit the orator Pausanias, a pupil of Herodes Atticus, and young Diodotus, cut off before his prime.[3]

Arrian's writings interlock with his official career. They ought to stand in some relation, so it is presumed. Apart from recourse to internal evidence, sundry experiences might be invoked, or the impact of notable transactions.

Arrian's major work narrated the wars between the Romans and the Parthians. Of the seventeen books of his *Parthica*, no fewer than ten were devoted to the campaigns of Trajan (114–17). Whether or no Arrian himself saw service, the Imperator evoked the conquering Macedonian.

Alexander, it is true, finds no mention in any fragment of the *Parthica*. The theme and parallel was not lost on Cassius Dio.[4] Like Arrian's *Parthica*, the *Anabasis* might fall in the sequel to Trajan's war, at no long interval.

Hesitations are enjoined. Authors do not always respond with due and prompt alacrity or leave clues for guidance. The governor of Africa Nova is not disclosed by Sallust's second monograph; and when Flaubert came back from his tour in the Orient it was not for the exotic *Salammbô*. His choice went to rural and bourgeois Normandy.

In the recent time preoccupation with Alexander has issued in a spate of writing: penetrating and subversive as well as erudite or fluent. Arrian suffered neglect, raw material for the industry or ending as a by-product. Compensation accrues from two recent studies of author and writings. A thorough investigation puts the *Anabasis* in the early years of Hadrian, not later than the year 125.[5] By contrast, an excellent book stands by a later dating.[6]

Interest in Arrian's person is now stimulated by three epigraphic discoveries, in close sequence. First, a fragmentary inscription at Corinth registers a legate of Cappadocia, styling him a philosopher. Second, at Athens the *praenomen* of Flavius Arrianus emerges as |

---

[3] Philostratus, *Vit. Soph.* 593 f.; 617. The latter is now disclosed as M. Acilius Diodotus (*Pergamon* viii, 3, no. 35). For his name and his kinsfolk, *Chiron* x (1980), 429 f. = *RP* iii (1984), 1318 f.

[4] Dio lxviii 29,1; 30,1.

[5] A. B. Bosworth, 'Arrian's Literary Development', *CQ* xxii (1972), 163 ff. For a firm pronouncement see his *Commentary* i (Oxford 1980), 6: 'The Alexander history, which demonstrably comes early in the sequence of his historical works, was composed when Arrian was in his thirties.'

[6] P. Stadter, *Arrian of Nicomedia* (1980), 184: 'after his consulship, in Cappadocia or in Athens.'

Observe also G. Wirth, *Historia* xiii (1964), 209 ff. (subsequent to the year 147); E. L. Bowie, *P&P* xlvi (1970), 24 ff. (in the early years of Marcus).

'Lucius'. Third, at Corduba Arrianus, a proconsul of Baetica, makes a dedication to Artemis in Greek verse.[7]

The present disquisition will eschew as far as possible the nature and content of Arrian's writings, their order of composition, the author's intellectual development. The design is to furnish a framework. Emphasis will concentrate on ages and stages in the service of the Caesars, on types and prospects of advancement, on comparison with other senators among Arrian's coevals.

Entering the Senate by the quaestorship at the age of twenty-five, the *novus homo* normally attains the *fasces* when forty-two. Two tiles with the stamp 'Arriano et Severo' assign Arrian's consulship to either 129 or 130.[8] A provisional device to facilitate the conduct of the enquiry may assume the former year and put his birth about 86.

Senators from the eastern provinces, that is a large theme and attractive, a long story.[9] They arrive sooner than might be expected, and more numerous. In the first place from the veteran colonies and from cities favoured by the Italian diaspora. Close behind follow the native aristocracies, promoted already by the Flavian rulers and on conspicuous show under Trajan with a whole cluster of consular magnates.

Bithynia's first senator was an equestrian officer adlected by Vespasian: he came from Apamea, a *colonia*.[10] Furthermore, Apamea (or perhaps Nicaea) is now claimed as the *patria* of a man who rose to abnormal eminence, namely L. Catilius Severus (*suff.* 110, *cos. II* 120).[11] The *nomen* 'Catilius' is very rare, even in Italy, and not borne by any previous senator.[12] |

Arrian's city was Nicomedia, where he held a priesthood; and he wrote a history of the Bithynian kingdom. Nicomedia, despite its rank and strategic advantages, shows few traces of Italian settlement.[13] As for Arrian's family, their Roman citizenship may go back

---

[7] *AE* 1968, 473; 1971, 437; 1974, 370.			[8] *CIL* xv 244; 252. Cf. *PIR*², F 219.

[9] For the full statement and catalogue, H. Halfmann, *Die Senatoren aus dem östlichen Teil des Imperium Romanum bis zum Ende des 2 Jh. n. Chr.* (1979).

[10] Halfmann, no. 18. That is, ']atilius L. f. Clu. Longus' (*CIL* iii 335, as emended by W. Eck). In Halfmann's view probably a Catilius. Add, also at Apamea, the slave of a Cn. Catilius Atticus (iii 337).

[11] Halfmann, no. 38. For his full nomenclature and *cursus*, *ILS* 1041 (Antium); *ILAfr* 43 (Thysdrus). The latter document furnishes the tribe, generally supplemented as '[Cla]u.' (cf. *PIR*², C 558): better '[Cl]u.,' cf. Halfmann.

[12] *TLL*, *Onom*. That repertory yields Κατιλλία Γαυριανὴ Νεικαηνή (*IG* xiv 790: Naples). Add further P. Catilius Macer from Nicaea (*SIG*³ 836: Delphi, dated to the year 125).

[13] In apparent contrast to Nicaea, cf. J. Hatzfeld, *Les Trafiquants italiens dans l'Orient hellénique* (1919), 134, 172 f. However, for rare names at Nicomedia, see K. F. Dörner, *Inschriften und Denkmäler aus Bithynien* (1941), no. 28 ('Numisienus'); 53 ('Ampilius'); 60 ('Tuccius' and 'Poppaeus'); 101 ('Oclatius').

a long way. The nomenclature 'L. Flavius Arrianus' invites
conjecture, although the *nomina* 'Flavius' and 'Arrius' are common
and indistinctive. With the latter nothing can be done, but attention
goes to L. Flavius, consul suffect in 33 B.C., at that time with Marcus
Antonius in the eastern lands.[14] For parallel, observe the *cognomen*
'Cocceianus', later on splendid attestation with Dio, the sophist of
Prusa, and with the consular historian Cassius Dio from Nicaea. As
partisans of Antonius both C. Cocceius Balbus (*suff.* 39) and
M. Cocceius Nerva (*cos.* 36) held commands and earned the title of
'imperator'.[15]

Along with the historian, Bithynian Cassii evoke Cassius Ascle-
piodotus, whose funeral monument stands outside Nicaea.[16] Also,
and relevant to the present theme, the fragmentary inscription of a
senatorial '[Cas]sius' who may be identical with Cassius Agrippa (or
Agrippinus), consul suffect in 130.[17]

Young Arrian is first discovered at Nicopolis of Epirus, attending
the lectures (or rather dialogues) of Epictetus. He wrote them up
many years later. One incident he reports gives the season of his
sojourn. A certain Maximus turned up, on his way to an
appointment in Hellas as *diorthotes* (that is, *corrector*). Maximus, of the
Epicurean persuasion, was enticed or forced into an interchange with
the relentless sage (*Diss.* iii 7).

Now Pliny happens to address a friend called Maximus, departing
'ad ordinandum statum liberarum civitatum' (*Ep.* viii 24, 2). The
letter belongs to 107 or 108. Persons of that name cause perplexity,
but an attractive identification is to hand: Sex. Quinctilius Maximus,
who in | 99/100 had been an exemplary quaestor in the province
Bithynia–Pontus.[18]

This man was in fact one of the better sort at the *colonia* Alexandria
in the Troad. That Pliny should equip him with copious admonish-
ment about the way to behave toward Greeks is no impediment. The
artful orator was emulating Cicero's epistle to his brother Quintus,
proconsul in Asia.

Next, Delphi. An inscription yields five members of a Roman
governor's *consilium*, among them 'Fl. Arrianus'.[19] The governor,

---

[14] Dio xlix 44,3.   [15] *PIR*[2], C 1214; 1224.

[16] *PIR*[2], C 486. See further on Cassii F. Millar, *A Study of Cassius Dio* (1964), 8 f.

[17] *AE* 1950, 251 (Nicaea). Strong doubts about identity are expressed by W. Eck, *RE, Suppl.*
xiv 86 f.; and this man has no separate entry in Halfmann, who notes him under no. 123 (M.
Cassius Apronianus, the parent of the historian). Cassius was admitted among the proconsuls
of Baetica by G. Alföldy, *Fasti Hispanienses* (1969), 168.

[18] *ILS* 1018 (Alexandria Troadis), cf. Pliny, *Pan.* 70,1. Doubt is voiced by Sherwin-White in
his *Commentary* (1966) on *Ep.* viii 24,6.

[19] *SIG*[3] 827. For the names see the revised text of A. Plassart, *Fouilles de Delphes* iii, 4 (1970),
no. 290.

C. Avidius Nigrinus, is styled 'leg. Aug. pro pr.'.[20] Caesar's legate
has thus replaced the proconsul in Achaea, as did Pliny and Cornutus
Tertullus in Bithynia–Pontus. Like them, Nigrinus (*suff.* 110) should
be presumed a consular, his post falling somewhere between 111 and
114.[21] He went on to govern Dacia, where he was superseded in 117
by the illustrious Pergamene C. Julius Quadratus Bassus (*suff.* 105).

There is an advantage in having Nigrinus in Achaea in 112 or 113.
He belonged to a cultivated and philhellenic family—and he was a
close friend of Hadrian. An anecdote asserts that Hadrian intended
Nigrinus for his successor.[22] At first sight dubious—but the item
may go back to an apologia in that emperor's autobiography.
Nigrinus was one of the Four Consulars put to death in the early
months of the reign, for a conspiracy not plausible.

In 112 Hadrian was elected archon at Athens. The ardent addict to
all things Greek would hardly fail to grace the city with his presence.
So far as known, he had never been previously in Achaea—and
escape from Rome was welcome for one whose personality was not
wholly congenial to the Imperator, apart from an uneasy kinship and
prospects at the mercy of hazard.

Going eastward or returning, many Romans put in at Nicopolis,
from veneration of the sage long established there, or from
curiosity.[23] Hadrian, averse from pomp and rank, was drawn to the
unconventional philosopher who had once been a slave; and
Epictetus, although a | Stoic, had marked affinities with Cynics
through his sharp criticism of society and government.[24]

The *Historia Augusta* transmits a precious item, deriving from the
basic source: 'in summa familiaritate Epictetum et Heliodorum
philosophos habuit' (*Hadr.* 16, 10). Heliodorus, otherwise C. Avidius
Heliodorus, Prefect of Egypt at the end of Hadrian's reign, was an
Epicurean.[25] These casual facts, it may be noted in passing, go far
toward invalidating much that has been alleged and written about
the beliefs of Hadrian.

Arrian is attested at Delphi in the company of Avidius Nigrinus.
Delphi evokes Plutarch of Chaeronea, holder of a priesthood and

---

[20] As on an Athenian inscription, published in *Hesperia* xxxii (1963), 4.
[21] Similarly L. Aemilius Juncus (*suff.* 127), cf. Halfmann, no. 55.
[22] *HA Hadr.* 7,1.
[23] Epictetus was among the philosophers banished by Domitian (Gellius xv 11,5). That is, in 93.
[24] See the illuminating paper of F. Millar, 'Epictetus and the Imperial Court', *JRS* lv (1965), 141 ff.
[25] *PIR*[2], A 1405 = H 50.

assiduous at the sanctuary. Also sundry friends of Plutarch, among whom the Avidii had been conspicuous.[26]

Arrian knew other cities, in the first place Corinth, a Roman colony and seat of the provincial governor. Lucius Gellius carries the dedication of the books devoted to Epictetus—and one of the new inscriptions reveals L. Gellius Menander as a friend of Arrian.[27] This person already stood on record as a fancier of Roman officials: dedications in honour of three imperial procurators.[28]

Likewise much in evidence at Corinth was Cn. Cornelius Pulcher, of an old Epidaurian family.[29] He paraded a collection of priesthoods and ceremonial titles.[30] Topics of varied interest radiate from this pretentious character. Pulcher became procurator in Epirus, a post created by Nero (in 67, when Hellas was liberated) or by Vespasian.[31] Nothing debars identity with the unnamed procurator whose ostentatious comportment at Nicopolis drew condign censure from Epic|tetus (*Diss.* iii 3). Pulcher, it is suitable to add, earned a treatise from Plutarch—on the technique for getting benefit from personal enemies.

So far the private existence of L. Flavius Arrianus. A larger theme unfolds, namely the season and the manner in which he made the transit to senatorial status. Various paths offered. Brief clarification may be useful.

When assuming the *toga virilis* with the broad stripe a senator's son duly enters the 'amplissimus ordo'. To other youths Caesar grants the *latus clavus* either at once (before minor magistracy and military tribunate) or just before the quaestorship. The first senator in a family tends to suppress the change of status. Few specify as did Quinctilius Maximus, 'lato clavo exornatus' by Nerva.[32] The negative side illustrates, since 'dignitas senatoria' can be discarded or refused. Thus Valerius Macedo declined when Hadrian offered 'latum clavum cum quaestura'.[33]

Some new men came to the quaestorship from equestrian service. Their acquisition of the *latus clavus* may be expressed by the

[26] For the Avidii, C. P. Jones, *Plutarch and Rome* (1971), 51 ff. Heliodorus presumably derives his Roman name from this family.

[27] *AE* 1968, 473 (Corinth), cf. G. W. Bowersock, *GRBS* viii (1967) 279 f.

[28] *PIR*², G 132.

[29] *PIR*², C 1424; Pflaum, *Carrières* etc. (1960), no. 81. Add now *AE* 1974, 593 (Athens). At Corinth he was honoured by Justus, the son of L. Gellius Menander (*IG* iv 1601).

[30] In those predilections Pulcher had a rival in another Epidaurian, Q. Alleius Epictetus (*IG* iv 691 = *AE* 1977, 775).

[31] The earliest procurator is patently Sex. Pompeius Sabinus (Pflaum no. 53). Next, after Pulcher, A. Ofillius Macedo (no. 112), to be presumed Hadrianic.

[32] *ILS* 1018 (Alexandria).   [33] *ILS* 6998 (nr. Vienna).

periphrasis 'adlectus in amplissimum ordinem'. Thus Ti. Claudius Quartinus (*suff.* 130) after a tribunate in the legion III Cyrenaica.[34] In most cases the quaestorship follows at once on military posts, without explanation. Thus Aemilius Arcanus of Narbo, after three tribunates—and also after all the local magistracies.[35]

Some of those promoted equestrians thus became quaestors well above the normal age. The striking and peculiar example is Statius Priscus (*cos.* 159): after five military charges and a procuratorship.[36]

In sharp contrast stand adlections to rank in the Senate. Admissions were conducted by the Caesars when censors (Claudius and Vespasian), by censorial powers (Domitian), by imperial prerogative (later rulers). By this device officers, procurators, or local worthies enter the Senate without having previously belonged to the 'amplissimus ordo'.

It has been expedient to register these distinctions and variations. | Misconceptions about Arrian's early career still occur.[37] Furthermore, emphasis on uncertainties all through. If Arrian was born in 86, and if he advanced by the quaestorship, he would be a senator in 112 or 113—when he is merely a member of a governor's *consilium*. Again, on the same hypothesis about Arrian's age, he would be too old for *tribunus laticlavius* in Trajan's Parthian War (114–17), too young for legate of a legion.

Equestrian service seems the answer. Here again there is a danger of misconceptions, fostered by the existence of a 'militia equestris' with a regular sequence of three posts. Ages of entry varied, likewise a man's tastes or his prospects.[38] Some, not ambitious for higher or civilian employment, might rest content with a single post. Municipal men looked to travel and exotic experiences, to acquiring a patron or local prestige.[39] Specimens abound in the western lands, to mention only Junius Columella, the Gaditane agronome, tribune in VI Ferrata.[40] For the context of Arrian, Cornelius Pulcher avails, tribune in IV Scythica.[41]

For Arrian himself the great war in the Orient may have marked a

---

[34] *CIL* xiii 1802 (Lugdunum): with, anomalously, 'splendidissimus' instead of 'amplissimus'. For the normal term, *ILS* 1064.

[35] *ILS* 1064 (Narbo). [36] *ILS* 1092 (Rome).

[37] Thus in P. Stadter, op. cit. 6 f. Arrian (he suggests) may have 'served several years in his early twenties in the equestrian military career.' After being commander of a cohort he may have been a *tribunus militum angusticlavius*. Then, after receiving the *latus clavus*, 'Arrian could have gone on as *vigintivir*, one of twenty minor administrative officials at Rome, then as *tribunus militum laticlavius*.' That process lacks parallel.

[38] E. Birley, *Roman Britain and the Roman Army* (1953), 135 ff.

[39] As emphasized through Spanish examples in *HSCPh* lxxiii (1969) = *RP* (1979), 748.

[40] *ILS* 2923 (Tarentum). [41] *IG* iv 795 (Troezen).

new turn in his fortunes as well as an incentive to authorship. His participation has been doubted or denied, it is true.[42] The evidence is imperfect. According to a passage in Johannes Lydus, Arrian in his *Historia Alanica*, in Book VIII, gave precise information about the Caspian Gates, having been put in charge of the region by Trajan.[43]

Some infer a military command, exercised in the direction of the Caucasus. Others disallow, supposing a confusion with the Cappadocian governorship under Hadrian. The item may be allowed to lapse.

A number of fragments from the *Parthica* have been adduced that | appear to disclose special knowledge or autopsy.[44] Caution is prescribed. Arrian was composing the ample narration of a contemporary war, with a wide theatre of operations. Whether or no present himself at some of the actions, the author needed much information from eye-witnesses.

If Arrian had not yet become a senator, the hypothesis is reasonable that he saw service as an equestrian officer in this period, and precisely in Trajan's campaigns. It would be a pleasing diversion to adduce persons whose acquaintance Arrian now made or reinforced, whose reminiscences he was able to exploit in the sequel.[45]

Most of the fragments are brief and tell little. One, of larger compass, concerns a general called 'Broutios'. Facing snow 16 feet deep, he rescued his force through help from native guides and the use of snow-shoes.[46] Identity was patent: Bruttius Praesens, the epigraphic record of whose career shows him commander of VI Ferrata.[47] Nor is the date and occasion beyond conjecture. Snow-shoes employed on Mount Masius and in Atropatene are mentioned by Strabo.[48] Therefore Praesens in the winter of 114/15 brought troops southward across the high Taurus that separates Armenia from the upper valley of the Tigris.[49]

After the charge of a minor road in Italy (the Via Latina) Praesens

---

[42] Firmly denied by E. Schwartz, *RE* ii 1236; and 'unlikely' for F. A. Lepper, *Trajan's Parthian War* (1948), 2. On the other hand, 'little reason to doubt' for P. Stadter, op. cit. 9, cf. 142 ff.

[43] Lydus, *De mag.* i 36 = Arrian, *Parthica* fr. 6 (ed. A. G. Roos, *Arrianus* ii [1928]).

[44] G. Wirth, *StudClas* xvi (1974), 189 f. Not so many are admitted by Stadter, op. cit. 144.

[45] Notably Catilius Severus, who governed Cappadocia along with the newly annexed Armenia from 114 to 117, when he took over Syria (*ILS* 1041). Catilius was still extant in 138 (*HA Hadr.* 24,6).

[46] *Parthica* fr. 85.

[47] *IRT* 545 (Lepcis); *AE* 1950, 66 (Mactar).   [48] Strabo xi 506.

[49] For this deduction, *Historia* xviii (1969), 352 = *RP* (1979), 774. Strabo in three other passages defined as 'Masius' the range north of Nisibis (522; 527; 747). That is, the Tur Abdin: not very high.

is discovered as governor of Cilicia when Trajan died at Selinus in August of 117. His long life and notable career was crowned by a second consulship in 139. There is something else, a small and neglected fact—he wrote a history of his own times.[50]

In the written record of the campaigns one name finds no mention: the heir-apparent whom the Imperator left in command of the army in Syria.[51] Imagination or fiction fills out his previous occupations. On one | estimate, Hadrian had been the chief of staff.[52] On another, he resided at Antioch.[53]

It fell to the new emperor to conduct back to Europe troops from the failed war. Ancyra and Nicomedia lay on his path. At Ancyra the Galatian magnate C. Julius Severus had generously facilitated the passage of armies to the seat of war.[54] Arrian, it is supposed, may have played a similar role in his city, either then or when they returned in the autumn of 117.[55] That is, if then resident at Nicomedia.

Arrian's friendship with Hadrian, which turns out to be closer and more congenial than conveyed by the word 'amicus' (at an early date it had become a kind of title), may go back several years. In any event, let it be conjectured that he was adlected to the Senate either during the Parthian war or in 118. That is well before Hadrian's first journey which took him to Gaul and Germany in 121, to Britain in the next year. There is no reason for retarding Arrian's admission.

If adlected *inter praetorios* Arrian stood in fair prospect of a consulship when ten or twelve years had elapsed. Not without employment by Caesar, at the minimum the command of a legion. The equestrian officers whom Vespasian promoted in 69 and 73 furnish useful parallels.[56] None happen to be available for the first quinquennium of Hadrian's reign.

---

[50] Nothing precludes identity with the Bruttius who according to Christian writers mentioned a Domitianic persecution (*PIR*[2], B 159). Praesens suffered retardation in his earlier career; and the language of Pliny shows him an Epicurean (*Ep*. vii 3). Cf. now *Studia Kajanto* (1985), 273 ff. = pp. 563 ff., below.

[51] Hadrian's epigram about Trajan's dedication on Mount Casius (*Anth. Pal*. vi 332) is quoted in fr. 36.

[52] W. Weber, *CAH* xi (1936), 299. Indeed, 'he was at the nerve-centre of all action.'

[53] M. Yourcenar, *Mémoires d'Hadrien* (1951), 80 ff. (allegedly appointed governor of Syria in 112).

[54] *OGIS* 544 (Ancyra).

[55] Thus A. B. Bosworth in his commentary on the *Anabasis* i (1980), 2. Hadrian might have spent the winter of 117/18 at Nicomedia or Byzantium.

Bosworth adds 'Hadrian also passed through Nicomedia and Nicaea on his first journey of 119–121 (Magie 613 f.).' To be discarded: Hadrian sojourned at Rome until spring or summer of 121.

[56] W. Eck, *Senatoren von Vespasian bis Hadrian* (1970), 103 ff.

For Arrian the only sign points towards a senatorial province. At
Corduba a proconsul of Baetica called Arrianus consecrates a Greek
poem to Artemis, declaring his gift better than gold and silver, better
than the products of hunting.[57] None other than the author of the
Cynegetica, the notion is highly attractive. A long way from home
and from familiar lands, it is true. For that matter, the Pergamene
historian | Claudius Charax was to visit Britain about the year 140, to
command the legion II Augusta.[58]

Arrian's writings lend no support. It is not safe to use the long
digression in the *Anabasis* which, devoted to the Tyrian Heracles,
happens to mention the shrine of Hercules 'at Tartessus' (i.e.
Gades).[59]

Again, the age knew other senators of the name, such as Arrianus
Severus, a *praefectus aerarii* under Trajan, or Arrianus, a *curator operum
publicorum* (epoch not determinate).[60]

Nor is it certain that one can claim for Arrian the small fragments
of a Hadrianic governor of Cappadocia, who was curator of the
Tiber.[61] The inscription carries the word 'H]ispa[niae'. That might,
however, be supplemented to give the legion IX Hispana.

If the dedicant at Corduba is held to be Flavius Arrianus (*suff.* ?129)
the date might invite curiosity. Sortition for proconsulates comes
five years after the praetorship. In Arrian's case perhaps toward the
year 124. A predecessor (perhaps immediate) would then be Tullius
Varro, who after commanding XII Fulminata in Cappadocia
brought VI Victrix from the Rhine to Britain (presumably in 122);
and who, after Baetica, proceeded by the charge of the *aerarium
Saturni* to a suffect consulship in 127.[62] Hadrian, it will suitably be
recalled, departing from Britain to Gaul and Spain, spent the winter
of 122/3 at Tarraco but omitted a visit to his *patria* in Baetica.

Engaging speculations are curtailed by the chance of a later date.
By anomaly a proconsulate can come late, after an imperial
governorship that was leading straight to the *fasces*. After a legion
and Lusitania both Oppius Sabinus and Javolenus Calvinus became
proconsuls of Baetica. Their consulates can be assigned *c.*140 and

[57] *AE* 1974, 370.

[58] *AE* 1961, 320.

[59] *Anab.* ii 16,4, with Bosworth's note. Stadter, however, sets value on the notice (op. cit.
10).

[60] *Dig.* xlix 14,42; *CIL* vi 31132. The former may be the consul Arrianus Aper Veturius
Severus (xiv 3587: Tibur). Nothing further is known about C. Statius Capito Arrianus, boy
ministrant to the *Arvales* in 117 and 118 (*CIL* vi 2076; 2078). The *nomen* 'Arrius' is extremely
common (about forty entries in *PIR*² A).

[61] From Caesarea Mazaca. Recalled by W. Eck, *RE, Suppl.* xiv 120, from *Mélanges Beyrouth*
v (1911) 309.

[62] *ILS* 1047 (Tarquinii).

*c.*143.[63] Earlier specimens can be discovered, and various reasons might be canvassed.

Of double relevance to Fl. Arrianus is the Cassius of the fragmentary inscription at Nicaea. After commanding a legion (XX Valeria Victrix, in Britain) he was proconsul of Baetica before the consulship. As | indicated, perhaps the *suffectus* of 130, Cassius Agrippa (or Agrippinus).[64]

As happens elsewhere, a new document can engross interest beyond its value for history. Let Corduba recede.[65] A proconsulate in Baetica has diverted attention from posts of another character likely to be held by a man who goes on as consular to one of the ten military commands in the portion of Caesar.[66]

The evidence about senatorial careers is so abundant as to constitute a subject in itself; and while system is to be deprecated (being liable to be overridden by social rank, by capacity, by patronage), types and patterns emerge. Even in the four minor magistracies a kind of predestination can be discovered.[67] The *tresviri capitales* have slender prospects, whereas patricians claim almost a monopoly among the *monetales*. Furthermore, under the Antonine rulers patricians are seldom *tribuni militum*, legionary legates, or governors of praetorian provinces. The rare exceptions are noteworthy.[68]

For a man's advancement and success, posts subsequent to the praetorship are crucial. One significant pattern takes shape under the Flavian emperors: the legionary command followed by the governorship of an imperial province, in some cases the sole praetorian posts, and with access to the *fasces* four or five years short of the standard age. The prime specimen is Julius Agricola (*suff.* 77), with XX Valeria Victrix and Aquitania; and there are good instances under Trajan.[69]

Although most consuls had commanded a legion, education and social gifts rather than military training opened the path to high honours; and a consular's experience with the armies had seldom been continuous and prolonged. Trajan numbered among his marshals

[63] *ILS* 1059 (Firmum); 1060 (Tusculum).
[64] *AE* 1950, 251, cf. G. Alföldy, *Fasti Hispanienses* (1969), 168. Also above, p. 24 n. 17. This senator might be a son of M. Cassius Agrippa, procurator in Baetica (*CIL* ii 2212: Corduba).
[65] Nine periodical articles are listed by Stadter (op. cit. n. 6, 195 f.), terminating with L. Koenen, 'Cordoba and no End', *ZPE* xxiv (1977) 35 ff.
[66] Ten, omitting Dalmatia, consular but lacking a legion since 85.
[67] For this, and for some other matters see E. Birley, 'Senators in the Emperor's Service,' *PBA* xxxix (1953), 197 ff.
[68] Thus the consul of 152, M'. Acilius Glabrio (*ILS* 1072). On whom see 'An Eccentric Patrician', *Chiron* x (1980) 427 ff. = *RP* iii (1984), 1316 ff.
[69] *Tacitus* (1958), 650.

men | of high cultivation such as Licinius Sura and Sosius Senecio (the most eminent friend of Plutarch).

A recent survey of consular legates, putting emphasis on diversities, goes all the way from 70 to 235.[70] A shorter span during which stability and routine obtained is more manageable and might prove more instructive. That is, the forty-four years from the death of Trajan to the accession of Marcus Aurelius.[71] Confined to those limits, the catalogue that was furnished is reduced to thirty-two names.[72]

Four should be added, viz.:

Ti. Claudius Quartinus (*suff.* 130). *PIR*[2], C 990. He held a legionary command in 123; his governorship of Lugdunensis, deduced from *CIL* xiii 1802, is now confirmed by an inscription at Lugdunum (*AE* 1976, 427).

(M.) Valerius Propinquus (126).[72a] *CIL* ii 6084 (Tarraco), cf. G. Alföldy, *RIT* (1975), 149. After the praetorship he had VI Victrix and either Arabia or Aquitania.

T. Flavius Longinus Marcius Turbo (*c.*150). *PIR*[2], F 305. He had in succession I Adiutrix and Lugdunensis: his sole praetorian posts.

C. Julius Severus (*cos.* 155). *PIR*[2], J 574. After the praetorship, legate of XXX Ulpia, *curator* of the Via Appia: no other praetorian posts.

In this total of thirty-six[72b] all except four commanded a legion. Each is exceptional in various fashions.

C. Popilius Carus Pedo (*suff.* 147). *ILS* 1071. Appointed to command X Fretensis (in Judaea), 'a cuius cura se excusavit.' His service as a military tribune had been passed in the same country with decorations from Hadrian, 'ob Iudaicam expeditionem'.

P. Salvius Julianus (*cos.* 148). *ILS* 8973. He acceded to the *fasces* after holding both treasury posts. Salvius was the great jurist of the age.

L. Dasumius Tullius Tuscus (*suff.* 152). *ILS* 1081 (Tarquinii). A legionary

---

[70] B. Campbell, 'Who were the "Viri Militares"?' *JRS* lxv (1975), 11 ff., with a catalogue of seventy names and three *Incerti*. One of the three *(ILS* 1057) is identical with no. 37, viz. Cn. Julius Verus, cf. *ILS* 8974. Further, to that rubric should accrue the *Ignotus* of Nemausus (*CIL* xii 3169), early Trajanic, with consular decorations; and likewise the acephalous *cursus* of a governor of Syria (*CIL* xiii 2662: Augustodunum), which should be assigned to the Flavio-Antonine period.

The argument concludes that 'in general there are no clearly discoverable patterns of promotion' (23). For temperate criticism of that thesis, G. Alföldy, *Konsulat und Senatorenstand unter den Antoninen* (1977), 375 f.

[71] For the detail see G. Alföldy, *Konsulat und Senatorenstand*, etc. (1977).

[72] It includes, be it noted, five legates in office when Trajan died, viz. Julius Quadratus Bassus (*suff.* 105); Minicius Natalis (106); Aelius Hadrianus (108); Pompeius Falco (108); Catilius Severus (110).

[72a] See further pp. 579 ff. below.

[72b] That is, together with the four extra names, the following from Campbell's list: nos. 1, 2, 6–8, 11, 17, 18, 20, 21, 24, 31, 35–7, 40, 43–5, 49, 50, 53–5, 58, 59, 62–5, 67, 70. (But for no. 17, cf. n. 76, below).

command may have been omitted from the inscription. Otherwise Tuscus is left with a single praetorian post.

T. Pomponius Proculus Vitrasius Pollio (?c.150). *ILS* 1112. This man | was a patrician; also married to Annia Fundania Faustina, a cousin of Marcus Aurelius. It is indeed an anomaly to find him governing Moesia Inferior, where he is attested in 157 (*AE* 1937, 247).

Next, the posts that qualify for the consulate. The total of praetorian provinces in the portion of Caesar, eight under the Flavians, had now risen to twelve; and in four of them the governor was at the same time commander of a legion.[73] Of the thirty-six senators here under review, twenty reached the consulate by this path.

The remainder may be summarily catalogued. For the patrician Vitrasius Pollio, a post was not requisite or normal; and Lollius Urbicus (*suff. c.*135) had a staff appointment during the Jewish War (*ILS* 1065). No fewer than ten held the prefecture of the *aerarium Saturni*, in a collegiate pair with a tenure normally triennial.[74] Like Salvius Julianus, Catilius Severus (*suff.* 110) had the two treasuries. His career is noteworthy for lack of promise until the vicinity of 108, when, so it may be conjectured, he married an heiress and attached himself to the potent Hispano-Narbonensian group, being known in the sequel as a 'great-grandfather' to Marcus Aurelius.[75]

Finally, three *curatores* in charge of the Via Flaminia or the Via Appia, combined with the charge of the *alimenta*.[76] These posts clearly rank as equivalents to the praetorian province or the *aerarium Saturni*.

For posts of this kind it would be superficial to postulate special aptitudes. While not such sinecures as the minor roads or the office of *praefectus frumenti dandi* (seldom found in epigraphical careers of the successful), they denote a patent privilege. Some of Caesar's friends thus dispense with a province and enjoy a spell at the capital after the legionary command.

A similar explanation may avail for the *cura operum publicorum*, held in this period immediately after the consulate. The tenure might be

---

[73] Viz. Numidia, Arabia, Pannonia Inferior, Dacia Superior. Judaea had been elevated to consular status, perhaps from 117.

[74] For the detail, M. Corbier, *L'Aerarium Saturni et l'Aerarium Militare* (1974).

[75] If Catilius married the widow of Cn. Domitius Tullus (*II suff.* 98), who is attested in Pliny (*Ep.* viii 18,8), he would become a step-great-grandfather to the boy Marcus. For this conjecture, *Historia* xvii (1968), 95 f. = *RP* (1979), 692 f.; *HSCPh* lxxxiii (1979), 305 = *RP* iii (1984), 1174.

[76] Namely Minicius Natalis (*ILS* 1061); Cluvius Maximus Paullinus (*AE* 1940, 99); Julius Severus (*ILS* 8829). Natalis was consul suffect in 139, Cluvius *c.*141, Severus the *ordinarius* of 155. As for no. 17 in Campbell's list, there is no evidence for the employment of Ti. Claudius Julianus (*suff.* 154) between legionary command and consulship (*PIR*[2], C 902).

assumed biennial.[77] Both Bruttius Praesens (*suff.* 118 or 119) and |
Metilius Secundus (123) were *curatores* before going to a province.[78]
A collegiate pair is not on direct attestation until Ti. Julius Julianus
and M. Ma[, dated to the consulate of Q. Insteius Celer (?128).[79]

Statistics combine helpfully. Of sixteen *curatores* between the years
136 and 161, no fewer than twelve proceed to consular provinces.
Seven of them had been *praefecti aerarii Saturni.*[80]

Some students of the Principate are prone to set a high value on
administration. The Romans did very little of it. It is a question how
arduous were the functions of the various *curatores.* When Julius
Frontinus was put in charge of the aqueducts he took his duties
seriously, and even compiled a technical handbook. Its accidental
survival should not mislead. Several of the earliest *curatores* held the
office for life. Further, Cocceius Nerva spent six years on the island
Capreae, and (under Claudius) Didius Gallus went away for some
years to be legate of Moesia.[81] After as before, experts of lower
station did the work. After the reign of Trajan the government may
have allowed the *cura aquarum* to lapse.[82]

On the evidence presented by thirty-two consular legates in office
under Hadrian and Pius, it would be premature and harmful to deny
Arrian the command of a legion; and he may well have governed one
of the twelve praetorian provinces. It will be of use to register ten of
his coevals by their modes of access to consulships during a
quinquennium.

Sex. Julius Maior (*suff.* ?126). Numidia. *PIR* ², J 397.
Ti. Julius Julianus (?126). Arabia, attested in 125. *AE* 1976, 691.
Sex. Julius Severus (127). Dacia, from 120 (or rather 119) to 126. *PIR* ², J. 576.
Q. Tineius Rufus (127). Thrace, in 124. *CIL* iii 14207³⁵ (a milestone).
P. Tullius Varro (127). *Aerarium Saturni. ILS* 1047. |
A. Egrilius Plarianus (128). *Aerarium Saturni. AE* 1955, 173.
M. Acilius Priscus Egrilius Plarianus (*c.* 130). *Aerarium Saturni. AE* 1955,
    171.[83]

---

[77] Annual tenure was assumed by G. Alföldy, op. cit. 26, cf. 289.

[78] Praesens to Cappadocia (*IRT* 545), Metilius to a province missing from the inscription
(*ILS* 1053), inspection of which (*CIL* xi 5718) might suggest Judaea.

[79] *AE* 1973, 36, cf. Halfmann, no. 53. Julianus had been legate of Arabia, attested in 125 (*AE*
1976, 691: Gerasa). The colleague baffles ascertainment.

[80] For these statistics, *Historia* xiv (1965), 358 f. = *Danubian Papers* (1971), 241 f.

[81] *History in Ovid* (1978), 124 (discussing the tenure of Messalla Corvinus).

[82] At least no *curator* on record between Neratius Marcellus under Trajan (*ILS* 1032) and
Caesonius Macer under Severus Alexander (1182).

[83] For the supplementing of that inscription see F. Zevi, *MEFR* lxxxiii (1970), 301. The
Egrilii of Ostia have caused much perplexity. For a clear statement, M. Corbier, op. cit.
164 ff., with a stemma.

L. Aurelius Gallus (*c*.130). *Aerarium Saturni*. ILS 1109.
Q. Fabius Catullinus (*cos.* 130). Numidia. *PIR*², F 25.
Ti. Claudius Quartinus (*suff.* 130). Lugdunensis, cf. above.

So far as known, five of the ten proceeded to consular provinces.[84] In contrast to the whole reign of Antoninus Pius, the Hadrianic evidence is capricious and defective. For example, for a whole decade (120 to 130) not one of the legates governing two of the four major commands (with garrisons of three legions) is on record, namely Pannonia Superior and Syria.

These ten consuls are heterogeneous. Various in origins as in attainments, they reflect the cosmopolitan recruitment of the upper order: the first two eastern, two of the others perhaps from the western provinces, while Julius Severus had for *patria* the colony of Aequum in Dalmatia.[85]

The limits have been indicated within which speculation should operate when discussing Arrian's employments anterior to his consulship. Turning to inferences from the writings, primary value adheres to a passage that describes the Indian rivers, with comparison of the Danube (*Ind.* iv.15 f.).

The author mentions two tributaries of the Danube, namely the Inn and the Save. He had seen them both. The Inn, he says, flows into the Danube in the border territory of Noricum and Raetia. A senator was not likely to see those provinces, which were governed by equestrian procurators.

Next, so Arrian states, the place where Save and Danube unite is called Taurunum. Compare the valuable notice in Pliny: 'Taurunum ubi Danuvio miscetur Savus' (*NH* iii 148). It may appear peculiar that Arrian should specify Taurunum (the modern Zemun) as the confluence of the two rivers rather than Singidunum (Belgrade), which in | his time was the camp of the legion IV Flavia. Taurunum was a port on the bank of the Danube; and, seen from Belgrade, the broad Danube flows gently into the rushing Save.

The facts about Taurunum were worth registering, whether to support or to deny autopsy. Taurunum was the boundary station of Pannonia Inferior. Not, however, valid to encourage a notion that Arrian had been governor of that province *c*.126–129.[86]

For the rest, appeal has been made to certain items about

[84] Namely Julius Maior (Moesia Inferior and Syria); Julius Severus (Moesia Inferior, Britannia, Judaea, Syria), Tineius Rufus (Judaea); Tullius Varro (Moesia Superior); Claudius Quartinus (Germania Superior). [85] *AE* 1904, 9; 1950, 45.
[86] Space is vacant well before L. Attius Macro (*suff.* 134), attested as *cos. des.* by *AE* 1937, 213 (Aquincum).

hunting.[87] Arrian in the *Cynegetica* refers in general terms to a variety of regions (23, 2). About two he is specific. He describes the practices of the Gauls (3, 19 f., cf. 34). Further, when the governor of Cappadocia he was able to compare the Caucasus (seen from the coast at Dioscurias) with the Celtic Alps (*Peripl.* 11, 5).

Next, 'a sight like nothing else', the African nomads hunting on horseback (24, 3). In the year 128 Hadrian visited the African provinces. There is no call, however, to suppose that the friend was in his company, admiring the technical skill that informed the imperial discourse to the troops at Lambaesis—and notably some remarks about cavalry.[88] As concerns the African nomads, Arrian might somewhere have seen in their recreations the Moorish horsemen led by their chieftain Lusius, active in both the Dacian and Parthian campaigns.[89]

Nor will other peregrinations of the Emperor be with safety invoked, although Arrian (if with him in 121) might have contemplated the Alps and visited Raetia. It is better to renounce—or fall back on experiences gathered by an equestrian officer, wider than what befell most senators.

A 'dira cupido' or conscientious endeavour attempts to wrest from ancient writers information they had no mind to furnish; and disputation of any kind about authorship and dates finds excuse or earnest commendation.

The other chronicler of Alexander is a palmary example, namely Q. Curtius Rufus. Dates have ranged from the Augustan age to the fourth century, with much ingenuity and industry expended in the contro|versy.[90] Meanwhile some historians were content to acquiesce in the belief that the historian of Alexander is identical both with the *rhetor* named by Suetonius (*De rhet.* 9) and with the legate of Germania Superior, to whose paradoxical destiny Tacitus devoted a delightful digression (*Ann.* xi 21).

Tacitus declined to state what he knew about the squalid origin of the consular, a gladiator's son, so some alleged: 'neque falsa prompserim, et vera exsequi pudet.'[91] It is no scandal, no surprise

---

[87] P. Stadter, op. cit. 16: 'Arrian seems to imply that he has been in both Gaul and Numidia.'

[88] Thus words of encouragement for cavalrymen attached to a cohort: 'difficile est cohortales equites etiam per se placere' etc. (*ILS* 2487); praise for the *ala Pannoniorum* (9134).

[89] *PIR*², L 439.

[90] Nineteen scholars are cited by J. E. Atkinson in his recent *Commentary* on Books III and IV (Amsterdam 1980), 19 ff. Add the Augustan dating preferred to Vespasianic by Tarn, *Alexander the Great* ii (1948), 113 f.

[91] One could adduce a Q. Curtius Rufus, *duumvir* at Arausio in Narbonensis (*CRAI* 1951, 238)—but the nomenclature is not distinctive.

that the Roman annalist chose to suppress the existence of the ten books entitled 'Historiae Alexandri regis Macedonum'.

By good fortune the latest investigation comes as close to proof as can reasonably be expected. It puts the compiler of the work under Caligula and Claudius—and Caligula's admiration for the Macedonian furnished an incentive.[92]

The *praenomen* of Rufus and his consular year (43) are now confirmed.[93] A thoroughgoing enquiry could hardly refrain from some speculation about the man's career. Rufus received the *latus clavus* while serving in the 'militia equestris', so it is suggested.[94] That notion is discountenanced by the language of Tacitus. After frequenting the quaestor in Africa, Rufus 'acri ingenio quaesturam . . . adsequitur' (xi 21, 1).

The disquisition failed to allude anywhere to posts between praetorship and consulate. Even the low-born orator Eprius Marcellus (*suff.* 62) had commanded a legion.[95] Further, he was legate of Lycia–Pamphylia, proconsul of Cyprus.[96]

Praetorian posts, that question concerns occupations surmised both for Arrian and for another literary gentleman, M. Cornelius Fronto (*suff.* 143). This African *novus homo* is the subject of a recent monograph, comprehensive yet admirable in its economy.[97]

Fronto in a letter to Marcus says that he has never governed provinces or commanded an army.[98] It therefore becomes expedient to devise for | him some suitable employments at the capital or in Italy. For example, one might think of one of the roads, which (combined with the *alimenta*) conveyed three senators to the consulate in the period 136–42.[99]

Instead is advocated the *aerarium militare* followed by the *aerarium Saturni*. For parallel, Pliny and Salvius Julianus are adduced, an orator and a jurist. Further, for Fronto's tenure the *sexennium* 126–31 is proposed.[100]

That proposal engenders a problem. Fronto should then have come straight to the *fasces*. How account for the long delay? Fronto, it is

---

[92] J. E. Atkinson, op. cit. 19 ff.
[93] *AE* 1975, 366 (a small fragment of the *Fasti Ostienses*).
[94] Atkinson, op. cit. 52.
[95] *AE* 1956, 186 (Paphos).
[96] Tacitus, *Ann.* xiii 33; *ILS* 992 (Capua).
[97] E. Champlin, *Fronto and Antonine Rome* (1980).
[98] Fronto, *Ad M. Caesarem* i 3,4 = Haines i 86.
[99] *ILS* 1061 (Minicius Natalis); *AE* 1940, 99 (Cluvius Maximus Paullinus); *ILS* 1069, cf. *AE* 1957, 135 (Caesernius Macedo). Compare later C. Julius Severus, the consul of 155 (*ILS* 8829).
[100] E. Champlin, op. cit. 80 f., cf. 164. Observe that M. Acilius Priscus Egrilius Plarianus (*suff. c.*130) also held the two prefectures in succession *c.*125–8 (M. Corbier, op. cit. 169 ff.).

argued, was born *c*.95, hence about five years beyond the standard age when he finally became consul, in 143.[101]

Fronto, it is a noteworthy fact, speaks of Hadrian with distaste and acerbity.[102] One could evoke the dark years before the ruler's decease. Hence a marked setback for the orator.[103]

Caesar's friend from Nicomedia was not likely either to suffer retardations (at least when well launched on the senatorial career), or, on the other hand, to benefit from abnormal favour. It is not easy to verify *novi homines* reaching the consulship under Hadrian before the age of forty.[104] After the praetorship and the command of a legion Sex. Julius Severus (*suff.* 127) passed seven years as governor of Dacia.[105] The promoted equestrian can take longer. Ti. Claudius Quartinus (130) was legate in Asia and *iuridicus* of Tarraconensis before the death of Trajan.[106]

Arrian was consul in 129 or 130 with a Severus for colleague. While that *cognomen*, along with 'Maximus' among the six most common, | deters any identification, a thought has gone to Herennius Severus, the patron of Philo of Byblos.[107]

In these pages the year 129 has been accorded a convenient preference. If consul in 129, Arrian might have been *curator operum publicorum* before his appointment to Cappadocia.[108] The post was attractive, as has been indicated. By the same token, Caesar might take pleasure if congenial friends or favoured adherents remained in the capital. Hadrian, however, after the African tour in 128 went eastward on peregrinations that lasted for six years.

On any count Arrian's governorship falls between the limits of 130 and 138. There are three fixed points. First, while Arrian was inspecting the coast of the eastern Euxine he learned at Dioscurias that Cotys, the ruler of the Bosporan kingdom, was no longer among the living (*Peripl.* 17, 3): the last coins of Cotys were struck in 131/2.[109] Second, the dedication made to Hadrian by Sebastopolis (in

---

[101] Champlin, op. cit. 97, cf. 81.   [102] Ibid. 94 ff.

[103] That depends upon the conjecture about the two prefectures—which not all may be disposed to find attractive.

[104] The two Caesernii, Macedo (*ILS* 1069) and Macrinus (1068) became consuls early in the next reign. For the careers of this favoured pair, G. Alföldy, *Konsulat u. Senatorenstand* (1977), 347 ff.

[105] *PIR*² J 576.

[106] *CIL* xiii 1802 (Lugdunum), cf. ii 2959 (Pompaelo, dated to 119).

[107] *PIR*², H 130.

[108] The Arrianus of *CIL* vi 31132 defies dating. The collegiate pair Ti. Julius Julianus (*suff.* ?126) and the enigmatic M. Ma[is attested by *AE* 1973, 36: probably of the year 128, cf. above, p. 34 n. 79.

[109] *PIR*², F 219.

Galatian Pontus), dated to the year 137, under the imperial legate
Fl. Arrianus (*ILS* 8801). Third, the successor Burbuleius Ligarianus
(*suff. c.*135), after holding the *cura operum publicorum*, arrives before
the decease of Hadrian (*ILS* 1066). Hadrian died in July of 138.

One scholar has Arrian's tenure begin in 130, another assigns
138–41 to Burbuleius.[110] No harm is done or deception entailed if
one allocates to Arrian the *sexennium* 131–7.

Along with Cappadocia, the large command embraced Armenia
Minor, Pontus Polemoniacus—and also Pontus Galaticus, with the
cities of Amaseia, Zela, and Sebastopolis. On the Euxine littoral
Roman posts went eastward beyond Trapezus across the river Phasis
as far as Dioscurias beneath the mountain of Caucasus. The kingdom
of Bosporus, however, fell under the supervision of the legate
governing Moesia Inferior.

Caesar's legate in Syria had charge of relations with the Parthians,
to face an intermittent threat of war or to conduct negotiations, and
he was sometimes invested with special authority. The role of the
Cappadocian command (instituted by Vespasian) should not be
neglected.[111] Two legions, stationed at Melitene and at Satala,
commanded the routes for | invading Armenia. The governor had
also a diplomatic function: not only Armenia but the vassal states
behind Armenia toward Caucasus.

Pharasmanes the Iberian had been recalcitrant, refusing to meet
Hadrian when he appeared on the frontier in 129.[112] The prince, who
controlled the Darial Pass, is under incrimination. In 135 he incited
the Alani. They came through the Caucasus, harried Armenia and
Media, menacing (so it seemed) the zone of the Roman frontier.[113]

Arrian mustered his army and deterred the Alani.[114] No battle
ensued; and there is no sign that Arrian seized the opportunity to
march through Armenia and approach the defiles of Caucasus.[115]

The governor has left a detailed account of the order of battle for
deployment against the Alani. The *Ectaxis* is variously instructive.
The legion at Satala, XV Apollinaris, is in prominence, and its legate
Vettius is named.[116] XII Fulminata had the left wing: the eagle is
mentioned, and the legion was under the command of its tribunes.[117]

[110] W. Eck, *Senatoren*, etc. (1970), 204; G. Alföldy, op. cit. 220.

[111] On which see A. B. Bosworth, 'Vespasian's Reorganization of the North-East Frontier,'
Antichthon x (1976), 63 ff.

[112] *HA Hadr.* 13, 9. Furthermore, he visited the coast of Pontus before Arrian's arrival, cf.
Peripl. 1,1 (Trapezus); 5, 2. Presumably not in 129 but in 131.

[113] Dio lxix 15, 1.

[114] E. Ritterling, *WS* xxiv (1902), 359 ff.; A. B. Bosworth, *HSCPh* lxxxi (1977), 217 ff.

[115] As argued by Bosworth in commentary on the *Anabasis*, 229 f. on the basis of a passage in
Themistius (*Or.* xxxiv 8 = test. 13 Roos).

[116] *Ect.* 5. That is, M. Vettius Valens (*CIL* xi 383: Ariminum).   [117] *Ect.* 6; 15; 24.

No word, however, of the legate, or of the *laticlavius* in either legion, although four commanders of auxiliary regiments earn a mention. Two years later the *laticlavius* of XV Apollinaris happens to be on record, namely M'. Acilius Glabrio (*cos.* 152). It is highly peculiar for a patrician to hold this appointment anywhere, let alone at bleak Satala on the edge of the Roman world. Hence legitimate curiosity.[118]

Anomalies crop up anywhere. They are recognized as such through regularities observed when evidence is abundant, as for example about the governors of several praetorian provinces under Hadrian and Pius.[119]

Cappadocia presents a welcome contrast to certain other consular provinces. After Catilius Severus who held the command from 114 to 117 (with Armenia briefly annexed), before proceeding to Syria and a second consulship in 120, there is a gap for three or four years. Then, thanks to recent accretions, there follows a complete run for two decades: |

?121–4. C. Bruttius Praesens (*suff.* 118 or 119). For his *cursus*, *IRT* 545; *AE* 1950, 66.
127/8 (L.?) Statorius Secundus (*suff.* ?c.123). *AE* 1968, 504 (nr. Sebastopolis).
129 T. Prifernius Paetus Rosianus Geminus (?125). *AE* 1976, 675 (Archelais).
?131–7 L. Flavius Arrianus (?129).
138 L. Burbuleius Optatus Ligarianus (*c.*135). *ILS* 1066.

Statorius Secundus is only a name. The others illustrate varieties of age and experience. Bruttius Praesens, a *laticlavius* with military decorations as early as 89, is found living at ease in Campania about the year 107, gently rebuked by Pliny for his Epicurean tastes (*Ep.* vii 3). His exploit in 114/15 and his governorship of Cilicia have already been noted. After the *cura operum publicorum* Praesens proceeded to Cappadocia: governor there when Hadrian in 123, breaking off his tour of the western provinces, came to the east and had a satisfactory interview on the Euphrates with the Parthian monarch.[120]

Prifernius Paetus, son by adoption to a consular, had been Pliny's quaestor in the year 100, under the name of 'Rosianus Geminus', as emerges from a petition of Pliny on his behalf a decade later (x 26). Nothing more is heard of the man until he becomes proconsul of Achaea *c.* 123 and survives to be proconsul of Africa in 141/2.[121] The

[118] *Chiron* x (1980), 427 ff. = *RP* iii (1984), 1316 ff. (discussing *ILS* 1072).
[119] *Historia* xiv (1965), 342 ff. = *Danubian Papers* (1971), 225 ff.   [120] *HA Hadr.* 12, 8.
[121] *ILS* 1067 (the *cursus* of his son-in-law Pactumeius Clemens).

surprise is to learn from an inscription that this unpromising person, coeval with Hadrian (*q.* 101), should have a military province in his middle fifties.

Burbuleius Ligarianus began as *triumvir capitalis*. This *novus homo* engages interest by the slow process of his career: no fewer than half a dozen praetorian posts (mostly minor) before acceding to the *fasces* in 134 or 135. He came from Africa, so it may be argued.[122] Comparable in certain ways is Ti. Claudius Quartinus (*suff.* 130), whose first post was equestrian. His tribe, the 'Palatina', may indicate libertine origin ultimately.[123]

Consular legates tend to be drawn from non-consular or equestrian families. Of some appointed by Hadrian, such as Praesens and Prifernius, one suspects that they had failed to win approval from his predecessor.

Other friends of the deceased Pliny may furnish instruction. About | the prospects of Erucius Clarus, Pliny, who had got him the *latus clavus* and the quaestorship (?99), was moved to express some disquiet (ii 9,2). Still only a legionary legate in 116, a vigorous exploit in Mesopotamia elevated him to a consulate the next year.[124] Erucius was the nephew of Septicius Clarus, whom Hadrian in 119 appointed to command the Guard as colleague of Marcius Turbo; and about the same time Suetonius Tranquillus (a diffident character in the letters of Pliny) became the secretary *ab epistulis*.[125]

A hostile tradition impugns Hadrian for ingratitude toward friends and allies. The indictment embraces a whole catalogue (*HA Hadr.* 15). Late in the year 136 Hadrian turned against his kinsfolk, choosing Ceionius Commodus as heir and successor, with dire consequences for old Julius Servianus and for the youth Pedanius Fuscus, the grandson of Hadrian's sister.

Hadrian had a propensity to omniscience (15,8). Conflicts with scholars and men of letters are duly reported—in some instances with manifest exaggeration.[126] Arrian had no further occupation after Cappadocia, so far as known. He is next discovered in retirement, archon at Athens.[127] Estrangement from the capricious ruler has been

[122] *Historia* xxvii (1978), 597 = *RP* iii (1984), 1113.
[123] *CIL* xiii 1802 (Lugdunum), cf. xiv 4473 (Ostia). Puteoli shows a *duumvir* of that name (x 1782 f.).
[124] Dio lxviii 32, 5.
[125] For the date of Turbo's appointment, recently contested, see *JRS* lxx (1980), 71 f. = *RP* iii (1984), 1287 f.
[126] G. W. Bowersock, *Greek Sophists in the Roman Empire* (1969), 51 ff.; R. Syme, *JRS* lxx (1980), 74 = *RP* iii (1984), 1291 f.
[127] In 145/6 (*IG* ii² 2055).

surmised.[128] Some may (or may not) have wondered about the attitude of Antoninus Pius. Bland but percipient, Pius could not quite suppress a distrust of sophists and philosophers.[129]

Before leaving Cappadocia Arrian wrote his *Tactica*. The manual divides sharply into two parts. The second, after a full exposition of cavalry tactics, praises military innovations due to the Emperor and concludes with a reference to his *vicennalia* (44, 3). That is, the anniversary falling in 136/7. The language conveys an unobtrusive solicitation for further employment, so it has been supposed.[130]

In fact, Arrian may have become legate of Syria not long after. According to Lucian, the notorious Peregrinus Proteus was once | released from prison by a governor of Syria who delighted in philosophy (*Per.* 14). Why not Arrian? The notion finds some favour.[131] It has also been deprecated.[132] However, to have Syria after Cappadocia is a natural and easy promotion, attested for Burbuleius Ligarianus and for others before or after.[133] Faint support may accrue from the new inscription at Corinth that designates Arrian as 'the philosopher'. Thus Arrian has recently been assigned Syria, c.138–141.[134]

That dating concerns other governors of Syria. Sex. Julius Severus (*suff.* 127), legate of Judaea and earning the *ornamenta triumphalia* for quelling the rebellion, proceeded to Syria. His inscription shows him there before the decease of Hadrian.[135] Account must also be taken of a fragment at Palmyra, bearing a date in April of 138 and disclosing the names of Bruttius Praesens and Julius Maior.[136] The former had been proconsul of Africa (133/4 or 134/5), the latter is attested as legate of Moesia Inferior in 134 and is further a known legate of Syria.[137] The two consulars, it can hardly be denied, were in succession governors of Syria in the last epoch of Hadrian.[138] Brief tenures are no bar. A senior consular like Bruttius Praesens, possessing diplomatic talents and eastern experience, may have been charged with negotiations with the Parthians.

[128] E. Schwartz, *RE* ii 1231.
[129] W. Williams, *JRS* lxvi (1976), 75.
[130] G. L. Wheeler, *GRBS* xix (1978), 351 ff.
[131] W. Hüttl, *Antoninus Pius* ii (1933), 156, following the opinion of G. A. Harrer.
[132] By A. Stein in *PIR*², F 219.   [133] *JRS* lxvii (1977), 46 = *RP* iii (1984), 1056.
[134] G. Alföldy, op. cit. 238 f.: 'mit grosser Wahrscheinlichkeit'.
[135] *ILS* 1056 (Burnum). The governorship of Syria (following 'Syria Palaestina') was unfortunately neglected in *PIR*², J 576.
[136] *AE* 1938, 137.
[137] *PIR*², J 397. Syria is certified by *IG* iv² 454 (Epidaurus).
[138] As assumed in *Historia* ix (1960), 575 = *RP* (1979), 490 f. See further *ZPE* xxxvii (1980) 10 f. = *RP* iii (1984), 1309 f., which registers different views about the position of Praesens and Maior.

A threat of hostilities is on record soon after the accession of Antoninus Pius, dispelled by a missive he sent to the Parthian monarch (*HA Pius* 9,6). Not before it provoked a display of energy from the tranquil ruler, as a casual piece of evidence proves. A legionary legate called Neratius Proculus was instructed to conduct reinforcements to Syria 'ob bellum Parthicum' (*ILS* 1076). Proculus, after holding the *aerarium militare*, was promoted to the consulate.

The 'prudentes', the men who know history and assess policy on a long view, may not have expected a war with a power that was normally | not aggressive. Yet it ensued early in the next reign, perhaps through miscalculations on both sides, the first action being the disaster incurred by a legate of Cappadocia, Sedatius Severianus (*suff.* 153), whom Lucian styled 'that silly Celt': a friend of the false prophet, a devotee of the sacred snake (*Alex.* 25).

The date of Arrian's *Parthica* now comes in again. As indicated, an easy assumption looks to the near aftermath of Trajan's war. Contemporary history is a hazardous enterprise, as Arrian stated in the exordium to the *Anabasis*. None the less, a loyal senator and a discreet expositor might be equal to the double challenge—the Imperator a great and glorious general, yet no disparagement of the actions and policy of Hadrian who renounced conquests that had already been lost or abandoned.

Later dates have been advocated, the question regarded as open. The *Parthica* might be a by-product of the Cappadocian governor-ship—or evoked by the Parthian War (162–6) which Lucius Verus conducted, or rather supervised.[139] The latter notion entailed for the historian a survival longer than most now contemplate. Moreover, a thought should have been spared for the crisis at the beginning of Pius' reign.

To sum up. On the hypothesis of a late dating, the *Parthica* might be regarded as comparable in some fashion to the *Discourses of Epictetus*, being in part recollection of a man's earlier years, especially if he had fought in Trajan's campaigns. On the other hand, those seventeen books were a major work of history—and the longest that Arrian wrote.[140]

Uncertainty also envelops the termination of Arrian's official employment. The chance has been noted that he was governor of Syria. Reflection may import a fairly strong doubt. Julius Maior may

---

[139] Thus P. Stadter, op. cit. 144. He there came to no conclusion, regarding the date of the *Parthica* as a puzzle. In a later place the early date is preferred (183).

[140] For a full and excellent appraisal, P. Stadter, op. cit. 135 ff.

have continued there for several years or have been replaced by Julius Severus before the death of Hadrian.[141]

Again, about the year 143 Arrian would become eligible for the | sortition for the proconsulates in Asia or Africa. For Asia the tenure 143/4 is available, preceding Claudius Quartinus (*suff.* 130) and (?Claudius) Julianus (?130).[142] For Africa, a long gap follows Tullius Varro (*suff.* 127), who should go in 142/3.[143] For the man of Nicomedia, Africa might appear less suitable. Not but that Africa rather than Asia may be the proconsulate of Julius Maior (*suff.* ?126), whose family was domiciled at Nysa and who traced a descent from Polemo, the king of Pontus, and Antonia Pythodoris.[144]

Some *viri militares* neither needed nor wanted a proconsulate—and a discreet hint from Caesar's friends could counsel withdrawal from the sortition. Again, age or health might deter. Cornelius Fronto, awarded Asia, hesitated before going there—and may never have left the shores of Italy.[145]

The proconsulates have been adduced, since they were the peak of a senator's ambition. Before that point Arrian may have made his decision. There are no grounds for attributing his Athenian retreat to supersession or frustration. After a *sexennium* in Cappadocia (double the normal tenure) either the senator or Caesar might conceive that he had had enough.

Parading as the modern Xenophon and even styling himself 'Xenophon' when governor of Cappadocia, Arrian in this reincarnation combines the author and the man of action.[146] He likewise exemplifies the double aspect of the times. The Hellenic renascence of letters, adumbrated by Plutarch and by Dio of Prusa, came to full bloom under Hadrian and Pius, producing the age of the sophists. The political aspect preceded. It exhibits eastern consuls of native

---

[141] There is a better solution. As follows. Severus died not long after passing from Judaea to Syria in 134 or 135. Hence the anomalous appointment of Bruttius Praesens. Julius Maior soon succeeded, holding Syria until 140 or 141. He was replaced by Burbuleius Ligarianus: 'in quo honor. decessit', as the inscription states (*ILS* 1066).

For mortality in the insalubrious province see 'Governors Dying in Syria', *ZPE* xli (1981), 125 ff. = *RP* iii (1984), 1376 ff.

[142] For those proconsuls, G. Alföldy, *Konsulat u. Senatorenstand* (1977), 212. The second of them is probably a Claudius Julianus rather than (as Alföldy) Ti. Julius Julianus.

[143] *ZPE* xxxvii (1980), 5 = *RP* iii (1984), 1306 (the proconsuls from 136/7 to 142/3).

[144] For that problem (Africa or Asia) see *ZPE* xxxvii (1980), 13 f. = *RP* iii (1984), 1312. Maior had been legate of Numidia, attested in 125 (*AE* 1950, 58) and in 126 (1954, 49).

[145] *Ad Antoninum* 8 = Haines i 236. Champlin, though cautious, inclines to believe that Fronto in fact went to Asia (op. cit. 164).

[146] The name is conveyed or implied already in *Peripl.* 1, 1; 12, 5; 25, 1. That is, perhaps a sign that he had already published the *Anabasis*.

stock, from Sardis and Pergamum, before the end of the Flavian dynasty.

Conventional history, built up largely on the biographies of emperors, was content for a long time to assign the main role and initiation to Hadrian. Facts emerging combine to declare a process, actions accelera|ted by accidents; and much credit is transferred from Hadrian to his martial predecessor. Trajan's reign is adorned by a group of four consulars, advertised on the inscription of their cousin Julius Severus of Ancyra, the descendant of kings and tetrarchs.[147] The conspicuous members of the nexus are A. Julius Quadratus, consul for the second time in 105, and the consul suffect C. Julius Quadratus Bassus. The latter, who commanded an army corps in Trajan's second war beyond the Danube, went on to govern Cappadocia, Syria, Dacia (dying on campaign in the winter of 117/18).[148]

Not all of the eastern magnates claim comparable splendour or merit. By lineage, in the forefront was C. Julius Antiochus Philopappus, grandson of the last ruler of Commagene (and with Seleucid ancestry), whose sepulchral monument stands on the Hill of the Muses.[149] A citizen of Athens, and archon, Philopappus was adlected to the Senate by Trajan and given a consulship in 109. Of active employment, no sign. Curiosity is aroused (and perhaps quenched) by the fact that Philopappus belonged to the priestly fraternity of the *Arvales*.[150]

The opulence and ostentation of these invaders may well have excited resentment, with enmity and feuds ensuing. Not even vestiges appear to survive. As elsewhere, the sparsity of the written sources has to be taken into account—and not least its character. To a satirist devoted to the Roman tradition the magnates of Asia would be an attractive target. Juvenal directs his shafts against the dead or the fictitious. Nor is illumination to be expected from Pliny. Approving of Greek culture with conventional and disciplined enthusiasm, he nowhere alludes to the eastern origin of any member of the 'amplissimus ordo'.

Hadrian himself, at divergence from Trajan in so many of his tastes and habits, may not have shared Trajan's liking for the descendants of kings and tetrarchs. There is a peculiar fact concerning the Galatian aristocrat C. Julius Severus (*suff.* ?138): late entry to the Senate through adlection *inter tribunicios* about the year 125.[151]

[147] *OGIS* 544 (Ancyra).   [148] *PIR*², J 508.   [149] *ILS* 845.
[150] As attested by the inscription—but no presence on the protocols of 101, 105, 110. Cf. *Some Arval Brethren* (1980), 113.   [151] *ILS* 8826 (Ancyra).

Hadrian's sympathies (it may be conjectured) went rather to Athens, to old Hellas, to the more modest and useful city aristocrats. Not that any sharp antithesis existed. Galatian tetrarchs had links with Pergamum long since; and Italian immigrants intermarried with dynastic families.[152] |

A dearth of evidence about consuls impedes the estimate. Apart from the years 127 and 128 (complete thanks to the *Fasti Ostienses*) hardly any *suffecti* are on record after 122 and before 138. Again, few governors of certain military provinces during the twenties.

Of the easterners, about ten consuls can be rounded up, a mixed bag. No *ordinarius* is among them, unless perhaps M. Antonius Rufinus (131) and M. Antonius Hiberus (133); and no *consul bis* apart from Catilius Severus in 120. By contrast, observe under Trajan the pair Julius Quadratus and Julius Candidus introducing the year 105.[153]

Hadrian paid special honour and deference to the Roman Senate, so it is averred. One of the proofs alleged is a mass of iterations in the *fasces*.[154] The facts refute.

After deplorable transactions in the first months (much worse than the dubious adoption) the new ruler stood in sore need of allies. It was also expedient to conciliate the whole senatorial order. By paradox, one method was to avoid exalting too many of the eminent with second consulates. Another would be to insist on regularity in the senatorial *cursus*.

In fact, Hadrian made no scandalous promotions, such as Trajan had—a Guard Prefect, Attius Suburanus, consul suffect in 101 and *ordinarius* two years later. Toward the end occurred other acts of flagrant favouritism, such as Terentius Gentianus, consul in 116 before he reached the age of thirty and Lusius Quietus, the Moorish chieftain, abruptly elevated in 117.[155]

Philhellenism has various and even contrasted facets—and so had the ruler himself: 'varius multiplex multiformis'. While certain features in Hadrian's conduct may disturb or repel, such as his infatuation with Antinous, the fact that he chose for friend a disciple of Epictetus acquires emphasis. Arrian, governor of Cappadocia and historian, is an attractive phenomenon in an age dominated by the sophists and

---

[152] As notably the Plancii of Perge, cf. S. Mitchell, *JRS* lxiv (1974), 27 ff.

[153] The latter, so it now appears, came from western Asia. Cf. Halfmann, no. 11; R. Syme, *Some Arval Brethren* (1980), 50 f.

[154] *HA Hadr.* 8, 4: 'tertio consules, cum ipse ter fuisset, plurimos fecit, infinitos autem secundi consulatus honore cumulavit.'

[155] *ILS* 1046a, inscribed on one of the Pyramids (Gentianus); Dio lxviii 32, 3 (Lusius).

paying homage to the pompous and verbose, to persons like Antonius Polemo, Aelius Aristides, Herodes Atticus.

Arrian selected Athens for domicile. That does not betoken estrange|-ment either from Rome and the Empire or from Nicomedia. Adequate reasons explain a predilection for Athens, and he had been away from Nicomedia for a long time.

It was to honour his *patria* that Arrian wrote about the antiquities and legends of Bithynia, the annals of the kingdom down to its annexation by Rome. Were it not for clear evidence in a passage of Photius, a temptation might have insinuated to suppose the *Bithyniaca* a late testimony of gratitude from an expatriate.[156]

Along with the *Bithyniaca*, the monographs on Dion and Timoleon are recognized among the earliest compositions of the polygraph.[157] If they concern Sicily, no special and personal interest in that island. Those biographies reflect rather the experience at Nicopolis, they bear upon the relationship between philosophical studies and the life of a general or a statesman.

Different avenues and complex motives lead to the writing of history. Not all authors begin with biography or local antiquities—and some go no further.

Soon or late in the reign of Antoninus Pius Arrian published the *Discourses of Epictetus*. When the elderly sage ended his days is beyond ascertainment: late or confused notices prolong his existence unduly.[158]

Unauthorized circulation of the books induced Arrian to publish at last, as an apologia explains in the letter addressed to L. Gellius Menander.[159] Another letter about Epictetus happens to be on record, to the address of 'Messalinus'.[160] That is, a personage of some eminence although known only from inscriptions: C. Prastina Pacatus Messallinus, the consul of 147.[161]

Friends of Arrian in the aristocracy of the consulars would be worth knowing. Speculation is legitimate but unproductive. Let it suffice to call up in passing Julius Maior (*suff.* ?126) or Julius Severus (?138), each of illustrious birth in Asia.

Matrimony created or reinforced alliances, some local, others

[156] Photius, reproduced in Roos ii 197 f. For the early date, A. B. Bosworth, *CQ* xxii (1972), 179 ff.; P. Stadter, op. cit. 182 f.
[157] Stadter, op. cit. 162.
[158] For the evidence, H. v. Arnim, *RE* vi 127 f.
[159] Reproduced in Roos ii 196.
[160] Roos, test. 4.
[161] This important and enigmatic person, known only from inscriptions, was legate of Moesia Inferior soon after his consulship. For the problems of his nomenclature and career, *Dacia* xii (1968), 336 = *Danubian Papers* (1971), 219 f.

transcending a province or a whole region in the world empire. No clue | leads to the wife or wives of Fl. Arrianus. There was issue, on record at Athens.[162]

While Hadrian made a painful exit during the ominous sixty-third year of life, Arrian enjoyed length of days and continuing productivity. Although not earning admittance to the intellectuals registered in Lucian's catalogue of 'Macrobii', he may have lived on into the reign of Marcus and Verus, reaching or surpassing the age of eighty. If outdoor pastimes contribute to longevity (that is a common belief), there is something to be said for addiction to polite studies, in defiance of sloth or mere recreation. Sustenance derives from writing—or even from compilation.

Estimates of Arrian's birth have exhibited a wide range, from 85 to 95.[163] The later year was never plausible. Better, between 85 and 90.[164] So far the present disquisition has operated with the year 86, for the manifest and avowed convenience of the 'suus annus' for a senator consul in 129. It was a further assumption (duly to be recalled) that Arrian entered the Senate during the Parthian War or soon after, by adlection.

The argument falls short of proof (and a retarded quaestorship is not excluded). There is something else. Parallel instances of promoted equestrians (whatever the mode of entrance), show them acceding to the *fasces* some years later than the standard age. A suspicion subsists that Arrian saw the light of day as early as 82 or 83.

Arrian's sojourn at Nicopolis in 107 or 108 will no doubt continue to be invoked—a student aged about eighteen, hence born about 89. That is, 'iuvenis admodum' to adopt the parlance of the Latins, referring to a *laticlavius* just before the military tribunate.[165] In that season a youth was liable to be captivated by teachers (or by doctrines and fashions), whether in oratory or in philosophy.[166]

Julius Agricola, when 'prima in iuventa', embraced philosophy with more ardour than was suitable in a Roman and a senator.[167] A vigilant mother curbed his ingenuous aspirations. Others may have had | a retarded approach to the hazards of conversion, among them

---

[162] Halfmann, no. 88.

[163] He was put 'c.95–175' in *CAH* xi (1936), 688.

[164] Stadter suggests 'born about A.D. 89, although perhaps as early as 85, or as late as 92' (op. cit. 3). Cf., in the chronological table (173), 'ca. 89'; and he is assumed to be about eighteen when with Epictetus at Nicopolis (5).

[165] Thus Cornelius Tacitus in *Dial.* 1,2 (assuming the year 75 as the dramatic date).

[166] Observe Helvidius Priscus: 'ingenium inlustre altioribus studiis iuvenis admodum dedit' (*Hist.* iv 5).

[167] *Agr.* 4, 3.

the country gentleman from Nicomedia who was devoted to horses and dogs. A rapid allegiance was not forsworn in the sequel although perhaps impaired by a senator's life and by experience of men and government.

3

Hadrianic Governors of Syria

WORSE things can befall a new emperor than a suspicious death-bed adoption—and Hadrian was the next of kin, left in charge of Syria when Trajan departed. Nor was his surrender of eastern conquests insuperable. Time would abate anger or disappointment, at least in some quarters. For another transaction, no apologia availed. In the first year of the reign four of Trajan's generals were put to death on charges of treason.

When the legate of Dacia, Julius Quadratus Bassus, died on campaign, Hadrian appointed a knight, Marcius Turbo. It was a special command, which embraced Pannonia Inferior. There is no sign of a military emergency that could not have been dealt with by a senator. Hadrian confronted a dire shortage of friends in the upper order. Of the other ten consular commands, the principal (three legions each) were Britain, Pannonia Superior, Moesia Inferior, Syria. To Britain Hadrian sent Pompeius Falco (*suff.* 108), from Moesia Inferior. Minicius Natalis (*suff.* 106) was in charge of Pannonia Superior when Trajan died: perhaps continued for a season.[1] Neither here nor in Moesia Inferior is the next governor on attestation. As for Syria, Hadrian appointed Catilius Severus (*suff.* 110), brought from the Cappadocian command and soon accorded a second consulate, in 120. Who took the place of Catilius in Cappadocia, and two years later in Syria, is not known. |

At different times the evidence about consular legates exhibits wide variations.[2] Fairly abundant hitherto, it now lapses for a long spell in a number of the commands. The lacuna is most to be deplored for Syria and for Pannonia Superior. For Syria the next legate to emerge after 119 is Publicius Marcellus in 132, when the rebellion broke out in Judaea. The other province is even worse served. After Minicius

[1] A new diploma shows him already there in 113 (as W. Eck informs me). Now published by K. Dietz, *RGK Ber.* lxv (1984), 159 ff.

[2] Recourse should be had all through to W. Eck, *Senatoren von Vespasian bis Hadrian* (1970); G. Alföldy, *Konsulat und Senatorenstand unter den Antoninen* (1977). Those excellent works obviate the need for much detail of annotation.

Romanitas–Christianitas. Untersuchungen zur Geschichte und Literatur der römischen Kaiserzeit Johannes Straub zum 70. Geburtstag . . . gewidmet, ed. G. Wirth (1982), 230–43.

Natalis (attested in 117) until the appointment of Aelius Caesar in 137 there is only Cornelius Proculus, disclosed by a military diploma in 133.

For Cappadocia two names have recently accrued, viz. L. Statorius Secundus (*suff.* ?*c.*123) and T. Prifernius Paetus (*suff.* ?125): a sequence thus stands complete, with five legates covering the period 121–41.[3] Elsewhere either a new discovery or the revision of a known text may subvert results accepted until then as the best obtainable. The repercussions are sometimes wide. Three specimens will furnish instruction.

(1) M. Cornelius Nigrinus Curiatius Maternus, known from inscriptions at Liria as legate of Moesia and of Syria (*CIL* ii 3783; 6013). The date long remained a vexatious problem. In the standard repertory Nigrinus was assigned to the first half of the second century (*PIR*[2], C 1407). Furthermore the twenties offered an easy lodgement, because of gaps both in Moesia Superior and in Syria.[4]

Another inscription yields the full career of this remarkable military man, now recognized as a consul suffect of 83 (*AE* 1973, 283: Liria). The consequences are multiple.[5] Briefly put, they concern the Dacian campaigns under Domitian and the identity of the Syrian governor during the crisis of the year 97.

(2) L. Neratius Priscus the jurist (*suff.* 97). An inscription at Saepinum registers two homonymous consulars (*ILS* 1034). The second was legate 'P[annonia]/inferiore et Pannonia [superiore]', hence taken for a son of the jurist and a Hadrianic governor of Pannonia Superior (*PIR*[1], | N 47). That fact was accepted and transmitted in standard works or in disquisitions on the Neratii.[6]

A recent revision of the document expels and suppresses the Hadrianic governor. The name and the posts appertain to the jurist. Consul in 97, he held Germania Inferior (?98–101) before proceeding to govern the undivided Pannonia.[7] Again, multiple consequences.[8] They concern:

(A) the army commander Priscus to whom Pliny in 100 wrote a letter commending his friend Voconius Romanus (*Ep.* ii 13).

---

[3] *AE* 1968, 504 (nr.Sebastopolis); 1976, 675 (Archelais). Statorius and Prifernius fill the space between Bruttius Praesens (?121–4) and Flavius Arrianus (?131–7), who was succeeded by Burbuleius Ligarianus. The five governors will find subsequent mention in this paper.

[4] As proposed in *Dacia* xii (1968), 332 = *Danubian Papers* (1971), 214.

[5] G. Alföldy and H. Halfmann, *Chiron* iii (1973), 331 ff.

[6] E.g. in the full discussion of the Neratii in *Hermes* lxxxv (1957), 480 ff. = *RP* (1979), 339 ff.

[7] G. Camodeca, *AAN* lxxxvii (1976), 19 ff., whence *AE* 1976, 195.

[8] Discussed in *ZPE* xli (1981), 141 f. = *RP* iii (1984), 1390.

(B) the career of Javolenus Priscus (*suff.* 86), governor of Germania Superior and of Syria (*ILS* 1015).

(C) the identity of Trajan's first legate of Syria, from 98 to 100.

(3) C. Ummidius Quadratus (*suff.* 118). An Ummidius Quadratus, governor of Moesia Inferior, emerged at Charax in the Crimea (*Arch. Anz.* 1911, 236). He was assigned to the reign of Antoninus Pius, on various grounds. For a long time no hesitations were voiced. Then came a conjecture: identity with the consul suffect of 118.[9] That is, holding the province (?121–4) in succession to the 'Se]rtorius' attested in 120 on two fragments of a bilingual inscription at Tomis (*CIL* iii 7539; 12493). The left-hand piece has now turned up, revealing the full nomenclature and one legate instead of two: C. Ummidius Quadratus Sertorius Severus (*AE* 1977, 745). Quadratus, being the grandson of Ummidia Quadratilla (Pliny, *Ep.* vii 24), had previously been assumed polyonymous.[10]

In this fashion two names recede from the rubric while a third receives endorsement; and the hazards inherent in this form of experimental science are sharply exposed.

The long gaps impair an assessment of Hadrian's government. Curiosity cannot be quenched about his selection of legates, their character and quality. Three friends have been noted above, in office | at the end of the previous reign, viz. Natalis, Falco, Catilius. As concerns new appointments, Hadrian's motives may be variously canvassed—with due respect to the sparsity of evidence in the first dozen years.

His notorious philhellenism is not on conspicuous show. Only two Greeks can be detected, viz. Sex. Julius Maior and L. Flavius Arrianus (on whom see further below). Nor is there any preponderance of the men from Spain and Narbonensis who contributed so powerfully to the ascension of the new dynasty. The excellent general Sex. Julius Severus (*suff.* 127), who held in succession four military provinces, came from Dalmatia (*ILS* 1056); and one might observe towards the end of the reign the earliest known consular legates from Africa.[11]

The collection is miscellaneous and it would take in a number of Italians of no great prestige. Statorius Secundus, the legate of

---

[9] *Historia* xvii (1968), 88 f. = *RP* (1979), 88 f.

[10] For a detailed enquiry about Quadratus, see *HSCPh* lxxxiii (1979), 287 ff. = *RP* iii (1984), 1158 ff.

[11] Viz. Lollius Urbicus (*suff. c.* 135), from Cirta (*ILS* 1065) and Burbuleius Ligarianus (*suff.* ?135). For an African origin for the latter, cf. the argument adduced in *Historia* xxvii (1978), 597 = *RP* iii (1984), 1113.

Cappadocia, is the first consul in his family, and the last, with no known kinsfolk.[12] His successor, Prifernius Paetus, had been slow to advance in the career of honours: he was the quaestor attached to the consul Pliny in 100.[13] Another friend of the orator, Bruttius Praesens, after earlier retardation, came back as legate of a legion in 114 and acceded to the *fasces* in 118 or 119 when aged about fifty.[14]

Praesens was an Epicurean, as the language of Pliny's letter demonstrates when he urged him to return to public life (vii 3). That would render him highly congenial to Hadrian. Other appointments (Septicius Clarus to the Guard, Suetonius Tranquillus to be secretary *ab epistulis*) show Hadrian's affection for writers or for cultivated persons in their ambiance.

As previously, it is not easy to discover an army commander from a consular family. The exception is the illustrious Ummidius Quadratus, | whose great-grandfather had been consul *c.*40. Quadratus first emerges as a young man of promise in eloquence about the year 106, matched to form an 'egregium par' with Pedanius Fuscus (Pliny, *Ep.* vi 11,1). In this season Fuscus married Julia, the niece of Hadrian (vi 26). The bride of his coeval (vii 24, 3) evades ascertainment. Quadratus formed, or perhaps reinforced, a link with a potent nexus in the alliance of Hadrian. His appointment to Moesia Inferior in 120, when aged about thirty-six, fits into an ample texture of fact and speculation.[15]

The value and significance of the Syrian command was political. In normal times it did not call for military experience. The Caesars preferred safe men, and often the elderly; and diplomatic talents might find useful employ. Trajan's second, legate from 100 to 104, was A. Julius Quadratus (*suff.* 94). The magnate from Pergamum (his *cursus* is extant) had never seen an army. Julius Quadratus may serve as an admonition. Routine develops in the imperial system, and regularities of promotion, but anything can happen. A recent survey of consular legates analyses the different paths of their access to

[12] The indistinctive *nomen* happens to be a rarity. It offers two specimens in *CIL* V, at Mediolanum (5869; 5888). Observe, inscribed by the same lapicide, *CIL* vi 16632 (Statoria M. f. Marcella); 16631 = *ILS* 1030 (Minicia Marcella, daughter of Fundanus). C. Minicius Fundanus (*suff.* 107) had married Statoria Marcella, so it appears. He came from Ticinum, cf. *Tacitus* (1958), 801.

[13] Pliny, *Ep.* x 26, 1. There as elsewhere he appears as 'Rosianus Geminus'. The full style of the consular, 'T. Prifernius Paetus Rosianus Geminus', indicates that he was adopted by T. Prifernius Paetus (*suff.* 96). The family is Sabine, from Trebula Mutuesca: cf. now *AE* 1972, 153.

[14] For his *cursus, IRT* 545 (Lepcis); *AE* 1950, 66 (Mactar).

[15] As developed in *HSCPh* lxxxiii (1979), 287 ff. = *RP* iii (1984), 1158 ff.

provinces, and it puts emphasis on civilian accomplishments.[16] That is no surprise. The rulers in the second and third dynasties emulated the aristocratic Caesars in predilection for the higher education.

That survey embraced a wide tract of time, from 70 to 235. A narrower approach (but not too narrow) can be variously instructive. While general competence and personal loyalty count for more than talent or special experience, patterns of promotion in the service of the Caesars may none the less be detected. For example, in the Flavio-Trajanic period a senator later found in charge of a military command has had a clear run to the consulate through two posts (a legion and a praetorian province), or through three at the most.[17]

Again, emergent under Hadrian and on full show under his successor, the role of the *cura operum publicorum* at Rome. That post is now held | immediately after the consulate, and it has become collegiate, the tenure (nowhere documented) to be presumed biennial.[18] A number of senators come to a consulship by way of the prefecture of the *aerarium Saturni* and after a spell as *curatores* go on to govern consular provinces.[19] Clearly a favoured category, being permitted to sojourn at the capital—and well suited to an epoch of peace and stability.

However, chance or accident intervenes all the time, patronage and personalities may decide. Caution is prescribed.

By the same token, variation in the length of governorships. According to a notion promulgated by the *Historia Augusta* (and sometimes accorded credence) Antoninus Pius kept good governors in office for periods of seven or nine years (*Pius* 5, 3). The facts refute.[20]

By good fortune and by irony, the reign of Hadrian produces two specimens lacking parallel under Pius: the one a praetorian legate, the other consular. First, Sex. Julius Severus (*suff.* 127). After the remodelling carried out by Marcius Turbo, Severus governed Dacia Superior from 119 to 126.[21] Second, L. Flavius Arrianus (*suff.* 129 or 130). He held Cappadocia for a *sexennium*, probably from 131 to 137.[22]

[16] B. Campbell, *JRS* lxv (1975), 11 ff.

[17] E.g. *Tacitus* (1958), 650. For 'predestination' in careers, E. Birley, *PBA* xxxix (1953), 197 ff.; cf. p. 31 above.

[18] For tenure just after the consulate, Bruttius Praesens (*IRT* 545) and Metilius Secundus (*ILS* 1053). The first attested pair comes up about the year 128 (*AE* 1973, 36).

[19] For revealing statistics, *Historia* xiv (1965), 365 = *Danubian Papers* (1971), 241.

[20] A. R. Birley, *Corolla Swoboda* (1966), 43 ff.

[21] Diplomas register him both in 120 and in 126, cf. *PIR*[2], J 576.

[22] Neither year is quite firm. Eck prefers 130 for the beginning (op. cit. 204). He was certainly still in Cappadocia in 137 (*ILS* 8801). The successor arrived before July of 138 (*ILS* 1066).

With these remarks for preliminary guidance, brief consideration can go to governors of Syria, in the first place to the lacuna subsequent to 119. Although no new name can be established, a digression of this kind need not be either vacuous or misleading. Factors of relevance can be brought up, or consulars in danger of being overlooked.

(1) Cappadocia. Transfer of a legate to Syria appears an easy and attractive device for the government in any season. Of four under Antoninus Pius whose antecedent province is on record, two came from | Cappadocia.[23] Hence a temptation to cast about for other or for earlier instances. For example, to occupy the vacancy between the death of Atilius Rufus in 84 and the next governor, P. Valerius Patruinus (*suff.* 82), who is attested in 88.[24]

The present enquiry led off with Catilius Severus, who passed from Cappadocia to Syria in 117, with no successor known in either post. The next legate of Cappadocia is Bruttius Praesens (*suff.* ?118), going there after the *cura operum publicorum* and proceeding to Moesia Inferior (?for the tenure 124–8).[25] In 123 Hadrian broke off his tour of the western provinces, came to Syria and had an interview with the Parthian monarch on the Euphrates. The identity of the governor in Syria would be worth knowing.

(2) C. Ummidius Quadratus (*suff.* 118). Since Hadrian by a notable decision chose to send Quadratus to Moesia Inferior in 120 (or, for all that can be known, in 119), why not to Syria in the sequel? The exordium of the reign presented an emergency. A second, following after no longer interval, leaves no trace in written history. Pedanius Fuscus shared the *fasces* with his wife's uncle in 118, not later to be heard of. On a painless assumption Fuscus and Julia succumbed together to disease or a pestilence.

The eclipse of the heir-apparent enhanced the value and the prospects of Ummidius Quadratus. He was to become patently 'capax imperii' during the intrigues and complications that infested the last *biennium* of the reign. In 136 or 137 his son married a sister of young Annius Verus (*HA Marcus* 4, 7, cf. 7, 4). Hadrian, frustrated by the decease of Aelius Caesar, chose for successor Aurelius Fulvus (*cos.* 120), a coeval of Quadratus. Fulvus, with no experience abroad save a year as proconsul in Asia, possessed a signal

---

[23] G. Alföldy, op. cit. 220; 239.
[24] Caesennius Gallus, legate of Cappadocia from 80 to 83, is admissible, cf. *JRS* lxvii (1977), 46 = *RP* iii (1984), 1056. The Caesennii were linked to the Flavian dynasty.
[25] *IRT* 545; *AE* 1950, 66.

advantage: no son. Hadrian was making provision for two boys, for the son of Aelius Caesar and for Annius Verus.

(3) P. Metilius Secundus (*suff.* 123). His rapid career after the praetorship (a legion and Numidia) indicated a future consular legate (*ILS* 1053). The name of the province to which he went after being *curator operum publicorum* is missing on the inscription. Hence at first sight | no grounds for conjecture, and Metilius tends to be left out of account. On recourse to the original publication (*CIL* xi 3718), the structure, in nine long lines, shows that the province should be a very short name. That is, either 'Iudaeae' or 'Syriae'.

The former is preferable. If accepted, Metilius was governor of Judaea (from 126 to 129 or 130): the predecessor of Q. Tineius Rufus (*suff.* 127), the legate in office when the rebellion began. The alternative is less plausible, although Syria as a consular's first province could not quite be excluded.

The above excursus was presented for a variety of avowed reasons, and not in the design or hope of certifying a new name anywhere in the long lacuna between Catilius Severus and Publicius Marcellus. The second problem is of a different order. It concerns identities and sequence in the last epoch, from 135 to 138.

When Publicius Marcellus (*suff.* 120) was governor in 132, he was called away to deal with insurgents in Judaea, Tineius Rufus having got into difficulties (*ILS* 8826). How long Marcellus had been in Syria, there is no means of telling. Three legates may have had the occupancy since 119. The short record of Marcellus' consular posts shows him previously governor of Germania Superior (*AE* 1934, 231): in fact the first on knowledge since the last years of Trajan.

Hadrian gave Marcellus the *ornamenta triumphalia*. The more remarkable since he was not generous with any military decorations: two praetorian legates in the Jewish War received less than the normal award.[26] Hadrian himself took one imperatorial salutation. It is not attested before the year 135. Warfare had dragged on. Marcellus may not have been superseded in Syria until 135. *Ornamenta* from Hadrian conveyed a due recognition, and they imply that a war has terminated.

Sex. Julius Severus (*suff.* 127) also received the award (*ILS* 1056). After Moesia Inferior and Britain he was brought to Judaea in 133.[27] The inscription shows that he acceded to Syria before the decease of | Hadrian (in July of 138). On the easy and natural assumption Severus

[26] Thus Lollius Urbicus (*ILS* 1045) and the *Ignotus* of Pisaurum (*CIL* xi 6339).
[27] The successor was P. Mummius Sisenna (*cos.* 133), cf. the comments of A. R. Birley, *The Fasti of Roman Britain* (1981), 110.

stayed in the East and went straight to Syria. He has been accorded a tenure lasting from 135 to 138.[28]

Perplexity now obtrudes: the Syrian governorship of Sex. Julius Maior, who became consul suffect after holding Numidia (attested in 125 and in 126: hence probably in 126).[29] The fragmentary inscription of his son enumerates his provincial governorships (*IG* iv² 454: Epidaurus). The list probably began with Numidia, to be supplied in the lacuna in line 5 which ends with Moesia, that word itself divided between two lines. In line 6 a gap then intervenes after Moesia, but ends by registering Syria and a proconsulate (i.e. either Asia or Africa).

The condition of the document does not reveal which of the two Moesian provinces Maior held. However, a diploma puts him in Moesia Inferior in April of the year 134 (*CIL* xvi 78). That is not all. There is much space in line 6 between Moesia and Syria. On one explanation, Maior governed in succession the two Moesian provinces.[30] Yet the registering of both is hardly sufficient to fill out the space. A longer word seems to be demanded. Perhaps therefore Pannonia. On a venturesome hypothesis, Julius Maior went on from Moesia Inferior in 134 or 135 to govern Pannonia Superior for two or three years.[31]

However, let that conjecture be waived for the present. The dating of the Syrian governorship is in question—and by ill fortune that governorship is not registered in the standard lists either under Hadrian or under Pius. Both reject it, despite the Epidaurian inscription. A reason may be divined, namely preoccupation with disallowing another piece of evidence. A fragment at Palmyra, dated to April of the year 138, disclosed two consulars, 'Bruttius Praesens' and 'Iulius M[' (*AE* 1938, 137). At first sight, successive legates of Syria.[32] Disquiet ensued, and | dissent. The pair, so it was suggested, were sent out on a special mission.[33] Their function defies any closer

---

[28] W. Eck, op. cit. 212; G. Alföldy, op. cit. 239.

[29] Thus *PIR*², J 397. With, however, the proper remark 'nisi remittendus est ad annum 129', E. Birley *JRS* lii (1962), 221 n. 9.

[30] Thus W. Hüttl, *Antoninus Pius* ii (1933), 22. But he got the order wrong. He supplemented Μυ|σίας τ|ῆς κάτω καὶ τῆς ἄνω καὶ] Συρίας. Maior could have had Moesia Superior c. 128–131, preceding P. Tullius Varro (*ILS* 1047), suffect in 127.

[31] That is, until the appointment of Aelius Caesar.

[32] A. Stein, *Die Legaten von Moesien* (1940), 67. Followed in *Historia* ix (1960), 375 = *RP* (1979), 490 f. (on Bruttius Praesens).

[33] W. Eck, op. cit. 232; G. Alföldy, op. cit. 241: 'zweifellos nicht als Statthalter, sondern vermutlich als Sonderlegaten'. Followed in his list of governors by J.-B. Rey Coquais, *JRS* lxviii (1978), 65.

definition, and the notion appears aberrant.[34] Epidaurus vindicates
Maior; and in the vicinity of the year 136 the young son of Praesens
(*cos.* 153) saw service as a military tribune in III Gallica, one of the
Syrian legions (*ILS* 1117).

In contrast to the period of dearth, Syria is beset by a plethora of
governors between 135 and 138. No cause for alarm. In certain
seasons a rapid change need not be enigmatic or defy explanation.
Alternatives offer. On the first, Severus did not go straightway from
Judaea to Syria: he was preceded by Praesens and by Maior. That
would entail abridged tenures for both governors. The second
acquires preference. It will be expounded in these terms.

(1) Sex. Julius Severus. He died in 135 or 136 soon after his
appointment.[35] At any time Syria was insalubrious or even lethal;
and pestilence follows in the train of warfare. Some are prepared to
assume that sequel to Trajan's Parthian War, the Imperator himself
being one of the early victims; and the decease of Quadratus Bassus
in Dacia will be suitably recalled.

(2) Bruttius Praesens. The death of a consular legate brings
annoyance to emperors and their counsellors, enforcing quick or
contestable decisions. Praesens was appointed, by anomaly, after a
proconsulate in Africa (133/4 or 134/5) had crowned a senator's
career.

Foreign affairs furnish a reason. Strained relations with Parthia
may be surmised. In 135 the Alani came over the Caucasus, raiding
Albania and Armenia. Rome's recalcitrant vassal Pharasmanes, the
ruler of Iberia, let them through the Portae Caspiae, so Dio states
(lxix 15, 1). To protect Cappadocia the legate Fl. Arrianus duly
mustered his army; and he was retained in his command for the next
two years (*ILS* 8801).

Further, a fragment of Dio shows the Parthian monarch raising
complaint to Rome about the behaviour of Pharasmanes (lxix 25, 2).
It | is uncertain whether the fragment belongs to the reign of Hadrian
or to that of his successor. However that may be, Antoninus Pius
had to face at once the threat of war. He deterred the Parthian by a
firm missive—but he also despatched reinforcements to Syria (*HA
Pius* 9, 1; *ILS* 1076).

Bruttius Praesens was endowed with valuable experience of
eastern affairs, having been legate of Cappadocia in 123. Furthermore, a close friend of Hadrian and capable of lending support and
comfort to the Emperor, now broken in health, vexed with the

[34] Cf. brief remarks in *ZPE* xxxvii (1980), 10 = *RP* iii (1984), 1309 f.
[35] As suggested in *HSCPh* lxxxvi (1982), 205 = p. 44, above.

problems of the succession, and ready to face extinction. Praesens did not stay long in Syria.

(3) Julius Maior. He followed Praesens either in 136 or 137, it may be supposed. That Maior or any other consular legates would be quickly superseded by Pius is not likely.[36] He may have continued in Syria until 141, when he became proconsul of either Asia or Africa. Maior had illustrious ancestry, going back to Polemo the king of Pontus and Antonia Pythodoris.[37] Asia was appropriate for one of its aristocrats, but Africa is not excluded.[38] Maior, unlike any of the eastern magnates hitherto, had been governor of Numidia before his consulship.

If Julius Maior held Syria from 136 or 137 until 141, consequences follow of some interest. He rules out a candidate who has found favour for the post, none other than Fl. Arrianus (*suff.* 129 or 130). Arrianus had a prolonged tenure of Cappadocia, probably from 131 to 137: he is attested there in the latter year (*ILS* 8801). His successor was L. Burbuleius Optatus Ligarianus (*suff.* ?135), who arrived before the death of Hadrian (*ILS* 1066). Burbuleius might be assigned Cappadocia until 140 or 141.

Burbuleius then went to Syria where he died, as the inscription states. How soon in his tenure, or how late, there is no sign. Nor is the successor known. He has been discovered in the person of D. Velius Fidus.[39] | A dedication to him, found at Heliopolis (his *patria*), was adduced (*CIL* iii 14387e). In error, it now seems clear. Velius Fidus was a governor not of Syria but of Syria Palaestina (the new name for Judaea).[40]

To return to Arrianus. In Lucian's essay on Peregrinus Proteus a friendly governor of Syria liberates the impostor from imprisonment: he is described as a man who took delight in philosophy (*Per.* 14). Why not Arrian, passing to Syria from his Cappadocian command? The notion conveyed a certain attaction, but not all scholars were disposed to concur.[41]

The notion has cropped up again, winning encouragement from an acephalous inscription at Corinth. A prominent citizen paid

[36] It is hardly necessary to adduce the *HA*: 'factus imperator nulli eorum quos Hadrianus provexerat successorem dedit' (*Pius* 5, 3).
[37] For the stemma, *PIR*², J 397 (from *IG* iv², 454).
[38] Asia is preferred by Alföldy, op. cit. 211.   [39] Alföldy, op. cit. 200; 263.
[40] As demonstrated by Eck, *ZPE* xlii (1981), 237 f. The man was governor of Syria Palaestina in 150 (*PSI* ix 1026 = *CIL* xvi, p. 146), cf. J. Rea, *ZPE* xxvi (1977), 217 f.
[41] Observe Stein in *PIR*², F 219: 'eum in Syria legatum Augusti fuisse G. A. Harrer Class. Phil. 11 (1916), 338 sq. coniectura plane incerta e Lucian. Peregr. 14 . . . efficere posse sibi visus est (cf. Hüttl 1. 1.).'

honour to a legate of Cappadocia who is styled 'the philosopher'. Patently Arrian.[42] Hence the firm hypothesis that Arrian held Syria from 138 to 141, to be succeeded by Burbuleius.[43]

Against which, Julius Maior comes into play: certainly a governor, and to be accorded without discomfort a tenure from 136 or 137 to 141. It looks as though Arrian has to lapse. Otherwise the only remedy is a retarded governorship inherited from the deceased Burbuleius.

To resume. On the reconstruction here advocated, the sequence runs as follows:

135	Julius Severus
	Bruttius Praesens
? 137–141	Julius Maior
141–	Burbuleius

Epilogue

In the first critical years of the reign, as in the last, Bruttius Praesens showed sterling worth. He was legate of Cilicia when | in August of 117 Trajan breathed his last at Selinus, a city of that province; and, it may be supposed, Praesens accompanied his friend to Rome in prospect of a speedy consulship (which perhaps ensued in the second half of 118 rather than in the next year). Before long two armed provinces advertised and confirmed his value (Cappadocia and Moesia Inferior). Finally, after Africa and Syria, Praesens became consul for the second time, in 139, sharing the *fasces* with Antoninus Pius. A scandalous tradition impugns Hadrian for base ingratitude towards friends and allies.[44] It is a pleasing thought that the honour may be recognition from the moribund friend, not from the new ruler.

Praesens was now aged about seventy. Thus terminated a paradoxical career that began with a tribunate (and military decorations) in 89 and proceeded, not without intermissions, until he commanded VI Ferrata in 114. Julius Severus, his junior by about fifteen years, took up the challenge, succeeding Praesens in Moesia Inferior soon after his consulship. When death cut him short Severus had run through no fewer than four provincial commands in seven or eight years. No previous military man had gone beyond three.

---

[42] *AE* 1968, 473, cf. G. W. Bowersock, *GRBS* viii (1967), 279 f. An Athenian inscription also attaches the label (*AE* 1971, 437).

[43] Alföldy, op. cit. 238: 'mit großer Wahrscheinlichkeit'.

[44] For a catalogue, *HA Hadr.* 15: presumably taken from Marius Maximus. Several items inspire distrust.

A third consular is now rescued from unmerited neglect. For Julius Maior two consular provinces are clear (Moesia Inferior and Syria). As has been shown, one more is needed, and perhaps two, to fill the gap on the inscription. Maior acceded to the consulate from Numidia, succeeding Metilius Secundus (*suff.* 123). No previous military post is discoverable. His coeval Julius Severus began as a tribune about the time of Trajan's second war against Dacia and commanded a Pannonian legion (XIV Gemina) before proceeding to take charge of Dacia Superior in 119.

The literary record for the reign is miserable and misleading. Dio happens to mention Julius Severus and his transference from Britain to Judaea (lxix 13, 2). Otherwise, only inscriptions reveal the governorships of the three consulars. Bruttius Praesens in his earlier and quiet existence had a letter from Pliny, but no author names Julius Maior. Epigraphy may hold in reserve persons who will amplify or modify, as before, the rubric of consular legates. It was not until 1932 that Pergamum surprised the learned world with Julius Quadratus Bassus | (*suff.* 105), leader of an army against the Dacians, legate of Cappadocia, of Syria, of Dacia.[45]

When evidence about Syria is abundant it shows mortality in high frequency. A survey of the century elapsing between the deaths of Germanicus and of Trajan registers four governors dying in the period 33–84 (as certified in the pages of Tacitus) and is emboldened to subjoin several conjectures.[46] The theme now expands to take in Burbuleius; and the decease of Julius Severus shortly after the end of the Jewish War will explain the anomalous emergence of Bruttius Praesens.

---

[45] On whom (*PIR*[2], J 508), see now Chr. Habicht, *Pergamon* viii 3 (1969), no. 21.
[46] 'Governors dying in Syria', *ZPE* xli (1981), 125 ff. = *RP* iii (1984), 1376 ff. The present paper may be taken as a sequel, in more ways than one.

4

Rome and the Nations

THE coming year introduces a notable name for commemoration—
Simón Bolívar. Since his birth only two centuries have elapsed, it is
true. Yet I propose to go back two millennia or more, to Rome:
imperial Republic and world empire.

The past is too much with us, so it may be objected anywhere, and
not least in the New World. Why bring up 'portions and parcels of
the dreadful past' (I adopt the phrase of an English poet)? The lessons
of history, it will pertinently be observed, are either obvious or
fallacious. That maxim need not deter rational enquiry. The
experience of antiquity offers valid comparisons, if and when the
social and political setting is similar. On that count, human history
becomes real, alive, intelligible.

There will be no call to indulge in vast and comprehensive
divagations in the manner of Arnold Toynbee. His vogue is passing,
he joins the company of others who created doctrines and systems.

On a modest exposition, Rome is strictly relevant to Latin
America, and congenial. To her conquests and colonies Spain gave
the language and religion, the institutions—and the cities, on the
Roman model. |

Bolívar himself can furnish a text for the present discourse.
Aristocrats or politicians are not in the habit of walking, in any
epoch. But on an August day of the year 1808 Bolívar went outside
the walls of Rome and climbed a hill in the company of Rodríguez,
his friend and mentor. The site, Monte Mario, evoked history—the
Mons Sacer, to which the rebellious plebeians made their secession.

Bolívar embarked on an oration. In the history of Rome, he
declared, everything had been seen—but Rome had done nothing for
human freedom. Liberty could only come from the New World.
Bolívar therefore announced a solemn pledge. He would destroy the
empire of Spain.

Like others in that generation, the Liberator drew encouragement
from the secession of the Thirteen Colonies. He might also have
given some thought to recent transactions in Europe—in a contrary

direction, and as a warning. Paris under the Revolution made lavish
appeal to classical antiquity, to its eloquence—and also to its forms
and institutions. Orators declaimed about liberty, parading like
tribunes of the plebs, and consuls were elected. In due course the
First Consul of the Republic became a despot and established a
monarchy.

Bolívar distrusted Rome. Other cities carried the torch of political
liberty through the ages, ranging from Athens or Florence to
London and Paris, to Philadelphia and Boston. On a surface view his
indictment receives powerful support. Internally Rome was a
republic, not a democracy, with an aristocracy ruling through
tradition and consent. In foreign affairs that aristocracy, after
subduing the peoples and cities of Italy, struck down the kingdoms
founded by the successors of Alexander and in short space acquired a
Mediterranean empire. As Cicero somewhere says, what condition is
better than abiding at the same time in liberty at home and dominion
abroad?

On a sober estimate, the *Libertas* in the name of which Cassius and
Brutus became assassins was the predominance of oligarchy | and
privilege. And, as for the conquered regions, Rome supervened only
to curb and repress, it should seem.

Distinctions have to be drawn. Of the kingdoms east of the
Adriatic, Macedon was a state built up around a nation, be it
conceded. Not so Ptolemaic Egypt or Syria of the Seleucids. The
true political units were the Greek cities, which went on to prosper
under Rome of the Caesars. Subject to the suzerain, and deprived of
an independent foreign policy, the cities enjoyed local autonomy.
That is, republics in the form of government, ruled by the wealthy
and educated class.

It is high time to return to the Roman West. Caesar's conquest of
Gaul has been deplored as a calamity: it destroyed the brilliant
civilization of the Celts and cut short the emergence of a great nation.
Thus Camille Jullian some eighty years ago, eloquent and patriotic.
Brief reflection dispels the engaging notion. Nothing in the previous
record of the Celtic peoples suggests that they possessed any
inclinations towards unity or talent for central government. But for
the Roman intervention (violent and murderous as it was) they
would have been subjugated by the Germans, who had already made
a firm beginning. They exploited the feuds and rivalries normally
obtaining between tribe and tribe.

As did the Romans. The Gaul which Caesar conquered comprised a vast expanse of territory, but it was permeated by river valleys, with ease of communications. A decade sufficed for the task.

By contrast, Spain: two whole centuries since armies first arrived in the Hannibalic War. It was left to Caesar Augustus to reduce the broad mountain zone of the North West, extending from Galicia to the Pyrenees. That was the earliest military achievement of his reign—and it took ten years.

Long rivers traverse the Iberian peninsula. They are of little use for penetration or for transit. In this respect as in others, Asia Minor offers a parallel (and the curious might further be moved to compare Madrid and Ankara, both cities of the central plateau). The land was broken and divided, with abrupt mountain masses | almost every-where. Hence a number of regions with diverse and distinct identities, as is all too apparent in the present season. Before the Romans came, those regions lacked cohesion, even in the civilized south (Andalusia). For the rest, most of the tribal units, otherwise than in Gaul, were very small and local. Add to which, diversity of languages, notably Iberian and sundry Celtic dialects.

Warfare and immigration introduced Latin, and along with it the habits and institutions of the imperial people. From the outset, Romans and natives began to fuse in certain areas. The process went on without abatement. In modern textbooks the term 'Romanization' is put to frequent employment. It is ugly and vulgar, worse than that, anachronistic and misleading. 'Romanization' implies the execution of a deliberate policy. That is to misconceive the behaviour of Rome, whether republican or imperial. The govern-ment encouraged city life, to be sure, converting tribes into towns, for ease of administration in the first place. But it was at no pains to impose the use of Latin everywhere.

A pair of paradoxes in history may now be disclosed. First, the name of Rome stands eternal for dominance and for government. In the national epic poem the supreme deity announces rule without limits of space or time: 'imperium sine fine dedi'; and the destiny of the Roman is proclaimed, 'tu regere imperio populos, Romane, memento'. To subsequent ages, authority and hierarchy are suitably perpetuated in the Roman Church; and the imprint of Rome subsists in the laws and institutions of diverse nations.

None the less, when the behaviour of the Roman people is put under inspection, a different picture begins to emerge. The constitu-tion of the Republic (if such that peculiar product deserves to be designated) depended upon a division of powers. The possession of an empire led to the demolition of the Republic; and centralized authority was installed as the only remedy to ensure stability. In view of which, supreme importance accrues to the policy of emperors and to problems of empire.

On a contrary estimate, so it can be maintained, the central | government of the Caesars lived largely by expedients. It preferred to ignore problems until they were brought to its notice or could no longer be avoided. Roman statesmen would have concurred in the maxim of the excellent Antonio de Mendoza, the first viceroy of New Spain: 'do little and do that slowly.' That was the lesson of their own experience through long ages. The diffusion of Latin civilization in the western lands was a long process, begun in violence but promoted by peace and prosperity, not by the deliberate actions of any government.

In studying empire and emperors, historians and others have been prone to assume policy, or to invent it; and they duly asseverate the importance of 'decision-making', as they call it. Doubt and hesitations will commend recourse from time to time to the admonition of Edward Gibbon: 'though we may suspect, it is not in our power to relate, the secret intrigues of the palace, the private views and resentments, the jealousy of women or eunuchs, and all those trifling but decisive causes which so often influence the fate of empires and the counsel of the wisest monarch.'

After policy, administration. It never fails to earn praise and honour in the modern age, for it appeals to routine and favours careerism. The Romans consented to have as little administration as possible. They were inspired by an ingrained dislike of interfering with the habits of individuals or communities. That healthy abstinence comes out in various ways, most clearly in their normal attitude towards foreign religions: no cause for alarm unless morality was impaired or public order endangered.

Through tolerance or salutary neglect the Caesars were able to superintend a world empire without elaborate regulations or a horde of bureaucrats. Spain can furnish a cardinal example. Of the three provinces into which the country was divided, the largest by far took its name from Tarraco, the earliest Roman base. West and south of the Pyrenees, Tarraconensis extended as far as Coruña, Toledo, Cartagena. In the last years of Caesar Augustus, a senator of consular rank had charge of the province with three legates under him, while a single procurator managed the finances.

The corollary to this economy of effort and personnel is patent: local autonomy. The city was the unit, not the province, despite the existence of a council of delegates, which convened once a year at Tarraco. |

After a time the fabric of the whole Empire, West and East, could be described as a federation of cities. A Greek orator from Asia proclaimed that edifying notion when speaking a panegyric on Rome before Antoninus Pius in the year 143. It will not be fancied that the orator in question (namely Aelius Aristides) was promulgating any kind of novelty.

In these terms imperial Rome can be regarded as a champion of freedom, even if that freedom be limited in that it reposed on a class structure. Furthermore, while the growth of separate nationalities was discouraged, the Caesars and their counsellors would not have conceived annoyance if some region or province developed a community of sentiments extending beyond local and parochial patriotisms.

Without devolution everywhere they would not have been able to manage the wide dominion that reached from Coruña and Cádiz as far as the edge of Caucasus and the river Euphrates. The system endured for long centuries. Its decline and fall will continue to furnish a theme of momentous debate. The phenomena, the process, and the results do not lie beyond ascertainment. To weigh and estimate the causes is another matter.

In those frequent and ample discussions, an indirect approach has seldom been accorded proper attention. During the middle years of the third century the Empire came close to ruin and collapse. It was expedient to ask how and why it held together.

The second paradox now comes into view. For brevity and convenience it may be styled 'the open society', a term taken from the book of Karl Popper nearly forty years ago. That essay in political science won wide renown, as it amply deserved, but it fell short of total recognition from students of history. For the period intervening between Aristotle and Augustine, Popper's theme had little to offer. The Romans deprecated political theory (it was alien and superfluous) and they seldom bothered to write about it.

Instead, they could point to facts, to the structure of their system, a product of change and of long development through the ages. To refuse them political science does not entail a deficiency in that | political thinking which emerges from their achievement.

Granting which, the term 'open society' applied to Rome can hardly fail to arouse disquiet or even scandal—at least on conventional beliefs. Roman society, however changing, continued to be based on clear distinctions of class and status: slave and free, citizen and foreigner, the upper order and the rest.

Some justification is required. It is found and declared in the nature of the Roman citizenship. The republics of old Hellas had been arrested in their growth because ungenerous with the franchise. By contrast, Rome was liberal, creating new citizens all the time as her dominion extended throughout Italy. A king of Macedon (Philip V) bore firm testimony. The Romans, so he proclaimed in an official document, even admitted freed slaves when they founded colonies.

That was only one symptom. Entrance to the governing class was not refused to municipal aristocrats, whatever their ultimate origin. When processes of peaceful change had been accelerated by violence (the secession of the autonomous Italian allies in 91 B.C. and the sequence of civil wars), the country seemed to be moving towards some kind of unity.

The slogan 'Tota Italia' might now be heard on the lips of politicians. It was still premature, but it was exploited with effect a generation later when the heir of Caesar, lacking legal authority in his contest for power with Marcus Antonius, appealed to the mandate of the nation and organized a plebiscite, with 'Tota Italia' swearing an oath of personal allegiance to its leader.

The Empire of Rome was then in danger of splitting into two kingdoms, as language and geography dictated. From the war against Antonius and the Queen of Egypt emerged a fervent Italian patriotism which found singular and eloquent expression in the epic poem of Virgil. However, that type of patriotism was not destined to last. It failed to issue in an Italian national state under the rule of Caesar Augustus. The reason is plain. The *populus Romanus* now extended far beyond the bounds of Italy.

What had begun with emigration and military colonies continued with native centres elevated to the rank of Roman towns. Southern France and certain regions of the Iberian peninsula thus come to resemble by their civilization the new land of Italy north of the river Po. Before long Narbonensis, the old *provincia* in | southern Gaul (an entity separate from Caesar's 'Gallia omnis'), could be styled more truly Italy than a province.

The dynamic and prosperous territories of the Roman West evoke without effort a modern term and an American theory of nation-building. That is, the zone of the frontier. From the far West to the head of the Adriatic it comprised, on a rough definition, Andalusia and Catalonia, Languedoc and Provence, Lombardy and Venetia.

Their earliest impact and visible sign was manifested in the field of Latin letters. Verse and prose, Virgil and Livy are the signal glories of Augustan Rome. Transpadanes both, they had come to manhood while Mantova and Padua still belonged to the sphere of a Roman proconsul. Then after an interval, follows the turn of Spain, with the omnicompetent Seneca and his nephew Lucan, who composed the epic on the fall of the Roman Republic. Cordoba was their *patria*, they represent ancient immigration of Italians—and a planter aristocracy.

With Martial and Quintilian the second dynasty of Caesars exhibits writers of more modest origins. They were Celtiberian, from the remote interior of Tarraconensis, and indeed of native stock. Each was fortunate to escape from his bleak and forbidding town: Calatayud and Calahorra.

So far the extraneous predominance in metropolitan literature. Meanwhile the governing order itself had been permeated by a steady invasion. As has been already stated, social rank was sharply defined. It was even visible and vestimentary. But there was no barrier that could block talent and energy when seconded by the patronage of Caesar and the friends of Caesar. Many of the new Romans of the West (Italian, native, or of mixed extraction) served as officers in the army or as financial agents. The Senate was normally accessible for their sons, and perhaps a consulship in the next generation and thereafter the command of an armed province.

When the dynasty produced Nero, a boy emperor, the government was superintended for a season in an admirable fashion (and largely negative) by Seneca, senator and consul, with the help of | the commander of the Guard, Afranius Burrus. The loyal and exemplary Burrus came from Vaison, in Provence. His ultimate extraction was indigenous, like that of the first consul from Narbonensis, namely Valerius Asiaticus, who, a magnate from Vienna of the Allobroges, outdistanced the descendants of Roman colonists.

The partnership between Seneca and Burrus shows Spain and Narbonensis mutually congenial. A pleasing but harmless fancy might evoke the pair in the role of precursors in government. The first extraneous emperor was Trajan, acceding to power through a veiled *coup d'état* three decades after the end of the first dynasty. Deriving from the ancient settlement at Italica (hard by Seville) Trajan, like Seneca, goes back a long way.

By rank and prestige (his father had governed the provinces of Syria and Asia) Trajan stood in the forefront of the imperial aristocracy. Elevation to the purple, he owed that to a potent nexus that had been forming at Rome between senatorial families from Spain and Narbonensis. The nexus continued valid, producing the dynasty of the Antonines. While Hadrian was the next of kin to Trajan, Antoninus Pius was Narbonensian (his family from Nîmes). Not that provincial origins mattered any more. Senators and their cities had been in symbiosis with Italy long since. And, for that matter, Italy declined into the semblance of a province.

In Rome of the Antonines the governing class was far from being merely an alliance of Romans new and old. One observes in passing that it exhibits a further development of the 'open society'. Victorious at Actium in confrontation with the Greek East, Rome could not disallow the parity of Greek civilization in the world empire now united. Results ensued that surpassed hope or fear or rational prediction. A renascence of the Hellenes might have been foreseen under the peace of the Caesars. It occurred in the second century; and by paradox it followed rather than preceded a political phenomenon. The new Romans of the West, the aristocracies of Asia could not be held back and kept out. They are discovered already as consuls and as provincial governors in an early season. Not friends of Hadrian, the notorious philhellene, but coevals of Trajan, introduced into the Senate under the second dynasty. Society and government thus became cosmopolitan, while imbued with an imperial and Roman patriotism. |

To revert to Spain and Narbonensis. The élite from the cities, conveyed to Rome by education and by ambition, chose to stay there, blending with comparable Italian families of substance and repute—and even intermarrying with the few surviving houses of the ancient aristocracy. For senators, no thought of going back to a drab and municipal existence. They soon lost interest in the old country. Their departure had an evident and not unwelcome consequence. It deprived the western provinces of potential leaders in secession or agents in the formation of separate units.

The Spanish Empire furnishes a parallel, instructive because contrasted and negative. Large estates, flourishing cities and high education (as witness early universities at Mexico City and at Lima) duly produced their aristocracies. Few members of that class managed to return to positions of prominence in the Peninsula. It was not only distance that impeded, but the set policy of the Spanish monarchy. Furthermore, the creoles suffered frustration in their aspirations to local office and power. Few viceroys or even governors, and not many bishops.

As concerns the provinces of the Roman West a clear exception now calls for brief scrutiny and assessment. The Gaul which Caesar subjugated and annexed defied complete integration, since its structure remained rural and tribal for the most part. By contrast, the urban civilization of Narbonensis, a Mediterranean territory—and further to be defined by the northward limits of the olive.

The Roman government was anxiously alert to the danger of insurrections in Gaul that might assume a nationalistic shape. Against which, Claudius Caesar devised a partial remedy. He brought into the Senate a number of Gallic barons. The design was clear. Not so much to secure 'representation' of their country in the governing class as to sever them from Gaul and weaken their local attachments and influence.

For various and known reasons, few Gallic senators are found in the sequel. The prime factor was an accident, twenty years later. One of the governors in Gaul, Julius Vindex, happened to provoke the revolt against Nero; the son of a Roman senator, but also a descendant of kings in Aquitania. A host of natives mustered to his call. |

It therefore becomes legitimate to look for signs or chances that a Gallic nation might come into being later on with the efflux of time, through processes of peace or the compulsion of warfare. During the crisis of the mid-third century, when Germans broke through the northern frontiers, when at the same time the resurgent power of Persia attacked the eastern provinces, the Empire seemed likely to split into a number of separate groups or kingdoms. No single emperor could master the multiple emergencies.

Military proclamations occurred in diverse regions. Generals or local magnates assumed the tasks of the central government, to repel the invaders and avert total disruption. Invested with the purple by the soldiers (and some of them perhaps reluctant), they bear the unfriendly appellation of 'usurpers'.

In fact, Gaul abode under emperors of its own for some fifteen years. To invoke alienation from Rome or conscious separatism is premature and erroneous. In due course the last ruler of the 'Gallic Empire' came round without much effort or discomfort. Submitting to Aurelian, he ended his days as a Roman senator, administering a part of southern Italy.

Unity was restored and enforced. In the classic definition of Gibbon, the Empire 'was saved by a series of great princes who derived their obscure origin from the martial provinces of Illyricum.' Those emperors are commonly called 'Illyrian'. The term is defective and misleading. Better, Danubian and Balkan, of mixed ethnic extraction.

To turn aside from race to geopolitics (a word likewise liable to misuse), their country is the land mass that held together an empire that otherwise had a perilously long extension west and east. To complete the conquest, to win balance and stability, was the prime achievement of Caesar Augustus. The central element in the design was not the Danube as a frontier but the route that links northern Italy to Byzantium and the East: by Zagreb, Belgrade, Sofia.

Those regions stand out as the latest accession to Roman civilization. Whereas the advent of the first provincial dynasty consecrated the success of education as well as prosperity and introduced a cosmopolitan government, Illyricum was harsh and impoverished, the emperors thence issuing rough and uncultivated, immune to the gifts of Hellas. They proudly proclaimed the 'virtus Illyrici', they combined ruthless energy with undeviating devotion to Rome. |

Hence the 'New Empire' founded by Diocletian and Constantine. It set out with fair prospects of enduring, although East and West were drawing apart in the course of.the fourth century. After the death of Theodosius in 395 their governments separated. That was not the worst. The western lands were afflicted by a fatal concatenation of invasions and calamities.

Catastrophe evokes anger or despair. At the conclusion of a noteworthy book (published in 1947) Piganiol declared: 'la civilisation romaine n'est pas morte de sa belle morte. Elle a été assassinée.' The peremptory verdict was extreme, deliberately so. It passed over the evidence for continuity and survivals in the following epoch; and it neglected the fact that Goths were already settled within the Empire, that German generals had commanded imperial armies long since.

The invaders caused enormous destruction. That was not the continuing purpose of all their leaders. The testimony of the Goth Athaulf, uttered about the year 415, is often cited. He had once hoped to establish a 'Gothia' in the place of 'Romania'. In vain. Experience taught him. His own people was recalcitrant to civic life. He now sought no nobler fame than to be a 'Romanae restitutionis auctor'. Athaulf was killed by some Goths at Barcelona not long after.

So much in human affairs being the product of chance, conjecture about what might have happened need not be condemned as idle or noxious. Admitted from time to time in a modest measure, it can contribute to the understanding of historical transactions.

What then might ensue if the barbarian invasions were repelled or diverted? Not perhaps a 'Romania' united in obedience to a single government, but rather a group of separate Latin realms. During the long centuries of Roman rule some of the features that distinguished Gaul from Narbonensis had become blurred or attenuated; and in

Spain, despite the barriers of geography, sentiments of a common identity may have developed. In each country the | Christian Church (for all its propensity to schism and heresies) was a potent factor for unity. The authority of bishops operated, and regional councils.

Speculation is deterred when it considers the hazards that beset the birth of nations, the bright prospects of their infancy annulled or perverted. The danger subsists of anticipating the achievement of long ages, through manifold vicissitudes. Modern France contemplates in just pride its shape and its boundaries, as though predestined: 'l'Hexagone', such is a recent appellation. A different area was once not inconceivable. For example, a Burgundian state, or Languedoc yielding to its deep affinities with Catalonia. Nor will the validity of Spanish regionalism be neglected—even without Catalonia and the Basques. And Portugal denies the specious unity of a peninsula that is almost an island.

The origins and character of the Spanish nation is a subject of perennial debate. Two theses stand in sharp opposition. Sánchez Albornoz embraced the Roman tradition, and he enhanced it. In his view, Seneca is already a Spaniard; and some have been tempted to go further, discovering an Aragonese character in authors as diverse as Martial and Quintilian.

Now Seneca (style as well as sentiments) has proved highly congenial to Spaniards, over a long period. The same might be said of Cornelius Tacitus, at least for the sixteenth century. His *patria* is not on record: it has been surmised either in Narbonensis or in Transpadane Italy. As for Seneca, he reflects education and fashion of the metropolis. When an infant, he was carried to Rome in the arms of an aunt. Spain (and Andalusia in particular) can hardly come into the reckoning.

One asks what is to be made of Hadrian. A German historian writing in the *Cambridge Ancient History* (vol. xi, 1936) came out with a pronouncement, adducing race and soil and climate: 'Hadrian's strength was born of the mingling in him of old Italian and Iberian and perhaps African-Semitic blood; the ocean, the plain, now luxuriant now sunstricken, and the sluggish river at the south western edge of the Empire left their mark on his family and | childhood.' A small fact can sometimes subvert doctrine or mysticism. Hadrian, like most sons of senators, was born at Rome.

The other thesis was expounded by Amerigo Castro. To understand the formation of Spain he went back to the Middle Ages, and he put special emphasis on Arab and Jewish components.

Epilogue

No student of imperial Rome can fail to regard Spain with affection. It was the 'oldest dominion', and its transmitted language is more archaic than Italian or French.

The present cursory essay has passed by many aspects and problems, among them Roman Africa, the curious fate of Balkan Latinity, or Britannia (marginal and ephemeral). Furthermore, empires and oligarchies have been allowed to engross the theme, not liberty, democracy, or popular movements. No attention has been accorded to what Gibbon somewhere calls 'the largest and more useful portion of mankind.' Nevertheless, Rome, Spain, and the Spanish Empire (which lasted for three centuries) retain primary relevance to the republics of Latin America.

5

Rival Cities, Notably Tarraco and Barcino

WHEN cities of ancient pride decline or perish, they evoke moving and melancholy testimony. Thus Propertius, iv 10, 25 f.:

> heu Veii veteres, et vos tum regna fuistis
> et vestro posita est aurea sella foro.

The site, so Propertius continues, was given over to the herdsman and the farmer:

> nunc intra muros pastoris bucina lenti
> cantat, et in vestris ossibus arva metunt.

A prosaic commentator might observe that Veii did not remain a total desolation. It was now reviving as 'municipium Augustum Veiens', and before long it annexed an eminent patron, namely M. Herennius Picens (*suff*. A.D. 1).[1] More significant perhaps of the new order in state and society, the town council advertised merit and loyalty by the lavish honours it bestowed on an imperial freedman.[2]

Some thirteen centuries subsequent to the imperfect renascence of Veii, the decline of cities (combined with a proper delight in place-names) inspired the famous lines of Dante:

> se tu riguardi Luni ed Urbisaglia
> come son ite, e come se ne vanno
> diretro ad esse Chiusi e Sinigaglia.
>
> (*Paradiso*, xvi 73 ff.)

In this instance nothing emerged to contradict the poet.

For a historian it will furnish instruction to assess cities in their vicissitudes, and to compare them when they belong to the same natural region. Economic factors enhance development, or curb it; and close vicinity, engendering emulation, leads to anger and enduring resentment. The lands of the Roman West offer prime specimens. In Transpadane Italy the reciprocal fortunes of Ticinum and Mediolanum would justify a chapter, or rather a whole book. Ticinum acquired early importance from a bridge across the Ticinus;

---

[1] *ILS* 922. For his buildings there, *CIL* xi 7746 f.   [2] *ILS* 6579

Ktèma vi (1981), 271–85.

and it was advantageous to pass over the Po above the confluence, before the Po received augmentation from the largest of its tributaries.[3] Mediolanum, however, soon benefited from the opening of routes across the Alps and from its central position in the Lombard plain. It was ringed about by other towns: Ticinum, Novaria, Comum, Bergomum, Laus Pompeia. Mediolanum may indeed be defined as a regional capital, dominating the eastern part of 'Regio XI' in the Augustan system. Along with the west of 'Regio X' it corresponds to the 'Pliny country'.[4] |

It is no surprise that Mediolanum prospered and became an imperial capital well before the last days. And again, geopolitics changing, Ticinum rose by contrast as Pavia in the early medieval epoch, to be depressed in the sequel by Milano.

Civil war sharpened old enmities. Neighbour cities took sides, some under compulsion but often with alacrity. Mantua's poet bears witness, deploring in the *Georgics* with solemn language the extreme evil in warfare that embraced the whole world:

> vicinae ruptis inter se legibus urbes
> arma ferunt, saevit toto Mars impius orbe.

> (i 510 f.)

Armed violence again assailed Transpadana when a century had elapsed, and twice in the same year. Of active partisanship caused by local rivalries, the narration of the historian Tacitus discloses hardly a trace. The cities became involved through the hazard of invading armies. However, one notes in passing the sinister rumour that envious neighbours set fire to the amphitheatre at Placentia.[5]

Recent events beyond the Alps, reviving the ancient feud between Vienna and Lugdunum, furnish a complete and murderous paradigm. When Julius Vindex raised rebellion against Nero (occasion and motives are obscure), he induced Sulpicius Galba, the legate of Tarraconensis, to lend his name and prestige to the movement. Since Vindex was not only a Roman senator governing the province Lugdunensis but a descendant of kings in Aquitania, with hosts of Gauls mustering at his call, his position became ambiguous. Hence easy confusion at the time, and misrepresentation in the sequel. Vienna in Narbonensis came out strong for Galba. How much for Vindex, that is a question.

[3] A. v. Hoffmann, *Das Land Italiens und seine Geschichte* (1921), 66 f.

[4] For this conception, *JRS* lviii (1968), 136 = *RP* (1979), 696.

[5] Tacitus, *Hist.* ii 21, 2, 'municipale vulgus, pronum ad suspiciones fraude inlata ignis alimenta credidit a quibusdam e vicinis coloniis invidia et aemulatione, quod nulla in Italia moles tam capax foret.'

Galba gave recompense and rewards to Vienna, and he confiscated revenues of Lugdunum, which had stood 'pertinaci pro Nerone fide' (*Hist.* i. 51, 5). When the Vitellian army arrived at Lugdunum in the early spring of the next year it brought the opportunity for revenge. Cornelius Tacitus supplies an alert and percipient account (i 65 f.).

The Lugdunenses made appeal to the troops. They asserted 'obsessam ab illis coloniam suam adiutos Vindicis conatus, conscriptas nuper legiones in praesidium Galbae'. Those were the 'causae odiorum'. Then they went on to hold out prospects of rich booty from the sack of Vienna: 'irent ultores, exscinderent sedem Gallici belli. cuncta illic externa et hostilia.' The allegations are suitably violent. There was more reason when the Lugdunenses declared 'se coloniam Romanam et partem exercitus'.

None the less, the incrimination abated. Vienna was spared 'vetustas dignitasque coloniae valuit' (not without the report that the general of Vitellius had been mollified by an enormous bribe).

As Tacitus concedes, there had been 'multae in vicem clades', far exceeding mere partisanship for Nero or for Galba (65, 1). And he was careful to add 'uno amne discretis continuum odium'.

In fact, the two cities stood in sharp contrast in every way. To put the matter in summary fashion, Lugdunum was a veteran colony whereas Vienna began as a town of the Allobroges, acquiring Latin rights, and only recently the status of a Roman *colonia*. Lugdunum possessed a small *territorium* | carved out of the land of the Segusiavi. That of the Allobroges was vast, extending from the Rhône to Geneva and Grenoble. The population of imperial Lugdunum, the capital of Tres Galliae, was mixed, commercial, and largely libertine. No senator is on attestation before the middle of the second century—and this man is an isolated phenomenon.[6] Vienna (like Nemausus of the Volcae) exhibits the indigenous aristocracy, with Valerius Asiaticus as the first Narbonensian consul (*suff.* 35).

The contrast suggests a number of criteria that can be adduced for assessing several pairs of cities in Spain. For example,

(1) Origin, status, function.
(2) Strategic situation in respect of roads or rivers
(3) The size of the city
(4) Public monuments and private constructions
(5) Epigraphical evidence: the varieties of its survival and quality
(6) The character of the citizen body

[6] *CIL* xiii 1803: cf. *PIR* [2], F 153. He carries the 'Galeria', the tribe of Lugdunum. The dedication was set up by the Lemovices, in Aquitania, of which province he was governor.

(7) The *territorium*: its extent and resources
(8) Persons of consequence. That is, the higher knights and the senators
(9) Education and culture: schools, professors, men of letters.

With this guidance the enquiry can proceed. It will have to be cursory, for various reasons, notably scarcity of evidence and economy of effort.

First, Italica and Hispalis. They were close neighbours, separated by hardly a dozen kilometres. Italica across the river Baetis (on an elevation above the village of Santiponce) commands a view on Seville.

Hispalis, a port on the river and a commercial centre, first enters history in 49, during the war of Pompeius and Caesar. After Gades had declared for Caesar, the *legio vernacula* deserted from Terentius Varro (the legate in charge of Ulterior), marched to Hispalis and took up its situation 'in foro et porticibus, sine maleficio'. The action and comportment of the troops earned warm approbation from the *cives Romani* established as a *conventus* in that town (*BC* ii 20, 4 f.).

The next year witnessed perturbations of some complexity, amply expounded in the *Bellum Alexandrinum* (49–59). Conspirators at Corduba tried to assassinate the Caesarian governor Q. Cassius Longinus, who had incurred their wide dislike for reasons various and adequate. At the core of the plot was a group of named Italicenses.[7] It is not clear that the incident denotes a revival of Pompeian allegiances.

A little later the *legio vernacula*, now stationed at Ilipa (not far to the north of Italica), raised mutiny. Joined by another Varronian legion, they chose for leader T. Torius of Italica. He conducted the force to Corduba, loudly proclaiming that he would win back the province for Pompeius Magnus.[8]

Hispalis and Ilipa are named in these disturbances. Never Italica itself, only some Italicenses. Nor is Italica on record three years later when the Pompeian cause enjoyed a formidable resurgence. | One episode in the fighting at Soricaria to the south of Corduba discloses on Caesar's side an *eques Romanus* from Italica, Q. Pompeius Niger. He challenged to single combat an opposing champion (*Bell. Hisp.* 25, 4).

Hispalis meanwhile had given help to the elder son of Magnus. The *Bellum Hispaniense* breaks off with a vigorous oration from

[7] *Bell. Al.* 52, cf. 54.
[8] *Bell. Al.* 58, 2: 'et forsitan hoc fecerit odio Caesaris et amore Pompei, cuius nomen multum poterat apud eas legiones quas M. Varro optinuerat.'

Caesar. He recounted past benefits and denounced the citizens for ingratitude and for foolish presumption. 'Did they not know that the Populus Romanus had legions that could tear down the very heavens?' (42, 7).

Though narrated in detail, all of these transactions are not enough to demonstrate dissidence between the two towns. Rather internal divisions and partisans.

Hispalis now acquired from Caesar the rank of a *colonia*, with the title 'Romula'.[9] Italica had a long past. It was founded by Scipio in 206 B.C., for invalid soldiers from his army. The choice of name is noteworthy, and it may indicate that most of the veterans had not been Roman citizens from the legions. The testimony of nomenclature lends support.

There are various problems concerning Italica. In the first place, its status as a *municipium*. Why not from Caesar, or even from Pompeius?[10] There is no sign that it was a large town in that season.[11] Imperial Italica rose to amplitude and magnificence.[12] In area (about 30 hectares) it equalled Emerita Augusta, and in the Spains only Corduba and Tarraco were bigger (the other capitals of provinces). One portion at least of Italica was laid out in fine style, with wide streets and handsome residences.[13]

That splendour is attributed to the agency of Hadrian.[14] Although the emperor never visited his *patria* again after a sojourn in youth, he paid especial honour to Italica, as Cassius Dio states.[15] Not but that some are disposed to deprecate the role of Hadrianus Augustus.[16]

Otherwise the source of that embellishment is not easy to divine. Italica had a small *territorium*. To the north-east lay Ilipa, barely 10 km. distant, whereas Osset was on the river itself, directly opposite Hispalis, so Pliny affirms.[17] That is, at or near Triana, the suburb of Seville.

Senators are 'boni viri et locupletes', the owners of wide domains,

[9] For the status of Spanish towns constant recourse is recommended to H. Galsterer, *Untersuchungen zum römischen Städtewesen auf der iberischen Halbinsel* (1971).

[10] The term 'municeps' (*Bell. Al.* 52, 4) will not be adduced.

[11] Strabo names Italica in passing along with Ilipa (iv 141), with no hint of its origin—which we owe to Appian.

[12] For all details, A. Garcia y Bellido, *Colonia Aelia Augusta Italica* (1960).

[13] For streets and houses, R. Thouvenot, *Essai sur la province romaine de Bétique* (1940), 410 ff.; 534 ff. For the vast amphitheatre, larger than those of Emerita and Tarraco, ibid. 444 ff.

[14] Thus A. Garcia y Bellido op. cit. 15 f. Followed by R. Syme, *JRS* liv (1964), 144 = *RP* (1979), 620 f.

[15] Dio lxix 10, 1.

[16] R. Nierhaus, *Corolla Swoboda* (1966), 151 ff., summarizing objections at 166 f. Also in *Les Empereurs romains d'Espagne* (1965), 188 f.; and further, *Madrider Mitteilungen* vii (1966), 189 ff.

[17] Pliny, *NH* iii 11: 'ex adverso Osset quod cognominatur Iulia Constantia'.

whatever might be the ultimate origins of their enrichment.[18] A negative test avails. Dalmatia had a string of *coloniae* or *municipia*, from the Liburnian cities down to Epidaurum and Risinium. But Dalmatia offers few senators. One reason is patent: no room along that littoral for large estates.

Italica produced a rich crop of senators. Not only Ulpii and Aelii, to supply rulers of Rome. The further search is seductive, but is attended with the danger of annexing far too many in the entourage of Trajan and Hadrian.[19] |

Hadrian's father is named in the *Historia Augusta*, but no grandfather. Instead, after mother, wife, and sister follows the insertion of the 'atavus Aelius Marullinus', described as the first senator of the family (*Hadr.* 1, 2). If authentic, Marullinus would take the Aelii back to the time of the Triumvirs, or even to Caesar the Dictator. Strong doubt is legitimate.

One falls back on M. Ulpius Traianus (*suff.* ?70), active in the elevation of Vespasian and going on to govern Syria and Asia. Then several further consuls on a cautious estimate. A. Platorius Nepos (*suff.* 119) carries the 'Sergia', the tribe of Italica (*ILS* 1052). He may be assigned without discomfort either to Italica or to Corduba. Finally, P. Coelius Balbinus (*cos.* 137), likewise with that tribe. Hadrian adlected him to the patriciate, and he was a *flamen Ulpialis* (*ILS* 1063). To be added is therefore his presumed parent P. Coelius Apollinaris (*suff.* 111); and, to convey the rubric as far as the death of Marcus Aurelius, the son of Platorius Nepos (*suff.* ?160) and the son of Coelius Balbinus (*cos.* 169).[20]

Hispalis, although fairly rich in inscriptions, is nowhere in the running.[21] Its earliest certified consul belongs somewhere in the Antonine age: a Q. Fabius, deduced from his daughter, Fabia Q. f. H[ispanil]la (*CIL* ii 1174). Certain Helvii, non-consular, come into the count, in the first place L. Helvius Agrippa, proconsul of Sardinia in 69 (*ILS* 5947). Hispalis honoured with a public funeral M. Helvius M. f. M. n. Agrippa (ii 1184). He has the 'Sergia'. The normal tribe of Hispalis is 'Galeria', but 'Sergia' is attested there several times, notably by a magistrate of early date.[22]

[18] See further 'La richesse des aristocraties de Bétique et de Narbonnaise', *Ktèma* ii (1977) 373 ff. = *RP* iii (1984), 977 ff.

[19] Thus R. Étienne, *Les Empereurs romains d'Espagne* (1965), 55 ff. See his map, ibid. 79. For the time of Trajan and Hadrian he claimed nine, among them Licinius Sura and Julius Servianus.

[20] The convenient terminus of the year 180 is adopted throughout in this paper.

[21] In *CIL* II they number 106: for Italica, seventy-six (many of them fragmentary).

[22] *CIL* ii 1176 (L. Blatius Ventinus). The 'Galeria' might belong to a second foundation, under Augustus. Observe both 'Sergia' and 'Tromentina' at Salona: cf. G. Alföldy, *Bevölkerung und Gesellschaft in der römischen Provinz Dalmatien* (1965), 103 f.

Curiosity is further aroused by M. Accenna M. f. Gal. Helvius
Agrippa, a senator of praetorian rank (ii 1262: near Hispalis), and by
M. Accenna L. f. Gal. Saturninus, praetor and proconsul of Baetica
(xiv 3585: Tibur). In the former the item 'Helvius Agrippa' probably
indicates the maternal ascendance.[23]

Finally, a word can go to Cutii. At Hispalis Cutius Balbinus set up
the funeral monument to his polyonymous son, deceased when
embarking on the senatorial career (ii 1172 f.). Cutii are involved in a
nexus with Messii Rustici and Aemilii Papi.[24] Apart from this one
item the epigraphical evidence points to Salpensa, about 25 km.
south-east from Hispalis (ii 1282 f., cf. 1371: Callet).

M. Aemilius Papus was consul suffect *c*.135.[25] To be assumed the
son of the Aemilius Papus who is recovered from the corrupt passage
in the *HA*, 'amicitia Sosi Papi' (*Hadr.* 4, 2).[26] A further step may be
taken, to identify Papus with L. Messius Rusticus (*suff.* 114), on the
assumption that he is a *polyonymus* like others in the group.[27]

So far senators down to the year 180, with emphasis on local
alliances or affinities. The record carries nomenclature attesting
immigrants from various regions. Thus Ulpii (Umbro-Illyrian),
Platorii (Illyrian), Accennae (Etruscan). And several other specimens,
such as Italicenses registered in the *Bellum Alexandrinum*;[28] and
Blattii, from south-eastern Italy, occur as magistrates both at |
Hispalis and at Italica.[29] As concerns relations between the two cities,
one is impelled to conjecture not enmity but a kind of symbiosis,
with prosperity accruing to Italica from the active emporium. Some
of the ample residences may have been occupied by opulent
magnates of Hispalis, in refreshment from the torrid city beside the
sluggish river.

From the valley of the Baetis, rich in inscriptions and in senators, it is
an abrupt declension to the valley of the Ebro, and a dearth all the

[23] Despite the 'Galeria', the Accennae are claimed for Italica by G. Alföldy, *Fasti Hispanienses*
(1969), 74; 171.

[24] H.-G. Pflaum, *Klio* xlvi (1965), 331 ff. For the stemma ibid. 337: reproduced by
M. Corbier, *L'Aerarium Saturni et l'Aerarium militare* (1974), 192. See now *PIR*[2], M 520b
(p. 329): the *patria* turns out to be Siara.

[25] Registered among Messii in *PIR*[1], M 376 (now *PIR*[2], M 526).

[26] H.-G. Pflaum, l.c. 331, following the intimation of E. Groag, *RE* iiiA 1187.

[27] For this conjecture see further 'Spaniards at Tivoli', *AncSoc* xiii/xiv (1982/1983), 248 f. =
pp. 100 f. below.

[28] Notably T. Vasius and L. Mercello (*Bell. Al. 52, 4*), the former non-Latin, the latter
Etruscan. Observe T. Mercello, a magistrate at Corduba (ii 2226); and a specimen of this
gentilicium at Caere (xi 3613) is adduced by W. Schulze, *LE* 301.

[29] *CIL* ii 1176 (L. Blatius Ventinus). Italica now produces the pair of magistrates L. Blattius
L.f. Traianus Pollio and C. Fabius C.f. Pollio (*Madrider Mitt.* xix (1978), 273): the earliest
occurrence of the name 'Traianus'.

way from Dertosa up to Turiaso and Calagurris, with other cities of the hinterland conforming, such as Bilbilis and Ilerda.[30] As for the pair here to be subjected to brief comparison. Celsa musters nine inscriptions in *CIL* II, Caesaraugusta twelve.

Celsa lay on the left bank (between Velilla de Ebro and Gelsa), about 55 km. below Caesaraugusta. It was founded by M. Lepidus (*cos.* 46), with the title 'colonia victrix Iulia Lepida', either in his first governorship (48/7), or in his second.[31] Preferably the latter—and also as parallel to Munatius Plancus, who in 43 established Lugdunum and Raurica at positions of strategic value. Strabo the geographer happens to record Celsa as a town, with a stone bridge across the Ebro.[32]

Caesar Augustus founded Emerita in 25, when he claimed to have subjugated the north-west (Callaecia, Asturia, Cantabria). Caesar-augusta was also a military colony, showing on its coins the emblems of three legions. The date is in dispute. Perhaps a dozen years later, so some argue.[33] In any event, a site higher up the Ebro had the advantage over Celsa, because of communications from Tarraco towards the west and the north-west. For roads and river crossings Narbonensis offers an instructive parallel on a smaller scale. The route from Spain made the passage of the Rhône at Ugernum (Beaucaire) and Tarusco (Tarascon), so Strabo states (iv 178), giving distances in Roman miles. That is, according to the Via Domitia.[34] Arelate comes in a later place, described as a trade centre (181). Now Caesar put a military colony at Arelate (a dozen km. downstream and close to the head of the Rhone delta). In the sequel Ugernum and Tarusco vegetated as small towns on the territories of Nemausus and Avennio—while the commerce of Arelate flourished at the expense of Massilia.

Caesar Augustus would not have been reluctant to impair the prospects of the Spanish colony established by Lepidus, his erstwhile associate in the supreme power. History duly complied. Celsa went into a decline. Some of its citizens may have departed before long.

The great Licinius Sura (*cos. III* 107) leaves his traces in the coastal zone of Tarraconensis. An arch on the road north of Tarraco bears

[30] The totals of inscriptions in *CIL* II are as follows: Dertosa (18), Turiaso (7), Calagurris (2), Bilbilis (5), Osca (8).

[31] For the coins of Celsa, G. F. Hill, *Notes on the Coinage of Hispania Citerior* (1933), 76 ff.; M. Grant, *FITA* (1946), 211 f.

[32] Strabo, iii 161. He calls Celsa, like Dertosa (159), an ἀποικία. Not evidence for its colonial status. As with Arelate, only an emporium (iv 181), the information is not recent.

[33] For a full discussion, J. Arce, *Caesaraugusta, ciudad romana* (1980), 19 ff.

[34] See F. Benoît, *REA* xl (1938), 133 ff; with a sketch-map of the region ibid. 134. For the role of Arles, ibid. 144.

his name;[35] and numerous inscriptions at Barcino (close on twenty) celebrate his agent L. Licinius Secundus, who was a *sevir Augustalis* both there and at | Tarraco.[36] Sura carried the tribe 'Sergia'. That suggests a different *patria*. Osca might have been suspected.[37] Better Celsa, with a pair of *duumviri* of early date, 'L. Sura' and 'L. Bucco'.[38]

Caesaraugusta was enrolled in 'Aniensis', which is distinctive: outside Italy only two other cities have it. In the quest for citizens of some status from that colony (the capital of a juridical *conventus*), the high priests of the provincial cult at Tarraco can furnish guidance. Between 70 and 180 (or not much later) no fewer than seventy-five *flamines* are on attestation.[39] Eight of them show 'Aniensis'.[40] It is legitimate to assume that most of the eight came from Caesaraugusta.

Senators are another matter. They have so far eluded enquiry. At first sight it might appear a remote recourse to rope in L. Funisulanus Vettonianus (*suff.* 78), who has 'Aniensis'. He is universally taken to be Italian: perhaps from Forum Popilii, where the inscription was set up (*ILS* 1006). However, the tribe of that town is not known—and Funisulanus had been *curator* of the Via Aemilia.

Two polyonymous consulars happen to append the item 'Funisulanus Vettonianus' to their names, viz. T. Pomponius Mamilianus (*suff.* 100) and T. Pomponius Antistianus (*suff.* 121). The former has 'Galeria'. The name 'Pomponius' is very ordinary, and it need not be held significant that Tarraconensis yields other senatorial Pomponii. Or for that matter, a *flamen* with 'Aniensis' called T. Pomponius Avitus.[41]

Regional alliances are a common phenomenon, but not with safety to be invoked in default of other signs. Observe therefore the early magistrate at Caesaraugusta, L. Funi. Vet.[42]

The *nomen* 'Funisulanus' is a choice specimen.[43] Colonies elsewhere, in the eastern lands as well as in the western, contribute non-Latin *gentilicia* rarely attested in Italy itself.

[35] *CIL* ii 4282.

[36] For a specimen, *ILS* 6956. The small acephalous fragment recording a *vir triumphalis* at Barcino belongs to Sura himself (ii 4508).

[37] Osca presents 'Sergia' and 'Quirina' (3003 f.). 'Galeria' has recently turned up with the magistrate M. Marius Nepos (*AE* 1966, 185).

[38] G. F. Hill, op. cit. 83: cited in *Tacitus* (1958), 791. Also 'L. Nep.' and 'L. Sura' as probably one of the earliest pairs, cf. M. Grant, *FITA* (1946), 210.

[39] See the masterly and comprehensive study of G. Alföldy, *Flamines Provinciae Hispaniae Citerioris* (1973). It duly includes twelve *flaminicae*.

[40] Ibid., nos. 17, 31, 34, 45, 52, 54, 61, 66.

[41] *CIL* ii 4235 = Alföldy, no. 52. Further, pp. 140 ff., below.

[42] Hill, op. cit. 93 (with pl. cli).

[43] Schulze, *LE* 86 f. He suggested a Sabine origin. Add Funisulana T. f. (*NSA*, 1896, 105: Forum Decii, near Bacugno).

From defective evidence at Celsa and Caesaraugusta, and from conjectures, it will be comforting to come to abundance of facts at Tarraco and Barcino. Although separated by about 90 km., they may be conveniently regarded as neighbour cities, and even as rivals, in view of the subsequent vicissitudes of Tarragona and Barcelona in European history. The theme can be set out in summary fashion under diverse rubrics.

(1) Origins. Like Caesaraugusta and Celsa, Tarraco began as a native settlement, the town of the Cessitani. The site is attractive and easily defensible, adopted as a Roman base in the early epoch.[44] The walls go back to the first half of the second century.[45] Eighteen inscriptions are claimed as pre-|Augustan, two of them bilingual.[46] Julius Caesar raised Tarraco to the rank of a colony, 'colonia Iulia Victrix Triumphalis'. Barcino bears the title 'Iulia Augusta Paterna Fidentia', which on superficial inspection would suggest a Caesarian origin.[47]

The foundation date is obscure, invested by a number of vexatious problems.[48] In Pomponius Mela, Barcino occurs in a list of 'parva oppida' along the coast towards Tarraco: Blanda, Iluro, Baetulo, Barcino, Subur, Tolobi (ii 96). As usual, Mela's information is a long way anterior to the time of writing (in the early years of Claudius Caesar). And no mention of Barcino anywhere in Strabo.

Coins are absent, and archaeology has not yet spoken to any conviction.[49] There is a lack of early finds within the circuit of the walls (the date not verifiable). In the search for the first Barcino attention has fixed on the adjacent high hill of Monjuich. Perhaps the site of an Iberian settlement, of the Laietani.[50] But not proved. The slopes of the Monjuich have revealed two important pieces of evidence. First, a handsome curved exedra, with, inscribed in large lettering (82 mm.), four names (not complete). The first is 'L. Licinius'.[51] The function of these persons is not clear, likewise the conclusions to be drawn.

---

[44] For Tarraco (all aspects), see G. Alföldy, *RE, Suppl.* xv 570 ff.

[45] Th. Hauschild, *Madrider Mitt.* xx (1979), 235 f.

[46] G. Alföldy, *Die römischen Inschriften von Tarraco* (1975), nos. 1–18, here to be cited as *RIT*.

[47] Compare 'Paterna' as a title of Arelate.

[48] See A. Balil, *Colonia Iulia Augusta Paterna Faventia Barcino* (1964); J.-N. Bonneville, *REA* lxxx (1978), 37 ff. (a long and thorough study).

[49] For the inscriptions, D. S. Mariner Bigorra, *Inscripciones romanas de Barcelona* (1973), here to be cited as *IRB*.

[50] Thus M. Tarradell, in *Symposium de ciudades augusteas* (1976), 297 f. Against J.-N. Bonneville, op. cit., 66 ff.

[51] *AE* 1959, 113 = *IRB* 71. See the discussion of A. Balil, *Ampurias* (1955/6), 273 ff. Also *Colonia . . . Barcino* (1964), 45 f., with the exedra on fig. 9.

Next, a building inscription, said to have been found not far away:

C. COELIVS. ATISI. F.
II. VIR. QVIN. MVR.
TURRES PORTAS
FAC. COER.

(*CIL* i² 2673 = *IRB* 51).

Everything points to an early date. Just how early, that is the question. Some epigraphists assumed the document pre-Augustan.[52] On the other hand most of the scholars who deal with Barcino put the foundation of the colony in the vicinity of 15 B.C.[53] The inscription of C. Coelius should be borne in mind as justifying certain hesitations.

By oversight a standard collection assigned the inscription to Ampurias.[54] That may have diverted attention—but the nomenclature demands it. The father of Coelius was a native: the name 'Atisius' or 'Atisus' is Celtic.[55] For comparison observe, at Clunia, C. Calvisius Aionis f. Galeria Sabinus (ii 2782). This man received citizenship from C. Calvisius Sabinus (*cos.* 39 B.C.), proconsul *c.*29.[56] As the source of the name no Coelius can be evoked. Nothing is known of C. Coelius L. f. | Caldus subsequent to his Cilician quaestorship in 50, and the next generation of the family is a blank.[57]

(2) The size of the cities. Tarraco was large, embracing about 75 ha. A lot of space was taken up by public buildings.[58] As elsewhere, one might wonder about suburbs. Vienna has recently come out with a welcome surprise. Across the river lay a residential quarter, with ample mansions and splendid mosaics.[59] In contrast to Tarraco, Barcino had 15 ha. at the most: smaller than Saguntum (20 ha.).

(3) Their territories. For Tarraco four other cities indicate rough limits. To the south-west the boundary marched with Dertosa near the mouth of the Ebro, to the north-west with Ilerda, thence with

[52] Thus L. Wickert in his report: 'dort sah ich auch die prächtige Mauerinschrift republikanischer Zeit' (*Berliner Sitzungsberichte*, 1929, 56). Therefore *CIL* i² 2673 and Degrassi, *ILLRP* 581.

[53] Thus A. Balil, J.-N. Bonneville, and others.

[54] *ILLRP* 581 had the note 'Emporiis Hispaniae Citerioris in muro'. Degrassi misunderstood Wickert's account of his visit to the Barcelona Museum (he had mentioned finds from Ampurias housed there).

[55] Schulze, *LE* 70. He cited specimens of 'Atisius' at Verona (*CIL* v 3406; 3499; 3593).

[56] *PIR*², C 352.

[57] The line of C. Coelius Caldus (*cos.* 94) ended with the *adulescens* who committed suicide after capture in the Varian disaster (Velleius, ii 120, 6).

[58] For a plan of Tarraco, Alföldy, *Flamines* (facing p. 60).

[59] For Saint-Romain-en-Gal, see P.-A. Février, *JRS* lxiii (1973), 14 (with air photograph, pl. iv).

Iesso and Sigarra. Further, the highway to Narbonensis, by the stations Palfuriana and Antistiana, reached 'm.p. XLVI' at Ad Fines.[60] That is, at Martorell in the river Rubricatus (Llobregat), about 25 km. north-west from Barcino.

That road avoided Barcino, which was constricted on the north by Egara (Tarrasa), and along the coast eastwards by Baetulo (Badalona), distant only a dozen km. Baetulo was a *municipium* of early date. Egara acquired that status under the Flavian emperors. Nor can Barcino's domain have extended very far beyond the Rubricatus in the direction of Tarraco. Mysterious Subur comes into the count, named by Mela and by Pliny, and reckoned by Ptolemy a town of the Cessitani.[61] The site evades ascertainment.[62] Not all scholars are ready to concede municipal rank to Subur. It is not quite proved by the dedication at Tarraco set up by 'Suburitani publice' (ii 4271).

(4) Their functions. According to Strabo, Tarraco was well suited to serve as a capital not only for the lands this side of the Ebro but for most of the peninsula; and, he adds, in population it now equals Carthago Nova. All that Tarraco lacked was a harbour, such as existed in Laietania and further up the coast (iii 159). That is the nearest that Strabo comes to mentioning Barcino.

Caesar's legate had his residence at Tarraco, likewise the procurator, along with governmental offices and a detachment of legionary soldiers. Nor will one neglect the prefects in charge of the *ora maritima*. Seven are on attestation, all except two of them holders of magistracies in the city.[63] Tarraco was also the capital of a *conventus* that extended from the Pyrenees as far as Valentia and Liria; and, most important, the seat of the provincial *concilium*.

Of the seventy-five *flamines* on record, six belong to Tarraco itself, perhaps a further seven. Whereas Carthago Nova has two, Barcino one (equalled in that by obscure Sigarra). The figures are instructive, but sometimes liable to deceive. No *flamines* are known before the accession of Vespasian; and in the course of the second century a decline of social rank sets in, with sporadic representatives from small places in the interior, and even from a number of new towns in

---

[60] The stations are on the Vicarello cups (*CIL* xi 3281). Also on *It. Ant.* 398, which followed the opposite direction, down the coast to Barcino and turning inland to Ad Fines.

[61] Mela ii 96; Pliny, *NH* iii 21; Ptolemy ii 6, 17.

[62] Some have sought it near Sitges. Thus Schulten, *RE* ivA 510. A place called Olérdala is proposed by Bosch-Gimpera, *ANRW* ii 3 (1975), 580.

[63] Viz. *CIL* ii 4138 (= *ILS* 2715); 4217; 4224; 4225 f. (= *ILS* 2714); 4264 (= *ILS* 2716); 4266 (= *ILS* 2717); *AE* 1956, 62. See now Alföldy, *RIT* (1975), 162–71; 288 f. Of the seven, Licinius Silvanus and Antonius Silo, *ILS* 2714 f., had not been magistrates at Tarraco.

the north-west, situated in the *conventus* of Asturica and Bracaraugusta (five and six respectively.)[64] |

With these advantages Tarraco quickly outstripped Carthago Nova. It also drew notables from other cities, not only for the conduct of official business but in permanent sojourn.

(5) The inscriptions. Tarraco offers about a thousand, in great variety and value.[65] The congregation of *flamines* is a unique document for both social and administrative history. They can be classified by their anterior posts, whether military or civilian and local.[66]

Barcino fails to respond adequately to its total of just under 280. The earliest emperor honoured with a dedication is Hadrian, and it is a minute fragment (*IRB* 19). As for provincial high priests, one, with the tribe 'Aniensis', is probably from Caesaraugusta (ii 6150), and the other has 'Tromentina' (4219, cf. 4515: Tarraco). Both had military service, but only as far as the post of *tribunus militum*. Otherwise the only equestrian is the truncated person with the tribe 'Teretina' who appears to be a *[praefectus f]abrum* (6147). Like Tarraco, Barcino was enrolled in 'Galeria'. The aberrant tribes excite interest. Notably 'Aniensis', with three specimens in addition to the *flamen*.[67]

Certain cities boasted a large number of persons with the equestrian census. Thus 500 at Gades and at Patavium according to Strabo (iii 169). The relative proportions of *equites Romani* and senators may show curious results. Thus at Patavium eight against six in *CIL* V. On the other hand Brixia, with hardly any knights, has about forty inscriptions registering members of senatorial families (male and female).

Tarraco displays (it is no surprise) twenty-three senators (of different epochs). Apart from the Minicii Natales (see below) Barcino has the following:

(a) The small acephalous fragment assigned to Licinius Sura (*CIL* ii 4508)

(b) The upper part of the base dedicated to C. Cilnius Ferox (*AE* 1956, 223 = *IRB* 28): an otherwise unknown member of the famous Arretine family

(c) A dedication honouring Nummius Aemilianus Dexter, a proconsul of Asia (*CIL* ii 4512): perhaps the consul of 259, perhaps of Theodosian date.

---

[64] For the statistics. Alföldy, *Flamines*, 20 f. For the social decline, ibid. 58 ff.
[65] In fact 934 in *RIT*, not reckoning Christian inscriptions.
[66] Alföldy distinguishes four types (*Flamines*, 28 ff.).
[67] Viz. 6150 (the *flamen*); 4532 and *IRB* 59 (magistrates); 4590. Note also the man from Barcino at Iluro (4617).

One of the longest documents at Barcino celebrates a retired centurion (extraneous by his tribe, the 'Papiria'), who settled there, held local offices—and lavishly advertised in advance his posthumous generosity (ii 4514). For the rest, apart from a number of magistrates, a mass of inconspicuous persons, either libertine or suspect of that origin. Along with the inscriptions of Licinius Secundus, twenty-seven of Pedanii comprise nearly one-sixth of the total harvest. The only other Spanish Pedanius is at Murgi (ii 5490).

Senators from Tarraco. Despite the precellence of Tarraco and its wide *territorium*, no great number of senators with that *patria* can be certified before the death of Marcus Aurelius.

(1) M. Raecius Taurus, attested as a senator in 49 (cf. *PIR*[1], R 9). A fragment of the *Acta fratrum arvalium* registers his membership (vi 2045): generally assigned to the reign of Nero, but better to the late months of 68, and to Galba's patronage of Spanish and Narbonensian senators.[68] The rare *nomen* is borne by five persons at Tarraco, among them Raecia M.f. and the adopted son of Taurus. It is regarded as Etruscan or Illyrian.[69] |

(2) M. Raecius Tauri f. Gallus (*RIT* 145, based on remarks in *AE* 1965, 236, etc.). Gallus was an equestrian adherent of Galba, holding the provincial priesthood before he entered the Senate as quaestor of Baetica: anomalous to the point of scandal.[70] He might be the Gallus who became consul suffect in 84.

(3) M. Fabius Priscus, legate of a legion in 70 (that is, amalgamating *PIR*[2], F 55 and 98). On the inscription, not now extant (*CIL* ii 4117). 'Fabius' should be read, not 'Fadius'; cf. *RIT* 134.

(4) *Ignotus*, adlected *inter tribunicios* by Vespasian (*CIL* ii 4130: his gravestone).

(5) Q. Licinius Silvanus Granianus (*suff.* 106). In 98 Baetulo elected him as *patronus* (*AE* 1936, 66), and Baetulo honoured his son, at the time a *tribunus militum laticlavius* (*ILS* 1028). The consul's homonymous father had been a provincial priest, also one of the *praefecti orae maritimae* (*ILS* 2714). A second inscription has 'orae maritimae Laeetanae' (*ILS* 2714a). He had not been a magistrate at Tarraco, and the chance might be admitted that Baetulo or Barcino (in Laietania)

---

[68] *HSCPh* lxxiii (1969), 229 = *RP* (1979), 767. See further *Some Arval Brethren* (1980), 8 f.

[69] Schulze, *LE* 44; 217.

[70] Commending his coeval friend Voconius Romanus to Priscus, an army commander *c.*100, Pliny, *Ep.* ii 13, 4, states 'citerioris Hispaniae . . . flamen proxime fuit.' That post should have impaired the admission to the Senate for which Pliny had recently addressed petitions both to Nerva and to Trajan (x 4, 2).

was his *patria*.[71] The consul ended as proconsul of Asia in 121/2. The further career of his son escapes knowledge.

(6) C. Calpurnius Flaccus (*suff.* ?125): *PIR*², C 268 and F 171 amalgamate without discomfort. Clearly the son of the homonymous *flamen*, who was well domiciled at Tarraco, with the functions of *curator templi* and *praefectus murorum* (*ILS* 6946). Their tribe, the 'Quirina', indicates extraneous origin.

So far no other senators can be certified during the period under review.[72] Gaps as well as uncertainties have to be allowed for. Neither Lerida nor Osca avows a senator. Dertosa, a place of some importance during the Republic, was made a *municipium* by Caesar. It could lay a claim to its *patronus* M. Aelius Gracilis, governor of Gallia Belgica *c.*56.[73]

It is not yet time to close the rubric of Tarraco. Two consuls call for attention. First, L. Antonius Saturninus (*suff.* 82), made a senator by Vespasian. A *flamen* crops up as homonym (*CIL* ii 4194), perhaps his father.[74] Due hesitations arose.[75] The date of the document is uncertain, the nomenclature not distinctive.

Second, P. Palfurius (*suff.* 56). The road station Palfuriana affords an indication, taking its name from a villa owned by Palfurii. Emerging in close vicinity to Seneca, to his brother Gallio, and to Narbonensian allies, his consulship will appear appropriate, albeit not in firm support. His son, Palfurius Sura, an orator of some consequence, came into personal notoriety.[76]

Again, some of the Tarraconensian Pomponii might derive from the chief city. Pliny, who had been procurator *c.*73, knew a Sextus Pomponius (one of the *principes* of the province), who had a | son of praetorian rank (*NH* xxii 120). A certain Q. Pomponius Rufus had been put in charge of the coasts of Tarraconensis by Galba for his war 'pro r.p.' (*IRT* 537: Lepcis). He reached a consulship in 95. His *patria* would be worth knowing, likewise that of C. Pomponius Rufus (*suff.* 98). The latter was polyonymous, one of the items being 'Coelius Sparsus' (*ILAlg* i 1230). The *cognomen* 'Sparsus' is abnormally

<hr>

[71] For the definition of the region Laietania see G. Barbieri, *Athenaeum* xxi (1943), 113 ff.

[72] The Alfii (*PIR*², A 534 f.) should be rated Severan, cf. Alföldy on *RIT* 127.

[73] *Eph. Ep.* ix 385 (Dertosa), cf. *PIR*², A 182. Of early date: Gracilis had been commander of a legion after his quaestorship. Possibly the ']rac[' who was *praetor peregrinus* in 37 (*Inscr. It.* xiii, l p. 299). Otherwise, with eighteen inscriptions in *CIL* II, Dertosa yields only a magistrate (4059).

[74] Thus *Tacitus* (1958), 596.

[75] Expressed in *HSCPh* lxxiii (1969), 230 = *RP* (1979), 768. And see now Alföldy, *Flamines*, 63 f.

[76] *PIR*¹, P 46, noting M. Palfurius Sura on an amphora at Tergeste (v 8812⁶⁴). The name is portentously rare. Schulze, *LE* 206, cites ix 4583 (Amiternum) and ii 934 (Caesarobriga). On the latter stone occur M. Palfurius Iasus and his son Laminius.

rare. On inscriptions from towns in Italy and the Roman West it is to be found once at Nemausus (*CIL* xii 3558), twice in Tarraconensis: the *flamen* L. Licinius Sparsus (ii 4198) and Licinia Sparsi f. (ii 2648: Asturica).[77]

Senators from Barcino. That city's prime exhibit is a pair of consuls, L. Minicius Natalis (*suff.* 106) and his homonymous son (*suff.* 139). Their careers are revealed by *ILS* 1029 and 1061, that of the son also by an acephalous document which carries testamentary dispositions in favour of the 'Barcinonenses, [apud q]uos natus sum' (ii 4511). They had already been given public baths. The father was holding Pannonia Superior when Hadrian came to the power. He ended as proconsul of Africa. Likewise the son who had governed Moesia Inferior.[78]

After the command of a legion, with military decorations in the first war against the Dacians, and the governorship of Numidia, the elder Natalis duly acceded to a quick consulship. His colleague was Licinius Silvanus. For both will be surmised the potent influence of Licinius Sura (*cos. III* 107). Observe furthermore the full nomenclature of their sons. The one has 'Quadronius Verus' for adjunct, the other (*ILS* 1028) 'Quadronius Proculus'. That *nomen* is portentously rare.[79] It proves a close relationship. On the easy and obvious explanation each had for a mother a Quadronia.

No product of Tarraco comes near the elder Natalis, who might have expected a second consulship from Hadrian. That is not the worst. Another family both anticipated and surpassed the Minicii.

Standing out from the pack of inferior Pedanii is the pedestal dedicated 'L. Pedanio / L.f. / Secundo / Iulio Persico' (4513: 'litteris elegantibus'). Some have identified him with L. Pedanius Secundus (*suff.* 43). Thus under *IRB* 34. Better perhaps another member of the family.[80]

Secundus was appointed to the prefecture of the city in 56, succeeding the aged and eminent Volusius Saturninus. He fell victim to assassination five years later. The first stage in his ascension is enigmatic, more so even than the appointment as *praefectus urbi*. On

[77] The other Sparsi are worth registering, viz. (*a*) Sparsus on an Augustan coin at Osca (M. Grant, *FITA* (1946), 167 f.); (*b*) the friend of Martial who owned a mansion within the walls of Rome (xii 57, 20 f.): probably Sex. Julius Sparsus (*suff.* 88); (*c*) Fulvius Sparsus the *rhetor* in Seneca (*PIR*², F 560); (*d*) Pliny's friend Sparsus, presumably a son of the consul (*Ep.* iv 5; viii 3); (*e*) C. Lusius Sparsus (*suff. c.*157).
[78] For a full and sympathetic appreciation of the two see E. Groag, *RE* xviii 1828 ff.
[79] The item 'A. Quadronius' occurs in the nomenclature of T. Julius Maximus (*suff.* 112), from Nemausus (*ILS* 1016). The name is nowhere registered in *LE*.
[80] For the Pedanii, Groag, *RE* xix 19 ff. Followed in *Tacitus* (1958), 480; 794. See further *HSCPh* lxxxiii (1979), 287 ff. = *RP* iii (1984), 1158 ff.

the lowest count he was opulent, like so many of the new nobility from the western provinces: 400 slaves in his Roman mansion.[81]

Barcino thus comes out as the *patria* of the first Spanish consul since the Cornelii Balbi. They had been doubly anomalous: from Gades (a foreign city) and new citizens.

In the summer of 61, the year of Secundus' catastrophe, a kinsman became consul suffect, viz. Cn. Pedanius Salinator. He had annexed a *cognomen* that pertained of old time to the aristocratic | Livii, which might inspire a doubt whether Pedanius Costa, designated for a consulship in 69, was a descendant of Pedanius Costa, a legate of Marcus Brutus.

As Tacitus reports the matter, Valerius Marinus (designated by Galba) was postponed by the Emperor, but Pedanius Costa was dropped from the list, 'ingratus principi ut adversus Neronem ausus et Verginii exstimulator' (*Hist.* ii 71, 2). Therefore to be assumed like Marinus one of Galba's nominations (cf. *PIR*[1], P 141)—and a plausible increment to the roll of his partisans from Spain and Narbonensis. Vespasian adlected the Pedanii into the patriciate.[82] Then follows Cn. Pedanius Fuscus Salinator (*suff.* c.84). About the year 106 his homonymous son acquired a splendid bride, none other than Julia, a daughter of L. Julius Ursus Servianus, consul for the second time in 102, with Licinius Sura for colleague.[83] Julia's mother was Domitia Paulina, the sister of P. Aelius Hadrianus (*suff.* 108).

Pedanius Fuscus shared the *fasces* with the new ruler in 118. If the dynasty subsisted, he stood next in the succession. Fuscus and Julia fade out quickly, with no trace in history—and scant regard in most modern narrations.[84] They left a son. The youth and his nonagenarian grandfather met their end when Hadrian, turning against his kinsfolk, adopted Ceionius Commodus.

Some paradoxes. New families commonly owe their ascension to equestrian merit displayed in the previous generation: and a *procurator Augusti* may be followed by a consular son.[85] Apart from Licinius Silvanus, few procurators are in evidence among the high priests at Tarraco. Furthermore, only three were progenitors of senators. In addition to Licinius Silvanus and Calpurnius Flaccus, there stands only M. Valerius Propinquus Grattius Cerialis from Liria of the

---

[81] *Ann.* xiv 42, 3.

[82] As shown by the youth honoured at Ephesus, L. Pedanius Secundus Pompeius Festus Munatianus (*AE* 1968, 482). If he survived he might have become a *consul ordinarius*.

[83] Pliny, *Ep.* vi 26.   [84] Nowhere in Cassius Dio or in the *Historia Augusta*.

[85] For a list of Spanish knights in the administrative posts see H.-G. Pflaum, *Les Empereurs romains d'Espagne* (1965), 87 ff. Not so very numerous in comparison with the high total of senators, cf. the remarks of Piganiol, ibid. 119.

Edetani, with excellent military service.[86] His son is probably to be identified as the polyonymous consular on an inscription at Tarraco, the third of whose four pieces of nomenclature is 'Grattius Cerialis'. The first, missing from the head of the document, is assumed to be 'Valerius Propinquus'.[87]

The inscriptions of Barcino (it will be recalled) disclose only three knights, and they by their tribes are extraneous. Yet Barcino is the *patria* of two senatorial families—and six consuls from 43 to 139.

In productivity of senators, cities of Italy and the west exhibit wide divergences. Reasons can sometimes be divined. From Narbo, that ancient citizen colony, no senator is discoverable until the time of Hadrian, and he is a person of small consequence or prospects (*ILS* 1065). Narbo, as its numerous inscriptions demonstrate, was permeated by the commercial class. By contrast, the aristocratic families of Vienna and Nemausus, old tribal capitals with wide territories.

A city may be marked by the dominance of a single house of ancient opulence. Thus the Ummidii at Casinum, confirmed by three monuments: a temple, a mausoleum, and an amphitheatre.[88] |

The mutual relations of Barcino's two consular families will arouse curiosity. Friendship reinforced by marriage or adoption in a city or a region is a constant phenomenon. By the same token, emulation or enmity. Between Minicii and Pedanii no links of blood or propinquity can be discovered. Before Julia's marriage, no wife of a Pedanius is on direct attestation. For that family two inscriptions disclose, it is true, a manifold nexus: perhaps it will never be unravelled.[89]

The large clear fact is the alliance with Julius Servianus. Minicius Natalis (*suff.* 106) belonged to the faction of Sura, such is the assumption. If correct, local rivalry was transferred to the larger scene. It is unfortunate that the province and city of Servianus should defy ascertainment.

The educated class. After cursory inspection of other features, the enquiry has concentrated on the upper order. The western aristocrats invade state and society, and when little more than a century has elapsed after the founding of the Principate the clients of the Caesars

---

[86] *ILS* 2711. For his military career in relation to that of his fellow townsman M. Cornelius Nigrinus (*suff.* 83) see G. Alföldy and H. Halfmann, *Chiron* iii (1973), 369 ff.

[87] *CIL* ii 6084, with Alföldy's comments in *RIT* 149; see further pp. 579 ff. below.

[88] *Historia* xvii (1968), 72 ff. = *RP* (1979), 659 ff.

[89] *CIL* iii 13826 (Doclea in Dalmatia); *AE* 1972, 578 (Ephesus). On these *polyonymi* see above all E. Champlin, *ZPE* xxi (1976), 84 ff.

impose one of themselves: M. Ulpius Traianus, a descendant of the old Italian emigration.

It was a victory for birth and wealth, for alert opportunism and mature strategy. Also a victory for liberal studies. Which impels to a question about Tarraconensis and the cities on the long littoral down to Carthago Nova. What might be their resources for education, their contribution to Latin letters?

At first sight precious little. For immigrants or for aspiring natives no benefit availed such as Narbonensians derived from long acquaintance with the university city of Massilia. At Tarraco, so the elder Seneca reports, the eloquent Gavius Silo extorted an equivocal appraisal from Augustus: 'numquam audivi patrem familiae disertiorem'.[90] Others of the eager adepts who congregated in the Roman schools may have originated from the province, such as Fulvius Sparsus, Licinius Nepos, Mamilius Nepos. Quintilian, so it happens, when discussing Romanius Hispo, mentioned an advocate called Fulvius Propinquus (vi 3, 100). Saetabis reveals a M. Fulvius Propinquus (ii 5978). That is a rare *cognomen*—but with nine specimens in *CIL* II.

The name of note is Curiatius Maternus, senator, orator, author of tragedies: known only from the *Dialogus* of Cornelius Tacitus. His *patria* might be sought in the region of Liria. Maternus was clearly close kin (perhaps maternal uncle) to an eminent governor of military provinces, M. Cornelius Nigrinus Curiatius Maternus (ii 3783; 6023). His date was for a long time a vexatious problem (cf. *PIR*[2], C 1407). His full career has now emerged at Liria, showing him identical with a suffect consul of 83.[91]

Next, Granius Licinianus, who wrote a history of the Roman Republic. He is generally supposed to fall in the time of Hadrian or Pius.[92] His nomenclature might give a hint of Tarraconensis. Thus 'Granianus', a *cognomen* of the Licinii Silvani, and a Granius magistrate at Egara, close to Barcino (ii 4494). One might also cast a glance much further to the south: to the region extending from Saguntum by Valentia to Dianium, with Liria and Saetabis not far from the coast. Granii were magistrates at Saetabis and at Dianium (3624; 5962); and 'Granius' is one of the *gentilicia* borne by Valerius Propinquus, the consular from Liria (6084 = *RIT* 149). |

Liria deserves a word in passing. This *municipium* was originally the town of the Edetani. Common *gentilicia* like 'Cornelius',

[90] Seneca, *Controv.* x, *praef.* 14.
[91] G. Alföldy and H. Halfmann, *Chiron* iii (1973), 331 ff., whence *AE* 1973, 283. Some of their opinions about the orator Curiatius Maternus (ibid. 346 f.) may be questioned.
[92] Thus N. Criniti in his edition (Teubner, 1981), v: 'aetate Antonino Pio proxima'.

'Licinius', 'Valerius', imply native extraction, whereas 'Curiatius' is Etruscan. Native and immigrant had blended long since along the littoral (although not so completely as in Baetica).

That concerns the interpretation of a vexed and perhaps corrupt passage in the *Historia Augusta*. During a convention held at Tarraco, Hadrian rebuked a group of persons styled 'Italici' in contrast to 'ceteri' (*Hadr.* 12, 4). Roman citizens of Italian origin, so some fancy or argue. No distinction obtained whether juridical or social. Behind 'Italici' of the text lies 'Italicenses'.[93]

Epilogue

By paradox, the contribution that the province made to literature issues from the far interior. It is resplendent—and from writers of native extraction ultimately, namely M. Fabius Quintilianus from Calagurris of the Vascones, high up the Ebro, and M. Valerius Martialis from Celtiberian Bilbilis. These were towns a man might be glad to escape from. The grandfather of the professor may well be the 'Quintilianus pater' in Seneca; and his father had certainly been in Rome.[94] Quintilian interrupted his own sojourn but was able to get back to the capital in the train of Galba.

Martial reverted to Bilbilis in the year 98, but not to contentment in his 'provincialis solitudo', as he styled it (xii, *praef.*); and when the illustrious orator Licinianus (a friend of Sura) revisited bleak Bilbilis he was not likely to pass the winter there.

> aprica repetes Tarraconis litora
> tuamque Laietaniam
>
> (49, 21 f.).

Tarraco exerted a strong appeal, as is evident from many items in the preceding pages.[95] The eloquent tribute comes from the poet P. Annius Florus, the author of the dialogue entitled *Vergilius Orator an Poeta*.[96] After long peregrinations and some disappointments, he was happy to settle there and superintend the education of 'pueri ingenui et honesti'. Florus did not fail to praise the wine, rivalling Italian vintages. That was also the verdict of Martial (xiii 118). By contrast, Barcino: 'a copone tibi faex Laietana petatur' (i 26, 9). For the earnest enquirer, Barcino is redeemed by six consuls.

[93] For this notion, *JRS* liv (1964), 145 f. = *RP* (1979), 622 ff.

[94] Seneca, *Controv.* x, *praef.* 2, cf. 4, 9; Quintilian, x 9, 73.

[95] Further, for immigrants cf. Alföldy, *RE*, *Suppl.* xv 626 f.

[96] He is generally held identical with Hadrian's poetical friend (*HA Hadr.* 16, 3)—and also (cf. *PIR*[2], A 650) with the Florus who wrote the *Epitoma*, or *Bella Romanorum*. On these questions see now P. Jal in his edition (Budé, 1967), vol. i, cxiii. For the historian he prefers the nomenclature 'L. Annaeus Florus'.

6

Spaniards at Tivoli

THE senator needs a mansion at Rome. Also, if his means permit, a villa in the suburban vicinity. The charm of Tibur is on abundant testimony: the fresh air, the cascades of the Anio, the groves and the orchards. In favour before the Republic ended and celebrated by Augustan poets, this salubrious resort rose to a summit of appeal in the epoch of the Antonines. It offered escape from metropolitan annoyances, not only 'fumum et opes strepitumque Romae' but the tedium of trivial or empty debate under the presidency of a benevolent autocrat—or often during his absence.

Access was easy, only 20 Roman miles away. That is, equidistant with Lanuvium. After a meeting of the Senate Annius Milo set out for his home town on a January afternoon. He rode in a 'raeda', a commodious four-wheeler with space for baggage and two companions (Fausta and an equestrian friend).[1] Rapid transport demanded lighter vehicles, various types of two-wheelers drawn by mules or ponies. Thus the bored and restless magnate 'currit agens mannos ad villam, praecipitanter'; or angry Cynthia in haste to disrupt an evening party at Lanuvium.[2] Driving along the Appia, she took the reins herself. On one occasion in the middle of the night Propertius received an urgent command to meet the lady at Tibur.[3] The poet alludes to the hazards of darkness and brigands. He does not specify the conveyance, an expeditious 'cisium' or 'covinnus'.[4] A cab-stand happens to be attested at Tibur, with an organized guild of 'cisiarii'.[5]

Among senators who elected Tibur for residence it is no surprise to discover 'boni viri et locupletes' from Spain. They had invaded society and government, on high show already under Claudius and Nero, a pack numerous enough without the Corduban Annaeus Seneca, | the minister of state, or Pedanius Secundus from Barcino (*suff.* 43), Prefect of the City from 56 to 61.

---

[1] *Pro Milone* 28; cf. Asconius 21.
[2] Lucretius iii 1063; Propertius iv 8, 15 ff.   [3] Propertius iii 14.
[4] The muleteer Sabinus could outstrip any 'volans cisium' (*Catalepton* 10, 3 ff.). For two very rapid journeys, *Pro Roscio Amerino* 19; *Phil.* ii 77.
[5] *CIL* vi 9485 (the monument of a member, Ti. Claudius Zosimus).

Ancient Society xiii/xiv (1982–3), 241–63.

In the next epoch, from the accession of Vespasian to the death of Marcus Aurelius, a whole collection musters at Tibur.[6] Epigraphy declares them, on various criteria. Nomenclature has to be solicited, and the tribe of their cities (primarily 'Galeria' and 'Quirina'). Hence sundry hazards in the procedure, and the recourse to casual or subsidiary phenomena which, while not amounting to direct proof, are none the less consonant with hypothesis about provincial or local origins.[7]

(1) L. Cornelius Pusio Annius Messalla (*suff.* 90). *AE* 1915, 60, set up by Cornelia Sabina, 'h(onoris) c(ausa)'. On his name follow 'cos., VII vir epul./procos.'. A senator L. Cornelius Pusio was known, legate of legio XVI and carrying 'Galeria' for tribe (*CIL* vi 31766): patently the Pusio who was *suffectus c.*73, with Pegasus for colleague.

This Vespasianic consular was amalgamated with the *polyonymus* in *PIR*², C 1425 (1936). Since then the *Fasti* of Potentia have imported a second L. Cornelius Pusio in 90 standing at the head of that notable collection of no fewer than eleven *suffecti*. That counsels a revision—and a proconsulate of Africa *c.*103.[8] The roll for Asia is complete about this time.

The inscription of a slave of L. Cornelius Pusio emerged not far from Gades.[9] Further, the piece of double nomenclature repays attention. Lepcis reveals M. Annius Messalla, legate in proconsular Africa (*IRT* 516). He was consul suffect with C. Fisius Sabinus *c.*83 (*AE* 1969/70, 6). A useful conclusion follows. The *suffectus* of 90 was an Annius Messalla by birth—or else the item reproduces maternal nomen|clature, a frequent habit. Annii from the province Baetica, that is a long story, culminating with M. Annius Verus from Ucubi (*cos. III* 126), the grandfather of Marcus Aurelius. It opened in 48 B.C. with Annius Scapula, 'maximae dignitatis et gratiae provincialis homo', who, so Q. Cassius Longinus learned with surprise and regret, shared in the plot to take his life.[10]

---

[6] Four were registered in *Tacitus* (1958), 602, with the adjunct 'and others'.

[7] For various reasons, among them economy, the Tiburtine inscriptions are cited by the numbers in *ILS* or *CIL* XIV, in preference to *Inscr. It.* IV 1 (1936) or IV IV 1 (1952), the second edition which adds nothing relevant to the present essay.

[8] E. Birley, *JRS* lii (1962), p. 221; cf. W. Eck, *Senatoren von Vespasian bis Hadrian* (1970), 161 (with a query). B. E. Thomasson, *RE*, *Suppl.* xiii 10, remains doubly agnostic: either Domitianic or Trajanic, either Africa or Asia.

[9] *Eph. Ep.* ix 214 (Jerez de la Frontera). Gades itself now adds M. Cornelius L. f. Pusio (*AE* 1971, 175).

[10] *Bell. Al.* 55, 2. Not in *RE* i. He shares the rare *cognomen* with certain Quinctii: probably from Lanuvium, cf. *Historia* xiii (1964), 112 = *RP* (1979), 590. Add the knight T. Quinctius Scapula who started a military revolt in Baetica (Dio xliii 29, 3) and perished after Munda (*Bell. Hisp.* 33, 3 f.). There are over twenty Quinctii in *CIL* II.

(2) L. Roscius M. f. Quir. Aelianus Maecius Celer (*suff.* 100). *ILS* 1025: set up after his proconsulate in Africa (116/17) by a friend, on ground provided by decree of the local senate.[11] The poet Martial, now back at Bilbilis, acknowledges the gift of a small cab to hold two persons in discreet company,

> o iucunda, covinne, solitudo,
> carruca magis essedoque gratum
> facundi mihi munus Aeliani.

> (xii 24. 1 ff.)

Identity with Roscius Aelianus has been surmised.[12] Something further is requisite. Spain exhibits Aelii well before the family from Italica that produced an emperor, as witness M. Aelius Gracilis from Dertosa (*PIR*[2], A 182), and Pompeius Aelianus, the youthful Spanish senator involved with a group that forged a will.[13]

The item 'Maecius Celer' in the nomenclature of the consular furnishes guidance. He is probably a brother of M. Maecius Celer, consul suffect in the next year. When this man was departing to take charge of a Syrian legion in 93 or 94, Statius hailed him as 'nobilis Ausoniae Celer armipotentis alumnus' (*Silvae* iii 2, 20). Some have supposed him Italian.[14] The word 'alumnus' should inspire doubts.[15]

One turns to Spain, to Ilici, where C. Maecius C. f. Celer made a dedication to Divus Augustus (*CIL* ii 3555). Moreover, early coins | of the colony show a C. Maecius as a magistrate.[16] The tribe of Ilici, not so far ascertained, might be 'Quirina'.

At this point a presumed son of Roscius Aelianus calls for passing comment, viz. 'L. Roscius L. [f. Quir. Mae]cius Celer' etc. The provincial council of Lusitania honoured him with a statue at Emerita (*ILS* 8972). That city (enrolled in 'Papiria') is patently not his *patria*; and there is no reason in favour of an origin elsewhere in Lusitania. Roscius is to be assumed a governor, and consul in the near sequel.[17] However, probably not identical with the Roscius Paculus *suffectus* with Papirius Aelianus *c.*135.[18]

---

[11] The inscription is peculiar in that it registers military decorations for Aelianus when a military tribune (in Domitian's war against the Chatti), but no praetorian posts.

[12] E. Groag, *RE* iA 1118.   [13] *Ann.* xiv 41.

[14] Thus apparently M. Fluss, *RE* xiv 234 f. No curiosity was evinced in Vollmer's commentary.

[15] See *Some Arval Brethren* (1980), 8 (discussing L. Maecius Postumus).

[16] M. Grant, *From Imperium to Auctoritas* (1946), 213.

[17] E. Groag, *RE* iA 1120. The shape of the inscription (see *Eph. Ep.* ix 302) indicates 'Aeliano' to be supplemented in line 1; and there is space for the governorship in line 6 after the man's command of a legion. The governorship was rejected by W. Eck, op. cit. 228, referring to G. Alföldy, *Fasti Hispanienses* (1969), 148.

[18] *CIL* xi 5178. He is considered 'wohl identisch' by E. Groag, *RE* iA 1119.

The second volume of *CIL* happens to yield only eight inscriptions of Maecii, four of Roscii. But the latter total includes the imprint on lead ingots: 'M.P. Roscieis M. f. Maic.' (i^2 2397 = *ILS* 8706). More than thirty specimens are extant. They document exploitation of the mines in the hinterland of Carthago Nova. The tribe 'Maecia' indicates Lanuvium.[19] That town parades Roscii in varied prominence— Gallus the actor, Otho tribune of the plebs in 67 B.C., Fabatus legate of Caesar in Gaul.

As has been shown, 'Maecius Celer' suggests Ilici, about 50 km. to the north of Carthago Nova. The Roscian name leads inevitably towards the nexus of problems that infest the polyonymous Q. Pompeius Falco (*suff.* 108). They would entail a more ample investigation than can here be accorded.[20]

For economy, it is advisable to segregate three pieces of nomenclature that accrue subsequent to his tenure of Moesia Inferior (from 115 or 116 to 118).[21] He was then registered as 'Q. Roscius Sex. f. Quir. Coelius Pompeius Falco' (*ILS* 1036: Hierapolis Castabala, in Cilicia). Other inscriptions add the *cognomen* 'Murena'. Thus *CIL* iii 7537 (Tomis), 12470 (Tropaeum Traiani). |

That is the suitable point of inception. First 'Coelius', indicating a link with Roscius Coelius, legionary legate in Britain in 69 (*Hist.* i 60), who turns up as M. Roscius Coelius, *suffectus* in 81. That is the form certified by the *Acta* of the Arval Brethren (*CIL* vi 2059). This man lacks a normal *cognomen*, carrying in its place a second *gentilicium*. As it happens, there are no Coelii at Lanuvium, but Spain has about twenty.[22]

Next, 'Murena'. That should attach to the Roscian name. It is preternaturally rare. Senators apart, it occurs on only five inscriptions throughout the world.[23] In passing will be noted another branch of Roscii, namely the family of M. Roscius Murena, proconsul of Bithynia *c.*160 (*ILS* 8834: Gortyn). They too carry the tribe 'Quirina'. The *cognomen* was rendered illustrious by the Licinii Murenae of Lanuvium, long extinct. It falls into place if taken up by

---

[19] Compare Turullii with that tribe, likewise on ingots. On whom, *Historia* xiii (1964), 124 = *RP* (1979) 602 f.

[20] See further remarks in *HSCPh* lxxxiii (1979), 294 f. = *RP* iii (1984), 164 f.; *Some Arval Brethren*, 48 f.

[21] Conveniently to be found in *ILS* 1035 (Tarracina): subsequent to Falco's proconsulate of Asia (123/4).

[22] Further, P. Coelius Balbinus Vibullius Pius (*cos.* 137), carrying the 'Sergia' (*ILS* 1063: Rome), may come from Italica, cf. *PIR*², C 1241.

[23] I. Kajanto, *The Latin Cognomina* (1965), 332. They occur in *CIL* II, VIII, X. Observe also Numitoria C. f. Murenilla at Firmum in Picenum (ix 5405). 'Murena' has nothing to do with the fish according to W. Schulze, *LE* 195 f.

provincial Roscii whose *ultima origo* was that city of Latium. That device of advertisement has parallels.

It is time to abbreviate. The *suffectus* of 108 stands as '[Q. Pompe]ius F[alco' on the *Fasti Ostienses*, as 'Pompeius Falco' in the superscription of the letter in which Pliny tendered advice about his comportment as tribune of the plebs in 97 (i 23). Later in the collection an episode of that year introduces him as 'Murena tribunus' (ix 13, 19).

Since practices varied, a man's 'real name' (that is, the paternal) is sometimes elusive. In this instance a Pompeius Sex. f. Falco was adopted by a Roscius Murena.[24] The tribe is often a valuable clue, since it is retained in testamentary adoption. But the 'Quirina', adhering to Roscii, may also belong to Falco's father. The origin of these Pompeii therefore remains uncertain: perhaps Spanish, perhaps even from the eastern lands.[25]

One of the three subsequent accretions to Falco's nomenclature is 'Iulius Eurycles Herculanus' (*ILS* 1035, Tarracina). It reproduces the Euryclid house of Sparta. Not that Falco should be deemed a descen|dant.[26] The chance subsists that he took over the item from his wife's father, Q. Sosius Senecio (*cos.* 99)—whose extraction is one more problem.[27] In the next generation the maternal ascendance wins pride of place over 'Roscius Murena'. The consul of 149 is styled 'Q. Pompeius Sosius Priscus' (*ILS* 1105 f.).

The above digression may appear inordinate. It is justified by the close attachment which Falco's grandson (*cos.* 169) acquired to Tibur (see below). Whereas the son abridged to 'Q. Pompeius Sosius Priscus', this portent of aristocratic nomenclature flaunts no fewer than fourteen *gentilicia*, beginning with 'Q. Pompeius Q. f. Quir. Senecio Roscius Murena Coelius' (*ILS* 1104: Tibur).

(3) P. Manilius P. f. Gal. Vopiscus Vicinillianus L. Elufrius Severus Julius Quadratus Bassus (*cos.* 114). *ILS* 1044: set up by N. Prosius Platanus, his wife Manilia Eutychia, and their three children.

A poet's testimony comes in happily. Statius gives a long and vivid description of the villa owned by a certain Manilius Vopiscus, beside the river Anio and sheltered by two rocky outcrops (*Silvae* i 3). The friend is extolled as 'vir eruditissimus', as a patron who 'praecipue vindicat a situ litteras iam paene fugientis' (i, *praef.*). Further, a performer himself, at least potential, in various types of

---

[24] The adopting parent, so some suppose, was M. Roscius Coelius (*suff.* 81).
[25] Perhaps from Cilicia, on the basis of *ILS* 1036. Thus A. R. Birley, in *Epigr. Stud.* iv (1967), 69; *Arh. Vestnik* xxviii (1977), 360.
[26] As by W. C. McDermott, *AncSoc* vii (1976), 244 f.
[27] For this hypothesis, *Historia* xvii (1968), 100 f. = *RP* (1979), 688.

verse, including satire (99 ff.); and a disciple of Epicurus, disclosed by 'fecunda quies virtusque serena' (91), with a precise reference to the sage of Attic Gargettus (93 f.).

A question of identity arises. In 60 M. Manilius Vopiscus was consul suffect. Statius vouchsafes no sign of any public occupations of his friend—who might have been elderly and in retirement. For what it may be worth, Statius at the end wishes him a survival beyond the normal: 'finem Nestoreae precor egrediare senectae' (110). Better perhaps Publius, the parent of the consul of 114. If so, he had eschewed public honours, opting for ease and retreat, intent to rescue polite letters from neglect and decline, an amiable role which was inherited by Pliny's equestrian friend Titinius Capito.[28] In that case the high distinction of an eponymous consulate for his son is something of an anomaly.

Multiple names are not always the product of ancestry or adoption. Advertising social success or aspirations, they may commemorate amity or a benefactor without any close tie of propinquity. The second member | in the consul's nomenclature reproduces L. Elufrius Severus: not a person of consequence since proconsul of Crete and Cyrene, in 100 (*AE* 1933, 7: Gortyn). The name is extremely rare. No specimens from any province, and in Italy confined to a narrow region of Umbria.[29]

By contrast, 'Iulius Quadratus Bassus'. None other than the *suffectus* of 105, governor in the sequel of Cappadocia, Syria, Dacia (*PIR*[2], J 508). A casual fact helps, though not much. Vopiscus (*cos.* 114) had been a military tribune. That was highly abnormal, since he was a patrician (the family had been adlected by Vespasian).[30] He served in the legion IV Scythica. That is, under the other Pergamene magnate A. Julius Quadratus (*cos. II* 105), legate of Syria from 100 to 104 (J 507).

The origin of Manilius Vopiscus is inferred from the tribe 'Galeria'. Spain offers about twenty Manilii, the most presentable of them being M. Manilius, magistrate of a small town in Baetica in 5 B.C.[31] The curious may recall Manilius Tusculus, who participated in the conspiracy at Corduba in 48 B.C.[32]

(4) L. Minicius L. f. Gal. Natalis Quadronius Verus (*suff.* 139). *ILS*

---

[28] Pliny, *Ep.* viii 12, 1: 'ipsarum denique litterarum iam senescentium reductor ac reformator'.

[29] *CIL* xi 5178 (Vettona) and 5526 (Asisium) were noted by W. Schulze, *LE* 129.

[30] Another remarkable exception is the consul of 152, M'. Acilius Glabrio (*ILS* 1072: Tibur). See *Chiron* x (1980), 427 f. = *RP* iii (1984), 1316 ff.

[31] *CIL* ii 1343 (Lacibula). There is a group of 'P. Manilii' at Epora (2173, 2082).

[32] *Bell. Al.* 53, 2. Along with Annius Scapula (cf. above), the group included T. Vasius and L. Mercello of Italica (52, 4), rare names.

1061: set up after his African proconsulate by the local senate, 'curante M. Tullio Blaeso'.[33] From Barcino. His father was consul suffect with Q. Licinius Silvanus Granianus in 106. The latter may come from Baetulo (on the coast, a dozen kilometres distant), of which he was *patronus* (*AE* 1936, 66); and Baetulo honours his son (*ILS* 1028). Like the younger Natalis, that son carries 'Quadronius', probably indicating the maternal line, hence cousins. The *gentilicium* is elsewhere on attestation only in Narbonensis. It belongs to the nomenclature of the senator T. Julius Maximus (*ILS* 1016: Nemausus), and three freedmen at Narbo carry it.[34]

The father of Natalis had a splendid career, governing Pannonia | Superior from 113 to 118 and acceding to Africa, but not granted a second consulship.[35] Natalis himself, Hadrian's quaestor in 121, went to join his father in Africa when the Emperor departed on his tour of the western provinces. He acceded to the *fasces* a little later than might have been expected.

The great house at Barcino was the Pedanii, emergent with L. Pedanius Secundus (*suff.* 43). Patrician by favour of Vespasian, they rose to abnormal eminence with Pedanius Fuscus (*cos.* 118), who had married Julia, the niece of Hadrian.[36]

(5) M. Messius M. f. Gal. Rusticus Aemilius Afer etc. *CIL* xiv 3516: a gravestone set up by his parents Aemilius Papus and Cutia Prisca. The polyonymous youth (two additional *nomina*) had perished at the inception of a senatorial career, having held only a minor magistracy.

The father rewards scrutiny. A passage in the *Historia Augusta* notes Hadrian's friends about the year 113 as follows: 'utebatur Hadrianus amicitia Sosi Papi et Platori Nepotis ex senatorio ordine' (*Hadr.* 4, 2). The first name, it was obvious, represents two persons, viz. Sosius Senecio (*cos.* 99, *cos. II* 107) and an Aemilius Papus.[37] The latter should be identified with the (M.) Aemilius Papus of the Tiburtine inscription.[38]

Further light is thrown by another son, *suffectus* c.135 and styled 'Aemilius Papus' when *curator operum publicorum* in 138 (*AE* 1934, 136), also on a fragment at Salpensa in Baetica (*CIL* ii 12826). Two

---

[33] A local notable, cf. *ILS* 5630, 6233.

[34] *CIL* xii 4414 f., 5081. Observe also, in Greek lettering, 'Toouta Kouadrounia' (*AE* 1903, 182: Ventabren, Bouches-du-Rhône).

[35] *ILS* 1029 (Barcino). A new diploma shows him in Pannonia in December of 113. For knowledge of which, I am grateful to Werner Eck. Now published by K. Dietz, *RGK Bericht* lxv (1984), 159 ff.

[36] Pliny, *Ep.* vi 26.   [37] E. Groag, *RE* iiiA 1187.

[38] For the family, H. G. Pflaum, *Klio* xlvi (1965), 331 ff. For a stemma, M. Corbier, *L'Aerarium Saturni et l'Aerarium militare* (1974), 192.

other inscriptions reveal his nomenclature and career (1282–3). He there stands as 'M. Cutius M. f. Gal. Priscus Messius Rusticus Aemilius Papus Arrius Proculus Iulius Celsus'. In this instance, the maternal name wins prominence. At Callet, however, he is 'M. Messius Rusticus Aemilius Papus' etc. (1371), and he is registered as *PIR*¹, M 376—and now as *PIR*², M 526.³⁸ᵃ

None the less, this consular is really 'M. Aemilius Papus' like his father, the husband of Cutia Prisca. Valid suspicion will claim the father as also a polyonymous senator. Hadrian's friend might even be identical | with L. Messius Rusticus (*suff.* 114), who would thus be 'L. Messius Rusticus M. Aemilius Papus'.³⁹

(6) M. Accenna L. f. Gal. Saturninus. *CIL* xiv 3585: set up by his wife Atilia L. f. Balbilla and giving his career as far as the proconsulate of Baetica. The Etruscan name excites interest, likewise his kinsman or son M. Accenna M. f. Gal. Helvius Agrippa, a senator of praetorian rank deceased at the age of thirty-four (ii 1262: nr. Hispalis). In relation to the second Accenna, observe M. Helvius M. f. M. n. Serg. Agrippa who earned a public funeral at Hispalis (1184). The 'Sergia' is the tribe of Italica, but it also occurs at Hispalis (where 'Galeria' appears normal): perhaps a result of symbiosis between those neighbour cities.⁴⁰

(7) P. Mummius P. f. Gal. Sisenna Rutilianus (*suff.* 146). *ILS* 1101: set up in 172 by the *Augustales* of Tibur, also *CIL* xiv 4244, by the Senate and People. The tribe has been taken to indicate Spain.⁴¹ The Peninsula shows over twenty Mummii, among them three magistrates in towns of Baetica.⁴² Further, a senatorial family. Mummia Nigrina, known to Martial (iv 75; ix 30), was the wife of L. Antistius Rusticus (*suff.* 90), himself presumed Spanish (cf. *PIR*², A 765): and there is L. Mummius Niger Valerius Vegetus (*suff.* 112),⁴³ whose father was Q. Valerius Vegetus (*suff.* 91), from Iliberris. The mother and the wife of the latter were honoured there (ii 2074, 2077).⁴⁴

---

³⁸ᵃ See further, on his son, *AE* 1983, 517, showing the young man prefect of the city during the *feriae Latinae*, in the consulship of his father Papus and father-in-law Burbuleius Ligarianus; and the *patria* was Siara rather than Salpensa.

³⁹ Although *Fasti* generally give the 'real' name. Apart from the Messii Rustici, *CIL* II shows only four Messii—and apart from senators (1172 f., 1282 f.) no Cutii at all.

⁴⁰ For the Accennae see further G. Alföldy, op. cit. 66, 171. He suggests Italica rather than Hispalis.

⁴¹ A. R. Birley, op. cit. 71: G. Alföldy, *Konsulat und Senatorenstand unter den Antoninen* (1977), 312.

⁴² *CIL* ii 1584 (?Itucci), 1684 (Tucci), 2025 (Singilia). Add a P. Mummius of Ugia (*AE* 1952, 49: Emerita).

⁴³ For his full nomenclature, *ILS* 5771 (Ferentum), *CIL* ix 948 (Aecae). On the *Fasti Ostienses* he is 'Q. Valerius Vegetus'. From a total of sixty-seven 'Vegeti', twenty-eight occur in *CIL* II, cf. I. Kajanto, op. cit. 247.

⁴⁴ The origin—from Osset in Baetica—is settled, with new evidence, by J. González, *ZPE* lii (1982), 172 f.

Mummius Sisenna enjoyed a successful career, ending as proconsul of Asia—and consigned to derision as a devotee of the prophet Alexander.[44a] His father deserves a brief word somewhere, *consul ordinarius* in 133 and passing rapidly to Britain in 134 or 135 (*CIL* xvi 82). The brief interval between consulships suggests that he came late to the *fasces*. Antecedents and earlier posts would be worth knowing. Conjecture might toy with the 'Publius' who governed Thrace at some | time between 128 and 136 (*IGR* i 785: Perinthus): that is, P. Mummius Sisenna *c.*129–132.

(8) Q. Pompeius Q. f. Senecio, etc. (*cos.* 169), the grandson of Falco. *ILS* 1104: set up by 'Senate and People'. Although the grandfather's origin is problematic, the old Roscian connection and close ties with the city permit his inclusion.

So far a rubric of senatorial families that echo back to various regions of the Peninsula. Four further items may be brought up, with credentials imperfect or disputable.

(1) Senecio Memmius Gal. Afer (*suff.* 99). *ILS* 1042: his gravestone, set up by his son L. Memmius Tuscillus Senecio. Since the homonymous grandson of that son receives honour from the priests of Ceres at Carthage (viii 24586), an African origin is assumed.[45] Only one city in the province carries 'Galeria', namely Hadrumetum. No consular descendant is discoverable of the *suffectus* of 99. Later senatorial Memmii tend to come from Bulla Regia or Gigthis.[46]

The *cognomen* 'Afer' falls short of support. It is borne, for example, by Hadrian's father; and the son of Aemilius Papus (presumably not the elder) is 'Aemilius Afer' (xiv 3516, cf. above). On the other hand, 'Tuscus' is fashionable in Spain, sometimes the assertion of an *ultima origo*.[47] Similarly 'Tuscillus'. *CIL* II yields five specimens.[48] One of them is Cn. Papirius Aelianus Aemilius Tuscillus (ii 2075: Iliberris): perhaps the consular (*suff. c.*135) who governed Britain in 146 (xvi 93), better perhaps a son.[49] Finally, eighteen Memmii on Spanish inscriptions.

(2) P. Marcius [?P.] f. Gal. Gallus. *Inscr. It.* iv iv 1 (1952), 159. The

---

[44a] Lucian, *Alex*, 30 ff.   [45] E. Groag, *RE* xv 622.

[46] Thus C. Memmius Fidus Iulius Albius (*suff. c.*191), from Bulla: cf. E. Groag, *RE* xv 623 ff.; M. Memmius Caecilianus, from Gigthis: ibid. 622 f.

[47] *CIL* II has 23, among them a Coranius (1060) and a Veienta (801). L. Fabius Tuscus, recently revealed as a suffect in 101 by a fragment of the *Fasti Ostienses*, is homonymous with a magistrate at Ulia (ii 1537).

[48] *CIL* ii 157, 236, 2075, 2279, 5175. Only the son of Memmius Afer is registered by I. Kajanto, op. cit. 188.

[49] Kept separate in *PIR*[1], P 80 f., they are amalgamated by Hofmann in *RE* xviii 1013.

first line ends with 'q.[', the second shows the man tribune in |
X Gemina p. f. and I Min. P. f. That is to say, subsequent to 96.
P. Marcius is disclosed as *pontifex* in 101 (vi 32445). Marcii are
frequent in Spain (over sixty), but 'Publius' is there to be discovered
only in the lady 'Marcia P. f. Postuma Messenia Lucilla Aemilia c. f.'
(ii 3740, Valentia).

The inscription of another Marcius at Tibur, reported in two
copies, begins with 'T. Marcio T. f. Falg. Le[' (xiv 3595). The tribe
'Gal.' might have been suspected. One remedy is to read 'Fal.
[C]le[menti'.[50] The document carries his career down to the
command of II Augusta: set up by Grania Tertull[a].

(3) Annius Faustus. A small piece reveals ']ius M. f./Faustus/trib.
mil./d. d.' (*Inscr. It* iv iv 1.166). Attention went to a man condemned
in 69, 'Annium Faustum equestris ordinis, qui temporibus Neronis
delationes factitaverat' (*Hist.* ii 10, 2). Perhaps identical, as suggested
in *PIR*[2], A 645.

The senator 'M. [......] Faustus' occurs, consul suffect in 121 as
colleague of Q. Pomponius Marcellus (vi 2080). A new diploma
discloses, with the same colleague. ']nnio Fausto'.[51] Not, however,
an Annius, so it has been proposed, but a Herennius.[52] Confidence
was premature. The spacing of the names on the diploma entails two
gentilicia for this consul.[53] Therefore an Annius Faustus is not ruled
out—perhaps 'M. Herennius Annius Faustus'. For the collocation,
observe as *suffecti* in the same year (85), P. Herennius Pollio and his
son M. Annius Herennius Pollio (*AE* 1975, 21).

Herennii as well as Annii evoke Spanish Romans. Thus Herennius
Senecio from Baetica (*PIR*[2], H 128) and the consul Herennius
Severus, the patron of Philo of Byblus (H 130).

The inscription of Annius Faustus was in fact found along with
that of L. Cornelius Pusio Annius Messalla (*AE* 1915, 60, cf. above).
Perhaps therefore related. As concerns the disreputable knight Annius
Faustus, it was the habit of the historian to bring up ancestors of the
notables in his own time.

(4) C. Popillius C. f. Quir. Carus Pedo (*suff.* 147). *ILS* 1071: set up
| by 'Senate and People'. His origin has not been ascertained. One
attempt invokes the second *cognomen* and suggests the zone of the
western Alps: of twenty-one specimens of 'Pedo', no fewer than

[50] Thus E. Groag, *RE* xiv 1557.
[51] Adduced in *Tacitus*, 792. See now M. M. Roxan, *Roman Military Diplomas 1954–1957*
(1978), no. 19.
[52] I. I. Russu, *Dacia* xvi (1972), 287 ff. He adduced the legionary legate M. Herennius
Faustus (*Apulum* iii (1949), 202).
[53] W. Eck, *RE, Suppl.* xiv 47.

eight are found in *CIL* XII, whereas the tribe 'Quirina' precludes the cities of Narbonensis.[54]

Waiving the *cognomen*, a thought might go to Spain, with about sixteen Popillii.[55] At Carthago Nova the 'porta Popillia' (*ILS* 5833 f.) commemorates, so it is held, M. Popillius Laenas (*cos.* 139 B.C.), who governed Citerior. Tarraco shows Popilia M. f. Secunda, daughter of a *flaminica* of the province (ii 4276); and Saguntum (enrolled in 'Galeria') can put up Popillii of the better sort, viz. Popillia L. f. Rectina, the wife of Pliny's friend and coeval Voconius Romanus (ii 3866). Also Popillia Avita, wife of a magistrate (3856, a Baebius), or M. Popillius, known from early coins.[56]

The Tiburtine document takes the career of Popillius Pedo as far as the governorship of Germania Superior (*c*.152–5). He ended as proconsul of Asia (*AE* 1924, 74). For presumed relatives one may cite M. (Popillius) Pedo Vergilianus (*cos.* 115) and Popillius Priscus (*suff. c*.134), the first Popillii to achieve rank under the Empire.[57]

After a haul so rich it might appear superfluous to rope in L. Baebius L. f. Serg. Balbus (xiv 3515), were he not incautiously labelled an 'Italicus'.[58] With a dense cluster at Saguntum, Baebii are common throughout the Peninsula. The tribe 'Sergia' does not rule out a city of Baetica—or even of Tarraconensis.[59] After the *cognomen* the inscription continues and concludes with 'trib. mil./leg. VIII, item trib./m[.' The absence of the legion's title *Augusta* speaks for a quite early date.

A Pedanius Rufus might arouse interest, friend of the imperial doctor Ti. Claudius Aelius Sabinianus (xiv 3641). Or again, the freedman of a Marcus Raecius (xiv 3790). M. Raecius Taurus, a senator already under Claudius, was co-opted among the *Arvales* (vi 2045). By Nero, that is the common assumption. A strong case can be made out for Galba.[60] His son by adoption, M. Raecius Gallus, was an active | partisan when the usurper was proclaimed in Tarraconensis. After being high priest of the provincial cult he passed by anomaly into the senatorial order.[61] These Raecii, as the inscriptions of several freedmen demonstrate, were domiciled at Tarraco.[62] The *nomen* is Etruscan or Illyrian.[63]

[54] G. Alföldy, op. cit. 313.

[55] And for that matter, two specimens of 'Pedo': the *duumvir* C. Iulius Pedo (ii 53: Pax Iulia) and a homonym at Coret in Baetica (1001).

[56] G. Alföldy, *Los Baebii de Saguntum* (1977), 77.

[57] The *suffectus* of 147 was alleged a patrician by R. Hanslik, *RE* xxii 65.

[58] H. Devijver, *Pros. Mil. Eq.* (1976), no. 22.

[59] A study of the 'Sergia' would be welcome, cf. below on Licinius Sura.

[60] *Some Arval Brethren*, 9 f.   [61] *AE* 1965, 236 = *RIT* 145.

[62] *CIL* ii 4304, 4401; *AE* 1929, 231. Note also Raecia M. f. (*AE* 1938, 19).

[63] W. Schulze, *LE* 44.

From epigraphy the discourse now turns to poetry. Martial shares with Statius several friends and patrons, notably Arruntius Stella (*suff.* ?101), Atedius Melior, and the enigmatic Blaesus, who is a senator of consular rank.[64] Of the cultivated Manilius Vopiscus and his Tiburtine villa, no sign.

In this fertile and well-documented epoch persons common to different writers (verse or prose) are an engaging theme. Likewise mutual silence between authors. Thus Martial and Statius—and some find it remarkable that Juvenal should be absent from the correspondence of Pliny.

To Martial he is 'Iuvenalis meus' (vii 24, 1), he is styled 'facundus' (vii 91, 1), he receives a missive at the end from Bilbilis (xii 18). Despite these tokens of affection, Juvenal makes no appearance until the year 92. Certain old Spanish acquaintances occur in Book I, half a dozen years earlier, viz. Decianus (i 24), Licinianus (49, 51), Canius Rufus (61, 69), Maternus (96).

Like most things about Juvenal's life, his age is a problem of contention. He may have been born in 67, precisely. If so, about twenty-five years junior to Martial, who was a close coeval with Quintilian, that other immigrant. Furthermore, the origin of Juvenal's family can be claimed provincial, from Spain—or even from Africa.[65] His late emergence in the poems cannot be invoked either way.

Juvenal might have been away from Rome for several years on military service as an equestrian officer. Not impossible. To go further is to go lower—to lapse into byways frequented by scholiasts and their modern disciples. |

The satirist, as he casually discloses, owned a property at Tibur (xi 65). Martial once described his own modest estate as a 'Tiburtinum' (iv 9). In truth Nomentum, as avowed on several clear statements (ii 38, xii 57, xiii 42, 119). They were contiguous. Tibur had the better name. Catullus declared it when amiably elucidating 'o funde noster seu Sabine seu Tiburs' (44, 1).

To proceed. Brief inspection of Martial's poems might elicit several persons with Tiburtine attachments.

(1) Lausus, addressed in a cluster of short poems devoid of individual features, good or bad (vii 81, 87 f.). No curiosity is excited. The fellow might appear fictitious, like so many in Martial. Lausus is the son of Mezentius in Virgil, of Numitor in Ovid (*Fasti* iv 54), and the name is authentically Etruscan, compare 'Lausenna' (vi 2684). An inscription brings a surprise: the son of a Licinius

---

[64] For the identity of Blaesus (a vexed problem), see *Some Arval Brethren*, 43 ff.

[65] For discussion of Juvenal's *patria*, *CP* lxxiv (1979), 1 ff. = *RP* iii (1984), 1120 ff.

Lausus from Saetabi buried at Tibur (xiv 3795). A minor character is thus certified, cf. *PIR*², L 136.

(2) Faustinus, with nineteen poems to his address (for the detail, *PIR*², F 127). He is an early entrant (i 25), honoured with the dedication of Books II and III and occurring for the last time in x 51. Frequent notice goes to his Tiburtine villa. Faustinus also had properties at Baiae, at Tarracina —and at Trebula Mutuesca, cooler in the summer than Tibur (v 71).

This person of patent opulence was not only a friend of polite letters but an author himself, gently rebuked for hesitance to publish (i 25). Only one poem brings him into relation with anybody else. It is with Marcellinus, to whom, in service on the Danube, Faustinus may despatch a book of Martial's poems (vii 80). Marcellinus himself is enjoined to restrain 'temerarius ardor': without that, 'tu potes et patris miles et esse ducis' (vi 25, 8). After the Danube, he is in prospect of seeing the Caucasus—'ecce Promethei rupes et fabula montis' (ix 45, 3). That is to say, the young officer has been transferred to the army of Cappadocia.

Addressing Marcellinus, Martial describes himself as a 'patrius amicus' (vi 25, 3). Hence the notion that Marcellinus is a son of Faustinus (cf. *PIR*², F 127). Faustinus might come from Spain—but it will not be safe in this context to adduce Marcella of Bilbilis, who presented the poet with an estate (xii 21, 31).

Through the years Faustinus is discovered only once at Rome (x 51). He does not look like a senator, and there is no call to evoke Cn. Minicius Faustinus (*suff.* 91), whose name, recurring in a *suffectus* of 117, is | prefixed to that of Sex. Julius Severus (*suff.* 127), from Aequum in Dalmatia (*ILS* 1056: Burnum, cf. *AE* 1904, 7).[66]

(3) Curiatius, who by paradox perished at the salubrious resort: when Death announces his advent, 'in medio Tibure Sardinia est' (iv 60, 6). Book IV belongs to the year 89, as is demonstrated by the reference to the failed usurpation of Antonius Saturninus, legate of Germania Superior (iv 11).

The name should arouse interest because of Curiatius Maternus, one of the four interlocutors in the *Dialogus* of Cornelius Tacitus, an orator and a dramatist. His fate engages some concern. According to Cassius Dio (under the year 91), Domitian put to death a 'sophist' called Maternus for declaiming against tyranny.[67] Identity still finds champions.[68] The notion should be discarded.

[66] Minicii are common (about twenty in Spain)—but only three in Dalmatia.
[67] Dio lxvii 12, 5.
[68] E. Paratore, *Tacito* (1951), 193 f.; K. Matthiessen, *AC* xxxix (1970), 166 ff. A violent end soon after 75 is inferred (from *Dial.* 11, 4) by A. D. E. Cameron, *CR* xvii (1967), 258 ff.

One theory enlisted Curiatius Maternus on the roll of the Gallic orators, by a misguided argument from the *cognomen* (twenty-eight instances in Gaul.)[69] Over sixty in Spain were neglected, likewise the consular M. Cornelius M. f. Gal. Curiatius Maternus.[70] Inscriptions at Liria in the hinterland of Valentia registered him as legate of Moesia and of Syria (ii 6013, cf. 3783). His date was long uncertain (cf. *PIR*[2], C 1407). The full *cursus* has recently emerged.[71] He is identical with 'M. Co[', consul suffect in 83.[72] Hence notable consequences for the Danubian wars of Domitian—and further for Syria and for transactions of the year 97, if he is none other than the governor whose attitude gave rise to rumours and alarm.[73]

The name 'Curiatius' is far from common in this epoch. Apart from the consular at Liria, Spain offers only three specimens.[74] The consular may be either a son of the orator, taken in adoption by M. Cornelius | Nigrinus, or a nephew; and the man who died at Tibur may be the friend and mentor whom the young Tacitus admired.[75]

(4) A certain Fuscus is addressed as a new acquaintance (i 54). The *cognomen* is indistinctive, but he might be the same as the Fuscus, an advocate of repute, who is enjoying a respite on his Tiburtine estate. The poet hopes that the product of his vineyard may prove equal 'Tartesiacis . . . trapezis' (vii 28, 3). The ornate epithet, although appertaining to Baetica, may merely stand for 'Spanish'. By a similar licence Martial, when writing to Maternus from Celtiberian Bilbilis, asks whether he has any message for the coast of Galicia: 'Callaicum mandas si quid ad Oceanum' (x 37, 4).

Martial's Fuscus is not a mere *causidicus* like Juvenal and others, but of high quality as a public speaker: 'sic fora mirentur, sic te Palatia laudent' (28, 5). The chance is not excluded that he was Cn. Pedanius Fuscus Salinator (*suff. c.* 84), the head of the leading family at Barcino. At this time the consul's son (*cos.* 118) was a small boy aged about seven, later to be praised for eloquence by Pliny (*Ep.* vi 26).

Like Pliny in his letters, the poet is seldom anxious to specify the origin and status of a friend. He refrains, especially with the eminent. Camonius Rufus, who died in Cappadocia at the age of twenty, happens to carry the label of his *patria*, namely Bononia (ix 30):

---

[69] Thus A. Gudeman in his edition (1914[2]), 66.
[70] As emphasized in *Tacitus*, 799 f.   [71] *AE* 1973, 283.
[72] He was conjectured to be a son in *Dacia* xii (1968), 331 ff. = *Danubian Papers* (1971), 214.
[73] Pliny, *Ep.* ix 13, 11, cf. the thesis of G. Alföldy–H. Halfmann, *Chiron* iii (1973), 331 ff. See further *ZPE* xli (1981), 136 ff. = *RP* iii (1984), 1386 ff.
[74] *CIL* ii 954, 1109, 2211 (of no consequence).
[75] The *praenomen* of some or all of these Curiatii may be revealed by the item 'C. Curiatius Maternus' in the nomenclature of C. Clodius Nummus, *suffectus* in 114 (x 1486, cf. *PIR*[2], A 83.

presumably an equestrian officer. Cappadocia is also impugned for
the death of Antistius Rusticus in 93 or 94: the widow Nigrina
brought the ashes back to Italy (ix 30). Nigrina had previously been
praised for concord with her spouse (iv 75). Neither was accorded
their Spanish provenance.

Sparsus calls for attention, on solitary mention at a late stage. He
owned the 'domus Petiliana' within the walls of Rome,

> cui plana summos despicit domus montis
> et rus in urbe est vinitorque Romanus.

> (xii 57, 20 f.)

The palace and vineyard bespeak a person of great wealth.[76]
Therefore | Sex. Julius Sparsus (*suff*. 88). The Sparsus who receives a
pair of inconspicuous missives from Pliny may be a son.[77] The
meagre epigraphic evidence for the name encourages a conjecture.
Once at Nemausus with a Sex. Domitius Sparsus (xii 3558), then
L. Licinius Sparsus, high priest at Tarraco (ii 4198) and Licinia Sparsi f.
at Asturica (2648).[78]

Again, Licinius Sura. His mansion beside Diana's temple on the
Aventine, once plebeian but now fashionable, earns a passing
reference (vi 64, 13). In 92 Sura nearly succumbed to a serious illness.
Martial salutes him as

> doctorum Licini celeberrime Sura virorum
> cuius prisca gravis lingua reduxit avos.

> (vii 47, 1)

Further, congratulating the orator on his escape, Martial incites him
to get pleasure out of life—'vive velut rapto fugitivaque gaudia carpe'
(47, 11).

The collection vouchsafes no sign thereafter. In 97 Sura had an
active part in the elevation of Trajan, the legate of Germania
Superior; and the poet lived long enough to hear about his second
consulship in 102. Book XII, written at Bilbilis, falls in 101 or
perhaps early in 102.[79] Martial died not long after.

---

[76] Perhaps property of the eminent Petillii, who fade out before the end of the Flavian
dynasty.

[77] *Ep*. iv 5; viii, 3. The two are amalgamated in *PIR*², J 586.

[78] For these Sparsi and for others, *HSCPh* lxxiii (1969), 232 = *RP* (1979), 769. Add 'Coelius
Sparsus' in the nomenclature of C. Pomponius Rufus, suffect in 98 (*ILAlg* i 230 etc.). Probably
Spanish, like Q. Pomponius Rufus (*suff*. 95), adlected by Galba or by Vespasian (*IRT* 537), and
the Pomponius of Pliny (*NH* xxii 120).

[79] Martial salutes the consulship of Arruntius Stella, which belongs in an October (*ILS*
6106). In *PIR*², A 1151 preference was given to 102 over 101. The book carries no reference to
the Dacian War beginning in 101.

In a Roman sojourn of thirty-four years (from 64 to 98) the ingenious Martial had solicited or enlisted a large and variegated company, taking in senators and consuls. The Spanish friends avow diverse or distant origins. Among the earliest to be put on display, emulating the glory of Corduba, are Canius Rufus from far Gades, Decianus from Lusitanian Emerita, Licinianus from Bilbilis (i 61).

Canius Rufus was a poet, adept in several measures. Decianus an advocate, and also a Stoic, while Licinianus had acquired fame in oratory.[80] Furthermore, Maternus (i 96; ii 74). He comes out towards the end as a man of Bilbilis and an expert in the law, 'iuris et aequarum cultor sanctissime legum' (x 37, 1). |

Martial went back in 98, to deplore in the preface of Book XII a 'provincialis solitudo' and petty malice in his home town, the 'municipalium robigo dentium'. Licinianus had anticipated him in retirement by a dozen years (i 49). Bilbilis was a place to escape from, for more reasons than one. The month of December will find Licinianus on the Catalonian coast, 'aprica repetes Tarraconis litora/tuamque Laietaniam' (21 f.). The poem concludes with praise of another orator, 'dum Sura laudatur tuus' (49, 50). Licinianus is a friend of Licinius Sura, perhaps a kinsman.

Sura had ties with both Tarraco and Barcino. Their tribe is 'Galeria', his 'Sergia'.[81] The *patria* is some other city, of the hinterland.[82] Perhaps Osca. Perhaps Celsa, 'colonia Victrix Julia Lepida', that foundation on the Ebro which was eclipsed by Caesaraugusta, perhaps from set purpose of the ruler.[83] The tribes of Osca and Celsa have not so far been ascertained.

As foreshadowed at the outset, the exposition conveys sharp relevance to the validity of arguments based on names and tribes. About the distribution or frequency of *nomina*, caution is expedient. Some comfort accrues when the Spanish provinces yield on average some twenty specimens each of Coelii, Manilii, Minicii, Memmii, Mummii, Popillii. On the other side, observe, apart from senators, Curiatii (three), Maecii (five), Messii (four), Roscii (four). Nor is the recourse to *cognomina* safe, as with 'Pedo', although 'Murena' and 'Sparsus' encourage speculation. Above all, account has to be taken of the sparse epigraphic harvest from certain cities. Thus Ilici, Osca, Celsa.[84]

To get value from statistics entails respect for proportions. The Tiburtine documentation is copious, the results remarkable. Of

[80] *PIR*², C 397, D 20, L 170.   [81] *CIL* ii 4282 (his arch near Tarraco).
[82] As argued in *Tacitus*, 791.   [83] On Celsa, see M. Grant, op. cit. 211.
[84] The totals in *CIL* II are Ilici (11), Celsa (9), Osca (4).

about twenty named senators belonging between 70 and 180, at least seven are shown to derive from the Spains. Rational conjecture has rendered others worthy of discussion.

It remains to assess the consequences. For comparison, other suburban resorts invite cursory inspection. Tusculum offered many owners of villas on attestation in the late epoch of the Republic, descending | from noblemen to Cornelius Balbus, that isolated and paradoxical precursor of the Spanish invasion. Few can be detected in the sequel.[85] One reason may be divined—palaces of the aristocracy annexed by the Caesars.

Lanuvium is less conspicuous but useful for parallel. The ancient *municipium* had contributed a large number of senators, among others Licinii, Roscii, Annii, Aquillii, Cornificii.[86] Of that order only two members can be discovered on inscriptions of imperial date— and they extraneous.[87] No Roscius of any class appears at any time.

The site was sheltered and attractive, nestling in the slopes of the Alban Hills close beside the Appia. It comes into the history of the third imperial dynasty. One of the rulers had a villa there, according to the *Historia Augusta* (*Pius* 1, 8); and Commodus, born at Lanuvium, displayed his skill in the arena (*Comm.* 1, 2; 8, 5). His father was seldom separated from Antoninus Pius—in the space of twenty-three years only two nights away (*Marcus* 7, 2 f.). A stray notice in Fronto declares that he found Lanuvium chilly in the early morning.[88] In the year 140 the young Marcus, returning with Pius from the vintage, turned aside to visit Pompeius Falco. They contemplated the tree of many branches (a 'catachanna') on which this elderly consular practised grafting.[89] No speculation can reach to the site of Falco's estate.

In contrast to Lanuvium and Tusculum, Tibur had a broad *territorium*. Coterminous with Nomentum on the north-west, it went a long way eastwards, taking in Sublaqueum (Subiaco).[90] Hence properties in the countryside, for profit as well as refreshment. A significant fact confirms: the number of inscriptions found at Castelmadama, about 10 km. to the east of Tivoli. Thus Cornelius Pusio (*suff.* 90), together with Annius Faustus, and Baebius Balbus (cf. above). The young son of Aemilius Papus was buried there (xiv 3516); and one will not miss an *Ignotus*, a senator who had

[85] For the list, G. McCracken, *RE* viiA 1487 f.

[86] T. P. Wiseman, *New Men in the Roman Senate* (1971), 185.

[87] *CIL* xiv 2095, 2107. Add the acephalous *Eph. Ep.* ix 612 (?Roscius Aelianus).

[88] Fronto, Haines i, p. 140.   [89] Ibid. p. 142.

[90] Dessau in *CIL* xiv, p. 368; S. Weinstock, *RE* viA 821. Estimates range from 350 to 500 square km.

commanded two legions in succession, viz. XI Claudia and I or II Adiutrix (3518).

A predominance of Spaniards comes out on another type of comparison. The core of the Antonine dynasty represents a coalescence of the notables | deriving from Spain and Narbonensis. Antoninus Pius, who married a daughter of M. Annius Verus (*cos. III* 126), is the third consul of the Aurelii Fulvi, Nemausus their *patria*. Not a single Narbonensian is disclosed at Tibur. Nor any of the alert and successful sons of provincial Italy, the Transpadana, except Novellius Atticus (*ILS* 950). As for Africa, rising fast in this period, if Senecio Memmius Afer (*suff.* 99) is reclaimed for Spain, there remains one senator at Tibur, the mysterious L. Uttiedius L. f. Afer, labelled as an augur, consul designate and patron of Carthage.[91] Nor can the opulent magnates from western Asia, whether dynastic or products of the Italian diaspora, make a showing, although they parade consuls before the death of Domitian. The nearest to the Greek East is the Pergamene item 'Julius Quadratus Bassus' attached to the nomenclature of Manilius Vopiscus (*cos.* 114) or a Euryclid affinity somehow annexed by Pompeius Falco (*suff.* 108).[92]

So far the general theme has for convenience operated with Spain, postponing the diversity of towns and of whole regions. Baetica exhibits early settlers in the train of the legions, some Italian before they became Roman, as witness Annaeii, Dasumii, Ulpii. Yet in Baetica, as in inner Tarraconensis, some of the names reflect proconsuls of the imperial Republic, and consequent fashions in nomenclature, such as Fabii, Licinii, Mummii, Popillii, Valerii.

Gades to Barcino, the Tiburtine congregation is highly heterogeneous. It includes an Etruscan from Hispalis (M. Accenna Saturninus), and the popularity of 'Tuscus' and 'Tuscillus' has not escaped notice. Other regions of Italy contribute, such as Picenum. The Aelii laid claim to Hadria (*HA Hadr.* 1, 1, cf. 19, 1). In choice of residence, some families of the returning emigrants may avow an *ultima origo*, whether authentic or invented, as happens in other times. The Annii, so it appears, asserted Lanuvium. Marcus Aurelius equipped one of | his daughters with 'Cornificia', recalling a reputable family long extinct. The Annius familiar from history and

---

[91] *CIL* xiv 3615. Dessau registered him as imperial in *PIR*[1], V 692. The consul designate in the Triumviral period called Tedius Afer, whom Octavian drove to suicide (Suetonius, *DAug.* 27, 3), continues to give trouble. Thus, firm for identity, T. P. Wiseman, op. cit. 268.

[92] However, one could add a Plancius Varus from Perge (*Inscr. It.* iv iv 1, 132 a-c), discussed in *Historia* xviii (1969), 365 = *RP* (1979), 788 f. He was probably a legate of Cilicia.

literature was too deleterious for resuscitation. 'Milo' could be resigned to persons of lower station.[93]

While in many respects bold innovators all the way from agriculture to the liberal arts, the immigrants from the western lands conformed to the Roman tradition; and some brought with them 'provincialis parsimonia' or 'antiquus rigor', along with other estimable habits or attitudes. The age of the Antonines evinced a strong tendency towards archaism in language and letters. Antiquarianism exercised a broad appeal. The towns of old Latium had plenty to offer in the way of relics. Anagnia captivated Marcus Aurelius: 'multas res in se antiquas et aedes sanctasque caerimonias supra modum'. The young man was moved to quote an inscription on one of the gates.[94]

Tibur had Hercules Victor for presidial deity. As custodians of the shrine no fewer than five consulars held office: Manilius Vopiscus, Minicius Natalis, Mummius Sisenna, Popillius Pedo, the third Pompeius Falco. Furthermore, Tibur like Rome had its dancing priests of Mars, the *Salii*. To that college belonged Roscius Aelianus, Mummius Sisenna, the third Falco. As the institution of the Arval Brethren demonstrates (although it had forfeited social prestige in this period), men derived much satisfaction from ceremony and ritual: no drawback if failing to correspond with inward convictions. Yet religion was now gaining ground. Minicius Natalis made a dedication to 'Hercules Victor and the other presiding gods' (*ILS* 3415); he also consecrated a temple to Asclepios Soter (*IGR* i 376); and he has left traces of his piety and wealth in other cities of Italy.[95]

Four of these consulars were *patroni* of Tibur, viz. Natalis, Sisenna, Pedo, the third Falco. Among their coevals only M'. Acilius Glabrio (*cos.* 152) had that honour, an aristocrat with lineage now out of the common (*ILS* 1072). Glabrio, it may be added, condescended to be a *quinquennalis* at Tibur.[96]

The functions thus assumed by families of the new imperial nobility imply a close attachment that may well go back several generations. | Natalis saw the light of day at Barcino, as he declared in a benefaction by his testament (ii 4511). Some of the others may have been born at Tibur or taken there in tender years.[97] The Roman *salius* enters the college in youth, and he normally retires when

---

[93] C. Annius Milo, a veteran from Luca (iii 14415: Oescus).

[94] Fronto, Haines i, p. 174.

[95] For his properties and benefactions, E. Groag, *RE* xv 1839 f.; personality and tastes, 1840 f. In 129, when praetorian in rank, he won a chariot victory (*SIG*[3] 840: Olympia).

[96] As did Natalis and the third Falco. The inscriptions at Barcino fail to show Natalis in that role.

[97] Thus Annaeus Seneca, carried to Rome by his aunt (*Ad Helviam matrem* 19, 2).

acceding to a magistracy or a superior priesthood. Tibur conformed, it may be presumed.

Nine consulars have been discussed. That is, including by conjecture the first Aemilius Papus (assimilated to L. Messius Rusticus) and Popillius Pedo, while the third Falco is added for convenience. Tibur thus furnishes no fewer than six complete senatorial careers, four of them concluding with Asia or Africa, while Falco declined Asia.

Apart from Minicius Natalis and the families of Accenna Saturninus (from Hispalis) and Aemilius Papus (Salpensa) none of the other senators finds honour in cities of the Peninsula.[97a] As elsewhere, the hazards of epigraphic evidence have to be allowed for—at Nemausus no Aurelius Fulvus, no Arrius Antoninus. Ambition took them away, the service of the Caesars, a life of decorative ease. They acquired new homes and turned into Italian senators, some with a strong predilection for Hellenic culture. Later generations tended to forget or ignore the old country.

Documented for the first time by consulars, most of them sons of consuls, the Tiburtine symbiosis presupposes ancestors of wealth and status, not neglecting the knights who founded their fortunes. Junius Columella will be recalled, the Gaditane agronome who possessed estates at Ardea, Carseoli, Alba, Caere.[98]

Suburban villas in the classic epoch served as meeting places for discourse on letters and philosophy, as congenial opportunity for political intrigue. Groups and factions are inseparable from the life of oligarchies in any age. In the present instance, a note of warning should be sounded. The Spanish consulars at Tibur are only a collection, not a group or a 'circle' of the type so often conjured up in the pages of literature. No ties of kinship or allegiance are perceptible, such as the alliances that formed at Rome between the rising families from Spain and Narbonensis. At the most (and it is not much), the Roscian connection may descend from Roscius Aelianus (*suff.* 100) to the grandson of Pompeius Falco (*cos.* 169). |

Epilogue

One name has been withheld until now, and one villa: the palace which Hadrian constructed on the slopes below Tibur, to delight him by memories of history and legend, and of his own peregrinations,

---

[97a] Cf., however, n. 44, above, for Mummius Sisenna (Osset).

[98] Columella iii 3, 3; 9, 2.

to ensure an island of seclusion in the manner of Capreae for old age.[99] Hadrian died in the course of the ominous sixty-third year.

The antecedents of the site are obscure. Hadrian himself was born at Rome, in January of 76, on the testimony, here unimpeachable, of the *Historia Augusta* (*Hadr.* 1, 3). In 90 he paid a visit to Italica: 'quinto decimo anno ad patriam rediit' (1, 5). He did not again see the city of his origin, although going on his first journey as far as Tarraco, where he spent the winter of 122/3. Estrangement has been surmised.[100] The evidence is imperfect, the notion not proved or disproved by the embellishment of Italica, by the dedication at Tibur celebrating *liberalitates* conferred on the province Baetica between the years 117 and 135.[101]

---

[99] *HA Hadr.* 26, 5, cf. Victor 14, 5: 'deinde . . . remissior rus proprium Tibur secessit, permissa urbe Lucio Aelio Caesari.' Nothing in Cassius Dio.

[100] For this debatable question, R. Syme, *JRS* liv (1964), 142 ff. = *RP* (1979), 617 ff.; R. Nierhaus, in *Corolla E. Swoboda* (1966), 151 ff.

[101] *ILS* 318 (Tibur), cf. Dio lxix 10, 1 (on Italica). What Hadrian did for his *patria* is extolled by A. García y Bellido, in *Les Empereurs romains d'Espagne* (1965), 7 ff.—and diminished by R. Nierhaus, op. cit. 167.

7

Partisans of Galba

THE seven months' rule of the patrician usurper declares few consequences not calamitous. The version of Tacitus is clear and condemnatory. The historian's insight was sharpened by the episode of Nerva three decades later, ominous but with a happy outcome imposed by the menace of civil war.

A new emperor requires firm allies and useful partisans. Galba was not well served. In demeanour a model of 'antiquus rigor' (and aged sixty-nine when he seized the power), he lacked decision or constancy, being dominated by a camarilla, narrow, nasty, and discordant. T. Vinius, legate of the legion in Tarraconensis, had incited Galba to make the proclamation; for his Guard Prefect he took Cornelius Laco, a mere legal officer attached to the governor; and the third member was the freedman Icelus.

Nor was Servius Galba equipped with support from family or kin. There was no substance in Cornelius Dolabella (grandson of his long dead brother) whom he passed over when looking for an heir and partner in January of 69.[1] Further, Galba refused to take a second wife on the decease of his Aemilia Lepida.[2] She is only a name. In the year 21 the excellent Marcus Lepidus had a nubile daughter—Lepidus (*cos.* 6), who is described as 'nomini ac fortunae Caesarum proximus'. Galba, born in December of 3 B.C., had now reached the season normal for marriage in the upper order.[3]

However, that daughter of M. Lepidus went to Drusus, the second son of Germanicus Caesar. Galba may have married a daughter of Manius Lepidus (*cos.* 11). She would carry descent from Sulla and Pompeius.[4]

---

[1] *PIR*[2], C 1347. As there indicated, the *praenomen* 'Cn.' in Suetonius (*Galba* 12, 2) is an error for 'P.'. His mother was probably a Sulpicia C. f. Galbilla (cf. *CIL* vi 9754); and he took over the first wife of A. Vitellius, namely Petronia (*Hist.* ii 64, 1).   [2] Suetonius, *Galba* 5, 1.

[3] The consular date for Galba's birth (3 B.C.) is furnished by Suetonius (4, 1); and he assumed the *toga virilis* on January 1 of the year 14 (Dio lvi 29, 5), about a week after his fifteenth birthday. Discrepancies about Galba's age elsewhere in the biographer and in other writers need not detain.

[4] As emerges from *Ann.* iii 21, 1 (the sister of Manius Lepidus). For the daughter of M. Lepidus and bride of Drusus, *Ann.* iii 52, 2; vi 40, 3: statements in *PIR*[2], A 421 f. are impaired by confusion between the consuls of 6 and 11.

Historia xxxi (1982), 460–83.

About the year 42 Galba lost Lepida, along with two children. The eminent consular thus became vulnerable, and not for the first time, to blatant | solicitation from Julia Agrippina, left a widow when Ahenobarbus died in 40.[5] His caution now resisted the hazards of a dynastic marriage—and he had lain low during the crisis caused by the assassination of Caligula.

In his own person Ser. Sulpicius Galba evoked a long span of history and manifold transactions. Legate of Germania Superior (40–2) and proconsul of Africa, he enforced discipline and conducted campaigns. Thereafter he lapsed into retirement. For which, some surmise the enduring enmity of Agrippina.[6] Otherwise it might be asked what more had Rome to offer. Fame accrued, the *ornamenta triumphalia*, three priesthoods. Galba might, it is true, have aspired to a second consulship in the early epoch of Claudius Caesar (a run of four from 43 to 46), but the Prefecture of the City was held (since 41) by Volusius Saturninus (*suff.* 3), who betrayed no sign of senescence.

That protracted secession did not foster the maintenance of a following or the enlargement of a faction. Galba possessed enormous wealth, but no inclination to disburse. His manner lacked amenity, he now shunned the company of women (whatever their rank), although he had once earned favour from Livia and from his stepmother, Livia Ocellina, whose name he was happy to take over.[7]

Of the civilian arts, Galba had not neglected to study the law. That went well with his pedantic temperament and habits; and his harshness enhanced among the ingenuous a belief that his military renown was deserved and authentic.

Of excellence in oratory, no trace despite the tradition of an illustrious ancestor (the consul of 144 B.C.). The family had recently come out with a historian: abnormal among the *nobilitas*, but no doubt his refuge during the years of tribulation.[8] In the next generation several Sulpicii bore witness to the amicable efforts of Caesar Augustus, eager to revive the decayed patriciate.

Nor would Ser. Galba be looked for anywhere in the vicinity of philosophers. Not but that the austerity of Stoic doctrines had a strong appeal for senators, sometimes in protest against the luxury of the Caesars. In dire need for an heir and successor, Galba chose Piso Licinianus, for long years an exile, who combined old-fashioned

---

[5] The pushful princess got more than a verbal rebuke from Lepida's mother at an assembly of matrons (5, 1). She quickly consoled herself with the opulent Passienus Crispus, who became consul for the second time in 44.

[6] M. T. Griffin, *Seneca* (1976), 243.

[7] On the *Fasti Ostienses* for 33 he is styled 'L. Livius Ocella Sulpicius Galba'.

[8] *RE* ivA 755 f.

principles with the tradition and memory of the Republic—and with descent from Crassus and Pompeius Magnus.[9] |

It was thus a remote and isolated figure who had the offer of Tarraconensis in the year 60. By whose decision, that is a question. According to Plutarch, Galba's mild disposition no less than his time of life inspired secure confidence in Nero.[10] Curiosity is impelled towards the imperial counsellors in this season when the authority of Seneca and Burrus was already on the wane. It succumbed two years later according to Tacitus (*Ann.* xiii 52, 1), who names Tigellinus in the context and goes on to demonstrate his influence (57 ff.). Other advisers will be suspected, superior in public station, and some superior in talent or resources.[11]

An answer, albeit partial and imperfect, might be sought in the Vitellian faction.[12] The potency of L. Vitellius embraced three reigns: consul in 34, consul twice again under Claudius (43 and 47). The nexus under the control of this paramount manager included in the first place the aristocratic Plautii and the rising Petronii. For example, on Vitellius in Syria followed P. Petronius (*suff.* 19). His wife, Plautia A. f., was the daughter of a Vitellia.[13] The next governor, Vibius Marsus (*suff.* 17), gave a daughter to a Plautius.[14] Furthermore, Aulus Vitellius (*cos.* 48), the elder son, had for his first wife a Petronia. She was transferred to Cornelius Dolabella.[15]

The artful Vitellius carried through the marrying of Claudius Caesar in 48, and three years later Agrippina intervened to rescue him from a prosecution (*Ann.* xii 42, 3) that may well appear paradoxical since Vitellius was still endowed with 'validissima gratia', so the historian asserts. Vitellius, compromised through the alliance with the freedman Narcissus, was now on the way out and soon to die, not needing an obituary notice (it had been anticipated by Tacitus in vi 32, 4).

While other influences prevailed during Nero's first quinquennium, as at once announced and confirmed by several names on the *Fasti*, about the year 60 a resurgence of the faction becomes verifiable on various signs. Four select items may suffice in this place.

---

[9] For the stemma, *PIR*[2], Vol. v, facing p. 40.

[10] Plutarch, *Galba* 3.

[11] Cf. *Tacitus* (1958), 387.

[12] M. T. Griffin, *Seneca* (1976), 453 f. Attention is there drawn to the unfriendly treatment of P. Petronius in *Apocol.* 14, 2.

[13] *Ann.* iii 49, 1, with *SEG* xiv 646 (Caunus). In *Tacitus* (1958), 386 (n. 5, l. 1) for 'Vitellius' read 'Vitellia'.

[14] *ILS* 964 (P. Plautius Pulcher, quaestor to Tiberius Caesar in 31).

[15] *Hist.* ii 64, 1.

(1) Petronius Turpilianus as consul in 61, the son of P. Petronius (*suff.* 19): said to be an old man when he perished in 68.[16] |

(2) Caesennius Paetus his colleague: the first *novus homo* to open the year since Q. Veranius and Pompeius Gallus in 49. Paetus was married to a Flavia Sabina.[17] Paetus was despatched to Cappadocia, Turpilianus to Britain.

(3) Flavius Sabinus (*suff.* ?47). Coming from Moesia (?53–60), he became *praefectus urbi* in 61 when Pedanius Secundus (*suff.* 43) was assassinated.[18] The Flavii could be described as clients of the Vitellii.[19]

(4) Flavius Vespasianus (*suff.* 51). Despite service in the invasion of Britain, with *ornamenta triumphalia*, no imperial province, but he became proconsul of Africa (?62/3). As Suetonius reports, 'in otio secessuque egit Agrippinam timens' (*Vesp.* 2, 2).

Galba's political and social isolation was intensified by eight years in Spain. As Princeps he faced an urgent and delicate problem, to find legates for several of the great military commands. He fell back on persons he had come to know in his earlier existence, in the thirties or forties, some of them close to himself in age, but none of high birth. The names come up in the Tacitean narrative of the year 69.

The new ruler saw no cause to disturb two consulars of recent appointment in the East: Licinius Mucianus (*suff.* ?64) in Syria, Flavius Vespasianus (*suff.* 51) conducting the war in Judaea. And, at the other extremity of the world, Trebellius Maximus in Britain (*suff.* 56) was not likely to provoke alarm, being elderly and torpid. He had been legate of a legion (presumably quaestorian) in Syria, under the governorship of L. Vitellius in 36. Sometimes doubted, identity has everything for it.[20] Provenance from Narbonensis is conjectured.[21]

For the rest, Galba when he vacated Tarraconensis put Cluvius Rufus in charge. This was a man of peace, lacking experience with the armies (*Hist.* i 8, 1), further described as 'perinde dives et eloquentia clarus' (iv 43, 1), and to be supposed well on in years. He

[16] Plutarch, *Galba* 15.
[17] *ILS* 995. For the Flavian stemma, G. B. Townend *JRS* li (1961), 62.
[18] For the dating of the two posts see *PIR*², F 352; M. T. Griffin, op. cit. 456 f. The consulate of Sabinus was generally assigned to 44 or 45. Thus, for 44 recently, P. A. Gallivan, *CQ* xxviii (1978), 420. Strong reasons now speak for 47, cf. A. R. Birley, *The* Fasti *of Roman Britain* (1981), 225.
[19] *Hist.* iii 66, 2: 'Vespasianus . . . Vitellii cliens cum Vitellius collega Claudio foret.' The author patently confused the consulates of father and son (47 and 48).
[20] C. Cichorius, *Römische Studien* (1922), 420. Followed by A. R. Birley, op. cit. 59 f. Hesitations were expressed by M. T. Griffin, op. cit. 446 f.
[21] For the evidence, *HSCPh* lxxiii (1969), 222 = *RP* (1979), 760 f.

was already a senator in 41.[22] After declaring for Otho in January of 69 he quickly turned to Vitellius and went away to join him (i 76, 1; ii 65, 1). Cluvius' origin might be Campanian. |

Central for fear or hope were the legates on the Rhine and in Illyricum. To Germania Superior, in the place of Verginius Rufus (*cos.* 63), went Hordeonius Flaccus, 'senecta ac debilitate pedum invalidus' (i 9, 1). His consular year baffles ascertainment, his origin appears Campanian, probably from Puteoli.[23] In the other command Fonteius Capito (*cos.* 67) had been killed through the agency of Fabius Valens, a legionary legate. After a fairly long interval A. Vitellius turned up towards the end of November. In allusion to the parent's prestige, Tacitus was content to state 'id satis videbatur' (i 9, 1). Enough, in truth, for the proud and angry legions. In the subsequent proclamation (or later) the historian failed to bring out the influence, still perceptible, of the Vitellian faction. Whatever the pressures, Vitellius was an unwise choice to the credit of Ser. Sulpicius Galba.

Next, Illyricum: 'Tampius Flavianus Pannoniam, Pompeius Silvanus Dalmatiam tenebant, divites senes.' Thus Tacitus, evoking for sharp contrast the active energy displayed by Antonius Primus, a legionary legate, and by the procurator Cornelius Fuscus (ii 86, 3). The two governors might be Neronian appointments, it is true. Nero would have reason to prefer age and inactivity. For example, Petronius Turpilianus in Britain, followed by Trebellius Maximus; and in 63 Cestius Gallus (*suff.* 42) went to Syria. On the other hand, observe some of Nero's latest appointments, who were recent consuls. In the forefront, Verginius Rufus and Fonteius Capito on the Rhine, Licinius Mucianus (*suff.* ?64) in Syria, Pomponius Pius (*suff.* 65) in Moesia (the successor of Plautius Silvanus Aelianus).[24]

For choice by Galba, nothing debars Tampius Flavianus and Pompeius Silvanus.[25] In Pannonia no legate is on record after Salvidienus Rufus (*suff.* 52), on attestation in 60 (*CIL* xvi 4). In Dalmatia the legate in 68 was either an *Ignotus* or Ducenius Geminus (*suff.* 60 or 61). On which problem, see below: the urban prefecture of Ducenius.

The consulship of Silvanus belongs to 45, that of Tampius, so it now appears, should go in 40 or 41.[26] For neither is a military post on

[22] *PIR*[2], C 1202; 1206 (discussing Josephus, *AJ* xix 91 f.). Cf. further *Tacitus* (1958), 294.

[23] J. H. D'Arms, *Historia* xxiii (1969), 497 ff.

[24] For Pomponius Pius, *SEG* i 329 (Histria).

[25] For Nero rather, G. E. F. Chilver, *JRS* xlvii (1957), 32 and 'probably' in his *Historical Commentary* (1979), on ii 86, 3.

[26] Thus, in comment on *AE* 1973, 162, W. Eck, *Historia* xxiv (1975), 339; P. A. Gallivan, *CQ* xxviii (1978), 418.

record before 69. Tampius, so it happens to emerge at a later stage, was a 'propinquus Vitellii' (iii 10, 2).

Tampius was Italian, although far from proved a citizen of Fundi, which yielded the inscription (*ILS* 985). For Pompeius Silvanus the colony of Arelate in Narbonensis looks like the *patria*.[27] |

Both benefited from an iterated consulship shared in the sequel (?76). A tribute due not so much to the rehabilitation of Galba, or a change of side in 69, as to wealth and influence.[28]

Finally, as fifth on the list of consular legates, M. Aponius Saturninus in Moesia. About his consular year, estimates have shown a wide divergence. A valid factor invoked was his proconsulate of Asia, generally put in 73/4.[29] A different hypothesis assigns him to 67/8, supposing him thence transferred to Moesia by Galba (to replace Pomponius Pius), and parallel to Fonteius Agrippa a year later. Hence a consulate *c.*55.[30] Aponius was a *frater Arvalis* by the year 57.[31] The fraternity was still fairly select, entry being confined either to *nobiles* (some of them quite young) or to ex-consuls.

Like the governors in Pannonia and Dalmatia, Aponius Saturninus was opulent beyond question. His presumed parent is a 'praetorius dives'.[32] Though acceding much later to the *fasces*, Aponius offers no sign of a consul 'suo anno' at forty-two. He came from Baetica, so it is surmised; and further, if consul *c.*55, a friend of Seneca.[33]

The praetorian provinces in the portion of Caesar (at this time six in number) should not forfeit attention. They normally led to consulships. In the forefront stood Numidia, the sphere of the legate commanding III Augusta (for a long time not to be defined officially as a province). After the disturbances provoked by Clodius Macer, Galba consigned it to Valerius Festus, an ambitious young man who had held no other post subsequent to the praetorship. Festus had a link with Vitellius, being later described as 'adfinitate Vitellii anxius'

[27] W. Eck, *RE*, *Suppl.* xiv 437 f. (revising *AE* 1952, 168 (Arelate) and producing designation to a third consulship).

[28] Tacitus was alert to this character: 'pecuniosa orbitas et senecta' (*Ann.* xiii 52, 1).

[29] *PIR*[2], A 937, cf. *Tacitus* (1958), 594; W. Eck, *Senatoren von Vespasian bis Hadrian* (1970), 119.

[30] For the argument, *Some Arval Brethren* (1980), 68 f. It is based on the career of his legate Servenius Cornutus (*ILS* 8817: Acmonia).

[31] *CIL* vi 2051.

[32] *PIR*[2], A 936.

[33] For his origin, *Tacitus* (1958), 785. The legate commanding the legion III Gallica in the autumn of 69 was Dillius Aponianus (*Hist.* iii 10, 1): honoured at Corduba (*AE* 1932, 78). Dillius Vocula carries the 'Sergia', the tribe of that city (*ILS* 983: Rome). The name is extremely rare: otherwise only *CIL* ii 287 (Olisipo).

(iv 49, 1). Tergeste honoured him as *patronus* (*ILS* 989). His *patria* is patently Arretium.[34]

For Lusitania no legate is discovered after Marcus Otho departed to join Galba, terminating ten years of virtual banishment. In the Gallic provinces the revolt against Nero took its origin in the action of Julius Vindex, the legate of Lugdunensis. The other two governors, not named, would be involved, in one | way or another. The legate of Aquitania wrote to Galba asking for help against Vindex.[35] Perhaps to be identified as that Betuus Cilo put to death 'in Gallia' by order of Galba.[36]

The early spring of the next year exhibits the three legates, viz. Julius Cordus in Aquitania, Junius Blaesus in Lugdunensis, Valerius Asiaticus in Belgica. For Cordus the *gentilicium* will suggest an origin from Narbonensis if not from Tres Galliae.[37]

In the eastern lands the command held by Domitius Corbulo until the winter of 66/7, namely Cappadocia–Galatia, had been broken up. Galba made a further change, implicit in the words 'Galatiam ac Pamphyliam provincias Calpurnio Asprenati regendas Galba permiserat' (ii 9, 1). What happened is clear. The province Lycia–Pamphylia had been split. Neither half was large enough to stand alone. The Lycians, it follows, had acquired freedom from direct rule. By whose decision? The common notion acclaims Nero, the liberator of Hellas. Better perhaps, not the histrionic philhellene but the archaic and Republican *princeps*.[38] The Lycians were a peculiar type of Hellene, commended to the Romans by civic virtue and conservative politics.[39]

Calpurnius Asprenas bore an illustrious lineage (his grandfather married a daughter of Piso the Pontifex). By his full style he is 'L. Nonius Calpurnius Asprenas'.[40] Two other praetorian governors also paraded high eminence. Valerius Asiaticus had for parent the famous Narbonensian from Vienna (*suff.* 35, *cos. II* 46). Vitellius gave him the hand of his daughter and designation for a consulship the next year (i 59, 2; iv 4, 3).

Concerning Junius Blaesus, the Emperor received a warning from

[34] Festus has the tribe of Arretium, the 'Pomptina'. Observe in confirmation *CIL* xi 1863 f.: quoted in *Danubian Papers* (1971), 181.   [35] Suetonius, *Galba* 9, 2.

[36] *Hist.* i 37, 3. Cf. Chilver in his *Commentary* ad loc., duly adducing for the rare name *ILS* 6615 (Perusia).

[37] The item 'Q. Iulius Cordinus' got prefixed to the name of (C.) Rutilius Gallicus (*suff.* ?70), cf. *CIL* xvi 23.

[38] As argued in *Klio* xxx (1937), 227 ff. = *RP* (1979), 42 ff.

[39] Strabo xiv 664: πολιτικῶς καὶ σωφρόνως ζῶντες.

[40] *IRT* 346 (Lepcis). He is there styled a grandson of Nonius Asprenas (*suff.* 6), and equipped with the 'Pomptina'. The tribe of that family, from Picenum, is 'Velina'.For remarks see *Historia* xvii (1968), 84 = *RP* (1979), 671.

his brother Lucius: 'in urbe ac sinu cavendum hostem Iunios Antoniosque avos iactantem' (iii 38, 3). This epoch offers no claimant to Antonian descent apart from Nero. An explanation can be ventured. Nero's aunt Domitia avows one husband only, Passienus Crispus. She may previously have been married to one of the 'duo Blaesi', who committed suicide in 36. That is, either Q. Junius Blaesus (*suff.* 26) or his brother (probably also a consul suffect).[41]

After the five praetorian governors here assumed to owe their posts to Galba, a brief search may turn to new commanders of legions. His partisan Caecina Alienus, the quaestor of Baetica, was sent to take charge of IV Macedonica at Moguntiacum on the Rhine; and he consigned to Antonius Primus the newly raised 'legio VII', despatching it to Pannonia. In this fashion a notable adventurer secured rank again, and rehabilitation. Seven years previously he was a member of the group that forged the will of an aged and opulent senator (*Ann.* xiv 40).

A certain curiosity attends upon I Italica, discovered at Lugdunum in the early spring of 69 (i 59, 2). Recruited by Nero in 66, this legion belonged to the force mustered in northern Italy in the summer of 68, under the command of the consulars Petronius Turpilianus and Rubrius Gallus.[42] It included detachments drawn from the armies of Illyricum. They were still there when they solicited Verginius Rufus, the legate of Germania Superior, to take the power (i 9, 3). That is, after Nero's suicide (June 9).

There is no sign that the legion I Italica had already crossed the Alps in the direction of Lugdunum.[43] It is strange, to be sure, that Galba should post the legion to a military colony notorious for Neronian sympathies.[44] However, if Galba did not send the legion to Lugdunum, he left it there—but perhaps not under Nero's legate, unless that person had earned credit for disloyalty and subversion.

The legate at Lugdunum is named, Manlius Valens. Hence a notorious problem. Is he to be held identical with Manlius Valens, commanding a legion in Britain in 50 (*Ann.* xii 40, 1)—and further, with C. Manlius Valens, the consul of 96 in his ninetieth year?[45]

---

[41] For this conjecture, *Antichthon* ix (1975), 62. The 'duo Blaesi' are registered in *Ann.* vi 40, 2. The consulate of the younger Blaesus, like that of Q. Sanquinius Maximus (*II suff.* 39), can be put in 28, although no vacancy was conceded by Degrassi, *I Fasti consolari* (1952).

[42] For those troops see Chilver in his *Commentary* (1979), 11 f.

[43] *AJP* lviii (1937), 11 f. = *Danubian Papers* (1971), 76 f.

[44] Thus Chilver (op. cit. 11 f.), arguing that Nero sent it there before he had the news of the battle of Vesontio.

[45] Thus A. R. Birley, *The Fasti of Roman Britain* (1981), 230. For strong doubts, Chilver on i 64, 4.

Either way, the legate of I Italica had far exceeded the age normal for the post. As might happen. T. Vinius, in command of VI Victrix in Tarraconensis was forty-seven when killed at Rome.[46] Further, Antonius Primus about fifty.[47]

Again, some of the seven legions on the Rhine would supply vacancies for Galba to fill, as a result of recent events. That is, friends of either Fonteius Capito or Verginius Rufus. In suppressing Capito, Fabius Valens had Cornelius Aquinus for ally (i 7, 1). The former, commanding 'legio I' at Bonna, was rancorous against Galba, and he impelled Vitellius to assume the | purple. The camp closest to Bonna was Novaesium ('legio XVI'). Cornelius Aquinus is not heard of after this exploit. The next commander is Numisius Rufus, left behind by Vitellius (iv 22, 1 etc.).[48]

The other two legions, V Alaudae and XV Primigenia, were brigaded together at Vetera. The latter remained there, its legate being Munius Lupercus (iv 18, 1), while Fabius Fabullus went with V Alaudae to Italy; and in the autumn the Vitellian forces on the Po chose him as their commander (iii 14, 1). The name 'Fabius Fabullus' has a Spanish flavour.[49]

As for Germania Superior, the new legate of IV Macedonica, namely Caecina Alienus, took it with him in the invasion of Italy. The other legion at Moguntiacum stayed behind. It was XXII Primigenia, under the command of Dillius Vocula. Perhaps appointed by Galba.[50]

The third, XXI Rapax, was stationed at Vindonissa. The name of its commander is absent from the ample narration which Tacitus devoted to the disturbances in the land of the Helvetii (i 67–70). Most peculiar, and an incitement to curiosity.[51]

As is likewise Pedanius Costa, designated consul by Galba but

[46] The figure 'quinquaginta septem annos' in i 48, 2 is clearly an error. Cf., on the career of Vinius, G. V. Sumner, *Athenaeum* liv (1976), 431.

[47] Martial x 23, 1 f.

[48] Cf. E. Ritterling, *RE* xii 1763. No fewer than thirty Numisii occur in *CIL* II, four of them high priests at Tarraco. For the detail, G. Alföldy, *Flamines Hispaniae Citerioris* (1973), 80 f. And one may note in passing Numisius Lupus, in 68/9 legate of VIII Augusta in Moesia (*Hist.* i 79, 1). In Italy the name points to Etruria or Campania (Schulze, *LE* 164).

[49] *CIL* II shows (including women) six specimens, all with 'L.' as praenomen or patronymic. Observe further, belonging to the period, M. Fabius Fabullus, legate of XIII Gemina (*ILS* 996: nr. Poetovio). According to Groag in *PIR*², F 32, 'neque igitur distinguendus' from the commander of V Alaudae (F 30). To be doubted—unless it be supposed that Galba brought him from Pannonia to the Rhine.

Add now to the rubric L. Fabius Fabullus, a magistrate at Liria (L. Martí Ferrando, *Arch. preh. Levantina* xiii (1971), 178).

[50] Dillius Vocula is patently from Corduba: compare Dillius Aponianus (above, n. 33), who commanded III Gallica in Moesia (iii 10, 1) after the departure of Aurelius Fulvus (i 79, 5), who had brought the legion from Syria shortly before Nero's end (Suetonius, *Vesp.* 6, 3).

[51] Which cannot be assuaged, cf. *MH* xxxiv (1977), 131 f. = *RP* iii (1984), 998.

dropped by Vitellius: 'ingratus principi ut adversus Neronem ausus et Verginii exstimulator' (ii 71, 2). Pedanius will be presumed without discomfort a legate of some influence and seniority. Observe in the other army Fabius Valens, who was 'inopi iuventa senex prodigus' (i 66, 3).

In this context the legionary legates in Illyricum during Nero's latest months offer scant encouragement for speculation. They were seven in number, for XIV Gemina is to be included: probably in Pannonia. Taken from Britain, XIV Gemina had been marching to the East.[52] Given this legion's devotion to Nero, as evinced in northern Italy in the last days (ii 27, 2), a change of commander might well be requisite. Despite its iterated prominence | in 69, no legate is on sight until Fabius Priscus in 70 (iv 79, 3), a senator from Tarraco.[53]

In 68 X Gemina was stationed at Carnuntum where it had gone from Spain in 63 to replace XV Apollinaris, taken away to join Corbulo's army under the command of Marius Celsus (*Ann.* xv 25, 3). Galba sent the legion back to its old province—for a brief spell until it departed again and for good. The interim produces a document. At Clunia a soldier of X Gemina set up a dedication to 'Iuppiter Augustus Ultor' (*ILS* 9239). Not without relevance to Galba and to Nero's end. It was at Clunia that Galba received the unexpected tidings.

It is time to revert to the governor of Tarraconensis, proclaimed at Carthago Nova on April 2 in response to the Gallic insurrection. Julius Vindex, a descendant of kings in Aquitania, had eager allies among the barons and he aggregated a host of 100,000 natives, so it is said.[54] His bold enterprise (the causes not verifiable, and accidents to be suspected) thus came to look like an indigenous rebellion, and misconceptions emerged in the sequel, some of them voluntary.[55]

The legate on the Upper Rhine saw his duty and mustered the army, defeating Vindex at Vesontio. Galba gave all for lost and retired in despair to Clunia, a town of inner Tarraconensis. In the confusion that ensued, enhanced by rumour, ignorance, and treachery,

---

[52] For the detail, Chilver, op. cit. 7; 10 f.

[53] *CIL* ii 1147, cf. *PIR*², F 55 and 98. Further, G. Alföldy in annotation on the inscr. (= *RIT* 134, now lost).

[54] Plutarch, *Galba* 8; Josephus, *BJ* iv 440: ἅμα τοῖς δυνατοῖς τῶν ἐπιχωρίων. That phrase should not be taken to cover magnates of Narbonensis, and especially of Vienna.

[55] For this interpretation see *Tacitus* (1958), 462 f., cf. (for Verginius Rufus) 179. In the ample writing which the imbroglio provokes there has been a temptation to discover coherence and a plot—perhaps widespread, perhaps even enlisting the legate of Tarraconensis.

the usurper was saved, first by Nero's ineptitude and then by his suicide, not without disquiet for a time. Of the legions in Germania Superior it is stated 'tarde a Nerone desciverant, nec statim pro Galba Verginius' (i 8, 2).

Meanwhile allies and agents accrued to Galba in Spain and in Narbonensis.[56] In Tarraconensis he had Vinius, but neither the *iuridicus* nor the procurator is on attestation. Lusitania came over with M. Otho, but there were hesitations in Baetica where the alert quaestor outstripped or circumvented the proconsul and his legate, with dire consequences for both. Among other deaths Galba | had to bear the discredit of 'occisi Obultronii Sabini et Cornelii Marcelli in Hispania' (i 37, 3).[57] The next proconsul of Baetica escapes record.[58]

For counsel and guidance Galba created an assembly of the notables, 'e primoribus prudentia atque aetate praestantibus velut instar senatus'.[59] Their class or type is clear on show, in the first place high priests of the provincial cult at Tarraco or *praefecti orae maritimae*. A single specimen will suffice: Q. Licinius Silvanus Granianus, who held both posts (*ILS* 2714). The provincial *flamines* are a topic variously remunerative.[60] And Tarraconensis already exhibited senatorial families, before all the Pedanii of Barcino.

Rapid promotion or honours therefore came to a number of Spanish partisans. As follows:

(1) Q. Pomponius Rufus, put in charge of the coasts of Tarraconensis and Narbonensis in the war 'quod imp. G[a]lba pro [re p.] gessit' (*IRT* 537: Lepcis). Entering the Senate, Rufus reached the *fasces* at length in 95, to end as legate of Moesia Inferior and proconsul of Africa.[61]

(2) M. Raecius Tauri f. Gallus. As an inscription of Tarraco declares (*RIT* 145), this youth began as a military tribune under Galba. He then became high priest and, a unique anomaly to come

---

[56] The theme was adumbrated in *Tacitus* (1958), 592 f.; and, for the Tarraconensian partisans, see *HSCPh* lxxiii (1969), 228 ff. = *RP* (1979), 766 ff.

[57] For the identifications, *AJP* lviii (1937), 9 f. = *Danubian Papers* (1971), 75, Obultronius Sabinus was a *quaestor aerarii* in 56 (*Ann.* xiii 28). For the rare *nomen*, which points to Casinum, see G. Alföldy, *Beiträge zur Namenforschung* i (1966), 145 ff.

[58] Not M. Ulpius Traianus (*suff.* ?70), as some supposed, among them G. Alföldy, *Fasti Hispanienses* (1969), 157 ff. And, as now becomes evident, Traianus was still in Judaea commanding X Fretensis in the second half of 69 (*AE* 1977, 829: Afula, near Scythopolis).

[59] Suetonius, *Galba* 10, 2.

[60] G. Alföldy, *Flamines Provinciae Hispaniae Citerioris* (1973). They are not drawn from senatorial families, and few equal Licinius Silvanus (*ILS* 2714) with a consular son (*suff.* 106).

[61] Not to be held identical with Q. Pomponius Q. f. Col. Rufus, prefect of an *ala* in 64 (*CIL* xvi 5). The nomenclature is indistinctive—and the tribe 'Collina' deters.

after that honour, entered the senatorial career as quaestor in Baetica.[62] After his praetorship Gallus was chosen *sodalis Augustalis* (a mark of imperial favour)—and he may have reached a suffect consulship in 84.

Gallus is manifestly the son by adoption of Raecius Taurus, attested in 49 as a senator of praetorian rank *PIR*[1], R 9). By their Etruscan name the Raecii declare an immigrant stock: in fact from Etruria, like other of the notables such as Caecina Severus (*ILS* 2716: Tarraco).

(3) Pompeius Propinquus, the procurator of Belgica, whose despatch in January of 69 announced trouble on the Rhine—and he was duly put to death by Vitellius (i 12, 1; 58, 1). The post was of prime importance, its holder being | paymaster-general to the Rhine armies. The identity of this man's predecessor would be worth knowing.

The *cognomen* 'Propinquus' exhibits an abnormal frequency in Spain, which yields nine of the thirty-five epigraphical instances.[63] Conspicuous among them are equestrian worthies from Liria and Dianium.[64] In due course they produce the polyonymous Valerius Propinquus on an inscription at Tarraco, who was a legate of Germania Inferior and proconsul of Asia (*CIL* ii 6084 = *RIT* 149): to be identified with the Propinquus consul suffect in 126.[65]

Furthermore, Galba usurped (or was granted) the powers of a censor, and he duly carried out adlections. The fact, often missed by scholars, is casually disclosed by

(4) 'Licinius Caecina nuper in senatum adscitus' (ii 53, 1). Pliny when procurator in Tarraconensis came to know the parent of P. Licinius Caecina: he decided to end his days by taking a dose of opium (*NH* xx 199).

(5) Praesens, on a fragmentary inscription at the legionary camp (*CIL* ii 2666: León). This man was adlected *inter praetorios*. He may have been an imperial procurator—perhaps the official absent from record in the year 68.

The *cognomen* is familiar from Bruttius Praesens (*suff.* 118 or 119) and his descendants. In the second *ordo*, it is represented only by Gargonius Praesens, an enigmatic *praefectus vigilum* (xi 629: Faventia)

---

[62] Relevant to the status and prospects of the Saguntine Voconius Romanus (Pliny, *Ep.* ii 13, 4 etc.), and to the chronology of the letters.

[63] I. Kajanto, *The Latin Cognomina* (1965), 303.

[64] G. Alföldy and H. Halfmann, *Chiron* iii (1973), 369 ff.

[65] L. Schumacher, *ZPE* xxiv (1977), 155 f. (on consular dates on brick stamps). Not without excuse, Propinquus had until recently been identified as colleague to L. Varius Ambibulus (*suff.* 132 or 133). Thus in *RIT* 149 (1975). See, conveniently, A. R. Birley, *The Fasti of Roman Britain* (1981), 240 f.; further, pp. 579 ff., below.

and by L. Pupius Praesens, procurator in Galatia in the year 54 (*ILS* 8848). Attention has been attracted towards the latter.[66]

Whether Praesens was admitted to the Senate by Galba or by Vespasian, that is a question. The same holds for the young knight Pomponius Rufus: the inscription (*IRT* 537) masks the fact of adlection, as happens.

Although the *nomen* is so common, other Spanish Pomponii ought not to be lost to sight. Pliny knew a Sextus Pomponius who hit upon a novel remedy against gout. He is termed 'praetorii viri pater, Hispaniae citerioris princeps' (*NH* xxii 120). The praetorian son of another 'princeps' in Tarraconensis (xx 215) carries no name. |

Consular Pomponii are on high frequency in the next epoch;[67] and one might wonder about the antecedents of other persons who rose to higher eminence.[68]

As often, Tarraconensis links and leads to Narbonensis. The old 'provincia' was quickly involved in the disturbances; and the standing feud between neighbour and contrasted cities (Vienna and Lugdunum) erupted in violence: 'multae in vicem clades, crebrius infestiusque quam ut tantum propter Neronem Galbamque pugnaretur' (i 65, 1).

When the Vitellian troops, bent on rapine, reached Lugdunum early in the next year, they were greeted by savage and encouraging aspersions on the recent activities of Vienna: 'obsessam ab illis coloniam suam, adiutos Vindicis conatus, conscriptas nuper legiones in praesidium Galbae' (65, 2). And further, 'sedem Gallici belli. cuncta illic externa et hostilia.'

Cornelius Tacitus exploits reported speech to convey exaggeration and dishonest pleas. The device comes out in a later place when a freedman is made to bring up Vienna in order to incriminate Valerius Asiaticus.[69]

As the whole context demonstrates, the historian insists on protecting Vienna, that opulent and conservative city, the *patria* of

[66] G. Alföldy, *Fasti Hispanienses* (1969), 115 ff. At the head of the inscription stands the isolated ']trix'. Alföldy suggests either I Adiutrix or VI Victrix, supposing Praesens to have commanded one or other legion. Yet one might read '[Nemesis Vic]trix', cf. *HSCPh* lxxiii (1969), 229 = *RP* (1979), 767.

[67] No fewer than five Pomponii between 94 and 100. The last of them, Mamilianus, a legionary legate at Deva, has for tribe the 'Galeria' (*CIL* vii 164 = *RIB* 445). See further pp. 150 ff., below.

[68] Notably the great Licinius Sura. The decayed colony of Celsa on the Ebro can be claimed as his 'ultima origo', cf. *Tacitus* (1958), 791.

[69] *Ann.* xi 1, 2: 'quando genitus Viennae multisque et validis propinquitatibus subnixus turbare gentiles nationes promptum haberet.' Appended to the ridiculous allegation 'didita per provincias fama parare iter ad Germanicos exercitus.'

senators long since. Vienna stood strong for Galba and the cause of 'senatus populusque' against Nero, rather than for Julius Vindex and the levies of Gallia Comata.[70]

Narbonensian adherents will now invite scrutiny, not without aid from rational conjecture. On that proviso, five names can be adduced.

(1) Sex. Julius Frontinus, praetor in 70, consul suffect in 73. His rapid passage indicates one of two things. Frontinus was either a patrician (a notion to be dismissed) or an equestrian officer of some standing and seniority, adlected by Galba. Frontinus, so it has been surmised, saw service under Domitius Corbulo. A passage in the *Strategemata* (a work not otherwise lavish of detail about personal experiences) reports an incident at the capture of Tigranocerta in 59.[71] The *patria* of Frontinus was perhaps none other than Vienna. Observe the senator Q. Valerius Lupercus Julius Frontinus (*CIL* xii 1859 f.). |

(2) M. Antonius Primus, put in charge of Galba's new legion, which was sent to Carnuntum in Pannonia. Tolosa was his home, and he retired there to enjoy a ripe old age. When he was a boy they gave him the unfriendly appellation of 'Becco'.[72] This character, energetic and highly vocal, may have had a role to play in 68. Tolosa is on the road into Aquitania.

(3) Cornelius Fuscus, in 69 procurator in Illyricum: 'idem pro Galba dux coloniae suae' (ii 86, 3). The historian chose not to specify the colony of Fuscus, irrelevant in the context and perhaps reserved for an obituary notice. That city, involved in the imbroglio of Galba's proclamation and the 'bellum Neronis', has not failed to arouse speculation. Perhaps Corduba, Vienna, or Aquileia.[73] Something speaks for Forum Julii, where the high road that linked Spain to Italy met the coast. The place, 'claustra maris' (iii 43, 1), did not forfeit strategic advantage when it ceased to be a naval base in the time of Claudius Caesar—and the position would have been worth capturing when the Othonian expeditionary force proposed to attack the Narbonensian coast early in 69. They did not get very far.

Fuscus, it will be recalled for paradox, had been induced 'quietis cupidine' to renounce the *latus clavus* of a senator's son. The parent would be worth knowing about.

---

[70] For this conception, *MH* xxxiv (1977), 139 f. = *RP* iii (1984), 996 f.

[71] Frontinus, *Strat.* ii 9, 5.

[72] Suetonius, *Vit.* 18. Tolosa itself happens to contribute that name: 'deo Silvano dom. Becco v. s. l. m.' (*CIL* xii 5381). Not noted in *PIR*[2], A 866—and not questioned by the editor.

[73] Those cities were canvassed in *AJP* lviii (1937), 8 ff. = *Danubian Papers* (1971), 74 ff. In any case not Pompeii, which for some had appeal because of the anonymous prefect on the Altar at Adamclisi (*ILS* 9107).

By initial rank socially, Fuscus had a parallel (and perhaps a close
coeval) in Cn. Julius Agricola, citizen of the 'vetus et inlustris
Foroiuliensium colonia', and later father-in-law to Cornelius Tacitus.
Prudent all through, Agricola when tribune of the plebs in 66
traversed that year of hazards 'quiete et otio' (*Agr.* 6, 3). The
praetorship in 68 (a noteworthy advancement) spared Agricola any
incentive to rapid or decisive actions when warfare spread to the
natal province. Galba rewarded discretion and integrity with a
civilian employment, 'ad dona templorum recognoscenda' (6, 5).

(4) Valerius Paullinus, procurator in Narbonensis, attested late in
the year 69; from Forum Julii (iii 43, 1). He had previously been a
tribune in the Guard and a friend of Vespasian. Paullinus might, it is
true, have owed his appointment either to Nero or to Vitellius. The
procurator in the summer of the previous year finds no mention—
neither does proconsul, legate, quaestor.

(5) Sex. Attius Suburanus Aemilianus. His career down to the
procuratorship of Belgica is on register (*AE* 1939, 60: Heliopolis).
The tribe 'Voltinia' seldom deceives; and one should not miss the
inscription at Rome that reveals Sex. Attius Atticus, citizen of
Vienna and provincial *flamen*.[74] |

Suburanus' first and only military post was the command of the
ala Tauriana. The abrupt promotion, passing over the two stages
now normal, evokes a season of disturbance. Early in the year 69 the
regiment is discovered at Lugdunum, precisely, in the company of
the legion I Italica (i 59, 2). The emergence of Suburanus can hardly
be divorced from the 'bellum Neronis', or from its near sequel.[75] To
the same period probably belongs Sex. Pompeius Sabinus, who after
commanding the *ala* (likewise a solitary post) went on to be a
procurator. His tribe may be read as 'V]o[lt'.[76]

Equestrian officers call for attention, notably tribunes in the
Praetorian Guard, and they share the vicissitudes of emperors. Galba
cashiered a pair of suspect tribunes (i 20, 3). On the day of January 15
three others find commemoration for loyal comportment. One was
Pompeius Longinus, styled 'non ordine militiae sed e Galbae amicis'
(31, 3). The nomenclature supports provenance from Narbonensis
(or perhaps from Spain). Compare the enigmatic C. Pompeius
Longinus Gallus, the consul of 49. The tribune may well be that
Cn. Pompeius Longinus who, legate of Judaea in 86 and consul

---

[74] *CIL* vi 29688. The student of provincial nomenclature may also note the officer Sex.
Attius Senecio, decorated in Hadrian's Jewish War (3505: without tribe or *origo*).

[75] *JRS* lxx (1980), 64 f. = *RP* iii (1984), 1276 f.

[76] *CIL* iii 12299 (in Epirus). Pflaum suggested 'P]o[ll.' for the tribe (*Les Carrières* i (1960),
123).

suffect in 90, advanced to the governorships of Moesia Superior and Pannonia.[77]

Of the Narbonensian partisans (documented or surmised), Antonius Primus after exploits and victory was discarded, but Cornelius Fuscus became Domitian's Guard Prefect, to perish at the head of a Roman army in the invasion of Dacia. Valerius Paullinus quickly acquired the prefecture of Egypt and duly left a consular son (*suff.* 107). Attius Suburanus attached himself to masters of patronage, namely Vibius Crispus and Julius Ursus. He served as an 'adiutor' to both, to the one in his governorship of Tarraconensis, to the other when *praefectus annonae* at Rome and then Prefect of Egypt.[78]

Suburanus was procurator in Belgica, a post that spelled either promotion or death in a time of crisis. The year was 97, on a fair conjecture.[79] Suburanus became Trajan's first Prefect of the Guard, to pass before long to a consulship in 101, to a second in 104, shared with the aristocratic Asinius Marcellus. Julius Frontinus then ended his days, having crowned his career as 'consul tertio' in 100 with the Emperor for colleague. |

Meanwhile and further, the consuls whom Galba was able to designate in the course of his brief tenure of the power. The year 68 had opened with a pair on high show for eloquence, Silius Italicus and Galerius Trachalus. Silius, so they later opined, blemished his fame by prosecutions, while Trachalus was to make up an oration for the Emperor Otho, his manner betrayed by pomp and resonance.[80]

When the news came of the rising in Gaul, Nero inserted himself in the place of Silius.[81] The next consuls to stand on the *Fasti* are P. Scipio Asiaticus and Bellicius Natalis, registered in October and in December.[82] The collocation, a high aristocrat and a man from

---

[77] A welcome accession puts him in the former province in July of 96 (M. M. Roxan, *RMD* (1978), no. 6).

Subrius Dexter, one of those three tribunes, earned promotion, but less conspicuous: procurator governing Sardinia in 74 (*CIL* x 8023 f.).

[78] Promoted to the Senate and a consul in 84, Julius Ursus ended as consul for the third time in 100. Cf. *JRS* lxx (1980), 66; 79 = *RP* iii (1984), 1279 f.; 1300. To be surmised Narbonensian and probably kin to the Julii Lupi.

[79] Pflaum, *Les Carrières* 134.

[80] *Hist.* i 90, 2, cf. Quintilian's verdict (xii 5, 5). The second wife of Vitellius was a Galeria (*PIR²*, G 33). She was able to protect Trachalus 'adversus criminantes' (ii 60, 2). Only Suetonius calls her 'Galeria Fundana', adding 'patre praetorio' (*Vit.* 6). Possibly 'Fundania'. No early imperial senators happen to offer that name—but 'L. Fundanius' is prefixed to Lamia Aelianus, the aristocratic consul of 116 (*AE* 1947, 4); and Annia Fundania Faustina (*PIR²*, A 713) is a first cousin of Marcus Aurelius.

[81] *CIL* vi 8639; 9190. According to Suetonius, 'consules ante tempus privavit honore atque in utriusque locum solus iniit consulatum' (*Nero* 43, 2): perhaps erroneous.

[82] Predecessors have not been looked for. No consul occurs at Rome in the episode of Nymphidius Sabinus, only the consul designate Cingonius Varro (Plutarch, *Galba* 14 f.). However, no *praefectus urbi* is mentioned either.

Narbonensis, advertises contrasted but congenial proclivities in Sulpicius Galba.

Natalis avows Vienna, patently (*PIR*², B 101). Scipio, in truth one of the Lentuli, was the son of P. Lentulus Scipio, consul suffect in 24 and proconsul of Asia. The *cognomen* 'Asiaticus' indicates birth in that province, and the father's proconsulate was conveniently assigned to 36/7 (*PIR*², C 1398, cf. 251), giving the son a youthful consulship.

In these studies a single fact can obtrude all of a sudden, with manifold consequences. An inscription found in Lydia dates Scipio's proconsulate to the reign of Claudius Caesar.[83] It can be lodged in 41/2.[84] The son, it follows, reached the *fasces* when only twenty-six or twenty-seven. That recalls the favour extended to *nobiles* in close propinquity to the dynasty—and it may have encouraged forecasts about an impending choice of heir.[85] Aristocrats who bore the 'magna nomina' were now a rarity.

For the next year both Nero and Galba had already designated several candidates. Otho and Vitellius imposed a number of changes in the *Fasti*. They | are reported in two passages of the *Historiae* (i 77; ii 71), which have been subjected to proper and exact scrutiny. Hence a list comprising designations as well as the numerous consuls who held office.[86] Such of the results as concern the present enquiry can be stated in succinct fashion. As follows,

(1) Nero designated Cingonius Varro and Arrius Antoninus.
(2) Galba substituted Marius Celsus for Cingonius Varro.
(3) Galba designated Valerius Marinus and Pedanius Costa.
(4) Otho added Pompeius Vopiscus.

The names and persons call for various annotation. First, Cingonius Varro, a total enigma, significant because he composed a speech for Nymphidius Sabinus, the Guard Prefect, shortly after Nero's end.[87] That sealed his fate. He was put to death at some stage on the ruler's journey to Rome, the 'tardum Galbae et cruentum iter'.[88]

---

[83] Noted under *Inschr. von Ephesos* iii 659.

[84] Otherwise the first half of 41 is not excluded. Shortly before his death Caligula revoked C. Cassius Longinus (*suff.* 30), the proconsul (Suetonius, *Cal.* 57, 3; Dio lix 29, 3). The new inscription liberates 36/7 for C. Vibius Rufinus (*suff.* 21 or 22). Cf. *History in Ovid* (1978), 85 f.; *ZPE* xliii (1981), 376 = *RP* iii (1984), 1435.

[85] Scipio's mother was the beautiful Poppaea (*Ann.* xi 4, 3), less on show than her daughter. The wife eludes.

[86] G. B. Townend, *AJP* lxxxiii (1962), 113 ff.: accepted and reproduced by Chilver in his *Historical Commentary* (1979), 140 f.

[87] Plutarch, *Galba* 14.

[88] *Hist.* i 6, 1. Tacitus accorded Cingonius a mention later. In 61 his harsh proposal in the debate following the murder of Pedanius Secundus was quashed by Nero (*Ann.* xiv 45, 2).

The name 'Cingonius' is a portentous rarity. The shape and root is patently Celtic.[89] Cingonius Varro may be assigned without discomfort to the Transpadane consuls emergent in the late Neronian epoch with Verginius Rufus (*cos.* 63), 'equestri familia, ignoto patre' (i 52, 4), from Mediolanum—and with the eloquent Silius Italicus (*cos.* 68). The 'Asconius' in his name links him to a clan at Patavium: his full style is 'Ti. Catius Asconius Silius Italicus'.[90]

Second, Arrius Antoninus and Marius Celsus, who in fact entered office on July 1. For aught that can be known, Antoninus might owe designation to Galba. Nemausus was his town, nowhere certified, but few have been found to doubt or disallow. Nemausus was also the *patria* of Marius Celsus, so it can be maintained.[91] Hence a pair suitably conjoined. Of which Cornelius Tacitus (praetor in 88, consul in 97) would be aware—even if his own Narbonensian origin be disputed.

Arrius Antoninus evades public notice, apart from a proconsulate in Asia and the second consulship that came at last in 97. A discreet and comfortable person of cultivated tastes, so it appears. Marius Celsus, legate of a legion under Domitius Corbulo, had a marked role in 69, emerging with credit—and | with sympathy—in the narrations of Tacitus and Plutarch.[92] In the sequel Celsus was governor of Germania Inferior, in the summer of 73, as a new document felicitously reveals.[93] He departed at once to Syria (*ILS* 8903), where death terminated a brief tenure of that insalubrious province. Before the next year was out, Ulpius Traianus succeeded (*suff.* ?70).[94]

Third, Valerius Marinus and Pedanius Costa, designated by Galba. This pair lapsed, with Marinus postponed and Costa thrown out, for stated reasons (ii 71, 2). The provenance of Marinus might be supposed Narbonensian or Spanish. The colleague offers an engaging problem. Some fancy descent from Pedanius Costa, a legate of Marcus Brutus. There is a better recourse: the dominant

[89] Schulze, *LE* 21, cf. 439 (citing no other specimens). In *TLL, Onom.*, only *CIL* vi 14823; 26362; viii 18068, A 5 (Lambaesis: a soldier from Cirta). For 'Cingius', 'Cingetorix', etc. see D. E. Evans, *Gaulish Personal Names* (1967), 177 ff.

[90] *MAMA* viii 411 (Aphrodisias). The item 'Asconius' is absent from the consular date (*ILS* 5025). For his origin, not Patavine, see the firm statement of G. E. F. Chilver, *Cisalpine Gaul* (1970), 109 f. The equestrian tribune C. Silius Aviola is from Brixia (*ILS* 6099).

[91] Thus in *Tacitus* (1958), 683.

[92] Celsus was perhaps an author himself. A military writer of that name alluded to Corbulo (Lydus, *De mag.* iii 33). Not noticed by scholars intent on the encyclopedist Cornelius Celsus. Thus K. Barwick, *Philol.* civ (1960), 236 ff.; W. E. Kaegi, *Athenaeum* lix (1981), 209 ff.

[93] Published by C. B. Rüger, *BJ* clxxix (1979), 187 ff. It gives his *praenomen*, 'Aulus'. Dessau in *ILS* 8903 had supplemented '[P.]': under influence from P. Marius (*cos.* 62) who, so it now turns out, lacks a *cognomen*, cf. W. Eck, *RE, Suppl.* xiv 276.

[94] See 'Governors Dying in Syria', *ZPE* xli (1981), 133 = *RP* iii (1984), 1384.

family at Barcino, which came up at Rome with Pedanius Secundus, consul suffect in 43 and *praefectus urbi* under Nero (from 56 to 61), and showed three more consuls down to the husband of Hadrian's niece (*cos.* 118). These Pedanii flaunted 'Salinator', a pseudaristocratic *cognomen*. It appertained to Livii in the old time.

Pedanius Costa can therefore be claimed for Tarraconensis, an adherent active for Galba as a senior legate in the army of Verginius Rufus.

Fourth, Pompeius Vopiscus. The Emperor Otho joined him as colleague to Verginius Rufus on pretext of old friendship. The historian adds alert annotation: 'plerique Viennensium honori datum interpretabantur' (i 77, 2). This eminent citizen of Vienna misses other record. The item 'L. Pompeius Vopiscus' is prefixed (for the first time in 80) to the nomenclature of an Italian consular, C. Arruntius Catellius Celer (*suff.* 77).[95]

Adding Bellicius Natalis late in 68, Vienna and Nemausus each come out with two consuls. A congenial tribute to the fame and opulence of those cities, and in no small measure a result of Narbonensian adhesion to Galba and to the tradition of the 'res publica'. The precellence accruing to the old tribal capitals (Allobroges and Volcae) against the colonies of Roman veterans admits no dispute, and it stimulates investigation.

Nothing (it is a melancholy defect) can be ascertained about the previous occupations of the four consuls, apart from the legionary command of A. Marius Celsus.[96] |

Along with consuls (and with the consular legates registered above) a word should go to the *praefectus urbi*, that peculiar and anomalous deputy to the Princeps, often changed when rulers changed, but otherwise in prospect of long duration. Galba declined to keep Flavius Sabinus, in office since 61 and with a brother at the head of an army. He chose Ducenius Geminus (mentioned only once, in i 14, 1).

Another candidate was to hand, congenial on a double count to the ruler's predilections. In his person Plautius Silvanus Aelianus (*suff.* 45) united descent from Plautii and Aelii Lamiae; and Nero had denied him the recognition earned for operations when legate of Moesia (?60–6), as a later emperor was not slow to declare and compensate (*ILS* 986: nr. Tibur).

Instead, Galba's favour went to a younger man, the first consul in his family. Like his claims, the earlier career of A. Ducenius Geminus

---

[95] On whom, *Some Arval Brethren* (1980), 18 f.
[96] In 63 Celsus took XV Apollinaris (from Carnuntum) to join Corbulo's army (*Ann.* xv 25, 3).

presents obscurities. His consulate was assumed to fall in 54 or 55.[97] Further, in 62 he was member of a committee of three set up to investigate taxation.[98] Finally, on an inscription at Narona in Dalmatia Ducenius appears as 'curator vectigalium publicorum' and governor of the province (*ILS* 9484).

That was not all. On a fragmentary dedication at Epidaurus stood an *Ignotus* who had the same two priesthoods as on the Narona inscription and was a legate of Dalmatia (*ILS* 963). Identity seemed close to certainty (cf. *PIR*[2], D 201). Epidaurus also contributed a proconsulate of Asia: to go suitably in 67/8, in consonance with the approximate consular year.[99]

Identity now comes under grave doubt. An Ephesian inscription registers the commissioners of the year 62 in their presumed order of rank, viz. A. Pompeius Paullinus (*suff. c.*54), L. Calpurnius Piso (*cos.* 57), A. Ducenius Geminus.[100] The consulate of Ducenius must belong either in 60 or 61, so it appears. Hence sundry perturbations.

What then is to be done with the *Ignotus* at Epidaurus? He is styled 'legatus Caesarum', when governing either Dalmatia or another imperial province prior to Dalmatia (as the structure of the truncated lines renders more plausible). The formulation applies to a governor who bridged two reigns. Thus Carminius Vetus in Lusitania under Caligula and Claudius (cf. *PIR*[2], C | 428). And Pomponius Rufus (*suff.* 95) is 'leg. imperatorum' in Dalmatia.[101] The emperors are Domitian and Nerva.

Alternatives offer. First, the *Ignotus* had Dalmatia in 54/5. He is therefore P. Anteius Rufus or his successor. Anteius, attested there in 51, was in Rome in 55 when he had some prospect of replacing Ummidius Quadratus in Syria (cf. *PIR*[2], A 731). Second, Nero's governor in 68.

In any event, waiving those hypotheses, Ducenius governed Dalmatia at some time between 63 and 68. If there in 68, he was summoned by Galba to assume the city prefecture—and old Pompeius Silvanus (*suff.* 45) took his place.[102] On that view Ducenius

---

[97] There was a consular pair shortly before 56, a M. Junius Silanus and 'A.[' (*CIL* xiv 3741: Tibur). For Ducenius, *Historia* v (1956), 210 = *RP* (1979), 322. This 'Aulus' should be A. Pompeius Paullinus, so it now appears. Cf. W. Eck, *ZPE* xlii (1981), 228 f.

[98] *Ann.* xv 18, 3.

[99] *PIR*[2], D 201 ('fortasse'): accepted to give a list of the proconsuls from 61/2 to 68/9 in *Some Arval Brethren* (1980), 69.

[100] Adduced by W. Eck, *ZPE* xlii (1981), 228. He proceeds to draw the consequences for Ducenius Geminus—and for *ILS* 963.

[101] On the inscription from Curictae published in their collection by A. and J. Šašel, *Situla* xix (1978), 141, no. 942. I owe knowledge of this to W. Eck. See further *ZPE* liii (1983), 196 ff. = pp. 353 ff., below.

[102] That conclusion would thus be doubly welcome and helpful. A governorship of

could still retain the Epidaurian dedication, and therewith a proconsulate in Asia, liberating 66/7 and advanced to 73/4. Which ejects Aponius Saturninus from the latter year, as had generally been accepted.[103] Saturninus on another argument had in fact been allocated the tenure 67/8, just before his governorship of Moesia.[104]

By good fortune the *patria* of Ducenius Geminus is exempt from doubt. The rare name points to Patavium.[105] An Asconius who happens to carry 'Ducenius' in his nomenclature (*PIR*[2], A 1207) evokes the Transpadane orator, Ti. Catius Asconius Silius Italicus. In the appointment of the *praefectus urbi*, an unabated influence of Silius is not out of question, although Patavium, conservative and Republican, harboured a different tradition, embodied in Thrasea Paetus, one of Nero's principal victims. Galba honoured that tradition, even if he lacked near affinities with friends of Thrasea.[106]

Another post at Rome carried ostensible prestige, the charge of the aqueducts. For the student of antiquity the *cura aquarum* is magnified by two facts. It was inaugurated by the illustrious Messalla Corvinus, and when Julius Frontinus was appointed by Nerva he proceeded to compose a whole treatise. The list of *curatores* transmitted by the author soon exhibited a social decline: | some *novi homines* appointed not long subsequent to a consulate.[107] Nor might absence from Rome be a bar.

In 68 the bland and alert Vibius Crispus acceded, with a tenancy lasting until 71. In the *Annales* the first entrance of this potent character occurs in the year 60. It is peculiar, being annotation on the equestrian Vibius Secundus, 'Vibi Crispi fratris opibus enisus' (xiv 28, 2). Vibius was later matched with Eprius Marcellus for skill and success as a political manager. Eprius became consul suffect in 62. It is a temptation to put the consulship of Vibius in the same season, marked (as shown above) by certain changes in the political

---

C. Calpetanus Statius Rufus (*PIR*[2], C 235) could be situated anywhere in the space of nearly twenty years (excepting only the tenure of Anteius Rufus).

[103] W. Eck, *Senatoren von Vespasian bis Hadrian* (1970), 119.

[104] *Some Arval Brethren* (1980), 68 f., cf. above.

[105] Schulze, *LE* 160, citing *CIL* v 5525 (Patavium); 3609 (Verona). It is also found in Campania.

[106] His adoption of Piso Licinianus was either 'propria electione' or, as some believed, under pressure from Cornelius Laco, 'cui apud Rubellium Plautum exercita cum Pisone amicitia' (i 14, 1). To be sure, Helvidius Priscus made search for the corpse of Galba and gave it burial (Plutarch, *Galba* 28); and one may note the verdict of Musonius Rufus on the fate of the Emperor, as reported in Arrian, *Diss. Epicteti* iii 15, 14.

[107] Frontinus, *De aq.* 102.

constellation.[108] It might fall earlier.[109] The question touches his proconsulate of Africa, best assigned to 71/2.[110]

However that may be, it is a comfort to discover Vibius Crispus exerting his arts as ever, to get a post from Galba; and Vespasian was to cherish both Vibius and Eprius.[111]

Senior ex-consuls suggest brief mention in this place for the proconsuls of Asia and Africa. Under influence at any time from Caesar, sortition and sequence were liable to be disturbed by civil war. In Numidia the legate Clodius Macer declared against Nero before the end, and his pretensions caused annoyance for some time until finally a procurator was able to put him to death.[112] The episode impinged on the period of transit from proconsul to proconsul. It may well have delayed the arrival of Vipstanus Apronianus (*cos.* 59). His predecessor is not mentioned in the little that is known of the rebellion of Clodius Macer. The name of Vipstanus occurs on a fragment of the *Acta fratrum Arvalium* which, so it can be argued, belongs to the month of October (see below under Raecius Taurus).

From Asia Aponius Saturninus, the retiring proconsul, was despatched to Moesia. His successor for the tenure 68/9 was Fonteius Agrippa (*suff.* 58), cf. | *PIR*[2], F 466. Fonteius and Vipstanus are both products of the sortition conducted at the beginning of 68—or perhaps not. One or other might be a replacement.

In Asia Rutilius Gallicus (*suff.* ?70) is on attestation as a proconsul's legate for two years (?68–70), equipped with a priesthood and with the title of consul-designate (*ILS* 9499; Ephesus). Previously for nine years legate in Galatia under Corbulo, Rutilius (from Augusta Taurinorum) was destined to a splendid career which ended with a second consulate and a brief occupance of the city prefecture.

Priesthoods declare a visible enhancement of social rank or political success, being accorded to aristocratic youths or to mature adherents

---

[108] Vibius by his full style shares the prefix 'L. Junius' with Caesennius Paetus (*cos.* 62), cf. *JRS* lxvii (1977), 45 = *RP* iii (1984), 1054. It may be hazardous to enlist in the 'Vitellian faction' a plethora of consuls in this vicinity. For example, T. Petronius Niger (*suff.* 62) may not have a close attachment to the consular Petronii. Nevertheless, the resurgence of the group is noteworthy—and its persistence in the sequel.

[109] An early Neronian date is suggested by A. B. Bosworth, *Athenaeum* li (1973), 70 f. Followed by Chilver in his *Historical Commentary* (1979), 173. On the other hand, 63 or 64 is advocated by P. A. Gallivan, *CQ* xxiv (1974), 307.

[110] It is put in 72/3 by Gallivan, who argues that Q. Manlius Tarquitius Saturninus, on his showing *suffectus* in 63, had the tenure 71/2 (op. cit. 306).

[111] Tacitus, *Dial.* 8, 3: 'ab ipso principe cum quadam reverentia diliguntur.'

[112] *Hist.* i 7, 1. The affair of Clodius Macer is most obscure. After Nero's death Nymphidius Sabinus incited him to hold up the corn ships (Plutarch, *Galba* 13). For the role of Calvia Crispinilla (73, 1) see *PIR*[2], C 363.

of the Caesars (often about the time of a consulship). Next to the 'quattuor amplissima' (the *sacerdotia* inherited from the old order) stood the *sodales Augustales*. Galba himself had been both a *XV vir sacris faciundis* and a *sodalis*. Like other emperors, Nero was an additional member of every priesthood, college, or fraternity. Three senators whom Galba put to death, all of status that warrants a priesthood, also offered welcome vacancies, viz. Petronius Turpilianus, Fonteius Capito, and the consul designate Cingonius Varro. Only one of the beneficiaries is certified, namely Rutilius Gallicus who, still absent in Asia, was honoured with Nero's place among the *sodales Augustales*.[113]

Attention is engaged by the inscribed record, albeit incomplete, of the Arval Brethren. Instituted by Caesar Augustus, and designed to be aristocratic and exclusive, the fraternity was restricted to either *nobiles* or ex-consuls, and it remained so for a long space. A relaxation crept in under Nero, with the obscure and enigmatic Tillius Sassius, admitted shortly before 63. In that year the protocol registers eight presences, and the absent four can be identified.[114]

In January of 69 three new names make their appearance, viz. M. Raecius Taurus, L. Maecius Postumus, P. Valerius Marinus.[115] Now Taurus occurs on a fragment which has been attributed to the reign of Nero.[116] None the less, a case can be made out for the previous autumn. The fragment also carries the names of Vipstanus Apronianus and M. Otho. At first sight Vipstanus appears to offer a clue. He was proconsul of Africa for 68/9. Yet he might not have gone there until October (cf. above).

The decisive name is that of M. Otho. An *Arvalis* in 57, he departed to Lusitania the next year, absent from Rome until he returned with Galba early | in October of 68. Not before then could both Otho and Raecius Taurus figure on the same document. Nor would 57 include the obscure Taurus, even were the list not complete.[117] The *novus homo* Aponius Saturninus belonged already—but he was consular by that time.

On this showing three adherents of Galba emerge without effort.

(1) M. Raecius Taurus, the old senator from Tarraco. On whom, see remarks above concerning his son Gallus.

(2) L. Maecius Postumus. Maecii of note are found at Ilici, a

---

[113] *ILS* 5025, cf. 9499. It would be idle to try to identify the ']onius' who was a priest in 68 (*CIL* xiv 2389: Bovillae).

[114] *CIL* vi 2043. For the complete list in 63, J. Scheid, *Les Frères Arvales* (1975), 286. For the list of 66 (vi 2044) see *Some Arval Brethren* (1980), 4 f.

[115] vi 2051.

[116] vi 2045, cf. J. Scheid, op. cit. 275 ff.

[117] vi 2038, cf. J. Scheid, op. cit. 286.

colony in the direction of Carthago Nova, and they contracted ties with Spanish Roscii.[118]

(3) P. Valerius Marinus, designated consul by Galba. The name is consonant with an origin in Spain or Narbonensis. His previous career is a blank: perhaps at some time a legate under Corbulo, who during a dozen years of command in the Orient had amassed quite a collection. Several consuls issued from that company, namely first of all Licinius Mucianus (*suff.* ?64), Vettius Bolanus (66), Verulanus Severus (?66). Then Marius Celsus (69); and Aurelius Fulvus was soon to accede to that honour (?70).

Search for Valerius Marinus might be attracted towards the 'Marinus' (or 'Marianus') who occurs, with the title of governor, on the Tariff of Palmyra.[119] He belongs somewhere anterior to the arrival of Mucianus. This item has not aroused much curiosity.[120]

Marinus, it is clear, was a praetorian legate who functioned during the lacuna between two consulars. Examples are to hand.[121] If Valerius Marinus be the man, alternatives occur. First, in 63, when by anomaly Domitius Corbulo had charge of the Syrian army, while Cestius Gallus (*suff.* 42) was on the way to take over the civilian administration (*Ann.* xv 25, 3). Second, in the early spring of 67, after the decease of Gallus. That unfortunate old man succumbed, 'taedio aut fato' (*Hist.* v 10, 1), not long after his retreat from the failed attack on Jerusalem (late November of 66).[122]

Vespasian had been with Nero on the Hellenic tour. He reached Syria after crossing the Hellespont and travelling through Asia Minor.[123] Licinius Mucianus, if not in that company, had the longer journey from Italy, arriving in Syria later than Vespasian.

Priesthoods reward an allegiance or solicit gratitude. In the place of the deceased Galba among the *Arvales*, Otho inserted Tampius Flavianus, at the | time legate of Pannonia.[124] The procedure invites a modest conjecture. Galba himself may have introduced Trebellius Maximus.[125] Further, Licinius Mucianus. A small piece of the *Acta* for 70 carries his name.[126] Not having to wait for the victory of the Flavian cause, Mucianus may have been brought in by some previous gesture designed to conciliate the commander in Syria.

---

[118] See further *Some Arval Brethren* (1980), 7 f.

[119] H. Seyrig, *Syria* xxii (1941), 159; 165 n. 3; 167.

[120] As emphasized by G. W. Bowersock, *JRS* lxv (1975), 182.

[121] *ZPE* xli (1981), 131 = *RP* iii (1984), 1381 (suggesting several alternative dates for Marinus).

[122] He survived long enough to make an attack on Sepphoris (Josephus, *Vita* 394).

[123] Josephus, *BJ* iii 8. Titus, 'after a swifter passage from Achaia to Alexandria than is normal in winter', joined his father at Ptolemais (iii 64).

[124] vi 2051.   [125] He was *magister* in 72 (2053).   [126] vi 2052.

Epilogue

The promotions made by Galba, in all their variety of status and local origins from equestrian officers to consuls, may not have much to tell about that emperor. Many facts and a number of conjectures, what does it amount to?

His character and habits are known. Likewise the predicament of a usurper in civil war, overcome by events and under constraint from allies and agents. And violence accelerates processes that had previously been moving under their own steady rhythm. Narbonensians and Spaniards owed signal advancement to Seneca and Burrus, the ministers of Nero. No great retardation ensued after they were superseded.[127]

Galba and his war deserve credit for three if not four consuls from Narbonensis: excellent men whom at the lowest another ruler would not be likely to retard or repress. By the same token, some of Vespasian's adherents active in his proclamation. Ulpius Traianus was a senior legionary legate; and Aurelius Fulvus in 64 had commanded III Gallica under Corbulo.[128]

Continuing to rise under the Flavian emperors, the magnates from Spain and Narbonensis coalesced to form the nexus which produced the dynasty of the Antonines.[129] Their epoch saw the culmination of another and parallel process that received a sharp impulsion from civil war. The accident of Vespasian's ascension promoted partisans in the eastern lands, with consulships ensuing under Domitian: for citizens of Sardis and Pergamum who were also descendants of kings and tetrarchs.

---

[127] M. Vestinus Atticus, a magnate of Vienna, held an eponymous consulate in 65; and one should not miss the discreet but alert Agricola, tribune in 66, praetor already in 68.

[128] *ILS* 232 (nr. Harput). In the spring of 68 Fulvus took the legion to Moesia. It there began the movement against Vitellius. Tacitus may later have recorded activities of Fulvus, no longer legate in the autumn of 69 (cf. iii 10, 1).

[129] Fulvus ended as *praefectus urbi* (*HA Pius* 1, 4): perhaps in the momentous year 97.

8

Spanish Pomponii. A Study in Nomenclature

RARE names are a rare delight, and often instructive. When non-Latin by shape or origin, they denote the immigrant in Spain, some going back to the epoch before certain regions of Italy received the Roman franchise. Baetica parades the prime exhibits, before all at Italica and Corduba. The litoral of Tarraconensis, from Barcino down to Carthago Nova, can also offer attractive specimens.

By contrast, the ordinary names in their plethora: Fabii, Licinii, and the like. The phenomenon reflects consuls or praetors of the imperial Republic, enhanced by choice or fashion. The two types combine in the nomenclature of M. Cornelius Nigrinus Curiatius Maternus (consul suffect in 83), the great man from Liria of the Edetani.

At the same time, the indistinctive *nomen* is ambiguous: either the enfranchised native or the immigrant. 'Pomponius' belongs to this class. Pomponii are common enough at Rome and throughout Italy. Yet, as it happens, no Pomponius can be discovered as a governor in the Spanish provinces.[1]

A catalogue has been presented of the names on highest frequency in *CIL* II, sixty specimens or more.[2] Pomponii do not much exceed a total of thirty; and they are not a promising collection. The most presentable is T. Pomponius Avitus, a high priest of the imperial cult at Tarraco. He carries for tribe the 'Aniensis', which points to Caesaraugusta as the *patria*.[3] |

No fewer than seventy-one of these *flamines* are on record, from the reign of Vespasian to the time of Commodus: precious documentation that has been analysed in an exemplary fashion.[4] Some of the results bring a surprise. Even amongst the earliest *flamines*, who come from cities on the coast or in its vicinity, the

---

[1] For names in Spain, Gallia Transalpina, and Africa that may reflect holders of *imperium* see E. Badian, *Foreign Clientelae* (1958), 309 ff.

[2] For the twenty names matched with Narbonensis, see *Tacitus* (1958), 783. And, for further statistics about frequency, R. C. Knapp, *AncSoc* ix (1978), 187 ff.

[3] *CIL* ii 4235. L. Pomponius Avitus of Tarraco (4395) cannot safely be adduced as a kinsman. The *cognomen* is desperately common in Spain: over a hundred specimens.

[4] G. Alföldy, *Flamines Provinciae Hispaniae Citerioris* (1973).

Gerión i (1983), 249–66.

social rank is not as high as might be expected. Only three produce sons who become senators and consuls.[5]

For Spanish Pomponii, meagre and sporadic compensation accrues from literature. Pomponius Mela, as he states, came from Tingentera, on the Strait of Gades; and Pliny, who had been procurator in Tarraconensis, relates how Sex. Pomponius, 'Hispaniae citerioris princeps', discovered by accident a remedy against gout.[6] For the rest, recourse is had to inscriptions found in other countries, not without inference, argument, conjecture.

When Galba made his proclamation in the spring of the year 68, he convoked an assembly of the provincial notables: 'e primoribus prudentia atque aetate praestantibus, velut instar senatus'.[7] To younger men the usurper allocated military rank or tasks. Thus Raecius Gallus was appointed a tribune (*RIT* 145); and the inscription on the arch at Lepcis recording the career of Q. Pomponius Rufus shows him in charge of the coasts of Tarraconensis and Narbonensis 'bello qu[od] imp. G[a]lba pro [re p.] gessit'.[8]

Some identified Galba's man with Q. Pomponius Rufus, commanding a cavalry regiment in 64 (*CIL* xvi 5). That was premature, and illicit. His tribe is 'Collina', not verifiable anywhere in Spain. Commonplace nomenclature engendered homonyms in all grades of Roman society. For example, Vibii Maximi cause a lot of trouble. No profit therefore to adduce a Q. Pomponius Rufus of the better sort, who was priest in a Samnite town.[9] And any who may be moved to seek the origin of a senatorial C. Pomponius Rufus will do well to neglect a freedman at Regium Lepidum.[10]

Galba's man earned adlection to the Senate, probably from Vespasian in his censorship. Pliny's friend Sex. Pomponius is styled 'praetorii viri pater' (*NH* xxii 20). Likewise another 'Hispaniae princeps' (no name) who cured himself of a disease by wearing round his neck the root of the herb purslane (xx 215).[11] Either son or both might however have acceded to the 'amplissimus ordo' by the normal path. |

Pliny collected friends from his occupations in the western provinces and bequeathed them to his nephew—whose 'circle', by

---

[5] Viz. Q. Licinius Silvanus Granianus (*suff.* 106); C. Calpurnius Flaccus (?125); M. Valerius Propinquus (126).

[6] Pliny, *NH* xxii 120.

[7] Suetonius, *Galba* 10, 3.

[8] *IRT* 537 (completing *ILS* 1014).

[9] *CIL* ix 2161 (Caudium), cf. 2189 ('litteris bonis').

[10] *AE* 1946, 210 (Regium Lepidum).

[11] Amalgamated with Sex. Pomponius in *RE* xxi 2335.

the way, acknowledges nobody from Baetica.[12] In August of 79 a Spanish guest was staying with the admiral of the fleet at Misenum. He upbraided the youth who quietly went on with his appointed task (reading Livy and making excerpts) long after the volcano had erupted (*Ep.* vi 20, 5).

Meanwhile the admiral, intent in any case on a close inspection of the phenomenon, had set out with warships, under added impulsion from a message sent by a lady called Rectina, whose mansion lay on the coast beneath Vesuvius (vi 16, 8). He could not land there, but he changed direction, with a firm command to the steersman: 'pete Pomponianum' (16, 11). Pomponianus, as the next sentence in the letter states, was at another part of the bay, at Stabiae. Pliny joined him, and they dined together.

Rectina perished (as the reader did not need to be told), and the admiral succumbed the next day in the vicinity of Stabiae. Rectina and Pomponianus arouse curiosity, and have aroused perplexity. Wife and husband, such is one incautious assumption.[13] Nothing in the narration speaks for it.[14]

The narration registers the husband's name in 'Rectinae Tasci'. That is the reading preferred by the latest text (OCT 1964). A 'Tascus' or a 'Tascius' is not inconceivable. He would have to be Celtic, on the analogy of various personal and place names.[15] But not in any way plausible. The plain answer is 'Cascus'.[16] That *cognomen* is preternaturally rare. It was borne by Cn. Pedius Cascus, consul suffect in 71: enigmatic in his prominence, for he stood next to the consuls who opened that year.

Rectina has some relevance to Spain. It is a rare *cognomen*. Spain exhibits nine out of fourteen specimens of 'Rectus', four out of six of 'Rectinus'.[17] Among the latter belongs Popillia L.f. Rectina, the wife of Voconius Romanus, the friend and coeval of the younger Pliny (*CIL* ii 3866: Saguntum). As concerns the provenance of Cn. Pedius Cascus, there is no call to adduce a pair of facts: Q. Pedius proconsul of Citerior in 45 B.C., and no Pedii in *CIL* II. The consul probably derives from old Latium.

Q. Pomponius Rufus made a spectacular entrance into history in the year 68—and he was to reach a consulate, not rapid or easy, in 95.

---

[12] *HSCPh* lxxiii (1969), 230 ff. = *RP* (1979), 768 ff.
[13] Thus A. N. Sherwin-White in his *Commentary* (1966), ad loc.
[14] C. P. Jones, *Phoenix* xxii (1968), 127: J. H. D'Arms, *Romans on the Bay of Naples* (1979), 222 f.
[15] For a number of specimens, *JRS* lviii (1968), 140 = *RP* (1979), 702.
[16] Adopted by M. Schuster (Teubner, 1952).
[17] I. Kajanto, *The Latin Cognomina* (1965), 252.

On the inscription (*IRT* 537), the first senatorial post is praetorian. That masks the fact of adlection, as can happen.[18] |

Briefly put, the career works out as follows. Rufus was *iuridicus* in Tarraconensis and thereafter commander of a legion.[19] For all that can be known, he might have taken up the first post as early as 75, the second as late as 90. In any event, many years have to be allowed for during which Pomponius Rufus was out of active employment.

The dating of the Spanish post, in itself a problem, is complicated by extraneous evidence. As shown by the *tabulae defixionum* that came to light at Emporiae, a man called Rufus held it when T. Aurelius Fulvus was governor of the province (*AE* 1952, 122). Like the identity of that Rufus, the tenure of Fulvus is in question.[20]

More important, the legion. Rufus is styled merely 'leg. leg. V'. Two legions bore that number. The one, V Macedonica, had its station at Oescus on the lower Danube, the other, V Alaudae, is also to be assigned to the garrison of Moesia. After 70 reinforcement of the frontier had become expedient. And another factor comes in. Evidence indicates that a Roman legion was wiped out in the invasion of Dacia conducted by Cornelius Fuscus, Domitian's Guard Prefect.[21]

Whichever the legion, Rufus may have been its commander at some time during the campaigns between 85 and 89, on and beyond the river. If it was V Alaudae, two phenomena find a single explanation. First, the omission of the legion's title from the inscription on the arch at Lepcis, dedicated by the proconsul Pomponius Rufus. Second, retardation in his career. A legate enjoying success or favour will proceed to one of the praetorian provinces, with clear prospect of a consulship.

In the face of seductive speculation, caution is prescribed. Rufus might have been appointed to the command of V Macedonica in 89, when the Dacian War terminated. Even so, that was late in the career of a man who had been adlected *inter praetorios* some fifteen years previously.

However that may be, Rufus acceded to a praetorian province in 92 or 93. A diploma dated to the latter year by the imperial titulature

---

[18] Thus *ILS* 1015 (L. Javolenus Priscus); 8819 (A. Julius Quadratus).

[19] On the inscription the order and formulation 'leg. Aug. pro pr. provinc. [M]oesiae Dalmat. Hisp.' caused trouble. Rufus was held for a time to be a consular governing Tarraconensis. For Rufus as a *iuridicus*, *Gnomon* xxxi (1959), 512 = *Danubian Papers* (1971), 193 f.; G. Alföldy, *Fasti Hispanienses* (1969), 71 ff.

[20] For one solution, Alföldy, op. cit. 19 ff. For present purposes the problem may be waived.

[21] E. Ritterling, *RE* xii 1569 f. For indications that V Alaudae was sent to Moesia in 70 see *Danubian Papers* (1971), 82, cf. 105 (a veteran at Scupi).

discloses him as governor of Dalmatia (xvi 38). Normally consular, that province had in fact forfeited its legion in 85. For its change of status at this juncture precisely some other reasons might be canvassed. For example, a shortage of consulars after a sequence of unhealthy seasons. Or again, emergency caused by the decease of a governor. In Cappadocia–Galatia Antistius Rusticus died, and the province was split for a brief season.[22] |

A further anomaly ensued. A fragmentary inscription at Curictae styles Pomponius Rufus 'leg. imperatoru[m]'.[23] The emperors in question must be Domitian and Nerva. Rufus held the *fasces* for the last four months of the year 95. He was consul in absence, it follows.[24] Moreover, Rufus continued in his mandate into the first year of Trajan. In 98 another governor, a certain Macer, went to Dalmatia, as is made clear by the language of Martial—and by the reference to his own imminent departure to Spain.[25]

From Dalmatia Rufus now passed to Moesia Inferior, where he is attested by two diplomas of 99 (xvi 44 f.). Not for long tenure. Another consular held the command in 100.[26] Despite his Danubian experience (a legion and Moesia Inferior), Rufus took no part in the Dacian campaigns that began the year after. Trajan had other friends and allies.

Rufus in the sequel held the post of *curator operum publicorum*.[27] When his year arrived for the sortition he became proconsul of Africa, for the tenure 110/11. He was then aged about sixty-five.

Emphasis has been put on the slow advance in the career of honours. It comes out on comparison with some of his coevals, such as Cornelius Nigrinus (*suff.* 83) or Javolenus Priscus (*suff.* 86), both adlected to the same rank.[28] A setback has been suspected, if he was legate of V Alaudae.

On the other hand, influences worked in his favour. They baffle detection. Cornelius Nigrinus held Moesia for a brief spell (85/6) early in Domitian's Dacian War, remaining in charge of Moesia

[22] As argued in *JRS* lxvii (1977), 42 = *RP* iii (1984), 1049 ff.: from *ILS* 1017 (Pisidian Antioch), the inscription of (L. Caesennius) Sospes, who had been a legionary legate in 92. Not all scholars accept this solution. Thus R. K. Sherk, *AJP* c (1979), 167 f.

[23] Published by A. and J. Šašel, *Inscr. Lat. Jug.* (1978), 942.

[24] For a parallel (or parallels) in 70, cf. *JRS* xlviii (1958), 6 f. = *RP* (1979), 387 ff. And see further below on T. Pomponius Bassus (*suff.* 94) in Cappadocia–Galatia.

[25] Martial x 78, cf. *Danubian Papers* (1971), 198. For problems of date and identity concerning the Dalmatian governorship of a Cilnius Proculus see W. Eck. *RE, Suppl.* xiv 97; 271 f.

[26] M. Laberius Maximus (*suff.* 87), cf. *CIL* xvi 48.

[27] The post was not yet collegiate or held in immediate sequence to a consulate.

[28] Nigrinus had been legate of a legion and governor of Aquitania (*AE* 1973, 283); Javolenus after a legion and Numidia was *iuridicus* in Britain (*ILS* 1015).

Inferior when the command was divided.[29] Nigrinus may have helped to promote the interests of a fellow Tarraconensian. Yet local ties are in some danger of being overestimated; the province included diverse regions—and no clue to the *patria* of Q. Pomponius Rufus.

However it be, luck or patronage served him well at two significant junctures. First of all, the praetorian province, which he acquired in 92 or 93. The latter year erupted in embarrassments for the government, when factional rivalries led to notable prosecutions for high treason. On the lowest count, senators from Spain and Narbonensis are not conspicuous in the ranks of Caesar's enemies or critics. Most of them remained firm adherents of the Flavian dynasty.

Next, when that dynasty ended abruptly, when from the crisis in Nerva's reign one of the generals came to the power, advantage accrued to Pomponius Rufus, the legate of Dalmatia. Among his early promotions (a | noteworthy company), Trajan advanced Rufus to the charge of Moesia Inferior: with three legions, ranking among the foremost military commands.[30]

No other consular Pomponius of the period demands or deserves a comparable exposition. About 'C. Pomponius[', consul suffect in 74 (*AE* 1968, 7) not a word can be said. A gap then intervenes, and in the vicinity of Rufus (*suff.* 95), the *Fasti* exhibit a cluster of four, from 94 to 100.

(1) T. Pomponius Bassus (94). His antecedents baffle enquiry. He first turns up in 79/80 as legate in Asia (*ILS* 8796). The proconsul was M. Ulpius Traianus (*suff.* ?70)—and Bassus later proved highly acceptable to the son of the proconsul. If he was a legate of praetorian status (some were quaestorian) he may have owed adlection to Vespasian. That entails a further consequence. Given the date of his consulship, Bassus suffered for a time a retardation comparable to that of Pomponius Rufus.

Yet merit, patronage, or luck spoke their word. Bassus was to hold one of the military provinces. The legates chosen for those commands had generally advanced by the command of a legion and a governorship in one of the eight praetorian provinces in the portion of Caesar. The employments of Bassus (as of sundry others) would be worth knowing. He clearly stood well with Caesar and Caesar's friends during more reigns than one. Domitian appointed him to

[29] See the demonstration by G. Alföldy and H. Halfmann, *Chiron* iii (1973), 356 ff.
[30] Britain and Syria had three legions each, and there were now four in Pannonia.

Cappadocia–Galatia. He remained there through a momentous season for a tenure longer than normal, until the year 100.[31]

Something new has recently come up. Coins of Caesarea register Bassus in Cappadocia in years 14 and 15 of Domitian. That is, October 93/4 and October 94/5.[32] Bassus' consulate embraced the last four months of 94. He therefore went to his province in 94, when still only consul designate. The parallel to Pomponius Rufus (continuing in Dalmatia although meanwhile consul) will be duly noted. In the case of Bassus, his appointment terminated the void caused by the death of Antistius Rusticus in 93 or 94.[33]

Returning from his province, Bassus in 101 was put in charge of the recently instituted *alimenta* (*ILS* 6106, cf. 6675). In a letter to Bassus, of 104 or 105, Pliny warmly commends the fashion in which he spends the leisure of retirement: 'ita senescere oportet virum qui magistratus amplissimos gesserit, exercitus rexerit' etc. (iv 23, 2). That would not preclude a change of mind, should a proconsulate offer, in 108 or 109. Asia is full, but there are vacancies in Africa.

(2) C. Pomponius Pius (98). Known only as a consular date, yet remarkable in that he shared the *fasces* with Trajan, in succession to four | 'consules iterum'. He is patently the son of the homonymous *suffectus* of 65, a person of some influence in the late Neronian epoch: he went rapidly to one of the important military commands, taking the place of Plautius Silvanus Aelianus in Moesia (*SEG* i 329: Histria).

The ostentatious *cognomen* declares loyalty to a family or to a political cause. This man might be a son of Q. Pomponius Secundus (*suff.* 41), who came to grief in the proclamation of Camillus Scribonianus (cf. *PIR*[1], P 564). The other consular involved was Caecina Paetus. The husband of his daughter took over the *cognomen*: P. Clodius Thrasea Paetus.

(3) C. Pomponius Rufus (98). To be identified as the Pomponius Rufus who prosecuted Julius Bassus and is styled by Pliny 'vir paratus et vehemens' (iv 9, 3). Otherwise on record only as a proconsul of Africa, in 113/14.

Thubursicu Numidarum yields the principal documents, viz. *ILAlg* i 1230; 1231; 1232; 1233; 1382. All fragmentary. There are also pieces of inscriptions at a place in southern Tunisia (*ILAfr* 13) and at Lares (*CIL* viii 1777).

The proconsul emerges as a *polyonymus*. In standard works he

---

[31] *CIL* iii 6896 f.

[32] P. R. Franke, *Chiron* ix (1979), 277 ff.

[33] The widow brought his ashes back to Italy (Martial ix 30). In the interim Caesennius Sospes had acted as governor in Galatia (as inferred from *ILS* 1017).

figures as 'C. Pomponius Rufus Acilius [?Prisc]us Coelius Sparsus'.[34] One is impelled to question the validity of the *cognomen* attached by conjecture to the second item of the nomenclature. It finds no justification at Thubursicu. The answer comes from the fragment at Lares, which has suffered strange neglect.[35] It reveals, as its last surviving line, the words ']scus Coe['.

Therefore not '[?Prisc]us' but '[?Pri]scus'. Curiosity is still not assuaged. Granting the need for a short *cognomen* (on one of the Thubursicu inscriptions), why 'Priscus'? Scholars, it appears, have allowed themselves to be influenced by the existence of an Acilius Priscus. That is to say, M. Acilius Priscus, the Ostian magnate (*AE* 1955, 169) whose name is prefixed to that of an Egrilius Plarianus, who was consul suffect *c.*129 (*PIR*[2], E 48).

Nothing commends the attachment of Pomponius Rufus to the well-documented nexus at Ostia. For the *cognomen*, 'Fuscus' or 'Tuscus' would do as well. The latter shows high frequency in Spain.[36] Passing comment may go to Pomponia Q. f. Tusca at Corduba (ii 2301). She was used to supplement (cf. *PIR*[1], P 568) the name of a senator as '[Q. Pomp]on[ius . . . T]usc[us' (vi 1557). Plain sense deters—and no need to counter the conjecture with, for example, Cn. Antonius Fuscus (*suff.* 109).

Acilii, with thirty-four specimens in *CIL* II, rank with Pomponii for frequency; and, as with Pomponii, no holder of *imperium* in the Spains is | available to explain the name. Baetica yields Acilii of the better sort. For example, Acilius Lucanus of Corduba, maternal grandfather of the poet (*PIR*[2], A 74) or P. Acilius Attianus of Italica, Prefect of the Guard in 117 (A 45). Again, P. Postumius Acilianus, procurator of Syria early in the reign of Trajan.[37] And one might wonder about the origin of L. Acilius Strabo (*suff.* ?71).[38] As concerns the other province, M. Acilius Rufus of Saguntum was an imperial procurator in the early epoch.[39]

Instructive on various counts, these Acilii from Spanish cities

[34] B. E. Thomasson, *Die Statthalter der römischen Provinzen Nordafrikas* ii (1960), 58; W. Eck, *Senatoren von Vespasian bis Hadrian* (1970), 176.

[35] Gsell duly referred to *CIL* viii 1777 in his annotation on *ILAlg* i 1230, but did not quote it, merely stating 'qui peut fort bien se rapporter au proconsul de nos inscriptions'. It was not printed by Thomasson along with the other six documents.

[36] I. Kajanto, *The Latin Cognomina* (1965), 188: of epigraphic instances 23 out of 48. He noted only one specimen of 'Tuscillus', i.e. L. Memmius Tuscillus Senecio (xiv 3597; *ILS* 1042: Tibur), the son of Senecio Memmius Afer (*suff.* 99). Add *CIL* ii 157; 236; 2279; 5175.

[37] *CIL* ii 2213 (Corduba); *IGR* iii 928 (Rhosus).

[38] His name recurs, along with 'C. Curiatius Maternus', in the nomenclature of Clodius Nummus, consul suffect in 114 (*PIR*[2], A 83); while the adoptive son (C 1423) and relatives (1450 f.) betray Spanish elements.

[39] *CIL* ii 3840; *ILS* 1376. Probably 'Marcus' not 'Manius' (as in *ILS* and in *PIR*, A 79), cf. *CIL* ii, Add. p. 967; *Ep. lat. de Saguntum* (1980), 41.

(more attractive than Ostia) offer no clear approach to C. Pomponius Rufus. One turns for succour to the third member of his nomenclature, 'Coelius Sparsus'.

Spain yields twenty Coelii, Narbonensis fifty-five. The name will be taken to reflect the presence in both provinces of C. Coelius Caldus, the consul of 94 B.C.[40] Some subsequent member of the family may also have contributed to spreading the name.

The prime document of early date at Barcino records walls, towers, and gates built by a *duumvir* (*CIL* i² 2673 = *IRB* 51). It has been the subject of abundant and lengthy discussion among those whom with justice the date and origin of that *colonia* preoccupies.[41] The nomenclature of the magistrate failed to excite attention. He is 'C. Coelius Atisi f.'. The father's name, 'Atisus' or 'Atisius' is Celtic. Verona supplies three specimens of 'Atisius'.[42]

In the context of Tarraconensis, M. Roscius Coelius deserves a brief mention (*suff.* 81). Roscii exploited the mines in the hinterland of Carthago Nova. Their tribe is 'Maecia' (*ILS* 8706), which indicates an ultimate origin from Lanuvium; and Lanuvium itself yields an acephalous fragment (*Eph. Ep.* ix 612), clearly belonging (cf. *ILS* 1025) to L. Roscius Aelianus (*suff.* 100). Along with 'Coelius', 'Roscius Murena' (that significant *cognomen*) turns up in the nomenclature of Q. Pompeius Falco (*suff.* 108).[43]

Next, 'Sparsus', which happens to be extremely rare: on epigraphic record in Italy and in the provinces of the West to be found (apart from xii 3558: Nemausus) only in Tarraconensis.[44] Licinius Sparsus was one of the high priests (ii 4198), and 'Licinia Sparsi fi(lia) Procilla' is on show at | Asturica. She married a man called L. Lusius.[45] Attention has duly been drawn to Lusius Sparsus, a procurator at Alexandria in 139, and to C. Lusius Sparsus, consul suffect in 156 or 157 (*PIR*², L 442 f.).

With this encouragement, three further items can be adduced.

[40] For his career, especially the Gallic command, E. Badian, *Studies in Greek and Roman History* (1964), 91 ff. Observe the coins of his grandson the *monetalis*, C. Coelius L. f. C. n. Caldus (who was quaestor in Cilicia in 50). On which, *BMC, R. Rep.* i 475; M. H. Crawford, *RRC* (1974), 457 ff. One type has the legend HISP. That is, an earlier proconsulate, in Citerior (?98) for the grandfather.

[41] A. Balil, *Colonia Julia Augusta Paterna Faventia Barcino* (1964); J.-N. Bonneville, *REA* lxxx (1978), 37 ff. (a lengthy study).

[42] W. Schulze, *LE* 70. Add now C. Atisius Pollio, *praefectus* of Drusus Caesar (*AE* 1955, 291).

[43] See further 'Spaniards at Tivoli', *AncSoc* xiii/xiv (1982/3), 244 ff. = pp. 94 ff., above.

[44] Attention was directed to 'Sparsus' in *HSCPh* lxxiii (1969), 231 f. = *RP* (1979), 769.

[45] *CIL* ii 2648, where the last three lines are reproduced as 'Luci/Lusi/Asturicae'; and so the last letter appears ('vidi'). Presumably the lady's second *cognomen*, 'Asturica'.
The city also discloses Lyde, slave of Q. Lusius Saturninus (2656). Elsewhere in Spain three Lusii, viz. 1003 (Ceret); 1490 (Astigi); 3479 (Carthago).

(1) Sparsus on a coin at Osca of Augustan date.[46]

(2) Fulvius Sparsus, a *rhetor* frequently mentioned and cited by Seneca (*PIR*[2], F 560). Perhaps, like others in the congregation, from Spain. The most conspicuous were from Baetica, but two or three from Tarraconensis should be conceded.

(3) Sparsus who owned a palace (along with a vineyard) inside the walls of Rome. Martial addressed him the one poem only, at a late date (xii 57). To be assumed Sex. Julius Sparsus, consul suffect in 88, otherwise only a name. The two letters which a Julius Sparsus received from Pliny (iv 5; viii 3) have little to say, and nothing to suggest a senior ex-consul.[47]

For 'Sparsus' as an epigraphic rarity one may compare 'Rarus' itself: only three specimens.[48] Or 'Densus', with only two, both in Tarraconensis (ii 2815; 2818), whereas Tacitus brings in Sempronius Densus, a centurion in the Guard (*Hist.* i 43, 1) and the knight Julius Densus (*Ann.* xiii 10, 2).

'Coelius Sparsus' disengages a Tarraconensian affinity in the consular. What does it amount to? Polyonymous senators are responsible for vexatious problems. Adoption or maternal ascendance, explanations diverge. To take the simplest, binary nomenclature. In most instances the second member recalls the mother. That is sharply relevant to M. Cornelius Nigrinus Curiatius Maternus (*suff.* 83): on this showing not a Curiatius either by birth or by adoption.[49]

As is abundantly clear, Pomponii Rufi can occur anywhere. For this consular the sole discoverable link is Tarraconensian (i.e. 'Coelius Sparsus', taken from the father of his mother or his grandmother). Let it be accorded provisional validity. And a chance could be admitted that he is a brother or cousin of Q. Pomponius Rufus (*suff.* 95).

One of the inscriptions conveys the name of his wife, Bassilla (*ILAlg* 1282). The *cognomen* 'Bassus' is extremely common.[50] It would be hazardous indeed to conjecture a relationship to T. Pomponius Bassus (*suff.* 94); and, as will emerge later on, more families than one of Pomponii Bassi should be postulated in the time of Trajan. |

If the tribe of any of the consular Pomponii so far under inspection

---

[46] M. Grant, *FITA* (1946), 167.

[47] He is equated with the consul in *PIR*[2], J 586.

[48] I. Kajanto, *The Latin Cognomina* (1965), 103. Add C. Cornelius Rarus Sextius Naso (*suff.* 93), a proconsul of Africa (*IRT* 523).

[49] It was assumed by Alföldy and Halfmann (op. cit. 346 f.) that the orator Curiatius Maternus (the main character in the *Dialogus* of Tacitus) took in adoption a Cornelius Nigrinus. Better, the consular general was the son of a Curiatia.

[50] About seventy entries in *PIR*[2], B.

were attested, their region might become apparent, and even the *patria*. By good fortune the next consul in the group avows a tribe.

(4) T. Pomponius Mamilianus (100). At Deva a dedication to Fortuna Redux defines him as 'leg. Aug.' (vii 164 = *RIB* 445). That is, not governor of Britain but the commander of XX Valeria Victrix.[51] Therefore towards the end of Domitian's reign or even as late as 97. Rapid promotion by way of a praetorian province might accrue to a legate in this season.

This man is found holding a military command about the year 108. Writing to Mamilianus, Pliny alluded to 'aquilas vestras' (ix 25, 3). A previous letter shows that he had been hunting (ix 16). The province eludes conjecture. Contrary to what students of administration might be prone to expect, legionary legates in Britain (or elsewhere) seldom return as consulars.[52]

For present purposes what matters is the full nomenclature disclosed at Deva. He is [T]. Pomponius T. f. Gal. Mamilianus Rufus Antistianus Funisulanus Vettonianus. Which is more than is convenient for interpretation.

The tribe 'Galeria' at once brings encouragement. It can often form the basis for rational conjecture about a Spanish origin.[53] Elsewhere only two provincial cities are enrolled in 'Galeria', viz. Lugdunum and Thysdrus.

Three items in the nomenclature invite inspection. First, 'Mamilianus'. Of ancient and legendary fame, the Mamilii had their last known praetor in 206 B.C. (Q. Mamilius Turrinus). Five Mamilii on Spanish inscriptions therefore go back to low-class immigrant stock. One of them is T. Mamilius Silonis f. Praesens, a high priest at Tarraco (ii 4227 = *ILS* 6934). Not of early date, and he came from Tritium Magallum in the far interior.[54]

Next, 'Antistianus'. Both provinces testify. C. Antistius Vetus was proconsul of Ulterior in 68/7 B.C.; and his son (*suff.* 30) served as legate under Caesar Augustus in the campaigns of 26 and 25. An origin from Baetica is assumed (and patent) for L. Antistius Rusticus (*suff.* 90).[55] Nor will | one neglect the station Antistiana on the high

---

[51] Thus *JRS* xlvii (1957), 122 = *Ten Studies in Tacitus* (1970), 112; A. R. Birley, *The Fasti of Roman Britain* (1981), 235 (registering two recent aberrant notions).

In *RE* xxi 2342 Mamilianus was described as 'Statthalter von Britannien und Kommandant der leg. [II Augusta]'.   [52] A. R. Birley, op. cit. 29.

[53] Even for Senecio Memmius Afer (*ILS* 1042), despite an inscription at Carthage in honour of his great-grandson (viii 24586).

[54] The others are all Tarraconensian, viz. 3371 (Aurgi); 6171 (Barcino); 4162 and 4388 (Tarraco).

[55] A homonym was magistrate at Corduba (ii 2242). Not noted in *PIR*[2], A 765. His wife, Mummia Nigrina (Martial ix 30), can be claimed for Baetica.

road eastwards from Tarraco, taking its name from a local owner of estates.[56]

Finally, the portentous 'Funisulanus Vettonianus'. It recalls L. Funisulanus Vettonianus (*suff.* 78), legate in succession of Pannonia and Moesia Superior in the Dacian campaigns of Domitian (*ILS* 1005). The rare *nomen* is Sabine, so it appears.[57] 'Vettonius' also turns out to be most uncommon.[58]

Funisulanus had for tribe the 'Aniensis'. He received a dedication at Forum Popillii on the Aemilia (xi 571). That town (tribe not verified) has been taken for his *patria*. The document permits a different explanation: Funisulanus had been a curator of the Via Aemilia.

The chance offers of something better, although it may seem remote. In Tarraconensis the tribe points to Caesaraugusta, where coins of early date disclose a magistrate called 'L. Funi. Vet.'[59] A citizen of that *colonia* entering the Senate at the beginning of Nero's reign is no scandal.

What then follows for Pomponius Mamilianus? His father, or better, his grandfather, may have married into that family. Local brides are often the choice of municipal aristocrats before they have attained to success at the metropolis, with superior alliances.

Funisulanus left no male heir, so far as can be ascertained.[60] Mamilianus could not obtrude on the *Fasti* the name of the eminent consular. He used it where he could, and he bequeathed it to his son (see below).

So far five Pomponii consuls in the period 94–100. For three of them an origin in Spain has been advocated, on various pleas. The next group arrives a generation later: four in the years 118–21. For convenience they divide into two pairs, the first of which presents no problems.

(1) T. Pomponius Antistianus (121). He is patently the son of Mamilianus. Shortly before his consulship he governed Lycia–Pamphylia. On the monument at Rhodiapolis that commemorates benefactions of Opramoas he appears as 'Pomponius Antistianus Funisulanus Vettonianus' (*IGR* iii 539, 14). Since the document is a

---

[56] Like Palfuriana, the preceding station. One is impelled towards P. Palfurius (*suff.* 56) and his son Palfurius Sura, a person of some notoriety (*PIR* ¹, P 46).

[57] Schulze, *LE* 86 f. Add Funisulana T. f. (*NSA* 1896, 105: Forum Decii, near Bacugno).

[58] No specimen in Schulze. In towns of Italy, only *CIL* v 751 (Aquileia); 1780 (Forum Iulium); 2090 (Aquileia).

[59] J. Vives, *La moneda hispánica* iv (1924), 82; G. F. Hill, *Notes on the Ancient Coinage of Hispania Citerior* (1933), 83.

[60] He died in 97 or 98 as is deduced from *AE* 1936, 95, cf. *PIR* ², F 570.

letter indited by the governor, the style of nomenclature should represent his own preference.

An Antistianus a generation later is in danger of being overlooked. The subject of the rescript he received from Antoninus Pius suggests the governor of a province.[61] |

(2) Q. Pomponius Marcellus (121). He was legate under his father, the proconsul C. Pomponius Rufus. One of the fragments at Thubursicu preserves his name entire: 'Q. Pomponio Rufo Marcello' (*ILAlg* i 1282). On another inscription, after the name (missing), was supplemented 'cos. d]esig. sodal[e] Titio' (1230). That a son had that seniority when his father was proconsul is highly dubious. Therefore 'pr. d]esig.'.[62] Hence a small fact, but valuable. Marcellus passed in seven years from praetor to consul. Not all were so fortunate. The intermediate stages might be worth knowing.

A Marcellus was on attestation as proconsul of Africa (*ILAfr* 591; *IRT* 304). Q. Pomponius Marcellus appeared the best candidate. An inscription recently discovered brings a revision and a welcome accession to knowledge. He was proconsul of Asia, to go in 136/7.[63]

A brother was legate along with him, viz. 'C. Pompo[nio . . .' (*ILAlg* 1230). The *cognomen* began with 'P' (1231), and apparently ended in '-tus' (*ILAfr* 13). Hence perhaps 'Potitus' or 'Pacatus'. The former is select, the latter at first sight unprepossessing, but not to be rejected for a senator in this period.[64]

And now, the second pair in the group.

(1) L. Pomponius Silvanus (121). Only a name, and no kinsfolk discoverable. Conjecture will add a son. A quaestor of Macedonia in 116 bears the name 'L. Pomponius Maximus Flavius [. . .]ianus'.[65] The last word can be read as '[Sil]vanus'.[66] As with C. Pomponius Rufus (*suff.* 98), the son's age indicates a father not consul until about fifty.

(2) L. Pomponius Bassus (118). Likewise only a name, but sometimes assumed a son of T. Pomponius Bassus (*suff.* 94). New and novel information has recently turned up on a fine marble slab at Albano:[67]

---

[61] *Cod. Just.* vi 24, 1: 'qui deportantur, si heredes scribantur, tamquam peregrini capere non possunt.' Not in *PIR*.

[62] E. Birley, *JRS* lii (1962), 222 f.

[63] Reported in *AS* xxiii (1973), 42, and adduced in a revision of African proconsulates in *ZPE* xxxvii (1980), 2 f. = *RP* iii (1984), 1304.

[64] As witness C. Ulpius Pacatus Prastina Messallinus (*cos.* 147). For 'Potitus', I. Kajanto, op. cit. 354.

[65] As published in *AE* 1947, 4 (Samothrace).

[66] Thus P. M. Fraser in *Samothrace* ii (1960), 51.

[67] The inscription was published by S. Panciera, *RPAA* xlv (1972/3), 105 ff., with

> L. Pomponio L. Bassi cos.
> et Torquatae filio
> Horatia Basso Casco
> Scriboniano, cos.
> auguri, fetiali, sodali
> [Tit]iali, praefecto urbis
> [f]eriarum La[tin]arum. |

This consul, a son of the *suffectus* of 118, demands a small excursus, for reasons that will soon become apparent.

His social distinction is declared in a triple fashion. First, the honorific post of *praefectus urbi*, held when the consuls departed to preside at the Latin Games on the Mons Albanus. It was restricted to youths of the high aristocracy. Exceptions are rare and remarkable. That P. Aelius Hadrianus was *praefectus urbi* (probably in 94) is powerful testimony to the influence accruing to a certain group in the last years of Domitian.[68]

Second, Torquata his mother. To be identified as a daughter of L. Nonius Calpurnius Asprenas Torquatus, the consul of 94, consul for the second time in 128. The line went back to Piso the Pontifex, whose daughter married L. Nonius Asprenas (*suff.* 6).

Third, the *cognomen* 'Scribonianus'. Given the resplendent pedigree of the mother, it should likewise reveal lineage. In the reign of Tiberius Caesar a notable match united M. Crassus Frugi (*cos.* 27) to Scribonia, with fateful consequences for their four sons, among them Crassus Frugi (*cos.* 64) and Piso Licinianus, whom Galba chose for son and successor.[69]

Two consular sons followed in the next generation. First, that Calpurnius Crassus who conspired against Nerva and Trajan in turn (so it was alleged), and who was killed by an imperial procurator when escaping from his penal island in the first days of Hadrian (*PIR*[2], C 259). He is identified as C. Calpurnius Piso Licinianus (*suff.* 87). Second, Libo Rupilius Frugi, now at last acquiring shape and substance from diverse testimony.

(1) Libo Frugi, a consular named by Pliny as a speaker in the year 101 (iii 9, 33).
(2) Frugi, discovered as a consul suffect of 88.
(3) Libo Rupilius Frugi, on a lead pipe at Rome.
(4) 'Rupili [Li]bonis' recuperated by a palmary emendation of *HA*

---

photograph and ample commentary. Whence *AE* 1973, 200. Duly noted by W. Eck, *RE*, *Suppl.* xiv 438 f.

[68] Registered on *ILS* 308 (Athens). Not in the *HA*.
[69] For the stemma, *PIR*[2], L (facing p. 40).

Marcus 1, 4.[70] Hence *PIR*², L 166: (?L. Scribonius) Libo (?Rupilius) Frugi.

From this aristocratic group therefore derives the ascendance of the new consul L. Pomponius L. f. Bassus Cascus Scribonianus. At first sight his father (*suff.* 118), had married a Scribonia. On the inscription she is styled 'Torquata', and is identified as a daughter of the eminent Nonius Asprenas (*cos.* 94). He, it follows, had for wife a Scribonia.

The new consul, however, also bears 'Cascus' in his nomenclature. That evoked the enigmatic Cn. Pedius Cascus, consul suffect early in 71. The maternal grandfather (i.e. Nonius Asprenas) had married his daughter, so it was conjectured.[71] That is legitimate, and may be the correct inference.[72] Yet 'Cascus' might go back a generation earlier in these Pomponii Bassi. |

A different explanation could be proffered. The inscription happily furnishes the tribe 'Horatia'. That points to Aricia. The family may have desired to advertise an origin from primeval Latium. Archaic writers like Ennius were coming back. Apart from that fashion, men might recall the line 'quam prisci casci populi tenuere Latini'.[73] Which, by the way, suggests that Pedius Cascus himself avows ancient Latin stock.

A new consul has emerged in the reign of Pius: for short, 'Cascus Scribonianus'. The tribe 'Horatia' enables another member of the family to be established. The fourth name on a decree of the Senate in the year 139 stood as 'Q. Pompeius Q. f. Hor. Bassianus' (*ILS* 7190: Cyzicus). Strong doubts could not fail to be conceived about the name as supplemented. Revision confirms.[74] This senator is a Pomponius (and perhaps polyonymous).[75]

Pomponius Bassianus may be assumed a close relative of Cascus Scribonianus, perhaps a first cousin, his father Quintus being a brother of L. Pomponius Bassus (*suff.* 118). Also perhaps to be added to the nexus is Pomponia Q. f. Bassila, owner of property that produced bricks in the suburban vicinity of Rome.[76]

---

[70] A. R. Birley, *Historia* xv (1966), 249 f.

[71] S. Panciera, op. cit. 114 f.

[72] The *cognomen* (not listed by Kajanto) being not merely rare but unique. *TLL* offers a 'Casco', a 'Casconius' and two Cascii. The *cognomen* 'Casca' is confined to a branch of the Servilii.

[73] Quoted by Varro, *De l. l.* vii 28: whence fr. 24 V.

[74] S. Panciera, op. cit. 111. He made careful inspection of Gradenwitz's photograph.

[75] Further, perhaps the ']sianus' who was consul suffect with L. Annius Fabianus, presumably in 141 (*AE* 1959, 38). See now L. Vidman (*Fasti Ostienses*, ed. 2, 1982), who suggests Q. Antonius Cassianus.

[76] *CIL* xv 1376–8: about the middle of the century. Otherwise she might be a daughter of Q. Pomponius Rufus Marcellus (*suff.* 121), whose mother was a Bassilla (*ILAlg* i 1282).

A further step was taken, not to be commended. As parent to Q. Pomponius Q. f. Bassianus (senator in 139) the stemma annexed Q. Pomponius Marcellus (*suff.* 121), supposing him a son of T. Pomponius Bassus (*suff.* 94).[77] That cannot be. Marcellus (with 'Rufus' in his nomenclature) is the son of C. Pomponius Rufus (*suff.* 98), proconsul of Africa.

The obtrusion of T. Pomponius Bassus arouses grave and general dubitation. The Pomponii of Aricia assert social pretensions. L. Bassus marries a Torquata; and the inscription of his son confines his public offices to consulate, priesthoods, and the function he exercised in extreme youth. Although only a Pomponius, that son is enrolled at once in the high aristocracy that was content with wealth and pomp and pedigree. Other senators had to make their way in the service of the Caesars.

T. Pomponius Bassus, legate for six years of Cappadocia–Galatia, looks like an isolated figure. Let him remain in that condition. The *cognomen*, although not as bad as 'Rufus', is very common. He might have come from anywhere.[78] To postulate unrelated families of Pomponii Bassi entails no | discomfort. Eggius Ambibulus of Aeclanum (*cos.* 126) carried 'Pomponius' in his nomenclature (*ILS* 1054), with M. Pomponius Bassulus for maternal uncle (2953, cf. *PIR*[2], E 6). His tribe is 'Cornelia'. A C. Pomponius Bassus somewhat later (*suff. c.*196) has the 'Veturia' (vi 31696).

Pomponius Bassianus and Cascus Scribonianus carry the theme into the early years of Antoninus Pius. It will be suitable to pursue it until the end of the reign.

(1) Q. Pomponius Maternus (*suff.* 128). Apart from the consulate known only as the owner of a villa on the bay of Puteoli.[79] The nomenclature appears indistinctive. Nevertheless, the *cognomen* could be brought into play. This Pomponius is the first consul to bear it. 'Maternus' is very frequent in Spain. In fact, that phenomenon was used to refute the notion that Curiatius Maternus, senator and orator, was a Gaul.[80]

(2) C. Pomponius Camerinus (*cos.* 138). That Camerinus held the eponymate in the last year of Hadrian is significant in itself. Origin, parentage, and descendants are out of reach. The *cognomen* stood for aristocratic descent, as Juvenal was well aware (vii 90; viii 38). It

---

[77] S. Panciera, op. cit. 111, cf. the stemma (ibid. 116).   [78] Spain not excluded.

[79] J. H. D'Arms, *Romans on the Bay of Naples* (1970), 233: discussing a lead pipe with his name (*Eph. Ep.* viii 378).

[80] *Tacitus* (1958), 798. Apart from the consular of Liria, Spain could show only ii 954 (Ilipula); 1109 (Italica); 2211 (Corduba).

recalled the patrician Sulpicii Camerini, extinct so far as known since the consul of 46 (*PIR*[1], S 713), and Scribonianus Camerinus (S 205), a son of Crassus Frugi (*cos.* 64), and therefore grandson of a Scribonia. The consul of 138 may well be related to his coeval, Scribonianus Cascus. His own *cognomen* took its origin from ancient Cameria, a colony of Alba Longa.

(3) Q. Pomponius Musa (*suff.* ?159). A homonym was *monetalis* in the last epoch of the Republic. His coins carry the head of Apollo on the obverse, on the reverse each of the Nine Muses in turn.[81] Only the ingenuous will fancy that his *cognomen* is Greek. Observe the *nomen* 'Musanus'.[82]

On a brick stamp the consul's name is 'Q. Pomponi Musses' (*CIL* xv 1375). He is attested at Velitrae (x 6568), along with Julia Magnilla (6584), presumably his wife. She also occurs at Tibur (xiv 3716).

Lineal descent from the *monetalis* is not easy to credit. Ancient *cognomina*, especially those of extinct families, were liable to be revived and annexed. The Pedanii of Barcino employ 'Salinator', which appertained to the Livii in the old time; and T. Julius Maximus of Nemausus (*suff.* 112) includes 'Servilius Vatia' in his nomenclature (*ILS* 1010).

Haste or pedantry might aggregate to the catalogue T. Pomponius Proculus Vitrasius Pollio (*suff.* *c.*151, *cos.* *II* 176), registered as *PIR*[1], | P 558.[83] Generally styled 'T. Vitrasius Pollio', he carries the prefix to his name on his earliest attestation when governor of Moesia Inferior *c.*157 (*AE* 1911, 11 and *SEG* ii 454: Histria), and much later, after the second consulate (*ILS* 1114: set up by his wife). For what reasons a senator who was adlected to the patriciate by Pius, who married a cousin of Marcus Aurelius, assumed and kept this drab and indistinctive piece of nomenclature, that is a question beyond an answer.

'Proculus' belongs along with 'Rufus' and 'Maximus' to the six most banal *cognomina*.[84] In default of other clues (or to corroborate them) appeal can sometimes be made to an ordinary *cognomen* when it happens, like 'Maternus' or 'Avitus' to be fancied in certain provinces. The hazards inherent in this procedure are obvious. On the other hand, as has been shown, 'Rectus' and 'Sparsus' turn out on

---

[81] M. H. Crawford, *RRC* (1974), no. 410 (437 ff.).

[82] *CIL* i[2] 2100 (Interamna). Observe the equestrian C. Musanus (*AE* 1954, 163: Lucus Feroniae), of early imperial date.

[83] The article in *RE* xxi 2344 ff. is riddled with errors; and the parent of the *bis consul* (*suff.* ?137) is not listed among the Vitrasii in ixA 416 ff.

[84] That is, going by the evidence of *PIR*. The other three are 'Priscus', 'Sabinus', 'Severus'. No account is here taken of African proliferations such as 'Fortunatus' or 'Victor'.

investigation to be much rarer than any might suspect. Hence a tempting recourse.[85]

Consuls engross the enquiry, and nothing can be done with C. Tullius Capito Pomponianus, *suff.* 84. A brief word may go to a pair of ladies of some minor interest. Pliny inherited from Pomponia Galla, widow of an Asudius (v 1, 1): a sister surely, hardly a daughter, of C. Pomponius Gallus Didius Rufus, proconsul of Crete and Cyrene in 88/9 (*AE* 1954, 188). As for Pomponia Galeria, who set up an altar at Rome in the year 107, she might well belong to a senatorial family.[86]

The enquiry bore upon two clusters of Pomponii, five in the years 94–100, four in 118–21; and in the sequel four were added, between 128 and 159 (including the new accession, Cascus Scribonianus). Among the first nine, no fewer than five have been claimed for the Peninsula. The result may appear paradoxical in view of the dearth of direct evidence from Spain itself. One is reduced to invoking the high priest from Caesaraugusta, T. Pomponius Avitus, and Sex. Pomponius, father of a senator of praetorian rank. However that may be, Q. Pomponius Rufus, the partisan of Galba, brings some comfort.

Those five consuls may stimulate (if it be necessary) sundry reflections in general on the rise of provincial aristocracies. Galba's proclamation brought | immediate benefit to Tarraconensis and to Narbonensis. It was enhanced by Vespasian. A long process, which civil war accelerated, was already well under way.

In the course of the next thirty years emergencies both military and civilian improved the prospects of the new senators. Despite generosity in the allocation of consulates early in the reign of Domitian, a blockage can be detected. It may have contributed to retard the career of Q. Pomponius Rufus.[87]

Domitian's wars were propitious for legionary legates. When they ceased in 92, various embarrassments of the ruler lent impulsion to intrigue and patronage. Pomponius Rufus managed to acquire the province of Dalmatia, hence his consulship assured.

Next, the crisis of the imperial succession. Pomponius Mamilianus, legate of a legion in Britain, was in good posture, although, as in 69, the decision rested with the army commanders on Rhine and Danube.

---

[85] And no call to reiterate warnings against a method which at the same time makes appeal to both the rare and the common.   [86] *CIL* vi 622.

[87] Or that of T. Pomponius Bassus (*suff.* 94), probably of praetorian rank before 79.

The *Fasti* of Trajan's first years proclaim his adherents, in all their variety of rank and origin. Spaniards were to be expected among the numerous consuls. A casual detail attracts. A new fragment of the *Ostienses* contributes L. Fabius Tuscus from Baetica, consul suffect in 100.[88]

By the same token, Hadrian's chief allies and kinsmen stand as *consules ordinarii* from 118 to 121. Among the *suffecti* is the second cluster of Pomponii.

'Spain' and 'Spaniards', those are comprehensive terms, and all too often deceptive. Baetica was a small country, easily defined, prolific in cities, and in senators, many of whom can be detected. Tarraconensis is a vast conglomerate, embracing heterogeneous regions. To establish (or at least render plausible) an origin from the Peninsula will not take the enquirer very far.

Of the five consuls here invoked and inspected, not one can be assigned a *patria*. Deplorable, but no surprise if some of them issued from Tarraconensis. Certain cities yield a paucity of inscriptions, notably the colonies Celsa and Caesaraugusta.[89] Another factor supervenes. The successful departed. The life of a senator detained them and broke their ties with the old country. A group, mainly from Baetica, took up residence in villas at Tibur.[90] |

Like the rise of families, their decline and extinction furnishes instruction. In these pages three Pomponii, consuls between 95 and 98, are assumed Spanish. Two sons followed in the next generation. Their posterity vanishes. The phenomenon finds parallel in other new families, whether provincial or Italian. On that note may terminate a modest and limited contribution to the constant renewal of the upper order in Rome of the Caesars.

---

[88] A homonym was magistrate at Ulia (ii 1537). Noted by W. Eck in *RE, Suppl.* xiv 117.

[89] The dearth at Celsa was emphasized in *Tacitus* (1958), 791: discussing the *patria* of Licinius Sura. As concerns Caesaraugusta, let it be observed that no fewer than six high priests at Tarraco have 'Aniensis' for tribe: G. Alföldy, *Flamines Provinciae Hispaniae Citerioris* (1973), nos. 17, 31, 24, 45, 52, 54.

[90] 'Spaniards at Tivoli', *AncSoc* xiii/xiv (1982/1983), 241 ff. = pp. 94 ff., above.

9

Clues to Testamentary Adoption

A DISCOURSE on the engaging topic of 'testamentary adoption' must open with an admonition. There was no such thing: the Roman jurists ignore it.

The phenomenon, of signal importance for social history, is merely the 'condicio nominis ferendi' imposed when an inheritance is taken up. There is a close and instructive parallel. A woman cannot adopt, but she may transfer her name.

A pair of examples affords some entertainment. They concern members of the patriciate who although avid and rapacious appear to have held attraction for women. | Publius Dolabella may have inherited from a lady called Livia.[1] There is no sign that he submitted to the condition. Ser. Sulpicius Galba, however, complied when 'adopted' (that is the term used by Suetonius) by his stepmother Livia Ocellina. Galba (*cos.* 33) stands on the *Fasti Ostienses* as L. Livius Ocella Sulpicius Galba.

The consequences are obvious and inexpugnable. No citizen by his last will and testament can change the legal status of his heir. He cannot transfer him from plebeian to patrician, or vice versa; and he cannot assign him to a different tribe.

That lay beyond the posthumous power of Caesar the Dictator. The designate heir was C. Octavius C. f. Scaptia from Velitrae. The youth needed to enter the *gens* of the patrician Iulii, acquiring thereby their tribe, the 'Fabia'. By what device that was achieved is no concern of the present investigation. Nor will anything be said about nomenclature and adoptions in the imperial dynasties.

When a proper and plenary adoption has been conducted, everything disappears: *praenomen, nomen,* filiation, and tribe. The only vestige is a *cognomen,* either inherited or constructed from the previous family name. The time of Augustus exhibits a clear specimen, viz. A. Licinius A. f. A. n. Nerva Silianus, consul suffect in A.D. 7. That

---

[1] Cicero, *Ad Att.* vii 8, 3.

Epigrafia e ordine senatorio i (Tituli iv, Rome 1982 [1984]), 397–410.

is, the second son of P. Silius P. f. Nerva (*cos.* 20 B.C.), taken in adoption by an A. Licinius Nerva not elsewhere on attestation.

It is by no means easy to establish from inscriptions any instances in the sequel. Testamentary adoption prevailed. It carried sundry attractions. Men of property are reluctant to renounce and disburse up to the end. For the indecisive the device left options open, wavering perhaps with reason between the aspirations of sundry kinsmen; and the malicious took pleasure in encouraging the hopes of *captatores*, to baffle their arts in the end. That was the comportment of the opulent Domitius Tullus (*II suff.* 98), one of the ancestors of the Antonine dynasty. Pliny tells the full story, disclosing more than is his wont about the less amiable features in the manners of high society.[2]

The criteria that declare testamentary adoption may now be stated. At the head of the nomenclature normally stand the new *praenomen* and *nomen* (which adhere closely together). This prefix, however, does not abolish a man's original paternity. The prime document is C. Plinius L. f. Ouf. Caecilius Secundus (*ILS* 2927). That is, a Caecilius L. f. adopted by his mother's brother C. Plinius.[3] In this instance, each had the same tribe, that of Comum. When the tribes are known to differ, valid clues sometimes emerge, determining who adopted whom. |

Study of the Roman tribes brings up sundry anomalies, for example changes of tribe or members of the same family in a different registration.[4] For present purposes it will suffice to point out a casual consequence of 'testamentary adoption'. The original tribe is retained (as is proper) but transferred and attached to the new *gentilicium*.

Three specimens afford various instruction.

(1) C. Laecanius C. f. Sab. Bassus Caecina Flaccus. *CIL* ix 39 (Brundisium). The tribe of the Laecanii, from Pola, is 'Velina' (cf. *PIR*[2], L 30), whereas the Caecina family avows Volaterrae, enrolled in 'Sabatina'. The father of this man, that is, C. Caecina Paetus (*suff.* 70), had assumed the name of the consul of 64, cf. *PIR*[2], C 104; L 37.

Caecina Flaccus (L 33) died at Brundisium at the age of eighteen. On the way to Asia, it may be conjectured, accompanying his father Caecina Paetus—whose proconsulate should be firmly assigned to

---

[2] Pliny, *Ep.* viii 18.
[3] Mommsen's exposition, prompted by the case of Pliny, will still be usefully consulted (*Ges. Schr.* iv 397 ff.)
[4] See the comprehensive study of G. Forni, in *L'Onomastique latine* (1977), 73 ff.

the tenure 80–1, next after M. Ulpius Traianus (*suff.* ?70).[5] It will not be fanciful to claim Caecina Flaccus as a victim of the great pestilence that raged under Titus, in the year 80.

(2) M. Gavius T. f. Vel. Appalius Maximus. *CIL* xiv 2607. This senator is patently the son of the knight T. Appalius T. f. Vel. Alfinus Secundus (*ILS* 1417). He was adopted by M. Gavius Maximus (G 104), Guard Prefect for about twenty years during the reign of Antoninus Pius. The tribe of Gavius Maximus was 'Palatina' (*ILS* 1325). He managed to discard it, wisely, in favour of the more resplendent 'Sergia', as a recent discovery reveals (*AE* 1972, 169: Hadria).

(3) L. Dasumius P. f. Stel. Tullius Tuscus (*suff.* 152). *ILS* 1081. The Dasumii derive from Corduba, enrolled in 'Sergia', though 'Galeria' might not be excluded. The 'Stellatina' carries a clear explanation. It goes back a generation, to a Tullius Varro of Tarquinii adopted by a Dasumius.[6] The *suffectus* of 152 is best regarded as a son of P. Dasumius Rusticus (*cos.* 119), rather than of P. Tullius Varro (*suff.* 127). His own son in turn is M. Dasumius L. f. Stel. Tullius Varro (*CIL* vi 1400).

This hazard (the transferred tribe) may affect other *polyonymi* and hamper the search for identities. A fragmentary bilingual recently found at Ephesus discloses a youthful aristocrat who flaunts no fewer than six *gentilicia* (*AE* 1972, 578). The first is Velleius, followed by the tribe 'Tromentina'. One of the items is Pedanius Fuscus Salinator. That links him to the family of Hadrian—and encourages legitimate speculation.[7] |

The three specimens here adduced demonstrate the retention of patronymic and tribe. The nomenclature has two members only. Before the Flavian dynasty was over, polyonymy in senators had begun to advertise one of the licences arrogated by the *amplissimus ordo*. On inscriptions *gentilicia* soon rise to three or four, to half a dozen.

The theme can seldom avoid coming to grips with Q. Pompeius Falco (*suff.* 108). When legate governing Moesia Inferior he has the style Q. Roscius Sex. f. Qui. Coelius Pompeius Falco (*ILS* 1036); and inscriptions set up in 116 and in 117 add the *cognomen* 'Murena', which adheres to 'Roscius' (*CIL* iii 12470; 7537). From which

---

[5] W. Eck, *Senatoren von Vespasian bis Hadrian* (1970) 84; 129. By anomaly only the first member of Caecina's binary nomenclature (indubitable, cf. *ILS* 9247b), stands on a dedication at Ephesus (*AE* 1977, 794).

[6] This is clear, despite the new piece of the *Testamentum Dasumii* (*CIL* vi 10229) published by W. Eck, in *ZPE* xxx (1978), 277 ff.

[7] See the excellent paper of E. Champlin in *ZPE* xxi (1976), 79 ff.

documents one deduces that a Pompeius Sex. f. Quirina had been adopted by a Q. Roscius Murena.

But Falco goes on to annex three more items of nomenclature, two of them taken from the Euryclids, the dynastic house of Sparta (*ILS* 1035).[8] Then, after the lapse of full testimony for a generation, Falco's grandson (*cos.* 169), parades as the prime and exorbitant exhibit: no fewer than fourteen *gentilicia* (*ILS* 1104). The second Bruttius Praesens (*cos.* 153) had about a dozen, it may be added (*ILS* 1107, incomplete).

Monstrosities of this order are not just a consequence of adoptions, of ancestry, of propinquity through blood or marriage. Many of the items reflect amity or gratitude for the share of an inheritance. To take a simple example. The developed style of Falco includes L. Silius Decianus: the elder son (*suff.* 94) of Silius Italicus.

For economy and for clarity in the search for a senator's original name and identity, it will be expedient to confine the enquiry for the most part to nomenclature with two members only—and, for obvious advantage, to personages of some notoriety in the time or ambit of Pliny.

Two preliminary observations are requisite. First, a convention to be respected: the name of the person who 'adopts' stands at the head of an inscription. That has sometimes suffered neglect. Three instances may be summarily registered.

(1) Q. Fulvius Gillo Bittius Proculus (*suff.* 98). Not, as in *PIR*[2], F 543 f., a son of M. Fulvius Gillo (*suff.* 76), adopted by Bittius Proculus.

(2) M. Cornelius Nigrinus M. f. Gal. Curiatius Maternus (*suff.* 83). *AE* 1973, 283. Not the orator Curiatius Maternus adopting a Cornelius Nigrinus.[9]

(3) Ti. Julius Candidus Marius Celsus (*suff.* 86). Not Marius Celsus (*suff.* 69) adopting a Julius Candidus.[10]

Second, the first member only comes to knowledge from inscriptions, sporadically. Thus, of paramount interest, A. Didius Gallus Fabricius Veiento (*ILS* 1010; *CIL* xvi | 158). Beside the great Veiento, and like him rising to a third consulship (presumably in 83), stands Q. Vibius Crispus. A piece of the *Fasti Ostienses* now registers him as L. Junius Vibius Crispus (*AE* 1968, 6). Another novelty

---

[8] For an evaluation of Falco's names, R. Syme, in *HSCPh* lxxxiii (1979), 294 ff. = *RP* iii (1984), 1164 f.; *Some Arval Brethren* (1980), 48 ff.

[9] As argued by G. Alföldy and H. Halfmann, in *Chiron* iii (1973), 345 ff.

[10] As assumed by H. Halfmann, *Die Senatoren aus dem östlichen Teil des Imperium Romanum* (1979), 107: 'sicher adoptiert'.

assigns the same prefix to L. Caesennius Paetus (*AE* 1973, 141 f.). Paetus (*cos.* 61) was in fact a P. Caesennius, so it may be argued. His putative son, the younger, is identified as [——] P. f. Stel. Sospes (*ILS* 1017; Pisidian Antioch).[11]

As has been demonstrated, the main clues are the retention of patronymic and tribe. Furthermore, the *praenomen* adhering to the new name tends to replace the original *praenomen*.

Other approaches furnish guidance, and often certitude.

(*a*) Evidence from literature, giving the name by which a senator was generally known. It will be variously instructive to put on record the more notable instances of *polyonymi* (with two or more *gentilicia*) as they stand abridged in the correspondence of Pliny.

Bittius Proculus (*suff.* 98); Bruttius Praesens (118 or 119); Catilius Severus (110); Domitius Tullus (*II suff.* 98); Fabricius Veiento (*III suff.* ?83); Javolenus Priscus (*suff.* 86); Julius Candidus (86); Lappius Maximus (86); Pompeius Falco (108); Salvius Liberalis (?85); Silius Italicus (*cos.* 68); Ummidius Quadratus (*suff.* 118).

The testimony is convincing and unexceptionable—but exceptions occur. Cn. Domitius Tullus, inheriting from the great orator Domitius Afer, declined to advertise his 'real name'. He was the son of a Sex. Curvius (*ILS* 990 f.).

(*b*) Epigraphic documents. For the Flavian period the protocol of the Arval Brethren registers three polyonymous consulars.[12] They are spelled out in full, many times, on the marble slabs. The pretentious fraternity saw no need to practise economy. There is a single exception of precious value. On one entry in the year 89 Ti. Julius Candidus Marius Celsus (*suff.* 86) is reduced to Ti. Julius Candidus (*CIL* vi 2066).

Drastic and proper abbreviation is imposed on consular *Fasti*. Some copies are liable to error, it is true. On those found at Potentia, 'M. Arrius Celsus' represents the *suffectus* of 86 (*AE* 1949, 33). The *Ostienses* claim respect. They present the abridged name, likewise for the second consulship he held in 105.

These *Fasti* can carry surprises, some instructive. Thus Ti. Caesius Fronto (*suff.* 96). That is, the orator Ti. Catius Caesius Fronto (*PIR*², C 194). He was a Caesius anterior to the decease and testament of Ti. Catius Asconius Silius Italicus, in 101. Pliny called him Catius Fronto (five times). That, it may be taken, was the style the orator |

[11] R. Syme, in *JRS* lxvii (1977), 44 = *RP* iii (1984), 1053.
[12] *Some Arval Brethren* (1980), 18. On the lists in question A. Julius A. f. Volt. Quadratus (*suff.* 94) had not yet acquired the prefix C. Antius.

himself preferred. Again, Q. Glitius Atilius Agricola (G 141). In his first consulate (97) he is Q. Atilius Agricola.

(c) Miscellaneous indications. For example, from descendants. Thus Pompeia Q. f. Falconilla (*AE* 1935, 26), the granddaughter of Falco. But not always: the daughter of Domitius Tullus is not a Curvia. Freedmen also come into the account. Falco deposited one of them at Oescus on the Danube (*CIL* iii 7433); and the freedmen of Catius Fronto are Caesii (cf. under C 194).

A disturbing factor in nomenclature can no longer be dissembled: the intrusion of items from the maternal ascendance. It goes through three stages.

First, a *cognomen*. Cn. Cornelius Cinna Magnus (*cos.* 5) avows descent from Pompeius. And Sex. Nonius Quinctilianus (*cos.* 8) had for mother a sister of Quinctilius Varus. That might prompt one to doubt about the two Quinctii, Sulpicianus (*cos.* 9 B.C.) and Valerianus (*suff.* 2). Not perhaps products of adoption.

Second, a *gentilicium* used as *cognomen*. A. Plautius M. f. Urgulanius (*ILS* 921) shows the name of his maternal grandmother, Urgulania, the mother of M. Plautius Silvanus (*cos.* 2 B.C.). Therefore doubt becomes legitimate about the *novus homo* P. Sulpicius Quirinius (*cos.* 12 B.C.), the earliest Roman of rank to carry that style. Perhaps not a Quirinius adopted by a P. Sulpicius.[13]

Third, a whole piece of nomenclature subjoined to what may be deemed a man's 'real name', the paternal. The phenomenon has sharp and sometimes alarming relevance when one interprets binary forms of nomenclature. These geminations may be ambiguous. That is, either (as discussed previously) adoptive name + paternal or paternal + maternal. Of the latter type half a dozen or so specimens will now be adduced on brief statement, several of them ignored or in dispute.

(1) M. Cornelius M. f. Gal. Nigrinus Curiatius Maternus (*suff.* 83). *AE* 1973, 283 (Liria). As the order shows, not a Curiatius adopting a Cornelius (cf. above). Therefore the reverse, perhaps. Another explanation offers. The father of Cornelius Nigrinus married a Curiatia, the sister of the orator who is the central figure in the *Dialogus* of Tacitus.[14]

(2) C. Salvius C. f. Vel. Liberalis Nonius Bassus (*suff.* ?85). *ILS* 1011. Pliny furnishes the real name of this distinguished orator. His mother was a Nonia: compare his presumed first cousin L. Flavius Silva Nonius Bassus (*cos.* 81).

---

[13] As supposed by Groag, in *RE* ivA 823.
[14] Thus R. Syme, in *ZPE* xli (1981), 137 = *RP* iii (1984), 1387.

(3) Ti. Julius Candidus Marius Celsus (*suff.* 86). *PIR* ², J 241. Pliny and epigraphy demonstrate his 'real name', therefore not an adopted Marius Celsus. His father may have married a sister of A. Marius Celsus (*suff.* 69). The latter family derives from Nar|bonensis, so it is argued.[15] Not so the Julii Candidi: from somewhere in western Asia Minor.[16] None of the Narbonensian notables was so recent as to be a 'Ti. Iulius' (i.e. citizenship acquired between the years 4 and 37).[17]

The alliance between Asia and Narbonensis is noteworthy. Not less startling the fortune vouchsafed to Iulius Candidus: consul for the second time with the Pergamene A. Julius Quadratus in 105—and Prefect of the City, as now proved by *AE* 1972, 591 (Ephesus).

(4) L. Julius L. f. Fab. Marinus Caecilius Simplex (*suff.* ?101). *ILS* 1026. His father had married the daughter of a Caecilius Simplex—as did likewise Julius Candidus, to judge by his son Ti. Julius Candidus Caecilius Simplex, attested among the *Arvales* in 105 (*CIL* vi 2075).

(5) C. Bruttius L. f. Pom. Praesens L. Fulvius Rusticus (*suff.* 118 or 119). *IRT* 545; *AE* 1950, 66. The parent is L. Bruttius Maximus, proconsul of Cyprus in 80 (*AE* 1950, 122). Pliny describes his friend as a Lucanian (vii 3, 1), and the tribe is in consonance. Later Fulvii Rustici occur on the territory of Comum, duly equipped with the tribe 'Oufentina' (*PIR* ², F 557, cf. 541).

(6) L. Minicius L. f. Gal. Natalis Quadronius Verus (*suff.* 139). *ILS* 1061. His father was suitably colleague with Q. Licinius Silvanus as consul suffect in 106. Tarraconensians both. And furthermore, related. The son of the latter carried the adjunct Quadronius Proculus (*ILS* 1028). Possibly each an adoptive son, better, maternal cousins. The parents had each taken to wife a Quadronia.

(7) P. Coelius P. f. Ser. Balbinus Vibullius Pius (*cos.* 137). *ILS* 1063. A person of high social distinction, elected to the patriciate by Hadrian—and probably from Italica in Baetica, cf. *PIR* ², C 1241. The adjunct excites no small interest. The mother of Herodes Atticus was a Vibullia; and Vibullius Pius is one of the two pieces of Euryclid nomenclature annexed by Pompeius Falco (*ILS* 1035).

(8) A. Junius P. f. Fab. Pastor L. Caesennius Sospes (*cos.* 163). *ILS* 1095. In this case testamentary adoption is precluded. The Caesennii, citizens of Tarquinii, are enrolled in the tribe 'Stellatina', cf. the Sospes of *ILS* 1017. The 'Fabia' indicates Brixia, in the 'Pliny country'. A block happens to reveal, in large lettering Iunius Pa[- - -]

[15] R. Syme, *Tacitus* (1958), 683.
[16] H. Halfmann, op. cit. 107. The exposition in *PIR* ², J 241, is unsatisfactory.
[17] Emphasized, along with the other arguments, in *Some Arval Brethren* (1980), 51.

(*NSA* 1950, 70). Pliny when young had defended a Junius Pastor in a law suit (i 18, 3).

For the contrary type of binary nomenclature it will be convenient to evoke Cn. Minicius Faustinus Sex. Julius (?Sex. f.) Serg. Severus (*suff*. 127). *ILS* 1056 (Burnum), cf. *AE* 1904, 9 (Aequum). The real name is clear, standing on the *Fasti Ostienses* and on military diplomata (*CIL* xvi 72 etc.). The prefix reflects Cn. Minicius Faustinus | (*suff*. ?117). It may be noted in passing that he is abbreviated to Cn. Iul. S[everus] on *AE* 1904, 9. This remarkable Dalmatian ended as legate of Syria after three other military provinces, viz. Moesia Inferior, Britannia, Syria Palaestina.[18]

This collection of eight, select and usefully heterogeneous, helps to reduce the appeal to adoptions and it will serve as a gentle admonition to scholars to be on the alert. It also illustrates the potency of extraction from women, especially when superior in rank and prestige. Indeed, the maternal ascendance may be strong enough to extrude and suppress in official nomenclature a senator's authentic *gentilicium*. C. Ummidius Quadratus (*suff*. 118) is certified by Pliny as the grandson of old Ummidia Quadratilla, daughter of an eminent consular (vii 24). Quadratus, it follows, must be a *polyonymus*—with the suspicion that his own father fell short of social parity (see below).

In support, a further phenomenon. A man may take over names from his wife's family, as happens with aristocracies in other ages. P. Clodius Thrasea chose to inherit Paetus, in dutiful remembrance of A. Caecina Paetus (*suff*. 37), who came to grief for conspiracy against Claudius Caesar. Observe also, for less laudable motives, P. Calvisius Tullus Ruso (*cos*. 109), when he annexed the heiress Domitia Cn. f. Lucilla, the daughter of the unamiable Domitius Tullus.

A further step may be taken, bold if not hazardous. At some time between 117 and his proconsulate of Asia (in 123) Pompeius Falco took to himself two pieces of Euryclid nomenclature (*ILS* 1035). Falco had married a daughter of Q. Sosius Senecio, perhaps on his decease.[19] His origin and family remain an arduous and exciting problem. In any event Falco himself cannot belong by birth to the dynastic house of Sparta.[20]

The main purpose of the present enquiry was to illustrate and define

---

[18] His governorship of Syria was by inadvertence omitted from *PIR*[2], J 576.

[19] As conjectured in *Historia* xvii (1968), 100 = *RP* (1979), 688.

[20] Although that was contended by W. C. McDermott, in *Ancient Society* vii (1976), 244.

practices current in the high imperial epoch. Emphasis has gone to regularities, even to rules; and sundry anomalies find admission. A senator could exercise wide freedom when choosing or varying the names he preferred to be known by—a freedom that can even extend to official or semi-official documents. The government did not mind, and it was no concern of the jurists.

There were certain limits. Patronymic and tribe adhere closely to *gentilicium* (for all that the tribe can change its position). And, once again, no testament can alter a man's tribe or legal status (patrician or plebeian). The enquiry thus conveys repercussions backwards, to the closing years of the Roman Republic, to the condition of Caesar's heir in spring and summer of 44.[21] |

The social consequences of adoption by testament are various and manifest. A question might subsist. Had it any political effects? At first sight, none.

Caesar Augustus lowered for *nobiles* the consular age by ten years, to thirty-two; and in the sequel, after election by the sovereign people had been abolished in September of the year 14, a differential obtains in favour of the sons of consuls.

On a strict and proper assumption, no benefit in access to the *fasces* for any product of testamentary adoption. None the less, the wealth and prestige accruing to a man like Fabricius Veiento, the heir of the eminent Didius Gallus might well earn some indulgence from Caesar and from the managers of patronage—to which company he duly acceded. Rules abate in the face of facts.

Epilogue

It is suitable to adduce in summary fashion three specimens that have aroused disquiet or perplexity.

(1) C. Silius P. f. P. n. A. Caecina Largus (*cos.* 13). Three sets of *Fasti* concern the colleague of L. Munatius Plancus.[22] (a) The *Antiates Minores* have the adjunct to the name of C. Silius, in the second line. (b) In the *Fasti Arvalium* all that survives is the three letters that may (or may not) represent the word Largus: the question of a suffect consul in 13 cannot be discussed in this place. (c) The *Capitolini* register Silius and Plancus, each with the filiation (father and grandfather). However, a peculiar phenomenon. While the name of the second colleague is continued with his *cognomen* put at the end of the second line, the rest of that line was erased. Hence various

---

[21] On which, W. Schmitthenner, *Oktavian und das Testament Cäsars*[2], (1973).
[22] For the documents, A. Degrassi, *Inscr. It.* xiii 1.

explanations. In Mommsen's view, the adjunct to Silius' name was held an impropriety and therefore deleted.

That is not all. There is testimony in Cassius Dio. The rubric of consuls attached to Book LVI has, albeit in an incorrect form, the equivalent of C. Silius C. f. Caecina Largus.

What then follows? A *polyonymus*, so Dessau held, with the explanation that a Caecina Largus may have adopted C. Silius (*PIR* [1], S 507).

More recently the contrary argument was espoused and advocated. Some scholars hesitated to accept the geminated nomenclature at so early a date. Not one person therefore but two.[23] That is to say, C. Silius, the son (the third son) of P. Silius P. f. Nerva (*cos.* 20 B.C.) and a consul suffect A. Caecina Largus, a member of the great Volaterrae clan not otherwise an attestation.

Disproof was slow to arrive. After a decade a Roman funerary inscription, long ignored, brought the solution. With a date in the month of August it revealed the con|sular pair, in abridged form as L. Planco C. Caec. cos.[24] The abbreviation corresponds to the nomenclature C. (Silius A.) Caecina (Largus).

One crux demolished, another abides and perplexes. Recourse is had to adoption. By testament, that is ruled out by an elementary fact. The consular C. Silius was still among the living until 24, when he ended by suicide after condemnation for high treason.

The alternative is an act of plenary adoption. Either way, if C. Silius was by birth a Caecina, a deduction of no small interest becomes unavoidable. When Claudius was at length induced to take action against Messallina and her paramour, the son of Silius, he derived ambiguous support and comfort from C. Caecina Largus (*cos.* 42), who was believed to incline towards clemency.[25] That is, presumably a brother or first cousin of the ill-starred Silius.

Against adoption a better solution avails: nomenclature from the side of the mother. The father of the consul C. Silius had married the daughter of an Aulus Caecina Largus.[26] A man called Largus occurs in the vicinity of A. Caecina, the son of Cicero's client.[27]

(2) Ti. Plautius M. f. Ani. Silvanus Aelianus (*suff.* 45). ILS 986. Although buried in the mausoleum of the Plautii, and labelled 'M. f.', Aelianus did not originate in that family. He is not a son born to M. Plautius Silvanus (*cos.* 2 B.C.), cf. Dessau, in *PIR* [1], P 363. The

[23] A. and J. Gordon, in *AJP* lxxii (1951), 283 ff. Followed by R. Syme, in *JRS* lvi (1966), 55 ff.: an unwise tribute to two excellent epigraphists.

[24] Published by S. Panciera, in *BCAR* 1963–4, (1966), 95, whence *AE* 1966, 16.

[25] Tacitus, *Ann.* xi 33; 34, 1.

[26] In 32 B.C. his wife was a Coponia (Velleius ii, 33, 3).   [27] Cicero, *Ad fam.* vi 8, 1.

Plautii were plebeian, whereas the career of Aelianus (quaestor to praetor) declares a patrician.

His veritable parentage will not elude: L. Aelius L. f. Lamia (*cos.* 3). It is confirmed by emergence in the nomenclature of L. Aelius Plautius Lamia Aelianus (*suff.* 80), to be deemed his son. There is a further inference. The family of L. Lamia had been brought into the patriciate by Caesar Augustus. Both particulars (it is strange) failed to get registered in *PIR*², A 206.

An Aelius taken in adoption, that is clear. But by what type of adoption? Aelianus saw the light of day about the year 10. Since he is patrician, plenary adoption would change that status. If it occurred, it would have to occur shortly after his quaestorship (held about 34), during the interval before he became praetor (or subsequently). In that late season the old consular was dead; and his homonymous son had encountered mishap and suicide when praetor in 24, having thrown his wife out the window.²⁸ A younger son, P. Plautius Pulcher, quaestor in 31, survived, to be adlected among the patricians by Claudius Caesar in his censorship (*ILS* 964). |

Therefore adoption by testament. Such appears the common assumption.²⁹ If so, by no normal procedure. For two reasons. First, this Plautius Aelianus has not retained Lucius, the *praenomen* of his parent. He is M. f. Second, not the tribe either. He carries the Plautian 'Aniensis', whereas the Lamiae, an ancient and even legendary house at Formiae, ought to be enrolled in 'Aemilia'.

Yet an Aelius has somehow secured integration into the family of the Plautii, as is declared both by patronymic and by tribe. By what method and device, that is a question. The problem has not often been discussed, let alone resolved.³⁰

In comparison his uncommon *praenomen* was a minor matter. Tiberius was not carried by any of the numerous Plautii in the past; and it was discarded by the son of Plautius Aelianus (*suff.* 80). A modest conjecture does no harm. The *praenomen* was conferred on the infant in compliment to Tiberius Caesar. Aelius Lamia, though not earning like Plautius Silvanus the *ornamenta triumphalia*, enjoyed high and conspicuous employment in the late Augustan years.³¹

(3) C. Ummidius Quadratus (*suff.* 118). Being the grandson of Ummidia Quadratilla, Quadratus must have owned another name, which he preferred to suppress. That is, either the name of

---

²⁸ Tacitus, *Ann.* iv 22.

²⁹ In *PIR*¹, P 363 Dessau eschewed elucidation. No help comes from W. Hofmann, in *RE* xxi 45.

³⁰ Aelianus, it will be recalled is M. f.—and he perhaps entered the Plautii after the decease of Marcus (the consul's son) in 24.

³¹ As Velleius amicably testifies (ii 116, 3).

Quadratilla's son or that of her daughter's husband. Both lay beyond ascertainment, the 'real name' of the young man an enigma.

Epigraphy brings succour. Briefly as follows. An Ummidius Quadratus stood on record as governor of Moesia Inferior. Not the son of Quadratus, as some opined. Rather Quadratus himself; and in that post he succeeded the Se]rtorius attested in 120 on two fragments of a bilingual inscription found at Tomis (*CIL* iii 7529; 12492).[32]

Another piece, from the left side of the document, has recently turned up. The fourth line comes out as 'C. Ummidio Quadrato S[evero Serto]rio leg. Aug. pr. pr.[33] Two legates thus reduce to one, the governorship of Quadratus finds confirmation, his geminated nomenclature is disclosed. To elucidate the second item one did not have to look far. Pliny delivers Sertorius Severus, a 'vir praetorius' towards the end of Domitian's reign (v 1, 1).[34]

The conclusion can be firmly stated. The alternatives are clear. Quadratilla either married a Sertorius Severus—or, whoever she married, she gave her daughter a Sertorius Severus for husband. Either way Quadratus himself is unmasked as a Sertorius Severus. |

How then explain the order of names in the binary nomenclature? Quadratilla might have 'adopted' her grandson. Or rather, he assumed the name of his preference. Who was there to stop him? To the 'Teretina', the tribe of his family, he would have no automatic right.[35]

As has been shown abundantly, the female line often commanded superior potency—and Quadratilla's father (*suff.* c.40) had been highly successful all through, terminating his life when governor of Syria for a decade. By contrast, no Sertorius certified as consul hitherto.

That name (it is no surprise) fails to reappear in the posterity of C. Ummidius Quadratus Sertorius Severus. In the year 136 his son acquired Annia Cornificia Faustina, the sister of the boy Marcus (*PIR*[2], A 708). By conjecture to be identified as C. (?Ummidius) Annianus Verus (?Quadratus), consul suffect in 146.[36] The grandson is C. Ummidius Quadratus, the consul of 167.

---

[32] As argued in *Historia* xvii (1968), 89 = *RP* (1979), 676.

[33] *AE* 1977, 745—where, however, the editors in scrappy comment neglect the essential and erroneously produce a son of Quadratus called Severus.

[34] See further in *HSCPh* lxxxiii (1979), 292 = *RP* iii (1984), 1162 f.

[35] To change the tribe would not be difficult; and it persisted for a long time on inscriptions of senators.

[36] For that conjecture, *Historia* xvii (1968), 98 = *RP* (1979), 686.

Discussion

DI VITA-ÉVRARD: Je voudrais simplement soumettre à Sir Ronald une hypothèse, s'il est permis de revenir encore sur le cas épineux du consul de l'an 13, C. Silius A. Caecina Largus. Si l'on considère qu'il y a eu adoption, il serait assez normal de penser que le polyonyme est un Caecina adopté dans la famille des Silii. Nous connaissons maintenant un C. Caecina Largus, qui pourrait fort bien être son père: c'est le deuxième dédicant de l'inscription du théâtre de Volterra, le frère de A. Caecina Severus, consul suffect en 1 av. J.-C. La filiation donnée par Dion Cassius pour le consul de l'an 13, C.f., ne serait alors ni une erreur ni une invention. A. Caecina Largus aurait été adopté par P. Silius, puisque les Fastes Capitolins donnent la filiation P. f., P. n.; or dans les Fastes, en cas d'adoption, nous avons non pas la filiation naturelle, mais la filiation adoptive: il suffit de se reporter au cas du deuxième fils de P. Silius, adopté, qui y est enregistré comme A. Licinius A. f. A. n. Nerva Silianus et dont nous savons, sans doute possible, par Velleius Paterculus, qu'il est bien fils de P. Silius. Je n'ignore pas que deux difficultés se présentent. La première, c'est que P. Silius a des fils, deux si nous lui enlevons C. Silius. Mais est-on sûr que, dans les années qui précèdent le consulat de 13, ces fils sont vivants? Sir Ronald lui-même avait remarqué que les fils des grands maréchaux d'Auguste étaient arrivés au consulat mais qu'on ne leur connaissait pas de gouvernements consulaires. Or P. Silius est consul en 3, après sa légation de Thrace-Macédoine, et nous ne savons plus rien sur lui après cette date; le deuxième fils, l'adopté, est consul en 7 et cette fois nous apprenons par Velleius Paterculus qu'il est mort peu de temps après, prématurément, sans avoir eu le temps de jouir de la haute position à laquelle il était parvenu. On peut dans ces conditions se demander si, dans les années 8–12, P. Silius ne s'est pas vu privé de postérité, du moins à la génération des fils en âge d'exercer une vie politique. La deuxième difficulté est constituée par le prénom. Il est anormal qu'un personnage adopté par un P. Silius porte le prénom Caius. Des anomalies de ce genre se rencontrent, semble-t-il, dans la nomenclature de l'adoption que donne D. Shackleton Bailey pour la fin de la République. D'autre part, il est vraisemblable que P. Silius Nerva, consul en 28, était le fils de P. Silius, le consul de 3; à l'époque de l'adoption présumée | de A. Caecina Largus, c'était un tout jeune homme, mais par égard pour lui A. Caecina Largus n'aurait pas ajouté au gentilice du père adoptif le prénom de ce dernier, Publius, choisissant alors peut-être le prénom de son propre père. Je dois reconnaître, honnêtement, que, si l'on considère que le deuxième volet de la nomenclature binaire du consul de l'an 13 correspond aux *tria nomina* du grand-père maternel, la formule raccourcie de la date consulaire, C. Caecina (on attendrait C. Silius ou A. Caecina), serait plus satisfaisante. Pour conclure, maintenant que nous connaissons un C. Caecina Largus qui, comme père du consul de l'an 13, 'fait l'affaire', puisque P. Silius a bien pu ne pas survivre longtemps à son consulat de 3 et que son père P. Silius a épousé—l'indication est de Velleius Paterculus—la fille d'un

Coponius, je préfère considérer C. Silius A. Caecina Largus comme un Caecina adopté par P. Silius après la mort de ses deux fils, dans les années qui précèdent immédiatement le consulat de 13.

FORNI: Movendo dalla nomenclatura dei senatori, che può palesare svariati rapporti tra famiglie, quali provengono da adozione o quali se celano dietro l'assunzione di nomi per gratitudine o per lascito o per derivazione dal nome materno, Sir Ronald Syme ha dischiuso orizzonti di estremo interesse. Le soluzioni possono apparire varie, complesse e congetturali, così come spesso sono le premesse, ma proprio per queste ragioni è probabile che si accostino alla realtà delle relazioni interfamiliari che semplici non sono mai. Nei casi illustrati di nomenclature susseguenti ad adozione testamentaria l'originaria tribù ricorre nella posizione propria fra l'originaria paternità e l'originario gentilizio o cognome dell'adottato. Poichè, come si sa, nei polionimi la tribù non segue sempre il primo elemento onomastico, è possibile che la sua posizione, se non dal capriccio di chicchessia, dipendesse da quella degli elementi onomastici con i quali era connessa? Potrebbe essere un'ipotesi di lavoro e di riflessione.

CASTILLO: Quisiera someter al juicio de Sir Ronald una hipótesis que me sugiere el análisis del tipo onomástico 'binario' según aparece en la nomenclatura de algunos senadores relacionados con la Bética, cuya cronología va de la época flavia a finales del s. II. Da la impresión de que existen dos fórmulas bien diferenciadas: (1) *Praenomen nomen–nomen cognomen*. A este tipo corresponden, por ejemplo, L. Dasumius Tullius Tuscus, M. Annius Herennius Pollio, M. Accenna Helvius Agrippa, Cn. Pinarius Cornelius Clemens. (2) *Praenomen, nomen, cognomen–nomen, cognomen/ -ina*. Fórmula a la que corresponden, entre otros, L. Cornelius Pusio Annius Messala, C. Iulius Pisibanus Papus. ¿Podría, en el primer caso, tratarse de una fórmula a la que refleja una adopción, mientras el segundo reflejaría de un lado la familia paterna y de otro la materna?

SYME: Mes Chers Collègues, je suis très touché par l'intérêt qu'a suscité ma communication en dépit, peut-être, de sa présentation un peu sommaire et un peu téléguidée. Évidemment, j'ai voulu mettre l'emphase sur les incertitudes: par exemple, avec ce type de nomenclatures binaires, il y a presque toujours des solutions alternatives. Par exemple, Salvius Liberalis Nonius Bassus: est-ce un Nonius adopté par un Salvius ou vice versa? Heureusement, nous savons que cet homme s'appelait couramment Salvius Liberalis. Donc, c'est le nom du père, le nom de famille, le patronyme. Mais, avec d'autres, manquent assez souvent les indices: j'ai pris comme exemple, naturellement, cet homme très important et un peu énigmatique qu'est M. Cornelius Nigrinus Curiatius Maternus; c'est ou, de naissance, un Curiatius Maternus adopté, ou bien le fils d'une Curiatia, c'est-à-dire, son père a épousé une Curiatia Materna, peut-être la soeur de l'orateur qui figure dans le Dialogue de Tacite.

Madame Di Vita-Évrard a soulevé cette horrible question de C. Silius P. f. P. n. (Nerva?) A. Caecina Largus. Je suis très reconnaissant de la solution qu'elle a proposée. Je crois qu'il y a quinze ans, précisément, j'étais pour, c'est-à-dire pour un Caecina Largus adopté ou entrant dans la famille des Silii; ce qui aurait des répercussions très intéressantes pour les événements de 48, c'est-a-dire la fin de Messaline et de son amant C. Silius, le fils, parce qu'avec Claude, dans sa voiture, venant d'Ostie à Rome, il y avait précisément un Caecina Largus qui l'a encou|ragé: peut-être un cousin de C. Silius l'amant de Valeria Messalina. Or, j'avoue franchement, il y a quinze ans, j'avais cru qu'il s'agissait d'une adoption; maintenant j'ai un peu changé. Je ne veux pas rester sur mes positions mais je veux assurer Madame Di Vita-Évrard que je suis un peu de son côté. Évidemment, je risque de sombrer dans l'équivoque, mais il y a tant d'incertitude dans la nomenclature d'un sénateur, comme dans la vie d'un sénateur, parce que c'est une occupation assez hasardeuse, nous le savons, n'est-ce pas?

Pour ce qui est de la position de la tribu, je prendrai le cas d'un consul sous Vespasien, Valerius Festus, qui est un polyonyme: C. Calpetanus Rantius Quirinalis Valerius P. f. Pomp. Festus. C'est intéressant: le gentilice Calpetanus est étrusque sans aucun doute, Rantius l'est probablement. Valerius Festus ne dit rien parce que des Valerii, on en trouve partout. L'inscription a été découverte je crois à Trieste. Or, il n'y a pas de lien apparent avec cette cité, mais la tribu 'Pomptina' amène à s'interroger: il n'y a pas beaucoup de Valerii dans les vieilles cités étrusques; mais la tribu 'Pomptina' est celle d'Arezzo. Voici donc quelque chose pour la liste de notre collègue Torelli. Valerius Festus paraît en fin de compte sur deux inscriptions d'Arezzo. Je crois que j'ai souligné ce petit détail il y a 20 ou 25 ans. Si on regarde, dans le *Corpus*, on peut les trouver (*CIL* xi 1863 f.). Dans ce cas-là, ce qui indique, c'est la tribu près du gentilice.

En résumant, je mets une fois encore l'emphase sur les incertitudes. Nous faisons de notre mieux, nous suivons une science expérimentale. Dans les vraies sciences, il y a toujours de la place pour l'hypothèse, autrement, s'il n'y a pas d'hypothèse, cela ne nourrit pas son homme. Pourquoi se préoccuper de choses où il n'y a rien de problématique? Merci.

Je crois que je n'ai pas esquivé de difficultés ni d'incertitudes. Merci bien.

10

Discours de clôture (Rome, May 1981)

Monsieur le Président, Mes Amis et Collègues,

Après ce qui a été exprimé avec tant d'élégance par notre Président, je me sens un peu à court; et d'ailleurs, résumer les résultats de notre colloque qui a duré une semaine, une bonne semaine, prendrait un peu trop d'espace.

J'ai été très content d'apprendre cet après-midi les idées de M. Patrick Le Roux. Pour ma part, je ne peux ajouter que des observations manquant peut-être un peu de méthode, un peu décousues. Car ce qui m'a frappé, ces jours-ci, ce sont précisément les incertitudes, les vides, les lacunes. C'est un peu la faute de notre méthode, ou plutôt de nos méthodes.

Par exemple, l'onomastique qui fait de tout bon poids, on peut le dire, ou un poids un peu ambigu. Primo, on trouve un gentilice très très rare: bon, c'est un indice, nous allons découvrir peut-être la patrie d'un sénateur ou la région. Dans d'autres cas le gentilice peut être assez commun, par exemple les Baebii. Comme Géza Alföldy, j'ai beaucoup d'affection pour les Baebii d'Espagne, avant tout pour ce nid de Baebii qui se trouve à Saguntum, mais, en Italie, on peut trouver des Baebii n'importe où. Donc, quel critère? Pour ma part, je suis tenté de faire appel assez souvent à la tribu, peut-être plus souvent que d'autres collègues. Par exemple, quand je trouve, dans une ville d'Italie, un Iulius portant la tribu 'Voltinia', je pense que c'est la Narbonnaise quand même, ou quand je trouve un Iulius à Athènes (C. Iulius, tribu Voltinia, Silvinus), je crois qu'il s'agit tout de même d'un homme de Narbonnaise.

Mais les vides, les lacunes . . . avant tout les villes où il n'y a presque pas d'inscriptions. Il y a des villes qui, évidemment, ont eu leur période de prospérité. Ainsi Saragosse, ou avant Saragosse, dirais-je, Celsa. Je crois que maintenant on ne peut plus douter que notre Licinius Sura, avec la tribu 'Sergia', quoiqu'assez connu à Tarragone et à Barcelone, n'ait cependant quand même pour patrie Celsa. Comme nous pourrions peut-|être dépister quelqu'un avec la tribu 'Aniensis' qui aurait pour patrie Saragosse, quoiqu'il n'y ait qu'une douzaine d'inscriptions latines dans cette grande ville.

Epigrafia e ordine senatorio ii (Tituli v, Rome 1982 [1984]), 789–91.

J'ai parlé de villes qui ont prospéré, d'autres, déchues. Une conjecture par exemple (parce que nous devons opérer avec des conjectures, nous n'avons pas assez de détails): 'colonia Julia Lepida', fondée par Marcus Lepidus, position stratégique avec un pont sur l'Ebre. Est-ce que nous avons besoin aussi de Caesaraugusta? Oui, du point de vue d'Auguste, car il voulait, je crois, entraver la colonie que son ennemi avait établie.

Ce serait une merveilleuse histoire de chercher les villes, comme les régions, qui n'ont pas de sénateurs, de voir la part du hasard ou du changement de routes, des changements économiques: un merveilleux thème, n'est-ce pas, les villes qui sombrent. Je crois que quelque part chez Dante, nous trouvons un conseil: 'Se tu riguardi Luni ed Urbisaglia, | Come sono ite e come se ne vanno | Diretro ad esse Chiusi e Sinigaglia.' Pour ce qui est de Senigallia, je ne suis pas sûr que nous ayons su y dénicher ces jours-ci un sénateur. Par le plus pur des hasards, il y a quand même un sénateur de Senigallia au livre IV des *Histoires* de Tacite, un certain Manlius Patruinus qui avait été quelque peu insulté par ses concitoyens et s'en était plaint auprès du Sénat.

Comme je le constate encore une fois, nos informations sont tellement éparpillées. Est-ce que nous devons désespérer? Je ne le crois pas. J'ai noté avoir lu à deux reprises dans les journaux anglais, il y a quelques semaines, l'*obiter dictum* de Thomas Mann; en anglais, c'était: 'Only the exhaustive is satisfactory.' En allemand, c'est peut-être 'nur das Vollständige befriedigt.' Eh bien, je m'inscris en faux, parce que notre science est une science expérimentale, imparfaite. Nous nous servons d'impressions, n'est-ce pas? Nous faisons de notre mieux. Il faut même espérer qu'on aura tort de temps en temps parce qu'alors on aura fait des progrès. Nous avons chacun, si nous jetons un coup d'œil sur le passé, fait une erreur de temps en temps, mais par un merveilleux hasard, quelqu'un d'autre a corrigé notre erreur et tout le monde est content. Je propose donc une science imparfaite comme nos sciences humaines, mais qui a quand même un côté optimiste. J'ai parlé des villes déchues. Évidemment c'est triste, des villes comme Pesaro, comme dit Catulle: 'moribunda ab sede Pisauri'. Mais quand même, sous l'Empire, nous avons la famille d'Arrecinus Clemens, *cos. II* sous Domitien, beau-frère de l'empereur Titus, qui est de Pesaro avec la tribu 'Camilia'.

Plusieurs des villes que nous étudions ont joui de beaucoup de progrès et de beaucoup de succès, Pergame par exemple. Comme les Romains ont dû admirer Pergame, sa situation, son architecture, Ephèse, et les grandes villes d'Asie, et d'autres!

Et avant tout je crois que ce sont précisément ces sénateurs de l'Orient qui peuvent nous encourager, parce que pour tant de villes de l'Ouest, au IIe siècle, villes d'Espagne ou de Narbonnaise, nous manquons tellement de documents. Je crois que c'est le collègue Barbieri qui a un jour attiré notre attention sur le fait que nous ne connaissons presque pas de légats des trois provinces de Gaule au IIe s., de légats de Belgica, Aquitania et Lugdunensis; beaucoup de ces légats seraient citoyens de villes d'Italie ou de villes de l'Ouest romain. Or, ce que les sénateurs des provinces orientales nous appren|nent, c'est que n'importe quel phénomène, à Rome, arrive un peu plus tôt que nous ne l'attendions. Par exemple, à l'époque d'Auguste, Auguste vient de préserver Rome et l'Italie contre la menace de l'Orient, n'est-ce pas, contre Antoine ou, plutôt, la reine (pour Virgile 'infandum'), avec toutes les ressources de l'Orient. L'Orient est vaincu à Actium. Est-ce qu'il en souffre? Pas du tout. Par la suite nous trouvons, au IIe s., la grande renaissance hellénique, quand un *imperator Romanus*, Marc-Aurèle, écrit en grec, écrit non pas des *res gestae*, des *commentarii*, mais écrit sur son âme. Renaissance culturelle des Grecs: évidemment, on ne peut les en écarter, les Romains savent que la culture grecque est supérieure, qu'elle est presque la seule culture.

Or, ce qui est remarquable chez nos amis des provinces d'Asie, les grands personnages, 'the big men' de Pergame, ou les membres des colonies romaines, c'est que l'essor des provinciaux d'Orient a précédé l'essor culturel. Évidemment, nous avons au Ier siècle, dans les personnes de Plutarque et de Dion de Pruse, les précurseurs d'Hérode Atticus et de toute la racaille des rhéteurs et des sophistes. Mais précisément, au Ier s. de l'Empire, nous voyons déjà sous Domitien des consuls de Sardes (Ti. Iulius Celsus Polemaeanus) et de Pergame; et, ce qui est encore pire, dirais-je, pour quelques-uns de nos gens d'Occident, sous Trajan en 105, les deux consuls ordinaires de cette année-là, consuls pour la deuxième fois, sont C. Antius A. Iulius Quadratus de Pergame et Ti. Iulius Candidus Marius Celsus lequel, pour M. Halfmann et pour moi-même, a son origine quelque part en l'Asie.

Voici déjà une espèce de symbiose. Je crois que nous pourrions résumer—de toute façon il est temps de résumer—en évoquant la question des périodes historiques: nous parlons assez souvent du siècle des Antonins, introduit au mois de septembre 96 par l'empereur Nerva, après Domitien, mais j'incline à croire moi-même que l'époque des Antonins commence avec Vespasien. Merci.

I I

The Marriage of Rubellius Blandus

IN all the principate of Tiberius Caesar one of the blackest years was A.D. 33. Rome mourned for Agrippina, the widow of Germanicus, for her son Drusus, and for the illustrious consular Asinius Gallus.

Confined to state custody for several years, they ended their lives by starvation, voluntary or imposed. To fill the tale of public woe came the marriage of the Emperor's granddaughter Julia. The historian Tacitus, whose indignation could scarcely find the words to denounce the misconduct of her mother Livia Julia (the wife of Drusus Caesar)—the affair with Aelius Seianus, that 'municipalis adulter'—now goes on to disclose the melancholy fate of the daughter. She married beneath herself. The husband elected for a princess of the line of Julii and Claudii was a senator of municipal extraction, Rubellius Blandus. Men recalled his grandfather, a person of mere equestrian rank from Tibur.[1]

They might have derived instruction, but no consolation, if they reflected that a proud disdain for the claims of blood and birth was no new thing among the patrician Claudii. Tiberius was running true to form.

If there was in the bridegroom Rubellius a disparity of years as well as of station, that was less to be reprehended, if at all, being a common feature of dynastic matches: the elderly Quirinius, a successful upstart who united diplomatic talent with military capacity, found himself rewarded more than a dozen years after his consulate with the hand of Aemilia Lepida, who was to have married Lucius Caesar, the adopted son of Augustus.[2] Not that Julia, the bride of Rubellius, was in her first youth, as the Romans reckoned these things. She had already been married, as long ago as the year 20, to Nero, the eldest son of Germanicus. A second match, to no less a person than Seianus, had recently been forestalled by a political catastrophe.[3] |

---

[1] Tacitus, *Ann.* vi 27, 1, cf. (for Livia) iv 3, 4.   [2] *Ann.* iii 23, 1.

[3] *Ann.* iii 29, 3. Julia's birth is put in A.D. 3 in *PIR*[2], J 636. Better, 5 or 6. Nero had just assumed the *toga virilis*, born presumably in 5. For the betrothal to Seianus, Dio lviii 3, 9 (Boissevain = Zonaras xi 2).

American Journal of Philology ciii (1982), 62–85.

To introduce the year 33 the historian had selected two other weddings. It was high time for the head of the family to find husbands for two daughters of Germanicus, namely Julia Drusilla and Julia Livilla. The former he consigned to L. Cassius Longinus, the latter to M. Vinicius: the consular pair who opened the year 30.

Now aged seventy-three, the recluse on the island Capreae had given long and anxious thought to the matter: 'diu quaesito'.[4] Five years previously he awarded Agrippina (the eldest of the three sisters) to Domitius Ahenobarbus (to be consul in 32). Ahenobarbus stood close to the power, being the son of the elder Antonia. Not perhaps a judicious choice, as Tiberius might be coming to see.

Of close kin to the dynasty, there was a Junius Silanus, now aged about nineteen.[5] Also his coeval, the son of that excellent Lepidus (*cos.* 6) who is designated 'nomini ac fortunae Caesarum proximus'.[6]

This time the Princeps decided on extraneous husbands. Cassius, the brother of the jurist, of the plebeian *nobilitas*, (but not a descendant of the tyrannicide), while Vinicius belonged to the new imperial aristocracy, grandson of M. Vinicius (*suff.* 19 B.C.). Both were congenial to Ti. Caesar, on various counts, notably their age, although his despatch to the Senate was couched 'levi cum honore iuvenum'.

The young senator takes his first bride when about twenty-two, not long before his quaestorship. Matrimony invites speculation, and sometimes repays it.[7] By a contrary phenomenon, marriages earlier and earlier had become manifest in the 'domus regnatrix'. Nero, the eldest son of Germanicus was united to Julia in 20, when he assumed the *toga virilis*.

In the past Tiberius Caesar had himself fallen victim to matrimonial arrangements in the dynasty; and after the decease of his son Drusus in 23 he suffered under the exacerbating presence and discords | of four widows.[8] A decade later he hoped to obviate vexations by selecting for the princesses three husbands of mature years, no obtrusive ambitions, and no previous attachment to the dynasty. For

---

[4] *Ann.* vi 15, 1. Drusilla was born in 16 or 17, Livilla in 18 (*PIR*[2], J 664; 674). For 'diu quaesito' compare 'saepe apud se pensitato' (iii 52, 3): taken by Tacitus from the exordium of the Tiberian missive to the Senate (53 f.).

[5] M. Junius Silanus (*cos.* 46), whose father (*cos.* 19) had married Aemilia Lepida, the great-granddaughter of Augustus.

[6] Velleius ii 114, 3 (writing in 30). For the son, *PIR*[2], A 371.

[7] For the peculiar case of Paullus Fabius Maximus, the consul of 11 B.C., still a bachelor about five or six years earlier (Horace, *Odes* iv 1), see *History in Ovid* (1978), 143 ff.

[8] Hence one reason for departing in 26, 'certus procul urbe degere' (iv 57, 1).

a time at least. For himself, he had no expectations of near extinction.[9]

So far motives nowhere documented but not evading rational conjecture. Cassius and Vinicius raise no problem. But what of Rubellius Blandus, over twenty years their senior (as will emerge in this enquiry), singled out to take over the granddaughter of Caesar?

Discredit adhered from Julia's adulterous mother (the mistress of Seianus) who committed suicide after the catastrophe of October 18, A.D. 31. It was expedient to excise Julia from the succession. Two ways of disposal offered. Either seclusion or an inconspicuous marriage to a tranquil man well on in life. Parallels occur in the annals of dynasties before or since.

It remains to investigate the extraction of C. Rubellius C. f. Blandus, his career as a senator, the identity of relatives, and the history of a municipal family through four generations. Hence a variety of problems, some of them resolved as epigraphic evidence accrues.[10]

First of all, the year of Blandus' consulship, giving a clue to his age. The gravestone of Calpurnia Donata registered September 3 under 'Blando et Pollione': Borghesi assigned the pair to the early years of Tiberius.[11] Blandus spoke in the Senate as a consular towards the end of the year 21; and for the colleague C. Annius Pollio was attractive, certainly a consul before 32.[12]

The *Fasti Ostienses* have now disclosed C. Rubellius Blandus, entering office on August 1 of 18, with M. Vipstanus Gallus (the first consul in a new family destined to long duration).[13] 'Blandus et Pollio' therefore recede. Where Annius Pollio should go remains a question: 21, 22, or 28.[14] As for the consular pair, Borghesi was moved by the | dating by *suffecti* which on funerary inscriptions quickly faded out in the early imperial epoch. However, a sporadic instance crops up in the reign of Hadrian.[15] Nothing debars a consulship for a son of Blandus.[16] The *cognomen* is not found in any other family, senatorial or high equestrian.

[9] The forecast of the astrologer Thrasyllus is recorded, but at a later date, by Dio lviii 27, 2 (cf. Suetonius, *Tib.* 62, 3).

[10] For Blandus and his father see the succinct account of U. Weidemann, *AClass* vii (1964), 64 ff., with a valuable table of the epigraphic documents (66 f.).

[11] *CIL* vi 14221, cf. Borghesi, *Oeuvres* iv 479.

[12] *Ann.* iii 51, 1; vi 9, 3. For C. Annius Pollio, *PIR*[2], A 627.

[13] *FO* vi = Degrassi, *Inscr. It.* xiii 1, p. 104 (first published in 1930).

[14] In any event a place has to be found for Q. Sanquinius Maximus, suffect for the second time in 39 and *praefectus urbi*.

[15] *ILS* 7912, in December, to be assigned to 125.

[16] That is, perhaps the Rubellius Blandus of Juvenal viii 39 ff. On whom see below, sub fine. But Blandus may have had a different son, by an earlier marriage.

Next, the Rubellii. The grandfather, the Roman knight from Tibur, passed into literary and social history as the first person of his rank to adopt the profession of teaching rhetoric.[17] He belongs with the first generation of the famous Augustan orators and declaimers who stand on abundant show in the pages of Seneca: coeval perhaps with Passienus, who died in 9 B.C., or with Q. Haterius, born about 63, and perhaps a dozen years older than Seneca and his friend Porcius Latro.

A further identity has been discovered and accepted for this Rubellius Blandus. Early in the year 43 Cicero commended to the good offices of Q. Cornificius, governing the province Africa Vetus, a group of six persons, left heirs by the businessman Q. Turius. He was a 'vir bonus et honestus', and they bore the same stamp.[18] One of the company was a C. Rubellius.[19] Another, Sex. Aufidius, earns praise in a second letter: 'splendore equiti Romano nemini cedit'.[20] Finally, a third letter concerning L. Aelius Lamia, otherwise known as 'equestris ordinis princeps' and a person of consequence already in 58 when the consul Gabinius ordered him to leave Rome.[21]

Rubellius and Lamia both left a firm imprint on their operations in Africa. An estate in the upper valley of the Bagradas is on ample attestation, known as the 'saltus Blandianus' adjacent to the 'saltus Lamianus'.[22] |

These knights of substance and repute were well qualified to be the founders of senatorial families.[23] Nor was business acumen incongruous with the teaching profession.[24] So far therefore an impeccable equation.

A small fact can overturn the obvious or the plausible. Tacitus gave no hint of any rank or occupation for the consul's father: 'patre praetorio' would not add anything of value. Two inscriptions reveal a C. Rubellius Blandus as proconsul of Crete and Cyrene. The first at Gortyn, calls for no comment.[25] The second is on the eastern part of

---

[17] Seneca, *Controv.* ii, *praef.* 5.

[18] *Ad fam.* xii 26, 1. For remarks on the whole group, *Historia* xiii (1964), 162 f. = *RP* (1979), 612.

[19] In his text (1977) Shackleton Bailey prefers 'Rubellinum' (the best MSS), citing in his commentary Schulze, *LE* 220: three sporadic instances: CIL vi 25501; ix 1738 (Beneventum); x 7212 (in Sicily).

[20] *Ad fam.* xii 27.   [21] *Ad fam.* xii 29.

[22] CIL viii 25943, cf. 26416.

[23] Senatorial in the next generation, the Lamiae (from Formiae) advance to the excellent L. Aelius Lamia (*cos.* 3).

[24] As witness the versatile Remmius Palaemon, profitably investing in vineyards (Suetonius, *Gram.* 23).

[25] *AE* 1930, 62 = *ICret.* iv 293.

the propylaeum of the Caesareum at Cyrene.[26] A recent revision produces 'C. Rubellius L. [f. Blandus]'.[27]

The consequence is noteworthy. Acquiring the *praenomen* 'Lucius', Rubellius the *rhetor* is disjoined from C. Rubellius the *negotiator*. The latter will be regarded as his brother, quite a lot older perhaps—at least some of that African congregation were well on in years.[28] The *praenomen* now acquires a further interest. At Marruvium was discovered a base dedicated to 'C. Rubellio L. f. / Cam. [B]lando'.[29] Perhaps the Augustan senator and proconsul. Not that it matters. Marruvium in the Marsian country avows more significant links with the Rubellii (see below).

Their own *patria* furnishes three dedications.[30] First, to Argive Juno, made by 'C. Blandus procos.'. By suppressing the *gentilicium*, | the man affects the aristocratic style of nomenclature, as did M. Agrippa and L. Plancus; and his brief title was the best a senator could manage if he had not reached a consulship. Second, the renovation of an ancient altar set up by the great god of Tibur: 'Iovi Praestiti / Hercules Victor dicavit / Blandus pr. restituit'. Whether the father or the son may be waived. The third, to 'Diva Drusilla', carries the name and filiation of the son, followed by his career '[q.] divi Aug., tr. pl., pr., cos., [pr]ocos., pontif.'. The enumeration is sober and dignified. It omits minor magistracy and military tribunate if he held either or both of those posts. Some may conceive surprise that in this season (the summer of 38 or not much later) Blandus chose not to specify Asia or Africa as the proconsulate.

The parent had not gone further than the governorship of Crete and Cyrene. Not on high estimation, avoided by the *nobiles* and almost furnishing a guarantee that the man would never become consul. Of seventeen during the reigns of Augustus and his successor only one achieved it.[31]

However, C. Blandus L. f. was amply endowed and he had done well otherwise, through socially resplendent matrimony. The facts emerge from later evidence, to combine and furnish a complicated

[26] J. M. Reynolds, *PBSR* xxvi (1958), 30, whence *AE* 1960, 266. The editor argued for Blandus the consul (*suff.* 18). Against, U. Weidemann, op. cit. 67 f.; W. Eck, *RE, Suppl.* xiv 588.

[27] L. Gasperini, *QAL* vi (1971), 7, with figs. 8 and 9.

[28] Q. Considius Gallus (*Ad fam.* xii 26, 1) may be identical with Q. Considius, the high-minded capitalist who refrained from calling in his loans in the crisis of 63 B.C. (Valerius Maximus iv 8, 3).

[29] *AE* 1975, 305. [30] *ILS* 3908; 3401; 196.

[31] For the list, W. Eck, *Zephyrus* xxiii–xxiv (1972/3), 245 f. The exception is Cornelius Lupus (*suff.* 42), a personal friend of Claudius—and not likely to be one of the patrician Cornelii, cf. *PIR*[2], C 1400.

family tree that extends to the epoch of Hadrian.[32] The cardinal documents are

(1) *ILS* 281 (Rome): Sergiae/Laenatis f./Plautillae/matri/imp. Nervae/Caesaris Aug.

(2) *ILS* 952 (Tusculum): [Rub]elliae/[Bla]ndi f. Bassae/Octavi Laenatis/Sergius Octavius/Laenas Pontianus/aviae optimae.

The construction is briefly as follows. Rubellius Blandus, the parent of the consul, had annexed a Sergia, presumed a daughter of the patrician L. Sergius Plautus. The Sergii, an ancient house, had not shown a consul for more than four centuries—and not to be retrieved by the desperate ambitions of L. Sergius Catilina. The next Sergius is disclosed by the dedication set up by a distant city: 'L. Sergio Regis f./Arn. Plauto q. /salio Palatino/patrono'.[33]

Something further is known about Sergius Plautus. He wrote about the doctrines of the Stoics.[34] Like the study of Roman legal and | religious antiquities, philosophy (though in a lesser measure) provided consolation for the decayed patriciate during evil days, not abandoned under the peace of the Caesars and before long to be enhanced. Plautus bequeathed a tradition to the grandson, Rubellius Plautus.

His time of life concerns the family tree. He might be identified as '[Sergius] Plaut(us)', *praetor peregrinus* in A.D. 2.[35] If so, perhaps the brother rather than the father of the Sergia who married the father of Rubellius the consul.

That is not all. Another Sergia married an Octavius Laenas, otherwise not on record. He is the father of C. Octavius Laenas, consul suffect in 33. In that year died the jurist M. Cocceius Nerva (*suff.* 21 or 22). Laenas took his place in the charge of the Roman aqueducts.[36] Not inappropriate. Laenas had given his daughter Sergia Plautilla to the son of Cocceius Nerva.[37]

Finally, the nexus with the Rubellii. Through his mother Sergia, Rubellius Blandus (*suff.* 18) was first cousin to Octavius Laenas (*suff.* 33). He duly tightened the link by bestowing his daughter Rubellia Bassa on a son of Laenas.[38]

Hence a large company of persons, known only from inscriptions

---

[32] E. Groag, *JŒAI* xxi–xxii (1924) 425 ff., with stemma (435 f.). The results are resumed in *Tacitus* (1958), 627 f.

[33] *ILS* 2922 (Urso, in Baetica).   [34] *PIR*[1], S 378.

[35] *Inscr. It.* xiii 1, p. 297. Groag, however, preferred to assume a son of the philosopher (op. cit. 432, n. 22).

[36] Frontinus, *Aq.* 102.

[37] As shown by *ILS* 281. There is no sign that this Nerva (*PIR*[2], C 1226) held a consulship.

[38] As shown by *ILS* 952: the (maternal) grandmother Rubellia Bassa celebrated by Sergius Octavius Laenas Pontianus (the consul of 131).

or as necessary postulates in a stemma. They illustrate the transmission of maternal nomenclature, and sometimes its predominance. It is no surprise that the *novus homo* Octavius Laenas preferred to exalt his daughter by the style 'Sergia Plautilla'.

The phenomenon is frequent enough—and useful for indagating maternal ancestry.[39] Another device of the new imperial nobility was ostentatious indeed. The latest character on the stemma is Sergius Octavius Laenas Pontianus (*cos.* 131). An earlier specimen of the *gentilicium* exploited in this fashion has turned up: Sergius Rubellius Plautus on a lead pipe at Rome.[40] No evidence attested a *praenomen* for Plautus, the son of Blandus and Julia. |

The Octavii Laenates are a reputable family deriving from the Marsian country. No need to seek help from 'Marso nescio quo Octavio, scelerato latrone atque egenti'.[41] An Octavius Laenas held a magistracy at Marruvium.[42] For Marsians the exit into Latium from the high country was Tibur, by the Via Valeria. Hence early relations to be surmised in forgotten history. Recently Marruvium paid honour to a C. Rubellius L. f. Blandus.[43]

The study of Roman families and senatorial careers was styled long ago a sheer delight.[44] If arduous, it can sometimes issue in valid results, not under contestation. Thus for the Rubellii, at least so far. A problem of ages and identities impinged that can no longer be postponed: a C. Rubellius Blandus was one of the *tresviri monetales*. He has often been taken to be the father of the consul.[45]

The post is held by young men two or three years short of the quaestorship. Clear indications are to hand. For example, two moneyers in a college firmly dated to 16 B.C. become consuls in 6 and 5.[46] Both had the benefit of consular parentage, hence able to accede to the *fasces* at thirty-two or not long after, according to the regulations ordained in the Republic of Caesar Augustus. The new man is in a different case, twenty years (and often more) elapsing before his consulship.

Blandus the *monetalis* is involved in the most intricate problem of

[39] Thus Servilia, the daughter of Q. Marcius Barea Soranus, and Fannia, daughter of P. Clodius Thrasea Paetus.
[40] *AE* 1954, 70: adduced in *Tacitus* (1958), 628.
[41] Cicero, *Phil.* xi 4. He had 'Marcus' for *praenomen* (Appian, *BC* iv 62.266).
[42] *ILS* 5364. [43] *AE* 1975, 305.
[44] Nepos, *Vita Attici* 21, 4: 'quibus libris nihil potest esse dulcius iis qui aliquam cupidinem habent notitiae clarorum virorum.' That 'honesta cupido' abated in the long sequel, with dire consequences for the understanding of Roman history.
[45] *PIR*[1], R 81; Nagl, *RE* iA 1158. And most in the sequel.
[46] Viz. C. Antistius Vetus and L. Vinicius, cf. *PIR*[2], A 771.

Augustan numismatics. He belongs to one of the four colleges who signed the small brass coins, the *quadrantes*. The group is otherwise anomalous, since one half has three members, the other four.[47] Dates for the four have been allocated in a range between the years 9 and 2.[48]

C. Rubellius Blandus had three partners lacking any clue of identity, although by exception all possess full nomenclature. For this college the dating varies, with a strong tendency towards the lower limit.[49] To cut short a long discussion, no harm or vexation ensues when Blandus is put in the vicinity of 3 B.C.[50]

If that is so, the *monetalis* comes out as the future consul. To argue for the parent would run into difficulties.[51] For example, not old enough to have a son consul in A.D. 18. In passing brief observations may be set on record. First, there is no call to put the moneyers of *quadrantes* in a close sequence. Second, the range might extend from 11 to 1. Third, Livineius Regulus, one of the three *suffecti* in A.D. 18. If he is supposed identical with the Regulus of one college, and with 'Reg[. . .]', who was *praetor peregrinus* in 2 B.C., he can hardly have held the post later than 9 B.C.[52] Therefore about fifty when consul. A casual notice shows Livineius an advocate of consequence. Along with M. Lepidus and L. Piso he undertook to defend Cn. Piso in 20.[53] The Livineii were already senatorial in the last epoch of the Republic.[54]

To have Blandus a *monetalis* in 3 or 2 B.C., hence born about 25, concords with the year of his consulship. That is, acceding to the *fasces* at forty-two. For a senator of non-consular parentage, earlier access cannot be established under Augustus or in the first epoch of

---

[47] In *BMC,R. Emp.* i, xcvii f., the four were numbered and ordered as follows:

IX Lamia, Silius, Annius
X Pulcher, Taurus, Regulus
XIII Apronius, Galus, Messalla, Sisenna
XIV P. Betilienus, C. Naevius Capella, C. Rubellius Blandus, L. Valerius Catullus

[48] Mattingly selected the years 9, 8, 5, 4. For K. Pink, however, a run from 10 to 7 (NZ lxxi [1946], 123). Again, adopting Mattingly's temporal order, 6, 5, 3, 2 in A. Kunisz, *Recherches sur le monnayage et la circulation monétaire sous le règne d'Auguste* (1976), 153. On the latter, observe that 6 B.C. will not do for L. Aelius Lamia (*cos.* A.D. 3).

[49] For the detail, references in U. Weidemann, op. cit. 64, n. 8. Add K. Pink (8 B.C.).

[50] Discord being evident among experts, and urgent need for constant regard to dates and ages in the careers of senators. Some of the *quadrantes* might belong in the period A.D. 10–14, so M. Grant opined, *The Six Main Aes Coinages of Augustus* (1953), 108 ff. He stated that 'prosopography affords virtually no aid'.

[51] U. Weidemann indicated a preference for the consul's father but remained inconclusive (op. cit. 65, cf. 68). For the consul, T. P. Wiseman, *New Men in the Roman Senate 139 B.C.–14 A.D.* (1971), 256.

[52] The praetor was not noted in *PIR*², L 290.   [53] *Ann.* iii 11, 2.

[54] From Campania, cf. T. P. Wiseman, op. cit. 237. To which, add *Ann.* xiv 17, 1.

his successor. A pair of items concerning Caecina Severus (*suff.*
1 B.C.) is consonant with birth *c*.44 B.C. In A.D. 15 he has forty *stipendia*
behind him, likewise in 21.[55] The first figure reckons from the
military tribu|nate, the second from the quaestorship. Caecina was
of good family, from Volaterrae. Some of the low-born military
such as Tarius Rufus (*suff.* 16 B.C.) and Sulpicius Quirinius (*cos.* 12)
may well have had to wait some years. Much longer might be the
delay if a man had only the arts of peace to commend him: that is to
say, law and oratory. When Q. Haterius, a speaker of some note,
won that distinction in 5 B.C. he was then close on sixty—nearly
ninety when he died in 26.[56] Another person of this type is C. Vibius
Rufus (*suff.* 16), frequently cited, like Haterius, in the reminiscences
of Seneca. A stray anecdote helps. Rufus affected high pretensions,
boasting that he owned the curule chair of Caesar the Dictator and a
wife who had once been married to the orator Cicero.[57] The lady
cannot be Terentia.[58] She is that Publilia whom her guardian married
in 46 B.C. and divorced the next year.[59] Therefore either Rufus was
quite inhuman in his passion for relics and antiques, marrying a
woman nearly old enough to be his grandmother, or else he was
considerably older, almost a generation older, than the date which
his consulship might indicate. In fact the retardation of Rufus is
confirmed once he is recognized as the parent of C. Vibius Rufinus,
consul suffect with M. Cocceius Nerva in 21 or 22.[60] Rufinus
acquires ample definition as a friend of Ovid, as an author writing
about herbs and trees and flowers, as a proconsul in Asia, to be
assigned the tenure 36/7.[61]

   The short interval after the consulship of a parent, an elderly *novus
homo*, here on attestation for the first time, recurs in the sequel,
predictably. Acquiring rank and privilege the son begins on parity
with the most eminent in the land.

   Though only the son of a praetor, Rubellius enjoyed early favour
from Caesar Augustus. As quaestor (*c*.A.D.2) he was one of the pair
allocated to the ruler.[62] They tend to be aristocratic. For parallel to |

[55] *Ann.* i 64, 4; iii 33, 1.   [56] Jerome, *Chron.* p. 172 H, cf. *Ann.* iv 61.
[57] Dio lvii 15, 6.
[58] Who became a subject of confusion and fable, allegedly transmitted 'per quosdam gradus
eloquentiae' to Sallust and to Messalla Corvinus (Jerome, *Adv. Iov.* i 48).
[59] A neglected inscription reveals M. Publilius Strato, freedman of Publilia and of C. Vibius
Rufus (*CIL* xiv 2556: Tusculum). On which, cf. *CQ* xxviii (1978), 293 f. = *RP* iii (1984), 1087.
[60] *CIL* vi 1539; 9005 = *ILS* 1795 (August). Thus Groag in *PIR*[2], C 1225 (the consular jurist).
Others have tried to put the pair in the vicinity of the year 40.
[61] For this argument, *History in Ovid* (1978), 85 f. Rufinus ended as legate of Germania
Superior, attested in 43 and in 45 (*ILS* 7076; 2283). The articles on Rufus and Rufinus in *RE* viii
A, 1979 ff. were in any case defective, variously.
[62] On which, M. Cébeillac, *Les* Quaestores Principis etc. (1973).

Blandus observe one of the four Vitellius brothers (sons indeed of a procurator).[63] Or Ummidius Quadratus, quaestor in 14.[64] Q. Vitellius was thrown out of the Senate in 17.[65] Quadratus, after a rapid advance to a praetorship in 18, had to wait about twenty-two years for the consulate.

Persons somewhat unlikely on a surface view may nevertheless have seen provinces and armies. A military tribunate omitted (like the post of *monetalis*) from the proud and sober presentation of Blandus' career on his Tiburtine inscription is no bar. Again, Blandus either before or after his praetorship may have been for a time with Ti. Caesar on the northern campaigns (from 4 onwards). Casual allusions in Ovid render that hypothesis plausible for a pair of his cultivated friends, viz. Pomponius Graecinus (*suff.* 16) and Vibius Rufinus (*suff.* 21 or 22).[66] In long absences from Rome the general needed congenial company.

When Caesar proposed to reward an aspiring new man with one of the four major priesthoods, the honour normally accrued about the time of his consulship. Blandus became a *pontifex*. Along with the augurs they stood highest in estimation.

In the *Annales* of Tacitus Rubellius Blandus makes two appearances as a speaker. In 20 he proposed a harsh penalty against Aemilia Lepida, the divorced wife of Sulpicius Quirinius; and in the following year, alone among the consulars, he supported Marcus Lepidus on the plea of mercy for Clutorius Priscus, the vain and incautious author of a premature funerary lament for the ailing Drusus Caesar.[67] Then nothing until wedlock with Julia.

Blandus had slipped unscathed through the season of hazard and peril that opened with Agrippina and her eldest son consigned to imprisonment in 29, to culminate in the destruction of Aelius Seianus and the dreadful aftermath. Meanwhile the Rubellii acquired a notable enhancement. In 29 L. Rubellius Geminus comes out as *consul ordinarius*, unique on the *Fasti* between Pomponius Flaccus in 17 and L. Vitellius in 34. Both enjoyed the friendship and confidence of the ruler. |

Geminus is only a name: a younger brother of Blandus, or perhaps a nephew. Curiosity should have been aroused by L.Rubellius T. f. Geminus Caesianus on a gravestone at Rome, a boy who died at the age of thirteen.[68] The *cognomen* 'Caesianus' admits of alternative

---

[63] Suetonius, *Vit.* 1, 2.   [64] *ILS* 972 (Casinum).   [65] *Ann.* ii 48, 3.
[66] Ovid, *Ex Ponto* i 6, 1 f. (Graecinus), iii 4, 5, and 64 (Rufinus).
[67] *Ann.* iii 23, 2; 51, 1.
[68] *CIL* vi 25503 (registered in *PIR*¹, R 84 under the consul Geminus).

explanations. First, the boy's father was a T. Rubellius Geminus who had married a Caesia. The *praenomen* 'Titus' deters. Not borne so far as known by the Tiburtine family—and in the whole of Italy only one T. Rubellius.[69]

Second therefore, and better, a product of adoption, to be assumed testamentary because of the retained patronymic. On that showing, L. Rubellius Geminus adopted the son of a T. Caesius. For adoption, recourse is had to relatives in the first instance. The boy Caesius looks like a nephew to the wife of L. Rubellius Geminus (*cos.* 29).

In any event, a link between the two families, hence a temptation to search for others, even if not to be proved of close propinquity. At first sight, scant prospect. Caesii are all too frequent throughout Italy.[70] None the less, Tibur has something to offer among the better sort. First, the family of the lyric poet Caesius Bassus, the friend of Persius.[71] He had an estate in the Sabine country, where he wrote poems in winter; and also a villa beneath Vesuvius, where he perished during the eruption.[72] An inscription found on the territory of Tibur concerns C. Caesius Bassus: a piece of property was sold in his absence, the proceeds to be paid to two men, a Scipio and a M. Silanus.[73]

Second, L. Apronius Caesianus, the son of L. Apronius (*suff.* 8): consul in 39 and proconsul of Africa. To him belongs without doubt the fragment at Tibur showing the tribe of that city. It begins with 'L. f. Cam. / [. . . . .]anus'.[74] The military man L. Apronius was a trusted adherent of Tiberius Caesar—and not likely to incur danger during the season of Seianus. He had married a Caesia: his daughter, the wife of Lentulus Gaetulicus, was called either Caesia or Caesiana.[75] |

Blandus owed social ascent to his father's acquisition of Sergia. It carried alliance with another rising family, the Octavii Laenates, and through them with the consular Cocceii. Of a previous marriage for Blandus himself, no trace survives. It would be peculiar indeed if this good man refused the social norm and failed to contract a match shortly before his quaestorship. For some of the municipal men local

---

[69] Viz. T. Rubellius L. f. Pudens (*CIL* v 3024: Patavium).
[70] Over three columns in *TLL, Onomasticon*.   [71] *PIR*[2], C 192.
[72] *Vita Persii* (twice); *Schol.* on Persius 6, 1.
[73] *CIL* xiv 3471 (between Varia and Sublaqueum). Accepted as the poet himself in *PIR*[2], C 192.
[74] *AE* 1916, 110 = *Inscr. It.* iv 1. 52. Not a Junius Silanus as there assumed. In *PIR*[2], A 972 Groag was unduly diffident: 'nescio an'. He is registered, but not as Apronius Caesianus, on the list of African proconsuls by B. E. Thomasson, *RE, Suppl.* xiii 3.
[75] *PIR*[2], C 976.

repute and opulence outweighed the advantages (often hazardous or oppressive) imported by an aristocratic bride.

It was an elderly gentleman, verging towards sixty, who won the hand of a princess, fifteen years subsequent to his consulship: a tranquil steady person, avoiding excess, remote from feuds and annoyance. Life under the Caesars entailed discretion. Some of the wealthy paraded antique parsimony, congenial as a protest against conspicuous expenditure; and an aristocrat might be disposed to conceal for safety his talent or ambitions, passing for dull or merely amiable.[76]

The qualities that Tiberius looked for when making his selection in 33 are not devoid of instruction. Cassius did not respond like his brother to a rigorous upbringing—'facilitate saepius quam industria commendabatur.' Vinicius is styled 'mitis ingenio et comptae facundiae'.[77]

Blandus was something of an orator, although not in the first rank for eloquence among the consulars. He might also have been a writer. The commentator Servius happens to cite 'Rubellius Blandus et Quadrigarius historici'.[78] Though linked to a late Republican annalist, this Rubellius Blandus may be an antiquarian researcher rather than a historian—and the *rhetor* rather than the consular (though anything can happen in a long life). Blandus is not likely to have neglected the traditions and cults of his *patria*. Blandus (and not his father) may have restored the Hercules altar at Tibur.[79]

It would be a pleasing fancy that Blandus, responsive to another kind of tradition (the maternal grandfather a philosopher), devoted anxious care to the education of his children. They came too late to | benefit from precept or example. Rubellius Plautus cannot be more than quaestorian in rank when he goes into exile in 60, while Blandus, absent from record subsequent to 38, may not have survived to complete the sixty-third year of his life (see below).

Before the end Blandus achieved the proconsulate of Africa. It is certified to 35/6 by inscriptions at Lepcis.[80] The abnormal delay since his consulship comes as a surprise, at first sight. The explanation is not far to seek.

Tiberius Caesar set out with the intention of maintaining a

[76] A certain Cornelius Sulla was alleged a 'simulator segnitiae' (*Ann.* xiv 57, 3). Falsely, cf. xiii 47, 3: 'nullius ausi capax natura'.

[77] *Ann.* vi 15, 1.

[78] Servius on *Georgics* i 103 (Gargara, in the territory of Thurii).

[79] *ILS* 3401. For the antiquarian writer Octavius Herennus, *RE* xvii 1830. He dealt with Hercules Victor and the Tiburtine guild of Salii.

[80] *IRT* 330 f., cf. also (not dated) 269; 540.

decennial interval, but the system encountered sundry disturbances. In Africa proconsuls had to be specially appointed or prorogued because of the seven years of warfare (17–24), and in Asia at least one tenure of two years intervened (26–8).[81] That was a tolerable phenomenon, unlike what soon became manifest.

In a general statement Cassius Dio alludes to consular proconsuls retained in office for a *sexennium*.[82] The names and dates are worth knowing. The process works out as follows. In 29 the lot awarded Asia to P. Petronius (*suff.* 19). About M. Silanus M. f. (*cos.* 19) there are certain problems: he went to Africa in 30, succeeding C. Vibius Marsus (*suff.* 17).[83] Both mandates were prolonged until the summer of 35.

It was high time for the ruler to break free from his morbid habits of procrastination. Prolonged tenures find apologists, it is true: a wise choice of governors, care for the well-being of the provincials, and so on. In this instance nine or ten ex-consuls were frustrated of legitimate aspirations—and the practice does not recur.

In 35 Tiberius had to reach back a long way for proconsuls. For Asia, to Cotta Messallinus (*cos.* 20).[84] Early in the next year the patri|cian C. Sulpicius Galba (*cos.* 22) debarred from the proconsular sortition by 'tristes litterae' from Caesar, committed suicide.[85] Asia, it appears, fell to Vibius Rufinus (*suff.* 21 or 22).[86] In Africa the successor to Rubellius Blandus has not been ascertained.[87] What else is known of Blandus can be briefly chronicled. When in 36 a conflagration laid waste the Aventine and a great part of the Circus Maximus, Caesar furnished funds to make good the damage, and a commission was appointed: the husbands of the three daughters of Germanicus (namely Ahenobarbus, Cassius, Vinicius), along with

---

[81] *AE* 1934, 87 (Cos): M. Lepidus (*cos.* 6), an anomalous appointment. For Lepidus and for other proconsuls of the period, *JRS* xlv (1955), 29 f. = *Ten Studies in Tacitus* (1970), 43 f.; *History in Ovid* (1978), 160 f.

[82] Dio lviii 23, 5 (under 33: no names).

[83] The tenure of Marsus was triennial (*ILS* 9375), i.e. from 27 to 30, but he may have been recalled before its expiry. As concerns Silanus, the dedication to C. Maenius Bassus comes in: 'praefecto fabrum/M. Silani M. f. sexto/Cathaginis' (*ILS* 6236: Tibur). The years may be calendar, not proconsular. A tenure for Silanus from 36 to 39 has found recent advocates, cf. B. E. Thomasson's list in *RE, Suppl.* xiii 3. On which, remarks in *Historia* xxx (1981), 196 f. = *RP* iii (1984), 1357 f.

[84] The year is not attested, but there is no other place.

[85] *Ann.* vi 40, 2.

[86] As argued in *History in Ovid* (1978), 85 f. A difficulty has since been removed. P. Lentulus Scipio, it seemed, should have that tenure (*PIR*², C 1398, cf. 251). A new document puts him under Claudius: from Hierocaesareia in Lydia, noted under *Inschr. Ephesos* iii 659.

[87] The next known is L. Piso (*cos.* 27), cf. Dio lix 27, 2. Tacitus was in error (*Hist.* iv 48, 1), cf. *Historia* xxx (1981), 197 = *RP* iii (1984), 1358.

Rubellius Blandus. Another senator was added to their number: P. Petronius, like Blandus a recent proconsul.[88] The last trace of Blandus belongs to the year 38 when he set up the dedication to 'Diva Drusilla'. His name does not occur in the context of dynastic plots or perturbations before or after the death of Caligula. Kinship with the dynasty might have conferred a public funeral.[89] In 43 the widow fell a victim to intrigues of Valeria Messallina.[90] Nor was much to be heard of the three noblemen who married the daughters of Germanicus. Cassius was compelled by Caligula to surrender his wife to the young Aemilius Lepidus, his coeval friend—and the designated successor to the throne. Cassius was an easy-going fellow. Vinicius, however, turned out to be a man of spirit. After the assassination of Caligula he was eager to make a bid for the power. Although Vinicius sought thereafter to appear harmless, and survived for a season with a second consulship in 45, he perished in the next year, poisoned, so it was alleged, by Valeria Messallina. Ahenobarbus had succumbed to a natural death in 40. |

Rubellius Blandus is not merely a Roman consular who gets attached to the stemma of the Julii and Claudii and serves, in his own person or by contrast with others, to illustrate vicissitudes in the dynasty. The rise of the Rubellii is one of those casual facts that dispel conventional notions about Roman political life and confirm the aristocratic Princeps as a steady patron of *novi homines*. Tiberius was a jealous custodian of 'pietas'. What obligation he honoured in promoting the Rubellii and in finally introducing this municipal strain into alliance with the dynasty, that cannot be known. Did he benefit when a young man from the lessons of the first knight to give public instruction at Rome?[91] Or were the Rubellii steady adherents of the Claudii Nerones in troubled times?

Other cities of Latium were drawn into the strife of Roman factions, and eventually into civil warfare. For Marcus Antonius the fabled descent from Anto, a companion of Hercules, indicates Tibur as the 'ultima origo' of the family.[92] And it was suitable that Caesar's

[88] *Ann.* vi 45, 2.

[89] As Caligula for Sex. Pompeius (Seneca, *De tranq.* 11, 10): to be presumed the son of the consul of 14.

[90] Dio lx 18, 4. Her memory was cherished for forty years by Pomponia Graecina, the widow of A. Plautius, the first governor of Britain (*Ann.* xiii 32, 2). Not irrelevant to the personal knowledge that accrued to the young Cornelius Tacitus.

[91] His model for Latin eloquence was Messalla Corvinus, cf. Suetonius, *Tib.* 70, 1: 'quem senem adulescens observarat' (with inadvertence to their respective ages).

[92] Plutarch, *Ant.* 4.

adherent should lay hands on the Tiburtine villa of Metellus Scipio.[93] Nor are partisans beyond detection.[94]

On the other side, the Coponii, who enjoyed wealth and esteem.[95] One of them, proscribed by the Triumvirs, owed salvation to his wife's intercession with Antonius.[96] This Coponius, or another member of the family, became a Caesarian by the year 32. He earned merit through the unfriendly comment uttered in the Senate about another | Tiburtine, the great Munatius Plancus, general and diplomat and the paragon of renegades.[97]

Political allegiances of the first Rubellius may have brought material damage during the civil wars, compelling him to turn his talents in another direction. Success in his new profession—or rather, perhaps, the reward of 'fides', for Tiberius did not forget the Republican and Pompeian allies of his family—repaired the fortunes of the Rubellii. Tacitus comments upon their wealth and refers to the ancestral estates: in Asia, not in Africa.[98]

Like other new names of note in the history of Rome, 'Rubellius' turns out on investigation to be rare and restricted in its provenance.[99] It was not carried by 'negotiatores' to the countries of the East, it is absent from the Illyrian and Balkan lands. In the western provinces it occurs once only in Spain, once in Africa, twice in Sardinia, not at all in Narbonensis. Nor are Rubellii at all frequent in the various regions of older Italy, from Etruria and Picenum down to Calabria.[100] It may be that this single municipal *gens*, with its clients and its freedmen, accounts for most of them: almost the only *praenomina* found are 'Gaius' and 'Lucius'.

Passienus the orator, a contemporary of the Tiburtine knight L. Rubellius Blandus, may serve for parallel. His name is patently Etruscan, and exceedingly uncommon.[101] The Passieni are a solitary family, extinct after the third generation: the last Passienus left no son. The match between C. Rubellius Blandus and the princess Julia

[93] Cicero, *Phil.* v 19; *Ad fam.* xii 2, 1 (on this villa, and a misconception about it, cf. *CQ* xxviii (1978), 294 f.).

Antonius held a military parade at Tibur on November 29 of 44, many senators attending (*Rom. Rev.* [1939], 126). Three years later, on the eve of the Perusine War, Tibur surrendered temple treasures (on loan) to Octavian (Appian, *BC* v 21, 97).

[94] In the first place, Munatius Plancus (*cos.* 42). For C. Geminius, *Historia* iv (1955), 62 f. = *RP* (1979), 282. For Manius (active in 41), *Historia* xiii (1964) 119 = *RP* 597 f.

For some hesitations, T. P. Wiseman, *New Men In the Roman Senate 139 B.C.–14 A.D.* (1971), 233, 239 f. Geminius has the 'Camilia', also the tribe of Pisaurum.

[95] For the Coponii, T. P. Wiseman, op. cit. 226.

[96] Appian, *BC* iv 40, 170.   [97] Velleius ii 83, 3.   [98] *Ann.* xiv 22, 3.

[99] Only one inscription is cited by Schulze, *LE* 220 (*CIL* xi 15539: Luca).

[100] Transpadana offers one (*CIL* v 3024: Patavium).

[101] Schulze, *LE* 213, citing *CIL* xi 2376 = *CIE* 868 (Clusium). No specimen in Wiseman, op. cit. 249.

was blessed with offspring, four children.[102] No grandchildren in the male line are attested. The termination of the Rubellii, however, is not caused by infertility: it was accelerated by the Emperor Nero.

A wider theme emerges, the social and political recompense now open to liberal studies. A few names suffice to declare the matter. Vibius Rufus got to the consulate in the end. Likewise old Haterius, an orator of portentous and proverbial fluency, commemorated by a saying of Augustus and condemned by an obituary notice in Tacitus.[103] |

He also married a daughter of M. Agrippa—his son, D. Haterius Agrippa is described as a relative of Germanicus Caesar.[104]

The original Passienus possessed a talent that could be named in the company of Pollio and Messalla.[105] His son, L. Passienus Rufus, became *consul ordinarius* (4 B.C.) and proconsul of Africa, while his grandson equalled and even surpassed the distinction of Rubellius Blandus. Adopted by the minister of state, Sallustius Crispus, he held two consulates and married two princesses, Domitia the aunt of Nero and Agrippina his mother: Agrippina, it is alleged, encompassed his end and inherited his fortune.[106]

On a surface view the orators whose purple patches adorn Seneca's compilation are a strange assortment of stylists and pedants, remote from the courts, the Forum, or the Curia. Some at least had their feet firmly planted on the ground—or on the political ladder. Others established a renown which their sons were able to exploit. Names like 'Passienus', 'Haterius', and 'Rubellius' exhibit the fine flower of municipal and Italian talent.[107] Provincials are already on the way. The Spaniard Porcius Latro was a notable declaimer. His friend, the Roman knight from Corduba, who preserved these memorials of the Augustan schools, had a son who became the dominant literary figure of his epoch, a *persona grata* at Court, a power behind the throne.[108]

---

[102] Viz. Plautus, Rubellia Bassa, the boy or child Drusus Blandi f. revealed by his brother (*CIL* vi 16057)—and, not attached to the stemma in *PIR*¹, R 80, the Rubellius Blandus of Juvenal viii 39 ff.

[103] Seneca, *Controv*. iv, *praef*. 7; Tacitus, *Ann*. iv 61: 'eloquentiae, quoad vixit, celebratae: monumenta ingeni eius haud perinde retinentur' etc.

[104] *Ann*. ii 51, 1.

[105] Seneca, *Controv*. iii, *praef*. 14.

[106] *Schol. ad Juv*. iv 81.

[107] None of those three names is found in *CIL* I² or in Degrassi, *ILLRP*.

Schulze in *LE* 269 cites for 'Haterius' only D. Aterius Arruntius (*CIL* vi 12450), but he notes 'Hatilius' and the Etruscan 'Hatile' (286). The name is infrequent. Observe three specimens in Etruria, *CIL* xi 2046 (Perusia); 2650 (Saturnia); 3208 (Nepet).

[108] For the elder Seneca, and for the other Spanish *rhetores*, see M. T. Griffin, *JRS* lxii (1972), 1 ff.

Brought into alliance with the dynasty, the Rubellii soon declare the fatal effects of that propinquity. Rubellius Blandus, it is true, had a peaceful end, but his son was among the illustrious victims of the Neronian tyranny. In the degree of descent from Augustus, Rubellius Plautus was the peer and equal of Nero, so Tacitus stated.[109] Hence suspect and vulnerable. The unobtrusive habits of the young man, his | attachment to the traditional virtues, gave no protection, his devotion to the teaching of the Stoics aggravated his nocivity.

Plautus came early into danger. The mother of Nero, angry at being thrust aside from the power, had designs on the young man, so it was alleged (*Ann.* xiii 19, 3). A short respite, and in 60 a comet appeared, portending change and alarming the ruler of the world; and experts or the credulous made public an ominous sign when a thunderbolt struck the country palace (Nero dining there) at Sublaqueum in the territory of Tibur (xiv 22, 1 ff.). Therefore Nero indited a letter to Plautus, encouraging him to depart from Rome to a retreat in Asia, where he possessed ancestral estates (22, 3). Plautus survived for five years, until a centurion arrived with the fatal mandate (57 f.).

The historian, refusing to let his exposition decline into the biography of a Caesar, concentrated emphasis in his third hexad on three victims of Nero: Annaeus Seneca, Thrasea Paetus, Domitius Corbulo. To that design Rubellius Plautus contributes an example of consummate artistry and structure. He is also a vital link in historical transactions.

On his first entrance the dynastic antecedents are alluded to (xiii 19, 3), and the episode concludes ominously with 'Plautus ad praesens silentio tramissus est' (22, 2). The second, evoking 'nobilitas per matrem ex Julia familia', conveys his unimpeachable morality and conduct (xiv 22, 1). Then, Seneca extruded, Tigellinus now emergent as the evil counsellor is employed to warn Nero against philosophy, citing Plautus as a pernicious specimen. Not only his affecting 'veterum Romanorum imitamenta' but 'adsumpta etiam Stoicorum adrogantia sectaque quae turbidos et negotiorum adpetentes faciat' (57, 3).

The historian's procedure is patent, and noteworthy: the first occurrence of the word 'Stoicus' in the *Annales*, the first signal to incriminate the sect and doctrine as a political menace to the security of ruler and government.

The account of Plautus' end in Asia brings up a rumour that he had

---

[109] *Ann.* xiii 19, 3: 'per maternam originem pari ac Nero gradu a divo Augusto'. Not by blood, on which some set store, as Agrippina: 'se imaginem veram, caelesti sanguine ortam' (iv 52, 2). Rubellius Plautus descended from Octavia, the sister of Augustus.

been in touch with Corbulo, at the head of a great army (58, 2). Likewise his wife's father, Antistius Vetus (*cos.* 55), who sent a messenger to Plautus counselling suicide (15, 3). Next, when at the end of 65 Vetus is prosecuted, the name of Plautus is duly adduced (xvi 10, 1).

In the following year Nero brought to destruction 'Virtus ipsa' in the persons of Thrasea Paetus and Barea Soranus (xvi 21,1). To charges against the latter the prosecutor added 'amicitia Plauti' (23, 1). More significant and totally revealing is the language in which Cossutianus | Capito (in a private interview) incites Nero to action against Thrasea. With appeal to past history he indicts 'ista secta' as subversion to all ordered authority (22).

No reader of normal alertness would miss the precedent (Tigellinus on Plautus), the development and climax of a theme, the devices of a coherent historian.

Tacitus conjured up all his resources to embellish, and to magnify, Rubellius Plautus, admirable in the conduct of his life, constant and courageous at the end, with philosophers in attendance: the Greek Coeranus and Musonius the Etruscan. A model and a lesson, breeding corroborated by doctrine—and not the sort of character Juvenal could use. The satirist presents for the scorn and delectation of his readers another Rubellius, the archetype of the stupid and incompetent aristocrat. He is a Rubellius Blandus, a son of Julia:

> his ego quem monui? tecum est mihi sermo, Rubelli
> Blande, tumes alto Drusorum stemmate, tamquam
> feceris ipse aliquid, propter quod nobilis esses,
> ut te conciperet quae sanguine fulget Iuli.
>
> (viii 39–42)

Blandus exhibits no merit in any arts of peace or war, only pedigree. He has neither hands nor feet, he resembles a stone image, a herm:

>   at tu
> nil nisi Cecropides truncoque simillimus Hermae.
> nullo quippe alio vincis discrimine quam quod
> illi marmoreum caput est, tua vivit imago.
> dic mihi, Teucrorum proles, animalia muta
> quis generosa putet nisi fortia?
>
> (viii 52–7)

In short, a lump of living statuary. If Juvenal is given credit, Blandus is a deleterious brother of the exemplary Plautus, an addition to the stemma of the Rubellii. The poem, be it noted, is strongly Neronian in tone, in matter, in personal names.

The inept *nobilis* is not certified outside the pages of Juvenal. He may well be genuine—decayed families survive unrecorded by historians or by the consular *Fasti*. Yet he might be only a plausible and malignant invention. To men who wrote under Trajan and Hadrian, | in recent memory of the brief and calamitous reign of Nerva, the claims of aristocracy, old and new, and the antithesis between *virtus* and pedigree, that was a theme of contemporary moment. The name 'Rubellius' bore a peculiar significance for a satirist, or for a historian.

Juvenal's choice of names demands careful scrutiny. Indeed, a full analysis is desirable.[110] There are traps for the unwary. In this satire he addresses a 'Ponticus' (viii 1, cf. 74 ff.); and a 'Creticus' comes in (38). They have been acclaimed as degenerate descendants of illustrious houses.[111] In fact, no *nobilis* had taken 'Ponticus' as a triumphal *cognomen*, and the Metelli were extinct long since.

Referring to characters in recent history, Juvenal normally employs a single name, as witness the ten members of Domitian's council in Satire IV. Apart from Rubellius Blandus, there are four exceptions. Rubrenus Lappa (vii 72) is defined as a dramatic poet; and Carrinas Secundus (viii 264 f.) is on ready identity. Nor is there cause for questioning Crepereius Pollio (ix 6 f.) as a person of some notoriety. Observe Crepereius Gallus (the companion of Agrippina), who perished when the vessel collapsed in the Bay of Naples.[112] Finally, Volusius Bithynicus, the friend to whom Juvenal dedicated one of his last poems (xv 1).

Rubellius Blandus therefore may be assumed a known figure in Roman society, a brother of Plautus, and perhaps named in the *Historiae* of Cornelius Tacitus.[113] That author would not miss the death of Junia Calvina in 79, the last in the descent from Divus Augustus. When the doors of the Mausoleum sprang open, Vespasian was not dismayed. The portent, he said, pertained to Junia Calvina.[114]

---

[110] See meanwhile the excursus in G. Highet, *Juvenal the Satirist* (1954), 289–94. For brief comments, *AJP* c (1979), 256 ff. = *RP* iii (1984), 1140 f.

[111] G. Highet, op. cit. 272 (Ponticus); 63 and 293 f. (Creticus).

[112] *Ann.* xiv 5, 1 To be presumed identical with, or related to, the imperial procurator C. Crepereius Gallus, cf. B. Levick and S. Jameson, *JRS* liv (1964), 98, whence *AE* 1964, 173 (Pisidian Antioch).

[113] Further, possibly the consul suffect in the pair 'Blandus et Pollio' (*CIL* vi 14221). But Blandus may have left a son by an earlier marriage.

[114] Suetonius, *Divus Vesp.* 23, 4. Calvina was a daughter of M. Silanus M. f. (*cos.* 19) and Aemilia Lepida.

M. Cocceius Nerva was produced somehow or other as emperor after the assassination of Domitian. Not a person of character or talent. | The line of the Cocceii (the grandfather and the father), had exhibited eminent jurists, but Nerva did nothing to perpetuate the tradition. His nobility was not Republican—the Cocceii derive from the Triumviral period—but conspicuous, now that four generations had passed since the Battle of Actium, sparse indeed being the old families that outlasted the first dynasty. Nerva himself had been a figure at Court and in high society, extravagantly honoured by Nero after the conspiracy of Piso.[115] Vespasian conferred on him an eponymous consulate, Domitian a second. Further, a link with the line of Caesar Augustus can be discovered, though not of consanguinity—his maternal uncle Octavius Laenas had married Rubellia Bassa, daughter of Blandus and of Julia.[116] Nerva already possessed the qualities, none of them resplendent, that made him an attractive candidate. How far the identity of his aunt by marriage can have counted is a question that must elude answer. Something was made of it when it had ceased to matter. The ashes of Nerva were consigned to the Mausoleum of the Caesars.[117]

When he had reigned for not much more than twelve months, Nerva adopted as his son and successor M. Ulpius Traianus, the legate of Germania Superior. That Nerva should have passed over his next of kin in favour of Trajan will surprise only those who fancy his action a free decision.[118] The hand of the political managers and the allies of the army commanders is surmised.[119] If pedigree and social prestige account for the elevation of Nerva, those prescriptions were firmly set aside in favour of the *virtus* of the new nobility when Trajan was chosen and imposed as emperor.

Nerva was effete and obsolete. The Italian *novi homines* had run their course. The Cocceii came from the old Latin colony of Narnia, in the south of the Umbrian country, the Octavii Laenates were Marsian, the Rubellii Tiburtine. Tacitus speaks for his own class, the magnates of Transpadana, Narbonensis, and Spain. If the message is often covert | and oblique, being disguised by Republican themes in his *Annales* and by his predilection for the 'magna nomina', it

---

[115] *Ann.* xv 72, 1 (*ornamenta triumphalia* and a *statua triumphalis* in the Forum).
[116] *ILS* 952, cf. above.   [117] *Epit.* xii, 10.
[118] Kinsmen are mentioned in Dio lxviii 4, 1. Nerva when emperor paid public honour to his mother Sergia Plautilla (*ILS* 281). Her brother, Octavius Laenas, married Rubellia Bassa, their son leaves no trace; he was first cousin to Nerva.
One of the *suffecti* of 97 was 'Se[', the colleague of Domitius Apollinaris (*AE* 1954, 220). Possibly a Sergius Octavius Laenas, better Sex. Hermetidius Campanus attested as legate of Judaea in December of 93 (*CIL* xvi, App. no. 12). On this question cf. *JRS* xliv (1954), 81 f.
[119] For this conception, *Tacitus* (1958), 13 ff.; 35 f.

sometimes emerges in a startling fashion. The indignation he proclaims at the misalliance of Julia the granddaughter of Tiberius Caesar seems exaggerated.

Tacitus emphasizes the equestrian grandfather, but is silent about the station of Blandus' father. Now another commoner had married a princess in the same year, M. Vinicius (*cos.* 30). How much better was he than Rubellius? The father and the grandfather of Vinicius had been consuls, but his extraction was municipal, from Cales in Campania (vi 15, 1). The facts are given, but extenuated. Anger is absent. Very different the comment on the marriage of Julia.

The placing of the item will furnish instruction. Tacitus carefully explained the death of the consular Cocceius Nerva, who, tired of life and tired of six years with Tiberius on the island, resolved to make an end by starvation, despite earnest entreaty from his friend (26, 1 f.). Then, after brief report about the extinction of Agrippina and Plancina (26, 3), he proceeds, with 'tot luctibus funesta civitate', to insert the marriage of Blandus and Julia (27, 1), and passes to the decease of the Prefect of the City, Aelius Lamia, 'extremo anni' (27, 2). Tacitus thus disjoins Julia from the other princesses (Drusilla and Livilla) with whose marriages the year opened (15, 1). The source followed by Cassius Dio grouped the three together, although not in initial prominence, and of them naming only Julia. They come up in sequence to a journey of Tiberius to the near vicinity of Rome.[120]

The disjunction operated by Cornelius Tacitus lodges the marriage of Blandus and Julia in a melancholy context—'pars maeroris fuit.' The consular historian (*suff.* 97) cannot be acquitted of a malicious design. He indulged in a subversive attack upon the pretensions of the Italian aristocracy in his own day. It has something to do with Nerva.

Similarly Juvenal. That he should set upon a relative of Nerva when launching his invective against birth and pedigree is by no means inappropriate. He lays emphasis on the dynastic blood of his Rubellius Blandus,

> tumes alto Drusorum stemmata, tamquam
> feceris ipse aliquid propter quod nobilis esses
> ut te conciperent quae sanguine fulget Iuli.
>
> (viii 40–42) |

He forgot, if he ever knew, how recent was the nobility of the Rubellii. Juvenal declaims about plebeian talent, eloquence coming

---

[120] Dio lviii 21, 1 (but cf. p. 233, below). In Tacitus the Emperor's absence from Capreae is first alluded to lower down: 'deviis plerumque itineribus ambiens patriam et declinans' (vi 15, 3). At the beginning of the previous year he got as far as the gardens beside the Tiber (vi 1).

out of the people, and a base-born advocate who might plead in the
courts on behalf of a dumb aristocrat and elucidate the law:

> gaudia longa feras, tamen ima plebe Quiritem
> facundum invenies, solet hic defendere causas
> nobilis indocti; veniet de plebe togata
> qui iuris nodos et legum aenigmata solvat.

> (47–50)

The satirist makes his point. He might have sharpened it with a
reference to the origin of the Rubellii. Juvenal's Rubellius Blandus is
not just any incompetent scion of the nobility. Luxury and torpor
dishonour the 'bonae artes' of an energetic ancestor, the municipal
knight who taught the art of public speech.

12

Tacitus: Some Sources of his Information

W HEN a consular turned to the writing of history he had full years of experience behind him; and the reminiscences of elderly survivors, not missed by an alert youth, carried a man nearly a century into the past. The mass of knowledge thus accruing has not always been taken into account by adepts of *Quellenforschung*.

A senator's employment could hardly fail to affect his beliefs and opinions. It might be expected to leave traces here and there in his writings. For Cornelius Tacitus ascertainment comes against impediments: reticence all through. He even proclaimed a distaste for 'iactantia' when adducing his praetorship and priesthood on the occasion of the Ludi Saeculares held in 88.[1] For occupations abroad he chose to reveal only the four years' absence from Rome not long after that season.[2] That disclosure was likewise made in strict relevance to his theme. The command of a legion will be assumed without discomfort.

That is not all. As with other new entrants to the *amplissimus ordo*, a military tribunate should be conceded, about the year 76. Anything further will tend to be deprecated by those who cling to a traditional verdict ('the most unmilitary of historians') or neglect the contemporaneous evidence about the consular legates selected to govern the nine armed provinces in the portion of Caesar.

Polite accomplishments (it is no secret) were high on show, attested by Licinius Sura and Sosius Senecio; and Fabius Justus, the friend of Tacitus and disciple in eloquence, went on to hold two of the eminent commands.[3] The case of the jurist Neratius Priscus is instructive, consul suffect in 97, the same year as Cornelius Tacitus. The recent revision of a familiar inscription brings novelty and a welcome surprise. Priscus, it emerges, had Germania Inferior soon after his consulship (?98–101), before proceeding to Pannonia.[4]

[1] Tacitus, *Ann.* xi 11, 1. [2] *Agr.* 45, 5.
[3] In 97 or 98 Justus (*suff.* 102) was absent from Rome (Pliny, *Ep.* i 11, 2), presumably as legionary legate; and with the armies in 105 or 106 (vii 2, 1 f.). That is, legate of Moesia Inferior (105–8) before going to Syria.
[4] *ILS* 1034 (Saepinum): the second of the two consulars whose careers are there briefly registered. See G. Camodeca, *AAN* lxxxvii (1976), 19 ff., whence *AE* 1976, 195. Instead of

Another document carried his whole career, beginning with a tribunate.[5] It is fragmentary and supplies space for the command of a legion and for another praetorian post.

In the sequel to the famous prosecution conducted to its termination early in 100 by Tacitus and Pliny, Tacitus finds no mention in the correspondence of the friend for about four years. In 104 or 105 a letter welcomes his return to Rome from a journey: 'salvum in urbem venisse gaudeo' (iv 13, 1). The phrase indicates a journey of some length.[6] Absence abroad was not unwelcome to one who, perhaps the foremost speaker of the time, renounced public oratory after the trial of Marius Priscus. It may be noted (though not as proof) that a prosecution in the early spring of 103 registers the names of five consulars participant (iv 9).

In this season Germania Inferior was held by Q. Acutius Nerva (*suff.* 100), the successor to L. Neratius Priscus.[7] For the other command on the Rhine, no evidence. Both had forfeited their former military primacy, being now reduced to two legions. The other gap is Moesia Superior, conveniently to be assigned to Sosius Senecio.[8]

A historian requires a spell of free time and continuous leisure, as Cicero pointed out when under earnest solicitation: 'historia vero nec institui potest nisi praeparato otio nec exiguo tempore absolvi'. A 'legatio libera' or some other form of 'cessatio libera atque otiosa' was just the thing, so his friend opined.[9] For Cornelius Tacitus the cares and duties of a provincial governor (often overestimated by the incurious) would be no bar. Rather the reverse, and a relief from tedious sessions in the Senate, the demands of social life, and the importunity of eager disciples.

'P[annonia]/inferiore et Pannonia [superiore]' Camodeca reads '[in provinc. Germania]/ inferiore et Pannonia'. The consequences are momentous and multiple, cf. remarks in *ZPE* xli (1981), 140 f. = *RP* iii (1984), 1389 f. Among them abolition of L. Neratius Priscus, governor of Pannonia Inferior and of Pannonia Superior in the reign of Hadrian. That is, *PIR*[1], N 47: accepted in *Hermes* lxxv (1958), 480 ff. = *RP* (1979), 338 ff., and elsewhere.

The two Neratii of *ILS* 1034, father and son, are the *suffecti* of 87 and 97. For the family stemma see now L. Vidman, *ZPE* xliii (1981), 377 ff.

[5] Published by O. Freda, *Contributi dell' Ist. di Fil. Class.* i (Milan, 1963), 239, whence *AE* 1969/70, 252 (Larinum). Both inadequate, as Freda's photograph (pl. 2) demonstrates.

[6] As proposed in Tacitus (1958), 71. Rejected by Sherwin-White in his *Commentary* (1966), 286, with a remark (highly pertinent) about the dangers of Italian travel. He further states that Tacitus' 'career as an advocate was in full swing'. The passage adduced is merely 'copia studiosorum quae ad te admiratione ingenii tui convenit' (iv 13, 10).

[7] *PIR*[2], A 101 (citing legionary tiles).

[8] Sosius (*cos.* 99) was in command of an army *c.*103 (*Ep.* iv 4). The Rhine would be a backwater for a man who went on to earn a 'statua triumphalis' and a second consulship (in 107). To Sosius (not to Sura) may belong the acephalous *ILS* 1022, cf. C. P. Jones, *JRS* lx (1970), 98 ff.

[9] Cicero, *De legibus* i 9 f.

Cicero and Atticus had contemporary annals in mind. The *Historiae* of Tacitus set out with the year 69 and much military narration. The original design embraced the fifteen years of Domitian. How much (if anything) Tacitus had written before changing the point of inception is a question that might come into account somewhere (as touching the time and rhythm of composition), but there is no call to obtrude this unknown factor.

Likewise unverifiable is a governorship in Germania Superior. However, the Helvetian episode invited inspection, for what is said—and for what is omitted (i 67–9). Omissions in a selective author are not to be taken as proof of ignorance. They may be caused by sheer familiarity with the theme or with the persons involved. For example, Tacitus nowhere alludes to the Narbonensian *patria* of Afranius Burrus.

In this episode the narrator decided to single out three notables of the Helvetii. He states that Caecina punished with death 'Iulium Alpinum e principibus ut concitorem belli'; and in conclusion he puts in prominence the artful performance of the eloquent Claudius Cossus. But nothing about the Helvetian general Claudius Severus, save that their levies made a poor showing in the field 'although they had chosen Claudius Severus to lead them'. No annotation is vouchsafed, such as service or exploits in the imperial armies to explain this general. He is treated as a known character.[10]

To revert to facts or dates in foreign occupations of the consular historian. Only the proconsulate in Asia is on attestation: an inscription assigned to the tenure 112/13.

Traces of the sojourn in Asia have been sought in the *Annales*. First, Germanicus Caesar consulting the oracle at Claros (ii 54, 2 ff.).[11] The procedure is described, with the detail that the officiant was not a prophetess as elsewhere but a man, drawn from certain families at Miletus. The historian, a *quindecimvir* for a quarter of a century, and custodian of the Sibylline Books, would not neglect Apollo's sanctuary. After long decadence, Claros had now revived to high fame. Trajan on his journey to Syria in the autumn of 113 may have applied to the oracle.[12]

Second, Rhodes. Coming upon the ruler's addiction to the science of the stars (at a late stage, through the prediction about Galba, the

[10] See further *MH* xxxiv (1977), 135 ff. = *RP* iii (1984), 991 ff. The alternative explanation is inadvertent copying of an excellent source.

[11] C. Cichorius, *Römische Studien* (1922), 386 f.: followed in *Tacitus* (1958), 469 f. 'All pure speculation, and in part, since this book was probably written by A.D. 112, misguided', so F. R. D. Goodyear observes in his *Commentary*, ii (1981), 359.

[12] Cf. Macrobius i 23, 14 ff. (the oracle at Heliopolis).

consul of 33), Tacitus recounts how Tiberius once subjected Thrasyllus to ordeal during a stroll along the cliffs: an astrologer found fraudulent met his fate after he returned, 'per avia ac derupta'. Tacitus adds the situation of the residence itself: 'nam saxis domus imminet' (vi 21, 1). Not essential for the story, the cliffs being already mentioned. The formulation looks like autopsy.[13]

A third sign can be evoked, not perceived by commentators on the event. Namely the earthquake which in 17 afflicted twelve cities of Asia, the severest in human memory according to Pliny.[14] Before cataloguing the cities and the measures of relief from the government (among them the mission of a senator of praetorian rank), Tacitus introduces the chapter with remarks of a general nature. The calamity struck during the hours of darkness. The normal habit of rushing out of doors was precluded by chasms that opened up. And a further particular: 'sedisse immensos montes, visa in arduo quae plana fuerint, effulsisse inter ruinam ignes memorant' (ii 47, 1).

The word 'memorant' and the tense should arouse some interest, no persons having previously been specified. Oral information therefore, perhaps from ostensible centenarians whose predilection it was to parade in front of travellers. In Britain Marcus Aper | encountered a native who avowed that he had fought against Julius Caesar; and Mucianus, visiting the island of Samothrace, saw Zocles, who at the age of 104 had grown a new set of teeth.[15]

The list of cities calls for passing annotation. It leads off with the principal sufferers, the Sardiani and the 'Magnetes a Sipylo'. After the next four occur 'quique Mosteni aut Macedones Hyrcani vocantur' (47, 3). At first sight the word 'aut' might appear misleading. No call, however, to emend to 'et'. The two communities stand in a certain antithesis (as a proconsul in his tour of duty might learn). Hyrcanis, the city of the Hyrcani, went back to the Persian period. The Seleucids introduced further colonists, as the label proclaims.[16] By contrast, Mostene. This city was proud to advertise an autochthonous origin by the Lydian name on its coinage and the emblem of the double axe.[17]

A small item of Asian toponymy will be suitably subjoined to this rubric. In the course of the year 22 the Senate heard a whole

[13] As briefly suggested in *Tacitus* (1958), 469.   [14] Pliny, *NH* ii 200.
[15] Tacitus, *Dial.* 17, 4; Pliny, *NH* xi 162.
[16] Pliny, *NH* v 120. For the Hyrcanian Plain, Strabo xii 629. For the site of Hyrcanis, L. Robert, *Hellenica* vi (1948), 16 ff. (with criticism of A. H. M. Jones).

    In the dedication set up by grateful cities in A.D. 30 (*ILS* 156: Puteoli) 'Hyrca[nis]' should be substituted for 'Hyrca[nia]'.

[17] Head, *HN*², 653 f.; Keil, *RE* xvi 379 f. For the site, L. Robert, *Bull. ép.* 1958, no. 433. Commentators, adequate or even ample on the familiar, neglect Mostene.

congregation of embassies from the cities asserting ancient privileges of asylum for their sanctuaries (iii 60–3). The Magnetes (i.e. Magnesia on the Maeander, as the historian did not need to specify) relied on decrees of L. Scipio and L. Sulla recognizing the shrine of Artemis: in the manuscript, 'Dianae Leucophinae perfugium' (62, 1). Recent editors have been content to print 'Leucophrynae'.[18] Beroaldus saw the plain remedy ages ago: 'Leucophryenae', which three Greek authors enjoin.[19]

A legitimate doubt may arise whether the correct form of a name, certified by other writers (and by coins or inscriptions), should be inserted into a text: the author was perhaps in error, not a scribe. About 'Thubuscum' (iv 24, 1) no doubt subsists. The town is patently Thubursicu (in Numidia). In the present instance the accurate Tacitus should not be defrauded.[20]

Not much on the score of autopsy or special knowledge, some will duly object. A large problem of a different order is in cause and dispute. Only a brief statement can here be accorded.[21]

Tacitus brought the *Historiae* to completion about the year 109, so it is generally held. Hence an interval before he resumed his labours when he came back from Asia in the summer of 113. That has been a fairly common assumption. The contrary thesis cuts down the interval and even abolishes it: Tacitus began the *Annales* in 109—or even in 108.[22] It has been lavishly expounded in the recent time. The main argument turns on the interpretation of a single passage in Book II. Germanicus Caesar in his peregrination reached the frontier of Egypt, 'Elephantinen ac Syenen, claustra olim Romani imperii quod nunc rubrum ad mare patescit' (61, 2). To Lipsius, to Gibbon, and to others in the sequel, the emphatic language, echoing Virgil, or oratorical pronouncements in Livy about the expanse of eastern empires, indicated Trajan's conquest of Mesopotamia in 116. For 'rubrum mare' the other side advocates not the Persian Gulf but the other inlet of the Indian Ocean, namely the Red Sea. Rome had recently annexed the kingdom of the Nabataean Arabs (in 105/6).[23] |

---

[18] H. Fuchs (1946); E. Koestermann (ed. 2, 1965).

[19] Strabo xiv 629; Pausanias iii 18, 9; Appian *BC* v 34 (who put the shrine at Miletus).

[20] *JRS* xxxviii (1948), 124 (in review of Fuchs): 'Tacitus should have known, having been proconsul of Asia'.

[21] In this matter as in others, economy enjoins a restriction of references—mainly to books or papers published in the last twenty-five years.

[22] Thus J. Beaujeu, *REL* xxxviii (1960), 232: 'commencées en 108–109'.

[23] The thesis is generously expounded by J. Beaujeu, *REL* xxxviii (1960), 200–35 and by F. R. D. Goodyear in his *Commentary*, ii (1981), 387–93. For five other proponents of the Nabataean thesis (since 1958), see *Ten Studies in Tacitus* (1970), 144 f.

The controversy finds a clear statement in S. Borzsák, *RE, Suppl.* xi 467 ff.

There is an inescapable corollary to the 'traditional view'. It entails belief (hence vulnerable) that the phrase 'quod . . . patescit' is an addition made by the author after he had finished either the first triad of the *Annales* or the first hexad.[24]

Additions enforced by subsequent knowledge are not beyond surmise. For example, in the comments on Tiberius' departure from Rome in 26. A sentence alluding to Rhodes and secret vice was misplaced (iv 57, 2).[25] It looks like an insertion by the author.[26]

Persian Gulf or Red Sea, the controversial topic ought not to be reserved or abridged in this place without considering the other two passages adduced for relevance. When Germanicus enters Armenia, Tacitus offers a statement summarizing the condition of that country at the time, regarded as permanent. Thus 'ambigua gens ea antiquitus'; and the Armenians are 'maximisque imperiis interiecti' (ii 56, 1). A description of this kind (it may be noted) could hardly have been avoided by the author, even if composed while Trajan was invading Armenia in 114. To allude to a sudden change in the status of Armenia would disturb the exposition of past events. The passage is relevant to what it describes and elucidates.

The author ran into trouble soon after, when explaining provinces and armies in Book IV. He then saw that he had to leave out the name of Armenia. After mentioning the functions of the army of Syria he proceeds 'accolis Hibero Albanoque et aliis regibus qui magnitudine nostra proteguntur adversum externa imperia' (iv 5, 2). As it stands, that passage must have been indited in or after the year 114. Precise detail (Iberia and Albania as Roman neighbours and vassals) combines with deliberate and portentous vagueness.

The two passages (in II and IV) provide a 'terminus ante quem', before 114, so it is contended.[27] Whatever be thought of the first, the second (Armenia not named) may be taken to imply the contrary.[28]

So far argumentation based on the text of the author. Two theses stand in sharp contradiction. Consensus or recantation being remote (but not the danger of fatigue or wilful nescience), the temptation occurs to try something else.[29]

In 108 or 109 Cornelius Tacitus (*suff.* 97) stood in near prospect of

[24] E. Koestermann in his *Commentary* (1963), 371.

[25] J. P. V. D. Balsdon, *CR* lxi (1937), 44 f.

[26] *Tacitus* (1958), 675, adducing for parallel *Ann.* i 4, 4.

[27] Goodyear, op. cit., 390.

[28] As argued in *Historiographia Antiqua* (Louvain, 1977), 260 f. = *RP* iii (1984), 1039 f. (in a restatement of the thesis).

[29] Brought up in *Historiographia Antiqua* 232 f. Not previously conceded a factor to admit or repulse.

a proconsulate in Asia or Africa. Those proconsulates are the peak of a senator's ambition, whatever be his previous career. Some, it is true, lacked keen incentive. Thus, among the consuls of Tacitus' year Annius Verus, of a tranquil and Epicurean disposition. Again, the two consular commands held by Neratius Priscus might be considered by others, or by himself, as eminence enough. Agents of the government persuaded Julius Agricola to withdraw from the sortition. They might have invoked the seven years in Britain and the grant of the *ornamenta triumphalia*, not conceded by Domitian to other generals, so far as known.

The list for Asia is complete for a long stretch after 103/4.[30] Not so Africa, but there is no sign that either Annius Verus or Neratius Priscus went there. Verus, had he wished, was a strong candidate, being close to the core of an influential nexus of alliances, which he proceeded to reinforce.

The only thing to deter Cornelius Tacitus was a second consulate, not likely perhaps from Trajan.[31] For Asia or Africa he had favourable prospects. The government inclined to honour civilian excellence as well as birth or military merit.

The interval after a consulship had recently become stable, at thirteen years. Tacitus could look forward to the tenure 110/11. Nonius Asprenas, the consul of 94, duly acceded to Asia for 107/8. A perturbation now impinged. Two of the *suffecti* went in succession to Asia, viz. Lollius Paullinus and A. Julius Quadratus: the former one of the high aristocrats, the latter a close friend of the Emperor, and anomalous because of his second consulship (in 105). |

The interval thus advanced to fifteen years, as shown by the next two proconsuls of Asia before the turn of Tacitus arrived, *suffecti* in 95 and 96. What is known of Africa confirms, viz. Q. Pomponius Rufus (*suff.* 95) in 110/11, C. Pomponius Rufus (*suff.* 98) in 113/14.[32] As these facts demonstrate, Cornelius Tacitus had to wait, until 112. In 108 or 109 he still had a rational prospect of going out as proconsul in the summer of 110.

It might appear dubious whether a writer in this season, instead of welcoming a respite and the enjoyment of fame, would be impelled to go on at once to another task, of magnitude and much more arduous, since narrating the past demands 'onerosa collatio', as the friend observed (*Ep.* v 8, 12). However, let that be waived. Who can

[30] W. Eck, *Senatoren von Vespasian bis Hadrian* (1970), 236.

[31] Nor the Prefecture of the City, which normally comported a second consulship. The double anomaly is the inconspicuous Q. Baebius Macer (*suff.* 103), in office when Trajan died (*HA Hadr.* 5, 5). The next *praefectus urbi* is Annius Verus (*cos. II* 121).

[32] Proconsulates dated by *IRT* 353; *ILAlg* i 1230.

tell? Nor will it be profitable to indulge in surmise about the author's time of life, his health or his temperament, or assume a rhythm for his writing, all of which, although seductive and not to be declined if the performance of a poet or historian is under assessment, should give way before the search for facts and for security of judgement.

The age of Tacitus has been adduced, it is true, to support the early date for the inception of the *Annales*.[33] On the other side, an entertaining and subversive parallel might be called up. Livy's prose epic devoted to the 'res populi Romani' found crown and culmination (so it can be argued) in the end of all the wars and the triple triumph of Caesar's heir in 29 B.C., with for sequel the nine books embracing the Republic down to 9 B.C., a point of termination not fortuitous but likewise a climax. That epilogue became a secure and attractive project in A.D. 4 when after a decade of seclusion Claudius Nero emerged to become Ti. Caesar.[34]

Livy's age is a question. Drawing on Suetonius, Jerome put his birth in 59 B.C., equated with Messalla Corvinus.[35] Wrong for Messalla, as was discovered nearly a century ago.[36] The consequences for the Patavine annalist were slow to percolate.[37] If 64 be accepted, the year of Messalla (*cos.* 31), Livy in A.D. 4 was aged about sixty-seven. When Cornelius Tacitus came back from Asia in 113 he was a dozen years younger.

From a digression in no way essential to the argument it will afford relief to revert to the *Annales*. First of all, a general impression not to be anxiously avoided if it comes straight out of the writing without solicitation. Beginning with the demise of Augustus, the historian had not devoted much time and study to the concluding decade of the reign. He was eager to break free from the metropolitan scene and embark on military narrative. The mutinies in Pannonia and on the Rhine and the ensuing campaigns of Germanicus gave scope for eloquence and drama, expounded in lavish and picturesque detail. They take up the greater part of Book I. That theme carries on into the next book, and the story of Germanicus soon resumes, amply related: a unitary narration, although exacting much more care and selection than the campaigns, where a single source might furnish most of the material. Before he had gone very far the historian became aware that the decision to begin with the death of Caesar

---

[33] Goodyear, op. cit. 388, concluding 'if T. finished the *Histories* by 108 or not much later, it would be surprising he should abandon history for five years or more.'

[34] For these estimates, *HCSPh* lxiv (1959), 27 ff. = *RP* (1979), 400 ff.

[35] Jerome, *Chron.* 164 H.

[36] H. Schulz, *De Valerii Messallae aetate* (Progr. Stettin, 1886), 6.

[37] No hint of the problem in *PIR*[2], L 292.

Augustus carried grave disadvantages. Leading topics ran continuous, such as the German war, the condition of the armies, complications in the eastern lands, prosecution for *maiestas*, senior consulars of weight and eminence, scandal in the dynasty. Many episodes and persons had echo and resonance backwards.

Coming upon a transaction in the Senate which evoked the banishment of the younger Julia, Tacitus could not refrain from making an announcement that contravenes his normal reticence: he would go back and recount that epoch, if life be vouchsafed (iii 24, 2). The declaration indicates that the writer, in whatever terms age be reckoned or held relevant, was robust and confident, imbibing energy and delight from the congenial task. |

Direct disclosures are not to be expected, and genius is elusive. How Tacitus worked upon his material is another matter. It should not baffle ascertainment. Content and structure reveal.

In the past, enquiry has been bedevilled either by analysis over-literary or by *Quellenforschung* often misapplied through pre-occupation with the theory of 'a single source'. Revulsion from which produced a firm challenge: the only single source pervading the first hexad is the *acta senatus*.[38] Another controversy therefore. The theme is large, it comports much detail. Concision will enhance clarity.

First, the orations and despatches of Tiberius Caesar. They declare the ruler in his manner, style, and language.[39] Further, the language influences the context. Whence derive these versions, from the *acta* or from a separate collection?

Of the reading matter of a later emperor it was averred 'praeter commentarios et acta Tiberi Caesaris nihil lectitabat.'[40] The passage gets put to constant employ. An item from Cassius Dio happens to be less in evidence. Among the ceremonies of the opening year certain orations of Augustus and of Tiberius were read out, to the fatigue and distress of senators, detained until evening. Claudius Caesar abolished the practice.[41]

Some scholars boldly and briefly postulate a published collection. Others hesitate about the *acta*, or deprecate.[42] One of them is impelled to restrict rigorously the historian's use of the Tiberian speeches.[43] Not all bother to cast their glance forward in the *Annales*

---

[38] *Tacitus* (1958), 278.   [39] N. P. Miller, 'Tiberius Speaks', *AJP* lxxxix (1968), 1 ff.
[40] Suetonius, *Dom.* 20.   [41] Dio lx 10, 2.
[42] B. Levick, *Tiberius the Politician* (1976), 222. And for R. H. Martin 'possibly in the *acta senatus*' (*Tacitus* (1981), 200).
[43] For D. Flach Tacitus used 'bestenfalls' only two 'Senatsreden' of the Princeps. He cited *Ann.* i 81, 1 and ii 63, 3 (*Athenaeum* li (1973), 92).

and consider the renderings of Claudius Caesar—and a discussion of the sources for that reign allocates scant notice to imperial orations in relation to Tacitus.[44]

Reflection will suggest that the hypothesis of collected and published orations is highly vulnerable. Of interest to enlightened students of oratorical style, such as was Cornelius Tacitus all through, they would be of imperfect value to a historian without the whole context, without the transactions that evoked them (sometimes casual or trivial) and the results (if any). He needed the *acta*.[45]

Next, structure and content. Continuous segments carry the report of senatorial business, interlarded with comment from the writer. For the year 15 the parallel with Cassius Dio is instructive. Dio went back to one of the annalistic predecessors of Tacitus who had made a selection notably different, and inferior in point and value.[46]

Significant for use of the *acta* are debates that resume after an interval. Even more so those which led to no conclusion. The choice of personal names is variously instructive. After the condemnation of Libo Drusus in 16, seven men of rank came out with proposals for revenge or for public thanksgivings (ii 32, 1 f.). At the head stands Cotta Messallinus, the younger son of Corvinus: the earliest entrance of an aristocrat whom Tacitus took care to indict for subservience later on. Cotta Messallinus gets placed first, before ex-consuls, although he was praetor-designate at the time.[47]

By contrast, obscure persons on solitary mention and sometimes in minor transactions. They certify research and documentation.

Because of the design he adopted for the Tiberian hexad, the historian had need of much material for Book III. Previous annalists marked a turn for the worse after the death of Germanicus Caesar.[48] Tacitus decided to postpone the declension and begin the second half of the hexad with the rise of Aelius Seianus. After the prosecution of Cn. Piso early in 20, he had to fill out undramatic annals down to the end of 22.

The challenge was gladly taken. The *acta* offered abundance, and freedom of choice.[49] | The selection in Book III discloses interests or

[44] D. Flach, *MH* xxx (1973), 101.
[45] By contrast Quintilian. The professor of rhetoric nowhere cited Asconius for the historical setting of Ciceronian orations. (His two references to Pedianus (i 7, 24; v 10, 9) were neglected in *CQ* xxxi (1981), 426 = *RP* iii (1984), 1421).
[46] A detailed comparison for 15 (and also for 16) is presented in *Gedenkschrift Pflaum, ZPE* xliii (1981), 365 f. = *RP* iii (1984), 1423 ff.
[47] The fragmentary name of Cotta can be discerned on the *Fasti Arvalium* (*Inscr. It.* xiii 1, p. 297).
[48] As emerges from Suetonius, *Cal.* 6, 2; Dio lvii 7, 1 f.; 13, 6; 19, 1.
[49] For a catalogue, *Historiographia Antiqua* (1977), 248 = *RP* iii (1984), 1028 f.

preoccupations of the author, among them sacerdotal antiquities and the condition of Gaul.

Africa and Asia conveyed personal concern for a consular. One episode explains how the sortition might be discussed or managed, how the Princeps intervened to secure a desired or suitable candidate. When warfare renewed in Africa, Caesar in a letter pointed out the need for careful selection (iii 32, 1). Asia then came into debate, the occasion being exploited by a consular for a personal attack on Manius Lepidus—who, defended by senators, was allowed to have that province. At the next meeting a despatch from Tiberius put forward two names for the senate to choose between: Marcus Lepidus and Junius Blaesus. Lepidus drew back on various pleas, and Africa went to the uncle of Seianus (iii 35).

Asia engrosses attention with the full-length prosecution of a proconsul (iii 66–8), the earliest in the *Annales*. It leads on to the helpful proposal of Cornelius Dolabella: no person 'vita probrosus et opertus infamia' should be admitted to the sortition, the Princeps to adjudicate. Tiberius sent a firm and sagacious answer, deprecating moral inquisition or regimentation (iii 69).

Asia also claims a long debate on its sanctuaries, with a plethora of names and of precedents from the old time. It afforded the high assembly a welcome 'imaginem antiquitatis' (iii 60–3).

Asia deserved high prominence in senatorial debates—and no proof that a recent proconsul reflects and renews his experiences. However that may be, those who advocate an earlier inception for the *Annales* have not been able to adduce any break in the exposition or any sudden novelties that could be ascribed to the year of the proconsulate.

Although a case may appear clear and valid in its own right, there is no harm in lending support on the flank, from negative indications. That is, things neglected by Tacitus because not to be found in the annual register. Phenomena of contrasted types cannot escape attention.

First, the Guard Prefect Seius Strabo departing to govern Egypt in 15 or 16, not long after he had been assigned his son as partner in that office.[50] Important, as revealing a stage in the rising ambitions of Aelius Seianus—and favour and confidence from the ruler. Imperial appointments would not normally be entered on the senate's protocol.[51] Hence facts or persons missing. It would be worth

[50] Dio lvii 19, 16 (apparently under A.D. 20).
[51] Poppaeus Sabinus, prorogued in Moesia, occurs because Achaia and Macedonia were then added to his province (i 80, 1).

knowing at what precise juncture began the absentee governorships of Aelius Lamia and L. Arruntius (in Syria and in Tarraconensis) which were noted under the year 33 (vi 27). Before censuring the historian, caution intervenes. Tacitus might have reserved Strabo's supersession in command of the Guard for more effective use later on, in relation to Seianus. Most of Book V is lost. It may not have omitted Strabo's successor in Egypt, C. Galerius, now terminating by death at sea a tenure of sixteen years.[52]

Second, noteworthy consulars on mention seldom or never. L. Piso was Prefect of the City for long years until his death in 32, and his personality conveyed amicable appeal to the author. Piso appears in the Senate only once (iii 68, 2). By the same token his successor in office: Aelius Lamia had made only one entrance, of no great moment (iv 13, 3). The reason is clear. These excellent men seldom raised their voices in the Senate. Likewise the next Prefect, Cossus Cornelius Lentulus, a 'vir triumphalis' but receiving no farewell notice from Tacitus when he died late in the reign.[53]

A diverse character and a different phenomenon will explain total silence about Domitius Ahenobarbus until the obituary in 25 (iv 44, 2). The husband of the elder Antonia was sullen, recalcitrant, or early senescent.[54]

Third, particulars about the private life and habits of Tiberius Caesar, and his earlier existence. Late awareness of his addiction to astrology has already been noted. Late also | the significance of Rhodes, so it can be argued. That is, on the hypothesis that an allusion in Book I to Rhodes and secret vice (i 4, 4), which interrupts a sequence bearing on pride and power, is a subsequent insertion (like iv 57, 2).

Indeed, growing interest in the person of the Caesar extends to a terrifying portrayal of his physical appearance in old age (iv 57, 2). The biographer is shown miserable by contrast. No hint of the shrunken form, the scarred face, the denuded summit.[55]

So far the case for the *acta senatus*. Tacitus happens to mention the protocol of the Senate once only, and at a very late stage: 'reperio in

[52] *PIR*[2], G 25. Tacitus was alert to prolonged governorships at an early stage, cf. i 80, 1 (Poppaeus Sabinus). He had appraised the sonorous eloquence of Galerius Trachalus, the consul of 68 (*Hist.* i 90, 2), probably a son or grandson of the Prefect of Egypt.

[53] Perhaps reserved for Book VII. Consulars had a keen interest in the *praefectus urbi*.

[54] For his detestable nature, Suetonius, *Nero* 4.

[55] Suetonius, *Tib.* 68, 1 f. The dreadful 'mentagra', an affliction that attacked the human face, arrived 'primum Ti. Claudi Caesaris principatu medio' according to Pliny, *NH* xxvi 3 f. Editors have failed to see that the word 'Claudi' is an intrusion. Neither Tiberius nor Claudius is designated elsewhere in the work by the reading innocently accepted and perpetuated. Cf. *ZPE* xli (1981), 125 f. = *RP* iii (1984), 1376 f.

commentariis senatus' (xv 74, 3). The solitary avowal of direct consultation is duly snapped up by the opposition.[56] That neglects two considerations of some relevance.

First, in what preceded (the fluent narration of Piso's conspiracy) Tacitus had not made much use of the *acta*, apart from the long catalogue of names at the end (xv 71), and the decorations for Nero's allies which disclose the *ornamenta triumphalia* for Cocceius Nerva (72). Second, it is by no means clear that he either completed the third hexad or revised the last Neronian books as extant. The note could have been omitted without damage, since the whole passage enumerates decrees of the Senate. The proposal in question, made by Anicius Cerialis, was abortive: a 'templum divo Neroni'. But Cerialis was of sharp concern—men remembered that this person had betrayed a conspiracy to Caligula, as soon emerges (xvi 17, 6).

In the matter of senatorial decrees the historian had asserted competence shortly before: 'neque tamen silebimus si quod senatus consultum adulatione novum aut patientia postremum fuit' (xiv 64, 3). And much earlier, 'exsequi sententias' etc. (iii 65, 1).

Another passage gave rise to misconceptions (vi 7, 4). Two men got involved in a treason trial: 'Iulius Africanus e Santonis Gallica civitate, Seius Quadratus (originem non repperi)'. Now Africanus belonged to a family of later fame for eloquence.[57] Why the profession of ignorance about Quadratus, it was asked. Tacitus, they said, had only to look in the *acta*. Confidence was premature. An enquirer would there find name and tribe but not the *civitas*.[58]

The episode concludes with an affirmation couched in solemn and Sallustian language: 'nobis pleraque digna cognitu obvenere, quamquam ab aliis incelebrata.' To deny it imports a grave charge. It impugns the integrity of the consular historian.

None the less, the strong disinclination has obtained to admit that Tacitus had any constant or continuous recourse to the protocol: from time to time (it is conceded) but we cannot tell how often.[59] That verdict carried weight and finds recent endorsement, express or through cursory treatment.[60] A more generous appraisal was still

---

[56] Thus for example A. Momigliano, *Gnomon* xxxiii (1961), 56: 'Tacitus hat zweifellos die Acta Senatus gelegentlich herangezogen (Ann. 15. 74), aber wir wissen nicht wie oft'; D. Flach, *MH* xxx (1973), 101: 'dass er sie häufiger einsah, lässt sich nicht beweisen.'

[57] *PIR*[2], J 120 f.

[58] A subsequent senator had 'Seius Quadratus' in his nomenclature, with the tribe 'Quirina' (*CIL* xiv 2381: Tibur). That Roman tribe, the most common of all, would not help an enquirer then or now. His other *cognomen*, 'Sittianus', happens to declare an African origin.

[59] Thus Momigliano, quoted above, n. 56.

[60] D. Flach, *Tacitus in der antiken Geschichtsschreibung* (1973), 71. There is not much about the *acta* in S. Borzsák, *RE*, *Suppl.* xi 482 f. In the phrase '. . . hat T. versäumt die acta senatus

hesitant: 'what we do not know is . . . whether, for instance, he used the *acta* to control his literary sources, rather than merely for variety from them.'[61]

To those doubts and uncertainties (how often the *acta* and for what purposes) a proper scrutiny of the text, if undertaken, might be expected to yield some kind of response. |

Other scholars betray a tendency to steer clear of the problem. They will derive benefit from the second volume of the new commentary on the *Annales*. A salubrious change has supervened. Thus, discussing the urban rubric of the year 15, 'substantial parts . . . rest on the *acta senatus* which in all probability he used directly'; and again for 18, 'his usual sources of information, in particular the *acta senatus*'.[62]

For ease and clarity a marked shift of opinion on a major and controversial topic ought to be registered somewhere. Some, but not many, have quite recently discovered a rift between philology and history and assert that it is widening.[63]

By paradox, a precise reference to the *acta* has been desiderated in a passage where they appeared not to belong. Adgandestrius, the chieftain of the Chatti, wrote to Tiberius offering to do away with Arminius if he were sent some poison. The letter was read out in the Senate. Tiberius Caesar composed an answer in consonance with the 'decus imperii' (ever his care); and, in the words of Tacitus, he put himself on a level with the 'prisci imperatores'.

Tacitus states the source of his information: 'reperio apud scriptores senatoresque eorundem temporum Adgandestrii principis Chattorum lectas in senatu litteras' (ii 88, 1). The introductory phrase has aroused some puzzlement. Without warrant. It may be rendered as 'contemporary writers who were senators'. No perplexity therefore. The statement was proffered for the precise reason that for once a transaction in the Senate did not derive from the Senate's protocol.[64]

sorgfältig zu studieren vgl. Mommsen' etc., the word 'nicht' should be inserted before 'versäumt'.

In relation to the *acta* Miss Levick stated that 'it would be impossible to show that the narrative of events in the House was based mainly on that record—an intermediate literary source may always be postulated, and can sometimes be demonstrated' (*Tiberius the Politician* (1976), 222).

[61] F. R. D. Goodyear, *Tacitus. Greece & Rome* New Surveys (1970), 26.

[62] Goodyear, ii (1981), 136; 352.

[63] Thus D. Flach, *Tacitus in der antiken Geschichtsschreibung* (1973), 13. He cited opinions (not recent) of Vogt, Klingner, and Büchner. 'À qui la faute?' No guilty men are named. He was presumably not indulging in self-incrimination.

[64] Compare Momigliano, *Gnomon* xxxiii (1961), 56: 'Syme gibt keine Erläuterung von Annales 2, 88. In diesem Fall ist es eindeutig, daß Tacitus die Acta Senatus nicht benutzt hat.'

The name 'Adgandestrius' excited alarm and distrust. More plausibly Germanic would be 'Gandestrius'. The text might be in corruption, extending beyond the name. Reinforcing a desire to find a reference to the *acta*, that notion elicited from Mommsen the remedy 'reperio apud scriptores senatoriisque actis Gandestrii . . . litteras'.

As earlier critics did not fail to observe, the adjunct 'eorundem temporum' was inept, the *acta* by nature and definition being contemporaneous with the event. However, another refinement now comes out with 'apud scriptores senatoriaque acta eorundem temporum'.[65]

Adgandestrius has caused more nuisance than he deserves. German princes sometimes betray Celtic nomenclature. Thus Maroboduus of the Marcomanni, flagrantly.[66] The curious may refer to Celtic types such as Adbucillus the Allobrogan or Adminius, a British chieftain.[67]

Doubts and hesitance were advertised about the reasons that might counsel Cornelius Tacitus to have recourse to the *acta senatus*. No mystery. He distrusted the historians of the first dynasty: adulation of the living and the dead defamed. Furthermore, Tacitus was anxious that his *Annales* should abide by the theme and tone of the Roman Senate, not degenerating into the biography of emperors. He was able to suffuse debates in the Senate with the real presence of the sombre and sagacious ruler, by orations and by curt sporadic comment such as 'castigatis oblique patribus' (iii 35, 1).

Recognition now accruing, albeit retarded, to the industry of the writer, equity demands that some attention should go to dangers incurred or even errors (suspected or proved) through employment of the *acta* when he blended them with other information, used them for supplement or transition, or added his own annotations. Nine specimens may be usefully put on exhibit.

(1) Augustus praised, incinerated, and consecrated, the Senate was permitted to discuss the position of his successor. When the debate of September 17 flagged and lapsed, they turned | to routine business. In the course of which, the Princeps 'Germanico Caesari proconsulare imperium petivit' (i 14, 3). At first sight the item, while instructive for assessing what preceded, provokes unease.

---

[65] Goodyear, ii 446, in a careful discussion of the text. Tacitus has 'senatorium album', once (iv 42, 3).

[66] Some now allege Ariovistus.

[67] Caesar, *BC* iii 59, 1; Suetonius, *Cal.* 44, 2. For the common Celtic prefix, D. E. Evans, *Gaulish Personal Names* (1967), 128 ff.

Germanicus was already invested with that *imperium*, indubitably. It is attested and enforced by his first imperatorial salutation, taken in the course of the previous year and concurrent with *imp. XXI* for Augustus, *imp. VII* for Ti. Caesar.[68]

A solution avails. The Princeps was merely re-affirming that *imperium*—which enabled him to make a friendly reference to Drusus, described as 'praesens' and consul designate.[69] Therefore two alternatives. The explanation of Tiberius either did not pass into the protocol or was misunderstood by a historian who had not studied the recent years. Another item in these transactions has attracted more urgent attention: 'candidatos praeturae duodecim nominavit' (14, 4). Some discover ambiguity or inadequacy. Yet it is a plain statement. The list of praetors up for election, by whatever devices established, was in the hands of Tiberius Caesar. He read it out to the Senate. Trouble comes up in the sequel, in the historian's comments, brief and studiously vague.

(2) As the first item of 15, introduced by the names of the consuls, occurs 'decernitur Germanico triumphus manente bello' (i 55, 1). In the late autumn of the previous year the Princeps had reported to the Senate actions of Germanicus, with firm commendation but without any hint of a triumph (52, 2); and the young prince did not then earn the prerequisite, an imperatorial acclamation. Hence a notion attractive on a surface view: Tacitus made a mistake. Facts are thrown in. Germanicus Caesar was acclaimed *imperator* in the course of 15, Tiberius concurring (58, 5). The vote of the triumph should fall at the end of the year when legates of the prince received military decorations (72, 1).[70]

A better solution is to hand. Germanicus was already equipped with the necessary salutation, taken in 13 (cf. above).

There is a further consequence, of no small value for the understanding of Tacitus, for the reconstruction of history and policy. Tiberius Caesar (one assumes) set his mind against warfare beyond the Rhine, from the first days of his reign. The offer of a triumph to Germanicus at the beginning of 15 conveys an easy and unobtrusive interpretation. That is, an honour to tempt the prince, conveying a gentle admonition to desist. The admonition became

---

[68] For Germanicus as *imp. I*, T. D. Barnes, *JRS* lxiv (1974), 24 f.; R. Syme, *History in Ovid* (1978), 56 ff.; *Phoenix* xxxiii (1979), 317 ff. = *RP* iii (1984), 1207 ff.

The 'imperatoria nomina' conceded to Tiberius and his brother (*Ann.* i 3, 1) presuppose *imperium proconsulare*: granted towards the end of 11 b.c., cf. Dio liv 31, 4; 33, 5; 34, 3.

[69] *Historiographia Antiqua* (1977), 241 = *RP* iii (1984), 1022.

[70] D. Timpe, *Der Triumph des Germanicus* (1968), 45 f., cf. 57. He found noteworthy followers, cf. *Phoenix* xxxiii (1979), 322, n. 67 = *RP* iii (1984), 1212, n. 67.

sharper at the end of the year when military decorations voted to the legates of Germanicus should have advertised not the end of a campaign, but the end of a war. Undeterred, the prince went on.[71]

(3) A proconsul of Bithynia prosecuted (i 74). The action was launched by Caepio Crispinus his quaestor, 'subscribente Romanio Hispone, qui formam vitae iniit quam' etc. A digression follows, describing the habits and vicissitudes of *delatores*. After which, the trial resumes with 'sed Marcellum insimulabat' etc., and the next sentence begins with 'addidit Hispo'.

A genuine perplexity. Does the parenthesis about *delatores*, introduced by 'qui', refer to Caepio the quaestor or to Hispo his adjutant? As one reads on in the passage it appears to be the former.[72]

Resort has been had to a small emendation. For 'insimulabat' Nipperdey proposed 'insimulabant'. That remedy has manifest attractions.[73] It would allow leaving Hispo as the *delator*.

To Hispo the label 'egens atque ignotus' (74, 2) attaches suitably, to Hispo the *subscriptor*. He crops up often in the pages of Seneca. Two passages are worth quoting. Hispo is defined as 'qui natura asperiorem dicendi viam sequeretur' (*Controv.* ix 3, 11); | and, further, 'maligne et accusatorie dixit' (ii 5, 20). Observe finally Hispo's employment of 'contumelia' (Quintilian vi 3, 100).

Therefore patently the better candidate, if one were compelled to make a decision.[74] If decision be waived, the passage retains its use, and an explanation. Tacitus, mindful of a leading theme, was incited to insert at once the portrayal of an archetypal *delator*, not waiting for Fulcinius Trio, a senator and a superior agent of evil.[75] In so doing he was not able to avoid an awkward suture.

(4) The Tiber floods. Asinius Gallus (perhaps not innocent) spoke for a consultation of the Sibylline Books. Caesar objected, and the Senate appointed two commissioners to investigate and report (i 76, 1). A later session discussed their proposals—and no action followed (79, 4). Cassius Dio registered the floods, to the accompaniment of portents such as earthquakes and thunderbolts (lvii 14, 7 f.). He subjoined a permanent board of five *curatores* now appointed. They

---

[71] For this interpretation, *History in Ovid* (1978), 59 ff.

[72] E. Groag, *PIR*[2], C 159; R. Syme, *Tacitus* (1958), 326, cf. 693 f.

[73] Sagacious reasons are produced by Goodyear, i (1973), 159.

[74] Goodyear, ibid.: 'on balance the arguments seem to favour Romanius' claims, but not so clearly as to preclude doubt.' The present writer is ceasing from doubt.

[75] *Ann.* ii 28, 3: 'celebre inter accusatores Trionis ingenium erat avidumque famae malae.' Trio, the prime prosecutor of Libo Drusus, reached a consulship in 31, a year fatal to many, and ended by suicide in 35 (vi 38, 2). His name is absent from the roll of declaimers in Seneca.

are on record, the first presided by L. Caninius Gallus (*suff.* 2 B.C.), the second by the elderly C. Vibius Rufus (*suff.* A.D. 16).[76] In the *acta* no doubt, but not in Tacitus, who is not drawn to administration, who eschews even the consulars in charge of the Roman aqueducts.

Furthermore, the innovation, though put under 15 in Dio, may belong to the next year. A small detail of this kind would not accord well with the technique there adopted by Tacitus: senatorial business grouped around central episodes in large sections.[77]

(5) Poppaeus Sabinus the legate of Moesia (i 80, 1). Continuing with 'id quoque morum Tiberii fuit', Tacitus explains the ruler's practice of leaving governors in their provinces for prolonged tenures, and some to the end of their days. The transition is abrupt. A link was there—but in the mind of the author. He knew that Poppaeus Sabinus died in Moesia twenty years later (vi 39, 3).

The phrase 'id quoque' may afford guidance to another passage a little earlier. Discussing criminal libels, Tacitus notes that the Princeps, consulted about the law of treason by the praetor Pompeius Macer, made an answer: 'exercendas leges esse' (72, 3). Tacitus adds 'hunc quoque asperavere carmina' etc. Among the topics of those poems he notes 'discordem cum matre animum'. Not perhaps relevant to the year 15. Discord between Tiberius and the Augusta is a motive that arises late in the hexad. The poems look like a subsequent addition, inserted between 'iudicia maiestatis' and the first prosecution for treasonable practices described as 'praetemptata crimina' (73, 1).

(6) Furius Camillus in Africa. The proconsul's campaign, with at the end the grant of *ornamenta triumphalia*, finds record under the year 17 (ii 52). Later, when the next proconsul, L. Apronius, turns up in 20, one reads 'eodem anno Tacfarinas, quem priore aestate pulsum a Camillo memoravi, bellum in Africa renovat' (iii 20, 1). A patent error in dating. Tacitus forgot.

Apronius had a tenure from 18 to 21. When Apronius awarded decorations, the Princeps added a 'corona civica'. That was within a proconsul's rights, so he pointed out, 'questus magis quam offensus' (21, 3). The *acta* again, as in the other two sections about Africa (iii 73 f., iv 23 ff.).

---

[76] *ILS* 5983; 5925. The order of the two colleges was inverted in *RR* (1939), 403. See further *ZPE* xliii (1981), 369 f. = *RP* iii (1984), 1427 f.

[77] Namely ii 27–32 (Libo Drusus); 33 (measures against luxury); 34 f. (L. Piso and Urgulania); 36 (a proposal of Asinius Gallus); 37 f. (the appeal of Hortensius Hortalus, with an oration from the Princeps).

(7) The ovation of Drusus Caesar. It was voted in 19 (ii 64, 1), celebrated in 20 (iii 19, 3), and also defined in 20 as 'ob . . . res priore aestate gestas' (11, 1). Those data | are involved in the notorious aporia that besets the Tacitean chronology of 18 and 19. A discreet approach from that basis may help to clarify the problem.

Before the end of 17 both princes had left Rome, Germanicus going to the eastern lands, Drusus to Illyricum, likewise invested with proconsular *imperium*—as a senatorial writer did not need to specify.

In the course of the year 18 Germanicus installed Zeno as ruler of Armenia. Drusus was sent out as 'paci firmator' (ii 46, 5). That is to say, to promote through diplomatic arts the disruption of the empire of Maroboduus.

Two considerations come into the debate. First, operations of Drusus and the fall of Maroboduus are related under the year 19 (62 f.). Suspicion has arisen. They ought to belong to the previous year. Second, that narration is introduced by the words 'dum ea aestas Germanico plures per provincias transigitur' (62, 1). As the text runs, that refers to Egypt, dated by the consuls of 19 (59, 1). The phrase 'plures per provincias' fits better the travels of the previous year.

Hence a bold solution. Transfer a large piece (62–7) to the year 18, to be inserted before the consuls of 19 (59, 1). Such was the proposal of Steup, in 1869. It has met with varied response.[78] Some scholars concur—or all but.[79] One has printed his own transposition in his edition of the text.[80]

Something has gone wrong somewhere. That is clear. The clue may reside in the date (sometimes postponed) at which certain transactions came to be discussed in the Senate and registered in the *acta*. The following passage under the year 19 is vital: 'simul nuntiato regem Artaxian Armeniis a Germanico datum, decrevere patres ut Germanicus atque Drusus ovantes urbem introirent. structi et arcus' etc. (64, 1). A conjecture can be proffered. Tacitus recounted the mission of Drusus and events beyond the Danube as a single episode, from Maroboduus and his demolition down to the establishment (a little later) of a client kingdom under Vannius of the Quadi (62 f.). In a speech to the Senate Tiberius extolled the achievement ('extat oratio') with emphasis on the formidable power of Maroboduus.

---

[78] Against, E. Koestermann in his *Commentary*, i (1963), 371 f.
[79] Thus, in a full and judicious discussion, Goodyear, op. cit. 394: 'there is a good chance that he is right, in spite of what follows.' He agrees with Koestermann, in thinking that Tacitus' annalistic structure has broken down (ibid. 395).
[80] H. Fuchs (1946).

The speech of Tiberius justifies the grant of an ovation to Drusus. At the same time it was easy and suitable to associate Germanicus in the abnormal honour (neither had taken the field), in recognition of the ceremony at Artaxata the year before.

The vote of the two ovations was simultaneous, but not the arrival of tidings at Rome. Tacitus by inadvertence fell victim to an error and wrote 'simul nuntiato' (64, 1).

On this showing an explanation emerges. No call therefore to acquiesce in Steup and transfer from 19 to 18 a large chunk which, along with Maroboduus (62 f.), comprises affairs in Thrace (64, 2–67, 3), firmly linked to the ovations and to Tiberius' satisfaction by 'igitur Rhescuporim' (64, 2). The narration in Tacitus follows the dating prescribed by the *acta senatus*—which is confirmed by the references in the next year to Drusus' ovation (iii 11, 1; 19, 3).[81]

(8) The descendants of Cn. Pompeius Theophanes. In 33 Pompeia Macrina suffered prosecution and exile on charges of *maiestas*. Whereupon her father and her brother under ominous prospects committed suicide: 'pater quoque inlustris eques Romanus ac frater praetorius, cum damnatio instaret' (vi 18, 2).

Names can be attached. Q. Pompeius Macer was praetor in 15, the praetor who consulted the Princeps about *maiestas*.[82] Macer's equestrian father, after being procurator of Asia under Augustus, stood high in favour with his successor. He was the son of Theophanes, the client and historian of Pompeius Magnus. Thus Strabo (xiii 618). | Macer was also a friend of the poet Ovid, sharing and guiding his early travels in Sicily and Asia—and related to Ovid's third wife.[83]

Tacitus' account of the affair is compressed and enigmatic. The incrimination appears unduly trivial. It brought up the famous ancestor, 'quodque caelestes honores Graeca adulatio tribuerat'. Tacitus styles him 'proavum eorum', perhaps a little awkwardly since the term includes the *eques Romanus*, the parent of the praetor and his sister.

Now that parent is the procurator of Asia, the son of Theophanes.

---

[81] That is, even if most of the Danubian portion in fact belonged to 18.

[82] For the *praenomen*, ILS 9349.

[83] For his occupations see H.-G. Pflaum, *Les Carrières procuratoriennes équestres* i (1960), 12 ff., with the *Addendum* in iii (1961), 957. He omitted however *Ann.* vi 18, 2. As did by wise and deliberate choice L. Robert, *CRAI* 1969, 48, n. 1 (discussing Theophanes).

Some harm has been caused by a failure to see that in Strabo Μάρκον Πομπήιον should be changed to Μακρὸν Πομπήιον. For the coin of Priene with the name of Macer and his presumed head, see M. Grant, *FITA* (1946), 388 f. He was disclosed as Cn. Pompeius Macer, with the title ὕπαρχος, on *Inschr. v. Priene* 247.

Theophanes should have been called 'avus' not 'proavus' in relation to Macer and Macrina. The historian has made a slip,[84] which many have failed to discern or refused to concede. It is no remedy to shove in another generation and a second *eques Romanus* between the client of Magnus and the praetor of A.D. 15.[85] Ages and chronology forbid.

Official documents are not immune from error. But there is no need to postulate a mistake in the contemporaneous protocol that recorded the prosecution of Pompeia Macrina. It may not have registered either word, 'avus' or 'proavus'. The reason is to be sought in Tacitus' annotation on the two suicides. He was well aware of the ancestor, and the memory of Magnus took him too far back into the past.

The more surprising perhaps because the family now came up again with a consul suffect in 115, previously governor of Cilicia when Tacitus was proconsul in Asia.[86] And another surprise. Tiberius Caesar made no move to rescue an old friend and close coeval. The annalist neglected an occasion to exemplify the fatalism of the ruler or his capricious temperament, who though enamoured of Greek letters turned against a scholar of elegant accomplishment.[87]

Fatigue ensued from the mass of prosecutions or deaths in this sombre year; and choice of emphasis bore on other persons and episodes.

(9) **A governor dying in Syria.** At the very end of 33 fell the decease of Aelius Lamia, with a public funeral (vi 27, 2). The tribute is splendid ('genus illi decorum, vivida senectus') but short, eschewing all but the absentee governorship of Syria from which Lamia had at last been released when he assumed the Prefecture of the City.

Then comes the death of Lamia's successor in Syria, Pomponius Flaccus (27, 3). It provoked a despatch from the Princeps complaining about the reluctance of consulars to take on provincial commands. Tiberius forgot that Arruntius had been detained at Rome for a decade and prevented from going to Spain, so Tacitus is careful to add. On which follows the decease of Marcus Lepidus: the annalist had postponed it (Lamia died 'extremo anni') in order to conclude

---

[84] Strongly suspected in *Tacitus* (1958), 749—and firmly stated in *History in Ovid* (1978), 73 f.

[85] Thus, following *PIR*¹, P 471 ff.: R. Laqueur, *RE* vA, 2099 f.; R. Hanslik, xxi 2277. The latter scholar failed to discern or state the problem presented by Tacitus—and no mention of the evidence from Priene.

[86] For the consulship of M. Pompeius Macrinus, styled 'Neos Theophanes', 100 or 101 was accepted in *Tacitus* (1958), 749. For the correct date, *Historia* xviii (1969), 355 f. = *RP* (1979), 777 f.

[87] Compare 'Iulius Montanus, tolerabilis poeta et amicitia Tiberii notus et frigore' (Seneca, *Ep.* 122, 11).

the evil year with a noble valedictory for a man who commanded much admiration.

To have Pomponius Flaccus dying in 33 imports a problem. Account has to be taken of Josephus and the long peregrination of Herod Agrippa.[88] If the story be given credit down to details of chronology, Agrippa had an interview with Flaccus not very long before he at last reached the capital. He arrived in the spring of 36. On this testimony, the tenure of Flaccus has been extended until 35, when L. Vitellius (*cos.* 34) turned up.[89] That estimate may be excessive.[90] A praetorian legate could function, as had occurred before | the appointment of Pomponius Flaccus. However that may be, the chance subsists that the historian made a mistake in disposing his material when he introduced Flaccus in juxtaposition to Lamia.

Epilogue

Tacitus has been under frequent assault from captious critics, overbold, overfleet. The more facts in an author, the greater danger of error or inadvertence. The nine specimens here on exhibit are intended to show how errors may arise, precisely during assiduous recourse to documents. By the same token, in the larger theme the very excellence of Tacitus' information about Tiberius Caesar (notably the orations) can be exploited to subvert (or at least modify) his portrayal of the ruler. It will be suitable to conclude with a pair of passages that illustrate his percipience and his technique.

When requesting the Senate to vote a public funeral for the unamiable *novus homo* Sulpicius Quirinius, Caesar recounted public services, with emphasis on personal loyalty during the sojourn at Rhodes; and he threw in a rancorous reference to Marcus Lollius, dead twenty years before (iii 48).

The version leads off with 'nihil ad veterem et patriciam Sulpiciorum familiam Quirinius pertinuit, ortus apud municipium Lanuvium.' The local origin of Quirinius might not be beyond reach despite the long efflux of time, but it carried no great value for Tacitus or for his readers: Quirinius left no issue from two aristocratic brides. Not therefore the product of research outside the *acta*. It is the noble and patrician who speaks, often at variance with his own class (not rivals and enemies only, but the idle or

---

[88] Josephus, *AJ* xviii 150 ff., cf. 126. Not noted by Koestermann ad loc., or by W. Eck, *RE*, *Suppl.* xiv 439 f.

[89] Thus in Schürer's *History of the Jewish People in the Age of Jesus Christ* (ed. 2, revised by G. Vermes and F. Millar, 1973), 264.

[90] On which see remarks in *ZPE* xli (1981), 129 f. = *RP* iii (1984), 1380 f.

incompetent) and eager, although with passing dispraisal of a municipal origin, to asseverate the claims of merit against birth.

In the year 33 Caesar had to find husbands for three princesses: for two daughters of Germanicus and for Julia, the daughter of Drusus. Cassius Dio curtly noted the occasion—and omitted to name the consorts (lviii 21, 1). Tacitus puts it on high show, to open the year (vi 15, 1). Drusilla was consigned to L. Cassius, her sister Julia to M. Vinicius. The extraction and character of the two husbands, standing in a certain contrast, is neatly indicated. Nothing, however, about the third princess, the daughter of Drusus Caesar.

In his missive to the Senate Tiberius evinced scant enthusiasm for his own choice. He wrote 'levi cum honore iuvenum'. That is significant for his manner. And something further. Tiberius had taken a long time to make up his mind. The passage opens with 'diu quaesito'. Observe for comparison 'saepe apud se pensitato' (iii 52, 3). That comes in the historian's preface to the long despatch in which the ruler evaded attempts to involve him in a programme of sumptuary legislation. The phrase, it appears, echoes Caesar's own exordium. Tacitus at an early point had singled out the 'anxium iudicium' which impeded and delayed the selection of governors (i 80, 2).

To resume. The third marriage Tacitus chose to segregate, to keep it until late in the year, before the decease of Aelius Lamia. It was a 'pars maeroris' (vi 27, 1). The sorrow was of a social nature. The daughter of Drusus 'denupsit in domum Rubelli Blandi.' Men recalled that his grandfather had been a Roman knight from Tibur.

Vinicius, the husband of the other Julia, avowed 'oppidanum genus', from Cales, it is true, but the son and grandson of consuls. Vinicius and Cassius shared the consulship of 30. In Rubellius Blandus (*suff.* 18) there was a certain disparity of age, not remarked by the historian: well over fifty when he got the hand of a princess. The explanations would be worth knowing, which Tiberius offered in his despatch. Julia was in fact about twenty-seven, and awkward to dispose of, having been married to Nero, the eldest son of Germanicus. An innocuous husband without birth and pretensions was a good solution, not without parallel in other dynastic arrangements.[91] |

---

[91] The Tiburtine grandfather may have counted with Ti. Caesar: illustrious in the schools of declamation and in fact the first Roman knight to teach rhetoric (Seneca, *Controv.* ii, *praef.* 5). For the match, see now 'The Marriage of Rubellius Blandus', *AJP* cii (1982), 62 ff. = pp. 177 ff., above.

The season remains a problem. Reasons can be adduced for questioning Dio's amalgamation with the other marriages early in the year (lviii 21, 1). The ceremony (perhaps discreet) may have ensued at some time in the summer, before Tiberius went back to Capreae (cf. *Ann.* vi 20, 1).

The disjunction of Julia's nuptials is an incentive to curiosity, likewise the placing of the last item but one (only the suicide of Munatia Plancina intervenes, on brief report). Tacitus had given full space to the decease of the jurist Cocceius Nerva, 'continuus principi comes' (26, 1). Despite earnest reproach from his old friend, Nerva resolved to end his days by starvation.

On any count, Nerva and Nerva's end called for emphasis and high relief. Something further is disclosed by the proximity into which Nerva and Blandus are cast. Descendants survived of Blandus and Julia. Not of great account, yet kinsfolk of the Emperor Nerva. His maternal uncle married Rubellia Bassa.[92]

Design is apparent, and malice suspected.[93] The enquiry comes round to its beginning: experience and knowledge acquired by Cornelius Tacitus, senator, consul, proconsul of Asia.

[92] *ILS* 232, cf. *PIR*[2], C 1227.
[93] As in the conjunction of Nerva and Tigellinus (xv 72, 1).

13

The Year 33 in Tacitus and Dio

IF authors diverge widely in talent and execution, there seems little profit in comparing them. Those who compose history are in another posture. On the lowest count their selection of facts brings them together for confrontation. Rome retained the fabric, 'annos a consule nomen habentes', and the recording year by year after the 'res publica' was annexed and subdued by the monarchy. The habit has been deplored, the various disadvantages duly indicted. On a contrary estimate, annals entailed order and accuracy, deterred the diffuse—and even impeded for a season the emergence of imperial biographies.

When diverse annalists preserve a parallel sequence, it is sheer felicity. Tacitus and Dio offer comparison in two portions of the reign of Tiberius Caesar, the first and the last. Inspection even cursory shows method and predilections, design and purpose.

In Tacitus the year 15, opening with a copious military narration, passes to Rome and the Senate with the vote of *ornamenta triumphalia* to legates of Germanicus (i 72, 1). The annual rubric then takes over, interlaced and linked by comments that disclose the principal themes or preoccupations (72–81). For example, *maiestas*. The praetor Pompeius Macer consulted the Princeps about the application of the law (72, 3), and two prosecutions are then reported (73 f.).

The section in Dio (lvii 14) comprises ten items, only three of them common to Tacitus. No prosecutions for treason, and no senator named (Tacitus has eleven). At first sight it hardly looks like the same year.[1]

For 16, Tacitus changed his technique. He operated with six episodes amply expounded (ii 27–38). They put certain of the consulars on prominence (notably Asinius Gallus), and they conveyed three orations in direct discourse. The Greek historian is again in sharp discrepance (lvii 15 f.). He followed an annalist who had made a different selection of senatorial business.[2]

---

[1] Thus *Tacitus* (1958), 691, cf. *ZPE* xliii (1981), 365 f. = *RP* iii (1984), 1423 f.
[2] For a comparison of both years in the two authors see now J. Ginsburg, *Tradition and Theme in the Annals of Tacitus* (1981), 67 ff.; 81 f.

Athenaeum lxi (1983), 3–23.

The text of Cassius Dio breaks off early in the next year, on brief mention of the great earthquake in Asia and measures of relief (17, 7 f.). It resumes in the summer or autumn of 31, and it proceeds to the catastrophe of Aelius Seianus, generously narrated. After that climax a compressed narration carries the reign from 32 down to the decease of the ruler in March of 37 (lviii 17–28). It is variously instructive—and seldom accorded much value. Tacitus pre-empts and occludes. |

The ample Tacitean exposition (*Ann.* vi 15–27) is a marvel of coherence and variety; and it obtains a central place between the fall of Seianus and the death of Tiberius. Indeed, on official promulgation the year 33 marked the liquidation of a whole episode. On a single day by Caesar's command the remaining adherents of Seianus were taken out and executed: 'iacuit immensa strages' (vi 19, 2).

The year was also of significance for the ruler's family and for the dynastic succession. Drusus and Agrippina perished in prison. The widow of Germanicus recalled past history, and so did the decease of the septuagenarian Asinius Gallus, close coeval and enemy of Ti. Caesar. On the other side, three princesses disposed in wedlock; and Caligula's marriage gave the historian an opportunity for ominous forecast about the youth, 'immanem animum subdola modestia tegens', supported by a witticism of the orator Passienus Crispus (20, 1). On which follows the prediction about a future emperor, namely the consul Ser. Sulpicius Galba, adumbrating an end to Julii and Claudii (20, 2).

Tacitus chose to divide his chronicle of events into two sections of equal compass, separated by a long digression.[3]

A.   VI 15, 1   The marriages of Drusilla and Julia (Livilla),
                   the daughters of Germanicus Caesar
             2   The Senate votes Tiberius a bodyguard
         16 f.   The financial crisis
         18, 1   Considius Proculus, arrested, condemned, and
                   put to death
             2   Pompeia Macrina prosecuted; her father and her
                   brother commit suicide
         19, 1   Execution of Sex. Marius
             2 f. Fate of the last adherents of Seianus
         20, 1   Caligula marries 'Claudiam M. Silani filiam'.

Tiberius' expertise in the art of astrology (20, 2) leads on to the story about Thrasyllus on Rhodes and the excursus about fate and free will (21 f.).

---

[3] For Tacitus on 33, J. Ginsburg, op. cit. 73 ff.

B.	23, 1	Death of Asinius Gallus
	23, 2–24, 3	Death of Drusus, likewise in prison
	25	Decease of Agrippina
	26, 1	Suicide of Cocceius Nerva
	2	Suicide of Munatia Plancina
	27, 1	Julia, daughter of Drusus Caesar, marries Rubellius Blandus
	2	Death of Aelius Lamia, the *praefectus urbi*
	3	Death of Pomponius Flaccus, legate of Syria; despatch of the Emperor to the Senate
	4	M. Lepidus (*cos.* 6) passes away.

This sombre year comprises, with little relief, the deaths of no fewer than twelve named persons. As concerns order and chronology, three dates are to hand. |

In the first section, the extinction of the 'Seianiani' is registered on the *Fasti Ostienses* (vii D): 'A]ug. coniur. Seian[i]/[exstincta e]t compl[ures]/[in s]calis [Gemoniis iacuer.].' That indicates the second half of July or the first part of August. Useful, since 'sub idem tempus' Caligula, 'discedenti Capreas avo comes', marries Claudia.

The next date is furnished by Agrippina's fate. It fell, so Caesar proclaimed, by singular felicity and to be suitably commemorated, on the anniversary of Seianus' doom. That is, October 18 (25, 3). Finally, the demise of the City Prefect, put by Tacitus 'extremo anni' (27, 2). The *Fasti Ostienses* confirm, two words surviving from the entry of his public funeral: 'D]ec. Lami[a' (*FO* ix). That is, late November or early December.

Those dates help to fix some other transactions. The first section terminates in August, it may be supposed. The second leads off with the death of Asinius Gallus, registered merely as 'isdem consulibus' (23, 1). But there follows 'Drusus deinde extinguitur' (23, 2), and that occurred not long before Agrippina's end: 'nondum is dolor exoleverat' (25, 1). Soon after which comes the suicide of Tiberius' friend, the jurist Cocceius Nerva: 'haud multo post' (26, 1). Then, with a pair of items interposed, Aelius Lamia dies close to the year's end.

Therefore, so far as can be ascertained, the annalist keeps to a temporal order. The only exception will not deceive. It is the concluding item, introduced with no need for precision as 'eodem anno'. Tacitus reserved for that place of honour and emphasis his tribute to the excellent Marcus Lepidus (27, 4).

Tacitus' earliest specimen of the obituary notice came in 20: 'fine anni excessere insignes viri L. Volusius et Sallustius Crispus' (iii 30,

1). In the next year the death and public funeral of Sulpicius Quirinius is 'sub idem tempus' only, the penultimate item (48, 1). In 22 the device passes over chronology: 'obiere eo anno viri inlustres Asinius Saloninus . . . et Capito Ateius' (75, 1). The mention of Capito evokes the rival jurist Antistius Labeo, Republican in sentiment, passing to Junia's decease sixty-three years after the Battle of Philippi, sister to Marcus Brutus and widow of C. Cassius (76). Thus ends the third book of the hexad. The three deaths may have occurred at any time in the course of the year.

Dio's account of the year can be summarized as follows:

LVIII	21,1	Tiberius approaches Rome; the marriages of three princesses
	2 f.	Tiberius insists on regular sessions of the Senate; he communicates through despatches to the consuls
	4	The fate of Vibullius Agrippa	
	4 f.	Nerva commits suicide through disapproval of Tiberius' measures to abate the financial crisis; the most notorious informers are put to death on a single day
	6	Centurions forbidden to practise delation
	22,1	Tiberius impugned for sexual divagations
	2 f.	Execution of Sex. Marius, with anecdotes about that person
	4 f.	Deaths of Drusus and Agrippina; Munatia Plancina killed
	23,1	Caligula appointed quaestor, with a five years' remission for other magistracies
	2	Tiberius and his grandson (Gemellus).
	3 f.	Anecdotes about Caligula and about Tiberius
	5 f.	Prolonged tenures for proconsuls
	6	Decease of Asinius Gallus.

Comparison with Tacitus will furnish manifold instruction. Not merely the divergence in selection and emphasis. Although Dio's exposition is abridged, it illustrates his methods and his preoccupations; and items from the other years (32 to 37) can be suitably adduced.

(1) *The interests of a senator.* For example, Tiberius' instructions to the consuls, a practice adopted in other matters also; but he consigned to the Senate both documents from informers and the results of inquisitions made by Macro, the Prefect of the Guard, so that all that was left to the high assembly was to pronounce condemnation (21, 3). Again, proconsuls prorogued for long periods. A valuable item, but Dio unfortunately assigned a reason:

the shortage of senators because so many had been killed (23, 5).
Under the previous year he described how the Princeps allocated
consulships and other magistracies, at some length (20, 1–4).

(2) *Predilection for the anecdotal*. On Sex. Marius the Latin historian
was brief and to the point: 'Hispaniarum ditissimus defertur
incestasse filiam et saxo Tarpeio deicitur.' He adds the detail that
Tiberius confiscated his mines of gold and silver (19, 1). An attentive
reader would know that Marius had been a close friend of the
Princeps, who angrily sent into exile a man who essayed an
indictment (iv 36, 1). Dio, referring to Marius as a notorious friend
(he may have been mentioned previously), allots space to his
opulence and pretensions, with the allegation that he tried to protect
his daughter from the lusts of the Emperor (20, 2 f.).

Further, stories about Caligula and Tiberius Gemellus—the latter
held illegitimate by his grandfather, who knew for a certainty that he
would not live long, that he would be killed by Caligula. And
sundry remarks of the ruler are quoted (23, 1–4).

This material occupies much room. By contrast the six deaths Dio
reports (apart from that of Sex. Marius) are managed in a cursory
fashion.

(3) *Confusion*. Nerva's resolve to end his life is assigned a precise
motive. He disapproved of the measures taken by the Princeps to
abate the financial stringency (21, 4 f.). Whatever Nerva may have
thought, those measures succeeded—and the jurist (not so labelled
by Dio) died late in the year.

In the item subjoined, Tiberius orders all the most notorious
delatores to be | executed on the same day. That is a misapprehension.
The victims were partisans of Seianus, as specified by Tacitus and by
the *Fasti Ostienses*; and they perished at a later date, in the summer
(cf. above).

(4) *Errors*. At an early point in the year Vibullius Agrippa, arraigned
before the Senate, took poison and succumbed at once
(21, 4). Tacitus has the same incident at the beginning of 36 (vi 40, 1),
followed by a sequence of prosecutions and deaths. It is told more
fully: the accused, 'prolapsusque ac moribundus', was hauled off to
prison by lictors and strangled there.

The date in Tacitus commands instant preference. He calls the man
'Vibulenus Agrippa'. There is a chance (but nothing more) that he
was a Vibullius.[4] However, no warrant for supposing a mistake of
scribe or author and altering the text.[5]

---

[4] As indicated in *JRS* xxxix (1949), 17 f. = *Ten Studies in Tacitus* (1970), 77.
[5] As done by Koestermann (ed. 2, 1965).

When a historian in any age operates with a plethora of personal names he is liable to inadvertence. For a clear case, observe 'Latinius Latiaris' (iv 68, 2), also 'Latinius' (71, 1). He crops up later as 'Lucanius Latiaris' (vi 4, 1).[6] To be accepted, deriving probably from the *acta senatus*, as the context indicates, whereas the previous narration issues from a written source (perhaps subsidiary). The incongruence should be allowed to stand in the text.

Next, the marriage of Caligula. Suetonius, vague and careless, put it before the catastrophe of Seianus (*Cal.* 12, 1). For Dio it is the first item in 35, with Antium as the place and Tiberius present (25, 2). He named neither the bride nor her illustrious parent. Antium was plausible, but not the year. There was no cause for postponing the ceremony: a prince born on August 1 of 12 was ripe for matrimony in 33, when, according to Tacitus, Caligula married Claudia on the way back to Capreae (vi 20, 1), in the summer of the year.

Another instance is variously instructive. Towards the end of 31 Tacitus inserted the story of the false Drusus (v 10). He describes the journey taken by Poppaeus Sabinus in pursuit of the impostor, all the way from Macedonia by Piraeus and Corinth to Nicopolis of Epirus, where, making for Italy, he was last heard of: he avowed identity as a son of M. Silanus.[7] Sabinus sent a report to Caesar, but the historian confesses himself at a loss: 'neque nos originem finemve eius rei ultra | comperimus'. Bafflement is shared by the reader: why so full a narration, and where did Tacitus light upon it?

Dio has the story, as the brief concluding item of the year 34, with a refinement: if the impostor had not been recognized and captured, he might have made his way to the army in Syria (25, 1). There is no call to redeem Dio's date or to speculate about a connection with certain events of the previous year.[8]

These phenomena inspire due curiosity about Dio's procedures in composition. If a compiler is rendering or abridging a unitary narration, he can go straight ahead and he need not bother with more than a single source. That is shown by Plutarch who converted a slice of history into the biographies of Galba and Otho. Very different the miscellany of transactions comprised in the chronicle of a year such

---

[6] Observe L. Lucanius Latiaris on a title (*CIL* xv 1245) and Q. Lucanius Latinus, praetor in 19 (*Inscr. It.* xiii 1, p. 305).

[7] That is, M. Junius C. f. Silanus (*suff.* 15), notable as a close friend of Ti. Caesar—and as the father of Caligula's bride. 'Claudia' in Tacitus, she is 'Junia Claudilla' in Suetonius (*Cal.* 12, 1).

[8] For speculation, B. Levick, *Tiberius the Politician* (1976), 211 ff. That scholar also states that 'it is tempting to jettison Tacitus' date for the false Drusus' (ibid. 213).

as 33. The author had licence to select and arrange, in accordance
with his tastes and purposes, supplying, if he had the requisite skill,
some links or explanations. Dio brought the suicide of Cocceius
Nerva into relation with the financial crisis, most detrimentally; and
a sentence blaming the morals of the ruler introduces the episode of
Sextus Marius. Again, Dio left the death of Asinius Gallus to the end
of the year, although it in fact preceded that of Drusus.

Some writers read well ahead before they put pen to paper (or
rather dictate). For the aftermath of Seianus, Dio followed that
practice (it may be assumed with no discomfort), going through to
the end of Book LVIII with the intention of producing a selective and
curtailed version. Ruthless abridgement is patent in the account of
eastern affairs in 35 (26, 1–4), which omits the role and actions of
Lucius Vitellius.

A small sign of anticipation may be put on record. Under 32 Dio
has a proposal that the Princeps when entering the Curia should be
escorted by a bodyguard of twenty senators (17, 3). A little lower
down, he subjoins (18, 5) what occurred in 33 (cf. *Ann.* vi 15, 2),
namely the ruler's request that the Prefect of the Guard along with
some tribunes and centurions should exercise that function.

The day-by-day operations conducted by prose writers often fall
beneath the notice of those who investigate historiography. Persons
of station or favoured clients of the wealthy did not have to spend
their time in anxious consultation of scrolls. Secretaries were
available. Josephus enjoyed their constant help, different styles
showing through. Trained adjutants would read out texts, while the
author | took notes—or better, relied upon his memory. Dio in fact
has the phrase ἤδη δ' ἤκουσα more than once, in reference (it
appears) to a subsidiary source.[9]

This hypothesis explains several of Dio's errors in chronology,
such as Caligula's marriage, the affair of Vibullius Agrippa, the false
Drusus (cf. above). There is a further consequence, of signal value.
The order of events produced by Dio for the year 33 cannot be taken
to correspond with that of his main source.

For a transaction that was at the same time contested and deemed
important, notably the decease of Caesar Augustus, Dio can cite
variant versions.[10] For the years 15 and 16 it is a question whether
more sources than one need be postulated.[11] Matter and treatment

[9] For that phrase, Dio liv 35, 5; lvii 3, 5; lviii 11, 7.
[10] F. Millar, *A Study of Cassius Dio* (1964), 85.
[11] However, Dio has τινές in lvii 14, 2.

appear fairly uniform. The same may hold for the last *quinquennium* of the reign.

Adepts of *Quellenforschung*, instead of being content to define the character and quality of a historical source, or its presumed date, are prone all too often to conjure up a known name. Much play has been made with Aufidius Bassus. At some time antecedent to his annalistic history Bassus had composed a *Bellum Germanicum*. The scope of the work is not certain: on one hypothesis, the wars between the years 4 and 16, a comprehensible unit and hence not to be recounted fully in his subsequent history.[12] Dio, so it has been observed, is scrappy on 4–6, and there is no sign that he had given much space to the campaigns of Germanicus Caesar.

Among the uncertainties about Bassus are both the inception and the termination of his annals. Pliny continued him, writing, so the nephew states, 'a fine Aufidi Bassi'. The phrase has evoked the attractive notion that Bassus ended not with the decease of an emperor but with the fall of Aelius Seianus.[13]

If that be so, Dio now had to look elsewhere. One text would serve most of his needs for what was only a minor section in a work of eighty books. His treatment of those years lacks a unifying theme. On the lowest estimate, few facts not in the Roman annalist and little instruction save negative.

The other named historian of the period is Servilius Nonianus, orator, consul, and proconsul of Africa, by those signs the authority likely to capture the preferen|ce of Cornelius Tacitus. His family was aristocratic, and Tacitus did not neglect the parent (ii 48, 2; iii 22, 2). Entering the Senate about the year 23, Nonianus, close coeval to Galba, stood in a similar relation of time to Augustus' end as Tacitus did to that of Nero.

Nonianus had friends or attachments to those of the Stoic persuasion.[14] In his writing he may not, however, have disdained anecdote or scandal. One repertory of revelations would not have been available to him, the memoirs of Nero's mother, to which Tacitus had recourse at least once (iv 53, 2), and perhaps several times.

Nonianus had been on Capreae.[15] He may have reported the

---

[12] For that hypothesis, *Tacitus* (1958), 697.

[13] Thus Mommsen, *Ges. Schr.* vii 677 ff.: followed by several scholars. Others have taken Bassus as far as 48 or 49.

[14] Of Persius it is stated 'coluit Servilium Nonianum ut patrem' (*Vita Persi*, OCT i 17). Much was made of the historian's Stoicism by F. Klingner, *MH* xv (1958), 200. Add perhaps the conjecture that his daughter married Barea Soranus—whose daughter is called Servilia (*Ann.* xvi 30, 2).

[15] To be identified as the 'vir consularis' of Suetonius, *Tib.* 61, 6.

motives that induced Cocceius Nerva, Caesar's old friend and constant companion, to end his days by starvation: 'ferebant gnari cogitationum eius' (vi 26, 2).

A highly literate society might well bring forth an *Ignotus* who served as Dio's principal source. Historians are sparsely certified by name in this epoch as in the next. Josephus affirms that many had written about Nero and about the year after Nero's end.[16]

Whatever the sources, Tacitus in ordering the annual rubric was able to operate with a bold hand—and with a purpose artistic or artful. Years tend to begin or end on strong emphasis—and often on an ominous note.[17] Some of his devices are peculiar indeed. To introduce 34 he inserted an erudite digression on the phoenix (vi 29). Now the Egyptian bird was reported in 36, according to Pliny (*NH* x 5), and Dio has the same date, presaging the decease of the ruler (lviii 27, 1). In Tacitus the exotic theme has no meaning—except that it usefully separates two years of urban transactions marked by many deaths, for the second year duly proceeds with 'at Romae caede continua' (29, 1).

By the same token, be it noted, his placing of the prediction about Servius Galba, to split the chronicle of 33. The standard tradition probably assigned it to the year 22, when Galba was taking a wife.[18] |

A more alarming divagation has been detected and with confidence declared. The year 15 begins with the vote of a triumph to Germanicus Caesar (i 55, 1). An error: the Senate's vote ought to go at the end of the year's campaigning, along with the *ornamenta triumphalia* to legates of Germanicus (72, 1).[19] The notion wins a wide measure of acceptance.[20] Brief reflection dissuades. Germanicus was already endowed with a salutation (requisite for the triumph), earned before the decease of Augustus.[21] The grant of a triumph is in its proper place, and highly significant, being a gentle admonition from the ruler (albeit clear enough) that the ambitious prince should desist from warlike adventures.

To revert to the year 33. It opens with husbands for two daughters

---

[16] Josephus, *BJ* iv 495 f.

[17] For the year endings, J. Ginsburg, *Tradition and Theme in the Annals of Tacitus* (1981), 31 ff.

[18] Thus Dio lvii 19, 4. The phrase employed by Tiberius recurs in lxi 1, 1. Tacitus has it ('degustabis imperium'), but Suetonius transferred it to Caesar Augustus (*Galba* 4, 1).

[19] D. Timpe, *Der Triumph des Germanicus* (1968), 45 f.; 57.

[20] Observe the five names cited in *Phoenix* xxxiii (1979), 322, n. 67 = *RP* iii (1984), 1212, n. 67. Add now J. Ginsburg, op. cit. 18, cf. 107. F. R. D. Goodyear in his *Commentary* (Vol. ii, 1981), 69, is 'not persuaded' by Timpe—'but his theory has its attractions'.

[21] T. D. Barnes, *JRS* lxiv (1974), 24 f.; R. Syme, *History in Ovid* (1978), 56 ff.; *Phoenix* xxxiii (1979), 317 ff. = *RP* iii (1984), 1207 f. As against an acclamation in 13, Goodyear accords preference to 11 (Vol. ii, 84).

of Germanicus. Tiberius, now in the vicinity of Rome (as emerges a little further on), made the selection with anxious care: 'diu quaesito' (vi 15, 1). Drusilla was consigned to Cassius Longinus, Julia (Livilla) to M. Vinicius.[22] Consuls together in 30, they were in a stable season of life. Further, not in propinquity to the 'domus regnatrix'. As this historian did not need to point out, a double departure from practices recently prevalent in the dynasty. Nero, the eldest son of Germanicus, married Julia, the daughter of Drusus Caesar, soon after assuming the *toga virilis* in 20 (iii 29, 4).[23]

The extraction and quality of Cassius and Vinicius are neatly indicated. In his despatch to the Senate Tiberius, so the historian observes, wrote with no great enthusiasm: 'levi cum honore iuvenum'. That was in his fashion—'non quidem comi via sed horridus ac plerumque formidatus' (iv 7, 1).

So far the exordium of the year. As has been shown, the order of public events appears to conform to chronology, at least down to the death of Agrippina (October 18). To that item Dio subjoined the end of Munatia Plancina (the widow of Cn. Piso). He explains that attachment. Tiberius detested her, not because of Germanicus but for some other reason; yet he allowed her to go on living lest Agrippina should conceive joy at her extinction; and so Plancina was now put to death also (lviii 22, 5).

Tacitus proffered a similar but more subtle explanation. The old Augusta had protected Plancina, and so did the hostility of Agrippina ('vix credibile'). Plancina | now became vulnerable to prosecution and she met a deserved end by suicide: 'ut odium et gratia desiere, ius valuit' (26, 3).

None the less, the historian chose to break the link between Agrippina and her enemy. After Agrippina he inserted, 'haud multo post', the suicide of Cocceius Nerva (26, 1).

The item that follows Plancina's exit is of another character: Julia, the daughter of Drusus Caesar, marries Rubellius Blandus (27, 1). It marks an interval (however short) and serves as a transition to three deaths in the course of nature. Next therefore Aelius Lamia, 'extremo anni', with a brief firm tribute and a reference to his absentee governorship of Syria. That brings in, 'exim', the decease of Pomponius Flaccus in the same province. On which the senators heard a missive from Caesar, complaining about consulars who were reluctant to undertake the command of armies. Tiberius, so the author is careful to point out, was guilty of inadvertence. He forgot

[22] In Tacitus 'Julia', she is 'Livilla' on her gravestone (*ILS* 188).
[23] Similarly, the marriage of Drusus to the daughter of M. Lepidus (cf. *Ann.* vi 40, 3) probably occurred about 23. The consular had a nubile daughter in 21 (iii 35, 2).

that for a decade he had been detaining at Rome L. Arruntius, the legate of Tarraconensis (27, 3).

The year comes to its conclusion with 'obiit eodem anno et M. Lepidus'. As the historian declared, the 'moderatio atque sapientia' of Lepidus had been established adequately in the earlier books, and the lineage needed no advertisement: 'quippe Aemilium genus fecundum bonorum civium, et qui eadem familia corruptis moribus, inlustri tamen fortuna egere' (27, 4).

The allusion to contrasts of morality among the resplendent Aemilii looks forward to the next year when Scaurus faced prosecution, 'insignis nobilitate et orandis causis, vita probrosus' (29, 3). He anticipated the verdict by suicide, 'ut dignum veteribus Aemiliis'.

A problem that carries manifold repercussions has so far been segregated. Tacitus opens the year with Drusilla and Julia Livilla, with annotation on their bridegrooms. In curt and cursory register Dio brings up three princesses, not two. To the daughters of Germanicus (not equipped with names) he adds Julia, the daughter of Drusus Caesar, but none of the three husbands is accorded a mention (lviii 21, 1).

If the Greek historian is correct, the consequence is clear. Tacitus has disjoined Julia, he has postponed her marriage by a long interval, until late in the year, shortly before the decease of Aelius Lamia. Such has been a fairly common assumption.[24] |

A further question arises. Was it Dio or his source who put that marriage at the beginning of the year? At first sight the source, since Dio is a compiler.[25] However, inspection of his procedures shows him operating rather freely in disposition of the material (cf. above). Hence a complication.

If Tacitus made the disjunction, his purpose and motives come in. He writes 'tot funeribus funesta civitate pars maeroris fuit quod Iulia Drusi filia, quondam Neronis uxor, denupsit in domum Rubellii Blandi, cuius avum Tiburtem equitem Romanum plerique meminerant' (27, 1).

The language is noteworthy. Prejudice is voiced. It adheres, not to the historian himself but to the society he is describing. Grief at the sad lot of Julia, made over to the grandson of a Roman knight from

---

[24] Thus recently J. Ginsburg, in reference to Dio: 'there is no good reason not to follow him on this point' (op. cit. 75). Koestermann in his *Commentary* (Vol. ii, 1965) failed even to cite the Dio passage when discussing *Ann.* vi 15, 1 and 27, 1.

[25] That was assumed, most incautiously, in 'The Marriage of Rubellius Blandus', *AJP* ciii (1982), 84 = p. 197, above.

Tibur, recalls the dispraisal incurred by her mother Livia, who, seduced by Aelius Seianus, succumbed to the embraces of a 'municipalis adulter' (iv 3, 4).

There is something else. Descendants of Blandus and Julia were on high show in the historian's own time. They avow a link with the Emperor Nerva. Rubellia Bassa, the daughter of Blandus and Julia, had married the maternal uncle of Nerva.[26]

Tacitus (it has not escaped notice) lodged the marriage of Julia in near vicinity to the Emperor's grandfather. Only the suicide of Munatia Plancina separates them, removed from what seems her proper position in the sequel to Agrippina's end. Design has been suspected, or even malice: Cornelius Tacitus, consul in 97, had contemporary persons in mind.[27]

Notions of this kind are not remote or aberrant when the author of the *Annales* is under scrutiny. Before the present specimen is conceded, alternatives deserve a thought. If Dio is correct, Tacitus may nevertheless have decided to withhold Julia for reasons of economy, to avoid a cumulation of six persons, two of whom might require to be specified by paternity, namely Julia the daughter of Germanicus and Julia the daughter of Drusus.

A different approach is expedient, with appeal to considerations that lie outside the text. It was high time for Caesar to make provision for the two daughters of Germanicus, 'postquam instabat virginum aetas'. Drusilla was born in 17, Julia Livilla in 18. By contrast, the daughter of Drusus Caesar, 'Neronis quondam uxor', | as Tacitus stated. Marrying Nero in 20, she was now aged about twenty-seven. Moreover, although Seianus had matrimonial designs on her mother, with a petition to Tiberius in 25 (iv 39), the chance subsists (and for some it is a belief) that the daughter was in fact the princess to whom Seianus secured betrothal in 31.[28]

That question may be waived. The widow Julia was something of an embarrassment, and perhaps in no good repute. They alleged that she had spied upon her husband for the benefit of Seianus (iv 60, 2); and discredit adhered from the adulterous mother. Two remedies offered, each with many parallels in the annals of dynasties: either seclusion or a safe and innocuous husband. Tiberius selected Rubellius Blandus (*suff.* 18), a worthy *novus homo*, eloquent and well educated, about thirty years senior to the bride.

[26] *ILS* 952, cf. the reconstruction of Groag, *JÖAI* xxi/xxii (1924), Beiblatt 425 ff. According to Dio, Nerva had kinsfolk whom he passed over when he adopted Trajan (lxviii 4, 1). The father of Sergius Octavius Laenas (the consul of 131) would be Nerva's first cousin.
[27] Thus *Tacitus* (1958), 576 (briefly); *AJP* ciii (1982), 83 f. = pp. 197 f., above.
[28] Thus, with no hesitation expressed, *PIR*², J 636. For her mother (Livia Julia), R. Seager, *Tiberius* (1972), 213; B. Levick, *Tiberius the Politician* (1976), 170, cf. 277.

On this showing, Dio lumped together Julia's marriage with that of the other princesses: for convenience, or writing from memory.[29] It was not Tacitus who disjoined them but the decision and act of Ti. Caesar, that 'sagacissimus senex'.

It remains to ask at what season of the year the nuptials of Blandus and Julia found their modest celebration. Very late, according to Tacitus. That is, about November. An earlier date is not out of the question, before Tiberius left the neighbourhood. In the summer Caligula took a wife when going back with him to Capreae (vi 20, 1). Indeed, Tiberius may have had all four marriages on his mind when he came close to Rome and hovered there for some seven months, 'deviis plerumque itineribus ambiens patriam et declinans' (15, 3).

Caesar had no cause to refuse his presence to the marriage of Blandus, whom he held in manifest esteem, not perhaps without recollection of the Tiburtine grandfather, on historic repute as the first man of equestrian status to teach the art of public speaking.[30] It is therefore permissible to argue that Tacitus reserved the marriage for a place late in the year—and further, for reasons not merely artistic.

Departure here or there from rigorous sequence in the annual rubric will not always issue in detriment to the understanding of a historical process. In a number of instances it mattered little at what juncture sundry isolated items found their mention. To the annalist fell the function and duty of bringing out value and significance. The skill of Tacitus in coherence and transition has been adequately documented. |

From Dio's compressed version of the year something percolates about the personality of Ti. Caesar. For example, he was pedantic and malicious, libidinous and savage; and he possessed foreknowledge of the future. Further, anecdotes; and a pair of sporadic remarks are brought together and quoted (23, 3 f.).

In Tacitus the absent Princeps suffuses and pervades the urban chronicle.[31] Tiberius was cautious and slow of decision, as in the search for husbands for two princesses ('diu quaesito'). He took pride in his public spirit, asserting 'offensiones pro re publica coeptas', but evasive in statement, 'redditis absentiae causis admodum vagis' (15, 3). Hypocrisy was revealed when he expressed regret that Asinius Gallus died before he could face his accusers—whereas Gallus had been held in custody for three years (23, 1). In criticism of consulars

---

[29] As elsewhere, inferences from Dio to the order of events in his source can be hazardous.
[30] Seneca, *Controv.* ii, *praef.* 5.
[31] Compare Koestermann's tribute in his *Commentary*, on the year 33 (273 f.).

the Princeps was aggressive, 'incusabat' (27, 3), brazen and careless of opinion when he published shocking details about Drusus' ordeal in prison, and savage towards the memory of the prince: 'invectus in defunctum' (24, 1).[32] Rancour against Agrippina exploded in anger, 'foedissimis criminibus exarsit', with the allegation that Gallus had been her paramour, and his death had driven her 'ad taedium vitae' (25, 2). The despatch to the Senate proclaimed her end as a happy anniversary; and Agrippina was lucky 'quod non laqueo strangulata neque in Gemonias proiecta foret' (25, 2).[33]

Finally, the fatalism of Ti. Caesar, a convinced believer in the science of the stars, as demonstrated by the forecast about Galba's destiny and the Rhodian episode thereto annexed. His addiction to astrology thus comes up for the first time in the *Annales*, overlooked hitherto, along with personal tastes and habits of the ruler, by the historian whose preoccupation resided in senatorial transactions.

On comparison with Dio's account of the *quinquennium*, Tacitus missed little of value. Due allowance will be made for the lacuna, most of book V being lost. Three items repay inspection.

First, two absentee governors. Aelius Lamia had earned a previous mention, as is proved by the phrase 'qui administrandae Syriae imagine tandem exsolutus urbi praefuerat' (vi 27, 2); and likewise no doubt L. Arruntius, the legate of Tarraconensis, still at Rome 'decimum iam annum' (27, 3). Both, it may be conjectured, received their mandates about the same time, in 23.[34]

Arruntius, facing prosecution in the summer of 31, had been rescued by the Princeps: Dio, omitting the name, refers to an enemy of Seianus who had been appointed governor of Spain ten years previously (lviii 8, 3). As for the other legate, Dio reported Lamia's absent governorship of Syria when in 32 he acceded to the City Prefecture on the decease of L. Piso, with the comment that Tiberius treated 'many others' in the same fashion, pretending thereby to pay them honour (19, 6). No others are on attestation anywhere.[35]

Second, prolongation of proconsuls, in Dio under 33: tenures of three years for ex-praetors, of six for consulars (23, 5). No names, but a reason alleged—so many senators had been killed. Tacitus can

---

[32] The other instances of 'invehor' in the *Annales* are confined to Tiberius, viz. i 13, 4 (against Haterius); v 3, 3 (against Nero). Compare 'increpo', frequent in Tacitus to be sure, but labelling Tiberius eight times.

[33] Not quoted by some apologists. F. B. Marsh was satisfied with 'it is to the discredit of the emperor that he heaped abuse upon her in the grave' (*The Reign of Tiberius* (1931), 209). However, Tiberius was 'neither suspicious nor vindictive' (ibid. 223).

[34] That is, shortly before or after Drusus died in September.

[35] Suetonius has 'unum et alterum consulares' (*Tib.* 63, 2), having specified 'Hispaniam et Syriam per aliquot annos' (41).

hardly have omitted the damaging item. For Asia and Africa it meant ten consulars thwarted of a legitimate ambition. The anomaly did not terminate until 35.[36] It may appear a little strange that the historian did not then register it.

Third, imperial legates inordinately prolonged. To the proconsuls Dio appended a brief vague sentence about them (23, 6).[37] Tacitus was aware of the practice at an early stage. Noting Poppaeus Sabinus, he inserted an anticipatory excursus, 'id quoque morum Tiberii fuit' (i 80, 1 ff.). It closes with a reference to legates detained at Rome. It would be suitable to revert to both themes in the year of Seianus—perhaps when passing in review the governors of the armed provinces, who were variously important, not least Lentulus Gaetulicus in Germania Superior.[38]

For the rest, what an author chooses to pass over is a test of his discernment no less than a sign of the information available. Several factors come into play.

(1) *Significance.* Unlike Dio, Tacitus omitted Caligula's quaestorship in 33. Further, Dio duly registered the first decennial celebration and the second (lvii 24, 1; lviii 24, 1). Tacitus disdained them both. Instead he split the reign and the hexad in 23, opening the book with 'nonus Tiberio annus'.

(2) *The anecdotal.* Tacitus eschewed a number of entertaining items. Beneath the dignity of his theme and manner. As appears from Dio, not all of his annalistic predecessors had been restrictive. |

(3) *Economy and structure.* As evident elsewhere, this author can refrain and postpone. When recording the decease of L. Piso, the *praefectus urbi*, in 32, Tacitus did not name the successor (vi 10, 3)—or again in the next year, when Aelius Lamia died. It was Cossus Lentulus, a *vir triumphalis* and a character of some note: perhaps reserved for somewhere in Book VII.[39] Tacitus evinces a keen interest in Prefects of the City.

(4) *The nature of the source.* This historian might miss or neglect

---

[36] The proconsuls had been P. Petronius (*suff.* 19) in Asia, M. Silanus M. f. (*cos.* 19) in Africa, with for successors Cotta Messallinus (*cos.* 20) and C. Rubellius Blandus (*suff.* 18). For sundry adherent problems see now *Historia* xxx (1981), 196 ff. = *RP* iii (1984), 1357 ff.

[37] According to Suetonius, the Emperor once installed on Capreae discarded all cares of government: 'usque adeo abiecit ut postea . . . non provinciarum praesides ullos mutaverit' (*Tib.* 41).

[38] Gaetulicus had been a friend of Seianus. Observe the peculiar story in vi 30. His father Cossus, intimate with Tiberius, intervened in 31 to rescue Arruntius, as is shown by *Dig.* xlviii 2, 12, *praef.*: 'hos accusare non licet: legatum imperatoris ex sententia Lentuli dicta Sulla et Trione consulibus.' Cf. R. S. Rogers, *CP* xxvi (1931), 40.

[39] Cossus is absent from the *Annales* as extant. His urban office is known only from Seneca, *Ep.* 83, 15; and only Josephus mentions the successor, L. Calpurnius Piso (*cos.* 27): in 36 and in January of the next year, cf. *PIR*² , C 293.

certain items not transmitted in the *acta senatus*. For example, Prefects of Egypt.[40] Nor is it clear that Caesar normally announced to the Senate the appointment of consular legates. An exception is L. Vitellius, charged with a special mandate to direct policy as well as warfare on and beyond the eastern frontier (vi 32, 3). Consular legates may crop up in the sequel when they enter the action, earn honours, or end their days. To obtrude the successor would spoil the effect of an obituary notice.[41]

Equity demands that the signal achievement of Tacitus in selecting and disposing his material should not be allowed to obscure defects that have been discovered in his treatment of the year 33. Asking how a historian goes about his work helps to explain mistakes.

(1) Considius Proculus, seized during his birthday festival, haled before the Senate, condemned, executed (18, 1). The charge was *maiestas* (not further defined), and his sister was sent into exile, being arraigned by Q. Pomponius. By actions of this kind Pomponius, 'moribus inquies', sought to win favour with the Princeps and help his brother, Pomponius Secundus, so he alleged.

That brother made his entrance towards the end of 31, impugned by Considius, a senator of praetorian rank, for complicity with a relative of Seianus and held in confinement for long years (v 8, 1 f.). Introduced as 'multa morum elegantia et ingenio inlustri', he is P. Pomponius Secundus, the author of dramas, later consul (in 44), and much admired by the historian (xii 28, 2).

There is a problem. Is the senator Considius, enemy of the dramatist in 31, the same person as Considius Proculus, executed two years later, with Q. Pomponius |in the context, named as the prosecutor of his sister? Identity has been denied, since Tacitus, normally so careful about persons, provided no reference backwards.[42]

One hesitates. Tacitus may have been inadvertent to a call for annotation, precisely because the whole history of the consular dramatist was so familiar to him. Pliny had composed a biography of Pomponius Secundus, his old commander in Germania Superior.[43] Which carries further relevance: a subsidiary source. Observe the personal note in what Tacitus chooses to say about the deleterious

---

[40] Dio under 32 registered the decease of Vitrasius Pollio—replaced by Hiberus, an imperial freedman (lviii 19, 6).

[41] To the decease of Poppaeus Sabinus in 35 Dio subjoined his successor Memmius Regulus (lviii 25, 4): a character of some interest to Cornelius Tacitus.

[42] Thus Koestermann on vi 18, 1. And in *PIR*[2], C 1278 identity is canvassed with L. Considius Gallus, praetor and *XVvir sacris faciundis* (*CIL* vi 31705).

[43] As the nephew reveals, *Ep.* iii 5, 3.

brother and his ostensibly helpful activities: 'haec et huiusce modi a
se factitari praetendebat.'

(2) Pompeia Macrina exiled, whereupon her father, an 'inlustris
eques Romanus', and her brother, a senator of praetorian rank,
expecting to be condemned, took their own lives (18, 2). They were
under incrimination because of their ancestor, Theophanes of Mytilene.
He had been a close friend of Pompeius Magnus; and further on his
decease 'caelestes honores Graeca adulatio tribuerat.'

The allegations are trivial, the affair remains totally obscure.
Pompeia Macrina offers an imperfect clue. Tiberius had brought
down her husband and his father: 'maritum Argolicum, socerum
Laconem e primoribus Achaeorum, Caesar adflixerat.' The ruin of
the Euryclids, the dynastic house at Sparta, that is a theme to excite
curiosity. Presumably at some time between 29 and 32 (the lacuna in
the Tacitean narration) but with no necessary link of any kind to
Aelius Seianus.[44] Conjecture has evoked the appearance of the false
Drusus, registered by Tacitus at the end of 31 (v 10, cf. above).[45] Not
to any acceptable solution.

The persons repay close attention. Macrina's parent comes out on
clear testimony: friend and travel companion of young Ovid,
librarian appointed by Caesar Augustus, also procurator in Asia.
And, equipped with a *praenomen*, he is Cn. Pompeius Macer.[46] His
son is Q. Pompeius Macer, praetor in 15.

Those facts are requisite. Tacitus styles Theophanes the great-
grandfather, 'proavum eorum'. Which most scholars have accepted.[47]
Chronology forbids. The standard notion entailed the insertion of
another generation between Theo|phanes, the client and historian
of Pompeius Magnus, and the 'inlustris eques Romanus' (the father of
the praetor and of Macrina).

The historian, it follows, has made a mistake.[48] His assumption
permits an explanation. Theophanes the client of Magnus took him
back into the Republican past—one generation too far.

After error, an omission. The Roman knight is enrolled among
conspicuous friends of Tiberius Caesar, so Strabo states (xiii 618).

[44] It is assigned to 33, precisely, by B. Levick, op. cit. 211.

[45] B. Levick, op. cit. 212 f., developing an idea of R. S. Rogers.

[46] *Inschr. v. Priene* 247. Not 'Marcus', as M. Grant, *FITA* (1946), 388 f., discussing the coin
of Priene with on obverse his head and part of his name (ibid. Pl. IX, no. 34). Likewise
J. M. C. Toynbee, *Roman Historical Portraits* (1978), 73.

[47] R. Laqueur, *RE* vA 2099 f.; R. Hanslik, xxi 2277 f.; Gow and Page, *The Garland of Philip*
II (1968), 468. And Koestermann, ad loc., is not adequate.

[48] As suggested in *Tacitus* (1958), 749—where in line 10 emend 'earlier than 15 B.C.' to
'later' (on the age of the praetor). For a firm statement, *History in Ovid* (1978), 73 f. Some still
hesitate. Thus F. R. D. Goodyear on i 72, 3: 'grandson or great-grandson of Theophanes'.

The vicissitudes or the fate of those friends was a theme not elsewhere neglected by Cornelius Tacitus.

(3) Pomponius Flaccus dying in Syria, subjoined to the death and funeral of Aelius Lamia (27, 3). A strong suspicion arises that Flaccus was still among the living when this year ended.[49] Governorships of Syria link the two consulars, and that may have led the historian into error.

Tacitus blended the *acta senatus* with historical narration and with his own comments. In that process, awkward sutures or even mistakes might well occur. A number have been detected or surmised.[50]

A larger question subsists. How far did Tacitus have recourse to the Senate's protocol, and for what purpose (variety or to check his predecessors)? That has been a subject of sharp contestation and extreme opinions. To many (advocates all too often of the 'single source'), his use of the *acta* was at best sporadic and infrequent, the solitary citation (xv 74, 3) being accorded decisive weight. On the contrary side, assiduous employment in the first hexad has been claimed, notably in Book III where the historian had to fill out the annals of quiet years between the prosecution of Cn. Piso and the death of Drusus Caesar.[51] Some will welcome a recent move in this direction.[52] It was to be commended and enjoined in the first place by the plain lesson of the text and by the study of structure. |

A disquisition on the year 33 cannot avoid some reference however summary to an engaging question that concerns Cassius Dio. How far was he familiar with the text of Tacitus? Attention fastens on the death of Augustus and the accession of Tiberius, with abundant discussion about resemblances between the two authors (which also takes in Suetonius).[53] Divergence is more significant.

The Greek historian duly advertised industry and the selection of 'digna memoratu'. He went back to the annalistic predecessors of Tacitus, as befitted a conscientious enquirer. He had looked into Tacitus. Not an easy or attractive text at this juncture, but painfully compressed and highly enigmatic (as readers in a later time can testify). And not indispensable. A vestige has been detected, namely

---

[49] See the argument of G. Vermes and F. Millar in Schürer's *History of the Jewish People in the Age of Jesus Christ* (ed. 2, 1973), 264. Further, observations in *ZPE* xli (1981), 129 f. = *RP* iii (1984), 1380 f.

[50] For nine specimens, *JRS* lxxii (1982), 76 ff. = pp. 213 ff., above.

[51] For Book III, *Historiographia Antiqua* (Louvain, 1978), 247 ff. = *RP* iii (1984), 1028 ff.

[52] Observe now F. R. D. Goodyear in his *Commentary*, Vol. ii (1981), 136: introducing *Ann.* i 72–81.

[53] See C. Questa, *Studi sulle fonti degli Annales di Tacito* (ed. 2, 1963), 35 ff.: not always easy to follow (in either sense of the word).

a pair of linked sentences that appears to be a personal contribution added by each writer.[54] Not therefore enough to enlist and specify Tacitus among 'the sources of Dio'. In those transactions both can be treated as independent testimony, and so can the biographer.

For what follows in 15 and 16 (and for 17, as far as Dio is extant) the contrast is striking. The annalistic report of the last quinquennium of the reign is in a different case. Though the same features recur as previously (for example, a propensity to the anecdotal, and few names of senators), the reader encounters a kind of blurred similarity to the Tacitean exposition.

Several close resemblances have been brought up. Notably for the year 32.[55] In the first place, two items related in sequence by Tacitus (vi 2 f.). First, the proposal of Togonius Gallus: the Princeps should choose an escort of twenty armed senators to go with him into the House. It was soberly assessed and gently declined by the ironical emperor—'ludibria seriis permiscere solitus' (2, 4). Next, Junius Gallio, with a motion that veterans from the Praetorian Guard be granted access to the fourteen rows of seats reserved for Roman knights. Tiberius took offence, 'violenter increpuit velut coram rogitans' (3, 1). They expelled Gallio. Making for Lesbos, his choice for exile, he was arrested and put under custody.

Dio recounts the two episodes (lviii 17, 2–18, 1; 18, 3–5). Derivation from Tacitus has been suspected or credited.[56] A note of caution should intervene. Had | other writers survived, close parallels might be apparent in the selection of material or even in the order of narration.[57]

The whole context repays inspection. As the first item of the year Dio inserted an innovation in the annual oath of allegiance, now to be taken by each senator in person. Introducing which provision, he describes it as 'most laughable' (17, 1). Next, the proposal of

---

[54] *Ann.* i 7, 7; Dio lvii 7, 3 f. The passage is introduced by Dio with ἤδη μὲν ἤκουσα. For that phrase, cf. above, n. 9. It might perhaps be contended that both authors were using a subsidiary source.

[55] H. Jaeger, *De Cassii Dionis librorum 57. et 58. fontibus* (Diss. Berlin, 1910), 55 ff., cf. 103. To be used with caution. Many of his conclusions are vulnerable. Thus the notion that Dio did not need Aufidius Bassus and Servilius Nonianus 'quod pleraque eorum, quae apud illos extabant, expedita repperit apud Tacitum' (ibid. 104).

[56] Jaeger, op. cit. 58 ff. Observe, e.g., R. Syme, *Tacitus* (1958), 692: 'it is difficult to resist the conclusion that Dio had Book VI before him' (in allusion to the two episodes, and to M. Terentius in vi 8).

[57] Five concordances from 34 and 35 are tabulated by R. Martin, *Tacitus* (1981), 205, remarking that 'it cannot be mere coincidence that Tacitus and Dio have so many items in common'. One item is instructive—but in the negative sense. Both authors relate in sequence the suicides of Pomponius Labeo and Aemilius Scaurus. Dio exhibits (not in Tacitus) Labeo's eight years in Moesia and the title of the drama for which Scaurus was incriminated (lviii 24, 3 f.). However, Martin is alert to discrepancies (ibid. 206).

Togonius Gallus (the name omitted) as 'even more laughable' (17, 3). A sense of the ridiculous, be it noted in passing, is a feature congenial to senatorial writers, though not always requiring to find explicit and verbal manifestation.

On that proposal follow marks of gratitude rendered by Caesar to the Praetorians, both money and words of praise (18, 2 f.). Next, Junius Gallio (18, 3 ff.). Dio then goes on to a subsequent measure (of the next year, cf. *Ann.* vi 15, 2), but not wholly irrelevant, namely the Guard Prefect and some tribunes as escort to the Princeps. He adds (not in Tacitus under 33) that the Senate augmented that decree: senators to be searched for weapons (18, 6).

The rubric now proceeds to friends of Seianus. Some escaped harm, among them Lucius Caesianus, a praetor of the year, and the knight M. Terentius. Presiding at the festival of Flora, Caesianus exhibited bald men in mockery of Tiberius, culminating in a torchlight procession of 5,000 boys with shaven pates. Hence the label 'Caesiani' attached to the bald (19, 1 f.).[58] On which follows M. Terentius (see below).

On this showing it becomes dubious that the Greek historian either needed to have recourse to the text of Tacitus or thence excerpted the episodes of Togonius and Gallio, blending them with other senatorial material which he possessed in abundance. Tacitus introduced the former with 'Togonius Gallus, dum ignobilitatem suam magnis nominibus inserit, per deridiculum auditur' (vi 2, 2). Dio found the proposal ridiculous. So may one of the predecessors of Tacitus, whether with or without the name. Tacitus expected his readers to be alert to 'Togonius' which is visibly and vocally Celtic.[59] |

So far resemblances that are either exalted or deprecated. There is one item of a different order. After noting the prosecutions of Julius Africanus and Seius Quadratus, Tacitus came out with a solemn pronouncement asserting the diligence of his researches: 'nobis pleraque digna cognitu obvenere, quamquam ab aliis incelebrata' (vi 7, 5).[60]

He continues with a specimen, 'nam ea tempestate' (8, 1). While

---

[58] The praetor is L. Apronius Caesianus (*cos.* 39), whose parent (*suff.* 8) had the confidence of Ti. Caesar all through.

[59] Dio's avoidance of personal names (due in part to a desire to spare the reader) was all too frequent. Note further 'multorum amoribus famosa Albucilla' (vi 47, 2), left anonymous without husband or lovers (lviii 27, 4).

[60] The Sallustian 'incelebrata' (cf. *Hist.* i 88) does not escape notice. Note also the stylish 'digna cognitu' replacing the common 'digna memoratu' which Tacitus had employed previously (*Agr.* 1, 2; *Hist.* ii 24, 1). He soon goes on to 'cognitu non absurda' (vi 28, 1).

others sought to deny friendship with Seianus, the knight M. Terentius, on trial before the Senate, essayed a courageous and well-reasoned defence. Tacitus renders it in direct discourse. The core of the argument conveyed an appeal to the consequences of the ruler's own behaviour—'ut quisque Seiano intimus, ita ad Caesaris amicitiam validus'. And he requited with due homage, 'tuum, Caesar, generum, tui consulatus socium' etc.

In a summary of the speech Dio reproduces the same line of argument, with quotation (lviii 19, 3 f.). The plea of Terentius has been regarded as both striking and novel. Hence taken from Tacitus. That has generally been conceded.[61]

So far, a curt statement. Brief allusion to further complications cannot be suppressed. The central argument devised by Terentius finds close parallel in a portion of the long oration of Amyntas in Curtius Rufus (vii 1, 26 ff.). Justus Lipsius did not miss it.

In the sequel various explanations have been proffered. They have a patent bearing on the date of that author—to whom it is not easy to deny identity with Q. Curtius Rufus, consul suffect in 43.[62] A recent enquiry suggests that Rufus was much impressed by the oration when he heard it in the Senate.[63] A temptation will be felt to fall back on the precedent set by an earlier historian: 'nos eam rem in medio relinquemus.'

In estimating the sources of a historian, and his technique, arguments from omission have a place, sometimes refused, sometimes admitted with eager generosity. Chance or sheer incompetence comes into the count. If Dio consulted Tacitus when compiling the transactions of 33, it is a strange paradox that, aware of the rancour and ferocity of Tiberius, he did not pounce upon what the Princeps said about Agrippina. Instead, a casual detail. Excluding from the Mausoleum the | mortal remains of Agrippina and Drusus, Tiberius had them buried in a site not likely to be discovered (lviii 22, 5). Nor was the senator from the Greek lands alert to the fate that befell the descendants of the Mytilenaean historian.

That theme moves towards a suitable conclusion with negligence betrayed by Suetonius, whose knowledge of Tacitus has been canvassed, as is proper, but not with much profit accruing. Tiberius Caesar, departing in 26, refused until the end to enter the City, although he came in sight of Rome several times. A noteworthy and

---

[61] Thus Koestermann in his *Commentary* ad loc. 'zweifellos'. Further, the muted concession in *Tacitus* (1958), 692 (quoted above, n. 56).

[62] J. E. Atkinson in his *Commentary* on Books III and IV (Amsterdam, 1980), 19 ff.

[63] A. M. Devine, *Phoenix* xxxiii (1979), 153.

morbid phenomenon. According to Suetonius, two attempts only: 'bis omnino toto secessus tempore Romam redire conatus' (*Tib.* 72, 1). That is, the first at the beginning of 32, certified by Tacitus: 'aditis iuxta Tiberim hortis' (vi 1, 1). The second, amplified by the biographer with much picturesque detail, fell in the last months. Not in Tacitus or in Dio.

Those historians disclose the ruler's presence not far from Rome on four other occasions in the *quinquennium*. As follows:

(1) At the beginning of 33, for the marriages. *Ann.* vi 15, 3, cf. Dio lviii 21, 1 (within 30 stades of Rome). A long sojourn.

(2) In 34/5, at Albanum and Tusculum. Dio lviii 24, 1.

(3) Early in 35, at Antium. Dio lviii 25, 2.

(4) Late in 35, 'urbem iuxta'. vi 39, 2.[64]

That is not the worst. Ever and again, inspection of Suetonius shows him hasty and careless—and impercipient. It was the design of this scholarly biographer to supply the public with curious information, often of a kind not to be found in senatorial annalists. Suetonius duly furnished full and precise particulars about the physique of the Emperor (68, 1–3). He ignored his appearance in old age, as depicted in the vivid passage of the consular historian (alien to that author's normal manner and avoidances): the shrunken frame, the scarred visage, the denuded summit.[65]

---

[64] These inadequacies are relevant to earlier movements of the Princeps: after the first two years of his rule never further than Antium, 'idque perraro et paucos dies' (*Tib.* 38). Now Tiberius went away to Campania in 21 and was still absent for much of the next year, as demonstrated by *Ann.* iii 31, 2–64, 1. Again, Suetonius (in conflict with Tacitus) has him on Capreae before the disaster at Fidenae in 27 (40, cf. 41, 1).

[65] *Ann.* iv 57, 2: 'quippe illi praegracilis et incurva proceritas, nudus capillo vertex, ulcerosa facies ac plerumque medicaminibus interstincta.' The Emperor, it appears, was one of the victims of the dreadful 'mentagra' that came out of Egypt and attacked the human visage (Pliny, *NH* xxvi 2 ff.). For this conjecture, *ZPE* xli (1981), 125 f. = *RP* iii (1984), 1376 f.

14

Tigranocerta. A Problem Misconceived

ERUDITE controversies can go on for a long time. Repetition or fatigue is no bar. Of some, notably in sacred history, there never was a solution. Problems in geography or topography are in a happier posture. Exploration or an inscription might enforce a decision.

Much turns on Tigranocerta. The monarch proceeded to build a capital at that place in Armenia where he first assumed the diadem. The ample city had high walls; and outside the walls Tigranes added for embellishment palaces, gardens, game-parks, and lakes. The population was captive, drawn from the lands he conquered and annexed. So far Appian.[1]

To maintain that broad dominion, Tigranes needed a second capital. He built the city about the year 80 B.C., as the counterpart to distant Artaxata on the Araxes, towards the frontier with Iberia.

Tigranocerta stands on high show in the annals of Roman warfare, attached to the performance of illustrious invaders. Lucullus captured it in 69, coming down through Sophene and crossing the Armenian Taurus. In A.D. 59 the city fell without a blow to Domitius Corbulo, at the term of the march that took him all the way from Artaxata. Two years later Tigranocerta, when held by the Roman vassal in Armenia, was besieged to no effect by a Parthian general.

In the torrid July of the year 1838 Moltke, when travelling westwards after the campaign in Kurdistan, passed over the Batman Su in the night. He duly admired the handsome bridge. Towards morning the company reached Meiafarkin: 'das alte Tigranokerta', so Moltke subjoined without further comment. The site is the later Martyropolis: now bearing the name of Silvan, to the north of the upper Tigris, some 40 miles north-eastwards from Diyarbakir (Amida in the ancient time). |

In 1883 the excellent Bunbury declared the identity 'most plausible'.[2] Three years before that pronouncement something

---

[1] Appian, *Mithr.* 285; 379 f.
[2] E. H. Bunbury, *A History of Ancient Geography* ii (1883), 104.

S. Mitchell (ed), *Armies and Frontiers in Roman and Byzantine Anatolia, Proceedings of a Colloquium held at University College, Swansea, in April 1981* (British Institute of Archaeology at Ankara Monograph No. 5: BAR International Series 156, 1983), 61–70.

sharply discordant had been brought up, a site in another region. Sachau advocated Tell Ermen, a modest elevation on the Meso-potamian plain, rising (they say) to about 150 feet.[3] The mound is situated a dozen miles south-west from Mardin, that lofty citadel, and about 40 miles to the west of Nisibis.

Hence the prolonged controversy, the echo and the annoyance of which is not yet mute. It serves no profit to retail opinions and arguments, to catalogue verdicts or even recantations. Enough to select a few names, variously significant—and especially such as laid claim to military expertise.

In Tell Ermen B. W. Henderson advertised explicit faith: 'I can feel no doubt at all.'[4] When seven years elapsed the journeys of Lehmann-Haupt contributed the powerful arguments that speak for Martyropolis.[5] Rice Holmes refused to be impressed. In lucid exposition and with spirited polemic in many directions, he concluded that in any event Tell Ermen was the Tigranocerta captured by Lucullus and by Corbulo. Duly perplexed by discrep-ancies (or rather contradictions) in the ancient evidence, he toyed with the notion of two cities carrying the same name.[6]

On the other side, when Anderson came to write about the campaigns of Corbulo, that sagacious and economical scholar eschewed any mention of Tell Ermen;[7] and the veteran Lehmann-Haupt, reverting to his theme, produced a long and elaborate statement.[8]

There the matter might rest but for two recent defenders of the mound in Mesopotamia. In a comprehensive and valuable book devoted to the historical geography of the region the author comes out in confidence all through, for Tell Ermen.[9] It also appeals to an editor of Strabo.[10]

---

[3] E. Sachau, 'Über die Lage von Tigranokerta', *Abh. der königl. Ak. der Wiss. zu Berlin* (1880).

[4] B. W. Henderson, *The Life and Principate of the Emperor Nero* (1903), 473. He could draw upon his detailed study: *Journal of Philology* xxviii (1903), 99 ff.

[5] C. F. Lehmann-Haupt, *Armenien einst und jetzt* i (1910). For the campaign of Lucullus he was followed by K. Eckhardt, *Klio* x (1910), 72 ff.; 192 ff.

[6] T. Rice Holmes, *JRS* vii (1917), 120 ff.: largely reproduced and not much modified in an appendix to *The Roman Republic* i (1923), 409 ff.

[7] J. G. C. Anderson, *CAH* x (1934), 764; of Tigranocerta he says: 'its exact site is still uncertain'. Anderson's caution and 'care for learning' survive in local anecdote. By the way, his *Map of Asia Minor* (1903) registered Tell Ermen. The second edition, by W. M. Calder and G. E. Bean (1957), printed both sites, with a query attached.

[8] *RE* vi (1937), 981–1007 (divided into 160 short sections).

[9] L. Dilleman, *La Haute Mésopotamie orientale et les pays adjacents* (1962), 252 ff., cf. 270 f.; 278. Observe the map facing p. 269.

[10] F. Lasserre, after mentioning Martyropolis and Amida, concludes with 'plus justement Tell Ermen' (Budé, vol. viii (1975), 137).

It is well to bear in mind the true nature of a problem. In many instances it is literary, for aught that exponents of warfare and strategy may have to say. The Spanish campaign of 26 B.C. is a pertinent example and admonition. Schulten devised an ambitious plan of operations for Caesar Augustus: three armies marching out for the | conquest of the north-west (Callaecia, Asturia, Cantabria) from bases widely separate, from Braga, from Astorga, from a point west of Burgos.[11] That defied the sources (the campaign embraced Cantabria only), as was seen and stated by an erudite cleric in 1768.[12] The authority of Schulten prevailed: with dire and lasting consequences for many scholars, not only in the Peninsula.[13]

There is another impediment. Manifold harm accrues when passages are culled from a large work without estimating the sources, structure, and habits of the author—often a compiler. That observation points towards Strabo, whose testimony is regarded as the crux or kernel of the Tigranocerta imbroglio.[14]

It is expedient to set forth the matters in a certain order, not that of Strabo's text. Begin therefore with Nisibis and Mons Masius.[15] The geographer defines the mountain as above the Mygdonians of Mesopotamia, whose city is Nisibis (xi 527). Now Masius is the range of the Tur Abdin, a sharp line when contemplated from the plain (with Mardin on a conspicuous promontory), as for example by Alexander's army when it marched past the 'Armenian mountains' —but less impressive from the other side: a sloping plateau area approached from Diyarbakir.

Next, two passages about the city and the mountain, but with another name inserted. First, Masius: τὸ Μάσιον, τὸ ὑπερκείμενον τῆς Νισίβιος ὄρος καὶ τῶν Τιγρανοκέρτων (xi 522). Second, in a later book, where Mesopotamia is described: Nisibis (styled Antioch of Mygdonia) lying thus: ὑπὸ τῷ Μασίῳ κειμένην καὶ Τιγρανόκερτα καὶ Κάρρας κτλ. (xvi 747).

Suspicion arises. Both references look like the author's additions to a basic text. Writers on geography tend to serve up obsolete information all too often. Their attempts to supplement sometimes betray their hand. Strabo's sources (it appears) were anterior to the foundation of Tigranocerta. Strabo inserted the name. In error, as will emerge without discomfort.

---

[11] F. Schulten, *Los cántabros y astures y su guerra con Roma* (1943), 136 ff.
[12] His *Cantabria* is reprinted with notes by R. Teja and J. M. Iglesias-Gil (Santander, 1981).
[13] Half a dozen names are registered by J. M. Echegaray in his *Cantabria a través su historia* (Santander, 1977), 80: himself a recent convert.
[14] The relevant passages are cited or quoted by Rice Holmes, *JRS* vii (1917), 134.
[15] The article in *RE* xiv 2069 f. omits two of the four Strabonian references to Masius.

The Tur Abdin extends between the upper valley of the Tigris and the plain of Mesopotamia. In terms of geography, however, the | line of division lies north of the Tigris. It is the Taurus, as Strabo states (xvi 744). It runs eastward from the Euphrates to the vicinity of Lake Van, arising in its central portion to about 9,500 feet above sea level.

Strabo is also of pertinent value when defining Sophene. That country lies in a hollow between Taurus and Antitaurus (xi 521); and the Taurus separates Sophene and the rest of Armenia from Mesopotamia (522). That is clear, once 'Mesopotamia' is recognized as an ambiguous term. In geography it includes the upper valley of the Tigris—which politically belonged to Armenia.

Trouble now intervenes, at first sight. According to another passage, Sophene lies between Masius and Antitaurus (xi 527). In this instance Masius is patently equated with Taurus. How so? Strabo (like others since) was not aware that 'Masius' represents the Armenian word for 'mountain'.

Taurus called 'Masius', that is no surprise. It is confirmed, vivid and visibly. Natives on the high mountains use sleds and snow-shoes. That occurs in Median Atropatene and on Mount Masius in Armenia (xi 506). Those would be peculiar practices, nay seldom possible on the Tur Abdin, which scarcely rises above 3,000 feet. The inadvertent compiler thus betrays a double use of 'Masius'—and a patent doublet in his location of Sophene.

It will be entertaining albeit superfluous to adduce an episode in Trajan's war, arising from delay, incompetence, or the orders of the wilful Imperator. Brutius, a Roman general, was in sore straits, confronted by snow 16 feet deep. Native guides saved him, and snow-shoes.[16] Identity and the occasion are beyond doubt: Bruttius Praesens, the legate of VI Ferrata, conducting troops in the winter of 114/15 across the Armenian Taurus to the valley of the upper Tigris.[17]

To conclude this rubric. Strabo, who had been a historian before he embarked on the vast enterprise, began as a classical philologist. That is deplorably evident in his treatment of Hellas, when he dishes up old lecture notes on Homeric geography.

The scholar from Pontic Amaseia contributes precious details | about Anatolia from his own time and memory, with no sign that his peregrinations had taken him further east than Cappadocia and Cilicia, let alone to the Euphrates. As concerns Armenia, doublets in

---

[16] Arrian, *Parthica* fr. 85 Roos.

[17] As argued in *Historia* xviii (1969), 352 = *RP* (1979), 774. For the habits and tastes of Praesens, Pliny, *Ep.* vii 3; for his long and paradoxical career, *IRT* 545 (Lepcis); *AE* 1950, 66 (Mactar). See further *Studia Kajanto* (1985), 273 ff. = pp. 563 ff., below.

Book XI attest an awkward amalgamation of two sources. Ignorance about Masius induced him to put Tigranocerta in the vicinity of Nisibis. And a further consequence, enormous but not always detected. Strabo compresses and occludes the whole valley of the upper Tigris, between the Tur Abdin and the Armenian Taurus. Ancient Amida has to wait until Ammianus for its earliest mention.

Strabo's methods, or rather habits, being elucidated, his testimony lapses—or can be turned against him to fortify the contrary thesis. Completeness and clarity demand that two other passages be put under brief inspection.

In the first, Tigranes harries Cappadocia. He took away all its inhabitants to Mesopotamia, using them to people Tigranocerta (xii 539). A careful reader will recall that according to Appian, also a compiler but reproducing a historical narration, the monarch established the city with an Armenian name on Armenian soil.

In the second passage corruption of the text has so far baffled emendation. After summarizing the conquests of Tigranes it proceeds to their corollary, the foundation of the new capital: ἐπὶ τοσοῦτον δ' ἐξαρθεὶς καὶ πόλιν ἔκτισε πλησίον τῆς Ἰβηρίας, μεταξὺ ταύτης τε καὶ τοῦ κατὰ τὸν Εὐφράτην Ζεύγματος, ἣν ὠνόμασε Τιγρανόκερτα (xi 532).

What has gone wrong, no mystery. The word Ἰβηρίας should not be altered or expunged but kept.[18] A reference to Artaxata, the former capital, has fallen out. The two cities stood in sharp antithesis. Pliny affords guidance. He notes 'in excelso autem Tigranocerta, at in campis iuxta Araxen Artaxata' (*NH* vi 26). Further he states the dimensions of Armenia. First the 'longitudo', extending 'a Dascusa ad confinium Caspii maris'. Then 'latitudinem dimidium eius a Tigranocerta ad Hiberiam' (vi 27).

Hiberia as a limit thus corresponds roughly to Artaxata in the | sentence that precedes. The supplement to be desiderated should be something like πόλιν ἔκτισεν ⟨ἀντίπαλον τῇ ἀρχαίᾳ τῇ⟩ πρὸς τῆς Ἰβηρίας.[19]

Tigranocerta, it follows, is situated in Armenia, approximately halfway between Artaxata and Zeugma ('Seleuceia on the Bridge').

Not very precise, to be sure. Even if Tigranocerta be not Martyropolis, the region is declared by Eutropius: in Arzanene (vi 9, 1). That is, the westernmost of the Five Satrapies, the 'regiones

---

[18] Dilleman emends to πλησίον τῆς Ἀρμενίας (op. cit. 256): that is, to support a Mesopotamian site for a capital of Armenia.

[19] I hit upon this notion nearly forty years ago when occupied with errors or gaps in the text of Strabo: unpublished. Something better may turn up in the sequel.

Transtigritanae' ceded to the Persians in 363 as Ammianus testifies (xxv 7, 9). Eutropius should have known, who participated in the expedition of Julian (x 16, 1).

Strabo disposed of, the head and front of the argument, brief epilogue can go to the other writer whose testimony was invoked on the same side, without proper caution, namely Cornelius Tacitus.[20] Problems of a different order are involved.

In A.D. 61 the Parthian monarch Vologaeses, provoked to anger by incursions of Tigranes (whom Rome had installed as vassal ruler in Armenia) threatened to renew the war, although not intending that it should go very far. He advanced to Nisibis, and his general Monaeses proceeded to invest Tigranocerta, held by Tigranes. Corbulo, having meanwhile taken measures to reinforce the frontier of the Euphrates, despatched an envoy to protest, the arrogant centurion Casperius. He had an interview with Vologaeses at Nisibis, 'septem et triginta milibus passuum a Tigranocerta distantem' (*Ann.* xv 5).

The distance from Tigranocerta brought comfort to the friends of Tell Ermen. That site lies about 40 miles to the west of Nisibis. Confidence was premature. Inspection of the transactions reported by Tacitus makes the whole situation peculiar indeed, if Tigranocerta was situated so close to Nisibis and in the same region. Coming from Zeugma, Corbulo's envoy would in fact encounter the besieged city on his path.

Tacitus was a careful and accurate historian. What then is to be done about the figure of 37 miles? Some assume it erroneous (as often happens to numerals in texts ancient and modern). The transmission is in question. The figure of 37 miles might go back to the source of Tacitus.[21] Numerical emendation, even if an easy recourse, is not the best way of dealing with this text. In any event, the passage is not valid to establish Tigranocerta on the plain of Mesopotamia instead of in Armenian territory north of the Tigris, as the campaigns of Lucullus and of Corbulo enjoin and impose.[22]

Even were the figure of 37 miles not held erroneous, it carries an anomaly that commentators fail to perceive and exploit. Milestones mark distances on Roman roads. What author could ascertain such precision about foreign lands or bother to register it when writing

---

[20] Observe J. Carcopino, *Histoire romaine* ii (1936), 541: 'pour moi il m'est impossible de sacrifier les indications de Tac., *Ann.* XV 4 et Strabo XI 12, 4 et XVI i, 23 aux récits plus ou moins fantastiques des campagnes de Lucullus.' And, on the other hand, H. A. Ormerod, *CAH* ix (1932), 366: 'if the testimony of Strabo and Tacitus may be disregarded'.

[21] H. Dessau, *Gesch. der r. Kaiserzeit* ii (1926), 195, suggesting the 'Urbericht' of Corbulo.

[22] R. Syme, *Tacitus* (1958), 396, cf. 747.

about Mesopotamia and Armenia? A round number was normal. It would not deceive, it would not impair the validity of a historical narration.

In sundry matters of warfare and topography the consular historian has been exposed to animadversion from eager or captious critics. Of Tigranocerta he happens to furnish a clear and vivid description: 'urbem copia defensorum et magnitudine moenium validam. ad hoc Nicephorius amnis haud spernenda latitudine partem murorum ambit, et ducta ingens fossa, qua fluvio diffidebatur' (xv 4, 1).

The river Nicephorius is a clue, if any require it: one of the affluents running from the north into the Tigris, as Pliny states (vi 129); and for Pliny, Tigranocerta stood 'in excelso' (vi 26). So much for Mesopotamia and the miserable mound.

Tacitus was composing Book XV after the impact of the Imperator's campaigns—or even (it can be argued) after their failure and Hadrian's renunciation. That influence might be variously surmised in large matters and in small, from the policy of emperors and the performance of generals to the Moschi, 'gens ante alias socia Romanis' (xiii 37, 3).[23] Tigranocerta does not occur in the fragmentary record of the warfare. But Bruttius Praesens, the paradoxical and Epicurean friend of the younger Pliny, had Tigranocerta as his goal (one may assume) when he crossed the snow-bound Taurus, as had Domitius Corbulo in the summer of 59.

Tacitus was alert to past history also, and responsive to a cherished and classical model. When Corbulo in 63 entered Armenia, to repair by a demonstration of force and vigour the disaster incurred by Caesennius Paetus (and to facilitate an accommodation through diplomatic arts), he duly followed 'iter L. Lucullo quondam penetratum'.[24] Plutarch in his biography of Lucullus took the general through Sophene and across the Armenian Taurus to victory beside a river a little below Tigranocerta.[25]

[23] *JRS* lxvii (1977), 47 (on Caesennius Paetus) = *RP* iii (1984), 1057 f.
[24] *Ann.* xv 27, 1. The same route had been taken by Paetus the year before (cf. xv 8, 1)—as the author did not state.
[25] Plutarch, *Lucullus* 24 ff. To insist on the harm done to Lucullus and to Corbulo these many years by Tell Ermen and by misconceptions about Strabo would be tedious and odious.
The present essay was designed as a fresh approach, without consultation of certain Strabonian studies composed nearly forty years ago: among them 'Tigranocerta', 'Taurus and Masius', 'Sophene and Gordyene'. In September of 1944 I had cursory autopsy of Martyropolis.

15

Domitian: The Last Years

FIFTEEN years of tyranny from 81 to 96, September to September precisely. The formulation imposed by Cornelius Tacitus in his first monograph attracts and detains: 'grande mortalis aevi spatium'. For generations indifferent to the Latin classics it is perpetuated in the novel of Proust, in a garbled fashion. Commenting on the long ordeal endured by Swann in servitude to a woman, the Sorbonne professor observes: 'ce que le poète appelle à bon droit *grande spatium mortalis aevi*'.

In the reigns of emperors as in their biographies a dichotomy is commonly advertised. Tiberius Caesar offers the standard example. The writers of annalistic history whom Suetonius and Dio followed made the cut either in 19 (the death of Germanicus) or in 26 (the ruler's departure from Rome). Although the latter date, half way through a reign of twenty-three years, was variously attractive, Tacitus decided on 23, with momentous consequences for the structure of the hexad and for his portrayal of Tiberius.

These dichotomies tend to be denounced as schema and artifice. On the contrary, if a Caesar outlasted an initial felicity he ran into trouble soon or late. The first Princeps was not exempt. In 6 B.C., twenty-five years from the Battle of Actium, the government of Caesar Augustus took a turn for the worse. Livy avoided vexation by setting the term of his great work three years previously.

To come to Domitian. According to Suetonius he was not able to abide by his early 'clementia' and 'abstinentia' (*Dom.* 10, 1). The declension to cruelty intensified: 'verum aliquanto post civilis belli victoriam saevior' (10, 5). That is to say, in the year 89 after the military proclamation of Antonius Saturninus, the legate of Germania Superior, which impinged on a season of acute embarrassment. The Dacian War was not yet over. Beginning in 85 with the defeat of Oppius Sabinus, it had brought another disaster in the field when Cornelius Fuscus, the Prefect of the Guard, met his end. However, in the late summer of 88 Tettius Julianus, the legate | of Moesia

Superior, won a signal victory at Tapae; and Decebalus might be ready to come to terms.[1]

Saturninus made his proclamation on the first day of January.[2] Time and place were ominous, evoking the mutiny of the two legions at Moguntiacum that led at once to the elevation of A. Vitellius (at Colonia Claudia) twenty years before. What ensued destroyed the parallel. Lappius Maximus, the commander of the other army, intervened with prompt decision.

Obscurity envelops the whole transaction. Conspiracy has been assumed.[3] Accident may be the answer, poor discipline, or evil counsellors among the officers, with Saturninus in the role of the 'reluctant usurper', as prefigured by Verginius Rufus in 68, as exemplified often by history or by fiction in the late annals of the Empire.[4]

No allies of Saturninus can be ascertained among the other army commanders.[5] And, so far as known, no partisans were indicted and punished at the capital. Saturninus (*suff.* 82), a new senator, was far from promising as a candidate for the purple—and perhaps a bad choice to have charge of four legions.[6] Whether Germania Superior was his first province after the consulship lies beyond knowledge.[7] The unfortunate Oppius Sabinus, by anomaly *consul ordinarius* in 84, had gone straight to Moesia, a province with the same legionary strength.

Lappius Maximus (*suff.* 86) won glory exorbitant for a senator, and dangerous prominence. Further promotion might be a problem. There was Syria, a command of eminent prestige, denied to Julius Agricola by the jealous emperor after he had conquered Britain. One might have been moved to wonder about Lappius.[8] None the less,

---

[1] To obviate the citation of some names and facts not in dispute see W. Eck, *Senatoren von Vespasian bis Hadrian* (1970).

[2] As reconstructed from the protocol of the *Arvales* by E. Ritterling, *Westdeutsche Zeitschrift* xii (1893), 218 ff.: widely adopted, as in *CAH* xi (1936), 172 ff.

[3] Thus in *CAH* xi (1936), 172 ff. Compare G. Walser, *Provincialia. Festschrift Laur-Belart* (1968), 498: 'hinter Saturninus stand eine größere Verschwörung aus Kreisen des Senats und der Generalität'.

[4] For this conception, *JRS* lxviii (1978), 20 f. = *RP* iii (1984), 1082 f.

[5] It cannot be assumed that Sallustius Lucullus (*Dom.* 10, 3) was legate of Britain in this season.

[6] Despite the governorship in Judaea (combined with a legion), as deduced from the erased name on a dedication set up towards the end of Vespasian's reign. Cf. *JRS* lxviii (1978), 12 ff. = *RP* iii (1984), 1070 ff.

[7] There is space for a legate, or rather for two, after Corellius Rufus, attested in 82 (*CIL* xvi 28).

[8] Observe, as a warning against premature assumptions, *Tacitus* (1958), 51 (on Lappius Maximus and Tettius Julianus): 'neither of those generals could with safety have been put in charge of Syria'—annulled rapidly for Lappius by a diploma of 91 emerging (*AE* 1961, 319); while death may have anticipated further employment and honours for Tettius.

Lappius went there, on attestation in 90.[9] That may be taken as a sign that | Domitian retained confidence in his generals—and further as some confirmation of doubts concerning the events at Moguntiacum.

The year 89 would command high relief in a narrative history, either to open a book dramatically or to close it: peace with Dacia and Domitian's double triumph. In the sequel the last Danubian campaign, waged on the Pannonian frontier against Suebi and Sarmatians, occurred in 92. A period of ease and security for the government might now seem vouchsafed.

In the autumn of the next year concord between the ruler and the high assembly was disrupted.[10] Hence for a senatorial historian a significant turning-point, introducing the last epoch of a doomed reign.

A sequence of prosecutions for treason brought death or exile to sundry persons of rank and to their adherents or clients. Calamity overtook a whole group, the relatives and friends who carried on the tradition of the illustrious Thrasea Paetus, a victim of Nero. Their opposition to Nero had been slow to take shape, and Thrasea was not prosecuted until 66, the twelfth year of the reign. The parallel is not without instruction in other respects.

About Thrasea Paetus the historian furnished a full and explicit exposition in the *Annales*. What happened in 93 depends almost entirely on recent testimony, highly favourable towards the incriminated group and standing in need of elucidation. Tacitus, writing when less than five years had elapsed, gave voice to horror and indignation in his biography of Agricola.[11] Next Pliny, ever alert for approbation. He showed courage during the prosecutions (he was praetor at the time), public spirit in aspirations for revenge when the exiles came back; and he continued to put emphasis on his ties with the deceased.[12]

The government thus came into conflict with educated opinion—and philosophers were banished. A grave consequence, it should seem,

---

[9] *AE* 1977, 827 = *SEG* xxvii 1009 (Gerasa).

[10] Subsequent to the decease of Julius Agricola on August 23 of 93 (*Agr.* 44, 1). A recent book puts these transactions in 94, Pliny's praetorship in 95 (H. Bengtson, *Die Flavier* [1979], 233 ff.).

[11] *Agr.* 45, 1: 'non vidit Agricola obsessam curiam et clausum armis senatum' etc. There is a chance that Tacitus was still abroad, despite 'mox nostrae duxere Helvidium in carcerem manus' (collective guilt).

[12] Observe, e.g., *Ep.* iii 11, 2 (help to a philosopher); ix 13 (an action in 97). Pliny now halted in his career, so he alleged (*Pan.* 95, 3 f.)—but he became prefect in charge of the *aerarium militare* before the death of the tyrant (*ILS* 2927: Comum).

but requiring sober estimation. Likewise the origin and nature of the crisis.

It was expedient for Caesar to hold the balance between rival combinations and factions, to avoid being beguiled by a powerful minister or entrapped by a helpful company of eager adherents. Assessment of these deplorable transactions should not neglect factional rivalries, though not perhaps provoked by the Emperor himself yet developing to his gratification. Freedom to prosecute was one of the last vestiges of Republican 'libertas'.

The senators under attack professed allegiance to a tradition of liberty, of integrity and courage; and they further paraded the teaching of the Stoics. While fortifying character in the evil days, that doctrine engendered arrogance and conceit, with a danger of incautious political activity or attitudes.[13] And some perhaps were thrust further into paths of opposition or 'contumacia' than they intended, through the zeal of younger partisans.

The group easily inspired animosity. For their own part, no recent or personal grievances can be discovered. On the contrary, Junius Rusticus attained to a retarded consulship in 92 (when tribune of the plebs in 66 he offered his intercession to Thrasea). The consulate of the younger Helvidius Priscus is not on record. If not previous to 87, it might fall in 93, precisely. To the second pair of that year belongs Avidius Quietus, once a friend of Thrasea: hence to be assumed a late consul, like Junius Rusticus.[14] Quietus is not named among the exiles, one of whom was Mauricus, the brother of Rusticus.

There is another factor. As happens elsewhere, hot weather or the plague may have exacerbated competition and enmities. From 89 onwards is detected a sequence of unhealthy seasons—or rather a pestilence, such as the Dacian War would easily cause or encourage. Cassius Dio has the revealing story of malefactors operating with poison pins at Rome and throughout the world: repeated later for the great plague in the reign of Commodus.[15]

For these years an adequate sum can be mustered of deaths among the young and middle-aged.[16] And at any time September is found more lethal at Rome even than August.

[13] As alleged by Tigellinus against Rubellius Plautus: 'veterum Romanorum imitamenta praeferre, adsumpta etiam Stoicorum adrogantia sectaque quae turbidos et negotiorum adpetentes faciat' (*Ann.* xiv 57, 3). Similarly, the prosecutor of Thrasea Paetus: 'ut imperium evertant, libertatem praeferunt' (xvi 22, 4).

[14] Pliny, *Ep.* vi 29, 1 (Thrasea and Quietus). His command of the legion VIII Augusta (*ILS* 6105) belongs about the year 82.

[15] Dio lxvii 11, 6; lxxii 14, 3 f.

[16] *Tacitus* (1958), 69; *Some Arval Brethren* (1980), 21 ff. Search for victims of the great plague under Titus is not so remunerative.

In this fashion might be excogitated reasons for modifying the impression conveyed by Tacitus and Pliny—and even for extenuating the ill fame of the ruler, at the expense of the prosecutors as well as their victims.[17] Is the historical significance of the year 93 thereby impaired?

The testimony of Suetonius now comes in. The biographer, who at this stage in his exposition was moving towards narrative, might have discerned and registered a second turn for the worse (subsequent to 89). He does not. Between the two notices concerning Domitian's cruelty (10, 1 and 10, 5) he inserted a catalogue of consulars put to death (10, 2–4). It comprises ten names, with no indications of time or order. The first three, leading off with Civica Cerialis the proconsul of Asia, are defined as 'quasi molitores rerum novarum'.[18] For the rest, trivial pretexts are registered: 'ceteros levissima quemque de causa'. In all, the ten names include four members of the high aristocracy, or what now counted as such.[19] But only two consulars who had held military commands.[20]

Junius Rusticus and the son of Helvidius Priscus figure as the eighth and ninth items, before Flavius Sabinus (*cos.* 82). The former was condemned 'quod Paeti Thraseae et Helvidi Prisci laudes edidisset appellassetque eos sanctissimos viros', the latter because in a mythological stage play he mocked Domitian's alienation from his consort Domitia Longina. The notice on Rusticus concludes with the phrase 'cuius criminis occasione philosophos omnes urbe Italiaque summovit.' That is all.

Suetonius, it will be salubrious to recall, was a sober and distrustful character. He nowhere betrays an affection for doctrines, let alone any propensity to hero-worship. In the company of his patron Pliny he no doubt heard more than he liked about the recent martyrs, the 'sanctissimi viri' whose memory was cult and veneration.

A brief glance at one of the earlier biographies furnishes various instruction on the score of omissions. Suetonius in the *Nero* passed over the fame and the fate | of Domitius Corbulo; and (also in the

---

[17] For a general rehabilitation of Domitian see K. H. Waters, *Phoenix* xviii (1964), 49 ff.; *AJP* xc (1969), 385 ff.

[18] Cerialis (*suff.* *c*.76) was presumably proconsul in 88/9: replaced temporarily by a Roman knight (*ILS* 1374). The offence of the other two baffles conjecture: Salvidienus Orfitus (*suff.* *ann. inc.*) and M'. Acilius Glabrio (*cos.* 91). The latter was killed in exile, in 95 according to Dio (lxvii 14, 3).

[19] Viz. Salvidienus Orfitus, Acilius Glabrio, Lamia Aelianus, Salvius Cocceianus (nephew to the Emperor Otho). There is no call to bring any of the four into relation with the faction of Junius Rusticus.

[20] Viz. Civica Cerialis, attested in Moesia in 82 (*CIL* xvi 26), where he succeeded his brother Sex. Vettulenus Cerialis (*suff.* *c*.73): on whom cf. now the diploma of 75 (M. M. Roxan, *RMD* [1978], no. 2); and Sallustius Lucullus, legate of Britain, who remains a total enigma.

Galba) he managed to recount the fall of Nero without mentioning Verginius Rufus. The short list of Neronian victims admits Thrasea Paetus, it is true, but in a trivial and miserable fashion, namely his 'tristior et paedagogi vultus', whereas Cornelius Tacitus had been impelled to celebrate Thrasea Paetus and Barea Soranus as 'virtus ipsa'.[21]

Some detect in the biographer not only a soured temper but a distance from senators and from senatorial historians, or even revulsion. The notion is not devoid of seductive appeal. It is not the whole truth. Suetonius is shown hasty and incompetent, perhaps in a hurry to polish off the lives of the first six Caesars. Friends no less than enemies should adhere to any biography, even were it not composed by a person of scholarly habits who was a government official, the secretary *ab epistulis*.[22] Along with Petronius and Lucan the *Nero* omits Ofonius Tigellinus and Nymphidius Sabinus.

To resume and conclude this rubric. Philosophers and their fanciers might earn dispraisal, as is manifest in the pages of Tacitus, despite eulogy for Thrasea Paetus as earlier for Helvidius Priscus.[23] The judicious Quintilian discovered pretence as well as pretention in the grim visages and heavy beards.[24] When Juvenal, near coeval to Suetonius, referred to Domitian's end, he put emphasis on the lower classes and on the fate of an aristocrat, namely Plautius Lamia Aelianus (*suff.* 80):

> sed periit postquam Cerdonibus esse timendus
> coeperat. hoc nocuit Lamiarum caede madenti.[25]

If somewhat abated, the significance of the year 93 does not have to be discounted. Yet it remains a question how far the government suffered damage or discredit in the eyes of the leading personages in the Senate, whether discreet relics of the old aristocracy (they were few, and counted little) or men who had risen through patronage and loyalty towards the new dynasty. Neither class was enslaved to principles or doctrines.

They wanted to be consuls, but legitimate aspirations were restricted by the Flavian habit of holding the eponymate, which

---

[21] Suetonius, *Nero* 37, 1; Tacitus, *Ann.* xvi 21, 7.

[22] The season in which Suetonius composed the biographies may here be waived.

[23] *Hist.* iv 5, 1: 'ingenium inlustre altioribus studiis iuvenis admodum dedit.' He was 'recti pervicax, constans adversus metus'.

[24] Quintilian, *praef.* 15; xii 3, 12.

[25] Juvenal iv 153 f. To balance 'Lamiae', 'Cerdones' is requisite. Thus (and also in viii 102) Mayor in his edition (1872), followed by Knoche (Teubner, 1950) and E. Courtney (1980): not so in OCT (1959). For this low-class *cognomen*, see *TLL*; and four at least of the thirteen instances in *ILS* are libertine.

Domitian continued.[26] However, | he was not reluctant to share the *fasces* with noblemen, as witness the two Volusii in 87 and 92. Safe men, whose grandfather lived unscathed until the age of ninety-three, 'inoffensa tot imperatorum amicitia'.[27]

Second consulates tended to fall to kinsmen of the Flavii or to their civilian agents and ministers. They are generally awarded early in a reign. Thus no fewer than four in 85 (and none again, save in 90 and 95).[28] Meanwhile in 83 Vibius Crispus and Fabricius Veiento exhibited their value by a third tenure.

For the rest Domitian had to make provision for those who benefited from his father's usurpation. The *Fasti* of 90 show eleven *suffecti*. Not solely the men loyal in the year of crisis. There had been a blockage in promotions—only five *suffecti* both in 87 and in 88 and four in 89. But later (in 92) perhaps as many as ten.[29]

After a time the Caesars of the first dynasty came to fear the conjunction of high birth and military achievement. In the sequel Sulpicius Galba, the legate of Tarraconensis, served as a warning lesson. Even sons of consuls (the new imperial nobility) are seldom permitted to govern the armed provinces.

Excellence in warfare was the 'imperatoria virtus'. Domitian had been careful to visit the Rhine and embark on a campaign against the Chatti in 83, assuming a triumphal *cognomen*; and he went to the Danube on three occasions (85, 89, 92). His selection of governors and generals demands attention. Likewise his relations with them.

Julius Agricola, anomalous by a seven years' tenure and by the conquest of new territory, earned the rare award of the *ornamenta triumphalia*. Two generals in the Dacian War received consular *dona militaria*, namely Funisulanus Vettonianus (*suff.* 78) and Cornelius Nigrinus (*suff.* 83).[30] About Tettius Julianus, no information.

Agricola might have aspired to a second consulate—and so might Tettius, if he survived long enough. That honour fell to Lappius Maximus in 95, subsequent to his governorship in Syria. Not, one supposes, without arousing surprise and envy among his peers and coevals. |

[26] With a remission after a time in five years (89, 91, 93, 94, 96).

[27] *Ann.* xiii 30, 2.

[28] Viz. Aurelius Fulvus with the Emperor, then Rutilius Gallicus, Catullus Messallinus, Arrecinus Clemens. Cf. F. Zevi, *RSA* iii (1973), 106, whence *AE* 1975, 131.

[29] *AE* 1975, 132 (reproducing Zevi's view). But only six according to L. Vidman, *LF* cii (1979), 97.

[30] *ILS* 1005; *AE* 1973, 283. For Nigrinus see below, Appendix. Funisulanus belonged to an important nexus, linked to Tettius Julianus: a Funisulana Vettulla married Tettius Africanus, the Prefect of Egypt (*ILS* 8759 c).

Prudent men supported the second dynasty, even when it came to avow the shape and substance of despotism. They saw no alternative, save civil war and disruption of the Empire. Prominent among the advocates of centralized government, though not always vocal, were senators and consuls who derived their origin from the zones of the 'old frontier': Transpadana, Narbonensis, and the two Spains.

Cornelius Tacitus, who denounced the excesses of the Domitianic tyranny, had already raised protest against excess in another direction: undue admiration of the martyrs who 'in nullum rei publicae usum ambitiosa morte inclaruerunt'.[31] There could still be great men under evil emperors, so he proclaimed. Referring to Julius Agricola, he had Ulpius Traianus in mind—and a defence of his own career and comportment.

Thrasea Paetus was a citizen of Patavium; and a northern origin is surmised for Junius Rusticus.[32] Not all Transpadani shared the sentiments and attitudes of the ostensibly dissident faction: not, for example, the aged Verginius Rufus, who after defeating Vindex had been reluctant to declare against Nero, or Silius Italicus, orator and poet, the last of the Neronian consuls (in both senses of the term). And the alert ambition of younger men was pressing forward.

Italia Transpadana was destined to be outshone by Spain and Narbonensis. Groups and combinations were quietly forming, with consequences to be made manifest at no long interval. First Narbonensis, a robust core issuing from the city of Nemausus. Aurelius Fulvus rose to a second consulate in 85. His son died untimely, not long after his consulship (*ordinarius* in 89), but Fulvus himself became *praefectus urbi* either on the decease of Rutilius Gallicus in 92 or a few years later.[33] The two Domitii also come in, the heirs of the opulent Afer: Lucanus, the younger brother, perished in 93 or 94, but Tullus had a long survival. On these families waited a resplendent future: the second Aurelius Fulvus married a daughter of the elegant and amiable Arrius Antoninus.[34]

Next Baetica, with Ulpius Traianus (*cos.* 91) in pride of place: the parent legate of Syria, a *vir triumphalis* and adlected into the patriciate by Vespasian. Nor was the other province negligible, with the Pedanii of Barcino, consular already (since the year 43) and neo-

---

[31] *Agr.* 42, 4.

[32] Pliny, discussing a reputable family of Brixia, appealed to 'illa nostra Italia' (*Ep.* i 14, 4: to Mauricus, the brother of Rusticus). The inference is not wholly secure.

[33] For the three Aurelii Fulvi, observe the precious details in *HA Pius* 1, 1 ff.

[34] For the group, and for the nexus with the Annii Veri from Baetica, see *Tacitus* (1958), 603 ff.; 792 ff.; *Some Arval Brethren* (1980), 82; 86.

patrician.[35] Somewhere in those parts of Tarraconensis lies | the *patria* of the enigmatic Licinius Sura, first on show as an orator;[36] and Domitian's general Cornelius Nigrinus came from Liria, in the far south of the province.[37]

That was not all. Domitian showed amity and favour towards the Hellenic lands. He took the archonship at Athens. More important, consuls from the dynastic houses of Asia, Julius Celsus of Sardis (*suff.* 92) and the Pergamene Julius Quadratus (94). Recent investigations add the name of a new senator not related to that group: Julius Candidus, consul suffect in 86 and governing the military province of Cappadocia (?89–92).[38] The magnates of Asia had no quarrel with government or ruler. Apart from his odious personality, state and society was already proto-Antonine as well as cosmopolitan.

The monarch requires subtle or courageous counsellors. They overcome his hesitations and fortify decision—and they protect him from impulses which even when generous or benevolent would have no good issue. In the Palace they intervene gently to maintain concord, in the high assembly they expound the policy of the administration and cover up errors or scandal.

Vespasian and Titus were well served, and Domitian on his accession refrained from changes in the privy council.[39] Declaring long continuity, the company of Caesar's friends still numbered substantial phantoms from the era of iniquity such as Montanus, the fat epicure: 'noverat ille/luxuriam imperii veterem noctesque Neronis'. Juvenal supplies the name, along with nine others.[40] He parodied the opening scene in the poem of Statius, *De bello Germanico*. That is, the council antecedent to Domitian's expedition against the Chatti in 83.

The first to make his entry is the jurist Pegasus, recently appointed Prefect of the City.[41] The bland Vibius Crispus follows, and the proces-

---

[35] For the family, E. Groag, *RE* xix 19 ff.; R. Syme, *Tacitus* (1958), 479 f.; *HSCPh* lxxxiii (1979), 287 ff. = *RP* iii (1984), 1158 ff.

[36] Martial vii 47 (recovering from a grave illness in 92). Sura's tribe is the 'Sergia' (*CIL* ii 4282: near Tarraco), which does not go with an origin from Barcino or Tarraco. Perhaps Celsa or Osca.   [37] *AE* 1973, 283.

[38] H. Halfmann, *Die Senatoren aus dem östlichen Teil des Imperium Romanum bis zum Ende des 2. Jh. n. Chr.* (1979), 107; R. Syme, *Some Arval Brethren* (1980), 90 ff.

[39] For the continuity, J. Devreker, *AncSoc* viii (1977), 223 ff.

[40] Juvenal iv 75 ff. Montanus is to be identified as T. Junius Montanus (*suff.* 81), cf. *AE* 1973, 500 (Alexandria Troadis): the first eastern consul, but from a Roman *colonia*. He came to the *fasces* after a proconsulate in Sicily. (Note, however, L. Sergius Paullus, perhaps *suff.* 70, from Pisidian Antioch: cf. *RP* iii (1984), 1328, n. 95).

[41] Pegasus (*suff. c.*73) now emerges as ']tius Pegasus', governor of Dalmatia (*AE* 1967, 355). Not therefore a Cornelius from Vasio in Narbonensis, as conceived possible in *Tacitus* (1958), 805.

sion terminates with Fabricius Veiento and Catullus Messallinus. |

The conclave furnishes various instruction as well as entertainment. Enough without speculation about absent members. The argument from silence is liable to be misused—or deprecated. Nevertheless it often leads without discomfort to conclusions of a certain value. For example, individuals or groups whom Pliny failed to honour with a missive.[42] In this instance, three characters should have invited curiosity.

First, Cocceius Nerva, the aristocrat whom Vespasian selected to share the *fasces* in 71. A favourite of Nero, he lent comfort and support on the occasion of Piso's conspiracy. Nerva was smooth and subtle—and, like Vibius Crispus, not one to go against the current.

Second, Arrecinus Clemens (*suff.* 73), a kinsman of the dynasty: his sister Tertulla had been the first wife of Titus, and mother to Julia.[43] Suetonius happens to call him a friend and agent of Domitian.[44]

Third, Julius Ursus. Juvenal registered one Guard Prefect, Cornelius Fuscus. There were normally two. A papyrus brings welcome elucidation.[45] It is a letter of Domitian inviting a Prefect of Egypt to become the colleague of Fuscus: he had transferred Julius Ursus 'in amplissimum ordinem'. The demotion of Ursus, at his own request (that was the formula), brought him a suffect consulship in 84. According to Dio he had tried to mediate in the quarrel between Domitian and his arrogant consort, and it was Julia's favour that secured him the consulate.[46] Her name implies a Julia for maternal grandmother, married to an Arrecinus—and presumably from the family of Julii Lupi.[47] Ursus had court influence—and kinship with Julia, so it may be supposed.

For these absences, explanations are not far to seek. Arrecinus was in fact governor of Tarraconensis, whence he came back to assume a second consulate in 85.[48] Further, one may note in passing that

[42] E.g. Annius Verus (*suff.* 97), Aelius Hadrianus (108)—or the third Aurelius Fulvus (*cos.* 120): some of whose coevals he did not neglect, viz. Pedanius Fuscus (*cos.* 118) and Ummidius Quadratus (*suff.* 118). On whom, *HSCPh* lxxxiii (1979), 287 ff. = *RP* iii (1984), 1158 ff.

[43] Suetonius attributes Julia to the second wife, Marcia Furnilla (*Divus Titus* 4, 2). An error, as now turns out. See the convincing arguments of H. Castritius, *Historia* xviii (1969), 492 ff.

[44] *Dom.* 11, 1: 'unum e familiaribus et emissariis suis, capitis condemnaturus'.

[45] *P. Berol.* 8334. The interpretation of Piganiol is followed in *Tacitus* (1958), 835 f.; *JRS* lxx (1980), 66 = *RP* iii (1984), 1279. For Ursus see further *PIR*², J 630; W. Eck, *RE*, *Suppl.* xiv 211 f.

[46] Dio lxviii 3, 1; 4, 2.

[47] Arrecinus Clemens, one of the Guard Prefects in 41, had for kinsman and friend a tribune called Julius Lupus (Josephus, *AJ* xix 191). His son is clearly Ti. Julius Lupus, dying as Prefect of Egypt in 73 (*PIR*², J 390). Close kinship with Ursus has been surmised, cf. *Tacitus* (1958), 636: perhaps indeed first cousins.

[48] *AE* 1947, 40 (Pisaurum), cf. G. Alföldy, *Fasti Hispanienses* (1969), 22 ff.

Flavius Sabinus (*cos.* 82) the husband of Julia would be an appropriate member of Domitian's *consilium*, and likewise Petillius Rufus (*cos. II* 83). On the other hand, Cocceius Nerva and Julius Ursus can hardly |have been left out by Statius. For Juvenal they jarred with a satirist's presentation. He could not use persons who survived to high eminence and a blameless reputation in public.

By the year 95 most of the ten 'amici Caesaris' put on parade by Juvenal were no longer among the living. Still extant, however, was 'prudens Veiento', the Nestor of the age, and not perhaps forfeiting the esteem of the despot. Otherwise curiosity goes short. A thought might be given to Aurelius Fulvus (*cos. II* 85), if successor in the Prefecture of the City to Rutilius Gallicus.[49]

Some earlier reigns had seen the emergence of a single potent minister, not without baneful consequences. While Domitian avoided recourse to a Seianus, he was trapped in his increasing isolation, and he came to distrust his near entourage. In 95 the two Guard Prefects were put on trial.[50] Their successors, Norbanus and Petronius Secundus, lacked the social prestige or senatorial relatives possessed by Cornelius Fuscus and Julius Ursus.

Domitian opened the year 95 as consul for the seventeenth time, with for colleague his cousin Flavius Clemens, the husband of Flavia Domitilla. Earning from the biographer the label of 'contemptissima inertia', this innocuous adjunct met his end in the spring shortly after he vacated the *fasces* (*Dom.* 15, 1).

When Vespasian seized the power he was in a happy posture to found a lasting dynasty. Not only a pair of sons, separated by a dozen years, and the elder embellished with military renown. He presided over a large family group, to be thinned and reduced by the course of nature or by actions of Domitian. Briefly as follows.[51]

First, his brother Sabinus (the *praefectus urbi*) left a son by a wife nowhere named: T. Flavius Sabinus, known only as *suffectus* in 69, *II suff.* in 72.[52] There was also a daughter.[53] The next generation is represented by Sabinus (*cos.* 82) and Clemens (95), grandsons thus of the City Prefect.

Sabinus (who married Julia, the daughter of Titus) was put to

---

[49] Gallicus (*II suff.* 85) died in 92 (Statius, *Silvae* i, *praef.*).

[50] Dio lxvii 14, 4. No names—but Casperius Aelianus, who turns up in 97, had been a prefect under Domitian (lxviii 3, 3).

[51] The stemma presented in *PIR*[2] (subjoined to F 398) has been modified in a thorough study by G. B. Townend, *JRS* li (1961), 54 ff. His own stemma (ibid. 62) is now fortified by having Arrecina Tertulla mother to Julia.

[52] He married an Arrecina, as conjectured by Townend, op. cit. 57.

[53] The wife of L. Caesennius Paetus, the consul of 61 (*ILS* 995).

death. The date is not clear, the trivial reason is reported in Suetonius' catalogue of the ten consulars: the herald at the election had inadvertently announced him as *imperator* (10, 4). That occasion, it has been supposed, might refer to a subsequent second consulate.[54] If so, perhaps the elections held in 87. |

Second, the Arrecini. The progenitor was M. Arrecinus Clemens, one of the two commanders of the Guard when Caligula was assassinated.[55] His wife can be specified without hesitation as a Julia.[56] The daughter, Arrecina Tertulla, married Titus (about the year 63), another daughter Flavius Sabinus (*suff.* 69), so it is plausibly conjectured: hence the *cognomen* of their second son, T. Flavius Clemens (*cos.* 95).[57] The son of the Guard Prefect is Arrecinus Clemens (*suff.* 73, *II suff.* 85).

This consular is absent from the Suetonian list. He occurs in a subsequent notice, with Domitian described as 'capitis condemnaturus' (*Dom.* 11, 2).

In September of the year 87 the *Arvales* offered thanksgivings 'ob detecta scelera nefariorum'.[58] Conspiracies do not always impose credence, as Domitian himself was in the habit of observing (21, 1). Whatever view he held of this transaction, it acquires singular value if it involved Arrecinus Clemens. Not only kin to the dynasty, but *praefectus urbi*, as now disclosed by the emendation of one letter on his inscription.[59] Flavius Sabinus (*cos.* 82) may also come in (cf. above). Valid conjecture assigned him an Arrecina for mother.

Despite some uncertainties the family nexus is shown to interlock tightly. By the same token, necessary reconstructions reveal the inadequacies of the written sources.

Third, the general Petillius Cerialis (*II suff.* 74) was linked to Vespasian by a 'propinqua adfinitas'.[60] He married a daughter, so it is presumed. Hence Petillius Rufus, consul for the second time in 83 as colleague of Domitian, was the ruler's close kin.[61]

---

[54] As suggested in *PIR*[2], F 355. Sabinus is normally identified as the eminent and ill-starred patron of Dio (*Or.* xiii 1). C. P. Jones puts his death 'perhaps early in the reign when many of Titus' friends came to grief' (*The Roman World of Dio of Prusa* [1978], 46).

[55] *PIR*[2], A 1073. His earlier career is now revealed by *AE* 1976, 200 (Ariminum)—where, however, the editors insert the tribe 'Ani(ensis)', ignoring the son's inscription at Pisaurum which duly certified 'Camilia'.

[56] As indicated above in the matter of Julius Ursus.

[57] Townend, op. cit. 57.   [58] *CIL* vi 2065.

[59] J. Devreker, *Epigraphica* xxxviii (1976), 180: on *AE* 1947, 40. Duly noted from Devreker by W. Eck, *ANRW* ii 1 (1974), 209.

[60] Tacitus, *Hist.* iii 59, 2. By his full style 'Q. Petillius Cerialis Caesius Rufus'.

[61] The identity of this consul is a problem. Cerialis himself, so it is argued by A. R. Birley, *Britannia* iv (1973), 186 f. Against, J. Devreker, *AncSoc* viii (1977), 233. He suggests a younger brother of the general.

The Petillii faded out, and after the killing of Flavius Clemens in 95 Domitian was left with the two boys, the sons of Clemens und Domitilla, to whom he allotted the names 'Vespasianus' and 'Domitianus'.[62] They were the survivors of seven children.[63] The facts of mortality at Rome, especially among the young, deterred | hopes for a long perpetuation of the dynasty—or, at the best, prudent men might be moved to exclaim 'dii avertant principes pueros!'[64]

Some may have wondered about an alternative, if Domitian died, to superintend the government as guardian to the boy princes. Caesennius Paetus, the consul of 61, had married a daughter of Flavius Sabinus.[65] Vespasian's brother was appointed *praefectus urbi* the same year—in a season of notable political changes and promotions.

Paetus left two sons. The elder, the homonymous consul of 79, went to Asia as proconsul in 92 or 93.[66] No evidence tells for or against his survival. The younger, Sospes (recalling by that name his preservation during the parent's invasion of Armenia), earned military decorations in 92, commander of the legion XIII Gemina in the campaign against Suebi and Sarmatae.[67] Sospes lived on, but he was not to be gratified by a consulship in the near sequel to his next post, namely Galatia: the province Cappadocia–Galatia was divided for a short time on the decease of the consular Antistius Rusticus, who died there in 93 or 94.[68]

In invoking any prospective role or aspirations for Caesennius Sospes, extreme caution is prescribed. By age, something like fifteen years separated the brothers. Since death or divorce was a common phenomenon, it is far from clear that the mother of Sospes was a Flavia Sabina.[69]

So far, the Flavian family and dynasty. By 95 Domitian had

[62] *Dom.* 15, 1. They had been entrusted to Quintilian for education (iv, *praef.* 2; vi, *praef.* 1).
[63] *ILS* 1839 (their nurse).
[64] *HA Tac.* 6, 5. A prospect to be feared in September of 6 B.C. when Caesar Augustus reached the age of fifty-seven.
[65] *ILS* 995.   [66] W. Eck, *Senatoren* etc. (1970), 226.
[67] *ILS* 1017 (Pisidian Antioch). For this reconstruction, *JRS* lxvii (1977), 38 ff. = *RP* iii (1984), 1043 ff.
[68] Martial ix 30. For the career of Rusticus (*suff.* 90), *AE* 1925, 126 (Pisidian Antioch). To be presumed legate from 92, in succession to Julius Candidus (*suff.* 86), attested by *CIL* iii 250 (Ancyra). T. Pomponius Bassus, the next governor (consul on September 1 of 94) reached the province while still consul designate. Cf., on the coin evidence, P. R. Franke, *Chiron* ix (1979), 277 ff.
[69] Sospes (it is assumed) came to a retarded consulship in the summer of 114. See the Thracian diploma, M. M. Roxan, *RMD* (1978), no. 14.

surmounted some of his preoccupations. The wars on the Danubian frontier were over. The Parthians, normally quiescent for good reasons, were alert to cause trouble if opportunity offered. In 88 and 89 they were lending support to a false Nero.[70] Diplomacy had recently induced them to surrender the impostor.[71] |

Domestic policy was not devoid of embarrassment. Domitian increased the pay of the troops, and he needed money for his buildings. Hence rapacity and confiscations, with resentment among the propertied class; and his rigour alienated the lower orders.[72] However, his building programme (much of it inherited from the reign of Titus) was close to completion, the imperial treasury now amply replenished, so at least it can be argued.[73]

Whatever the situation at the capital, the security of the ruler depended on the armies and their commanders. It was a favourable sign that in 95 he conferred a second consulate on Lappius Maximus, the governor of Syria: an abnormal honour, none since 85 apart from Cocceius Nerva in 90.[74]

On the other hand, the ruin of an army commander, the solitary specimen on Suetonius' list. It was Sallustius Lucullus, the legate of Britannia.[75] His identity and full nomenclature is a problem.[76] Likewise the period of his tenure, the date of his prosecution and death.

Although crafty and rancorous, Domitian was arrogant and impulsive. The destruction of Flavius Clemens was a fatal mistake.[77] A propensity to erratic behaviour became manifest shortly before, when, to encourage cereal production in a season of famine, he promulgated an imperious decree: no new vineyards in Italy, in most regions abroad half of them to be torn up.[78] Protests arose, leading to

---

[70] Suetonius, *Nero* 57: 'tam favorabile nomen eius apud Parthos fuit ut vehementer adiutus et vix redditus sit.'

[71] Statius, *Silvae* iv 3, 110: 'Eoae citius venite laurus.' The opening poem in the book celebrates January 1 of 95 (the ruler's seventeenth consulship).

[72] *Dom.* 12, 1: 'exhaustus operum ac munerum impensis, stipendioque quod adiecerat' etc. He was 'super ingenii naturam inopia rapax, metu saevus' (3, 2).

[73] *JRS* xx (1930), 55 ff. = *RP* (1979), 1 ff. Against which, C. H. V. Sutherland, *JRS* xxv (1935), 150 ff. For a middle view, A. Garzetti, *Nerva* (1950), 60 ff. See further *Tacitus* (1958), 629 f.

[74] Perhaps a reward for successful diplomacy in the matter of the false Nero.

[75] *Dom.* 10, 3: 'quod lanceas novae formae appellari Luculleas passus esset.' Not sufficient to demonstrate much previous military experience.

[76] P. Sallustius Blaesus (*suff.* 89) might be polyonymous, cf. *Tacitus* (1958), 648. But never thus registered on the lavish protocol of the *Arvales*. For an intricate and inconclusive discussion see now *Some Arval Brethren* (1980), 42 ff. Add now A. R. Birley, *The Fasti of Roman Britain* (1981), 82 f.

[77] *Dom.* 15, 1: 'quo maxime facto maturavit sibi exitium.'

[78] *Dom.* 7, 2, cf. 14, 2. In 94 or perhaps even in 93, cf. 'sobria rura' in Statius, *Silvae* iv 2, 37 along with 3, 11 f. For this abortive measure see now B. Levick, *Latomus* xli (1982), 66 ff.

an eloquent embassy from Asia, and Domitian dropped the notion.

Otherwise the men of substance and repute in the provinces east or west had little to complain about. The ruler was vigilant, intent to curb exactions and malpractice of the governors.[79]

Domitian's edict about the vines would put elderly senators like Fabricius Vei|ento in mind of an earlier emperor. Nero came out with an idea of genius: to abolish indirect taxes and thus confer 'pulcherrimum donum generi mortalium'. Imperial counsellors, the 'seniores', restrained the juvenile impulse, after due praise for 'magnitudo animi'.[80]

Nero became contemporary and visible in matters of grave import. After Flavius Clemens the next victim was the freedman Epaphroditus, killed (it was alleged) for ingratitude because he deserted his patron and friend in the supreme emergency.[81] After the suppression of Piso's plot Epaphroditus had received military decorations.[82] Some may have remembered that Cocceius Nerva on that occasion was honoured with the *ornamenta triumphalia*, and also with statues in triumphal garb. In the transactions of 68 and 69 (so far as recoverable) Nerva escaped any mention for good or ill.[83] However, it is an idle fancy that Nerva now went in fear of his life.[84]

As consuls to introduce the next year Domitian designated the aristocratic Antistius Vetus, with as colleague the almost nonagenarian Manlius Valens.[85] Selection of that relic could scarcely have been taken by the high assembly as other than affront and contempt, comparable to the one-day consul appointed by Caesar the Dictator— or to Rosius Regulus by Vitellius on the last day of October in 69, saluted by derision.[86] Manlius Valens brought up Nero's end, the rapid sequence of pretenders, the invasions of Italy. In the winter of 68/9 he commanded the legion I Italica, then stationed at Lugdunum.[87]

---

[79] So much that 'neque modestiores umquam neque iustiores extiterint: e quibus plerosque post illum reos omnium criminum vidimus' (8, 2). Suetonius may be guilty of exaggeration. The notorious case was Marius Priscus, proconsul in Africa. Many will now concede that the *patria* of Suetonius was in fact Hippo Regius (*AE* 1952, 73).

[80] *Ann.* xiii 50, 2.

[81] Dated by Dio before the killing of Flavius Clemens (lxvii 14, 4), therefore late in 94. Suetonius also puts it before Clemens, and proceeds 'denique Flavium Clementem' (15, 7); and, after 'maturavit sibi exitium', follow the celestial phenomena of the first eight months of 96 (15, 2). Suetonius thus abridges unduly the interval between the end of Clemens and the end of Domitian.

[82] *ILS* 9505 (his large sepulchral monument on the Esquiline). On which (against Stein in *PIR*[2], E 69), W. Eck, *Historia* xxv (1976), 382 ff.

[83] *Ann.* xv 72, 1.

[84] Alleged by an anecdote in Dio (lxvii 15, 6). In the fiction of Philostratus, Nerva is exiled along with (Salvidienus) Orfitus and an unidentified Rufus (*Vita Apollonii* viii 8).

[85] Dio lxvii 14, 5.   [86] *Hist.* iii 37, 3.   [87] *Hist.* i 64, 4.

Juvenal styled Domitian a 'calvus Nero'. Clearly not a coinage of the satirist. Men of the time might with propriety adduce a more formidable predecessor, likewise a | bald head.[88] The state papers of Tiberius Caesar were the sole reading matter of Domitian, so they opined.[89]

Tiberius, who distrusted the medical profession, lived to seventy-seven. Curious particulars show him delicate in his diet. He liked pears and cucumbers, asparagus and broccoli.[90] Not enough perhaps to certify a vegetarian in the last years on the island. Tiberius had previously been addicted to strong drink. That consolation in his vicissitudes might have abated with old age and tranquillity on the island retreat.

Something is known about Domitian's habits. At noon he took a substantial meal, but nothing much in the evening, only an apple and 'modicam in ampulla potiunculam'; and when he gave banquets they were not extended to long hours of drinking.[91] In short, he was careful and abstemious. No court doctor happens to be on record—and for that matter no astrologer or philosopher, all standard equipment of the Palace, and sometimes potent influences.

Domitian was now completing his forty-fourth year and surpassing his corpulent brother who died at forty-one.[92] As far as bodily health went, a firm candidate for survival or even longevity, apart from the hazards of a pestilence. But he might fear poison or an assassin.

Domitian's mind was clouded, his spirits in depression. He was dangerously isolated, he felt the fears he inspired, 'terribilis cunctis et invisus' (*Dom.*14, 1). During the first eight months of the next year celestial anger was manifested by much thunder and lightning (15, 2). Many buildings were struck, including the Templum gentis Flaviae—and even the Palace and the imperial bedchamber. Other portents supervened. While some members of the educated class might renounce traditional beliefs or superstitions, few remained impervious to the science of the stars. The Chaldaeans (it was said) warned Domitian in his youth, hence no danger from eating mushrooms. He knew the year destined for his end, the day and even

[88] While furnishing valuable particulars about the physique and complexion of Tiberius, the biographer missed the 'nudus capillo vertex' (*Ann.* iv 57, 2). Likewise the 'ulcerosa facies ac plerumque medicaminibus interstincta'.

[89] *Dom.* 20: 'praeter commentarios et acta Tiberi Caesaris nihil lectitabat.' Not meant for praise. The modern scholar will interpret in a contrary sense.

[90] Pliny, *NH* xv 54; xix 64; 145; 137. He even had 'siser' brought from Germany (xix 90): presumably parsnips.

[91] *Dom.* 21. Compare Statius, *Silvae* v 1, 121 f. (on the wife of Abascantus): 'ipsa dapes modicas et sobria pocula tradit/exemplumque ad erile monet'. Domitian's habits were duly traduced by Pliny, *Pan.* 49.

[92] Suetonius, *Divus Titus* 11. In 2, 1 the biographer was in error by two years.

the hour. He was 'pavidus semper atque anxius', he became 'sollicitior in dies' (14, 2; 4). |

On September 14 Domitian completed his fifteenth year in the purple. Four days later he succumbed in the Palace. The chamberlain Parthenius arranged the murder. Even when a plot succeeds, not all of the facts become public; and the passage of time brings embellishment or misconceptions. Suetonius furnished the essential names and particulars, prefixed with a cautious phrase: 'haec fere divulgata sunt' (19, 1). He had already assumed the complicity of Domitia Longina (14, 1). But he omits the commanders of the Praetorian Guard.

Dio has a lengthy account, composite and of unequal value.[93] Three items deserve brief attention, though not for the same reason.

First, the Empress Domitia along with the Guard Prefects Norbanus and Petronius Secundus had foreknowledge, 'so at least it is said'.[94]

Second, Domitian wrote down the names of those he intended to do away with, and he put the tablet under his pillow when taking his siesta. A small boy noticed the object and innocently gave it to the Empress. The persons endangered at once went into action.

Circumstantial (as fiction has to be), the story betrays a precise and damaging parallel to what occurred (or was believed) in the lifetime of the historian. Namely when Commodus was assassinated on the evening of the last day of December 192[95] That has been duly noted. Curiosity or pedantry may observe that another small boy was in fact present when they killed Domitian. He gave a report on one particular (*Dom.* 17).

Third, the conspirators did not go to work before making sure of a candidate for the power. After vain approach to others, they had recourse to Cocceius Nerva, and he complied, having been himself in dire peril yet preserved because an astrologer told Domitian that he would die anyhow within a few days.

Dio's exposition concludes (it is highly suitable) with the anecdote about the notorious sage and charlatan of Tyana. On that September day Apollonius had a vision at Ephesus, and he joyously ejaculated the name of Stephanus, the author of the deed.

A large measure therefore of fable as well as speculation and surmise. Conspirators, it should seem, ought not to have gone ahead without enlisting the Prefects of the Guard or deciding on the choice

[93] Dio lxvii 15–18.   [94] Dio lxvii 15, 6.
[95] Herodian i 17. On which, F. Grosso, *La lotta politica al tempo di Commodo* (1964), 400 ff. That scholar was sceptical about both stories.

of the next emperor.[96] Conspirators are not always given the requisite leisure. However, if acting on chance and sudden impul-|sion, Parthenius and his agents may well have managed to get in touch with the commanders of the Praetorians.[97] Cocceius Nerva was likely to be elusive.

Provinces and armies created the monarchy. Dissembled or forgotten for a time, the alarming truth came out in 68 and 69—and it had to be faced by a civilian usurper emergent at the capital. Furthermore, an assessment of Domitian's rule during the last *triennium* bears heavily on his relations with the legates governing the military regions.

Despite the events of 93 and a sequence of consulars put to death (sporadic, however, and a highly miscellaneous list), Domitian was able to find loyal adherents, so it appears. Caesar and his counsellors had to manage a system of promotions without undue disturbances. Regularity was expedient, and it appealed to the convenience of most senators.

Long tenures were a dubious benefit. Apart from Agricola, prorogued for a task of conquest at the outset of the reign, they are not easy to establish later. For the most part three years, or sometimes four. Many of the legates had previously governed one of the eight praetorian provinces in the portion of Caesar. That type of promotion was acquiring stability. Further, some of the ex-consuls went out to take up their commands quite soon.

Active warfare ended with the end of 92. In the near sequel governors may have been replaced, and perhaps again in the summer of 96.[98] The identity of nine consular legates in office in September of 96 would be worth knowing. Not merely for the intensive, albeit sometimes hazardous, investigation of senators and their careers.[99] Domitian's policy is in question, and the prospects awaiting his successor.

For an armed proclamation, distance and time hampered consensus among the legates. Britain and Syria (along with Cappadocia) lay on the far edges of the Roman dominions. Likewise Spain, and not likely to repeat with a single legion the fateful elevation of Sulpicius Galba.

The armies now comprised twenty-eight legions. Of that total fifteen stood on Rhine and Danube. Though the two Germanies had

---

[96] Thus S. Gsell, *Essai sur le règne de l'empereur Domitien* (1894), 327 f.

[97] *Dom.* 23, 1: 'miles . . . paratus et ulcisci, nisi duces defuissent'.

[98] A certain temptation must be confessed, to assign important changes of governors to 89, 93, 96.

[99] W. Eck, *Senatoren* etc. (1970). Since then valuable discoveries or revisions accrue.

fallen from eight to six, they carried heavy and historic prestige. Recent warfare shifted the balance of military power: four legions in Pannonia, five in the two Moesian commands.[100] |

Search for those nine legates encounters lacunae in the evidence and intricate problems going back to 89 or 93; and constructions are liable to be overturned by the emergence of new inscriptions. Confined to Rhine and Danube, the enquiry takes the following shape and procedure.

For Germania Inferior the gap of a decade intervenes after Lappius Maximus, who defeated Antonius Saturninus. In Germania Superior the successor to Saturninus is on record: the jurist Javolenus Priscus (*suff.* 86), attested by a military diploma of 90.[101] He can be allocated the period from 89 to 92 or 93. Then another lacuna. In both Germanies the next known legates are men appointed after the death of Domitian.[102]

Moesia is more helpful. The successor to Tettius Julianus is missing, but a diploma of 93 disclosed Pompeius Longinus (*suff.*90) in Moesia Superior;[103] and new testimony shows him still there on July 12 of 96.[104] In the other province Octavius Fronto (*suff.* 86) is attested in July of 92.[105] Perhaps towards the close of his tenure. If so, the successor should be an *Ignotus*. The next document is dated to January of 97, not without problems, and perhaps instruction.[106] The auxiliary troops are registered as 'sub Iulio Mar['. He is identified as Julius Marinus, proconsul of Bithynia *c.*89 and presumed a consul suffect of 93.[107] Given the season and the region, he is more likely to have been appointed by Domitian than by his successor.[108]

Julius Marinus should engage some interest—from the eastern lands and probably from the Roman colony Berytus.[109] Though put in charge of three legions, Marinus may not have had much military

---

[100] *JRS* xviii (1928), 43 ff.; *CAH* xi (1936), 177; 187. Mainly following E. Ritterling in the article 'Legio' (*RE* xii). For Moesia the vital document is *ILS* 2719: a tribune of II Adiutrix commanding detachments of five legions and receiving decorations in Domitian's Suebo-Sarmatian campaign (of 92). Of those five, three were allocated to Moesia Superior in *JRS* xviii (1928), 48 f. For various reasons I now believe that to be erroneous.

[101] *CIL* xvi 36, cf. *ILS* 1015 (Nedinum: his *cursus*).

[102] Viz. Ulpius Traianus and Julius Servianus. On whom see below.

[103] *CIL* xvi 39 (issued on September 16, 94).

[104] *AE* 1977, 104 = M. M. Roxan, *RMD* (1978), no. 6.

[105] *CIL* xvi 37.   [106] *CIL* xvi 41.

[107] The proconsulate, the only known detail in the career of Marinus, emerges from the inscription of his son (*ILS* 1026). For some uncertainty about the *cognomen*, A. Stein, *Die Legaten von Moesia* (1940), 59. Further, proposing to read Mar[in xvi 41, *Some Arval Brethren* (1980), 54 f.

[108] The next legate is Pomponius Rufus (*suff.* 95), in 99 (*CIL* xvi 44 f.).

[109] For the evidence and the arguments, H. Halfmann, *Die Senatoren aus dem östlichen Teil* etc. (1979), no. 14. The family has the tribe 'Fabia'.

experience in his favour. That was not in demand for legates in a quiet period.

Pannonia is the crux, by its central and strategic position in the world empire, by its garrison of four legions. No other province now had more than three. After Funisulanus Vettonianus (*suff.* 78),[110] who left in 85 when the Dacians invaded Moesia and became the first legate of Moesia Superior, no governor is on direct | attestation for a long space of time, through the years of Danubian warfare and the ensuing cessation until Pompeius Longinus at the beginning of 98.[111]

A new inspection of an important document brings supplement. Two consular Neratii stand together on an inscription, both governors of Pannonia.[112] The elder was identified as Neratius Priscus the jurist, consul suffect in 97 (and the brother of Marcellus, *suff.* 95).[113] The younger, a homonymous son, was assigned to the reign of Hadrian.[114] Then the *Fasti Potentini* revealed a Neratius Priscus, consul suffect in 87.[115] Not but that conviction persisted in the existence of three Neratii Prisci.[116]

The revision reduces them to two, consuls in 87 and in 97.[117] The Pannonian governorship of the former is therefore assigned somewhere in the period 90–6. There are notable consequences for the career of the latter, the jurist.[118]

If accepted, Neratius Priscus (*suff.* 87) may belong without discomfort to 93–6. Pompeius Longinus now comes in, attested in Pannonia at the beginning of 98. He went there from Moesia Superior. The date of transition therefore demands close attention. Perhaps before September of 96—and he may in fact have already left before the diploma was issued in July of 96.[119] Delays in these documents are not without parallel. For example, Funisulanus had probably been called to Moesia by the Dacian invasion before September of 85.[120]

The gaps in the evidence for 96 are painful and discouraging. Two names of note and consequence have not failed to arouse hopes:

---

[110] *ILS* 1005.   [111] *CIL* xvi 42.   [112] *ILS* 1034 (Saepinum).

[113] *PIR*[1], N 46. The document showed the prefecture of the *aerarium Saturni*—but no priesthood.

[114] Because of the supplement 'leg. Aug. pr. pr. P[annonia]/inferiore et Pannonia [superiore]'. Pannonia was divided in 106, with Aelius Hadrianus (*suff.* 108) the first legate. This Neratius Priscus, be it noted, was *septemvir epulonum*.

[115] *AE* 1949, 23.

[116] A full statement of the thesis was rendered in *Hermes* lxxxv (1957), 480 ff. = *RP* (1979), 339 ff.

[117] G. Camodeca, *AAN* lxxxvii (1976), 19 ff., whence *AE* 1976, 195.

[118] See below, Appendix.

[119] *AE* 1977, 104 = M. M. Roxan, *RMD* (1978), no. 6.   [120] *CIL* xvi 31.

Ulpius Traianus (*cos.* 91), and Julius Servianus (*suff.* 90), neither with known consular occupations before the death of Domitian. For Traianus the first on record is Germania Superior (he was appointed in the summer of 97); and Servianus took his place there in the winter of 97/8.[121]

Resort has been had to an indirect approach. Tribunes commonly saw service in | an army commanded by a consular kinsman. Aelius Hadrianus was the son of Traianus' cousin, and Servianus had married his sister. Hadrianus passed through three tribunates, abnormally.[122] His movements ought to reveal something. Early in 98 he joined Julius Servianus in Germania Superior. Before that he had served in II Adiutrix (Moesia Superior, it is presumed) and in V Macedonica (stationed at Oescus in Moesia Inferior). Hence a Moesian command held by either consular, or perhaps by both.

The search has not been attended with success. For Traianus, Moesia Superior seemed plausible.[123] It is annulled by Pompeius Longinus now emerging as still there in 96—unless Traianus had after Longinus a tenure of a dozen months before going to Germania Superior.[124]

Traianus acquired the power without needing to make a proclamation. Nerva's government ran into trouble, and in October it was pushed to the verge of collapse. Casperius Aelianus fomented a tumult of the Praetorian Guard and compelled Nerva to surrender to their vengeance the assassins of Domitian—assigning his colleague Petronius to that company.[125]

In discredit and dire emergency, Nerva mounted the Capitol and declared Traianus his partner and heir. An orator later invoked guidance from divine providence. Pliny and others would not underrate secret influences and strong pressures; and Pliny conceded that Nerva's decision was tantamount to an abdication.[126] The ingenious (and among them the erudite) are prone to discover design where chance or accident operates. There are clear temptations. The conspiracy that removed Commodus has not failed to provoke

[121] *HA Hadr.* 2, 6. Thence to Pannonia in 98, cf. Pliny, *Ep.* viii 25, 3 (a tribune who shared the transit).

[122] *HA Hadr.* 2, 2 ff.; *ILS* 308.

[123] For this conjecture, *Arh. Vestnik* xix (1968), 101 ff. = *Danubian Papers* (1971), 204 ff.

[124] Rapid changes in this season (97) are not excluded (likewise in 98).

[125] The fate of Petronius occurs only in a late source (*Epit.* 12, 8). Norbanus had lapsed—perhaps extruded by Casperius.

[126] Pliny, *Pan.* 8, 4: 'nam quantum refert, deponas an partiaris imperium?' Further, 7, 6: 'quem constat imperaturum fuisse etiamsi non adoptasses.' That Nerva abdicated was assumed in Lactantius, *De mortibus pers.* 18; Victor, *De Caes.* 12, 2.

surmise, notably the role of the Guard Prefect Aemilius Laetus. He
was able to impose quickly his candidate, an elderly military man
who was in the near vicinity, being *praefectus urbi*: namely Helvius
Pertinax. Ulterior plans have even been suspected: Septimius
Severus had been installed in a key position, the governorship of
Pannonia.[127]

Without conjecture to excess, missing facts and persons encourage
sundry questions about the elevation of Ulpius Traianus. In 97 army
commanders had time to weigh their chances and enter into
negotiation anterior to a provocative crisis in | the government.
Germania Superior and Pannonia offered routes for a rapid invasion
of Italy.[128]

At Rome Traianus could reckon on friends and allies among senior
consulars, notably the Narbonensians, like himself adherents of the
Flavian dynasty. Aurelius Fulvus may (or may not) have held the
urban prefecture.[129] Significant iterations of the *fasces* were soon
manifest: Domitius Tullus, followed by Julius Frontinus and Julius
Ursus.[130] Furthermore, a decisive role for Licinius Sura is registered
by a late epitomator.[131] The position Sura held so far evades
ascertainment.[132]

Trajan lacked resplendent kinsfolk, but he enjoyed high social
prestige, being patrician and *consul ordinarius*, son of a *vir triumphalis*.
He stood at the peak of the new imperial aristocracy, already visible
and solid as 'capax imperii' in the terminal epoch and malady of an
upstart dynasty.

APPENDIX: SYRIA

In a season of hazard Syria would not be expected to make the first
move; and if the legate chose to intervene in a civil war, he needed

---

[127] A. R. Birley, *Septimius Severus* (1971), 134 f.

[128] Emphasis therefore on Pompeius Longinus.

[129] In 69 Fulvus may have encouraged the Moesian army to declare for Vespasian. He had recently brought III Gallica from Syria.

[130] The fourth was T. Vestricius Spurinna. Of two *consules tertio* in 100 (i.e. Frontinus and Ursus) Pliny observed 'utriusque cura utriusque vigilantia obstrictus es' (*Pan.* 60, 6). The *Fasti Ostienses* have recently disclosed the honour of Ursus, expelling Spurinna. For the iterations in 98 and 100, F. Zevi, *PP* clxxxvi (1979), 189 ff.

[131] *Epit.* 13, 6: 'Surae cuius studio imperium arripuerat.'

[132] For his consulship opinions vary between 93 and 97. An earlier date is advocated by T. D. Barnes, *Phoenix* xxx (1976), 76 ff. An added complication is the *Ignotus* of *ILS* 1022: Licinius Sura—or perhaps Sosius Senecio (*cos.* 99). For the latter, C. P. Jones, *JRS* lx (1970), 98 ff.

support from Cappadocia and from Egypt (two legions in each).[133]

In the course of 97 the alleged prospects of the Syrian governor caused disquiet.[134] Rumour exaggerates, but the sequel shows a solid basis of fact. The governor departed or was removed, young Larcius Priscus (quaestor in Asia) being despatched to take over his functions, as legate of IV Scythica.[135] |

The identity of the *Ignotus* continues to aliment curiosity and speculation, for valid and various reasons. On short statement as follows.

In the first place, Javolenus Priscus. Subsequent to Germania Superior he held Syria.[136] At what date, that was a question. An epistle of Pliny, which should belong to the year 100, addresses a consular legate called Priscus, then close to the end of his tenure.[137] No other Priscus being then available in that office, Javolenus was the man. That is, Trajan's first governor of Syria, from 98 to 100.[138]

The argument seemed coherent, and it was widely accepted.[139] As is amply apparent in studies of this kind, a new fact emerging may result in manifold perturbations. The Neratii Prisci now come up again. The revision of the evidence gave the elder (*suff.* 87) a Pannonian governorship before the end of Domitian's reign (cf. above). It extends to the younger (*suff.* 97). By a different reading of the obscured letter that opens the gap in the inscription (*ILS* 1034) he is presented as 'leg. Aug. pr. pr. [in provinc. Germania] inferiore et Pannonia'.[140] That is to say, an unsuspected consular command (?98–101), preceding Pannonia. Neratius Priscus there took the place of Glitius Agricola (*II suff.* 102), being thus the last governor before Pannonia was divided.

The revision is welcome indeed, for many reasons.[141] Noteworthy consequences ensue. Neratius Priscus in Germania Inferior denies to

---

[133] Pomponius Bassus (*suff.* 94) was in Cappadocia–Galatia from 94 to 100. He had been legate in Asia to Trajan's parent, proconsul in 79/80 (*ILS* 8797). Likewise continuous, in Egypt, was Junius Rufus, from July of 94 to June of 98 (*PIR*², J 812).

[134] Pliny, *Ep.* ix 13, 10 f.

[135] *ILS* 1055. At the same time Julius Proculus, after being *quaestor Augustorum*, was appointed tribune in that legion (*ILS* 1040). Those measures convey a crisis, genuine or believed such, not the mere decease of a governor.

[136] *ILS* 1015.

[137] Pliny, *Ep.* ii 13, 2: 'longum praeterea tempus quo amicos tuos exornare potuisti.'

[138] *Historia* ix (1960), 365 = *RP* (1979), 480 f.

[139] Thus Eck, *Senatoren* (1970), 153. Conceded with some hesitations (he preferred to date the letter ii 13 before the decease of Nerva) by Sherwin-White in his *Commentary* (1966).

[140] G. Camodeca, *AAN* lxxxvii (1976), 19 ff.: with photograph, ibid. 20. That is, Germania Inferior instead of Pannonia Inferior, thus abolishing the supposed third Neratius Priscus, hitherto assumed governor of both Pannonias (under Hadrian).

[141] Cf. remarks in 'Governors Dying in Syria', *ZPE* xli (1981), 140 f. = *RP* iii (1984), 1389 f.

Javolenus Priscus the notice in Pliny's letter.[142] Javolenus' Syrian governorship falls earlier than 98, subsequent to Germania Superior (from 89 to 92 or 93). He therefore succeeded Lappius Maximus, who entered on his second consulship on May 1, 95. Lappius (it was a convenient assumption) went straight from Syria to that signal honour. Yet it | might not be so. The two items admit of a partial dissociation. Lappius might have left earlier, in 93. If so, 93–6 for Javolenus, to be followed by the *Ignotus*.[143]

That is not all. The *Ignotus* himself now acquires name and substance—as M. Cornelius Nigrinus Curiatius Maternus (*suff.* 83). Three fragments found at Liria in Tarraconensis fit together, and although not complete, they reveal the essentials of a splendid career. The document has been interpreted in a long and thorough investigation.[144]

Nigrinus, adlected by Vespasian *inter praetorios*, commanded the legion VIII Augusta and had Aquitania for praetorian province. Further, not long after his consulship he became governor of Moesia, earning in the Dacian War military decorations: indeed, a double set.[145] Of that, a convincing explanation avails.[146] In 85 Nigrinus took the place of the dead Oppius Sabinus; and then, the command being divided, he continued and fought in the war as legate of Moesia Inferior.[147] Since the emperor who awarded the decorations is not named, the dedication to Nigrinus was set up subsequent to the death of Domitian. Finally, Nigrinus was legate of Syria (the concluding item on the inscription).[148]

Cornelius Nigrinus held that post, it is argued, in succession to

---

[142] Previously no letter to Neratius Priscus could be certified in the collection, though Pliny (without the names) paid handsome tribute to Priscus and Marcellus (*Ep.* iii 3, 1), along with the grandfather of Corellia's son (M. Hirrius Fronto Neratius Pansa, *suff. c.*75). As concerns the *suffectus* of 97, two items should here be added for brief record. First, Larinum disclosed the first part of his career (*AE* 1969/70, 152): it showed him plebeian. Second, the monumental inscription (in four pieces) that had been standing for some time in the forum at Saepinum: published by G. A Pentiti, *StudRom* xxvi (1978), 343 ff. Plates xviii and xix show its structure. That scholar, however, assigned it to the 'third Neratius Priscus'. Camodeca (in 1976) was apparently not aware of this document.

[143] A faint chance might appear to subsist that Javolenus was still there in 97. Imprudent political ambitions will not lightly be ascribed to jurists.

[144] G. Alföldy and H. Halfmann, *Chiron* iii (1973), 331–72. Whence *AE* 1973, 283.

[145] Otherwise exhibited on *ILS* 983 (Carthage), probably Sex. Vettulenus Cerialis (*suff. c.*73), and by *ILS* 1022 (Sura or Senecio).

[146] Alföldy and Halfmann, op. cit. 356 f.

[147] With Funisulanus governing Moesia Superior (*ILS* 1005).

[148] Moesia and Syria were already shown by the abridged inscriptions, *CIL* ii 3783; 6013 (Liria), with a wide range in dating, cf. Groag in *PIR*², C 1407; Eck, *Senatoren* (1970), 239; 242; and, supposing the governor a son of the *suffectus* of 83, the twenties under Hadrian (gaps in Moesia Superior and in Syria) was suggested in *Dacia* xii (1968), 322 = *Danubian Papers* (1971), 214.

Lappius Maximus from 94 or early in 95. About the initial term a
difficulty intervenes, not to be avoided if Javolenus Priscus shifts,
moving back from 98–100 to the last years of Domitian.[149] There is
an instant remedy. Nigrinus need not have arrived in Syria before the
summer of 96.

Even if not the *Ignotus*, Nigrinus excites interest on several counts,
for example the relationship to the senator and orator Curiatius
Maternus. His binary nomenclature carries alternative explanations.
In short, the father of the consular general either adopted a Curiatius
Maternus or had married a lady of that family (to be deemed
Spanish).[150] Either way, a close link. |

More important, the pervading theme recurs of Domitian's
relations with the legates in the closing *triennium*. Sending Nigrinus
to Syria, the ruler exhibited a double anomaly. He went back to a
consul from the earliest years of the reign (which traversed the
normal scheme of promotions); and he chose a consular of military
renown. Again, no sign that Cornelius Nigrinus belonged to any
potent group or faction.

Brief reflection brings some abatement. After the termination of
warfare on the frontier, employment offered for safe men with little
previous experience of provinces and armies. Thus Neratius Priscus
in Pannonia (*suff.* 87), who acceded to the consulate from an urban
post, the prefecture of the *aerarium Saturni*.[151] Another example may
be Julius Marinus in Moesia Inferior, if appointed by Domitian
rather than (in winter) by his successor.[152]

Syria with three legions, confronting the Parthians, cannot be
denied military importance. Yet the Parthians were normally averse
from acts of aggression, and Syria should be regarded as a political
appointment. The Caesars tend to choose the elderly and torpid, or
their own close friends. Thus Trajan's second governor A. Julius
Quadratus (*suff.* 94), in Syria from 100 to 104.[153] In any event,
Cornelius Nigrinus therefore enjoyed the confidence of Domitian.

[149] The emergence of Neratius Priscus (*suff.* 97), as legate of Germania Inferior, affecting the
Plinian letter, came several years later than the *Chiron* paper.

[150] Alföldy and Halfmann assumed that the orator Curiatius Maternus adopted a Cornelius
Nigrinus (op. cit. 345 f.). And further, that Maternus came to a bad end not long after 75.
Thus A. D. E. Cameron, *CR* xvii (1967), 258 f. On the decease of Maternus, see further
'Spaniards at Tivoli', *AncSoc* xiii/xiv (1982/1983), 255 = p. 94, above.

[151] *ILS* 1033 f.

[152] Or again, perhaps Sallustius Lucullus in Britain, at some time between the departure of
Agricola in 85 and 93 or 94. Domitian's last legate was P. Metilius Nepos (*suff.* 91). Whose
previous career is a blank. A diploma of 98 (*CIL* xvi 43, month not given) shows him replaced
by Avidius Quietus: the latter appointed late in Nerva's reign, it might be supposed. He was
still at Rome when the name of the Syrian governor was mentioned (Pliny, *Ep* ix 13, 15).

[153] No trace in his career of any military post.

So far the powerful case for Nigrinus as the portentous *Ignotus*. The preceding pages had reason to put hazards and uncertainties on high relief. It will be suitable before the end to indicate alternative dates for the tenure of Cornelius Nigrinus.

First, he went to Syria from Moesia Inferior in 89 and died soon after. A pestilence was abroad in this season, and death in office was the fate all too frequent of Syrian legates. Facts and conjecture accumulate a formidable total.[154]

Second, if Javolenus Priscus (as seems plausible) recedes into the late years of Domitian, Nigrinus might assume the place as Trajan's first governor.[155] |

Hence a chance to be conceded that Nigrinus, although prepollent on the known evidence, is not the *Ignotus*. The revelation manifested at Liria brought a surprise and new information about the Dacian Wars. Gaps subsist—thus no legates of Pannonia between 85 and 93.

Sundry great generals of the period escape all mention in the written record. They owe existence to epigraphy. Thus Glitius Agricola, legate of Pannonia, honoured for action in Trajan's first campaign with military decorations and a second consulate; thus Julius Quadratus Bassus the Pergamene, a general on the Danube after his consulship (in 105) and going on to be legate of Cappadocia, Syria, Dacia.[156]

As Sir Thomas Browne pronounced when reviewing in *Hydrio-taphia* the famous nations of the dead, 'who knows whether the best of men be known? Or whether there be not more remarkable persons forgot than any that stand remembered in the known account of time?'

---

[154] *ZPE* xli (1981), 125 ff. = *RP* iii (1984), 1376 f. The list covers a century, from Germanicus Caesar to the fatal malady of Trajan. It is convenient to subjoin the decease of Burbuleius Ligarianus *c.*142 (*ILS* 1066). And problems about the governorships of Bruttius Praesens and Julius Maior (cf. *ZPE* xxxvii [1980], 10 f. = *RP* iii (1984), 1309 f.) would be resolved by the conjecture that Sex. Julius Severus (*suff.* 127) died shortly after going to Syria from Syria Palaestina after the termination of the Jewish insurrection (*ILS* 1056). On which, *HSCPh* lxxxvi (1982), 205, n. 141 = p. 44, n. 141, above.

[155] This alternative was not recognized in *ZPE* xli (1981), 140 ff. = *RP* iii (1984), 1899 ff. It is not very plausible. That Nigrinus was like Trajan 'a Spaniard' will not safely be adduced.

[156] *PIR*[2], G 181; J 508. Glitius, although Transpadane (from Augusta Taurinorum), finds no mention in the letters of Pliny; and Quadratus Bassus did not burst upon the world until A. D. 1932.

16

Antistius Rusticus, a Consular from Corduba

LOCAL aristocrats from Spain and Narbonensis had been on steady advance through the patronage of the first imperial dynasty. The ministers of Nero lent encouragement, Annaeus Seneca and Afranius Burrus in firm alliance. Their influence was already on the wane when Burrus died and Seneca asked for release, but other agents who emerged lacked the power to retard the process, even if such were in their conscious purposes.

Civil war sharpens ambition and accelerates change. When in the spring of 68 Sulpicius Galba, the legate of Tarraconensis, cast off his allegiance, he turned for support to men of substance and repute in the province, convoking an assembly of the notables. Their type and class is evident. To two young men the usurper allocated military rank, as inscriptions reveal. For his war 'pro re publica' he put Q. Pomponius Rufus in charge of the coasts of Spain and Narbonensis; and M. Raecius Gallus of Tarraco was made a tribune.[1]

The proclamation of Galba had repercussions in Baetica. Of the proconsul and his legate there is no precise record at this conjuncture. A little later two murders in Spain are brought up, to discredit the new ruler, in the oration of Otho (*Hist.* i 37, 3). The names indicate two senators, and identities can be supplied.[2] Nor is the agent beyond reach. The quaestor in Baetica, Caecina Alienus, came out for Galba, energetically (i 53, 1).

Corduba or its vicinity may have witnessed some disturbance. Although a 'provincia inermis', Baetica had a regiment for coastal defence. It comes up in a letter of the younger Pliny. In epilogue on his prosecution of a proconsul the orator mentions a certain Stilonius Priscus 'qui tribunus cohortis sub Classico fuerat' (*Ep.* iii 9, 18). Epigraphy supplements. On an inscription at Corduba the regiment is styled the 'cohors maritima' (*ILS* 6905).

Appeal has duly been made to the unique 'cohors Baetica' on the fragmentary bronze tablet found at Bergomum (*CIL* v 5127). It carries the decree of a 'colonia' (not named) which testifies to the

---

[1] *IRT* 537 (Lepcis); *RIT* 145 (Tarraco).

[2] Obultronius Sabinus, *quaestor aerarii* in 56 (*Ann.* xiii 28, 3) and (?L.) Cornelius Marcellus (cf. *PIR*[2], C 1403).

Historia xxxii (1983), 359–74.

excellence of the commander, M. Sempronius Fuscus. A proconsul of Baetica now turns up, Sempronius Fuscus (*AE* 1962, 288: Munigua). He held the province for the tenure 78/9, preceding C. Cornelius Gallicanus (*suff.* 84). At first sight, | identity seemed plausible: Fuscus was one of the equestrians adlected by Vespasian in his censorship.[3]

Identity was vulnerable, since the nomenclature is not distinctive: compare Q. Pomponius Rufus (*IRT* 537) who has for homonym a cavalry commander attested in the year 65 (*CIL* xvi 5). Above all, the document: items of phraseology indicate the time of Hadrian.[4] The roll of new senators has to forfeit a member, so it appears.

Galba himself had usurped the prerogatives of a censor. That is proved by a casual and often neglected item in Tacitus. An incident of late April in 69 discloses Licinius Caecina, described as 'novus adhuc et in senatum nuper adscitus' (*Hist.* ii 53, 1). Pliny's uncle, who had been procurator in Tarraconensis, knew about 'P. Licini Caecinae praetorii viri patrem in Hispania'. He ended his days and his malady by taking opium (*NH* xx 199).

Adherents of Galba in every class or rank, that is a theme to excite curiosity.[5] To take one example, legionary legates on the Rhine. Recent transactions brought vacancies. Verginius Rufus, commanding in Germania Superior, had been slow to declare for Galba. The legate of IV Macedonica was replaced by Galba's eager partisan, Caecina Alienus the quaestor of Baetica. In the next year Dillius Vocula (a senator from Corduba) had charge of the other legion at Moguntiacum, namely XXII Primigenia: perhaps likewise appointed by Galba.[6]

In the other army, the consular Fonteius Capito had been suppressed by a pair of legionary legates. Another legate, the commander of V Alaudae, happens to evade mention until the autumn of 69. He is Fabius Fabullus.[7] The name is characteristic of Baetica.[8]

---

[3] G. Alföldy, *Fasti Hispanienses* (1969), 159 (on verbal suggestion there stated from E. Birley and R. Syme); W. Eck, *Senatoren von Vespasian bis Hadrian* (1970), 105.

[4] See the full and careful discussion of A. Garzetti, *Revista de la Universidad Complutense* xviii (1979 = *Homenaje a García Bellido* iv), 66 ff. That scholar is reluctant to concede that the unnamed 'colonia' belongs to Baetica (ibid. 78).

[5] 'Partisans of Galba', *Historia* xxxi (1982), 460 ff. = pp. 115 ff., above.

[6] For the *patria* of Vocula, observe his cousin Dillius Aponianus (*AE* 1932, 78: Corduba).
A senior legate in that army, Pedanius Costa, had been designated to a consulship by Galba. He is described as 'adversus Neronem ausus et Verginii exstimulator' (*Hist.* ii 71, 2).

[7] *Hist.* iii 14, 1. On his identity, observe M. Fabius Fabullus, legate of XIII Gemina (*ILS* 996: near Poetovio): to be presumed the same, according to Groag in *PIR*[2], F 32. That was premature.

[8] Most with 'Lucius' for *praenomen*. Add L. Fabius Fabullus, a magistrate at Liria in Tarraconensis (L. Martí Ferrando, *Arch. preh. Levantina* xiii (1971), 178).

Some of the notables of Baetica who looked for promotion to Galba (and soon to his successors in competition for the power) had already embarked on the career of a senator. One of them is the youth L. Antistius Rusticus (*suff.* 90). His *patria* is Corduba, which exhibits a homonymous magistrate.[9] |

Rusticus was known from the pair of poems in which Martial bestowed praise on his wife (iv 75; ix 30). A city far away furnishes the prime document. At Pisidian Antioch the governor of the province Cappadocia–Galatia issue a remedial edict in a season of dearth and famine. According him honour as 'patronus coloniae, quod [ind]ustrie prospexit annon(ae)', the community prefixed the detail of his career.[10] As follows:

L. Antistio [L.] f. | Gal. Rustico cos. | leg. imp. Caes. [Domitiani] Aug. [Germanici] ‖ pro pr. provinciarum | Capp. Galat. Ponti Pisid. | Paphl. Arm. Min. Lyca. praef. | aer. Sat. procos. provinc. Hisp. | [u]lt. Baetic. leg. divi Vesp. et divi Titi ‖ et imp. Caesaris [Domitiani] Aug. | [Germanici] leg. VIII Aug. cura | tori viarum Aureliae et Corne | liae adlecto inter praetorios | a divo Vespasiano et divo Tito ‖ donis militaribus donato ab isdem | corona murali cor. vallari | corona aurea vexillis III | hastis puris III trib. mil. leg. II | [A]ug. Xvir. stlitibus iudicand. ‖ patrono coloniae quod | [ind]ustrie prospexit annon.

The first post, a minor magistracy, shows that Rusticus was either a senator's son or acquired 'dignitas senatoria' through grant of the *latus clavus*. The posts in the vigintivirate were allocated in a far from random fashion. First of all, social distinction. The *tresviri monetales* and the *tresviri capitales* stand at notorious extremes. There was something else. Future prospects seem adumbrated. The *IVviri viarum curandarum* are better than the *Xviri stlitibus iudicandis*: a number go on to important positions in the service of the Caesars.[11]

Rusticus (it will here be assumed) was born about the year 48. The tribunate in II Augusta took him to Britain: whether Nero or Galba made the | appointment cannot be known, and matters little. Early in 69 the army, though distant from the wars and proclamations, suffered disturbance. The consular Trebellius Maximus lacked authority. Lapsing into a feud with Roscius Coelius, legate of XX Valeria Victrix, he was driven to depart from the island (*Hist.* i 60). In the sequel that legion was tardy in swearing allegiance to Vespasian (*Agr.* 7, 2). However, II Augusta took the lead; and men

---

[9] *CIL* ii 2242. Not registered in *PIR*², A 675.
[10] Published in *JRS* xiv (1924), 180, whence *AE* 1925, 126.
[11] E. Birley, *PBA* xxxix (1953), 202.

recalled that the new emperor had been its commander in the invasion of Britain.[12]

A decisive role was played by young Rusticus. That is proved by the military decorations he was awarded: those appropriate to a legate of praetorian rank. The *laticlavius* is the deputy to the legionary commander. In the course of these transactions the legate of II Augusta might have gone away.[13] Or perhaps he died.

The beginning of Vespasian's reign offers a close parallel. A mutilated inscription at Arretium reveals the praetorian *dona* earned by a tribune called Firmus, who went on to be *quaestor Augusti*. Firmus had been 'tr. mil. leg. IIII [. . . . v]ic. leg. Aug. Vesp.' (*ILS* 1000: Arretium). On an easy explanation, the legion was IV Scythica. In the year 70 its legate Pompeius Collega was acting-governor of Syria until the consular turned up.[14]

At one level higher, Valerius Festus, the legate of Numidia, was treated like a consular (*ILS* 989), for minor exploits in the year 70 (*Hist.* iv 50, 4), and for prompt adhesion to the Flavian cause; and by a double but rational conjecture Neratius Pansa is assigned the command of VI Ferrata in the expeditionary force that went from Syria in 69 and consular decorations as a reward.[15]

Proclaimed by the eastern armies in July of 69, Vespasian at once accorded senatorial status to a number of his partisans: some excellent men who rose high, whereas 'quibusdam fortuna pro virtutibus fuit' (ii 82, 2). Three can be certified among subsequent consuls, now given the rank of aediles or tribunes, namely

(1) Salvius Liberalis (*suff.* ?85): *ILS* 1011[16]
(2) Plotius Grypus (88): *Hist.* iii 52, 3; he was abortively elected to a praetorship in 70 (iv 39, 1)
(3) Julius Celsus Polemaeanus (92): equestrian tribune in III Cyrenaica at Alexandria (*ILS* 8971). |

The large batch supervened in Vespasian's censorship.[17] For Antistius Rusticus, given his youth, adlection *inter tribunicios* might have

---

[12] *Hist.* iii 44, with the excellent *Commentary* of K. Wellesley (Sydney, 1972), ad loc. He missed however the significant role of Antistius Rusticus.

[13] A. R. Birley, *The Fasti of Roman Britain* (1981), 270.

[14] Josephus, *BJ* vii 58, cf. E. Ritterling, *RE* xii 1560. For other interpretations of *ILS* 1000 (not here to be discussed), see E. Birley, *Britannia* ix (1978), 245 f.; A. B. Bosworth, *ZPE* xxxix (1980), 267 f.

[15] For Neratius Pansa, M. Torelli, *JRS* lviii (1968), 170 ff.: whence *AE* 1968, 145.

[16] The inscription registers a double promotion, first 'inter tribunicios', then 'inter praetorios'. Both are attributed to Vespasian and to Titus, hence both perhaps in the course of the censorship.

[17] For the list and for comments, W. Eck, *Senatoren von Vespasian bis Hadrian* (1970), 103 ff.; J. Devreker, *Latomus* xxxix (1980), 70 ff.

seemed adequate. None the less, all of the promotions in that season (whether senatorial already, or new entrants) appear to be *inter praetorios*.

The first post accruing to Antistius Rusticus as a senator of praetorian rank was the charge of a road: the Via Aurelia (along with its minor adjunct, the Cornelia). He is the earliest known *curator*. The fact is devoid of significance. For two other long arteries, the Appia and the Flaminia, epigraphy offers none before the last years of Hadrian.[18]

The *curatores* of the Italian roads provoke sundry questions.[19] First, as the statistics indicate, appointments may have been casual and intermittent. Second, the duties. As with certain other occupations designed for senators (such as notably the post of *praefectus frumenti dandi*), to be presumed negligible. Third, value and prestige. The upper order was enamoured of titles and emblems. Of which the government took due cognizance. For example, the minor priesthoods or membership of the Arval Brethren in this period. Senators in scant prospect of high reward found there a satisfaction.

By corollary, the charge of a road is often absent from careers of marked success. To conclude, the duration of the mandate. It is nowhere stated. A *biennium* might be assumed without discomfort. It filled an interval before serious employment. On the other hand, the Via Aurelia was both honorific and useful for the advancement of Antistius Rusticus.

Rusticus next proceeded to take command of VIII Augusta: stationed at Argentorate in Germania Superior, and not at this time offering action in the field. The inscription, naming three emperors, enables a close delimitation, between 78 or 79 and 81 or 82. Moreover, by good fortune Rusticus fits neatly between two other legates of VIII Augusta, diverse in their careers. Namely M. Cornelius Nigrinus (*suff.* 83) and T. Avidius Quietus (*suff.* 93).[20]

Legionary legates are sparse on attestation in the decade 75–85. Of promoted equestrians, praetorian by 74 and subsequently consuls, five can be adduced. |

(1) M. Cornelius Nigrinus (*suff.* 83). VIII Augusta, *c.*75–8. *AE* 1973, 282.

[18] Namely *ILS* 1069; 1061.
[19] W. Eck, *Die staatliche Organisation Italiens in der hohen Kaiserzeit* (1979), 37 ff.
[20] For the career of Cornelius Nigrinus see the ample discussion of G. Alföldy and H. Halfmann, *Chiron* iii (1973), 331 ff.; for the dating of the legionary command, ibid. 352 f. Quietus is registered as legate of VIII Augusta by *ILS* 6105.

(2) C. Salvius Liberalis Nonius Bassus (?85). V Macedonica, ?78–81. *ILS* 1011.[21]

(3) L. Javolenus Priscus (86). IV Flavia, *c.*78–81. *ILS* 1015.

(4) C. Caristanius Fronto (90). IX Hispana, under Vespasian. *ILS* 9485.

(5) Ti. Julius Celsus Polemaeanus (92). IV Scythica, ?80–3. *ILS* 8971.

Two others may be added, on imperfect testimony, but likewise useful for various comparisons. First, Q. Pomponius Rufus (95), Galba's partisan in Tarraconensis. The inscription (*IRT* 537), suppressing the fact of adlection, goes on to list two praetorian posts.[22] Rufus was *iuridicus* in Tarraconensis and legate of a legion, which is styled merely 'leg. V'. That is, either V Alaudae or V Macedonica. The former met its end in 86 when a Roman army under Cornelius Fuscus was defeated in an invasion of Dacia.[23] If the latter, Rufus could have assumed command in any year between 81 and 89. His governorship of Dalmatia, at the time a praetorian province, began in 92 or 93.[24] Until that the career of Pomponius Rufus betrays retardation—or a suspicion of vicissitudes.

Second, L. Antonius Saturninus (*suff.* 82). According to a late author, he was adlected to the Senate by Vespasian.[25] An inscription at Jerusalem carries the erased name of a governor of the province Judaea.[26] No other candidate can compete (Saturninus the legate of Germania Superior made a proclamation at Moguntiacum on the first day of January, 89). Hence in office *c.*78–81. An antecedent legionary command will be surmised.

For convenience a new senator of a different type may be subjoined. After receiving the *latus clavus* P. Baebius Italicus (*suff.* 90) began as quaestor in Cyprus (*ILS* 8818). As legate of XIV Gemina he earned military decorations in Domitian's war against the Chatti in 83.

No commander of any of the four legions in Britain is on record during the seven years of Agricola's campaigns, which brought *ornamenta triumphalia* to the general. To have named any of them was alien to the purposes of the consular biographer.

[21] For the dating of his career see *JRS* lxviii (1978), 18 = *RP* iii (1984), 1079 f.; *Some Arval Brethren* (1980), 25 f.
[22] For problems presented by his career see G. Alföldy, *Fasti Hispanienses* (1969), 71 ff.; R. Syme, 'Spanish Pomponii', *Gerión* I (1983), 250 ff. = pp. 140 ff., above.
[23] E. Ritterling, *RE* xii 1278; 1569.
[24] Attested by a diploma dated to 93 by the imperial titulature (*CIL* xvi 38).
[25] Aelian, fr. 112 Hercher.
[26] Discussed in *JRS* lxviii (1978), 12 ff. = *RP* iii (1984), 1070 ff.: whence *AE* 1978, 825.

For another reason (hazards of documentation), no legate happens to be attested during the Dacian War of Domitian, which began in 85 and lasted until 89. |

After an interval, Rusticus became proconsul of Baetica. A new inscription dates this post to the year 84.[27] Since Domitian's titulature does not carry 'Germanicus', the tenure should be 83/4.

The seven proconsulates exhibit a wide range in rank and honour.[28] When, for example, Cyprus or Crete with Cyrene figure in a senator's career, they declare poor prospects for a consulship. Baetica is in posture of esteem, along with Macedonia and Achaia; and it can fall at a late stage in a senator's advancement.[29]

Which raises a question that baffles a clear answer: how was the sortition managed? Manifold complications adhere.[30] In theory, a man qualified five years after the praetorship. In fact, evidence shows senators able to acquire a province after a much longer interval. Rusticus accedes to Baetica when he had enjoyed praetorian status for a decade. In this instance conjecture permits a solution congenial to a society where convention mattered more than regulations: age as well as rank could be taken into account. In 83 Rusticus was about thirty-five, hence on parity with proconsuls who became praetors five years previously.

Another phenomenon has a bearing upon the working of the lot. Rusticus got one of the better provinces. It was Baetica—as if by choice and preference. More natives of that province go there as proconsuls than might be expected.[31]

For a senator at this stage who stood well with Caesar (and with the managers of patronage) the next post would beckon towards the consulate. One path led through the praetorian provinces in the portion of Caesar. They had risen to a total of eight, and a regular scheme of promotion was taking shape.[32] Few of the governors miss the *fasces*. Some accede promptly.[33]

Rusticus did not advance that way. He became prefect of the *aerarium Saturni*. The post was collegiate, and it normally foretold a consulship. That comes out clearly in a notorious incident of the year

[27] *AE* 1977, 440 (Cisimbrium).
[28] For a full analysis, W. Eck, *Zephyrus* xxiii/iv (1972/3), 233 ff. For praetorian proconsuls under Domitian, B. W. Jones, *Historia* xxiv (1975), 631 f.
[29] Thus Macedonia for Salvius Liberalis (*ILS* 1011), immediately before his consulship (?85).
[30] Illustrated by G. Alföldy, *Fasti Hispanienses* (1969), 267 ff.
[31] Alföldy, op. cit. 269 f.
[32] For details, *JRS* xlviii (1958), 1 ff. = *RP* (1979), 378 ff.; *Historia* xiv (1965), 342 ff. = *Danubian Papers* (1971), 225 ff.
[33] Thus Cornelius Nigrinus: Aquitania following on the legionary command.

97. When Pliny launched his attack on Publicius Certus, prudent friends told him to stop and think. As one of them said, 'lacessis hominem iam praefectum aerarii et brevi consulem' (ix 13, 11). In the event, Certus was passed over: 'collega Certi consulatum, successorem Certus accepit' (13, 23). |

The prefects normally held office for a full *triennium*.[34] One of the pair preceding Antistius Rusticus (*suff.* 90) was L. Neratius Priscus (*suff.* 87).[35] Rusticus therefore occupies the years 87–9. Two pairs should intervene for the *sexennium* before Certus and his colleague entered office in January of 96. The political situation in the next year enhanced competition, and might in any case have abridged the tenure of the two *praefecti*. As it happened, the next pair were Pliny himself and his friend Cornutus Tertullus. They continued in office till the end of 100 although they had meanwhile assumed their consulates in September of that year.[36]

That excites the suspicion that the charge of the Treasury was normally the reward for civilian aptitudes. The next prefect on clear record is L. Catilius Severus (*suff.* 110). His career hitherto lacked distinction. For example, he had been for two years a legate in Asia, and at Rome a *praefectus frumenti dandi*.[37] Men of the time would not have seen Catilius as governor in the sequel of two military provinces.

For all that, Neratius Priscus (*suff.* 87) went to Pannonia: probably in 93. Instructive evidence about the prefecture accrues during the reigns of Hadrian and Pius. It is held by a number of men who not long after their consulships go on to consular commands. The procedure can be described as providential. Caesar makes provision for servants of state and empire, compensating them for absences abroad with an easy sojourn at the capital.[38]

Antistius Rusticus assumed the *fasces* early in 90, with Ser. Julius Servianus for colleague: in a company of no fewer than eleven *suffecti*. Long consular lists tend to occur in the early years of a reign. The present phenomenon will evoke (and combine) diverse explanations.

(1) Honour for persons of conspicuous fidelity to emperor and dynasty. Domitian had recently faced and surmounted a sudden crisis. In 89, on the first day of January, Antonius Saturninus, the

---

[34] M. Corbier, *L'Aerarium Saturni et l'Aerarium Militare* (1974), 652 ff.

[35] *ILS* 1033 (Saepinum). To be assigned to this Neratius Priscus, not to the homonym (*suff.* 97), as demonstrated by G. Camodeca, *AAN* lxxxvii (1976), 19 ff.

[36] As emerges from *Pan.* 92, 1.   [37] *ILS* 1041, cf. *PIR*², C 558.

[38] *Historia* xiv (1965), 358 = *Danubian Papers* (1971), 241.

legate of Germania Superior, had made a proclamation at Moguntiacum.

(2) A blockage resulting from the numerous adlections carried out by Vespasian. There had not been many suffect consuls in 87, 88, 89. Caristanius Fronto and Baebius Italicus were held back until 90, the former a legionary legate in the reign of Vespasian (*ILS* 9485); the latter | in 83 (8818). They governed in succession the province Lycia–Pamphylia, where Baebius is on attestation in 85.[39]

(3) The age factor. While certain consulars qualified through governorships (and some enjoyed rapid promotion) others had to wait their turn until they reached the standard age of forty-two, or not far short of it. Thus might seniority and equity dictate.[40] Julius Servianus in fact arrived 'suo anno': he was born in 47.[41] Antistius Rusticus was a close coeval.

The notion of deferment without dishonour gains support from several pieces of evidence. L. Flavius Silva Nonius Bassus was already a senator when adlected *inter praetorios* in 73/4 (*AE* 1969/70, 183). Legate of Judaea, he terminated the rebellion in 73. He was not consul until 81—but he then opened the year as *ordinarius*.

The case of Caristanius Fronto and Baebius Italicus has been noted above. Baebius, not an adlected equestrian, was presumably the younger man.

Two *suffecti* of the year 115 furnish a clear and useful testimony. As a diploma reveals, Juventius Celsus and Statilius Maximus governed Thrace in succession.[42]

It may be of various advantage to set forth the consular years of those adlected equestrians who possessed praetorian status by the year 74.

?79 Q. Aurelius Pactumeius Clemens[43]
 80 Q. Aurelius Pactumeius Fronto
 82 L. Antonius Saturninus
 83 M. Cornelius Nigrinus
    M. Annius Messalla
?85 C. Salvius Liberalis Nonius Bassus
 86 L. Javolenus Priscus

[39] *IGR* iii 548.
[40] As argued in *JRS* lxviii (1978), 14 f. = *RP* iii (1984), 1073 f.
[41] In his ninetieth year when perishing in 136 (Dio lxix 17, 1).
[42] A copy of this important document (kept for long years in the Museum at Sofia) is published by M. M. Roxan, *RMD* (1978), no. 14.
[43] The Pactumeius of *ILS* 1001 (Cirta) was universally held to be Fronto (*suff.* 80). Rather Clemens (attested also by *CIL* viii 7057), cf. T. D. Barnes, *CR* xxi (1971), 332.

88 D. Plotius Grypus
90 C. Caristanius Fronto
92 Ti. Julius Celsus Polemaeanus
94 A. Julius Quadratus
95 Q. Pomponius Rufus.

The range is wide indeed. In some instances to be explained by diversity of age on entry to the high assembly. Several of the earliest on the list were then | probably over thirty. Again, variety of merit or patronage. Both political and personal vicissitudes will be allowed for. Domitian promoted Julius Celsus from Sardis, Julius Quadratus from Pergamum. Their eventual ascension was hardly contemplated twenty years before.

Plotius Grypus, adlected *inter tribunicios* in 69, became consul only in 88, but then with honour, for he replaced the Emperor. A clearer case of retardation at some stage is Q. Pomponius Rufus (*suff.* 95). His fortunes declared a signal improvement when he became legate of Dalmatia (now a praetorian province) in 92 or 93 (*CIL* xvi 38, of 93). For a parallel of late emergence one may observe two members of a group not in high favour with the government: Junius Rusticus (*suff.* 92) was tribune of the plebs in 66; and Avidius Quietus (93) had been a friend of Thrasea Paetus.[44] Rusticus succumbed to the prosecutions for treason in the autumn of 93.

The palmary specimen is Cornutus Tertullus (*suff.* 100). Already an aedile when given praetorian rank in 73/4. His career (*ILS* 1024) shows him only legate in Crete–Cyrene and proconsul of Narbonensis until the prefecture of the *aerarium Saturni* indicated that consulship to which he attained when about fifty-five.

As was to be expected, the eleven consuls suffect in 90 comprise a highly heterogeneous collection. Pride of place belongs to L. Cornelius Pusio, succeeding the Emperor. He came from Gades, his father a consul *c*.73 (as colleague of the jurist Pegasus). By his full style, L. Cornelius Pusio Annius Messalla.[45] Pusio is clearly close kin to M. Annius Messalla (*suff.* 83), who owed adlection to Vespasian (*IRT* 516).

There follow Antistius Rusticus and Julius Servianus. Collocations

---

[44] Pliny, *Ep.* vi 29, 1.

[45] *AE* 1915, 60 (Tibur). Assigned to the Vespasianic *suffectus* in *PIR*[2], C 1425—and that must be so, according to R. Hanslik, *RE*, *Suppl.* xii (1970), 190. The son (*suff.* 90) should have the preference, cf. E. Birley, *JRS* lii (1962), 220 f. It follows that he was proconsul of Africa, since Asia is complete.

in consular pairs sometimes appear appropriate or even intentional.[46] The origin of Servianus is a problem. Spain is generally conjectured or assumed.[47] About this time Servianus married the sister of young Aelius Hadrianus.[48]

The next year opened with M. Ulpius Traianus, son of an eminent consular, and neo-patrician. A potent nexus was forming (it embraced Narbonensis also) | with results momentous in history. When Antistius Rusticus is under inspection, curiosity will fasten, as is venial, on friends and allies from the natal territory. And curiosity will have a pertinent question to ask about the next stage in his career.

Many senators (old families or recent) whom birth or luck elevated were content with their station, and with the chance of a proconsulate in Asia or Africa to crown their eminence about thirteen years later. New men could aspire to an imperial province, earned by modest merit or constant allegiance—and Caesar preferred them.

The consular commands now numbered nine (excluding Dalmatia, which in 85 had surrendered its sole legion to Moesia). Competition might be keen. The cessation of the Dacian War in 89 precluded action and glory—and also the hazards. In virtue of their previous careers, two consuls of 90 possessed claims, viz. Caristanius Fronto and Baebius Italicus. Likewise Cn. Pompeius Longinus, governor of Judaea in 86.[49] Further, one might wonder about the earlier occupations of Ser. Julius Servianus. On the other hand, ex-consuls senior by several years stood in expectance.

Whatever the influences that prevailed, Antistius Rusticus took up a province. It was Cappadocia–Galatia, a vast conglomerate of regions that extended from the borders of Pamphylia and Cilicia to the river Euphrates. Two legions were the garrison, on the frontier that faced Armenia. Which for the governor entailed diplomatic as well as military functions.

The predecessor was Ti. Julius Candidus (*suff.* 86). There has been some uncertainty about the dating. He went to the province in 89, so it can be argued.[50] Therefore he was probably in office until 92.

---

[46] In 85 P. Herennius Pollio and his son M. Annius Herennius Pollio formed a pair. And observe in 69 Arrius Antoninus and Marius Celsus: probably both from Nemausus.

[47] He was even presumed a citizen of Italica by R. Étienne in *Les Empereurs romains d'Espagne* (1965), 61.

[48] Deduced from the marriage of the daughter to Pedanius Fuscus *c.*106 (Pliny, *Ep.* vi 26). Given the age of Servianus, a wife (or wives) previous to Hadrian's sister will be assumed.

[49] *CIL* xvi 33. He is attested in Moesia Superior in 93 (xvi 39).

[50] *Some Arval Brethren* (1980), 27 f. Tenure from 87/8 to 90/1 was proposed by W. Eck, *Senatoren* (1970), 239; from 89 to 91 by R. K. Sherk in *ANRW* ii 7 (1980), 1011 f.

In the spring of 93 (if that was the year), Rusticus received an urgent letter from the magistrates and council of Antioch, asking for his intervention: there was extreme dearth 'propter hiemis asperitatem'. Rusticus complied. He issued a firm edict. It forbade, among other things, the hoarding of grain, and it fixed a maximum price (double the normal).

When full and explicit testimony accrues, it conveys the temptation to exploit it to the utmost. Hence (despite diversities from region to region) the notion of a famine prevailing throughout Asia Minor. None the less, heterogeneous evidence can be mustered, indicating world-wide shortages and famine. Not enough land, it seemed, was under cultivation for cereals, too much for vineyards. Domitian was impelled to make an imperious ordinance, | 'ad summam quondam ubertatem vini, frumenti vero inopiam'.[51] The date of the measure is not on adequate report. A reference made by Statius does not occur until a poem published in 95.[52]

In this context it may seem harsh to refuse the Book of Revelation. When the black horse appears, a voice announces savage prices for wheat and barley (6, 6). In the wake of famine comes pestilence: 'and behold a pale horse, and his name that sat on him was Death, and Hell followed with him' (6, 8).

Warfare is prolific of epidemics, and they produce alarming stories. Malefactors went about using poisoned pins, not at Rome only but throughout the world. Thus Cassius Dio under the year 90, a notice that has suffered undue neglect.[53]

Pestilence in the sequel of the Dacian campaigns, that assumption will cause no discomfort. At the lowest estimate a sequence of unhealthy seasons at Rome can be enlisted in support, with many deaths ensuing.[54] It is not enough, to be sure, that Agricola passes away in August of 93 at the age of fifty-four. Evidence accumulates and converges. For example, the poet Martial nearly perished in 91 (vi 58, 3), Licinius Sura the year after (vii 47); and young people were carried off.

In 91 Martial had mourned a victim of the 'impia Cappadocum tellus', namely Camonius Rufus at the age of twenty, the son of a friend at Bononia (vi 85); and now death overtook Antistius Rusticus in that province. Nigrina his wife brought the ashes to Rome, as

[51] Suetonius, *Dom.* 7, 2. On which see now B. Levick, *Latomus* xli (1982), 66 ff.
[52] Statius, *Silvae* iv 3, 11 f. Miss Levick (op. cit. 68) opts for 90 (the date for the edict given by the *Chron. Paschale*).
[53] Dio lxvii 11, 6. Describing the great plague under Commodus, Dio proffers the same explanation, with an explicit reference backwards to the time of Domitian (lxxii 14, 4).
[54] *Tacitus* (1958), 69; *Some Arval Brethren* (1980), 21 ff.

Martial relates (ix 30). The publication of Martial's ninth book is generally assigned to the year 94. An item in the previous book referring to the same year has duly been noted. It is the consulship of the elder son of Silius Italicus (viii 66). L. Silius Decianus and T. Pomponius Bassus assumed the *fasces* on the first day of September. There is a chance that the poem alludes to the designation of Decianus. It mentioned the prospects of Severus, his brother. They were annulled by death before the end of 94 (ix 86).

The decease of Rusticus (ix 30) cannot be dated as closely as an enquirer might wish: the next poem refers to a certain Velius, absent on the staff of Domitian in Pannonia for eight months until December of 92.[55] |

The death of Antistius Rusticus might have supervened before the end of 93 (hence a very short tenure). However it be, the interim arrangements for the double province engage close attention. The next consular governor was Pomponius Bassus (*suff.* 94).

The inscription at Antioch of L. Caesennius Sospes (*ILS* 1017), much vexed in its interpretation, has been brought into play. Commanding XIII Gemina in 92, a legion of Pannonia, Sospes earned decorations in the campaign against Suebi and Sarmatians. He is next discovered in Galatia. The inscription enumerates nine regions of the complex, beginning with Galatia, but omits Cappadocia, which on other documents stands without exception at the head. The precise position he occupied was a question. Some fancied him a *iuridicus*, taking authority when the governor died. Against which, he is styled 'leg. Aug. pro pr.'; and his rank (a previous legate of a legion) forbids. Therefore the province had been split.[56]

The division did not last for long. New evidence has been adduced. Coins of Caesarea show Pomponius Bassus in Cappadocia for the year of Domitian reckoned from October 93 to October 94.[57] Bassus was consul suffect for the last four months of 94. The consequence is clear. Bassus went out to the province while still consul designate. A consulship held in absence is no scandal, or even an innovation.

Pomponius Bassus was not disturbed by the fall of the Flavian dynasty or by the crisis in the reign of Nerva. Continuing in office,

[55] Book VII was published in 92, Book X in 95. The intervening books may both have appeared in 94.

[56] Suggested as 'possible' by B. Levick, *Roman Colonies in Southern Asia Minor* (1967), 230. For a firm statement of the thesis, R. Syme, *JRS* lxvii (1977), 40 f. = *RP* iii (1984), 1046 ff. Not all accept. Thus R. K. Sherk, *AJP* ci (1979), 167 f.

[57] P. R. Franke, *Chiron* ix (1979), 277 ff.

he completed a *sexennium*, a tenure of unusual duration. Death at the age of about forty-five frustrated Rusticus of a second imperial province. In a successful career that opened with the early and abnormal promotion of a *tribunus laticlavius* one thing appears to be lacking, namely rcognition through a priesthood. One of the 'quattuor amplissima sacerdotia' often fell to a *novus homo* about the time of his consulship. Seasons of high mortality would help. Not but that the meritorious might have to wait. The alert Pliny did not become an augur until 103 or 104.

Rusticus either received the *latus clavus* or began as the son of a senator who had entered the 'amplissimus ordo' about fifteen or twenty years earlier. Claudius Caesar as censor in 47 made adlections, but none of the Spaniards or | Narbonensians later so eminent can be proved to have come in by that promotion.

The ultimate extraction of Baetican senators is a fascinating topic.[58] By their rare or regional names a number go back to the old Italian diaspora. Thus Annaei, Ulpii, Dasumii. Others are indigenous, reflecting proconsuls of the imperial Republic. Antistii may belong to either class: an Antistius Vetus was governor of Ulterior in 68/7 B.C. A soldier or veteran of a legion in Britain who came from Corduba may be registered in passing.[59]

The Aponii are clearly immigrant.[60] On prominence in the season of Rusticus' début was M. Aponius Saturninus, the son of an opulent senator.[61] The year of his consulship is in dispute. If it is *c.*55, the influence of Seneca will be suitably invoked.[62] In 69 Saturninus is discovered as governor of Moesia, perhaps one of Galba's appointments. The legion III Gallica was commanded by Dillius Aponianus (*Hist.* iii 10, 1), patently a close kinsman. Corduba yields his inscription (*AE* 1932, 78). Further, the heroic Dillius Vocula, left in charge of XXII Primigenia on the Rhine, may be assumed his cousin.[63] He likewise carries the 'Sergia' for tribe (*ILS* 983: Rome). It is on clear attestation at Corduba, along with 'Galeria' (the tribe of Antistius Rusticus).[64]

Baetica was conspicuous on the *Fasti* of 90, as has been pointed

---

[58] For seventeen families on prominence in Baetica see Carmen Castillo García in *ANRW* ii 3 (1975), 631 ff.

[59] *RIB* 518 (Deva). He has for tribe the 'Sergia'.

[60] *Tacitus* (1958), 758 (where for 'L. Aponius' in l. 10 read 'Q. Aponius').

[61] The parent is *PIR*², A 936 + 937: with properties in Egypt.

[62] For that approximate year, *Some Arval Brethren* (1980), 68 f.

[63] Vocula is 'A. f.', Aponianus 'L. f. A. n.'.

[64] Only one specimen (ii 2286) was adduced by W. Kubitschek, *Imperium Romanum tributim discriptum* (1889). Others have accrued, among them ii 5523 and *RIB* 518—and the two Dillii.

out. Conspicuous, even were Julius Servianus to be waived: the chance subsists of Narbonensian origin both for Servianus and for the great Julius Ursus (consul for the third time in 100) whose nomenclature he took over.[65]

In the next year (that of Ulpius Traianus), Q. Valerius Vegetus of Iliberris was consul suffect, in 93 L. Dasumius Hadrianus, a wealthy citizen of Corduba. The Dasumii are linked in some way or other to Servianus and to the Annii Veri (of Ucubi).[66] Momentous alliances were developing.

The theme leads on to kinsfolk of Antistius Rusticus. At first sight there is only his wife. An inscription of one of their slaves declares her name as 'Mummia Nigrina'.[67] That entails a brief disquisition: not only Mummii, but in the first instance Valerii Vegeti.

Iliberris supplies Cornelia P. f. Severina, the mother of the consul Valerius Vegetus (*CIL* ii 2074), Etrilia Afra the wife (2077), which was welcome and satisfactory (cf. *PIR*[1], V 150); and observe an Etrilius Afer at Tucci (1624).

Complications arose when a second Q. Valerius Vegetus emerged on the *Fasti Ostienses* as consul suffect in 112. How should the ladies be apportioned? On one view, Cornelia Severina married the first consul, Etrilia Afra the second.[68] A further step was taken. The *suffectus* of 112 had for colleague a Cornelius Severus, to be supposed a close relative because of his mother, Cornelia Severina.[69] That is aberrant. The lady is 'P. f.', the consul 'Cn. Pinarius Cn. f. Cornelius Severus' (*PIR*[2], C 1453). Profit seldom accrues from dealing with nomenclature as indistinctive as 'Cornelius Severus'.

It is better to suspend judgement, or revert to the original assumption (cf. *PIR*[2], E 105). On the latter position, Q. Valerius Vegetus (*suff.* 112) forfeits a wife. A further uncertainty threatens on the flank: more wives than one for either consul, or for both.

Polyonymy now takes a hand, to vex and perplex. An important document concerning property and property rights in southern Etruria has for its subject 'Mummius Niger Valerius Vegetus consular(is)': *ILS* 5771 (near Viterbo). First of all, hardly the consul of 91: the document happens to include a mention of P. Tullius

---

[65] *Tacitus* (1958), 636; *JRS* lxx (1980), 79, n. 151 = *RP* iii (1984), 1300, n. 152.
[66] *Tacitus* (1958), 792.
[67] *CIL* vi 27881.
[68] Thus Carmen Castillo García in *ANRW* ii 3 (1975), 648.
[69] First cousins, as assumed by H.-G. Pflaum, *Les Carrières procuratoriennes* (1960), 634: discussing the family in relation to the 'Kalendarium Vegetianum' of *ILS* 1405 (Osqua, in Baetica).

Varro (*suff.* 127). Better, the son.[70] He had prefixed the name of a relative to his own.

Students of nomenclature will not overlook the alternative explanation. It can be briefly stated. This Mummius Niger is a hitherto unattested consul, to go somewhere in the reign of Hadrian. The adjunct carries the maternal ascendance (it happens often). His father had married the daughter of a Valerius Vegetus.

That is not the end of trouble. A member of the next generation appears on an Apulian inscription as 'L. Mummius Niger Q. Valerius Vegetus Severinus Caucidius Tertullus'.[71] The nomenclature may be taken to support the alternative which has just been mooted. 'Mummius Niger' is the paternal name, the annexed items being all maternal. 'Severinus' recalls Cornelia P. f., while 'Caucidius Tertullus' may be the maternal grandfather, whose daughter married the first *polyonymus*, viz. the consular Mummius Niger Valerius | Vegetus (*ILS* 5771). The item 'Caucidius Tertullus' recurs in the nomenclature of the wife of Herodes Atticus (*PIR*[2], A 720), and in that of two consular kinsmen: one is a Vigellius (*ILS* 1116), the other an Atilius Bradua, disclosed at Lepcis (*IRT* 517). The *nomen* is preternaturally rare, and not otherwise on attestation.[72]

To revert to Mummia Nigrina, the wife of Antistius Rusticus. His link with Valerii Vegeti of Iliberris may turn out not to be as close as had been suspected. That family was no doubt among the wealthy. They had a house on the Quirinal.[73] Nigrina for her part shared her inheritance with her husband, so Martial states (iv 75). He need not be deemed impoverished to begin with.[74] And, for that matter, Nigrina may not be his first wife.

Twenty-two Mummii are to be found in *CIL* II, among them three magistrates in towns of Baetica.[75] And one will add the local worthy at Corduba, L. Julius M. f. Q. n. Gal. Gallus Mummianus, tribune commanding the 'cohors maritima' (*ILS* 6905). Their name goes back (it is assumed) to L. Mummius, the consul of 146 B.C., governor half a dozen years previously.

[70] E. Groag, *RE* xvi 528. In consequence Degrassi in his *Fasti consolari* (1952) printed the *suffectus* of 112 as polyonymous. Followed in 'Spaniards at Tivoli', *AncSoc* xiii/xiv (1982/1983), 249 = p. 94, above.

[71] *CIL* ix 948 (Aecae). In *PIR*[1], M 515 he was supposed a grandson of Q. Valerius Vegetus (*suff.* 91), and the same person as the consular Mummius Nigrinus Valerius Vegetus of *ILS* 5771.

[72] No specimen in *TLL, Onom.*, which has a Caucideius (x 5340: Interamna Lirenas) and six Caucii (among them i[2] 113: Praeneste). Caucilii occur only in *CIL* VI. Add P. Caucilius in 49 B.C. (*Bell. Hisp.* 32, 7). [73] *CIL* xv 7558.

[74] Donations between consorts were forbidden (unless for helping the census of the husband in his career). See the lengthy disquisition, *Dig.* xxiv 1, 1–67.

[75] *CIL* ii 1584 (Itucci); 1684 (Tucci); 2025 (Singilia).

No inspection of the upper order in Rome of the Antonines will neglect P. Mummius Sisenna, the consul of 133, soon after legate of Britain.[76] No antecedents or kinsfolk are discoverable. His son Rutilianus (*suff.* 146), a successful person but blemished by superstition, was one of the immigrants, from Baetica in the main, who took up residence at Tibur.[77]

---

[76] An origin in Baetica is assumed by A. R. Birley, *The* Fasti *of Roman Britain* (1981), 249. He adduces P. Mummius Ursus, a magistrate of Ugia in A.D. 6 (*AE* 1952, 49: Emerita). J. González, *ZPE* lii (1982), 172 f., confirms: their *patria* was Osset.

[77] *ILS* 1101, cf. 'Spaniards at Tivoli', *AncSoc* xiii/xiv (1982/1983), 249 = p. 94, above.

17
Hadrian and the Senate

SENATORS liked funerals. For some the style of the laudation invited expert appraisal. Others would be intent on the matter—and alert for what was not said. An emperor's obsequies furnished rare entertainment for the men of judgement, the 'prudentes', with comments normally sharp and subversive.

On the Senate's vote of consecration followed another and necessary ceremony when the Princeps made suitable remarks about his own position, or about principles of government now to be respected. Tiberius Caesar ran into trouble. Nero, after discourse on a blameless past and allusion to felicitous prospects, went on to delineate 'formam futuri principatus' (*Ann.* xiii 4, 2).

Some of the accession formalities had to be modified or postponed when an emperor initiated his reign far from Rome. Thus Vespasian and Trajan. Trajan's successor was proclaimed by the army in Syria on August 11th of the year 117, the news arriving that Trajan had died at Selinus. The gist of Hadrian's first despatch to the Senate can be gleaned from the *Historia Augusta*. Requesting the consecration of his predecessor, the new ruler proffered an avowal: the 'auctoritas patrum' had been anticipated by the troops 'quod esse res publica sine imperatore non posset' (*Hadr.* 6, 2). Whether he embarked on edifying pronouncements about government and policy has not been disclosed. No harm would be done if detail was eschewed—and several topics were best avoided.

In his speech from the throne, Nero declared that he arrived with a clean sheet: 'nulla odia, nullas iniurias nec cupidinem ultionis adferre' (*Ann.* xiii 4, 1). Hadrian's earlier existence had incurred enmities or detraction. The young man was the next of kin to Trajan, and he acquired the hand of the grand-niece shortly before his quaestorship in 101. By character and tastes, Hadrian was far from congenial to the Imperator, and an autocrat is seldom at ease with a predictable heir. Astute men in the dynastic entourage might be disposed to venture sundry calculations and reckon with hazards of mortality.

Athenaeum lxii (1984), 31–60.

For a season some may have wondered about Licinius Sura, whom Trajan's favour elevated to a third consulship.

In ostensible deference to the 'res publica', Trajan until the end refrained from taking the step that would annul speculation and confirm the succession. According to idle fancies current in a later age, Trajan proposed to emulate Alexander the Macedonian or leave the choice to the Senate; and some spoke of a preference for Neratius Priscus.[1]

Hadrian went to the East with Trajan in 113. No evidence shows him active in the field or deciding policy.[2] Various frictions or recriminations may have ensued in the high command. However, some of Hadrian's firm partisans were now emerging. When the Imperator, ailing in mind and body, departed to celebrate a Parthian triumph, he consigned to Hadrian the charge of the army in Syria.

Suspicions arose about the death-bed adoption, not diminished by the despatch that bore the signature of Plotina Augusta. That was not the worst. The Imperator had sent lavish bulletins of victory. He may have failed to render to the Senate an honest or adequate explanation of the retreat from Mesopotamia. The inheritor had to shoulder blame for the surrender of eastern conquests that had already lapsed.[3] He was fortunate in not having to confront the high assembly until ten months had passed.

Journeying from Syria, Hadrian spent the winter at Nicomedia or Byzantium. A dutiful ruler could find in military tasks a pretext for further delay. Beyond the lower Danube the Sarmatians were in disturbance: only a 'tumultus', and no expedition followed. So far the *HA* (6, 6 ff.). An inscription supplies a valuable fact. A Roman governor of Dacia, the illustrious Julius Quadratus Bassus (*suff.* 105), died there on campaign.[4] Hadrian, when departing for the capital, left behind a Roman knight, Marcius Turbo, with an anomalous command that embraced both Dacia and Pannonia Inferior (6, 7; 7, 3).

The emergency was more than local or military. A grave and tragic embarrassment had supervened. On charges of treason the Senate ordered (or rather had to approve) the execution of four consulars (two of them *bis consules*), who had been generals of Trajan. That was not done by Hadrian's wish or decision, 'ut ipse in vita sua dicit' (7, 2).

---

[1] *HA Hadr.* 4, 8 f. Marius Maximus has been suspected as the source of the anecdote.
[2] He was 'at the nerve-centre of all action', according to W. Weber in *CAH* xi (1936), 299.
[3] M. I. Henderson, *JRS* xxxix (1949), 129 (reviewing F. A. Lepper, *Trajan's Parthian War*).
[4] *Pergamon* viii 3, no. 21.

Apologia in the autobiography of an emperor is an invitation to disbelief. This specimen cannot evade scrutiny, but may enlist a measure of acquiescence. Agents at the capital had been zealous and incompetent.[5]

On arrival the new Princeps had to combat the 'tristissimam de se famam' | as well as justify his foreign policy—and rumour added that he was giving up Dacia. A variety of pronouncements reassured the high assembly. Thus the solemn oath affirming that no senator should suffer the death penalty (7, 4).[6] Again, no knights permitted to sit in justice on senators (8, 8 f.), and so on.[7] And there ensued a vast remission of debts owed to the Treasury.

Hadrian demonstrated a prince not autocratic or avid for honours. He duly deprecated the title 'pater patriae', not for the first time (cf. 6, 4); and, as he was frequently heard to declare, he proposed to manage the State as 'populi rem, non propriam' (8, 3).

When a ruler's relation with 'the Senate' is in question, distinctions should be drawn: deference towards the institution or active response to the desires of individuals and groups. Membership comprised a wide diversity in category and status, with social eminence no less pervasive and influential than official rank: the broad mass, which took tone and guidance from aristocrats or from ex-consuls, might not happen to concur with their leaders all the time. Nor would the 'prudentes' be of one mind when they discussed 'per circulos et convivia' the débâcle in the East and the new policy of peace and conciliation. It is therefore difficult to assess the repercussions provoked by the removal of the Four Consulars.

First of all, Lusius Quietus.[8] No grief or regrets ushered out this person. He was in fact a Moorish chieftain, signalized when commanding his own force of cavalry in the campaigns of Domitian and Trajan. In 116 he recaptured Nisibis and Edessa; and in the next year Trajan abruptly shoved him into a consulship with the charge of coercing rebellious Judaea. Hadrian at once dismissed him.

Two of the four are in a different case, namely Cornelius Palma and Publilius Celsus. Each had been *consul iterum* (109 and 113), and honoured by Trajan with a public statue: they are named together

---

[5] That is, the Guard Prefect Acilius Attianus.

[6] In Dio the item occurred in a despatch (lxix 4, 2).

[7] Whether authentic or not, this item may have inspired *Alex.* 21, 4: 'Alexander autem idcirco senatores esse voluit praeff. praet. ne quis non senator de Romano senatore iudicaret.'

[8] *PIR*[2], L 439. The evidence for a number of facts and dates in the present paper will be found in *PIR* or in W. Eck, *Senatoren von Vespasian bis Hadrian* (1970).

with Sosius Senecio (*cos. II* 107).[9] Palma stood prominent early in the reign, opening as colleague of Sosius the year 99. He then governed Tarraconensis; and when holding Syria he carried out the annexation of Arabia, which earned the *ornamenta triumphalia*.[10] |

Publilius Celsus (*suff.* 102) is the total enigma among the marshals of Trajan. No exploit of war is on record, and no consular province.[11] None the less, the statue and the iterated consulship put him on a level with Sosius Senecio. During the first war against the Dacians Sosius governed Moesia Superior; and according to a further conjecture he commanded an army corps in the second war (105 and 106).[12] A post of that kind was certainly held by Julius Quadratus Bassus (*suff.* 105), and it brought him the *ornamenta triumphalia*.

Palma came from Etruscan Volsinii. Celsus will be presumed likewise Italian. No earlier Publilius stands on the imperial *Fasti*, and none is discoverable under the Republic who might have transmitted the name to a client in the provinces.

Kinsfolk or allies of both Palma and Celsus elude enquiry. A certain amount is known about the fourth victim, Avidius Nigrinus (*suff.* 110). The *patria* was Faventia on the Aemilia, the family highly cultivated (friends of Plutarch), and Nigrinus benefited from a consular uncle (Quietus, *suff.* 93).

Nigrinus first comes to notice when tribune of the plebs in 105 (Hadrian's year). He took an independent line in senatorial transactions both then and the year after, and his style of oratory won praise from an expert.[13] Nigrinus' accession to the *fasces* five years later was abnormally rapid on comparison with certain of his coevals who did not lack merit or favour.[14] Not long after the consulate Nigrinus was put in charge of the senatorial province of Achaia as Caesar's legate.[15] Hadrian, it may be observed, held the archonship at Athens in 112/13. In the sequel Nigrinus went on to govern Dacia, replaced there before the death of Trajan.[16]

In the late season of the reign both Palma and Celsus came under suspicion from Trajan, so a passage in the *HA* alleges (4, 3). Not to

[9] Dio lxviii 16, 2. One might have expected a fourth name, that of Licinius Sura. Perhaps deceased by that time.

[10] *ILS* 1023 (acephalous and fragmentary) was attributed to him by Borghesi.

[11] Britain or Pannonia Superior might be conjectured, within the period 107–12.

[12] Moesia Superior has been inferred from Pliny, *Ep.* iv 4 (written about 103). Except for Germania Superior, the other frontier commands have occupants at this time.

[13] Pliny, *Ep.* v 13; 20; vii 6, 2 ff.

[14] Pompeius Falco (*suff.* 108) was tribune of the plebs in 97 (*Ep.* ix 13, 9): he married the daughter of Sosius Senecio, himself son-in-law to Julius Frontinus (*cos. III* 100).

[15] *SIG*[3] 827 (Delphi); *Hesperia* xxxii (1963), 24 (Athens).

[16] *ILS* 2417 (Sarmizegethusa). Succeeded by Julius Quadratus Bassus, before the death of Trajan, as is generally held, cf. *PIR*[2], J 508.

be accorded credit. It also states that they had always been hostile to Hadrian. Which might be true, but cannot be assumed authentic.

By contrast, Avidius Nigrinus, a close friend, and congenial. That is confirmed by the imputation of ingratitude which the Autobiography conveyed. Hadrian intended to make Nigrinus his successor (7, 1).

Furthermore, Nigrinus belonged to a nexus of some consequence in the new nobility. It centres on an aristocratic lady called Plautia, nowhere named in any | document of history or epigraphy but acquiring an identity through the names of her descendants.[17] Plautia's first husband was Ceionius Commodus (*cos.* 106), the second Avidius Nigrinus (*suff.* 110); and after Nigrinus' death she reverted to Vettulenus Cerialis (*cos.* 106). The son of Ceionius Commodus (*cos.* 136), otherwise Aelius Caesar, was at the same time stepson and son-in-law of the ill-starred Nigrinus.

The destruction of Nigrinus was a blow to the new emperor in more ways than one. It alienated an influential group, which happened to be Italian (the Ceionii from Bononia, not far distant from Faventia, the *patria* of Nigrinus, the Vettuleni Sabine).[18] For the rest, nothing shows a compact, let alone a conspiracy that enlisted Lusius Quietus. At the most perhaps friction or discontent, fatally enhanced by rumour or malice.[19] A single charge and the same doom united the Four Consulars. They perished in separate localities: Faventia, Baiae, Tarracina, and Lusius Quietus on a journey (7, 1).[20]

A 'primum facinus novi principatus' introduced the reigns of Tiberius and of Nero, removing a rival of dynastic blood or pretensions. No such rival existed to alarm Hadrian, and he could count on support from powerful interlocking factions. Significant names are published among the *consules ordinarii* of the first four years.

> 118 Imp. Caesar Hadrianus Aug. II: Cn. Pedanius Fuscus Salinator
> 119 Imp. Caesar Hadrianus Aug. III: P. Dasumius Rusticus
> 120 L. Catilius Severus II: T. Aurelius Fulvus
> 121 M. Annius Verus II: Cn. Arrius Augur.

Alliances had been forming for some time between families from Baetica and Narbonensis, with results apparent when Trajan came to

---

[17] As established by Groag, under *PIR*², A 1408. For the stemma see now *Athenaeum* xxxv (1957), 314 = *RP* (1979), 331.

[18] For the origins of Vettuleni and Ceionii, *RP* (1979), 330 ff.

[19] Discontent with Hadrian's renunciation of the eastern conquests has commonly been surmised.

[20] A brief vague statement in Xiphilinus gives little guidance: some of the four plotted to kill Hadrian while he was hunting, others succumbed on different charges (Dio lxix 2, 5).

the power.[21] In the sequel that unobtrusive gentleman Annius Verus (*suff.* 97) occupies a central position through mastery of matrimonial stratagems. He annexed two families of Nemausus, the Domitii and the Aurelii. For one of his sons, Annius Verus acquired Domitia P. f. Lucilla, heiress to the fortune originally founded by the orator Domi|tius Afer. His daughter went to Aurelius Fulvus (*cos.* 120). This young man was the third consul of that name. His parent (*cos.* 89) had married a daughter of Arrius Antoninus (*suff. II* 97), who is presumed likewise from Nemausus.

Cn. Arrius Augur, selected to share the *fasces* with Annius Verus in 121, avows nothing to elucidate that eminence. He is only a name, and not safely to be taken for a relative of Antoninus.[22] Nor is Dasumius Rusticus, although identifiable by parentage and descendants, a character in history. The Dasumii (an opulent family from Corduba) come into the nexus somewhere, linked probably both to Hadrian and to the Annii Veri (deriving from Ucubi in Baetica).

Nor does the other *bis consul*, Catilius Severus, lack an attachment, albeit tenuous and peculiar. Catilius (*suff.* 110) is styled the 'proavus' on the maternal side of Marcus, the grandson of Annius Verus; and the boy (born in 121) carried his name for a time. How the term 'proavus' can be interpreted has been a tiresome problem.[23]

One tentative solution opined that Catilius might be regarded as a 'substitute grandfather' to Marcus. That is, if Catilius married his grandmother (Domitia Cn. f. Lucilla) on the decease of her husband P. Calvisius Tullus (*cos.* 109).[24] A better path lay open.[25] About the year 107 Cn. Domitius Tullus died (*II suff.* 98). While most of the property went to Domitia Lucilla, his daughter (by adoption), the widow received a handsome endowment. This lady, nowhere named, had married for money and was 'aetate declivis'.[26]

That was no bar in this society. If Catilius seized the opportunity, he later became, as step-great-grandfather, a 'proavus', to the boy Marcus. His career, showing no promise hitherto, now took a sharp

---

[21] For the detail, *Tacitus* (1958), 603 ff., with App. 86 f.

[22] This man may well be polyonymous. Arrii are common, but no senator with the *praenomen* 'Gnaeus' except Cn. Arrius Cornelius Proculus (*suff.* 145). Groag suggested a link (under *PIR*[2], C 1422). Observe also the polyonymous Q. Cornelius Proculus (*suff.* 146), with 'Senecio' in his nomenclature, and Q. Cornelius Senecio Annianus (*suff.* early in the reign of Pius). The latter comes from Carteia in Baetica (*CIL* ii 1929). A third Cornelius Proculus was legate of Pannonia Superior in 133 (*CIL* xvi 76).

[23] Groag once suggested that a son of Catilius Severus might have married Domitia Cn. f. Lucilla, the grandmother of Marcus (in *PIR*[2], C 357): not with any confidence, and ages debar.

[24] *Tacitus* (1958), 793, n. 3.

[25] *Historia* xvii (1968), 95 f. = *RP* (1979), 638; *HSCPh* lxxxiii (1979), 305 = *RP* iii (1984), 1174.

[26] Pliny, *Ep.* viii 18, 8.

turn for the better. He acquired the charge of the *aerarium Saturni*, a post which conveys a senator straight to the consulship.[27] |

One consul remains, Pedanius Fuscus, chosen to inaugurate the reign as colleague of the Emperor. A dozen years previously he emerged for the first time in the written record (and the last) as a youth of high promise, betrothed to the daughter of Julius Servianus, who about the time of his first consulship (in 90) had married Hadrian's sister.[28] The consul of 118 thus reproduces Hadrian's own role under Trajan. The husband of Julia became the heir apparent, to succeed if Hadrian perished—or to be suppressed.[29]

The Pedanii derive from another part of Spain, from the colony of Barcino in Tarraconensis, consular long since, and also patrician. No evidence has so far revealed the origin of Ser. Julius Servianus.[30] He went on to annex the nomenclature of the great Julius Ursus, consul for the third time in 100. Ursus is probably one of the Narbonensians.[31]

Servianus and Sura stood foremost among the marshals of Trajan, opening the year 102 together as consuls for the second time. Neither was exempt from envy or enmities, and there is no sign that they abode in concord. The ruler would have to be on guard against rumours or calumny.[32]

In 107 Sura outdistanced Servianus with a third consulship. He died not long after. According to the *HA*, Sura made a portentous revelation to Hadrian when the latter became consul (in May of 108): Trajan proposed to adopt his kinsman (3, 10). The item should be declared dubious, whatever the source. If it derives from the Autobiography, it carries a pertinent meaning.[33] Far from being a rival, Licinius Sura was well disposed towards the prospects of Hadrian. Which might be the case, despite Hadrian's alliance with Servianus. Like Licinius Mucianus, the ally of Vespasian, whom he

---

[27] *ILS* 1041 (Antium); *ILAfr* 43 (Thysdrus). The latter document carries the tribe, which should be supplemented as 'Cl[u', giving the colony Apamea in Bithynia as his *patria*. On which see H. Halfmann, *Die Senatoren aus dem östlichen Teil des Imperium Romanum* (1979), no. 38, cf. no. 18.

[28] Pliny, *Ep.* v 26 (the betrothal of Fuscus and Julia).

[29] On the son of Fuscus see E. Champlin, *ZPE* xxi (1976), 84 ff. (on *AE* 1972, 578: Ephesus).

[30] And an earlier wife or wives might be allowed for, before he married Domitia Paulina, Hadrian's sister. Servianus was connected with the opulent Dasumii from Corduba.

[31] *Tacitus* (1958), 636; *JRS* lxx (1980), 79, n. 151 = *RP* iii (1984), 1300, n. 152.

[32] For hostility towards Sura, Dio lxviii 15, 4.

[33] Compare the statement about the prospects of Avidius Nigrinus (*Hadr.* 7, 1): not specified as coming from the Autobiography.

resembles in so many ways, Sura may not have wanted the power for himself.

Much remains enigmatic about Sura. No parent is known, no wife, no heir—and even the date of his first consulship is in dispute.[34] His *patria* lies in Tarraco|nensis, probably Celsa, and he had interests both at Tarraco and at Barcino.[35] One might look for local adherents. Minicius Natalis and Licinius Silvanus occur, consuls suffect as colleagues in 106. The pair were related.[36] Natalis came from Barcino, Silvanus perhaps from Tarraco.[37] Natalis is attested as legate of Pannonia Superior in 113, and he was holding the province when Trajan died.[38] Of the career of Silvanus only the proconsulate of Asia is known: in 121/2, parallel with Natalis in Africa.

Despite Barcino, the common *patria*, there is no call to assume that Minicius Natalis owed advancement to the Pedanii; and nothing is known to connect the Pedanii with Sura. However, Hadrian perhaps inherited some of the following of Sura, such as Natalis.

From Sura the enquiry moves to Sosius Senecio, who in 107 shared the *fasces* with the *consul tertio*, but is not thereby proved either close or congenial. Yet one wonders.[39] Sura was an orator before rising to the political summit, and Sosius is the most conspicuous of Plutarch's Roman patrons.[40] A valuable notice in the *HA* happens to register Sosius along with Platorius Nepos as friends of Hadrian in the year 113 (4, 2). He may have enjoyed no long survival thereafter. In 116 his son-in-law Pompeius Falco (*suff.* 108) held Moesia Inferior, passing thence to Britain. Both for Sosius and for Falco an origin from the eastern lands has been suspected.[41] Hence important and intricate problems.

The identity of the legates in the armed provinces at this juncture excites legitimate curiosity. Along with Natalis and Falco goes Catilius Severus (*suff.* 110), who vacated Cappadocia for Syria when Hadrian departed, holding it for the *biennium* before his second

---

[34] The years 93 and 97 have been variously canvassed. For an earlier date, T. D. Barnes, *Phoenix* xxx (1976), 76.

[35] For Celsa or Osca, *Tacitus* (1958), 791.

[36] 'Quadronius' (very rare) occurs in the nomenclature of their sons (*ILS* 1061; 1028).

[37] For Silvanus, Baetulo (close by Barcino) is not excluded, cf. *ILS* 1028; *AE* 1936, 66.

[38] *ILS* 1029. A new diploma shows him legate in December of 113 (information from W. Eck).

[39] Few have been tempted to adduce *ILS* 7854: 'libertor. / et famil. / Seneci. Surae'. As Dessau duly observed, 'nomen videtur indicare hominem nobilem'.

[40] C. P. Jones, *Plutarch and Rome* (1971), 54 ff. etc.

[41] *Historia* xvii (1968), 100 = *RP* (1979), 688; *Some Arval Brethren* (1980), 48 f.; A. R. Birley, *Epigraphische Studien* iv (1967), 69; *The Fasti of Roman Britain* (1981), 97 f.; C. P. Jones, *JRS* lx (1970). 103.

consulship. The immediate successors in all four consular commands baffle ascertainment. For compensation, albeit imperfect, three names can be adduced of *suffecti* in the first two years.

First Platorius Nepos. Coming from the governorship of Thrace and consul | early in 119 (perhaps in absence), he was despatched to Germania Inferior. He stayed there until 122, when he replaced Falco in Britain.[42]

Second, Bruttius Praesens (*suff.* 118 or 119). After holding the *cura operum publicorum* he governed Cappadocia (?121–4) and Moesia Inferior (?124–8).[43] His early career had encountered delay or vicissitudes (see below). At some time subsequent to 107 Praesens married the daughter of Laberius Maximus, who won glory in warfare against the Dacians and acceded to a second consulship in 103 as colleague of the Emperor.[44] The *HA* discloses Maximus residing in exile on an island when Trajan died (5, 5). It would be worth knowing why and when he was sent there. The best piece of testimony implying discord among the marshals cannot be exploited.

Third, Ummidius Quadratus (*suff.* 118). A senator of this name was legate of Moesia Inferior.[45] Date and identity were not clear. One recent estimate put this governor *c.*121–4, succeeding the 'Se]rtorius' attested in 120 by an inscription at Tomis.[46] A new piece of the document shows them identical, supplying the nomenclature 'C. Ummidius Quadratus Sertorius Severus'.[47] Which is welcome, for more reasons than one. It had been taken for certain that he was a *polyonymus*. The descent from a consul (*c.*40) ran through the grandmother, Ummidia Quadratilla. The family was ancient, with impressive monuments at Casinum.

The notable members of the expanding Hispano-Narbonensian nexus have already been put on show. Ummidius Quadratus makes his first entry in the company of Pedanius Fuscus. They are styled an 'egregium par'.[48] Perhaps already related in some way, the conjecture is not idle. The aristocratic Quadratus is anomalous and peculiar among commanders of armies now or previously.

Platorius Nepos conforms, patently a *novus homo*. From the country of the Ulpii and Aelii, but not on social parity with other

---

[42] *ILS* 1052; *CIL* xvi 69.   [43] *IRT* 545 (Lepcis); *AE* 1950, 66 (Mactar).

[44] Laberius Maximus came from Lanuvium, cf. *ILS* 6194. His daughter, Laberia Hostilia Crispina, is disclosed by *AE* 1964, 106 (Trebula Mutuesca). About the year 107 Praesens had an 'uxor Campana' (Pliny, *Ep.* vii 3, 1).

[45] *AA* xxvi (1911), 236 (Charax, in the Crimea).

[46] *Historia* xvii (1968), 89 f. = *RP* (1979), 676 f.

[47] *AE* 1977, 745 (with inadequate commentary) = *SEG* xxvii 400. See further *HSCPh* lxxxiii (1979), 291 f. = *RP* iii (1984), 1162 f. (correcting and supplementing the original publication). The editors had missed the Sertorius Severus of Pliny, *Ep.* v 1, 1.

[48] Pliny, *Ep.* vi 11, 1.

members of the group.[49] Bruttius Praesens was Lucanian, with a mother from Mediolanum or Comum.[50] His | first known wife was Campanian, the second (the daughter of Laberius Maximus) had for *patria* Lanuvium in old Latium.[51]

Along with three army commanders attested in 117 (Natalis, Falco, Catilius), the three additional names illustrate the heterogeneous company aggregated by the new ruler, from personal affinities or under necessity and previous obligations.

Emphasis has been put on the embarrassments confronting Hadrian on his accession. One of them was a shortage of loyal allies to occupy the consular commands. Reliance on a few persons carries manifest disadvantages, and even danger. Likewise prorogation of tenure, beyond the normal three or four years. No example of the latter expedient is discoverable at the outset of the reign, unless it be supposed that Minicius Natalis went on for some time more in Pannonia Superior. For the next dozen years, conjecture is baffled at all points by a singular dearth of evidence.

It becomes sharply perceptible in the four major commands, each with a garrison of three legions. In Moesia Inferior there is a gap after Pompeius Falco, but Ummidius Quadratus supervenes, then Bruttius Praesens, to be followed by Sex. Julius Severus (*suff.* 127).[52] In Britain, however, the tenure of Platorius Nepos is a problem, no successor verifiable before Julius Severus in 130.[53]

Above all, Syria and Pannonia Superior. After Catilius Severus the next legate of Syria is Publicius Marcellus (*suff.* 120), in office when Judaea raised rebellion in 132.[54] In Pannonia Superior the gap extends from Minicius Natalis to Cornelius Proculus (otherwise unknown) whom a diploma attests in 133.[55]

Epigraphy may bring help one day. One recalls how recent is knowledge about the career of Bruttius Praesens or the Moesian governorship of Ummidius Quadratus. It may also come up with some surprises, to impair conventional notions or establish the unpredictable.

Two legates of Cappadocia now accrue, furnishing various

---

[49] He had for tribe the 'Sergia' (*ILS* 1052), but his city is not certified. The rare *nomen* exhibits a solitary specimen in Baetica (*CIL* ii 1861: Gades).

[50] As indicated by the second item in his name, 'L. Fulvius Rusticus', cf. *PIR*², F 541; 557.

[51] Above, n. 44.   [52] *ILS* 1056.

[53] The *Ignotus* of *RIB* 995 may belong here, cf. A. R. Birley, *The Fasti of Roman Britain* (1981), 105 f.

[54] *ILS* 8826. For Hadrianic legates in Syria see now *Romanitas–Christianitas* (*Festschrift Straub*, Bonn, 1982), 230 ff. = pp. 50 ff., above.

[55] *CIL* xvi 76.

instruction. Namely Statorius Secundus (*suff.* *c.*122), attested in 127/8, and Prifernius Paetus (*suff.* ?125) in 128/9.[56] Their tenures fill the lacuna between Bruttius Praesens and Fla|vius Arrianus (?131–7).

Statorius Secundus is the first consul in his family, and the last. Prifernius Paetus turned up in the correspondence of Pliny under the name of Rosianus Geminus, the recipient at a late stage of six letters. Writing from Bithynia, Pliny solicited Trajan to accord him advancement of some kind or other.[57] As the petition states, Rosianus had been quaestor to Pliny the consul (in 100).

Nothing ensued to the benefit of Rosianus through a long efflux of time. The inscription of his son-in-law contributes two facts.[58] Rosianus became proconsul of Achaia (*c.*122) and he ended as proconsul of Africa (?140/1), hence to be presumed consul suffect in 125. His full style runs as 'T. Prifernius Sex. f. Paetus Rosianus Geminus'. By birth the son of a Sex. Rosius Geminus, he took by adoption the name of a *suffectus* of 96. The Prifernii are patently Sabine. The same may hold for Rosii, another rare *nomen*.[59]

The *gentilicium* of Statorius Secundus, though not local or distinctive, happens also to be uncommon. Obscurity envelops this person. It lifts, but only a little, if he be supposed a relative of Statoria Marcella, the wife of Minicius Fundanus (*suff.* 107).[60] The *patria* of Fundanus is Ticinum.[61] Of 'Statorius' the sole specimens in Transpadana occur at the neighbour city of Mediolanum.[62]

Pliny slipped in a tribute to the eloquence of Fundanus (not of his own brand); and Plutarch dedicated a treatise to him.[63]

So far the two new legates of Cappadocia. For promotions both to consulates and to governorships Hadrian's freedom of choice was inhibited by various factors. Three of the early consuls (Pedanius Fuscus, Ummidius Quadratus, Aurelius Fulvus) are eminent members of the group on which he relied for political support. Apart from that, they belonged to the new imperial aristocracy, in prospect of acceding to the *fasces* at thirty-two, or not long after. No ruler in his senses would refuse | homage to birth and influence. At the same

---

[56] *AE* 1968, 504 (nr. Sebastopolis); *AE* 1976, 675 (Archelais).

[57] *Ep.* x 26.

[58] *ILS* 1067 (the *cursus* of Pactumeius Clemens).

[59] For the local origins of both families see *Historia* ix (1960), 372 f. = *RP* (1979), 488. Trebula Mutuesca has recently yielded the *cursus* of the polyonymous T. Prifernius T. f. Paetus, consul suffect in 146 (*AE* 1972, 153).

[60] The same lapicide inscribed *CIL* vi 16632 (Statoria M. f. Marcella) and 16631 = *ILS* 1038 (Minicia Marcella, the daughter of Fundanus).

[61] Inferred from the tribe 'Papiria' on his inscription found at Šipovo in Bosnia, cf. *Tacitus* (1958), 801.

[62] *CIL* v 5869; 5888.   [63] Pliny, *Ep.* vii 3; Plutarch, *De cohibenda ira.*

time, it was prudent to do something for the inconspicuous—and personal affinities might come into play.

Rosianus Geminus was a close coeval of Hadrian. Few can have expected that this unpromising person would turn up as governor of a military province in his middle fifties. Bruttius Praesens affords a firmer basis for deductions or speculations. He avowed adherence to the precepts of Epicurus, as is made patent by the language in which Pliny gently deprecated a senator's abstention from political life.[64]

About Hadrian's own beliefs some uncertainty obtains. It is fostered by his catholic curiosities and taste for the exotic. Those features attract and seduce writers of history or fiction. In some particulars hesitation is enjoined. Before all, his alleged addiction to astrology and expertise in that science.[65]

Full weight should be accorded to a brief statement in the *HA*, which happens to be unimpeachable in this instance: 'in summa familiaritate Epictetum et Heliodorum philosophos . . . habuit' (16, 10). Epictetus, born in slavery, was a Stoic by his teaching, or rather a Cynic, repelled by the arrogance of high society, and sharp in criticism.[66] Heliodorus (otherwise C. Avidius Heliodorus, Hadrian's secretary, rising to the prefecture of Egypt) adhered to the Epicurean persuasion.[67]

The conjoined names agree well with other evidence about Hadrian's habits and predilections. He paraded hostility to distinctions of nation or class, he took delight in converse with persons of low degree, 'detestans eos qui sibi hanc voluptatem humanitatis quasi servantes principis fastigium inviderent' (20, 1). Above all, he disliked pomp and pretension.

Epicureanism prescribed tolerance, charity, the claims of friendship. Trajan's wife, who lent support to the sect, viewed Hadrian with favour; and Hadrian himself may have been well disposed towards senators of the less ambitious type, not least if they had suffered retardation during the previous reign. The prime exhibit is Bruttius Praesens, who had made a splendid début as military tribune in 89, with military decorations. Nearly twenty years later he is discovered living at ease in Campania. Pliny was not perhaps the only friend who urged him to take up the career of honours again. In 114

---

[64] *Ep.* vii 3, 2: 'quin ergo aliquando in urbem redis? ubi dignitas honor amicitiae tam superiores quam minores.'

[65] For a fabulous item observe *Hadr.* 16, 7, certified for Marius Maximus by *Ael.* 3, 9. The character and the distribution of the notices about astrology repays analysis, cf. *HAC 1972–4* (1976), 291 ff. = *Historia Augusta Papers* (1983), 80 ff.

[66] F. Millar, *JRS* lv (1965), 141 ff.

[67] *PIR*², A 1405 = H 51. Some scholars have failed to recognize identity.

Praesens emerged as commander of the legion VI Ferrata.[68] |

Another Epicurean is detected in Pliny's ambience. His coeval Calestrius Tiro, praetor in 93, did not seek a proconsulate until 107, when he proceeded to Baetica. Pliny struck a warning note. Calestrius must observe the 'discrimina ordinum dignitatumque' and not neglect the better sort in the province out of kindness towards those of lower station.[69]

It is a pleasing thought that Calestrius, if he survived, might have earned some recognition from Hadrian. A near kinsman, T. Calestrius Tiro (brother, nephew, or cousin) became consul suffect in 121.[70]

Like Pliny's admonitions, his comments on the behaviour of senators tend to be bland or improving. A certain Licinius Nepos stands out as an exception. During his praetorship in 105, Nepos displayed an excess of zeal; and when he persisted with efforts for reform the year after, the praetor Juventius Celsus was moved to style him an 'emendator senatus'.[71] A bad mark that took time to erase. Licinius Nepos turns up as a consul suffect in 127.[72] Other offenders against the conventions may have benefited from sympathetic or tardy indulgence.

To a wilful temperament and the habit of opposition Hadrian joined the perils of a sophisticated education. Prone to omniscience, he was not reluctant to assert superior talents. According to a noteworthy verdict in the *HA*, 'professores omnium artium, ut doctior, risit contempsit obtrivit' (15, 10). The Emperor's quarrels with sundry intellectuals adorn and diversify a hostile tradition, with manifest exaggerations.[73]

In fact, a predilection for men of letters was advertised the year after Hadrian's arrival in Rome when he changed the Guard Prefects. Releasing Sulpicius Similis and Acilius Attianus (he blamed Attianus for the destruction of the Four Consulars, so it is alleged), Hadrian chose Marcius Turbo and Septicius Clarus (9, 3 ff.). Turbo is the trusted friend with long military experience, now brought from his special command on the Danube frontier. Of Septicius, no previous occupations are on record, and everything points to a contrast with Turbo. Septicius is the man to whom Pliny had dedicated his

---

[68] In Armenia. He led the legion southwards across the snow-bound Taurus, as shown by Arrian, *Parthica*, fr. 85, taken together with Strabo xi 506 (snow-shoes on Mount Masius).

[69] *Ep.* ix 5, 3, cf., also to Calestrius, an incident as a warning to all 'qui se simpliciter credunt amicis' (vi 22, 1).

[70] For his career, *AE* 1965, 320 (Cestrus in Cilicia).   [71] *Ep.* vi 5, 4.

[72] Reflection about ages will show that this consul is the praetor of 105, not a son, as assumed in *PIR*[2], L 220 f.

[73] G. W. Bowersock, *Greek Sophists in the Roman Empire* (1969), 50 ff.

selection of letters, and before he vacated the prefecture of the Guard Septicius was to be honoured in like fashion, with imperial biographies composed by Suetonius Tranquillus. About the time of Septicius' appointment Sue|tonius, known already as a scholar and an author, became the imperial secretary *ab epistulis*.[74]

Suetonius belongs in the company of friends on whose behalf Pliny made unsuccessful petitions.[75] In the event, Hadrian took up some of them. Whether or not that amiable prepossession issued in wise choices is far from clear.

Lovers of the paradox will observe that Hadrian (*suff.* 108) got no missive, or even a passing mention. The nearest Pliny came was the letter announcing the betrothal of Servianus' daughter to Pedanius Fuscus. The consular Annius Verus is likewise absent, also young Aurelius Fulvus, coeval with Pedanius Fuscus and with Ummidius Quadratus.

Hadrian was thus able to combine personal tastes or affinities with obligations towards the governmental nexus. He had also to be careful about his attitude towards other groups, some aristocratic or aloof, others eager and pushing. In honours for himself the Princeps imposed strict moderation. A second consulship followed by a third, and then no more. To which matter the *HA* subjoins a portentous pronouncement: 'tertio consules, cum ipse ter fuisset, plurimos fecit, infinitos autem secundi consulatus honore cumulavit' (8, 4).

The facts refute (see below). The presuppositions call for rigorous scrutiny. On a surface view, iteration in the *fasces* declares honour to the high assembly, recompense for signal merit in the arts of war or peace. Reflection suggests a detrimental feature that would be painfully apparent to men of the time. The benefit went to a minority, to the political allies of the ruler and the military men. A number of other senators were debarred from giving their names to the Roman year.

Trajan's first *ordinarii* were Cornelius Palma and Sosius Senecio. Then, between 100 and 107 the iterations monopolized twelve places (including three for Trajan). Only four were left for other senators. By contrast, Hadrian's first decade (118 to 127) exhibited few iterations, with fourteen senators acquiring the eponymate.

In consequence men of distinction would not now have to put up with a suffect consulship, and senators of non-consular families had a

---

[74] The precise year is not certain.

[75] For that category, *Historia* ix (1960), 362 ff. = *RP* (1979), 477 ff. The notorious specimen is the Saguntine Voconius Romanus: too old, for one thing, when his coeval friend solicited both Nerva and Trajan for adlection to the Senate.

chance of the supreme honour. After the *ordinarii* of 118–21 (dealt with above), noblemen occupy the next four years.[76] |

New names then obtrude, Epidius Titius Aquilinus (125), Eggius Ambibulus (126). And after a time follows a run of consuls with no discoverable ancestry, among them Antonius Rufinus (131), Trebius Sergianus (132), Mummius Sisenna (133). Some of the five here adduced might be sons of *suffecti*, as is normal—but hardly all of them.[77] The obscure Trebii, who show *suffecti* in 121 and 125, are the first and last consuls of that name.

Hadrian's policy offers an interpretation. He wished to spread patronage more widely and win support outside the groups dominant in the Senate. In due course that aim was furthered by admissions at the outset of the reign (by the *latus clavus* or by adlection). A large influx was not liked. In casual and laudatory comment the *HA* alleges of Hadrian 'difficile faciens senatores' (8, 7). There is however no means of telling.[78]

As elsewhere, dearth of precise evidence deters. Admissions to the privileged order of the patricians are documented by a solitary name.[79] Nor can anything be said about awards of the higher priesthoods. Hadrian had no cause to alter the standard practice of the Caesars, unless his predecessor had been over-generous. As concerns the Arval Brethren, that fraternity, select under the first dynasty, became under Domitian and Trajan a haven of nonentities, though sometimes disturbed by accidents or by brilliant anomalies.[80] Under Hadrian the congregation conforms. It eschewed birth, talent, or success.[81]

It will be appropriate to insert brief remarks about the iterations. The earliest have been noted, Catilius Severus in 120, Annius Verus in 121. Next, in 125, comes Lollius Paullinus Saturninus (*suff.* 94). Then, in 128, Nonius Calpurnius Asprenas (*cos.* 94). That year was designed to open with a pair of *consules iterum*. Two papyri register a

---

[76] Viz. 122, M'. Acilius Aviola and Corellius Pansa; 123, Q. Articuleius Paetinus and L. Venuleius Apronianus; 124, M'. Acilius Glabrio and C. Bellicius Torquatus.

[77] Mummius Sisenna, who passed rapidly to Britain (attested early in 135 by *CIL* xvi 82), may be a promoted equestrian officer.

[78] The earliest on direct attestation appears to be Julius Severus (*suff.* ?138), adlected *c.*125 (*ILS* 8886). However, Flavius Arrianus (*suff.* 129 or 130) had perhaps been an equestrian officer; and the obscure Aemilius Arcanus may have received the *latus clavus*, with admission to the quaestorship, in 122 after service as tribune in II Augusta (*ILS* 1064: Narbo).

[79] P. Coelius Balbinus, the consul of 137 (*ILS* 1063): unfortunately ignored by the author when discussing patricians in *Chiron* x (1980), 436 = *RP* iii (1984), 1324 f.

[80] *Some Arval Brethren* (1980), *passim*.

[81] Lists are registered, viz. *CIL* vi 2078 (in 118); 2080 (120); 2081 (*c.*124). Observe in the third, recent entrants: M. Valerius Junianus, Cornelius Geminus, P. Vitellius Saturninus.

colleague with the sign of iteration, namely P. Metilius | Nepos.[82] This consular, it is inferred, died before taking office. His identity is a problem. Perhaps the Metilius who had been legate of Britain long ago (*suff.* 91).[83] Better, the *suffectus* of 103.[84]

The aristocratic *bis consules* of 125 and 128 invite inspection. Both stood on eminence of ancestry, going back to Triumviral or Augustan consuls, hence among the few survivors whom contemporaries could recognize as *nobiles* (the Republic witnessed its legal demise in September of the year 14).

For Lollius Paullinus the prefecture of the City explains the honour. Annius Verus decided to resign an office that normally terminated with death or with a change of ruler. For Hadrian, no fancier of birth and pedigree, an incident had to be lived down, from the opening days of the reign. Crassus Frugi (*suff.* 87), a Piso descended from Pompeius and Crassus, tried to escape from his penal island. He was put to death by a procurator (5, 6).

For Lollius Paullinus and for Nonius Calpurnius (both consuls in 94) personal regard or gratitude perhaps counted. Young Hadrian went for a visit to Baetica in 90 (2, 1). After his return and before departure to the first of his three military tribunates, 'extremis Domitiani temporibus', Hadrian held a minor magistracy at Rome. He was also the *praefectus* appointed when the consuls were absent, celebrating the Feriae Latinae.[85] The year may be 94, precisely. The honorific post, be it noted in passing, was generally reserved for young aristocrats.[86]

The next *consules iterum*, who open the year 129, represent the new nobility, namely Neratius Marcellus (*suff.* 95) and Juventius Celsus (*suff.* ?115). Marcellus was the son (by adoption) of Neratius Pansa (*suff.* c.75).[87] His brother Priscus (*suff.* 97), the illustrious jurist, did not reach that distinction, although he is registered among the counsellors of Hadrian (18, 1).

Neratius Marcellus had been legate of Britain (?101–4), with no other trace of his subsequent survival apart from the charge of the Roman aqueducts.[88] Juventius Celsus, jurist and son of a jurist,

---

[82] Reported in *IEJ* xii (1962), 269. For discussion of the identities of Metilii, *JRS* lviii (1968), 138 = *RP* (1979), 699 f.

[83] A. R. Birley, op. cit. 84.

[84] W. Eck, *RE, Suppl.* xiv 282.

[85] *ILS* 308: omitted (a useful clue) by the author of the *HA*.

[86] A noteworthy exception is the jurist Aburnius Valens (of no known ancestry), who held the post in 118, and then *triumvir monetalis* and *quaestor Augusti* (*ILS* 1051): a certain consul, if he survived.

[87] For the stemma of the Neratii see now L. Vidman, *ZPE* xliii (1981: *Gedenkschrift Pflaum*), 384. Further, W. Eck, *ZPE* l (1983), 154 ff.

[88] *ILS* 1032 (Saepinum).

proceeded (anomalous for a *bis consul*) to the proconsulate of Asia (129/30). Hadrian was peregrinating the eastern lands in that season. |

Finally, two *consules tertio*. First, Annius Verus in 126, as compensation when he vacated the office of *praefectus urbi*, although enjoying good health and a tranquil temperament. Verus may be presumed Epicurean in his tastes. In most ages there were more of them about than made public profession of the creed. Next, in 134, the honour fell at last to the aged Julius Servianus: close to the power and grandfather to the son of Fuscus and Julia.

The total is not large, and it is diversified agreeably. Trajan offers a contrast. If four *suffecti* of 98 be included (although one or other of them might have been designated by Nerva),[89] eleven consulars down to 107 benefited from iterations, among them three becoming *ter consules*. As in earlier reigns, the practice tails off. Only Palma and Celsus augment the company, in 109 and 113. Their claim was military. No *nobilis* was permitted to achieve parity.

Under Hadrian the rubric comprises eight consulars (including Metilius Nepos). His successor, a ruler whom senators liked, was much more restrictive. Only Bruttius Praesens in 139, Erucius Clarus in 146. The latter was *praefectus urbi*. Praesens had meanwhile been governor of Syria for a short spell *c*.136, after his proconsulate in Africa.[90] There is a chance that Antoninus Pius appointed him to the urban office.

Negative phenomena often furnish instruction, even without firm answers of any kind. In the early Hadrianic epoch Calvisius Tullus (*cos*. 109), the second husband of the elder Domitia Lucilla, would appear highly eligible. The latest sign of Tullus' survival is the fact that Herodes Atticus (*cos*. 143) passed some of his boyhood in his household.[91] Tullus may have predeceased the accession of Hadrian or died in its near aftermath.[92]

Again, a second consulship for Catilius Severus after his governorship of Syria, but none for Minicius Natalis, legate of Pannonia Superior in 117. And none for the jurist Neratius Priscus, or for Pompeius Falco (who lived on into the next reign).

Less surprise attends upon the aristocratic Ser. Cornelius Scipio Salvidienus (*cos*. 110). During the terminal crisis of the reign, Hadrian, annoyed by the pretensions of Catilius Severus, demoted him from the prefecture of the City and appointed Scipio, who did

---

[89] Especially the aged Vestricius Spurinna.

[90] *AE* 1938, 137 (Palmyra), cf. A. Stein, *Die Legaten von Moesien* (1940), 67 (on Julius Maior). See further below, n. 133.

[91] As Marcus Aurelius stated (Fronto, vol. i p. 60, Haines).

[92] In 117 he would not be much over forty. Pestilence might be surmised at Rome, and other deaths, in the wake of campaigns in the Orient.

not last long enough to attain to the second consulate. Antoni|nus Pius accorded him retreat, 'petenti', for that is the phrase that by custom veiled demotion.[93]

Pius was averse from change or disturbance. As the *HA* affirms, 'factus imperator nulli eorum quos Hadrianus provexerat successorem dedit.'[94]

Ambiguity is normally inherent in the comportment of an emperor towards the actions and policy of his predecessor. It was advisable to assert continuity in government—and at the same time to imply a change for the better. Nero in the oration from the throne, announcing a programme in studied terms, was able without discomfort to allude to abuses of the previous dispensation: 'ea maxime declinans quorum recens flagrabat invidia' (*Ann.* xiii 4, 2).

Hadrian was precluded from using one powerful argument. The Parthian War could have been exposed and denounced as sheer folly from first to last. Instead, he had to shield the fame of the Imperator and allow the wisdom as well as the necessity of his own decisions to percolate gradually.

About warfare Hadrian at once made his position clear: none if he could help it, and he deprecated military glory. After grave disturbances in Britain he refrained from taking an imperatorial salutation either about 120 or in 130 when 'his best general', Sex. Julius Severus (*suff.* 127) was despatched from Moesia Inferior.[95] He only relented when the Jewish War was brought to an end in 134.[96] On that occasion the *ornamenta triumphalia* were granted to Publicius Marcellus and Julius Severus.[97] Praetorian legates, it is worth noting, got decorations a little lower than what was standard.[98] Hadrian's restraint may not have been to the liking of all senators.

As has been shown, Hadrian resisted the temptation to ingratiate himself with the eminent by a generous award of second consulates. In certain other respects he might derive profitable lessons from exaggerations or imprudence on the part of his predecessor. |

(1) Abrupt or scandalous promotions. The Danubian command which Hadrian conferred on Marcius Turbo was perhaps an unwise expedient. It is difficult to believe that the new emperor was in such

---

[93] *HA Pius* 8, 9. The successor may well be Bruttius Praesens (*cos. II* 139)—unless that consulship be tardy gratitude from Hadrian.

[94] *Pius* 5, 3. Compare Hadrian's testimony to his character (Dio lxix 20, 4 f.).

[95] Dio lxix 13, 2.   [96] For the Parthian War Trajan took seven (VII–XIII).

[97] *AE* 1934, 231 (Aquileia); *ILS* 1056 (Burnum).

[98] Thus Lollius Urbicus (*ILS* 1065) and the *Ignotus* from Pisaurum (*CIL* xi 6339). Nor did equestrian officers come off well, cf. E. Birley, *Roman Britain and the Roman Army* (1953), 24. For the complete list of Hadrian's awards, M. Corbier, *MEFRA* xciii (1981), 1037.

straits that he could not have employed a consular legate, or even a praetorian, with competence equal to any military tasks. However, Turbo's command had no long duration: perhaps no more than eight or nine months.[99]

On the other side, observe a pair of Trajan's actions, one early in the reign, the other towards the end. His first Prefect of the Guard, Attius Suburanus, was admitted to the Senate and given a suffect consulship in 101. There was a precedent—Julius Ursus under Domitian, involved in palace intrigues but protected by Julia the daughter of Titus. His demotion was covered and compensated by a consulship (in 84).[100] Suburanus, however, went on with short delay to open the year 104 as *consul ordinarius*. That elevation must have come as a shock to many senators. None could foresee Lusius the Moor made a consul in 117.

When Hadrian removed Acilius Attianus, he transferred him to the Senate (8, 7). No consulship followed. According to a different (and dubious) passage in the *HA*, the Emperor both wanted to kill Attianus and encountered a difficulty because Attianus did not petition for release (9, 3 f.).

(2) The Prefecture of the City. In 117 it was held by Baebius Macer, as disclosed by the valuable passage that names the two eminent exiles, Laberius Maximus and Crassus Frugi (5, 5). On his arrival in Rome Acilius Attianus wrote to Hadrian requesting authority to put Macer to death 'si reniteretur eius imperio'. Hence further imputations about the Guard Prefect—and doubts about the allegation.

For Baebius Macer (*suff.* 103), in contrast to the other *praefecti* under Trajan, no marks of any distinction can be claimed.[101] His appointment is a mystery—and perhaps a mistake.[102] Annius Verus (one is happy to assume) was a more acceptable choice.

(3) Youthful consuls. By a poem inscribed on one of the Pyramids, the sister of | Terentius Gentianus (*suff.* 116) paid honour to his

[99] Turbo's name on a peculiar diploma issued on August 23 of 123 aroused premature speculation, cf. the annotation on *AE* 1973, 459. See, however, M. M. Roxan, *RMD* (1978), no. 21; and, for explanations, G. Alföldy, *ZPE* xxxvi (1979), 233 ff.; R. Syme, *JRS* lxx (1980), 70 f. = *RP* iii (1984), 1287.

[100] Dio lxvii 3, 1; 4, 2. In the sequel Ursus became consul for the second time in 98—and for the third in 100 (succeeding Julius Frontinus), as the *Fasti Ostienses* have recently revealed. Cf. L. Vidman in his new edition (Prague, 1982).

[101] The others were *bis consules*. After Aurelius Fulvus (*cos. II* 85), perhaps in office in 97, the next on record are Ti. Julius Candidus (*II* 105), and Q. Glitius Agricola (*II suff.* 103). For the former, *AE* 1972, 591 (Ephesus), for the latter *CIL* v 6980 (Augusta Taurinorum). Add perhaps Q. Fabius Postuminus (*suff.* 96), cf. *PIR*[2], F 54.

[102] Baebius Macer was a friend of Pliny: perhaps a Transpadane, like Baebius Italicus (*suff.* 90), whose tribe, the 'Oufentina' (*ILS* 8886), indicates Comum or Mediolanum.

memory. It states that he became consul when not yet thirty (*ILS* 1046a). His career shows him *legatus Augusti*, with no other post after the praetorship (which must likewise have come early). Gentianus was the son of Scaurianus (*suff.* 102 or 104), Trajan's first legate of Dacia, and to be deemed one of the Narbonensians.[103]

Among Hadrian's first promotions Pedanius Fuscus (*cos.* 118) and Ummidius Quadratus (*suff.* 118) were young consuls, as befitted their extraction, as is deduced from the season in which they entered on matrimony.[104] There is no reason for putting them under thirty-two; and another member of the group, Aurelius Fulvus (*cos.* 120), assumed the *fasces* when aged thirty-three.

In Terentius Gentianus is discerned a favourite of the Imperator, a general in the campaigns, and presumably a consul in absence. Hadrian decided not to let him have a military province.[105]

Ummidius Quadratus was despatched to Moesia Inferior when in his middle thirties. That fact furnishes useful information. The Caesars seldom took legates from the consular families. The exceptions under Trajan are not numerous. They comprise the two Neratii in the first place.[106] Then the parent of Pedanius Fuscus (*suff.* ?84), who held a command *c.*109 (anomalous because of seniority), and the parent of Calvisius Tullus.[107] Under Hadrian, apart from Ummidius Quadratus, there is only Metilius Secundus Pontianus (*suff.* 123), so far as can be known.[108]

Terentius Gentianus is not registered in the catalogue of the twelve friends and allies Hadrian treated with ingratitude, or worse (15, 2–8). His name crops up in a later passage concerning the intrigues and turmoil provoked by the problem of the succession. Hadrian execrated any potential candidates, among them Platorius Nepos and Terentius Gentianus—and Gentianus the more, 'hunc vehementius quod a senatu tunc diligi videbat' (23, 5).

How long Platorius Nepos, the old friend, survived, there is no evidence. Gentianus at this juncture was no longer among the living. The memorial verses of his sister were indited in 130 when she

[103] Even if not the *Ignotus* of Nemausus (*CIL* xii 3169).

[104] Pliny, *Ep.* vi 26; vii 24, 3.

[105] In 120 he governed Macedonia as a *censitor* (*ILS* 1046, cf. *AE* 1924, 57).

[106] Priscus (*suff.* 97) held Germania Inferior before Pannonia. See the revision of *ILS* 1034 (Saepinum) conducted by G. Camodeca, *AAN* lxxxvii (1976), 19 ff. Whence *AE* 1976, 195 (with inadequate annotation). The consequences are manifold, cf. remarks in *ZPE* xli (1981), 141 f. = *RP* iii (1984), 1390 f.

[107] For Pedanius Fuscus Salinator, Pliny, *Ep.* x 87, 3; for Calvisius Ruso, *AE* 1914, 267 (Pisidian Antioch). [And see further pp. 397 ff., below.]

[108] His consular province, at the truncated end of l. 2 of the inscription (*CIL* xi 3718 = *ILS* xi 1053: no longer extant), is probably Judaea or Syria. Cf. *Festschrift Straub* (Bonn, 1982), 236 f. = pp. 50 f. above.

visited Egypt in the company that included Vi|bia Sabina and the poetess Julia Balbilla.

(4) High honour for Greeks. The peak was reached in 105, with a pair of *consules iterum*. A Julius Quadratus (*suff.* 94), coming from the governorship of Syria, had for colleague Ti. Julius Candidus Marius Celsus (*suff.* 86). The Pergamene notable Quadratus was a close personal friend of the Emperor. Less is known about Candidus, whose *patria* lies somewhere in western Asia.[109] The Ephesian inscription of a descendant reveals the fact (some had surmised it) that he was *praefectus urbi*.[110] Then, in the summer of the year the other notable of Pergamum, Julius Quadratus Bassus (*suff.* 105), went out to command an army corps on the Danube.

Two *bis consules* and a consular general, the impact must have been startling. No echo is perceptible in the pages of written history or in any contemporary author, Roman or Greek.

Nothing comparable was to be seen during the reign of Hadrian. Indeed, it is not easy to detect consuls from the Greek East among the *ordinarii*, unless Antonius Rufinus (131) and Antonius Hiberus (133) be assigned to that rubric. The former is only a name, the latter goes back, so it is presumed, to an imperial freedman of the first dynasty.[111]

If Hadrian reserved his exuberant philhellenism for other spheres and countries, sparing the *Fasti*, that was all to the good: a mark of tact and prudence. Personal motives and choices may also be operant. Philhellenism has various aspects or components, and senators from eastern lands fall into different categories.[112] Trajan's favour went conspicuously to a dynastic group: the descendants of kings and tetrarchs revealed by the inscription of C. Julius Severus, the magnate of Ancyra. He had for cousins four senators of consular rank.[113]

Hadrian was not reluctant to set himself at a distance from the habits or policies of his predecessor, and he was unresponsive to pomp and pedigree. Indeed, if the general Quadratus Bassus had survived, legate of Cappadocia, Syria, Dacia, he might, like other marshals, have become an embarrassment. His kinsman Julius

---

[109] H. Halfmann, *Die Senatoren aus dem östlichen Teil des Imperium Romanum* (1979), no 11; R. Syme, *Some Arval Brethren* (1980), 50 f.; 92. His verdict on Greek volubility was cited by Pliny, *Ep.* v 20, 5.

[110] *AE* 1972, 591.

[111] The freedman Hiberus took the place of the deceased Vitrasius Pollio as Prefect of Egypt in 32 (Dio lviii 19, 6).

[112] On summary statement, Italians of the diaspora; Roman colonists; native dynasts or urban aristocrats. They blend and intermarry.

[113] *OGIS* 544 (Ancyra).

Severus was not persuaded to enter the Senate until the vicinity of the year 125, when he was adlected *inter tribunicios*.[114] |

Severus did not suffer any setback (*suff.* ?138), and marked success attended upon Julius Maior (*suff.* 126 or 129), of illustrious ancestry in western Asia (see below). However, some of the eastern magnates were far from arousing enthusiasm, even in a fancier of all things Hellenic. It does not pass belief that Hadrian had seen no value in a decorative nonentity like Julius Antiochus Philopappus (*suff.* 109), of the regal line of Commagene.[115]

Hadrian's preferences (the surmise is easy) went to the cultivated class in the cities. Flavius Arrianus is the man. He had attended the lectures of Epictetus, and he was to prove congenial to Hadrian in all ways. His entry to the Senate may have followed service as an equestrian officer in the Parthian War.[116]

The interests of emperor and senator came together in the recruitment of the high assembly; and their mutual involvement grew tighter through the career of honours. Routine appeals in any age. Regular and predictable advancement means less trouble for the government, it abates strife or anguish among aspirants. The stability that pervades the reign of Antoninus can be shown in firm process of formation under Hadrian.

At any time merit or patronage intervenes, luck or mishap. None the less, several types of promotion can be detected and defined. First of all, the posts held after the praetorship, largely determinate for access to the consulate.[117] Furthermore, of especial significance for the consular commands, and analysis is requisite. One useful enterprise takes in a very long period.[118] More manageable results can be achieved by concentration on the reigns of Hadrian and Pius.[119]

A noteworthy pattern, emergent under the second dynasty, continues valid. A praetorian province in the portion of Caesar leads

[114] *ILS* 8886 (Ancyra).
[115] *ILS* 845 (Athens): adlected *inter praetorios* by Trajan, and a *frater Arvalis* (not registered at any meeting).
[116] For this conjecture (not novel), *HSCPh* lxxxvi (1982), 188 f. = pp. 21 f., above.
[117] For praetorian posts and careers see W. Eck, *ANRW* ii 1 (1974), 181 ff.; G. Alföldy, *Konsulat und Senatorenstand unter den Antoninen* (1977), 40 ff.; A. R. Birley, *The* Fasti *of Roman Britain* (1981), 15 ff.
[118] Consular legates from 70 to 235 have been discussed by B. Campbell, *JRS* lxv (1975), 11 ff.: with a catalogue of seventy-three. That scholar took a firm stand against regular patterns of promotion. For temperate criticism, G. Alföldy, op. cit. 375 f.; A. R. Birley, op. cit. n. 18.
[119] See now observations in *HSCPh* lxxxvi (1982), 193 ff. = pp. 21 ff., above (including legates of the period missed by Campbell).

straight to a consulship, and a governor can secure designation thereto before his mandate expires. For one category, after the command of a legion one post follows (or two at the most) before | the consulship. A man could reach the *fasces* four or five years short of forty-two, the standard age.

The signal precursor is Julius Agricola (*suff.* ?77), who had been legate of a legion and governor of Aquitania; and the time of Trajan provides adequate documents.[120] Thus, proving abridgement of the normal interval, Julius Proculus, *quaestor Augustorum* in 97, consul suffect in 109.[121]

These men tend to go on to military commands. The *Ignotus* of *ILS* 1022, with double military decorations and the *ornamenta triumphalia*, had been legate of I Minervia and governor of Belgica before the consulate: Licinius Sura, or perhaps Sosius Senecio.[122] Again, the *Ignotus* of Nemausus, with consular decorations. He had been legate of a legion under Nerva, governor of a praetorian province under Trajan (*CIL* xii 3169). Fabius Justus will occur, the friend of Cornelius Tacitus (*suff.* 102) or Terentius Scaurianus (*suff.* 102 or 104).[123]

Facts of this order encourage conjecture. Fabius Justus was away from Rome in 97, according to Pliny (*Ep.* i 11, 2): the command of a legion, to be followed by a praetorian province. In due course Justus became governor of Moesia Inferior and of Syria. Similarly Neratius Priscus (*suff.* 97): the structure of his inscription at Larinum offers space for two praetorian posts before the consulate.[124]

At the same time a contrary tendency can be discerned. The text of a Thracian diploma of 114, now accessible at last, registers as governors Juventius Celsus (praetor in 106) and Statilius Maximus (*suff.* 115).[125] The document carries various and valuable consequences. The consulate of Celsus might go in 117, so it had previously been supposed: for 115 the *Fasti Potentini*, showing two pairs of *suffecti*, offered no place.[126] Those *Fasti* were defective, it appears. Advantage

---

[120] *Tacitus* (1958), 650.

[121] *ILS* 1040. Another Narbonensian, T. Julius Maximus, did not move so quickly: military tribune in 89, consul suffect in 112 (*ILS* 1016: Nemausus).

[122] For the latter, C. P. Jones, *JRS* lx (1970), 98 ff.

[123] *JRS* xlvii (1957), 134 = *Ten Studies in Tacitus* (1970), 115. The Moesian governorship of Justus, detected on *BM Pap.* 2815 and assigned to 105–8 (but doubted by some), now finds confirmation in an inscription of 106 (*Dacia* xxv (1981), 357).

[124] Not allowed for in *AE* 1969/70, 252.

[125] M. M. Roxan, *RMD* (1978), no. 21: a copy pending publication of the 'official version'. The document has lurked in the Museum at Sofia for about thirty years.

[126] *Hermes* lxxxv (1957), 493 n. 2 = *RP* (1979), 351 n. 8. That was based on a verbal report of the Sofia diploma—and, in ignorance and error, the order of the two governors was there inverted.

accrues: 115 for Celsus accords with his proconsular year in Asia, namely 129/30.

Successive governors of a praetorian province thus become consuls in the same year. Celsus, praetor in 106, was either the first or the second legate when Thrace | improved its status in the sequel of the Second Dacian War; and his consulship, with an interval after Thrace, was none the less quite rapid.

For a parallel case soon after, observe two legates of Lycia–Pamphylia, viz. Trebius Maximus and Pomponius Antistianus.[127] The latter was consul suffect in 121. The former shared the *fasces* with T. Calestrius Tiro, probably in the same year.[128] Tiro's career has turned up.[129] It shows him governing Cilicia before Trajan took the title 'Parthicus'. His tenure therefore falls between Pompeius Macrinus (*suff.* 115) and Bruttius Praesens, in office when Trajan died. A delay of four or five years after Tiro's vacating the province is thereby certified.

Again, there is Julius Maior, attested as legate of Numidia in 124/5 and in 126.[130] He followed Metilius Secundus (*suff.* 123), whose only other praetorian post was the command of a legion (*ILS* 1053); and he preceded Fabius Catullinus (*cos.* 130). It was easy and natural to have him consul in 126 (cf. *PIR*[2], J 397). However, the inscription of 126 does not style him 'cos. des.'. He might not have been consul until 129 (127 and 128 are complete).[131] Which affects problems in his subsequent career. At the lowest estimate, Julius Maior was certainly governor of Moesia Inferior and of Syria before a proconsulate in either Asia or Africa.[132] A diploma lodges him in Moesia Inferior in 134 (*CIL* xvi 78); and he went to Syria in 136 or 137, after the brief and anomalous command of Bruttius Praesens.[133]

A further instance is variously instructive. Minicius Natalis, *quaestor Augusti* in 121, was transferred to Africa to be legate to his father the proconsul when Hadrian departed for his tour of the western provinces (*ILS* 1029; 1061). He did not reach the consulate until 139. Eighteen years had elapsed. Hardly to be expected for the

[127] *IGR* iii 739, §7 = *TAM* ii 3, 905.
[128] The consulate of Trebius Maximus and Calestrius Tiro (*CIL* xvi 169) is generally put in 122: 121 is preferable, cf. Nesselhauf's note. See further *Historia* xviii (1969), 357, n. 33 = *RP* (1979), 779, n. 2.
[129] *AE* 1965, 320 (Iotape).
[130] *AE* 1954, 149; 1950, 58.
[131] Thus E. Birley, *JRS* lii (1962), 222.
[132] Syria is shown without doubt on *IG* iv[2] 1, 454. (Epidaurus, very fragmentary).
[133] *AE* 1938, 137 (Palmyra). That both consulars were legates of Syria has been disputed. Thus W. Eck, *Senatoren von Vespasian bis Hadrian* (1970), 232; G. Alföldy, *Konsulat u. Senatorenstand* (1977), 240 ff. See however *ZPE* xxxvii (1980), 10 f. = *RP* iii (1984), 1309 f.; and, for a full statement, *Festschrift Straub* (Bonn, 1982), 238 ff. = pp. 50 ff., above.

son of a consular—and perhaps to be explained by estrangement from Hadrian.[134]

The ruler (so it might be conjectured), wishing to introduce uniformity, enjoined a retardation for praetorian legates in the approach to consulships, even if | some of them held only two or three posts. At least it is not easy to establish consuls in this category under the age of forty. The Caesernii brothers (from Aquileia) enjoyed favour with Hadrian. One estimate of their parallel careers has the elder, Macedo, born in 101, consul in 138.[135]

Regularity in the duration of governorships was desirable on every count. Hadrian's men were kept in office by his successor, so the *HA* states. It then adds a comment: 'fuitque ea constantia ut septenis et novenis annis in provinciis bonos praesides detineret' (*Pius* 5, 3). Seven to nine years, that is startling indeed. Recourse to the facts (fairly abundant for the whole course of the reign) dispels the silly notion.[136]

The origin of that notion will engage due curiosity. At first sight the passage looks like an insertion. If so, from the author of the *HA*, although he has not tampered much with this *Vita*, as the structure shows so clearly. Yet the item may well belong to the basic source. In that case, relevant to a question of authorship. It is far from certain that a senatorial writer would be moved to commend prolonged governorships.[137]

Either way, internal evidence elsewhere in the *HA* imports discredit. According to one of the fictional biographies, the exemplary Pescennius Niger conceived disquiet about frequent changes. He indited despatches both to Marcus and to Commodus conveying a sagacious proposal: 'ut nulli ante quinquennium succederetur provinciae praesidi vel legato vel proconsuli' (*Pesc.* 7, 2).

As in a comparable piece of fantasy, namely Hadrian's generosity with iterated consulships, it is useful to put the presuppositions under sharp scrutiny. Prolonged tenures continue to find advocates among the ingenuous: the welfare of the provincials, and so on. Brief reflection suggests manifold disadvantages.

The notorious practices of Tiberius Caesar impelled the historian Tacitus to curiosity and sundry speculations, at an early stage (*Ann.* i 80). No sign that he approved. While prorogations appeal to a ruler

---

[134] Observe by contrast Pactumeius Clemens, quaestor ?122, consul suffect in 138 (*ILS* 1067).

[135] G. Alföldy, op. cit. 350 (on *ILS* 1069). Yet 139, or 140, is not excluded.

[136] A. R. Birley, *Corolla Swoboda* (1966), 43 ff.

[137] So perhaps not Marius Maximus.

slow to make decisions and hating change, less thought goes to the governors themselves, liable to be marooned interminably in a distant or uninviting country; and other consulars took annoyance when legitimate ambitions were frustrated.[138] The high commands carried honour and prestige. They were also burdensome. Consulars might evince reluc|tance—and Tiberius complained about them, in a moment of inadvertence.[139]

It was bad for administration if choice or necessity imposed reliance on a small minority of allies and agents. That may have been Hadrian's plight for a time after his accession. As has been shown, scarcity of evidence for the first dozen years impedes the enquiry. The lacunae for Syria and for Pannonia Superior have already been noted. As for Britain, Platorius Nepos might have remained there after 122 for five or six years, for all that can be known. No predecessor is verifiable for Julius Severus (*suff.* 127) who went from Moesia Inferior to the island, probably in 130.

By suitable irony for the benefit of the *HA*, it is not Pius but Hadrian who contributes the specimens of long tenures. First, Julius Severus after the command of a legion went to the new province of Dacia Superior in 119 and held it for seven or eight years before acceding to the *fasces* in the autumn of 127.[140] Second, Flavius Arrianus (*suff.* 129 or 130) had Cappadocia for a term double the normal, probably from 131 to 137.[141] Emergency on and beyond the frontier may have continued after the threat from the Alani in 135.

Under Trajan the praetorian provinces rose from eight to twelve, and the total subsists, Judaea now governed by consular legates while Dacia forfeited that rank. In four of them the provincial governor is at the same time commander of a legion.[142]

Equipollent for advancement to the *fasces* is the collegiate pair of *praefecti* holding the *aerarium Saturni* for a term of three years. Statistics, although imperfect, disclose a remarkable fact. In a period of thirty years, from Tullius Varro (*suff.* 127) to Servilius Maximus (158), no fewer than ten *praefecti* go on to consular commands.[143] A parallel feature may be noted that emerges towards the end of

---

[138] Two proconsuls in Asia and Africa for a *sexennium* excluded ten others.

[139] *Ann.* vi 27, 3. As the author points out, the Princeps forgot L. Arruntius, the legate of Tarraconensis, detained at Rome 'decimum iam annum'.

[140] For his *cursus*, *ILS* 1056; for the duration of his Dacian command (succeeding Marcius Turbo), the diplomata cited in *PIR*[2], J 576. That of 126 is now *RMD* (1978), no. 27.

[141] His successor Burbuleius Ligarianus (*suff. c.*135) was in Cappadocia before the death of Hadrian (*ILS* 1066).

[142] Viz. Numidia, Arabia, Dacia Superior, Pannonia Inferior.

[143] See the list in M. Corbier, *L'Aerarium Saturni et l'Aerarium militare* (1974), 540 ff.

Hadrian's reign: the charge of the *alimenta* combined with the Via Flaminia or Via Appia.[144] Hence sixteen praetorian posts now normally leading to consulships.

The consular provinces are eleven in number (including Dalmatia, with no | legion). A noteworthy phenomenon in the careers of legates develops under Hadrian. The *cura operum publicorum* is now held in immediate sequence to the consulate. The first examples are Bruttius Praesens (*suff.* 118 or 119) and Metilius Secundus (123). Furthermore, by the year 128 the *curatores* are discovered as a collegiate pair.[145] The tenure, nowhere on direct record, might be supposed biennial.[146]

That is not all. A pattern can be established. Of the ten prefects of the *aerarium Saturni* registered above, seven held the *cura operum publicorum* before proceeding to a consular province. Of the three remaining, two had analogous posts. Tullius Varro (*suff.* 127) was in charge of the banks and bed of the Tiber (*ILS* 1047), while Mummius Sisenna Rutilianus (*suff.* 146) was *praefectus alimentorum per Aemiliam* (*ILS* 1101). The tenth is Julius Verus (*suff.* ?151), to be styled a *vir militaris*: governor of Germania Inferior, Britannia, Syria (*ILS* 1057 and 8974).

A plain reason can be divined. Caesar has devised a provision for the benefit of those senators likely to become consular legates. In compensation for absence abroad they enjoy a continuous sojourn at the capital, both before and after the consulate—some no doubt were highly congenial to the person of the Princeps.[147] Sporadic evidence enlists a number of senators assumed close friends of Hadrian. Not many of them can be discovered as his companions in the peregrinations that took up half of the reign (from 121 to 125, from 128 to 134). That is, apart from Caesernius Macedo (*ILS* 1069, cf. *AE* 1957, 135); and one will not neglect the governors in office when he decided to visit a certain region, such as Platorius Nepos.

Another consular post was now accorded a regular grade in the senatorial *cursus*. It is the charge of the Tiber banks. In 121 and in 124 a senior consular, Messius Rusticus (*suff.* 114), is on attestation.[148] The successor in 124 may be Vitrasius Flamininus (*suff.* 122). That is,

---

[144] *ILS* 1061 (Minicius Natalis); 1069 (Caesernius Macedo).
[145] *AE* 1973, 76, namely Ti. Julius Julianus (*suff.* ?126) and M. Ma[, not identifiable. The consular date is that of Q. Insteius Celer, probably the 'Q. [' at the end of 128 on the *Fasti Ostienses*.
[146] An annual tenure was assumed by Alföldy, op. cit. 26, cf. 289.
[147] E. Birley, *PBA* xxxix (1953), 209. Civilian accomplishments and polite studies among consular legates are no surprise.
[148] *CIL* vi 1240; *AE* 1917/18, 108.

previous to his governorship of Moesia Superior.[149] Then Valerius Propinquus fits in, since his consulship is now assigned to 126 instead of 132 or 133.[150] A sequence of four thus concludes with Tullius | Varro: prefect of the *aerarium* and then consul suffect (in 127), he occupied this *cura* before proceeding to Moesia Superior (*ILS* 1047).

It would be premature to assume that any duties entailed by these urban occupations were arduous or even necessary. Dignified leisure stands on premium. As in other ages, work is less important than title or office.

Hadrian thought up a further employment for ex-consuls. Three passages in the *HA* (here unimpeachable) and one in another writer reveal a peculiar fact. Hadrian appointed consulars, four in number, to hold jurisdiction throughout Italy.[151] One of them was Aurelius Fulvus (*cos.* 120), chosen 'ad eam partem Italiae regendam in qua plurimum possidebat, ut Hadrianus viri talis et honori consuleret et quieti' (*Pius* 2, 11).

No other name is on clear record, but something might be said about Vitrasius Flamininus, described as 'leg. pr. pr. Italiae Transpadanae' (*CIL* x 3870: Capua). He should be held identical with the consul suffect of 122, not an unattested person in the time of Marcus Aurelius, as a number of scholars have assumed or argued. The inscription is not altogether easy to interpret.[152] Since it appears to be in descending order, three successive consular posts are attested, viz. the Tiber curatorship, Moesia Superior, Italia Transpadana. Hence Vitrasius is one of the four 'consulares Italiae', perhaps among the earliest, *c.*128.

[149] Assuming the posts on his inscription (*CIL* x 3078) to be in descending order. See below, n. 152. That order was adopted by Alföldy, op. cit. 204.

[150] This polyonymous consular (*CIL* ii 6048) suffered neglect. Recently, however, because of the tiles with 'Propinquo et Ambibulo cos.' he was taken for the colleague of L. Varius Ambibulus (*ILS* 9486), consul suffect in 132 or 133. Cf. W. Eck, *Senatoren* etc. (1970), 45, n. 15; G. Alföldy in his revision of the document in *RIT* (1975), no. 149 and in *Konsulat u. Senatorenstand* (1977), 212 f. Meanwhile, intricate but convincing argument from tiles shows the colleague to be Eggius Ambibulus, in 126. Thus L. Schumacher, *ZPE* xxiv (1977), 155 ff.: clearly summarized by A. R. Birley, op. cit. 240 f.
The career is noteworthy. Coming to his consulship by way of VI Victrix and Aquitania, Propinquus governed Germania Inferior and ended as proconsul of Asia. See further pp. 579 ff., below.

[151] *HA Hadr.* 22, 13; *Pius* 2, 11; *Marcus* 11, 6; Appian, *BC* i 38, 172. Cf. W. Eck, *Die staatliche Organisation Italiens in der hohen Kaiserzeit* (1979), 247 ff.

[152] *CIL* x 3780 (Capua, not extant): L. Vitrasio L. f. Pos. /Flaminino cos. procos. provinciae Africae / leg.pp.pr. Italiae Trans / padanae et provinciae Moesiae Superioris et / exercitus provinciae / Dalmatiae curatori / alvei Tiberis riparum / cloacarum urbis / . . . Instead of 'Pos.' in 1. 2 read 'Pob(lilia)', the tribe of the Vitrasii, who come from Cales. [See now *Epigrafia e ordine senatorio* ii (1982), 529 ff.: the stone rediscovered.] For detailed criticism of the views of Zwikker, adopted by Jagenteufel, see *Gnomon* xxxi (1959), 513 f. = *Danubian Papers* (1971), 196 f. The governorship of Moesia Superior is attested by *CIL* iii 14499 (Ratiaria).

Otherwise he would have to be a praetorian legate. Compare Julius Proculus (*suff.* 109), who was 'leg. Aug. p.p. region. Transpadanae' (*ILS* 1040). Proculus occupied the post after the command of a legion and antecedent to his consulship, as the exact equivalent of a praetorian province in the portion of Caesar. Nor will one omit to wonder about the person called Priscus who in letters of Pliny appears to exercise judicial functions in Transpadana about the year 106.[153] |

Hadrian's innovation was open to damaging criticism—Italy reduced to the condition of a province. Such was the protest heard when in the time of Augustus the proconsul L. Piso sat in judgement at Mediolanum.[154]

Furthermore, it was perhaps imprudent to risk the authority of a senior statesman in local feuds or lawsuits. To be sure, apprehensions would not be conceived about the excellent and vigilant Aurelius Fulvus—who, however, abolished the four *consulares* when Antoninus Pius. Which is significant, since that ruler was disinclined to modify or desert any policies of his predecessor. However, *iuridici* of praetorian rank make their appearance early in the reign of Marcus.[155]

Hadrian's initial professions have been alluded to in summary fashion, likewise measures he then adopted to conciliate the upper order. While providing for friends and allies, he did not neglect the broad mass of senators; and he showed himself responsive to the duties of his station.

In 119 Hadrian continued in the *fasces* for four months, he never missed a regular session of the Senate, he was assiduous in dispensing justice (8, 6).[156] In consonance therewith, his comportment was modest and civil: 'omnia denique ad privati hominis modum fecit' (9, 8).

When nearly three years had elapsed since his arrival, Hadrian had surmounted many of the early embarrassments, so it may be supposed. It was time to go away before fresh annoyances supervened. Constant attendance in the high assembly was liable to be burdensome. Senators had been happy to dispense with Trajan recently, for four years; and a Princeps with decided views about law

---

[153] *Ep.* vi 8; vii 8. A friend of Pliny called Saturninus was on his staff (vii 7 f.; 15). See further *Hermes* lxxxv (1957), 488 f. = *RP* (1979), 347.

[154] Suetonius, *De rhet.* 6.

[155] *HA Marcus* 11, 6. The first of them, in Transpadana and expressly so styled, is Arrius Antoninus *c.*165 (*ILS* 1118: Concordia).

[156] Dio asserts that he discussed with the Senate all matters of highest import and urgency (lxix 7, 1).

and equity, distrusting general rules and frequent in the courts, exposed his person to malevolence or ridicule. Senators in the habit of comparing past and present were easily put in mind of Claudius Caesar, or the formidable Domitian.

Hadrian left Rome in the early summer of 121. The eastern lands presented no problems, thanks to diplomatic arts exercised on the vassal princes. He turned to the western provinces, not having seen the Rhine since service as a tribune under Julius Servianus at Moguntiacum in 98. And Britain was an obvious emergency or pretext, though nothing perhaps to exceed the capacity of Pompeius Falco, who had been a legionary legate in Trajan's first war against the Dacians. But Hadrian | was eager as ever to see things for himself and make his own decisions about frontier policy, down to all details of defence.

Ummidius Quadratus stood on the lower Danube, and Bruttius Praesens now went to the zone that faced Armenia. Syria and Pannonia Superior were managed by loyal consulars (whose identity defies ascertainment).

On departure the Emperor took with him, as was normal, one of the two Guard Prefects. The literate Septicius Clarus promised congenial company on travels that might well last for several years, as did Suetonius Tranquillus, the secretary *ab epistulis*, a necessary adjunct.[157]

Marcius Turbo remained at Rome, happily devoid of the ambition or the aristocratic kinsmen that converted Aelius Seianus into a menace during Caesar's absence. The formal presidency of the government reposed upon the consuls and upon the *praefectus urbi*, the sagacious Annius Verus. Behind him stood the *bis consules* Julius Servianus and Catilius Severus (perhaps far from concordant), along with younger members of the dynastic nexus.

A momentous question subsisted, ostensibly in abeyance. The literary sources betray no awareness, they fail to mention anywhere Pedanius Fuscus, the heir apparent. Hadrian might, or might not, have thought of taking him to the Rhine or sending him like Ummidius Quadratus to apprenticeship in a military province. That is, if Fuscus survived for any time. All is obscure. Fuscus and Julia fade out together. The easy surmise might not be idle: a pestilence coming out of Syria and Mesopotamia in the train of defeated legions and their despondent leaders.

---

[157] For Suetonius' presence in Britain, often ignored or denied, see *Tacitus* (1958), 799; *Hermes* cix (1981), 109 f. = *RP* iii (1984), 1340 f.

18

The Proconsuls of Asia under Antoninus Pius

MERE proconsuls of Cyprus have their uses. Asia and Africa declare social eminence or political success. In an age that turned away from the writing of history to biographies of emperors (and modern accounts conform) consulars and their careers add ample substance, above all Caesar's legates governing the armed provinces.

Decorative in their day and sometimes useful, the proconsuls of Asia and Africa now serve diverse functions. At the lowest they furnish a date for a public building, an official document, or even, it may happen, for some historical transaction. There is something better. In periods void of good written sources, these proconsuls are a powerful aid to the study of society and government, and some impinge on literature.

For the twenty-one years of Hadrian, only four gaps in Asia remain on the roll, according to the latest enquiry.[1] As elsewhere, sporadic items accrue, bringing new persons or dates and entailing revisions in an experimental science that has recourse to combinations and to conjecture. The consulate of Gargilius Antiquus emerges, in 119.[2] That fixes his proconsulate and throws Aurelius Fulvus (*cos.* 120) a year forward to the tenure 135/6. Next, an inscription reveals Pomponius Marcellus (*suff.* 121).[3] Therefore to go in 136/7. He had previously been held identical with the Marcellus on attestation from two African documents.[4]

It will be convenient to append the list for the last nine years of Hadrian, as it now stands.

129/30   P. Juventius Celsus (*suff.* 115, *cos. II* 129)
130/1   P. Afranius Flavianus (*suff.* ?115)
131/2   L. Lamia Aelianus (*cos.* 116)

---

[1] W. Eck, *Senatoren von Vespasian bis Hadrian* (1970), 237. For the sequence 126/7 to 132/3 observe Chr. Habicht, *Pergamon* viii 1 (1969), 56 ff.

[2] Q. Gargilius Antiquus and Q. Vibius Gallus, on May 27 of 119 (*AE* 1979, 62). Gargilius was previously governor of Arabia (*AE* 1973, 531: Bostra).

[3] Reported in *AS* xxiii (1973), 42; *AJA* lxxviii (1974), 122.

[4] *ILAfr* 591 (Aunobaris); *IRT* 304 (Lepcis).

Zeitschrift für Papyrologie und Epigraphik li (1983), 271–90.

132/3   C. Julius Alexander Berenicianus (*suff.* 116)
133/4
134/5   Q. Gargilius Antiquus (*suff.* 119)
135/6   T. Aurelius Fulvus (*cos.* 120)
136/7   Q. Pomponius Rufus Marcellus (*suff.* 121)
137/8

At the end, one gap.[5] Then, with Venuleius Apronianus (*cos.* 123), the | reign of Antoninus leads off; twenty-three proconsular years, summer to summer. By good fortune a comprehensive study of consuls and governors in now available, from 138 to 180.[6] It permits an economical treatment.[7] Though recent, the list demands one supplement. Flavius Tertullus (*suff.* 133) turns up as proconsul: in 148/9, precisely.[8] Furthermore, some tenures have to be altered. And sundry problems subsist, with vexatious complications.

As the evidence enjoins, the proconsulates divide into three sections (ten years, five, eight):

(A) 138/9–147/8. Beginning with Venuleius Apronianus (*cos.* 123).

(B) 148/9–152/3. From Flavius Tertullus (*suff.* 133) to Julius Severus (?138) inclusive.

(C) 153/4–160/1. Down to Mummius Sisenna Rutilianus (*suff.* 146): the next five proconsuls form a sequence in the early years of Marcus Aurelius.

The first section can now be set forth. The ten years take in five attested proconsuls. Only the essential or decisive items of evidence need be cited.[9]

(A) 138/9. L. Venuleius Apronianus (*cos.* 123). *OGIS* 493. Further, Ephesus congratulating the Emperor on his birthday (*SEG* xv 695). That is, September 19.

---

[5] The last Hadrianic proconsuls of Africa are P. Valerius Priscus (*suff.* ?121), in 136/7; L. Vitrasius Flamininus (122), in 137/8. See *ZPE* xxxvii (1980), 5 = *RP* iii (1984), 1306.

[6] G. Alföldy, *Konsulat und Senatorenstand unter den Antoninen* (1977).

[7] In what follows the book will be cited by the author's name only. A number of proconsuls were discussed by C. A. Behr, *Aelius Aristides and the Sacred Tales* (1968). For his eccentric methods and queer results, see Alföldy, op. cit. 211, n. 27, and in other footnotes. A list of proconsuls from 145/6 to 153/4 was produced by L. Schumacher, *ZPE* xxiv (1977), 24: variously vulnerable.

[8] On a military diploma of the province Asia published by B. Overbeck, *Chiron* xi (1981), 267 f.

[9] Much of the evidence was quoted by W. Hüttl, *Antoninus Pius* i (1933). Two of his twelve proconsuls have lapsed, viz. L. Aemilius Juncus (*suff.* 127), and Glabrio.

139/40. After Venuleius, aristocratic and patrician, a *suffectus* of 124 or 125 would be suitable.[10]

140/1 (or perhaps the next year). (M.?) Valerius Propinquus (*suff.* 126). *CIL* ii 6084 = *RIT* (1975) 149. This polyonymous senator (with three more sets of names), from Liria in Tarraconensis, and registered as a Grattius (*PIR*[2], G 221), has only recently acquired his shape and date. It took two stages. First, invocation of three bricks with the stamp 'Propinquo et Ambibulo cos.'. The colleague offered in the person of a known consul, L. Varius Ambibulus: legate of Numidia (*ILS* 9498: Cuicul), attested in 132 (*AE* 1950, 59: Gemellae). Consul suffect therefore in 132 or 133. Valerius Propinquus was proconsul of | Asia *c*.147. That seemed clear and firm.[11]

Second, a small fact was brought to notice. One of the three stamps (*CIL* xv 1228b) continued with a formula identical with that on 'Vero III et Ambib.' (1228a). Therefore Valerius Propinquus took the place of Annius Verus early in 126 as colleague of Eggius Ambibulus—despite the incorrection of a *suffectus* preceding an *ordinarius* in 'Propinquo et Ambibulo'.[12] Hence the whole career of the eminent *polyonymus* to be revised, with manifold consequences.[13]

141/2. ?Sex. Julius Maior (*suff.* ?126). The fragmentary inscription of his son showed him proconsul of either Asia or Africa (*IG*[2] iv[2] 454: Epidaurus). The former generally wins preference, for a patent reason. Julius Maior belonged to the high aristocracy of Asia (the ancestors being Polemo the ruler of Pontus and Antonia Pythodoris), and he resided at Nysa (cf. *SEG* iv 402 ff.). Yet Africa is not excluded.[14] Maior had been governor of Numidia, attested in 125 (*AE* 1950, 58: Thamugadi) and in 126 (1954, 149: Gemellae). That is, after Metilius Secundus (*suff.* 123) and before Fabius Catullinus (*cos.* 130). Numidia normally carried designation to a consulship—and for 127 and 128 the *Fasti Ostienses* allow no vacancy.

The document of the year 126 does not accord Maior the title of 'cos. des.'. On that ground the chance has been admitted that his

---

[10] In Africa the names for 138/9 to 140/1 are T. Salvius Rufinus Minicius Opimianus (*suff.* 123); M'. Acilius Glabrio (*cos.* 124), introduced by conjecture based on his son's career (*ILS* 1072); T. Prifernius Paetus Rosianus Geminus (*suff.* ?125). See *ZPE* xxxvii (1980), 12 f. = *RP* iii (1984), 1310 f.

[11] Thus, citing the present writer, W. Eck, *Senatoren von Vespasian bis Hadrian* (1970), 45, n. 15; *RE*, *Suppl.* xiv 819 f.; G. Alföldy commenting on *RIT* 149 (1975); op. cit. 212 f.

[12] L. Schumacher, *ZPE* xxiv (1977), 155 ff. For a brief clear statement, A. R. Birley, *The Fasti of Roman Britain* (1981), 240. The new dating of Propinquus was overlooked in 'The Career of Arrian', *HSCPh* lxxxvi (1982), 193 = p. 21, above.

[13] See 'The Career of Valerius Propinquus', *AEA* (forthcoming) = pp. 579 ff., below.

[14] *REA* lxi (1959), 313 = *RP* (1979), 464.

consulship fell in 129.[15] In that event, his tenure would have to go in 143/4 or 144/5.

142/3. ?Q. Insteius Celer (*suff.* ?128). Quoting from Ulpian, *De officio proconsulis*, the *Digest* adduces a rescript from Pius to Insteius Celer (xxvi 5, 12, 1 f.). Asia or Africa might be kept in mind.[16] If Africa, a place is open for Celer after Tullius Varro (*suff.* 127).[17] The year of Celer's consulship has recently emerged, recording Ti. Julius Julianus (*suff.* ?126) as *curator operum publicorum* (*AE* 1973, 36). The last name on the *Fasti Ostienses* for 128 happens to be 'Q.['.[18]

143/4. ?Ti. Julius Candidus Celsus (if accepted, *suff.* 129). Coins of Harpasa bear the head of the young Marcus on the obverse, the name of Candidus Celsus on the reverse (*BMC, Caria* 114). For Waddington long ago a proconsul, but | deprecated in *PIR*[2], J 242.[19]

There is a plethora of persons called 'Iulius Candidus'. First of all, Ti. Julius Candidus Marius Celsus (*suff.* 86), a member of the Arval Brethren in the year 75, if not earlier.[20] The maternal grandson of a Marius Celsus and marrying the daughter of a Caecilius Simplex, he had been able to introduce two sons into the fraternity by 105 (the year of his second consulship), namely Ti. Julius Candidus Caecilius Simplex (*PIR*[2], J 237) and Ti. Julius Candidus Capito (J 239). The latter was consul suffect in 122, the former should have acceded to the *fasces*, if he survived. Homonymous sons followed. The former (J 238) is attested by his full nomenclature as legate in Asia in 139 (*AE* 1966, 428: Ephesus), the latter is presumably the Julius Candidus who was proconsul of Achaia *c.* 136 (*IG* vii 70 ff.: Megara). They too were enrolled among the *Arvales*. A fragment of the protocol that can be assigned *c.* 150 shows a Ti. Julius Candidus Capito.[21] A son of the proconsul of Achaia, so it is suggested in *PIR*[2], J 240. Better perhaps, the proconsul himself. Anyhow, no more of them.

Another Ti. Julius Candidus has now turned up, a praetor of the year 121 (*AE* 1965, 337). Easy and harmless conjecture will identify him as a third son of the *bis consul*, and perhaps a decade younger than the two who were already with the fraternity in 105. If the praetor of 121 be held the same as 'Candidus Celsus', the presumed proconsul

---

[15] E. Birley, *JRS* lii (1962), 225.

[16] W. Hüttl, *Antoninus Pius* i (1936), 372 (noting, likewise from the *Digest*, Julius Candidus).

[17] For Varro's proconsulate (?142/3), ILS 1047.

[18] For the consulate, and for other items bearing on Insteius Celer, see H. Halfmann, *Arh. Vestnik* xxviii (1977), 157 f.

[19] Following Groag, *RE* x 539.

[20] *Some Arval Brethren* (1980), 16. For his extraction and nomenclature, ibid. 50 f.; 92 f.

[21] *AE* 1947, 59, cf. *JRS* xliii (1953), 160 = *RP* (1979), 254. The piece (with two fragmentary names of consuls) was assigned to 120–40 by the editor, to 155–60 in *PIR*[2], J 240.

of Asia, and the Julius Candidus who received a rescript from Pius (*Dig.* xlviii 2, 7, 3), a suitable year is discovered for his consulate.[22] When a senator cannot achieve the eponymate, the next best is to come in after the *ordinarii*. The year 129 opened with a pair of iterations (Neratius Marcellus and Juventius Celsus), which some may have found a disappointment. The parent was illustrious indeed. He became not only *consul iterum* but Prefect of the City, as Groag divined, as is confirmed by the inscription of a later descendant, which discloses his region but not his city (*AE* 1972, 591: Ephesus). The second consulship, shared in 105 with the Pergamene magnate Julius Quadratus, throws vivid illumination on the epoch as well as on the Emperor. His successor, notorious as a philhellene, was less obtrusive.

144/5. (Ti. Claudius?) Julianus (*suff.* 129 or 130). The proconsul Julianus is attested by a letter of the Emperor which he conveyed to the people of Ephesus, rebuking them for inadequate recognition of the irreproachable Vedius Antoninus. It is dated to 145 (*SIG*³ 850). Hence the standard date for his | tenure, 145/6 (cf. *PIR*², J 76). The previous year is as good, if not better.

The question comes into relation with the movements of Aelius Aristides. Not perhaps a promising omen. The sophist held his panegyric before Caesar either in 143 or 144. The former year now receives strong approbation.[23] Aristides returned to Smyrna late in the year (*Or.* xlviii 49). Then, when a year and several months had elapsed he went to Pergamum, to hold the chair of rhetoric (xlviii 70, cf. 7). At some time during that sojourn (duration not specified) the proconsul Julianus turned up (*Or.* l 107).

Identity has been under dispute. Some opt for a Julius Julianus.[24] Against which, Ti. Julius Julianus Alexander now comes in, attested as governor of Arabia in 125 (*AE* 1976, 691: Gerasa), to be lodged as consul suffect in 126.[25] Brick stamps carry the consular date 'Iuliano et Casto' (on which, cf. *PIR*², J 75). Senators called 'Iulius Castus' had tended to suffer neglect.[26] The collegiate pair Julianus and Castus

---

[22] The *cognomen* 'Celsus' reflects the grandmother, as 'Caecilius Simplex' the mother. Celsus may (or may not) have had a different mother.

[23] J. H. Oliver, 'The Ruling Power', *TAPhS* xliii 4 (1953), 886 f.

[24] Alföldy, 212 (with a query).

[25] For identity and career see H. Halfmann, *Arh. Vestnik* xxviii (1977), 153 ff. He was also *curator operum publicorum*, attested in the consulate of Q. Insteius Celer (*AE* 1973, 36): that is, 128.

[26] *Historia* xviii (1969), 364 f. = *RP* (1979), 786 f. As there argued, the name of the Cilician governor on the milestone of 120 (*AE* 1898, 59 = *CIL* iii 13635: near Elaeussa) is either 'Iulius Castus' or 'Iulius Gallus'. C. Julius Gallus was consul suffect with C. Valerius Severus in 124 (xvi 70).

might be assigned to the year 126. Otherwise, if the first is not a Julius Julianus but a Claudius Julianus, to 129 or 130.

On present knowledge the proconsul is Ti. Claudius Julianus (*PIR*[2], C 896), the grandnephew of Ti. Julius Celsus Polemaeanus (*suff.* 92). His homonymous son held the *fasces* as colleague of Sex. Calpurnius Agricola in September of 154.[27] For the parent the dates 129 and 144/5 concord with the next item, a recent and welcome accession.

145/6. Ti. Claudius Quartinus (*suff.* 130). Coins of Aezani and one of Smyrna carry the name of Claudius Quartinus.[28]

146/7. From this year has to be expelled a tenant after long and tranquil occupation. That is, T. Atilius Maximus (*PIR*[2], A 301). He was proconsul when the prince Marcus Aurelius sent a letter to a confraternity at Smyrna, dated March 28 (*SIG*[3] 851). The titulature of Marcus carries the *tribunicia potestas* without a number. On the same stone was inscribed a letter from Antoninus Pius, dated to 158, precisely.

The formulation on the letter of Marcus was defective, it appears. A pertinent reason disallowed the date in March of 147.[29] Therefore the pro|consulate of Atilius Maximus has to be displaced, and it might have to be moved forward, perhaps by as much as a decade.[30]

The case has recently found a firm and explicit advocate. The proconsulate of Atilius Maximus, so it is argued, should fall between 153/4 and 156/7.[31]

The demonstration was welcome, and the result seemed highly satisfactory. Studies of this kind proceed by experiment and are subject to hazard. A fresh inspection of the document comes out with a signal innovation. The proconsul is not T. Atilius Maximus. He is none other than T. Statilius Maximus, the consul of 144: probably proconsul of Asia in 157/8.[32]

---

[27] For this consular pair see now M. M. Roxan, *RMD* (1978), no. 47. Previously the diploma xvi 110 had been assigned to 159.

[28] Alföldy, 212.

[29] The people at Smyrna had congratulated Marcus on the birth of a child—which however died. Now a daughter was born to Marcus on November 30 of 147, as the *Fasti Ostienses* disclosed (*FO* xxviii). That is, the eldest daughter, Annia Galeria Aurelia Faustina (*PIR*[2], A 699). It has taken some time for the bearing of that fact to be appreciated.

[30] As suggested in *Danubian Papers* (1971), 190: 'the dating of his proconsulate of Asia (*SIG*[3] 851), generally allocated to 146/7 (cf. *PIR*[2], A 1301), is in fact highly insecure: it might belong *c.*157. If so, he was consul *c.*142.'

[31] J. Krier, *Chiron* x (1980), 456.

[32] To be argued by G. Petzl in *Chiron* xiii (1983), as I am informed by Werner Eck. To him and to Dr. Petzl I am grateful for permission to insert and use this important item.

It will be noted that *ILS* 1062 should be attributed to Claudius Maximus, not to Statilius Maximus (*cos.* 144), cf. J. Fitz, *AAntHung* xi (1963), 258 ff. Followed in *Historia* xiv (1965),

At one stroke a Roman consular is thus blotted out. No other testimony spoke for his existence. In any event, the proper dating of *SIG*³ 851 rendered vacant the tenure 146/7.

147/8. L. Antonius Albus (*suff. c.*132). *SEG* iv 533; xix 684 = *AE* 1967, 480. Aelius Aristides now comes in again. He was at Pergamum in 146, not prevented by his malady from delivering an oration to celebrate the birthday of the young Apellas: the subscription to the speech states that he was then twenty-nine (xxx, p. 211K). Next at Smyrna, when great earthquakes ravaged several cities in the province. Warned by a dream, Aristides sacrificed an ox to Zeus. He saw a bright star flash through the agora—and the calamity at once abated. Albus was proconsul at that time (xlix 38).

An attempt has been made to transfer proconsulate and earthquake to 160/1.[33] It ran against impediments. First, the strong case for another proconsul in that year, viz. Mummius Sisenna Rutilianus (see below). Second, the age of Antonius Albus. He was admitted to the *Arvales* in 111 or 112 (cf. *AE* 1964, 70). Albus was the son of a consul (*suff.* 102), and it was the practice to co-opt senators at a quite early stage in their careers.[34] |

For the proconsulate recent estimates range between 146/7 and 148/9.[35]

The third of these dates is now ruled out. It is a provisional convenience to stand by 147/8, leaving the previous year open.

To sum up. Of the ten years, five exhibit proven proconsuls. There are two gaps; and three names are enlisted on varying grades of plausibility, viz. Sex. Julius Maior (*suff.* ?126), Q. Insteius Celer (?128) and the resurrected Ti. Julius Candidus Celsus (?129).[36] To keep them at hand entails no deception.

---

352 = *Danubian Papers* (1971), 235. For hesitations, A. R. Birley, *Marcus Aurelius* (1966), 125, n. 1. Alföldy accepted the attribution as 'zweifellos richtige', dating the consulship of Claudius Maximus to 142 (op. cit. 143).

[33] G. W. Bowersock, *HSCPh* lxxii (1968), 289 ff. Approved by L. Robert, *Bull.ép.* 1968, no. 171; T. D. Barnes, *JRS* lviii (1968), 38. The important document appealed to concerns the harbour at Ephesus (*AE* 1967, 480 = *Inscr. Eph.* 23).
[34] W. Eck, *Epigraphische Studien* ix (1972), 22 f.: discussing the inscription at Corinth (fragmentary) that furnishes the career of Albus. Whence *AE* 1972, 567. Further, *RE*, *Suppl.* xiv 50 f. Followed by Alföldy, op. cit. 213 (with ample annotation).
[35] Thus 146/7 (*Inscr. Eph.* 23: 'wahrscheinlich'); ?148/9 (Alföldy); 147–9 (Eck). Hüttl had opted firmly for 147/8.
[36] Two other names have been canvassed. On the basis of *IGR* iv 1275 (Thyatira) Hüttl advocated L. Aemilius Juncus (*suff.* 127). That is now discountenanced by a dedication set up by his son (*AE* 1967, 452: Athens). For the son's consulship Alföldy suggests 154, with Asia in 171/2 (op. cit. 165 f.). As for L. Flavius Arrianus (*suff.* 129 or 130), the notion is kept for a footnote by P. Stadter, *Arrian of Nicomedia* (1980), 198. Arrian would be an obvious nuisance if proconsul in the period 143–5.

The next section is shorter and highly satisfactory. Five proconsuls follow in a tight sequence from 148/9 to 152/3.

(B) 148/9. Q. Flavius Tertullus (*suff.* 133). The new military diploma of the province Asia, dated by the last consular pair of 148, establishes this proconsulate: published in *Chiron* xi (1981), 267 f.

149/50. Popillius Priscus (*suff.* ?134). *IG* xii 325 = *SIG*³ 852. This decree of Thera records the completion of a public building under the proconsulate of Mummius Sisenna. A prominent citizen, Flavius Clitosthenes, had made the vow and promise on July 18 of the year 149. Another decree had been passed on that same day: it yields the name of the proconsul Popillius Priscus (*IG* xii 326).

That proconsul is not otherwise known. A Priscus colleague of L. Aurelius Gallus was registered on a diploma belonging between 129 and 132 (xvi 173). The consulship of Popillius Priscus might fall in 132, it was supposed.[37] That appears too early for his proconsular date—and the pair can be assigned to 129 or 130. Popillius Priscus goes rather in 134, with no discomfort so far.

150/1. P. Mummius Sisenna (*cos.* 133). *SIG*³ 852 (Thera). The year being certified, the interval of seventeen years from the consulate (no parallel under Hadrian or Pius) presents an acute problem. Ill health might be surmised, or a changed decision, with later admittance to the sortition by special indulgence of Caesar for a consular of marked merit. Another reason can be canvassed, namely occupation elsewhere. For example, Lentulus the Augur (*cos.* 14 B.C.) did not accede to Asia until 2 B.C. (*SIG*³ 781). Rational conjecture brought up the command of the Balkan army *c.*9 B.C., in succession to Piso the Pontifex, who won a great war in Thrace.[38] |

Mummius Sisenna was governor of Britain, attested in 135 (xvi 82), but probably going there almost at once after he laid down the *fasces*.[39] For a legate of Britain the next promotion, and the ultimate, is Syria. But Syria was blocked all the way, it appeared, and notably in 147 or 148, when Sisenna's year for the sortition came up. There was D. Velius Fidus to be reckoned with (*CIL* iii 14387e: Heliopolis), assigned a tenure in the vicinity of 146; and next, Sulpicius Julianus, on attestation (so it appeared) in 149 (*IGR* iii 1274: Soueida).[40]

However, 'volvenda dies', or rather sharper science, brings a

---

[37] Alföldy, 214.   [38] *JRS* xlv (1955), 30 = *Ten Studies in Tacitus* (1970), 43.
[39] To take the place of Sex. Julius Severus (*suff.* 127), sent to Judaea to deal with the rebellion (*ILS* 1056, cf. Dio lxix 13, 2).
[40] Alföldy, 239.

happy solution. The dedication at Heliopolis honours Velius Fidus as 'leg. Aug. pr. [pr.'. That city was his *patria*. He governed not Syria but Syria Palaestina.[41]

No impediment therefore to Mummius Sisenna as legate in Syria *c*.147. The appointment of a senior consular, perhaps for a brief tenure, is not without parallel. Bruttius Praesens (*suff.* ?118) was there, *c*.136, preceding Julius Maior.[42] Tension with the Parthians might be surmised—and Pius at the outset of his reign had to take prompt measures (diplomacy backed by mobilization of troops). Again, at the end the moribund ruler spoke in fever and delirium 'de his regibus quibus irascebatur' (*HA Pius* 12, 7). Vexations recurring after an interval in the middle years of the reign should occasion no surprise.

The antecedents of Sisenna (anomalous as an eponymous consul) arouse interest. He might have been adlected after service as an equestrian officer, and a consul later than usual: his son was *suffectus* in 146. Further, his passage to the consulate. A 'Publius' is on attestation as legate of Thrace at some time between 128 and 136 (*IGR* i 785).

151/2. T. Vitrasius Pollio (*suff.* ?136). This proconsulate is known only from Aristides, who now turns up for the first time since the earthquake. The fourth of the Hieroi Logoi is a confused and repellent piece of composition. It takes its inception from Severus (i.e. the successor of Pollio), advances a long way forward to Quadratus (a later proconsul), then Severus again, then Pollio, and at the end Julianus (who was anterior to Severus by seven or eight years). In this imbroglio, curt statement will suffice. The sophist was in trouble, | trying to evade the post of fiscal inspector to which the people of Smyrna had elected him (*Or.* l 96 ff.). He wrote letters of protest both to the proconsul's legate and to Pollio himself. A certain Glabrio, styled 'the illustrious Glabrio', impinged on those transactions (l 97). Under influence from another passage (l 100), some took him for a proconsul.[43] He is patently M'. Acilius Glabrio (*cos.* 152), legate in Asia not long previous to his consulship (*ILS* 1072). He was there before Pollio, well before. That has now become clear. An

---

[41] As shown by W. Eck, *ZPE* xlii (1981), 237 f. Velius Fidus was legate of Syria Palaestina in 150 (*PSI* x 1026).

[42] *AE* 1938, 137 (Palmyra), dated to April of 138. For this interpretation, *Historia* ix (1960), 375 = *RP* (1979), 490 f. Not all have accepted it. Thus Eck, *Senatoren* etc. (1970), 232; Alföldy, 240 f. See now *Romanitas—Christianitas* (*Festschrift Straub*, 1982), 238 f. = pp. 50 f., above.

[43] For a succinct exposition, G. W. Bowersock, *Greek Sophists in the Roman Empire* (1969), 36 ff.

Against, Groag in *PIR*², A 73. Nevertheless an Acilius Glabrio has been conjured up, an unknown uncle of the consul of 152. Thus H. J. Mason, *CP* lxviii (1968), 121 ff.

inscription reveals a surprising fact. This aristocrat stayed on to occupy the post of *logistes* at Ephesus.[44]

As concerns the proconsul of 151/2, T. Vitrasius Pollio was legate of VII Gemina in Tarraconensis, as shown by a soldier's gravestone in another province (*ILS* 2404: Nemausus); and a Vitrasius Pollio governed Lugdunensis under Hadrian (*Dig.* xxvii 1, 15, 17). The combination produced a Vitrasius Pollio to be deemed consul suffect in 136 or 137.[45]

152/3. C. Julius Severus (*suff.* ?138). *ILS* 8826 (Ancyra). He is mentioned several times by Aristides (l 12; 71 ff.). The sophist soon caused more annoyance, objecting when they tried to make him chief of police at Hadrianutherae, his native town (73).

The year of Julius Severus determines the chronology of the prolonged and habitual illness of Aelius Aristides. The tenth year of that affliction now came round (l 1, cf. 12), and the season was winter. Therefore the beginning of his woes falls in the winter of 143/4 (that is, soon after his return from Rome).

Items concerning the age of Aristides confirm the dating of the proconsulate. He supplied astrological information about the season of his birth (l 57 f.) which points to 117, late in the year.[46] When Aristides made a speech at Baris, Severus being governor, he was aged thirty-five years and one month: that item is supplied by the subscription to the hymn in honour of Athena (xxxvii, p. 312 K).

The tenure 152/3 for Julius Severus is inexpugnable.[47] It closes a sequence, with two nasty problems (heterogeneous) to emerge before long in | the eight concluding years.

(C) 153/4.

154/5.

155/6. ?M. Peducaeus Priscinus (*cos.* 141). He found admission to the authoritative encyclopedia, supported as proconsul by the most excellent of sponsors.[48] The claim cannot be substantiated. It depended on an inscription from the Great Theatre at Ephesus,

---

[44] *Inschr. Eph.* 611. On which, *Chiron* x (1980), 446 ff. = *RP* iii (1984), 1334 ff.

[45] *JRS* xliii (1953), 159 = *RP* (1979), 231 f. Not to be found among the Vitrasii catalogued by R. Hanslik in *RE* ix A (1961), 416 ff.

[46] A. Boulanger, *Aelius Aristide* (1923), 465 ff.; W. Hüttl, *Antoninus Pius* ii (1933), 36 ff.

[47] By mishap *PIR*[2], J 573 has 'anno 151/52 ut videtur'. The sequence from Popillius Priscus to Julius Severus (149–53) was established by W. Hüttl, op. cit. 49 ff. (albeit in error about the identity of Vitrasius Pollio). For a brief restatement, *Chiron* x (1980), 434 = *RP* iii (1984), 1322 f.

[48] Groag, *RE* xix 54.

supplemented long ago in a fashion all too optimistic.[49] Later finds put the inscription in its place: one of six dedications to Antoninus Pius set up under the supervision of P. Gerellanus Flavianus—but neither space nor need for the name of a proconsul.[50]

Peducaeus Priscinus therefore lapses.[51] With him goes an item that would have helped to narrow the dating of Statius Quadratus, troublesome in more ways than one.

156/7. L. Statius Quadratus (*cos.* 142). *IGR* iii 175 (Magnesia ad Sipylum). An Athenian, and presumed son of L. Statius Aquila (*suff.* 116).

So far, the year seems acceptable. A fresh factor supervenes. If Peducaeus is disallowed, the tenure 155/6 becomes admissible. That entails a shorter interval than the normal fourteen or fifteen years. Thirteen is not excluded. Accident could convey benefit, especially to an *ordinarius*. Proconsuls sometimes fell out, either before or after the sortition. Three examples from the vicinity of Quadratus are variously instructive.

(1) Herodes Atticus (*cos.* 143). From a confused passage in Philostratus, when rationally interpreted, it appears that Herodes declined the result of the sortition.[52]

(2) Cornelius Fronto (*suff.* 143). He had been awarded Asia, he made preparations, mustering friends, as related in a letter to Pius. No sign that Fronto went to Asia. The letter breaks off on the condition of his health: 'ingruit deinde tanta vis valetudinis quae mihi ostenderet omnem spem illam ⟨frustra fuisse⟩.'[53]

(3) Cluvius Paullinus (*suff.* ?143). He died before taking up the proconsulate: 'pr[oc]onsuli sortito pro[v]in[c. Asiae]' (*AE* 1940, 99). The season of his consulship emerges from a comparison between two of his praetorian posts | (a legion and the charge of the Via Flaminia) with those held by three coeval senators.[54] If not 143, the year might be 142: it can hardly be earlier.

---

[49] Wood, *Discoveries at Ephesus. Inscriptions from the Great Theatre* (1877), 53, no. 7. See remarks by Hicks on *IBM* 502. The inscription (it appears) had been supplemented by Wood on the basis of *CIG* 2966, which showed Peducaeus Priscinus (i.e. the Hadrianic proconsul, *cos.* 110) honouring Sabina.

[50] *Forsch. in Ephesos* ii 50. Furthermore, the pendant to *CIG* 2966 has turned up: the base of a statue of Hadrian set up in the proconsulate of M. Peducaeus Priscinus (*JÖAI* xlv (1960), Beiblatt 83, no. 10, whence *AE* 1966, 427).

[51] Thus Hüttl, op. cit. 33 ff. He is kept, without the query, by Alföldy, 214.

[52] Philostratus, *Vit. soph.* p. 556, cf. Groag in *PIR*², C 802.

[53] Fronto, *Ad Antoninum Pium* 8, 2. = Haines i, p. 238.

[54] Namely L. Minicius Natalis (*suff.* 139), T. Caesernius Statianus (?141), L. Aemilius Carus (?144). Their careers are given by *ILS* 1061; 1068; 1077. For Caesernius and his brother, Alföldy, 347 ff.; for Cluvius Maximus, 146.

To prosecute the case for a thirteen-year interval for Statius Quadratus. It happens to stand firm for Lollianus Avitus (*cos.* 144) in Africa. On him follows a run of five proconsuls, all comporting the standard interval from their consulships. For the list, see below. And, for that matter, two further African examples can be cited from the middle sixties.

The proconsul Quadratus in the notorious fourth discourse of Aelius Aristides has been withheld until this point. Aristides called him a *rhetor*, and a friend (*Or.* l 63, cf. 71). Another passage, much later, refers to Quadratus, so it can be argued. The item might seem trivial, but it has a bearing on the author's methods, or rather habits, of composition. After narrating the episode under the proconsulate of Pollio, which includes a reference to Glabrio (97), the author states that he is going back in time, and he relates another incident: 'the sophist whom I mentioned a little earlier was governor' (100).[55]

Who then is this 'sophist'? None other than Glabrio (cf. 97), so it has been held.[56] He was not a proconsul, but the difficulty could be turned: legate in Asia, he held authority for a short spell before the arrival of Vitrasius Pollio in the summer of 151.[57]

That is not all. It is strange that a Roman aristocrat, whom the author had previously singled out by an honorific appellation should now be summarily designated as 'the sophist'. An explanation has been essayed: Aristides is boldly enlisting the nobleman in the 'aristocracy of the intellect'.[58] Better, the proconsul Statius Quadratus. Philostratus happens to bring up a consular Quadratus who as a sophist went in for the fashion set by Favorinus.[59]

And the end is not yet. For this proconsul Aristides furnishes a statement that looked for once more or less precise. He had mentioned Quadratus (63 ff.). Then, referring to Severus, he says that Severus was governor 'a year, I suppose, before my friend' (71).[60] The friend is Quadratus.

What then is to be done? To redeem Aristides, scholars have been impelled | to lodge Statius Quadratus in the near sequel to Severus (the proconsul in 152/3). Hence even in 153/4.[61] Others opt for

---

[55] Aristides, *Or.* l 100.

[56] E. Groag, *PIR*[2], A 73; G. W. Bowersock, *Greek Sophists in the Roman Empire* (1969), 37; R. Syme, *Chiron* x (1980), 435 = *RP* iii (1984), 1324.

[57] Since, before departing to hold the consulate of 152, he had been not only legate but *logistes* of Ephesus.

[58] Thus in *Chiron* x (1980), 435 = *RP* iii (1984), 1324.

[59] Philostratus, *Vit. soph.* p. 576.   [60] Aristides, l. 71.

[61] Thus L. Schumacher in his list, *ZPE* xxiv (1977), 162. It appears to be implied by the phrases 'Quadratus' predecessor Severus' and 'Quadratus, who seems to have succeeded Severus' (Bowersock, op. cit. 37; 40).

154/5.[62] Against which, a single sharp admonition avails. No proconsul under Hadrian or Pius is likely to go to Asia eleven or twelve years after his consulship. The alternatives for Statius Quadratus stand as 155/6 or 156/7.[63]

Aristides is beyond redemption. Writing about these transactions many years later, he was faulty of memory, occluding the gap of two years, or even three, between the proconsulates of Severus and Quadratus.

Out of that labyrinth, no need to enter another. The martyrdom of Polycarp has duly engendered debates long and anxious.[64] The Appendix to the document supplies a double dating, viz. Philippus of Tralles high priest of Asia, Statius Quadratus proconsul of Asia. The former item is more than vulnerable, the latter cannot be used to date the proconsul.[65]

157/8. T. Atilius Maximus was under constraint to forfeit the standard tenure of 146/7. Not only that. As was briefly indicated, that consular has now given way before the claims of T. Statilius Maximus, the consul of 144.

Nothing, so it appears, forbids allocating Statilius to 157/8. In that case, thirteen years' interval from the consulate. That is acceptable— and relevant to Statius Quadratus.

The remaining years under Antoninus Pius are therefore:

158/9 ⎫
159/60 ⎭ for consuls suffect in 143–5.

160/1. P. Mummius Sisenna Rutilianus (*suff.* 146). *ILS* 1101: the son of the remarkable consul of 133. For the run of five proconsuls in the sequel, see below.

To sum up. The twenty-three proconsular years work out as follows:

(A) 138/9 to 147/8. Five certified proconsuls, two gaps, three conjectural names, viz. Sex. Julius Maior, Q. Insteius Celer, Ti. Julius Candidus Celsus. Of them Celer is the weakest, Maior has clear attractions—and Candidus Celsus (the new importation) has at the least a claim not inferior to Claudius Quartinus.

(B) 148/9–152/3. Five proconsuls firmly fixed.

[62] Hüttl, op. cit. 52.
[63] For 156/7, Alföldy, 214 f.
[64] For a clear exposition, Hüttl, op. cit. 53 ff.
[65] For a firm and sceptical approach, T. D. Barnes, *JThS* xviii (1967), 433 ff.

(C) 153/4–160/1. Three proconsuls, five gaps (expelling Peducaeus Priscinus), sundry problems of date and order. |

As concerns the last section, three names may be put under brief scrutiny.

(1) M. Cornelius Fronto (*suff.* 143). Despite the letter to the Emperor, it has been supposed that Fronto might after all have gone to Asia, for the conjectured tenure 157/8.[66]

(2) Gratus, the proconsul when Montanus arose in Asia, according to Eusebius.[67] Other sources indicate a year: Epiphanius 157, Eusebius in his Chronicle *c*.172. Hence eager debate on inadequate evidence, or some fairly positive statements. Thus *PIR*[2], G 224: 'eo anno (156/7 vel 157/8) igitur Gratus Asiam videtur rexisse'. On the other hand, a strong case has been made out for the vicinity of the year 170.[68]

Only the proconsular year of Gratus could decide. As concerns the late years of Pius, 157/8 does not look at all propitious, and there are complications enough in that vicinity.[69] Nomenclature can sometimes help. The *cognomen* 'Gratus' is unprepossessing. In the senatorial order it is documented for the first time with C. Vettius Gratus Sabinianus (*cos.* 221). *Ordinarii* tend to have ancestors, and a *suffectus* two generations back is not out of the question. Asia is fecund in epigraphy. A Vettius Gratus may come to light one day.

(3) Vibius Bassus, proconsul of Asia, attested by *Forsch. in Ephesos* iii no. 72. The editor put the inscription in the third quarter of the century. But it would demand faith to assign this proconsul to the end of Pius' reign; and, on the other hand, little profit in asking whether he may not be Bassus, City Prefect in 193 (*HA Severus* 8, 8).[70]

At this point it may be of use to pursue the proconsuls for five years into the next reign. On Mummius Rutilianus (*suff.* 146) follow

    161/2 Q. Cornelius Proculus (*suff.* 146); *ILS* 1089
    162/3 C. Popillius Carus Pedo (*suff.* 147); *SIG*[3] 867
    163/4 Q. Sosius Priscus (*cos.* 149); *CIL* vi 31753: the name of the
           province missing, but cf. his son, quaestorian legate in Asia
           (*ILS* 1104)

---

[66] Thus E. Champlin, *Fronto and Antonine Rome* (1980), 164. Not, however, with any conviction. The letter, he suggested, 'may simply be an elaborate plea for extending the orator's stay in Rome'.

[67] *HE* v 16, 7.   [68] T. D. Barnes, *JThS* xxi (1970), 403 ff.

[69] For 157/8, Alföldy, 215, cf. 143 f.

[70] His proconsulate is put in the period 155–75 by Alföldy, 194, cf. 112.

164/5   M. Gavius Squilla Gallicanus (*cos.* 150); in *OGIS* 512 his son (*cos.* 170) figures as a legate

165/6   D. Fonteius Fronto (*suff. c.*150); a new milestone dated to 165.[71]

By the same token, comparison with Africa comes in, from the late epoch of Antoninus Pius.[72] |

157/8. L. Hedius Rufus Lollianus Avitus (*cos.* 144). *IRT* 372 (Lepcis) with the date 157, cf. 533 f.[73] The tenure 157/8 cannot be refused (note also the following proconsuls). Hence an interval of thirteen years certified, the sole specimen so far as ascertained for Africa under Hadrian or Pius—and relevant to the assessment of Statius Quadratus in Asia.

158/9. Claudius Maximus (*suff.* ?143), the successor of Lollianus Avitus (Apuleius, *Apol.* 94). If his consulship were assigned to 142, that would extend the interval to sixteen years.[74]

159/60. Q. Egrilius Plarianus (*suff.* ?144). *CIL* viii 800 + 1177, the consular colleague of L. Aemilius Carus (vi 30868), who is attested as legate of Arabia (*ILS* 1077), in 142/3 (*AE* 1909, 237: Gerasa).

160/1. T. Prifernius T. f. Paetus Rosianus Geminus (*suff.* 146). *CIL* vi 1449.

161/2. Q. Voconius Saxa Fidus (*suff.* 146). *AE* 1949, 27 (Gigthis); *CIL* viii 22691 (Carthage).

162/3. Sex. Cocceius Severianus Honorinus (*suff.* 147). *CIL* viii 1030 (Thagora); 24535 (Carthage).

163/4. Ser. Cornelius Scipio Salvidienus Orfitus (*cos.* 149). *IRT* 232 (Oea).

This run of seven proconsuls in order of seniority is determined, one repeats, by the tenure of Lollianus Avitus. At the end a blank year ensues, formerly occupied by M. Antonius Zeno (*suff.* 148). He now lapses.[75] But there should follow in 165 M'. Acilius Glabrio (*cos.* 152), cf. *IRT* 21 (Sabratha), in 166 C. Bruttius Praesens (*cos.* 153), his proconsulate established by a revised reading of *IRT* 91 (Sabratha).[76]

---

[71] Published by D. French, *AS* xxvi (1976), 11 f., and noted by Alföldy in his *Addenda*, 379.

[72] For this list, see *REA* lxi (1959), 318 f. = *RP* (1979), 468 f.

[73] Discussed by J. Guey, *REL* xxix (1951), 307 ff.

[74] That consular year was advocated by Alföldy, 143. It suited the career of the Maximus of *ILS* 1062 better than did 143 or 144.

[75] The fragment at Thugga (viii 1480) was assigned to the *suffectus* of 148, cf. *PIR*², A 883. Wrongly: it belongs to his son (as shown by *AE* 1966, 511), proconsul in 183/4 or 184/5.

[76] F. Jacques, *ZPE* xxii (1976), 438: followed in *Chiron* x (1980), 438 = *RP* iii (1984), 1327.

Hence a noteworthy fact: the earliest proconsuls since Lollianus Avitus to show the shortened interval of thirteen years—and, like him, eponymous consuls.

Epilogue

When the fine flower of Antonine society is mustered and put in line, it is a pity if the operation stops short with matters of chronology and order. The thirteen proconsuls respond to interrogation.[77] The questions arrange themselves under eight headings.

(1) *The interval from the consulate.* From thirteen years early in Trajan's reign and until 106, it extended to fifteen, since three consuls of 94 went to Asia. Rational expectations were frustrated.[78] When at the end it got to seventeen, the consequences were unfortunate. A *novus homo* would be close on | sixty, if he survived—and death in the middle fifties of life was fairly common.

By 120, with the proconsulate of Cornelius Priscus (*suff.* ?104), the sagacious ruler had cut the interval to fourteen years, and he kept it there for 124, 125, 126.[79] The next two years offer room for conjecture. On one reconstruction, a blank in 127/8, then Lollianus Avitus (*cos.* 114).[80] Now a proconsul called Messalla was disclosed by the inscription of Claudius Chionis (*ILS* 8860: Didyma). Of uncertain period, and some gave a thought to L. Vipstanus Poplicola (*cos.* 48). A later member of this illustrious house might occur, viz. L. Vipstanus Messalla (*cos.* 115).[81] If so, Messalla would occupy 128/9, with Lollianus thrown back to the previous year. On that showing, two more proconsuls at the term of thirteen years.

The next consul to go to Asia is the jurist Juventius Celsus (*suff.* 115), anomalous because he opened that year as consul for the second time.[82] Afranius Flavianus followed (*suff.* ?115). Then Lamia Aelianus (*cos.* 116), but his successor, Julius Alexander Berenicianus (*suff.* 116), carries the term to sixteen years—not again exhibited under Hadrian or Pius, apart from the anomalous seventeen of Mummius Sisenna.

---

[77] Thirteen proconsuls, since several have been either rejected or held in suspense.

[78] As notably for Cornelius Tacitus (*suff.* 97). Relevant to the inception of his second work. Cf. remarks in *JRS* lxxii (1982), 71 f. = pp. 204 f., above.

[79] For the sequence, Eck, *Senatoren* (1970), 237.

[80] Chr. Habicht, *Pergamon* viii 1 (1969), 58: adopted by Eck.

[81] As suggested in *Historia* xi (1962), 152 = *RP* (1979), 535 f.

[82] For a time 117 seemed plausible for the consulship of Celsus (praetor in 106), no room being available for 115 on the *Fasti Potentini*. A text of the long-unpublished diploma in the Sofia Museum is now available: M. M. Roxan, *RMD* (1978), no. 14. It shows that, as legate of Thrace, Juventius Celsus preceded Statilius Maximus (himself a *suffectus* of 115).

For the rest, the norm of fifteen years obtains more often than not, into the reign of Marcus. Perturbations supervened: deaths from the pestilence and senior ex-consuls called back into service as governors, generals in the wars, and *comites* of Verus or Marcus.[83]

(2) *The sortition.* How it was managed is a delicate and engaging topic: privilege or favour, and various stages of preliminary selection or renunciations under unobtrusive pressures.[84] Some aspirants came to see that they had scant hope. Little was reserved for chance, and the thing works out in a providential fashion. For example, proconsuls of Africa during the reign of Hadrian. They tend to come from Italy and from provinces of the West—and *novi homines* in preponderance.[85] Asia exhibits contrasts, not beyond the understanding.

(3) *Eponymous consuls.* Four have been noted in Asia, sharply diverse characters: the Italian aristocrat Venuleius Apronianus, the military man Mummius Sisenna, Statius Quadratus a sophist from Athens, T. Statilius Maximus, probably from Berytus. |

(4) *Praetorian careers.* An epigraphic *cursus* is extant for five of the thirteen. A significant avenue of approach to the consulship is opened by one of the twelve praetorian provinces in the portion of Caesar, especially if the only post before it is the command of a legion.[86] Thus Valerius Propinquus (*suff.* 126) by way of VI Victrix and Aquitania (ii 6084 = *RIT* 149).

As equivalent to the imperial province now counted the charge of the *aerarium Saturni*. It enabled favoured senators to spend a *triennium* at (or near) the capital.[87] Julius Severus (*suff.* ?138) was legate in Asia. Next, commanding IV Scythica in Syria in 132 he acted as deputy when the consular legate was called to Judaea by the rebellion; then, after the proconsulate of Achaia, Severus governed by special mandate from Caesar the province Bithynia–Pontus (*ILS* 8826). Sisenna Rutilianus, however (*suff.* 146), went straight after his praetorship and a legion to the *aerarium Saturni* (*ILS* 1101).

The other two careers are totally diverse. Claudius Quartinus (*suff.* 130), an equestrian officer, received *latus clavus* and quaestorship from Trajan (*CIL* xiii 1802: Lugdunum; xiv 4473: Ostia).[88] After becoming praetor he was legate in Asia, *iuridicus* in Tarraconensis in 117 and still there late in 119 (cf. ii 2959). The next post was a command of two eastern legions when trouble arose with Parthia. Finally, legate of Lugdunensis, as once surmised and now certified

---

[83] Alföldy, 118 f.   [84] Alföldy, 119 ff.
[85] *ZPE* xxxvii (1980), 14 ff. = *RP* iii (1984), 1312 ff.
[86] For some of the praetorian provinces under Hadrian and Pius see *Historia* xiv (1965), 342 ff. = *Danubian Papers* (1971), 225 ff.
[87] See remarks in *Historia* xiv (1965), 358 = *Danubian Papers* (1971), 241.
[88] Alföldy, *Fasti Hispanienses* (1969), 79 ff.

(*AE* 1976, 427: Lugdunum). Legion and praetorian province thus declare their value, although in a career slower than might have been expected.

Quartinus the new senator advanced through merit and service. Statilius Maximus (*cos.* 144) was the son of T. Statilius Maximus Hadrianus (*suff.* 115). Antonius Albus (*suff. c.*132) was also the son of a consul. As restored, the fragmentary inscription at Corinth shows him legate in Asia, curator of a group of minor roads in Italy, proconsul of Achaia.[89] And nothing in the sequel. In 129/30 Albus was *magister* of the Arval Brethren (vi 2083): the sole of the thirteen to belong to a congregation that was decorative, a haven of nonentities, and not held in great esteem.

Finally, missing information. The earlier career of Mummius Sisenna (*cos.* 133) would be worth knowing. All that avails is the conjecture that he had been governor of Thrace. For Vitrasius Pollio (*suff.* ?136) sporadic evidence contributed a legion with Lugdunensis following.

(5) *Consular commands.* Four of the above-mentioned proconsuls had been governors in the ten military provinces. Mummius Sisenna, it has been proposed, had Syria at a long lapse after Britain. That would explain the retarded proconsulate in 150/1. Valerius Propinquus had Germania Inferior *c.*129–132; | and Claudius Quartinus is attested in the other command by a diploma early in 134 (xv 80). He may have proceeded thence to Britain.[90] Julius Severus was legate of Germania Inferior *c.*141–4. Rutilianus, the son of Sisenna, went to Moesia Superior *c.*149. Finally, regret will be conceived that the excellent Julius Maior (*suff.* 126) does not aggregate to this company, his proconsulate of Asia remaining short of proof. Maior held Moesia Inferior with three legions *c.*130–4 (cf. *CIL* xvi 78), and he went to Syria not long before the decease of Hadrian.[91] On the other hand Peducaeus Priscinus (*cos.* 141), who lapses, was only an Italian aristocrat, and perhaps patrician by now: no career in the service of the Caesars.

(6) *Extraction and origins.*

(a) *Italy.* Venuleius Apronianus (*cos.* 123) came from an ancient and opulent house at Pisae, showing senators in the last epoch of the Republic, a senator again under the first dynasty, and a consul suffect in 92.[92] Of Vitrasius Pollio, Cales in Campania is the *patria*. High

---

[89] Eck, *Epigraphische Studien* ix (1972), 21, whence *AE* 1972, 567.

[90] Thus, adducing *RIB* 1997 f., A. R. Birley, *The Fasti of Roman Britain* (1980), 110 ff.

[91] *AE* 1938, 137 (Palmyra). His Syrian governorship had been registered on *IG* iv² 454 (Epidaurus).

[92] For the history of the family, *Some Arval Brethren* (1980), 57.

equestrian, with two Prefects of Egypt, the Vitrasii lapse from notice for two generations, to emerge again with L. Vitrasius Flamininus, consul suffect in 122, honoured at Capua (x 3870). The son of Pollio the proconsul married a cousin of Marcus Aurelius and ended as consul for the second time in 176. Until the parent was discerned the pair suffered a crude amalgamation.[93]

Ti. Claudius Quartinus presents indistinctive nomenclature, and a foreign origin might have been suspected. However, he carries for tribe the 'Palatina', and a magistrate of that name is discovered at Puteoli (*ILS* 5919).

(b) *Spain.* Valerius Propinquus had for *patria* Liria of the Edetani. His father, given equestrian rank by the Emperor Titus, pursued a successful military career and ended as a provincial high priest at Tarraco (*ILS* 2711). The inscription of Propinquus (*RIT* 149) discloses no post before the praetorship. He had probably been adlected to senatorial rank.[94] That is, after service in the *militia equestris*. The same may well hold for Mummius Sisenna—and the more remarkable in that he became an eponymous consul. The *patria* of these Mummii (Sisenna and his son) has been sought in the province Baetica.[95]

Next, Popillius Priscus (*suff.* ?134). The first temptation is to renounce, cheerfully. He lacks lineaments—or any attachments unless to C. Popillius Carus Pedo, consul suffect in 147, whose tribe is 'Quirina' (*ILS* 1071). Evidence about Popillii in Spain might attract a hopeful enquirer.[96]

(c) *Eastern provinces.* Such is the origin of no fewer than five, in their variety extreme and attractive. Athens claims the sophist Statius Quadratus (*cos.* 142), the western region of Asia both Claudius Julianus (*suff.* 129 or 130) and Antonius Albus (*c.*132); and Statilius Maximus (*cos.* 144) derives from Berytus, a Roman *colonia*, so it can be argued.[97]

Julius Severus (*suff.* ?138) is in himself a whole chapter of history, the descendant of kings and tetrarchs, and styled 'the first of the

---

[93] At the hand of Lambertz, *RE* xxi 2344 ff. (with numerous errors). Nor was the parent recognized by Hanslik, *RE* ixA 416 ff.

[94] Thus Alföldy, in annotation on *RIT* 149. See further *AEA*, forthcoming = pp. 579 ff., below.

[95] A. R. Birley, op. cit. 249, n. 8.

[96] See 'Spaniards at Tivoli', *AncSoc* xiii/xiv (1982/3), 252 = p. 94, above.

[97] For the detailed evidence see H. Halfmann, *Die Senatoren aus dem östlichen Teil des Imperium Romanum bis zum Ende des 2. Jh.n.Chr.* (1979), nos. 67; 57, 24. Halfmann, however, remains dubious about the Statilii (ibid. 211 f.). Julius Maior, it will be recalled, has to be omitted from the present rigorous rubric. Likewise the conjectural consul and proconsul Ti. Julius Candidus Celsus (*suff.* ?129). The Iulii Candidi and the Antonii Albi both avow attachments to Ephesus—but the earliest Ephesian consul is much later (Halfmann, no. 101).

344   The Proconsuls of Asia under Antoninus Pius   [288

Hellenes'. Despite four cousins of consular rank (*OGIS* 544),
Severus eschewed normal entry to the Senate for some time. Hadrian
adlected him 'inter tribunicios' (*ILS* 8826).

There remains Q. Flavius Tertullus (*suff.* 133), proconsul in 148/9:
a welcome accession to the catalogue, in a fixed place, but not
remunerative to any who make search for antecedents or for local
origins. In a host of consular Flavii no 'Quintus' is perceptible apart
from Q. Flavius Balbus in the age of the Severi (*ILS* 3388). Some of
the other proconsuls, it will be suitably recalled, are only names or
not much better.

By region or province the other twelve divide into three portions.
Too neatly perhaps, and not without conjecture, as duly and clearly
avowed, for example for Popillius Priscus. The company, or rather
collection, is highly variegated. In a cosmopolitan empire that is no
surprise—and none that Africa should be absent although Africa was
now coming out with consular legates.

(7) *Continuity.* Taking in consuls from 123 to 146, the list bridges
two reigns. It is a question whether it can yield results bearing on the
policy or personalities of emperors. Probably not a great deal.
Recruitment of the Senate and promotion to office reflect a process
and deep strong forces that a ruler cannot do much to modify. It is
Caesar's duty to recognize birth, wealth, and legitimate ambitions,
to recompense loyalty or merit. He holds the balance between
competing groups, and it is in the interest of all concerned that the
path of honours should be clear and smooth, with advancement
almost predictable, at least in certain categories.

Hadrian, so it can be argued, took especial care to regularize the
senatorial career in notable aspects, to render it exempt as far as
possible | from hazards or caprice. Hence the steady rhythm that
characterizes the reign of Antoninus Pius.

Stability and concord were congenial to Hadrian's second choice
for the succession. No changes to be feared. Yet a mild paradox can
be divined. Hadrian prudently refrained from obtruding upon the
capital his Hellenic predilections. One sign should not be missed. It is
not easy to discover a senator from the Greek East introducing as
consul the Roman year.[98] By contrast, Statius Quadratus in 142,
Herodes Atticus in 143. The curious or the superficial will be aware
that Antoninus Pius (proconsul in Asia, 135/6) bore no great
affection to talkers and thinkers.[99] He was endowed with a gift for
quiet irony.[100]

---

[98] Apart from M. Antonius Hiberus (133), and possibly M. Antonius Rufinus (131).
[99] Incidents involving Polemo and Herodes are reported by Philostratus, *Vit. soph.* pp. 534
and 554.   [100] *Dig.* xxvii 1, 6, 2, 7 f., cf. W. Williams, *JRS* lxvi (1976), 75.

(8) *Society and letters.* After Tacitus and Juvenal the literature of the Latins went into an abrupt decline. The pride of the next age is Cornelius Fronto, from Cirta. Fronto had never governed a province, even as proconsul of praetorian rank. Concerning Asia, he spread himself on exertions for the abortive peregrination. They are not devoid of instruction. Elsewhere Fronto fails to allude to any proconsul of Asia as such.

For Africa compensation accrues from another sophist, of inferior station and dubious repute. Apuleius names several proconsuls. On Lollianus Avitus he lavished praise for style and eloquence, evoking for parallel the diverse virtues of the classic performers from Cato down to Hortensius and Cicero.[101] A sober tribute went to Claudius Maximus, before whom Apuleius spoke his defence in 158/9. The proconsul was at the same time a military man and an adept of the Stoic persuasion. He earns a firm commendation: 'virum tam austerae sectae tamque diutinae militiae'.[102] The reference to 'militia' may be carried and covered by the governorship of Pannonia Superior, where Maximus is on attestation in 150 and in 154 (xvi 99; 104). To look further back, one might ask whether Maximus had not been an equestrian officer, adlected to the Senate by Hadrian.

Like Flavius Arrianus (*suff.* 129 or 130), who wrote histories, Claudius Maximus serves to commend the education and taste of the age in its better aspects. The detrimental side is more on show.

Greek writers offer valuable sidelights on folly and superstition. Rutilianus, the son of Sisenna, worshipped the sacred serpent whom the prophet Alexander produced for a variety of the devout. Lucian showed up both of them; and no need to enlarge on Aelius Aristides, assiduous at oracles and | devout in reverence towards 'our lord Serapis' who causes the Nile to rise.

Aristides introduced five of the proconsuls, one at least a friend (Statius Quadratus), although not much emerges about their personalities, apart from Julius Severus. Aristides was not happy with the descendant of kings and tetrarchs. He described Severus as proud in temper, decisive in his manner;[103] and he let slip a damaging revelation. As Severus declared, 'it is all very well to parade as the foremost of the Hellenes for eloquence. You have to work and teach pupils.'[104]

---

[101] Apuleius, *Apol.* 95.
[102] *Apol.* 19. Maximus was cherished by Marcus Aurelius (*Ad se ipsum* 15, 1; 17, 10).
[103] Aristides, 1 71.
[104] Aristides, 1 87.

APPENDIX

The following list can be presented in the belief that it rests on a fairly firm basis. Certain conjectural or disputed names are omitted.

138/9	L. Venuleius Apronianus (*cos.* 123)
139/40	
140/1	M. (?) Valerius Propinquus (*suff.* 126)
141/2	
142/3	
143/4	
144/5	Ti. Claudius Julianus (129 or 130)
145/6	Ti. Claudius Quartinus (130)
146/7	
147/8	L. Antonius Albus (*c.*132)
148/9	Q. Flavius Tertullus (133)
149/50	Popillius Priscus (?134)
150/1	P. Mummius Sisenna (*cos.* 133)
151/2	T. Vitrasius Pollio (*suff.* ?136)
152/3	C. Julius Severus (?138)
153/4	
154/5	
155/6	
156/7	L. Statius Quadratus (*cos.* 142)
157/8	T. Statilius Maximus (*cos.* 144)
158/9	
159/60	
160/1	P. Mummius Sisenna Rutilianus (*suff.* 146).

19

Problems about Proconsuls of Asia

A BOOK eagerly awaited through long years has now appeared. It registers the proconsuls of Africa and Asia from 14 to 68, and it discusses, in lavish detail, family and kinsfolk, careers and political roles.[1] Asia should command the primary attention: more names on record by a third, a more illustrious company, and a number of intricate problems.

The most recent catalogues for Asia were published in 1941 and in 1950.[2] They betrayed certain inadequacies even then, and will seldom require to be cited. Improvements normally derive from epigraphy. As it happens, no new proconsuls of the period have thence accrued in the course of the last forty years.[3] However, a variety of documents turns up to entail revisions in dating. Proconsulates are determined or surmised from consulates, and conversely. Hence an abundance of hazards in the game. A number still subsist.

There is a further cause for annoyance, namely tampering with the procedure of sortition. For a time Tiberius Caesar was happy to enjoin or respect an interval of about ten years from a man's consulship. That is made clear by four proconsuls who fall between 20 and 26, namely

C. Junius Silanus (*cos.* 10)	20/1
M'. Aemilius Lepidus (11)	21/2
	22/3
C. Fonteius Capito (12)	?23/4
Sex. Pompeius (14)	?24/5
	25/6

---

[1] U. Vogel-Weidemann, *Die Statthalter von Africa und Asia in den Jahren 14–68 n. Chr. Eine Untersuchung zum Verhältnis Princeps und Senat* (1982), pp. 718. Here to be cited as 'V.-W.'

[2] S. J. de Laet, *De Samenstelling van den Romeinschen Senaat* etc. (1941), 240 f.; D. Magie, *Roman Rule in Asia Minor* (1950), 1581 f.

[3] Apart from two modifications. From *AE* 1933, 265 Ursula Weideman herself retrieved Sex. Nonius Quinctilianus (*cos.* 8), in *AClass* iii (1960), 93 ff.; and, instead of C. Pompeius Longinus Gallus (*cos.* 49), now stands Messalla Vipstanus Gallus (*suff.* ?48), cf. J. Devreker, *ZPE* xxii (1976), 202 ff.

Zeitschrift für Papyrologie und Epigraphik liii (1983), 191–208.

Concerning these four, it was noted that Fonteius Capito might go a year earlier. Further, that a *biennium* was not excluded for Sextus Pompeius.[4]

Then, by exception, in 26 M. Aemilius Lepidus (*cos.* 6) went out to Asia, to be prorogued for a second year (*AE* 1934, 87). In 29 began the sexennial tenure of P. Petronius (*suff.* 19), with for parallel M. Junius M. f. Silanus (*cos.* 19) in Africa. The conduct of the Princeps was highly de|trimental. He frustrated the legitimate aspirations of no fewer than ten ex-consuls. Consequences became apparent in the sequel. Of eight proconsuls in Asia from M. Aurelius Cotta Messallinus (*cos.* 20) in 35/6 to C. Sallustius Crispus Passienus (*suff.* 27) in 42/3, all but two suffered a long retardation, to find only two parallels before the last years of Trajan.

Trouble has been caused by several problems of identity in the high aristocracy. Cotta Messallinus, the younger son of Messalla Corvinus, comes up four times in Tacitus. For Borghesi, the same person as M. Aurelius Cotta, the consul of 20. Groag conceived strong doubts and accorded separate entries (*PIR*[2], A 1487 f.). Those doubts were soon dissipated.[5]

More vexatious in every way was the case of Marcus Lepidus, the consul of 6. He earned renown and the *ornamenta triumphalia* during the war in Illyricum, and Velleius styled him 'vir nomini ac fortunae Caesarum proximus' (ii 114, 5). That should have been enough. Marcus is patently the consular named *capax imperii* in the notorious anecdote concerning the last hours of Caesar Augustus (*Ann.* i 13, 2).

The axiom was firmly announced.[6] Little heed was paid in the sequel. Manius Lepidus (*cos.* 11) retained the preference, with resultant confusion about the dates of their proconsulates.[7] It became expedient to furnish a full exposition, which redistributed drastically the Tacitean references to the two Lepidi.[8]

The operation entailed an emendation of the text. Early in the year 21 a despatch from Caesar led to a discussion about proconsulates. Sex. Pompeius (*cos.* 14) exploited the occasion to launch an attack on 'Marcum Lepidum'. He derided Lepidus as 'socordem inopem et maioribus suis indecorum' (iii 32, 2). Whereupon senators came out

[4] *History in Ovid* (1978), 161.
[5] S. J. de Laet, *AC* vi (1937), 137 ff. With, however, the aberrant date 'rond 26/6' in his book (op. cit. 240).
[6] *Rom. Rev.* (1939), 433; *JRS* xxxix (1949), 7 = *Ten Studies in Tacitus* (1970), 60.
[7] Notably in D. Magie, op. cit. 1581, cf. 1362 f.
[8] *JRS* xlv (1955), 22 ff. = *Ten Studies in Tacitus* (1970), 30 ff. It affects *PIR*[2], A 363; 369; 422.

in defence: Lepidus was 'mitis magis quam ignavus'. And so Lepidus went to Asia.

Attack and defence are alike ludicrous if Marcus Lepidus was in cause. A *vir triumphalis* might be denounced as harsh or cruel, vicious or rapacious. On no account can he submit to the epithets of 'socors' or 'mitis'.

With the illustrious Sex. Pompeius, a kinsman of the dynasty, whom Ovid admired, two other authors come in. Valerius Maximus accompanied his patron to Asia (ii 6, 8). Not long after, Valerius had to mourn his decease (iv 7, *Ext*. 2).[9] The term and limit is given by the reference to Livia, still extant | among the living (vi 1, 1). She passed away at the beginning of 29. The denunciation of Seianus towards the end of the work (ix 11, *Ext*. 4) is a patent insertion, perhaps added on a second edition.

For the proconsulate of Pompeius a wide margin was at first left, from 27 to 30, and incautiously perpetuated.[10] Much too late, as indicated by his consulship in 14 and by the dates of some predecessors; and the *biennium* of Marcus Lepidus (*AE* 1934, 87) intervened to preclude. Therefore the tenure 24/5 seems the best choice.[11] It is worth stating that 23/4 is also available for Pompeius. One recalls his eager attack on M'. Lepidus (*cos*. 11) in 21—and in the near sequel ex-consuls happen not to be numerous (see below).

Next, identity and parentage. A standard work of reference came out with a consul suffect of 5 B.C., who never was.[12] Finally, the death of Sex. Pompeius, which Valerius Maximus reports, was overlooked. Seneca describes how Caligula reduced to death by starvation in the Palace an opulent Pompeius, his own kinsman—whom he accorded a public funeral (*De tranq*. 11, 10). The victim is manifestly a son of the consul, not often recognized and not elsewhere on attestation.[13] Inadvertence (to use no other word) has transferred Caligula's crime to the year 33.[14]

Lepidus and Pompeius show what can happen when scholars neglect to read texts with due attention. Lepidus serves also to illustrate anomalies in the accession to proconsulates. First, Lepidus stood high in favour with the ruler. Second, he was otherwise employed when his turn arrived, being Caesar's legate in Tarraconensis; and later on, in 21, he had declined an appointment to

---

[9] Not noted in *PIR*[1], P 450; V 82. Death subsequent to that of Livia was assumed by R. Helm, *RE* viiiA 92.

[10] Thus *c*.27 in *RE* viiiA 90; *OCD*[2] (1970), 1186.

[11] *History in Ovid* (1978), 161.   [12] R. Hanslik, *RE* xxi 2060; 2265.

[13] As suggested in *AJP* lxxix (1958), 21 = *Ten Studies in Tacitus* (1970), 82, cf. 143. That notion had in fact been put out in 1876, cf. R. Helm, *RE* viiiA 92.

[14] R. Hanslik, *RE* xxi 2267.

Africa, for adequate reasons, the best of which he chose not to avow (iii 35, 2). Third, a shortage of ex-consuls manifest in the year 26. Of those who held office in 13, C. Silius, under prosecution in 24, committed suicide; and Munatius Plancus may have been governing Pannonia.[15] Further, as it now appears, there were no suffect consuls in 13.[16] As for the next year, Sex. Appuleius was no longer among the living;[17] while Sex. Pompeius had Asia (probably for 24/5). The consuls of 15 were Drusus Caesar and Norbanus Flaccus. The latter is not heard of subsequently. There remains the | suffect, M. Junius C. f. Silanus. If Silanus wanted Asia, they could not have stopped a nobleman who exercised great 'potentia' (iii 24, 3), whom Caesar liked and admired (Dio lix 8, 5).

The consuls from the first *quinquennium* of the reign of Tiberius (the years 15 to 19 inclusive) exhibit a curious phenomenon.[18] Seventeen in number, but scant signs of success. Only one was selected to govern a province in the portion of Caesar, namely Pomponius Flaccus (*cos.* 17), and that not until the year 33. Ti. Caesar kept a rigorous preference for consuls from the last decade of the previous reign. As concerns proconsuls in Asia and Africa, only four. The sexennial tenures of P. Petronius and M. Silanus have already been registered. The other two proconsuls are Vibius Marsus (*suff.* 17) and Rubellius Blandus (18), both in Africa.

At this point it will be convenient to insert the Tiberian proconsuls down to P. Petronius, according to the new catalogue.[19] Also expedient, since one of them (Favonius) has to be dealt with in an excursus later on.

C. Vibius Postumus	(*suff.* 5)	12–15
		15/16
Sex. Nonius Quinctilianus	(*cos.* 8)	?16/17
Q. Poppaeus Secundus	(*suff.* 9)	?17/18
		18/19
C. Junius Silanus	(*cos.* 10)	20/1
M'. Aemilius Lepidus	(11)	21/2
C. Fonteius Capito	(12)	?22/3
		23/4
Favonius		24/5 (or 25/6)

---

[15] *CIL* vi 1743, as interpreted by J. Morris, *BJ* clxv (1965), 88 ff.

[16] S. Panciera, *BCAR* 1963/4 (1966), 94 ff.

[17] As argued in *History in Ovid* (1978), 152; 159.

[18] For these consuls, *Historia* xxx (1981), 189 ff. = *RP* iii (1984), 1350 ff.

[19] V.-W. 582. It is unfortunate that the lists of proconsuls are not equipped with their consular dates.

Sex. Pompeius	(*cos.* 14)	24/5 (or 25/6)
M. Aemilius Lepidus	(*cos.* 6)	26–8
		28/9
P. Petronius	(*suff.* 19)	?29–35.

The repertorium presents thirty-nine names, which yield some valuable sequences. They are interrupted by nine vacant years. As follows. Under Tiberius 15/16, 18/19, 19/20, 23/4; under Claudius 44–8; under Nero 60/1.

At the same time, two additional years had to be borne in mind. First, 28/9. M. Lepidus might have been prorogued for a third term, so it is conjectured.[20] That is most attractive. For parallel stands Vibius Marsus in Africa for a *triennium* (*ILS* 9375): perhaps 27–30, better 26–9.[21] The conse|quence is not without interest. Installed on Capreae in 27, the ruler at once began these prorogations. As for the prudent Lepidus, no need to add a personal reason for absence from the noxious atmosphere of the capital. His daughter was married to Drusus, the second son of Agrippina—who along with Nero was put under arrest at the beginning of 29.

Second, 41/2. Passienus Crispus (*suff.* 27) is assigned to 42/3 (consul for the second time in 44). The notion was canvassed that he held the province for the previous year as well.[22] It is now annulled. A tenant for that year has since come to light, viz. P. Lentulus Scipio (*suff.* 24). On whom, see below.

Diligence is baffled by time as well as chance. Since the large book was consigned to the printer, a *quinquennium* elapsed. During that period several revisions of accepted dates emerged, and two notable inscriptions. The author has therefore been under constraint to furnish a substantial addendum.[23] The most significant changes can be resumed under two names.

First, C. Vibius Rufinus. His consular colleague was M. Cocceius Nerva: to be identified with the jurist, who was appointed to the charge of the Roman aqueducts in 24. Thus Groag with no indication of doubt (*PIR*[2], C 1225). A vacancy is available for this pair in either 21 or 22. Degrassi and others dissented. They preferred the son of the jurist (not yet attested as a consul), and assigned the pair to the vicinity of 40. Rufinus' proconsulate of Asia therefore fell a decade later. The tenure 50/1 was suggested in this book.[24]

---

[20] V.-W. 268.   [21] V.-W. 92 f.   [22] V.-W. 326 f.
[23] *ZPE* xlvi (1982), 271–94: with revised lists for the periods 35–43 (ibid. 291) and 61–9 (293).
[24] V.-W. 362 ff.

Meanwhile Rufinus was acquiring clear identity as a friend of Ovid who had served under Tiberius in the northern wars (*Ex Ponto* iii 4, 5, cf. 64). He is the son of the elderly Vibius Rufus (*suff.* 16), and nothing precludes a consulship in 21 or 22.

As for Asia, there stood impediments: Cotta Messallinus (*cos.* 20) presumably in 35/6, P. Lentulus Scipio (*suff.* 24) in 36/7, C. Calpurnius Aviola (*suff.* 24) in 37/8. Indeed, Scipio and Aviola were considered firm and fixed.[25] That held for the latter, but not for the former.

Despite these difficulties, declared not insuperable, a case was made out for Vibius Rufinus as proconsul in 36/7.[26] Asia has recently come up with a welcome surprise. An inscription from Lydia shows that Lentulus Scipio was proconsul in the reign of Claudius Caesar.[27] The revised list as now printed runs as follows:[28] |

M. Aurelius Cotta Messallinus	(*cos.* 20)	?35/6
C. Vibius Rufinus	(*suff.* 21 or 22)	?36/7
C. Calpurnius Aviola	(24)	37/8
C. Asinius Pollio	(*cos.* 23)	?38/9
M. Vinicius	(30)	?39/40
C. Cassius Longinus	(*suff.* 30)	40/1
P. Cornelius Lentulus Scipio	(24)	?41/2
C. Sallustius Crispus Passienus	(27)	?42/3

The wide variations in consular seniority will duly be noted, as conveying the caprice of the Caesars or the influence of their ministers.[29] The next proconsul will be presumed Paullus Fabius Persicus (*cos.* 34). Then a gap is assumed of four years, until Memmius Regulus (*suff.* 31), ?48/9, followed by Didius Gallus (39), ?49/50. A long sequence then took over—that is, until broken now by the expulsion of Vibius Rufinus from the tenure 50/1.

Rufinus removed, it is permissible to suggest a revision in dates for four proconsuls and put them in a regular order between Didius Gallus and Iunius Silanus, proconsul in 54. As follows:

A. Didius Gallus	(*suff.* 39)	49/50
Cn. Domitius Corbulo	(39)	50/1
P. Suillius Rufus	(?41)[29A]	51/2

[25] V.-W. 292; 296. Cf. 582.
[26] *History in Ovid* (1978), 85 f.; *ZPE* xliii (1981), 374 f. = *RP* iii (1984), 1433 f.
[27] From Hierocaesareia. Now *Inschr. von Ephesos* iii, no. 659.
[28] V.-W., *ZPE* xlvi (1982), 291.
[29] Oberve also, in the vicinity of some retarded aristocrats, Q. Marcius Barea Soranus (*suff.* 34) going to Africa in 44 and prorogued for a year (V.-W. 135 f.).
[29A] The date of Suillius' consulship may require revision, perhaps to 44 or 45, cf. A. R. Birley, *The Fasti of Roman Britain* (1981), 41; 225.

L. Pedanius Secundus	(43)	52/3
Ti. Plautius Silvanus Aelianus	(45)	53/4
M. Junius Silanus	(*cos.* 46)	54

In support of which notion, it may be observed that a decennial interval has now resumed at last and finds fairly close observance in the sequel down to 68, though minor variations occur—and premature certitudes are to be deprecated all through.

In the foregoing list of proconsuls, not proposed from any sense of conviction, occurs Plautius Aelianus, transferred from 55/6.[30] At this point it is advisable to insert a warning note. Between M. Silanus, who as 'prima novo principatu mors' perished from poison in Asia towards the end of 54, and 58/9, which is occupied by Vipstanus Poplicola (the consul of 48), various problems subsist, or newly arise. They will be discussed lower down. For the rest, only one gap after 59 (namely 60/1) until Nero's end.

Second, A. Ducenius Geminus. His consular year was indeterminate (*PIR*[2], D 201), but a temptation emerged to discover him in the 'A[' disclosed by an inscription at Tibur as colleague of a M. Junius Silanus (otherwise | unknown) in 54 or 55.[31] In 62 Ducenius was one of three consulars appointed to report on taxation (*Ann.* xv 18, 3). An inscription at Narona showed him legate of Dalmatia (*ILS* 9484). Finally, Galba made him Prefect of the City (*Hist.* i 14, 1) in the place of Flavius Sabinus.

That was not all. An acephalous and fragmentary dedication at Epidaurus (*ILS* 963) revealed a senator, proconsul of Asia, who had been governor of Dalmatia, who held the same pair of priesthoods as certified at Narona. It was not easy to resist those plain facts. Thus Groag in *PIR*[2], D 201. It remained to establish a date for Ducenius' tenure of Asia. Highly plausible seemed 67/8, and it tended to be adopted.[32]

However, 66/7 was not excluded, and a new candidate for 67/8 found recent sponsorship, namely M. Aponius Saturninus.[33] His consular year had been a subject of various debate. Several reasons speak for the vicinity of 55. In 57 Aponius was one of the Arval Brethren, a company still select and not easily accessible to senators

[30] Thus placed in V.-W. 405.

[31] *CIL* xiv 3741 (Tibur), cf. *Historia* v (1956), 210 = *RP* (1979), 322.

[32] V.-W. 462, with a query. *PIR*[2], D 201 had 'fortasse'. Firm and confident, P. A. Gallivan, *CQ* xxiv (1974), 300.

[33] *Some Arval Brethren* (1980), 67 ff.; *Historia* xxxi (1982), 465 = p. 120, above. It is there argued that he proceeded from Asia to Moesia in 68, by appointment from Galba. Aponius Saturninus had previously been supposed a proconsul under Vespasian (?73/4).

other than the nobility, unless already consular. He originated from the province Baetica. As with other promotions in this season, the patronage of Annaeus Seneca will be suitably invoked.

Whichever the proconsular year of Ducenius Geminus, it is now thrown forward, if not annulled. A document at Ephesus registers the three commissioners in order of rank: A. Pompeius Paullinus (*suff. c.*54), L. Calpurnius Piso (*cos.* 57), A. Ducenius Geminus.[34] The consulship of Ducenius has to go in 60 or 61, so it appears. No proconsulate therefore in the late years of Nero. And further, the attribution of the Epidaurus inscription becomes dubious and may well have to be discarded.[35]

By good fortune, the revised catalogue was able to take account of the new document. Ducenius Geminus goes out. He is replaced in 67/8 by Aponius Saturninus. The last Neronian years now present the following pattern:[36]

Q. Marcius Barea Soranus	(*suff.* 52)	?61/2
P. Volasenna	(?54)	?62/3
L. Salvius Otho Titianus	(*cos.* 52)	63/4
L. Antistius Vetus	(55)	64/5
M'. Acilius Aviola	(54)	65/6
M. Aefulanus	(*suff. c.*55)	?66/7
M. Aponius Saturninus	(?55)	?67/8.

So far three lists concerning the reigns of Claudius and Nero have been set forth. The first conveys a firm sequence (but highly variegated) from 35 to 43. The second introduces four proconsuls in strict order of seniority (but only hypothetical). The third takes its inception after the gap in 60/1.

All of the nine original vacancies remain open. Vibius Rufinus, expelled from 50/1, adds a tenth. Moreover, as already indicated, there is trouble lurking early in the first half of Nero's reign.

For a variety of reasons it may now be useful to subjoin several conjectures or hypotheses. The study of consuls and provincial governors avows an experimental science. It proceeds by trial and error. No harm or deception ensues if it is seen for what it is. Previous experience declares the inherent hazards. One way or another, an inscription may vouchsafe a decision. As has been amply

---

[34] W. Eck, *ZPE* xlii (1981), 227 ff.
[35] Ibid. 230. For the present he prefers an *Ignotus*. See further below.
[36] V.-W., *ZPE* xlvi (1982), 293.

demonstrated, a single document can have wide and manifold repercussions.

Under that proviso, the following items will be put up for inspection.

(1) *Favonius.* This proconsul was disclosed by an acephalous inscription found near Ipsus in Phrygia (*JRS* ii (1912), 240, whence *ILS* 9483)

....
FAVONIO COS. PRO
COS. ASIAE XV VIRO
SACR. FACIENDIS SODA
LI AUGUSTAL. IIIVIR. CEN
TUR. EQUIT. RECOGNOSC.
CENSORIA POTESTAT.
LEG. DIVI AUGUSTI ET TI.
CAESARIS AUGUSTI
....

Favonius is plagued with problems of singular complexity, and he failed to attract much attention since the year 1912. Which can be understood. In the present place only a rigorously compressed treatment can be offered.

Favonius is a consul from the late years of Caesar Augustus or the early epoch of his successor, in any case not later than 18, for the latest year he could occupy as proconsul of Asia is 28/9 (assuming that M. Lepidus did not prolong his *biennium*). But not necessarily a consul hitherto unknown since 'Favonius' is a *cognomen*, indicating the maternal ascendance.[37]

Favonius earns a full discussion in the new repertorium. At the head of the entry stands 'cos. suff. 13 (?)' with for the proconsulate '24–5 (25–26?)'.[38] The following remarks are pertinent. |

(1) A consulship in 13. Consuls suffect in this year have caused much vexation. Was C. Silius P. f. A. Caecina Largus, opening the year as colleague of L. Munatius Plancus, one person or two?[39] The problem has recently found a precise answer. A neglected funerary inscription at Rome carries the date 'L. Planco C. Caec. cos.'.[40] C. Silius was in fact polyonymous, carrying the item 'A. Caecina

[37] As to be presumed (rather than adoption) for P. Sulpicius Quirinius (*cos.* 12 B.C.).

[38] V.-W. 253, for the consular year, following A. Degrassi, *Epigraphica* viii (1946), 34 ff. For the proconsulate, the same alternate years as assumed for Sex. Pompeius (*cos.* 14).

[39] Following A. E. and J. S. Gordon, the case for two persons was argued in *JRS* lvi (1966), 56 ff. Favonius was discussed—and there rejected as a *suffectus* of 13 (59 f.).

[40] S. Panciera, *BCAR* 1963–4 (1966), 95, whence *AE* 1966, 16.

Largus' either through adoption (and if so in an anomalous position) or because it was the name of his mother's father.[41] The notion of suffect consuls in 13 appears to lapse entirely.[42]

(2) The post of 'IIIvir centur(iis) equit(um) recognosc(endis) censoria potestat(e)'. For which, observe Suetonius, *Divus Aug.* 37, 1. It should be consular. Compare the similar post registered by Tacitus in the obituary notice of L. Volusius Saturninus (*suff.* 12 B.C.), namely 'censoria etiam potestate legendis equitum decuriis functus' (*Ann.* iii 30, 1).

(3) Favonius as legate of Augustus and Tiberius. When Augustus died, all of the legates in the seven consular commands are on attestation. Hence the suggestion of Groag (*PIR*², F 121). Favonius commanded an army in the northern campaigns between 4 and 12: Ti. Caesar is wrongly styled 'Augustus'.

That was a harsh and extreme remedy. An alternative offered.[43] In the campaigns of 15 Germanicus Caesar had with him another consular legate, apart from the commanders of the two armies (C. Silius and Caecina Severus). A casual mention brings in L. Apronius (*suff.* 8), left behind in an invasion of Germany to build roads and bridges (*Ann.* i 56, 1)—and only named (it is a fair inference) because he was to receive the *ornamenta triumphalia* at the end of the year (72, 1).

That fact encourages one to look at the year 13. A campaign of Tiberius and Germanicus, almost missing record and not to be deemed important, issued in imperatorial acclamations.[44] If Favonius was a legate, say from 12 or 13 until the beginning of 15, his occlusion is no surprise. He may well have left for Asia (see below).

(4) Identity. Marcus Favonius is on high exhibit in history (and in literature) as a stubborn and fanatical adherent of Cato. He perished when the Republic went down at Philippi, executed after insulting words to the | address of Caesar's heir.[45] The *nomen* is extremely rare.[46] The consul can be claimed without discomfort as a descendant.

---

[41] See now the full discussion in *Epigrafia e ordine senatorio* i (1982), 405 ff. = pp. 159 ff., above.

[42] Thus Panciera, whom the author in fact cites as having 'festgestellt, daß im Jahre 13 nur zwei consules ordinarii fungierten' (253, n. 273).

[43] Adduced in *JRS* lvi (1966), 60.

[44] As argued in *History in Ovid* (1978), 53 ff.; *Phoenix* xxxiii (1979), 317 ff. = *RP* iii (1984), 1206 ff. That campaign explains the 'novies' of *Ann.* ii 36, 3. Namely 8 and 7 B.C.; A.D. 4–6 and 10–13.

[45] Suetonius, *Divus Aug.* 13, 2; Dio xlvii 49, 4. Favonius' absence from the list in Velleius ii 71, 2 f. has aroused speculation. It should be noted that Velleius is exemplifying a carnage of aristocrats, *clarissimi viri*.

[46] M.Favonius was municipal, from Tarracina (cf. *ILS* 879). In 'Sallust', *Ep.* ii 9, 4, he belongs to 'inertissimi nobiles'.

Of late Augustan consuls, it is not easy to bring up one to whom the *cognomen* 'Favonius' might suitably adhere. Hardly a *nobilis*. Attention diverts to Lucilius Longus, consul suffect in 7.[47] He died in 23, having been an intimate friend of the ruler, 'omnium illi tristium laetorumque socius'. In fact, the sole senator with him at Rhodes. And so, abnormal honour: 'quamquam novo homini censorium funus' (*Ann.* iv 15, 1). A link has been surmised with Lucilius, that devoted friend of Brutus who stayed with Antonius in long loyalty till the end.[48] Republican allegiances and predilections in Ti. Caesar need no illustration.

Neither do the hazards in this sort of reconstruction. A hypothesis has here been propounded that conflicts with no known evidence. A new proconsul might wreck it.

(5) The date of the proconsulate. After the *triennium* of C. Vibius Postumus (*suff.* 5), assigned to 12–15, follows a year's gap, then Sex. Nonius Quinctilianus (*cos.* 8), and Q. Poppaeus Secundus (*suff.* 9). The vacant tenure 15/16 is highly suitable for a suffect consul of 7. Of the consuls of 6, M. Lepidus was absent governing Tarraconensis (cf. *PIR*², A 369), while L. Arruntius was occupied in 15, charged with reporting on the Tiber floods (*Ann.* i 70, 1; 79, 1), and the suffect L. Nonius Asprenas had Africa. As concerns 7, Lucilius Longus was the sole *suffectus*. A. Licinius Nerva Silianus had perished soon after his consulship (Velleius ii 116, 4), and Q. Metellus Creticus was now Caesar's legate in Syria. Observe Africa for parallel, viz. L. Nonius Asprenas (*suff.* 6) from 12 to 15; L. Aelius Lamia (*cos.* 3), retarded, in 15/16; A. Vibius Habitus (*suff.* 8) in 16/17.[49]

To conclude. Dates appear to fit. Unless another consul suffect can be established for A.D. 7, Favonius should be held identical with Lucilius Longus. He was a legate on the Rhine (in 14 for certain), proceeding in 15 to Asia. Some civic distinction was desirable to justify a public funeral for Longus, exorbitant if only to commend 'amicitia' and 'fides'. Young Asinius Saloninus was in a different case, being close kin to the dynasty: 'fratre Druso insignis Caesarique progener destinatus' (iii 75, 1). |

(2) C. Stertinius Maximus (*suff.* 23). No provincial post is on record, but an official occupation in the Aegean lands at some time or other

---

[47] Probably from Aricia, cf. *Eph. Ep.* vii 1236: a decree of the local senate with his name in large letters towards the end. The editor observed 'nomen eius quid hic sibi voluerit nescio'.

[48] Plutarch, *Brutus* 50; *Antonius* 69. Cf. *Rom. Rev.* (1939), 434 f.

[49] When Lamia's year arrived, he was occupied 'in Germania Illyricoque' (Velleius ii 116, 3). Perhaps, when on the Rhine, comparable to L. Apronius and to Favonius.

has been surmised.[50] He left his name by a double imprint. First,
C. Stertinius Xenophon, the imperial doctor (*SIG*[3] 804: Cos).
Second, C. Stertinius Orpex, his freedman, 'quondam scriba
librarius' (*AE* 1935, 169: Ephesus).

Nobody takes Stertinius for a proconsul of Asia. No place seemed
open. An expedient is to hand—a proconsul dying or removed half-
way through his tenure. There is the case of C. Cassius Longinus
(*suff.* 30). Caligula shortly before his end, warned by a prediction of
menace from a Cassius, had him brought in chains to Rome (Dio lix
29, 3, cf. Suetonius, *Cal.* 57, 3).

This vacancy was in fact briefly adduced in discussion about the
vexatious problems caused by proconsulates between 35 and 42.[51]
The normal deputy is the senior legate in the province. Nevertheless,
in this painfully crowded period ambition might not disdain six
months in Asia, if Caesar or the managers of patronage concurred;
and a governor of low rank was no compliment to the cities of
ancient pride.

Hence sharp relevance to what happened after M. Silanus was
poisoned in November or December of the year 54 (*Ann.* xiii 1): see
below, on the rank and the dating of Marius Cordus. And a parallel
obtains. M. Plancius Varus, legate in Asia, has his name on coins of
Apamea: presumably acting governor when Fonteius Agrippa was
called to Moesia in the autumn of 69.[52] But certainly not for the
whole remaining tenure. M. Suillius Nerullinus (*cos.* 50) supervenes,
followed by the triennial governorship of Eprius Marcellus, from 70
to 73.[53]

Finally, Minicius Italus, 'proc. provinciae Asiae quam mandatu
principis vice defuncti procos. rexit' (*ILS* 1374). That is, after the
suppression of Civica Cerialis, probably in the winter of 88/9. No
sign of how long the scandalous anomaly lasted.

A peculiar phenomenon calls for passing mention. Through more
than two centuries from the Battle of Actium to the decease of
Marcus Aurelius no proconsul of Asia happens to be certified as
dying a natural death, even in seasons of pestilence. Asia was not so
insalubrious, it is true, as Syria, which contributes a whole
catalogue. And mortality at the capital corresponds: youthful
aristocrats in sure prospect of the *fasces* and consuls succumbing
either in office or soon after.

These facts comport a useful consequence. If at any time it appears

[50] *RE* iiiA 2455.
[51] *ZPE* xliii (1981), 374 = *RP* iii (1984), 1433 f.
[52] S. Jameson, *JRS* lv (1965), 58.
[53] W. Eck, *Senatoren von Vespasian bis Hadrian* (1970), 83.

difficult to fit in some plausible proconsul, the hypothesis of a providential death may be cheerfully entertained. |

(3) P. Memmius Regulus (*suff.* 31). Like a number of predecessors, a retarded proconsul. He was assigned by conjecture to 48/9.[54] That is, at the end of the lacuna between Paullus Fabius Persicus (?43/4) and Didius Gallus (?49/50), leading on to the sequence of five as now by innovation proposed, from Domitius Corbulo to M. Silanus in 54 (cf. above).

A neglected document from Tusculum can be brought into play (*CIL* xiv 2612). Of the three fragments, the first two belong together,

> PRO·COS·Asiae·per·TRI
> HIC·LECTUS EST·AB·DIVO CLAUDI

That is to say, a consular who had been adlected by Claudius Caesar (either to rank in the Senate or to the patriciate), and was also proconsul of Asia for three years. To cut the matter short, Eprius Marcellus seemed the man (*suff.* 62), proconsul of Asia from 70 to 73 (*ILS* 992, cf. *PIR*[2], E 74).

No dissent ensued. By mishap, the third fragment had been overlooked, namely ']REM OPTINUI['. It indicates a fairly long and explicit recital, in the manner of an *elogium*, compare *ILS* 918 (Tibur), for many years a cause of 'inextricabilis error'.

Two provinces and two only come into the reckoning. First, Hispania Citerior. In the year 41 Claudius Caesar recalled Ap. Silanus (*cos.* 28) from Tarraconensis to take on as husband the mother of Valeria Messallina.[55] No other governor is discoverable for two decades until Ser. Galba went there in 60. Galba's tenure excludes a consul of 62, and Eprius in particular.

Nothing is known to disallow a brief governorship of Tarraconensis by Regulus when he vacated Moesia in 44 (after a tenure of nine years). Only the fact that, if Regulus had held two consular provinces, it was ignored by Pergamum and by Delphi when they paid him honour during or after the proconsulate in Asia. Not conclusive, since both documents register only the essential titles. Thus, along with consulship and priesthoods, 'legat. Augu[storum propr.' (*ILS* 962, cf. 8815).

Yet due hesitation will be conceived about Tarraconensis. Hispania Ulterior also comes in, a praetorian province. If admitted, a proconsulate of Baetica at once rules out Eprius Marcellus. His

---

[54] Because of the 'littera Claudiana' in the text of *ILS* 962 (Pergamum). It was introduced in 47 (*Ann.* xi 13, 2). Therefore 47/8 is as good as 48/9.   [55] Dio lx 14, 3.

province was known. Subsequent to his governorship of Lycia–Pamphylia (?53–6), and not discredited by the ensuing prosecution (*Ann.* xiii 33, 3), Eprius went on to annex as proconsul gratitude from Cyprus (*ILS* 992: Capua; *SEG* xviii 589: Paphos). |

Eprius Marcellus engrossed early success, shoved into the praetorship for the last day of 48 through the potent influence of L. Vitellius (xii 4, 3). If he were awarded the Tusculan fragments, he might have been an *adlectus inter tribunicios*.[56] The notion that Eprius was admitted to the patriciate by Claudius Caesar will not enlist fanciers. That honour may now accrue to Memmius Regulus, patently in high esteem from four Caesars in succession, and not needing the testimony proffered by Nero in an anecdote that adorns the necrological notice (xiv 47, 1).

Tusculum discloses a *triennium* in Asia, either for Regulus or for an *Ignotus*. If an *Ignotus*, this proconsul had either 44–7 or 45–8. If Regulus, 46–9. Or better perhaps 45–8, since *ILS* 962 (with the 'littera Claudiana') can belong to 47. Either hypothesis (*Ignotus* or Regulus) might help to explain why the eminent Regulus, consul in 31, is not sooner discovered in Asia after vacating the Moesian command in 44.

Finally, the *triennium* reduces to either one year or to two years the interval between Fabius Persicus (43/4) and Didius Gallus (49/50). If one opts for Regulus, he was proconsul from 45 to 48 or from 46 to 49.[57] Hence two late Tiberian consuls were denied Asia. Africa provides the next parallel. M. Pompeius Silvanus (*suff.* 45) baffled prosecution in 58 through wealth and influence (xiii 50, 2). He had been proconsul from 53 to 56.[58]

(4) Marius Cordus. He was not a consular, so it is argued, but a praetorian, occupying in 54/5 the last six or seven months vacated by M. Silanus.[59] The list following down to Barea Soranus (after which it is continuous till Nero's end) was thus presented:

Ti. Plautius Silvanus Aelianus	(*suff.* 45)	?55/6
M. Vettius Niger		?56/7
Q. Allius Maximus	(*suff.* 49)	57/8
L. Vipstanus Poplicola	(*cos.* 48)	58/9
Messalla Vipstanus Gallus	(*suff.* ?48)	59/60
Ignotus		60/1
Q. Marcius Barea Soranus	(*suff.* 52)	?61/2.

---

[56] Thus, discussing the Paphian inscription, K. R. Bradley, *SO* liii (1978), 174.

[57] For African prorogations about this time observe Q. Marcius Barea Soranus (*suff.* 34) in 41–3 and Ser. Sulpicius Galba (*cos.* 33), presumably 44–6.

[58] *IRT* 338; *AE* 1968, 349 (Lepcis).   [59] V.-W. 400 ff.

Several comments are called for. First Plautius Silvanus can be thrown back two years, to 53/4 (cf. above), hence by the way parallel to the first year of Pompeius Silvanus (*suff.* 45) in Africa.

Second, Marius Cordus could have 55/6, M. Vettius Niger retaining the next year. Their consulships may fall in 47 (the list for 46 is full). |

Third, Cordus and Niger are known only from coins of the κοινόν of Phrygia struck at Apamea: the reverses are closely similar.[60] It might be contended, it is true, that neither was a proconsul of consular rank, the analogy being the coins of M. Plancius Varus of late 69.[61] In that instance, however, the consular Suillius Nerullinus, as has been shown, turned up to occupy the first half of the year 70, preceding Eprius Marcellus.

Fourth, for present purposes both Cordus and Niger will be assumed consular proconsuls, falling within the period 55–8—since a proconsul now has to be expunged. That is, the next item.

(5) Q. Allius Maximus (*suff.* 49), claimed for 57/8. It is awkward that the fellow should come in ahead of Vipstanus Messalla, the aristocratic consul of 48. That is not the worst.

This proconsul is equipped with a firm date—and no query. The source of certitude is worth looking for. According to the *Acta Timothei*, Paul installed Timothy as bishop of Ephesus in the reign of Nero when Maximus was proconsul; and Usener[62] over a century ago supplied identity with the consul suffect of 49. Credit, albeit not always complete, was accorded in the sequel.[63] *PIR* (both editions) had 'fortasse'. That was going too far.

'Maximus' is one of the commonest of all *cognomina*. The *Historia Augusta* duly dishes up a centurion of that name to serve as father for an emperor (*Prob.* 3, 2). For the Ephesian document, let an expert enquirer be heard: 'les hagiographes n'ont jamais été embarrassés pour recruter leur personnel. Ne nous extasions donc pas devant la précision chronologique, très illusoire, de nos Actes.' And further, 'notre hagiographe est donc un simple compilateur et de plus un faussaire.'[64]

So much for Q. Allius Maximus. The document has caused further ravages. After furnishing curious particulars about the life of

[60] V.-W. 400 f.; 419.

[61] Thus S. Mitchell, *JRS* lxiv (1974), 79. Both are expelled from the rubric of Claudian consuls by P. A. Gallivan, *CQ* xxviii (1978), 411, n. 14.   [62] H. Usener, *Acta S. Timothei* (1877), 16.

[63] De Laet, with no query (op. cit. 147; 241); Magie, with a query (op. cit. 1582).

[64] H. Delehaye, *Anatolian Studies . . . Buckler* (1939), 80; 82. He had missed the article of J. Keil, *JÖAI* xxix (1935), 82 ff. Keil, putting emphasis on the author's topographical knowledge, was disposed to accept Q. Allius Maximus in 57/8 (ibid. 83)—and further to support 'Peregrinus' as proconsul under Nerva.

the bishop (notably the genesis of the first three gospels) the narration tells how he came to grief when trying to interrupt a pagan festival at Ephesus. He died on January 24, in the reign of Nerva, Peregrinus being proconsul.

Peregrinus was not allowed an entry in *PIR*[1]: the editor, Hermann Dessau, had a fine nose for names, and for bogus characters. None the less, name as | well as date has aroused amicable solicitude.[65] And scholars became aware of the item 'P. Delphius Peregrinus' in the nomenclature of Nonius Mucianus, consul suffect in 138 (*CIL* v 3343: Verona).

If the foregoing remarks were to be accepted, the untenanted years in the reigns of Claudius and Nero would stand as follows: (*a*) two years in the period from 44 to 49 which includes the conjectured *triennium* of Memmius Regulus; (*b*) in 55–8 either one year or two, according to whether Marius Cordus had a normal full year. (*c*) 60/1, before Barea Soranus.

(6) The *Ignotus* at Epidaurus (*ILS* 963). He was held identical with Ducenius Geminus (*PIR*[2], D 201), one reason being the pair of priesthoods, as attested on the inscription at Narona (*ILS* 9484). As explained above, the new Ephesian document recording the three consular tax commissioners entails 60 or 61 for his consulship. Further, if Ducenius was proconsul of Asia, that post moves forward to displace Aponius Saturninus (*suff. c.*55), who can be assigned the tenure 67/8 instead of ?73/4.[66]

The assignment of the Epidaurian inscription thus became dubious.[67] Not but what a claim could be put up. The text is reproduced by Dessau as follows:

```
. . . . . [Aesculapio?] . . . .d. d.
q. prov. Cretae et Cyren]arum, trib. pl.
. . . . . . . [XVvir s]acr. fac., sodalis
[Augustalis] . . . . . . . leg. Caesarum
                    [D]almatiae et exercitus
[Illyrici, procos.]provinc. Asiae
```

A variety of points arises. First, structure of the document. Recourse to *CIL* iii 7267 shows that the reproduction is inadequate and

---

[65] Peregrinus occurs in the senatorial rubric of 'certi' in A. Garzetti, *Nerva* (1950), 148; and he finds support from Keil, followed by B. Kreiler, *Die Statthalter Kleinasiens unter den Flaviern* (Diss. Munich 1975), 65: 'es ist deshalb anzunehmen, daß im Jahre 96/97 ein bisher nicht identifizierbarer Peregrinus Prokonsul in Asien war.' Not, however, to be found in the repertorium of W. Eck.

[66] As in *Some Arval Brethren* (1980), 69; *Historia* xxxi (1982), 465 = p. 120, above.

[67] W. Eck, *ZPE* xlii (1981), 230, as noted above.

misleading. The second line demands name and tribe of the dedicant, if not pre-quaestorian posts as well. Hence ll. 2 and 5 comport close on fifty letters, with half a dozen fewer for ll. 3 and 4. Several tentative restorations will bear this out. Furthermore, the last line exhibits abnormally wide spacing, namely 'provinc.   Asiae'.

Second, in l. 3 the praetorship and some praetorian post or posts no doubt led up to the consulate and the first priesthood. After the third, ample space avails in l. 4 for 'curator vectigalium public.' |

Third, the imperial governorships. The term 'leg. Caesarum' furnishes a clue. In the first place for economy, when a governor bridged two reigns. Compare, for three, Memmius Regulus, 'legat. Augu[storum' (*ILS* 962).

For a tenure beginning under Caligula, there offers 'legat. Caesarum provinciae Lusita.' (*CIL* vi 1544). That is, Carminius Vetus (*suff.* 51), attested in Lusitania in 44 (*AE* 1950, 217). Again, Pomponius Rufus (*suff.* 95) as 'leg. imperatorum' in Dalmatia.[68] He entered office there as praetorian, but went on into Nerva's reign, so it appears. Like 'Caesarum' the economical formula 'imperatorum' conveniently masks the name of a condemned ruler.

In the present instance therefore Nero, to whose late epoch belongs the Dalmatian governorship of Ducenius Geminus. Indeed, Galba summoned him thence in 68 to be Prefect of the City, so it can be argued; and Galba appointed in his place one of the 'divites senes', namely Pompeius Silvanus (*suff.* 45).[69]

So far Dalmatia. What of the missing province that preceded? Not consular. It is absent from the Narona inscription, which registered Ducenius as 'curator vectigalium publicorum'. Further, for a consular to proceed to Dalmatia as his second province was a declension in this season. Dalmatia had forfeited one of its two legions. VII Claudia went to Moesia, either to replace IV Scythica, transferred to the East in 57—or perhaps a decade earlier.

Therefore one of the praetorian provinces in the portion of Caesar. The collocation is economical and defensible, provided the temporal order was respected. In descending order Pomponius Rufus shows 'M]oesiae, Dalmat., Hisp.' (*IRT* 537).[70] Compare Didius Julianus at a much later date, 'German]iae, Dalmatiae, Belgica[e' (*ILS* 412: Rome).

No problem therefore. One can supplement l. 5 with a praetorian

[68] On the new fragment from Curictae, published by A. and J. Šašel, *Situla* xix (1978), no. 942.

[69] *Historia* xxxi (1982), 464; 479 = pp. 120, 134, above. On this hypothesis both he and Aponius Saturninus owed their commands to Galba, not to Nero (as most had assumed).

[70] The Tarraconensian post of Rufus was that of *iuridicus* only, cf. G. Alföldy, *Fasti Hispanienses* (1969), 71 ff.

province: *exempli gratia* Aquitania, which was likely to destine a man for the consulate (Tacitus, *Agr.* 9, 1), as recently Duvius Avitus, between praetorship and 'leg. pro pr. exerc[it.] Germ. infer.' (*ILS* 979: Vasio). Furthermore, instead of 'D]almatiae et exercitus/ [Illyrici', a longer formula, if it suits the space. The inscription of Popillius Pedo (*suff.* 147), set up nearly a century later, preserves old-fashioned terminology: 'legato........pro pr. Germaniae super. et exercitus in ea tendentis' (*ILS* 1071: Tibur). However, if Ducenius is conceded, 'praef. urbi' follows suitably.

That is not the end of the matter. Another copy of the inscription as printed in *IG* iv² 439 shows wide spacing between each and every item. In reference to that copy, and with due and necessary reservations, the last three lines could be supplemented as follows:

leg. Caesarum
pro pr. provinc. Aquitanicae et D]almatiae et exercitus
Illyrici praef. urbi procos.] provinc. Asiae

This disquisition does not issue from conviction, or aspire to proof. Still less should it be censured for conjuring up a new legate of Aquitania. On its own terms the inscription deserved an excursus, even if one cannot assert, in the phrase of Ammianus, 'ad scientiam proficiet plenam'.

It is time to cast a glance at other governors of Dalmatia during the reigns of Claudius and Nero. Salvius Otho in 42 succeeded the ill-fated Camillus Scribonianus. For a very short tenure: he was back in Rome the year after.[71] Only four known names intervene before Ducenius Geminus.[72]

(1) Piso, legate at some time before the departure of VII Claudia.[73] For identity avails only L. Piso Cn. f., the consul of 27, so it seems. Prefect of the City at the accession of Caligula, and not long after proconsul of Africa, he is assumed successor in Dalmatia to Salvius Otho (cf. *PIR*², C 293). C. Piso, the conspirator of 65, incurs dispraisal—no mention of the governorship in the *Laus Pisonis*, which describes him as a man of peace. And he was with the *Arvales* in 44 (*CIL* vi 2032). However, the chance subsists of a consular Piso otherwise unknown.

(2) C. Ummidius Quadratus (*suff. c.*40). The inscription shows him legate of Claudius Caesar 'in Illyrico' (*ILS* 972: Casinum). Dalmatia

---

[71] Suetonius, *Otho* 1, 3, cf. Dio lx 18, 4.

[72] For the detail, A. Jagenteufel, *Die Statthalter der römischen Provinz Dalmatia von Augustus bis Diokletian* (1958), 28 ff.; J. J. Wilkes, *Dalmatia* (1969), 443 f.

[73] *ILS* 5952. The legion departed to Moesia. Perhaps not until 57, to replace IV Scythica—or better, a decade earlier. For this problem, J. J. Wilkes, *Dalmatia* (1969), 96.

or Pannonia, that is a question.[74] Ummidius may have held Dalmatia from 46 or 47 until 50, when he went to Syria.[75]

(3) P. Anteius Rufus (*suff. ann. inc.*). Attested by inscriptions in 50 and in 51/2.

(4) C. Calpetanus Rantius Sedatus (*suff. ann. inc.*). Attested by only a small fragment, he gets thrown between 54 and 63. He was of praetorian rank in 46.

Sharp attention should fix on Anteius Rufus. If he was still in Dalmatia after October of 54, he qualifies for 'legatus Caesarum' on *ILS* 963. Late in the following year he stood in prospect of Syria when they tried in vain to edge out old Ummidius (*Ann.* xiii 22, 1). Eleven years later, denounced by an astrologer who knew him 'caritate Agrippinae invisum Neroni', Anteius escaped condemnation by suicide (xiv 14). |

There is a chance that Anteius by way of consolation for Syria was allowed to go to Asia in 56 or 57. A place is vacant. For what it is worth (not much) a tie with the eastern lands is revealed by the name of the Cilician doctor P. Anteius Antiochus (*PIR*[2], A 730).

A proconsulate *c.* 57 would accord well, if Anteius' consulship is assigned to 47 (compare lists adduced above). Otherwise an *Ignotus* could be evoked, consul in that same year and governor of Dalmatia as successor to Anteius from 52 or 53 to 56, thus bridging the two reigns.

Significant gaps subsist in provincial *Fasti*, and several consuls hitherto totally unknown have recently turned up. It is safer to renounce, and remit the problem of *ILS* 963—while bearing in mind the fact that it discloses a proconsul of Asia, either *c.* 57 or (if Ducenius Geminus) in 73/4.

---

[74] Both Jagenteufel and Wilkes refrain from a decision.

[75] For Quadratus (and for Piso) see further 'Lurius Varus, a Stray Consular Legate', *HSCPh* lxxxviii (1984), 165 ff. = pp. 366 ff., below. Lurius (*Ann.* xiii 31, 1, cf. Suetonius, *Otho* 2, 2), so it is there argued, was legate of either Dalmatia or Pannonia from 43 to 46, with some slight preference accorded to Pannonia.

20

LuriusVarus, A Stray Consular Legate

NOTHING much occurred in 57. Tacitus introduces the year with scathing comment on authors who, contrary to the 'dignitas populi Romani', fill out their pages with a lavish account of the dimensions and materials of an amphitheatre (*Ann.* xiii 31, 1). The consular historian was able to put on deserved record some transactions and persons also of interest to himself, such as the charges brought against Pomponia Graecina (the wife of A. Plautius) and the prosecutions of Cossutianus Capito and Eprius Marcellus.

Nor did he omit the consular Lurius Varus, now regaining the place in the Senate he had forfeited 'avaritiae criminibus olim perculsus' (32, 2). Suetonius employed the item (without the name) to illustrate the 'potentia' exercised by young Otho, and a profitable operation. He restored to the Senate 'damnatum repetundis consularem virum, ingens praemium pactus' (*Otho* 2, 2). Testimony thus accrues to confirm, in an equivocal fashion, the acclaimed felicity of the new dispensation.

The sphere and function in which Lurius was able to practise extortion fails to arouse much curiosity. Some take him for a proconsul of Asia or Africa.[1] The recent large and comprehensive volume disallows, firmly.[2]

Alert to persons, and above all to criminal proconsuls, the historian had no doubt related the prosecution of Lurius Varus somewhere in the narration now missing. That is, previous to the second half of 47. Moreover, observe the word 'olim': hardly suitable for an interval of less than a decade. If he was a proconsul, then at the latest for the tenure 45/6, and therefore in any event a Tiberian consul. Which is not at all likely.

For the consulate of Lurius, one can do better than 'before 54'.[3] It

---

[1] P. A. Brunt, *Historia* x (1961), 225: with a query, but no hint of an imperial province.

[2] U. Vogel-Weidemann, *Die Statthalter von Africa und Asia in den Jahren 14–68 n. Chr.* (1982), 467 f.

[3] The term adopted by P. A. Gallivan, *CQ* xxiv (1974) 300 f.; xxviii (1978) 426. Lurius is absent from his Caligulan list in *Antichthon* xiii (1979), 66 ff.

Harvard Studies in Classical Philology lxxxviii (1984), 165–9.

should fall under Caligula or at the very beginning of the next reign. The peccant consular, so it appears, held one of seven commands in the portion of Caesar, at some time between 40 and 46. Of | four the occupants are known, viz., the two Germanies, Moesia, Syria. Tarraconensis exhibits a vacancy after Ap. Silanus (*cos.* 28), recalled in 41 to marry Domitia Lepida.[4] Hence at first sight a place for Lurius Varus. An obscure person, yet perhaps in benefit of abnormal favour from Claudius Caesar, like Q. Curtius Rufus, legate in Germania Superior (cf. *Ann.* xi 21). On the other hand, Tarraconensis had hitherto been reserved for the eminent—at least to judge by the names on record, although few in a long stretch of time.[5] Even after the garrison fell to a single legion the province retained high prestige.[6]

Next, Dalmatia.[7] In 42 Camillus Scribonianus (*cos.* 32) made his abortive proclamation. To restore order, Claudius Caesar despatched L. Salvius Otho (*suff.* 33). His task fulfilled, Otho was back in Rome the year after. He then reinforced the ruler's trust by detecting in conspiracy a Roman knight—who was thrown down from the Tarpeian Rock.[8]

A brief tenure therefore in Dalmatia, and Suetonius in fact refers to 'extraordinaria imperia' in the career of Otho. Hence Lurius Varus might have been the next legate, from 43 to 46.

There was an impediment. A fragmentary inscription discloses a Piso as governor, along with the legion VII Claudia, which departed to Moesia in 57 at the latest—and perhaps a decade earlier.[9] Calpurnii Pisones cause vexation all too often. Identity and date are in question.

First, C. Piso the Neronian conspirator. Co-opted by the *Arvales* in 38, he was probably consul suffect early in the reign of Claudius.[10] This Piso is ruled out because of the *Laus Pisonis*, so it has been with confidence decreed. The poem styles him a man of peace, unlike his ancestors (l. 25). As concerns the succession to Salvius Otho, C. Piso was at Rome with the *Arvales* in 44.[11] |

---

[4] Dio lx 14, 3 (under the year 42).

[5] After Paullus Fabius Maximus, attested in 3/2 B.C., only Cn. Piso, M. Lepidus, L. Arruntius (governing in absence, ?23–33). Ap. Silanus, with the *Arvales* in 38 and 39 (*CIL* vi 2028 f.), had not been long in Tarraconensis. His predecessor would be worth knowing about.

[6] G. Alföldy, *Fasti Hispanienses* (1969), 207.

[7] For the detail, A. Jagenteufel, *Die Statthalter der römischen Provinz Dalmatia von Augustus bis Diokletian* (1958), 21 ff.; J. J. Wilkes, *Dalmatia* (1969), 443 f.

[8] Suetonius, *Otho*, 1, 3; Dio lx 18, 4.

[9] *ILS* 5952. For the date of the legion's departure, J. J. Wilkes, op. cit. 96.

[10] *CIL* vi 2028. No season for his consulship is proposed by P. A. Gallivan, *CQ* xxviii (1978), 426.

[11] *CIL* vi 2032.

Second, a Piso not otherwise on attestation. In this period the only Pisones whose ancestry is verifiable descend from Cn. Piso (*cos.* 7 B.C.); but his brother, L. Piso the Augur (*suff.* 1 B.C.), is relevant. Like the parent of the conspirator, his relations have missed all record, apart from L. Piso, the consul of 57, described as a 'consobrinus' of his son.[12] C. Piso, it has been supposed, might be a descendant of L. Piso the Augur or a son of M. Piso (who was the younger son of Cn. Piso, the consul of 7 B.C.).[13]

Attention has been drawn to L. Piso, the praetorian legate in Tarraconensis assassinated by a native in 25 (*Ann.* iv 45). He was probably a son of the Augur.[14] Further, to a missing but necessary C. Calpurnius. Acilius Aviola, legate of Lugdunensis in 21 (*Ann.* iii 41, 1), reappears soon after as C. Calpurnius Aviola, consul suffect in 24. Aviola, it is conjectured, was adopted by a C. Piso.[15]

Third, L. Piso the consul of 27 (*PIR*[2], C 293), elder son of Cn. Piso (*cos.* 7 B.C.). He has been the firm and uncontested choice, going to Dalmatia in 43. On first inspection he might appear all too illustrious. Prefect of the City at the accession of Caligula, he went on to be proconsul of Africa. Apprehension of his ambitions induced Caligula to remove the legion from the charge of the proconsul.[16]

Nevertheless, L. Piso retains a potent claim when the policy and motives of Claudius Caesar are put under brief scrutiny. The new and insecure ruler was anxious to conciliate the leading consulars and annex families equipped with rival or dynastic claims to the power. Two alliances devised in his first year are significant. Claudius gave his daughter Antonia in marriage to Pompeius Magnus, the son of Crassus Frugi (*cos.* 27); and the infant Octavia was betrothed to L. Silanus, who through his mother, Aemilia, carried the blood of Caesar Augustus.[17] |

Not only that. Crassus Frugi was appointed to a military command as legate 'in M[auretania]' (*ILS* 954) and awarded the *ornamenta triumphalia*—soon to have them by anomaly a second time when he went to Britain in the company of the Emperor.[18]

[12] Tacitus, *Hist.* iv 49, 2.

[13] Thus Groag in *PIR*[2], C 284. The presumed ages of M. Piso (C 296) and C. Piso tell against the notion of father and son.

[14] For that hypothesis, *AJP* ci (1980), 334 = *RP* iii (1984), 1227 (discussing sons of L. Piso the Pontifex). If correct, his ancestor was Cn. Piso, quaestor in 65 B.C., with the same fate—and with similar imputations against his character (Sallust, *Cat.* 19, 4). The language of Tacitus (iv 45) is suitably Sallustian.

[15] As argued in *AJP* ci (1980), 335 = *RP* iii (1984), 1227. The identity of legate and consul was not noted in *PIR*[2], A 47 and C 251.

[16] Dio lx 20, 7. To be given preference against Tacitus, who has M. Silanus, the consul of 19 (*Hist.* iv 48, 1). See remarks in *Historia* xxx (1981), 196 f. = *RP* iii (1984), 1357 f.

[17] Dio lx 5, 7. One may subjoin the marriage of Ap. Silanus to Domitia Lepida, the mother of Valeria Messalina (lx 14, 13).   [18] Suetonius, *Claudius* 17, 3.

In this context and season, L. Piso accords admirably as legate of Dalmatia (?43–6), although (or even because) he was the son of Cn. Piso—who had been the enemy of Germanicus, the brother of Claudius Caesar.

A later date for this senior consular is not likely—and it might well collide with the tenure of another governor. Before going to Syria in 50 Ummidius Quadratus (*suff. c.*40) had been Caesar's legate 'in Illyrico' (*ILS* 942: Casinum). Dalmatia or Pannonia, that is the question. Proper caution will hesitate to pronounce.[19] Further, Pannonia carries that appellation on a diploma of the year 60 (*CIL* xvi 4).

None the less, Dalmatia was the original province 'Illyricum'; and when Illyricum was divided it stood at first as 'Illyricum superius'.[20]

To resume. As a consular province for Lurius Varus, Tarraconensis seemed in no way plausible; and the foregoing remarks can be taken to reinforce the standard assignment of Dalmatia to L. Piso (*cos.* 27), succeeding Otho in 43, precisely. Despite which, the chance of another Piso should not be lost to view. Members of aristocratic families, and even consuls, sometimes stand on solitary attestation. Thus M. Junius Silanus, consul suffect in the vicinity of 54.[21]

Of the seven commands there remains Pannonia. In 43 A. Plautius (*suff.* 29) departed to undertake the invasion of Britain. Lurius Varus can be accommodated in the ensuing *triennium*.

The next legate on record is Palpellius Hister, discovered there in the year 50 (*Ann.* xii 29, 2). His successor was Vipstanus Gallus (*suff.* ?48), revealed by a fragment with the imperatorial salutation of Claudius indicating 52, 53, or 54.[22]

Arguments based on a duration deemed appropriate for consular commands are invalid in this period. Legate 'in Illyrico' (*ILS* 972), Ummidius Quadratus can have either Dalmatia or Pannonia before 50. | If hesitations about the date and identity of Piso are discounted, Lurius Varus takes Pannonia, in 43.

Epilogue

The name 'Lurius', strangely absent from the repertorium of

---

[19] Thus both Jagenteufel and Wilkes.

[20] *ILS* 938 (Epidaurum): 'civitates superioris provinciae Hillyrici'.

[21] *CIL* xiv 3471 (Tibur).

[22] *CIL* iii 4591 (Carnuntum). The Vipstani were not well treated by R. Hanslik in *RE* ixA (1961). See remarks in *Historia* xi (1962), 149 ff. = *RP* (1979), 533 ff. And Vipstanus Gallus is missing from P. A. Gallivan, *CQ* xxviii (1978), 407 ff. For his consulship see now J. Devreker, *ZPE* xxii (1976) 205 f.

Wilhelm Schulze, is (like 'Lusius') unprepossessing and fairly common. It first came to notoriety with M. Lurius, who tried to hold Sardinia for Caesar's heir in 40 B.C.—and who commanded the right wing at the Battle of Actium.[23] Unlike the low-born Tarius Rufus, also an admiral in that campaign, this partisan did not reach a consulship, even in the late sequel. And nothing is known of P. Lurius Agrippa, save that he was a *monetalis*. Later ages fail to reveal any other senatorial family.

The Dalmatian coast happens to register eight Lurii, among them 'Publius' as the only *praenomen*.[24] The surprise is Africa, with about sixty. Some might be tempted to discover a sign of official occupations held by M. Lurius in those parts, on valid parallels. To no result—not one of them is a 'Marcus Lurius'. It will be suitable to terminate on uncertainties. The problem subsists: either Pannonia or Dalmatia as the consular province of Lurius Varus.

---

[23] Dio xlviii 30, 7; Velleius ii 85, 2.

[24] G. Alföldy, *Die Personennamen in der römischen Provinz Dalmatia* (1969), 95. Cf. also *AClass* xxviii (1985), 41 = p. 634, below (adducing the new inscription that reveals a M. Lurius Varus at Reate).

21

Eight Consuls from Patavium

No city of Italy save Patavium equalled far Gades with its total of five hundred knights. Thus Strabo, reporting a census that had been held recently.[1] Otherwise the geographer's information about Transpadana (it is no surprise) goes back quite a long way. While Strabo accords Patavium an especial primacy along with Aquileia, credit also goes to Verona and Mediolanum. About the latter city his testimony confirms the value early apparent of its central situation in the Lombard plain. Cremona should perhaps be added, which Strabo placed south of the Po, misled no doubt by its vicinity to Placentia.[2]

The prosperity of Patavium is on ample attestation. Strabo's plethora of knights will arouse interest on sundry counts. For example, totals of knights as against senators in any city. Senators presuppose equestrian status and wealth in the previous generation. At Brixia some forty inscriptions disclose members of the *amplissimus ordo*, both male and female. Knights are not much on sight. Only three can be discerned who had military service; and there is a solitary procurator.[3] Patavium registers three in the *militia equestris*, all of early date.[4]

Of senators, there is a paucity: six all told.[5] They comprise two consuls, two praetors, a fragmentary name, and an anonymous proconsul of Bithynia. Extraneous evidence augments the total in a marked degree. It contributes to a chapter of social and political history, with wide repercussions. The Transpadane zone had come up with sporadic senators before Caesar's heir advertised 'tota Italia'. Even a consul, if the jurist P. Alfenus Varus (*suff.* 39) were conceded. The notion that he derives from Cremona is more than dubious.[6] Cremona, it is true, was an ancient colony of the Latin right. Likewise Aquileia. More significant are the new *municipia* that took

[1] Strabo v 213, cf. iii 169. [2] Strabo v 216.
[3] CIL v 4368; 4372 f. (military knights); 4123 (L. Arrius Secundus: no occupation specified).
[4] CIL v 2791; 2828; AE 1953, 33. Each had the sole post of *tribunus militum*.
[5] CIL v 2819–25.
[6] Since alleged by Porphyrio on the 'Alfenus vafer' of *Sat.* i 3, 130. Against, E. Fraenkel, *Horace* (1957), 89 f.

Papers of the British School at Rome li (1983), 102–24.

their origin from native towns, notably in Venetia. P. Sepullius Macer was one of the *monetales* in 44. In Transpadana the rare and distinctive name is confined to Patavium and Ateste.[7]

The figures for the region are variously instructive.[8] City can be matched against city—and curiosity can extend with profit to Narbonensis or to Spain. For convenience and economy the present enquiry is restricted to consuls. The list leads off in fine style, and not to be predicted, with a *consul ordinarius*. |

(1) Sex Papinius Allenius (*cos.* 36). *PIR*[1], P 76. The *cursus* provides valuable clues: 'Sex. Papinio Q. f./Allenio/tr. mil., q., leg./Ti. Caesaris Aug. / tr. pl., pr., leg./Ti. Caesaris Aug./pro pr., cos., XVvir./sacr. fac./d. d.' (*ILS* 945: Patavium).

(2) P. Clodius Thrasea Paetus (*suff.* 56). *PIR*[2], C 1187. Of signal fame but leaving no trace in the natal city.

(3) A. Ducenius Geminus (60 or 61). D 201. The standard dating for his consulate was *c.*55: by error, as now emerges, cf. below.

(4) M. Arruntius (66). A 1134. On *CIL* vi 2044 the *cognomen* (i.e. 'Aquila') has perished. Arruntius and his colleague, M. Vettius Bolanus, are attested on 25 September and on 23 November of the year 66.

Another pair presents a problem, namely 'M. Arru[ntius' and 'L. Nonius' on an inscription at Samothrace carrying for date either 1 September or a day in the second half of August.[9] The consulate of L. Nonius Calpurnius Asprenas must fall early in the reign of Vespasian, since he was proconsul of Africa in 82/3 (*IRT* 346: Lepcis). The pair at Samothrace could be assigned to 66—but only on the hypothesis that a different L. Nonius died before entering office. There are parallels.

(5) M. Arruntius Aquila (77). A 1139. The last word of the document shows him son of the foregoing. As follows: 'M. Arruntio M. f. Ter. Aquilae / IIIviro a. a. a. s. f. / quaest. Caesaris / trib. pl., pr., cos. / XVviro sacr. fac. / filio' (*ILS* 980: Patavium).

(6) C. Ducenius Proculus (87). D 202. Only a name and a date.

(7) P. Ducenius Verus (95). D 203, cf. 200. Known as a consul from the *Digest* (xxxi 29, *pr.*). The *praenomen* was inferred from his *servitor* among the *pontifices* of 101 and 102 (vi 32445; 31034):

---

[7] W. Schulze, *LE* 277: to which add P. Sepullius P. f. Tacitus (v 3037). For the *monetalis*, T. P. Wiseman, *New Men in the Roman Senate* (1971), 392. For the amphora stamps of the Sepullii, M. H. Callender, *Roman Amphorae* (1965), 217; W. V. Harris, *ZPE* xxvii (1977), 287.

[8] For the full detail see now G. Alföldy, *Epigrafia e ordine senatorio* ii (1982), 309 ff.

[9] *AE* 1947, 2. Observe however *Samothrace* ii 1 (1960), no. 40. For these consulates see also P. A. Gallivan, *CQ* xxxi (1981), 200.

confirmed, along with the date, by the *Fasti Ostienses* (xiii d), first
published in 1939.

(8) L. Arruntius Stella (?101). A 1151. For his consulate (with
L. Julius Marinus Caecilius Simplex) Groag expressed a marked
preference for 102. Better, the previous year.[10]

Six out of eight from two families, that helps the enquiry, at least on
one count. Kinship comes in powerfully, but local rivalries are not
excluded. By the same token, while mutual aid was often reciprocated
between the ambitious issuing from the same region (and even from
the same province), neighbour cities were not always on terms of
amity. |

Under those provisos, the ascension of the Patavine consuls may
be subjected to scrutiny. First, Sex. Papinius Allenius (*ILS* 945). His
second name may be presumed maternal. It is documented at
Patavium by two equestrian officers of early date, viz. M. Allenius
Crassus Cossonius and Al]lenius C. f. Strabo.[11]

Papinius' own service as military tribune may antedate possession
of the *latus clavus*.[12] That is relevant to his age. Papinius was praetor
in 27, acceding to the *fasces* when an interval of only eight years had
elapsed. It will not be easy to discover in this period a *novus homo*
who became consul before forty-two, the standard age.

The question has a bearing on a notice in Pliny. Two kinds of
exotic fruit were brought to Italy, from Africa and from Syria: 'Sex.
Papinius, quem consulem vidimus, primus utraque attulit divi
Augusti novissimis temporibus, in castris sata' (*NH* xv 47). Papinius
was military tribune in Syria, quaestor in Africa, so Borghesi
conjectured.[13] Better, tribune in both provinces towards A.D.
14—and if so a retarded entrant to the Senate as quaestor.[14]

After the quaestorship Papinius was 'legatus Ti. Caesaris'. That is
to say, commander of a legion. Then, after the praetorship, with no
other post intervening (such as a proconsulate), Papinius governs one
of the five praetorian provinces in the portion of Caesar.

In 31, the fateful year of Aelius Seianus (or in that vicinity),
praetorian as well as consular provinces might engage the anxious
care of Tiberius Caesar. One observes in passing the anomalous

---

[10] R. Syme, *Tacitus* (1958), 655, n. 3; W. Eck, *Senatoren von Vespasian bis Hadrian* (1970),
148 f.

[11] *CIL* v 2828; *AE* 1953, 33.

[12] Compare M'. Vibius Balbinus (*ILS* 937).

[13] As noted under *PIR*[1], P 76.

[14] It would be hazardous to invoke a Syrian legion, XII Fulminata, in turbulent Africa for a
time in the last decade of the reign (*ILS* 8966: Thugga).

tenure of the aristocratic Ser. Galba (*cos.* 33), governor of Aquitania for less than a year.[15]

Long prorogations were the characteristic habit of that ruler. In 31 Fulcinius Trio returned from Lusitania to become consul: Ummidius Quadratus may be the immediate successor, attested there in 37.[16] For the rest, the list for Galatia is probably complete in these years. One of 'Tres Galliae' might offer for Papinius—to be held perhaps for much longer than a *triennium*.

Papinius had a swift clean passage to the *fasces*.[17] A long sequence of eminent *ordinarii* was broken by a peculiar run of new men: L. Vitellius (34), C. Cestius Gallus (35), Sex. Papinius (36), Cn. Acerronius Proculus (37). Two of the names invite curiosity but do nothing to repay it—unless Acerronius be none other than the jurist Proculus. The one thing clear is the influence that Lucius Vitellius commanded, and continued to exert during the next two reigns.

Vitellius not only enjoyed the confidence of Tiberius Caesar. Along with Valerius Asiaticus (so it is said) he was assiduous in cultivating old Antonia, the | mother of Claudius, who had a court of her own.[18] Operations of the potent manager may be detected in a consulate for Asiaticus in 35.

The Papinii met a rapid and melancholy end. Early in 37 the young Sex. Papinius committed suicide to escape advances from his mother. The lady was arraigned before the Senate. The notice in Tacitus, introduced by 'isdem diebus' (*Ann.* vi 49, 1), concludes a sequence of prosecutions (with a plethora of names). It derives from the *Acta*, so one presumes.[19] Whatever the sources, the historian would not miss her name. He chose to suppress it. The last of the family was another son, cruelly put to death by Caligula.[20]

The consulship of Thrasea Paetus falls in the concluding months of 56. This man had no cause to cherish the Caesars. His wife's father A. Caecina Paetus (*suff.* 37), who in 42 had gone to join Arruntius Scribonianus (insurgent in Dalmatia), earned fame by a suicide which his consort Arria encouraged and shared. Thrasea declared honour and 'pietas' by taking 'Paetus' into his own nomenclature,

---

[15] Suetonius, *Galba* 6, 1.   [16] *ILS* 190. For Fulcinius Trio, *AE* 1953, 88.
[17] Comparable to C. Laecanius Bassus from Pola (*suff.* 40), praetor in 32 (*PIR*[2], L 30). For the idle fancy that Papinius had been an adherent of Seianus, observe, with other inadequacies, *RE* xviii 983.
[18] Tacitus, *Ann.* xi 3, 1.
[19] To be added to other instances, now reiterated in *JRS* lxxii (1982), 76 ff. = pp. 213 ff., above.
[20] *PIR*[1], P 75. For the interpretation of Dio lix 25, 5 b see E. Grady, *RhM* cxxiv (1981), 261 ff. The passage also concerns Anicius Cerialis (*suff.* 65).

and 'Clodius' is extruded except when the consulate is registered.

A consulship at the inception of a new reign advertises conciliation; and Thrasea may have been awarded a priesthood about the same time.[21] The patronage dispensed by Annaeus Seneca and Afranius Burrus in their useful alliance is suitably apparent in the vicinity: as witness the Narbonensians A. Pompeius Paullinus (*suff.* ?54), M. Trebellius Maximus (56), L. Duvius Avitus (56).[22]

P. Clodius Thrasea avows no kinsfolk at Patavium. His daughter was called Fannia (*PIR*[2], F 118), no doubt the name of his mother. Fannii are fairly frequent in *CIL* V (about sixteen). Verona exhibits one of the better sort, viz. P. Fannius M. f., magistrate and equestrian officer (3366); and Pliny devoted a letter to C. Fannius, a busy advocate who before his decease was able to finish three books commemorating the victims of Nero (*Ep.* v 5).[23]

Among the company who carried on the tradition of Thrasea Paetus the most prominent were Helvidius Priscus (who married Fannia) and his consular son.[24] The Helvidii came out of the Samnite country. Next, the two brothers Junius Mauricus and Arulenus Rusticus. The latter, tribune of the plebs in 66, showed himself eager and impulsive when Thrasea faced prosecution (*Ann.* xvi 26, 4). The nearest trace of propinquity is a casual fact in Pliny. Junia, one of the virgins of Vesta, was related to Thrasea's daughter (vii 19, 1). |

The provenance of these Junii is a problem. When Mauricus sought a husband for his niece, Pliny had the man, namely Minicius Acilianus, an admirable senator from the north: 'patria est ei Brixia, ex illa nostra Italia' (i 14, 4). The assumption is easy that Mauricus pertains like the author to Italia Transpadana. Doubt intervenes.[25] Perhaps Pliny is enrolling Mauricus as a kind of 'honorary Transpadane', for a patent reason (Thrasea Paetus).

The *cognomen*, by the way, is ambiguous. With Hosidius Mauricus from Histonium it recalls the exploits of an ancestor in Mauretania (H 220, cf. 216). In the case of Pliny's friend it is 'Maurĭcus', as the poet Martial demonstrates (v 28, 5). The word has a native flavour. Observe M. Valerius Bradua Mauricus (*cos.* 191), from Albingaunum in Liguria.[26]

---

[21] That Thrasea was one of the *XVviri sacris faciundis* emerges at a later stage (*Ann.* xvi 22, 1).

[22] For the origin of Trebellius Maximus, *HSCPh* lxxiii (1969), 222 = *RP* (1979), 761; A. R. Birley, *The* Fasti *of Roman Britain* (1981), 60.

[23] For what it may be worth, Patavium yields freedmen of a C. Fannius (v 2951).

[24] Fannia was his second wife, cf. *PIR*[2], H 59 f.

[25] For appropriate caution, G. E. F. Chilver, *Cisalpine Gaul* (1940), 105; R. Syme, *Tacitus* (1958), 559, n. 1; A. N. Sherwin-White in his *Commentary* (1966), ad loc. On the other hand 'videtur' in *PIR*[2], J 771, cf. 730 (on the brother).

[26] *CIL* v 7783. Observe also C. Atilius C. f. Bradua, who paved the forum at Libarna (7427

Nor does light percolate from 'Arulenus', the name of the brother. This *gentilicium* is extremely rare.[27] By strange coincidence it is prefixed to another senator, the jurist Cn. Arulenus Caelius Sabinus (*suff.* 69). On the *Fasti Ostienses* Rusticus is styled 'Q. Aru[lenus Rusticus'. Men of rank preferred to get away from common *gentilicia* such as 'Junius' or 'Clodius'.

Finally, the link with A. Caecina Paetus (*suff.* 37). The great *gens*, almost eponymous of Volaterrae, had wide and distant ramifications. Thus L. Caecina of Volsinii, a senator of early date; Caecina Alienus from Vicetia; or even an equestrian Caecina Severus at Tarraco.[28] Again, the *cognomen* of Caecina Tuscus (C 109) indicates only the ultimate provenance of an ancestor, not for himself a *patria* in Etruria.

The faint chance has found a mention that Caecina Paetus was a Patavine.[29] Paetus was an enemy of Claudius Caesar, but C. Caecina Largus enjoyed abnormal favour, sharing the *fasces* with the Emperor in 42 and continuing in office until the year's end. During the emergency provoked in 48 by Messallina and C. Silius, Largus was ready with needed support for his wavering friend (*Ann.* xii 33 f.).

The Etruscan *cognomen* 'Largus' is not of frequent occurrence. A poet of that name celebrated Antenor and the foundation legend of Patavium; and a Largus can be found among its magistrates.[30] Further, the Patavine scholar, with a unique reference to a contemporary personage, mentions the historic mansion at Rome: | 'possidet eam nunc Largus Caecina qui consul fuit cum Claudio' (Asconius p. 23). The useful item serves to date the Ciceronian commentaries of Q. Asconius Pedianus to the beginning of Nero's reign. By 57 the consular was no longer among the living.[31]

So far, nothing to enlist valid support—and Caecina Largus has firm lodgement at Volaterrae. First, a tile found in the theatre offers two names, 'A. C]aecin. Sever.' and 'C. C]aecin. Larg.'.[32] The former is patently the consul suffect of 1 B.C., the latter the parent of the *ordinarius* of 42. Second, in large letters on the architrave of the

= *ILS* 5354). Senators apart, that *cognomen* is portentously rare. The same holds for 'Barea' (enigmatic) and for 'Chaerea' (Etruscan).

[27] In towns of Italy only libertine persons at Mediolanum (v 5762), Fanum (xi 6269), Puteoli (x 2106)—and an African sailor at Misenum (x 3244).

[28] *CIL* i² 2515 (Volsinii); Tacitus, *Hist.* iii 8, 1; *ILS* 2716 (Tarraco).

[29] *Tacitus* (1958), 559, n. 3.

[30] Ovid, *Ex Ponto* iv 16, 17 f.; *CIL* v 2973 (*gentilicium* not preserved).

[31] Since the full list of the *Arvales* can be established. See J. Scheid, *Les Frères Arvales* (1975), 254 ff.; 285 f.

[32] *CIL* xi 6689[54].

theatre itself: 'A. Caecina A. f. S[everus]/C. Caecina A. f. [Largus'.[33]

What then remains to be said about Caecina Paetus? Not much perhaps. His daughter married Thrasea—and she was also related to the Volaterran poet Persius.[34]

On the other side, the son of Caecina Paetus (*suff.* ?70) was taken in adoption by C. Laecanius Bassus (*cos.* 64) a northern magnate from Pola (L 31, cf. 33). He kept the 'Sabatina' which is the tribe of Volaterrae.[35] A Patavine parallel is noteworthy. M. Arruntius Aquila (*suff.* 77) is enrolled not in 'Fabia' but in 'Teretina' (*ILS* 980), which proves that these Arruntii are immigrant, from Atina in Latium.[36] The chance subsists that the family of Caecina Paetus had left Volaterrae for the north—and had found there a residence superior to Vicetia, for example (the *patria* of Caecina Alienus). It is not clear that Caecina Paetus was close kin to Severus and to Largus.

The first Neronian years bring Patavines on show in more ways than one. Not much should perhaps be made of the sporadic item that reveals an Arruntius Stella given charge of imperial games in 55 (*Ann.* xiii 22, 1). He had 'Lucius' for *praenomen*, and is identified as father (or rather grandfather) of the *suffectus* of 101, cf. *PIR*[2], A 1150.

Towards the end of the previous year the prince made a double request to the Senate: a statue for the deceased parent Ahenobarbus and *ornamenta consularia* for Asconius Labeo, who had been his guardian.[37]

That occupation could lead a long way in social ascent. A striking parallel is now to hand. Q. Veranius, the 'tutor' chosen by Augustus for Drusus (the father of Germanicus Caesar), is revealed by an inscription at Xanthos.[38] The next | Veranius was a legate of Germanicus in the eastern lands. The third, praetor in 42 or 43, went out to govern the new province Lycia–Pamphylia—and returned to be *consul ordinarius* in 49 and enter the patriciate.[39]

A more modest function could prove remunerative. The mother of C. Caecina Tuscus was the 'nutrix' of the child Nero.[40] In alarm

[33] *NSA* 1955, 123, with fig. 9b (whence *AE* 1957, 220). See further M .Torelli, *Dialoghi di archeologia* iii (1969), 295 f., with n. 43 (ibid. 349).

[34] *Vita Persii* (OCT, p. 32).

[35] The tribe is borne by his young son, who died at Brundisium (ix 39): that is, in 80, on the way to Asia with his parent (*suff.* ?70), the proconsul.

[36] Atina is the *patria* of the illustrious L. Arruntii, the consuls of 22 B.C. and A.D. 6.

[37] *Ann.* xiii 10, 1. To *PIR*[2], A 1205 can be added the gravestone of 'As]coni Q. f. Labeonis', a local *pontifex*, a boy who died at the age of fifteen (v 2848).

[38] A. Balland, *Fouilles de Xanthos* vii (1981), 82. He had been a tribune in a 'legio IV'.

[39] For his career, *AE* 1953, 251. And see now A. R. Birley, *The Fasti of Roman Britain* (1981), 50 ff.

[40] Suetonius, *Nero* 35, 5.

and panic after the murder of Britannicus, Nero thought of putting Tuscus in command of the Guard (xiii 20, 2). Tuscus, so some opine, was a 'Greco-Oriental'.[41] Most unlikely. Tuscus, it will be added, later became Prefect of Egypt—and was sent into exile about the time of Thrasea's end (cf. *PIR*[2], C 109).

Two Asconii, Pedianus and Labeo, have already made their entrance. Both erudition and teaching brought ample recompense. Thus Remmius Palaemon, of servile extraction from Vicetia, who invested in vineyards, to no small profit.[42] Superior in all respects (including morality) was the provincial professor of rhetoric, Quintilian from remote Calagurris. He ended as the tutor of boy princes. More significant for the student of social history, Quintilian made a late marriage into a senatorial family. The elder son, betrothed to his cousin and adopted by an ex-consul, perished at the age of nine—along with his mother and brother during a sequence of unhealthy seasons (90–3).[43]

Asconius addressed youthful sons in his treatise (p. 38). Their age suggests a question about his own. In one at least of his writings Asconius evinced an interest in protracted lives.[44] He was to reach 85 according to Jerome. The source was Suetonius, who was in a position to know. Jerome adds the year 75 for his *floruit*. Perhaps the year of his decease.[45]

Conjecture can indagate a wife for Asconius. A Roman inscription conveys 'Mutia Festa Pediani'.[46] The name is rare, and restricted in Transpadana to Brixia and Patavium. Three specimens: one is a *praefectus fabrum* and magistrate at Patavium.[47]

As they move upwards, scholars like senators transcend local attachments and gain access to superior matrimony. Asconii had formed a resplendent connection long since. The formidable Ummidia Quadratilla, recalling by her habits the 'old empire', received a handsome portrayal from Pliny when she died at the age of eighty (vii 24). | She was the daughter of Ummidius Quadratus (*suff. c.*40). The amphitheatre at Casinum paraded her full name in

---

[41] Thus in *CAH* x (1934), 727,

[42] Suetonius, *De gramm.* 25.

[43] Quintilian vi, *praef.* 4; 13.

[44] Viz. Sammulla, dying at 110 (*NH* vii 159): possibly local. It is a diminutive of 'Sammo', or of 'Sammus'. For the former name, cf. *CIL* iii 1765 (Lugdunum); 7120 (Moguntiacum); xii 1889 (Vienna). On these items see E. Evans, *Gaulish Personal Names* (1967), 252 f.

[45] For the items bearing on Asconius' age see Wissowa, *RE* ii 1524 ff.

[46] *CIL* vi 22784. Even without a long existence, Asconius may have had offspring by more wives than one.

[47] *CIL* v 2835 (T. Mutius Gracilis). The Brixian specimens are 4131 (a magistrate); 4659.

large letters: Ummidia C. f. Quadratilla Asconia Secunda.[48] The consular had married an Asconia: perhaps not his first or only wife. He was born about 12 B.C.[49] The influence of Quadratus was not impaired by a decennial absence in Syria or by his decease there in 60.

If sons of Q. Asconius Pedianus survived (one bears in mind the great pestilence of 65), they had a fair prospect of entering the high assembly—unless a prudent parent deterred, fearful of the later Neronian years. A dedication at Patavium registers the first known senator in the family: 'Q. Asconiu[s] Gabinius Modestu[s]/ praetor, procos./ praef. aerari Saturn[i] / dedit' (v 2820). Attention has been drawn to the consuls P. Gabinius Secundus (*suff.* 35) and A. Gabinius Secundus (*suff.* 43). A Gabinius, it is suggested, was adopted by a Q. Asconius.[50] Another explanation avails: nomenclature from the maternal side. Often valid when adoption has been incautiously assumed.[51]

That is not all. The inscription is acephalous. The first line is missing, of the second three isolated letters survive. That line may have carried another name with the filiation and probably the tribe as well. In *polyonymi*, those two items adhere to the 'real name' of a man, that is, the paternal name. On that showing, the man was not the son of an Asconius. Because of the treasury post, the inscription is assigned to the period 55–95, and the plain (but emphatic) formulation looks fairly early.[52] This proconsul refrained from naming the province he governed. And nothing antecedent to the praetorship. He may be suppressing a fact: he was *adlectus inter tribunicios*. If so, by Vespasian, one presumes. Further, the collegiate post of *praefecti* in charge of the *aerarium Saturni* soon became equipollent with legates governing the praetorian provinces, hence normally leading to a consulship.

One branch of the clan carries the *cognomen* 'Sardus'. Thus the local worthy in the Flavian period C. Asconius C. f. Sardus. His mother is styled 'Cusinia M. f.', his sister 'Asconia C. f. Augurini, sacerdos divae Domitillae' (*ILS* 6692). 'Cusinius' is not a common name.[53]

The husband of the sister cannot evade. He is T. Mustius C. f.

---

[48] *NSA* 1929, 29. For this important document, often overlooked (but not by Groag, cf. *PIR*[2], A 1207), see further *Historia* xvii (1968), 77 = *RP* (1979), 664.

[49] Quadratus was quaestor in A.D. 14 (*ILS* 970: Casinum).

[50] M. Corbier, *L'Aerarium Saturni et l'Aerarium militare* (1974), 110. Groag refrained from any comment on names and relationships (A 1204).

[51] For examples, see 'Clues to Testamentary Adoption', *Epigrafia e ordine senatorio* i (1982), 397 ff. = pp. 159 ff., above.

[52] M. Corbier, op. cit. 110 f.

[53] *TLL, Onom.* No specimens in *CIL* V, apart from 6956a (Augusta Taurinorum). M. Cusinius, the Caesarian senator (*ILS* 965: Tusculum), has the tribe 'Velina', which suggests an origin from Picenum, cf. T. P. Wiseman, op. cit. 228. The tribe would not exclude Aquileia.

Hostilius Medulla Augurinus, adlected *inter tribunicios* by Nerva (v 2822: Patavium). Another wife of the same man (or perhaps his father's wife) is registered on tiles in the territory as 'Sab[. . .] Quinta C. f. Must. Aug.'.[54] |

Hostilii abound, with over forty in *CIL* V. The rarity is Mustii, otherwise only two in that volume, one at Patavium, the other at Atria.[55] The *cognomen* 'Augurinus' carries a slight and adventitious relevance. Pliny's friend the poet Sentius Augurinus is presumed Veronese because of 'meus Catullus' (iv 27, 4). Perhaps to be identified as Q. Gellius Sentius Augurinus, proconsul of Macedonia under Hadrian (G 135). Quinti Gellii are not common. One of them was a magistrate at Patavium (v 2861).

To revert to Mustii. Pliny indited an amicable but vague epistle conveying instructions to Mustius, his architect (ix 39). He also wrote to Sardus, in gratitude: Sardus composed a book in which he was 'percopiosus' on a proper and felicitous theme, praise of the orator (ix 31). There is no sign that this Sardus was a person of rank. He may be identical with C. Asconius C. f. Sardus (*ILS* 6692). An Asconius Sardus who entered the Senate under Domitian calls for separate treatment (A 1207, see below).

In Transpadana the *cognomen* is confined to Patavium. Although at first sight unprepossessing, it has nothing to do with natives of an ill-famed island. Compare the *nomen* 'Sardius', likewise a rarity.[56]

Asconii cannot fail to evoke the Transpadane orator and poet Ti. Catius Silius Italicus (*cos*. 68). In the *Punica* the author gave some care to the choice of leaders for Italian peoples and he duly allotted a heroic role to a Pedianus from Patavium (xii 212 ff.). On an edict at Aphrodisias of Silius, the amiable proconsul, 'Asconius' turns up in his nomenclature.[57] Clearly the maternal side, 'Silius' being paternal.[58]

The precise *patria* continues to evade search. The *nomen* happens to be infrequent in Transpadana. Four specimens only, all at Brixia or in its territory.[59] One of them belongs to the better sort: C. Silius Aviola, an equestrian tribune in the reign of Tiberius (*ILS* 6099).

The item 'Ti. Catius', an adoptive prefix, may inspire a certain

---

[54] *CIL* v 8810[288] (twelve specimens). The lady is a Sabinia. For that name, Schulze (*LE* 222) cited *CIE* 869 = xi 2420 (Clusium); and for 'Sabo', *CIE* 4840 (ibid.). Other explanations avail.

[55] *CIL* v 2998; 2368.

[56] In *CIL* v, Verona (3253), Aquileia (3615), and eastwards at Capodistria (503). Observe two obscure persons in Fronto (*PIR*[1], S 140 f.).

[57] *MAMA* viii (1962), 411. See now J. Reynolds, *Aphrodisias and Rome* (*JRS* Monograph no. 1, 1982), 172 f.

[58] Thus, firmly, G. E. F. Chilver, *Cisalpine Gaul* (1940), 109 ff.

[59] *CIL* v 4181; 4296; 4401; 4419–22 (= *ILS* 6099: Val. Trompia). By inadvertence Silius Italicus was assumed Patavine in *Some Arval Brethren* (1980), 79.

curiosity. The *nomen* is indistinctive, not borne hitherto by any senator of the imperial epoch. No Ti. Catii occur in *CIL* V, and nothing can be done with Catius Lepidus, correspondent of Pliny and citizen of a town not far from Comum (iv 7, 6).

Another letter deserves brief scrutiny. It concerns the Epicurean Catius, whom Cicero when writing to Cassius (a recent convert) styled 'Insuber' (*Ad fam.* xv 16, 1). On request from a senatorial friend eager to embellish his library, Pliny asked | Vibius Severus to comply and furnish 'imagines municipum tuorum Corneli Nepotis et Titi Cati' (iv 28, 1). On the basis of which, the Transpadane philosopher is equipped with the *praenomen* 'Titus'.[60] Hesitation impinges. To spell out the *praenomen* is not customary in Latin authors save for persons of some note or notoriety such as Marcus Agrippa or Marcus Lepidus.[61] The Insubrian (Ticinum or Mediolanum) might be a Ti. Catius.[62]

Silius Italicus shares the prefix with another consular orator (*suff.* 96) who is styled 'Catius Fronto' in Pliny's letters, 'Ti. Caesius Fronto' on the *Fasti Ostienses*.[63] Possibly a son by adoption of old Silius, who died in 101. He had lost his younger son Severus (Martial ix 86), but the elder survived, namely L. Silius Decianus (*suff.* 94), *curator aquarum* subsequent to 102.[64] However that be, a relationship might be surmised. Caesii are common enough.[65] None the less, it is worth registering L. Caesius, *praefectus aerarii militaris* under Tiberius (v 8845: Verona), presumed parent of L. Caesius Martialis (*suff.* 57).

Silius Italicus died at the age of seventy-five, the last of the Neronian consuls, in both senses of the term. Hence born about 26, and a close coeval of Ummidia Qudratilla. In fact, as now emerges from nomenclature, probably her first cousin.

Silius damaged his reputation by undertaking prosecutions under Nero, so it is averred (*Ep.* iii 7, 3). His consular colleague P. Galerius Trachalus was a speaker of public note and performance. When the Emperor Otho was leaving Rome he delivered an oration in which the audience (so Tacitus subjoins) detected the manner of Trachalus, 'crebro fori usu celebre et ad implendas populi aures latum et sonans'.[66]

---

[60] No *praenomen* in *RE* iii 1792. But the Epicurean is 'T. Catius' in the commentary of Shackleton Bailey on *Ad fam.* xv 16, 1.

[61] See *JRS* xxxix (1949), 124 f.: *praenomina* written out by Tacitus but abridged by a recent editor (H. Fuchs).

[62] As assumed, with no supporting argument, in *Tacitus* (1958), 88, n. 7.

[63] His freedmen are 'Ti. Caesii', cf. *PIR*², C 194.   [64] *CIL* xv 7302.

[65] For the distribution of the name, A. R. Birley, *Britannia* iv (1973), 181 (on Petillius Cerialis).

[66] Tacitus, *Hist* i 90, 2. Compare the verdict in Quintilian (xii 5, 5). The Galerii come from Ariminum, cf. Pliny, *NH* x 50. Not noted in *PIR*², G 25 or G 30.

Another coeval was Cingonius Varro, with no testimony to his quality. He composed a speech for Nymphidius Sabinus.[67] Consul designate, he was put to death by Galba in the course of his march to Rome. The *nomen* 'Cingonius' looks Celtic, and is a portentous rarity. Cingonius Varro may well be Transpadane.[68] | Silius Italicus entered the Senate as quaestor late in the reign of Claudius Caesar. The first Ducenius takes one back to that epoch. The consulate of A. Ducenius Geminus was commonly assigned to 54 or 55, on what seemed adequate grounds.[69] A new document imports a sharp revision. In 62 Ducenius Geminus was one of the three commissioners appointed to investigate indirect taxes (*Ann.* xv 18, 3). An Ephesian inscription now supplies the names in order of seniority, viz. A. Pompeius Paullinus (*suff.* ?54), L. Calpurnius Piso (*cos.* 57), A. Ducenius Geminus.[70]

The consulate of Ducenius should be assigned to 60 or 61. That season marked a decisive turn in politics and patronage. The influence of the ministers Seneca and Burrus (abruptly broken in 62, according to Tacitus) was already verging towards eclipse. A resurgence of the Vitellian faction can be detected.[71] To it belonged, for example, the consuls of 61, Petronius Turpilianus and Caesennius Paetus. Perhaps likewise Eprius Marcellus (*suff.* 62) and Vibius Crispus (*c.*62)—the latter already described as potent in 60 (*Ann.* xiv 28, 2).[72]

Political significance has been attributed to Verginius Rufus, *consul ordinarius* in 63.[73] Verginius came into subsequent renown, legate of Germania Superior in 68 and a potential candidate for the purple after Nero's end, with long and tranquil survival—and with a funeral oration from one of the consuls in 97.

Verginius came from Mediolanum. Styled 'equestri familia, ignoto patre' (*Hist.* i 52, 4), Verginius is not himself a force. Rather a product of certain promoters. One turns to another type of *novus*

---

[67] Plutarch, *Galba* 14 f.

[68] Assumed Celtic by Schulze (*LE* 21), but with no other specimens. The name is absent from the Italian volumes of *CIL*. Sporadic examples occur elsewhere. Thus xii 2591 (Geneva); iii 2279 (in Dalmatia).

For parallel one notes the (ridiculous) Togonius Gallus (*Ann.* vi 2, 2). Curiosity should attach to the early senator C. Mocconius C. f. Fab. Verus (vi 1463), whose tribe suggests Brixia or Patavium. No specimen in other Celtic zones (III, XII, XIII), but observe 'Moccius' (v 7147; 7835; 7936; 7947). By contrast, 'Cervonius', with fifteen specimens in *CIL* V, among them one at Patavium (2926).

[69] Thus, on the basis of xiv 3471 (Tibur), in *Historia* v (1956), 210 = *RP* (1979), 322.

[70] Adduced by W. Eck, *ZPE* xlii (1981), 227 f.   [71] *Tacitus* (1958), 386 f.

[72] Both Vibius Crispus and Caesennius Paetus share the unexplained prefix 'L. Iunius', cf. *JRS* lxvii (1977), 45 = *RP* iii (1984), 1054.

[73] Thus G. E. F. Chilver, *Cisalpine Gaul* (1940), 86.

homo, to the bland and subtle Vibius Crispus from Vercellae. In the complicated play of ambition and patronage it is expedient to bear in mind Transpadanes not in concordance for habit or allegiance with Thrasea. Especially should they happen to be Patavine.

An inscription at Narona shows Ducenius Geminus governing Dalmatia (*ILS* 9384). That is, at some time between 63 and 68. Another document, an acephalous dedication at Epidaurus, had been assigned with some confidence to Ducenius (*ILS* 963, cf. *PIR*², D 201). At first sight the new consular date (60 or 61) might appear to deter.

Reflection suggests the contrary, at least on a provisional estimate.[74] The *Ignotus*, who held the same two priesthoods as Ducenius, is styled 'legatus Caesarum' as governor of Dalmatia. The formulation would fit Nero or the transition from Nero to Galba.

Ducenius was Galba's *praefectus urbi*, named once in the *Historiae* (i 14, 1), but not again, even when superseded by Flavius Sabinus (46, 1). Galba brought him from Dalmatia, it may be conjectured. If so, the legate Pompeius Silvanus | (*suff.* 45), one of the 'divites senes' (ii 86, 3), owed his place to Galba, not to Nero.

The new emperor's choice for the urban prefecture may arouse some perplexity. Other candidates were to hand, such as the aristocratic Plautius Silvanus Aelianus, recently governor of Moesia (?60–6), with some credit (*ILS* 986).

Aged sixty-nine when he seized the power, Galba was archaic and rigid. Not but that Tacitus could apply the term 'mobilitas ingenii' (i 7, 2), which some find peculiar. No problem. Galba was liable to be swayed by his entourage. Which influences dominated at this point, it might be idle to speculate. Perhaps friends of Thrasea Paetus now coming back from exile. Or, for that matter, the consular Silius Italicus, who should not too readily be discounted, despite his recent and questionable activities.

Ducenius fades out—apart from a proconsulate in Asia, which the attribution of the inscription at Epidaurus would entail.[75] He got no second consulship from Vespasian, in contrast to a number of careerists who weathered the stormy seasons and, if 'fluctibus rei publicae iactati', managed to keep an even keel. Notably Vibius Crispus and Eprius Marcellus.

Two more consulates accrued to Ducenii, in 87 and in 96. In between, in the autumn of 93, catastrophe overtook the party that honoured the memory of Thrasea Paetus. The causes are obscure, less so the publicity later accorded by writers on the flank such as

[74] See 'Partisans of Galba', *Historia* xxxi (1982), 478 f. = pp. 134 f., above.
[75] That is, in 73/4, succeeding the triennial tenure of Eprius Marcellus (*ILS* 992).

Pliny and Tacitus, from whom as from others the Emperor earns incrimination. Sundry ambitions, conflicts, exacerbations might be surmised. Arulenus Rusticus had come at last to a consulship in 92, and Avidius Quietus (one of their friends) held the *fasces* early in the next year.

For balance of judgement and for the assessment of groups and factions, attention will suitably divert to senators who kept out of trouble and found a defence or pretext in service to state and empire whoever the ruler might be. The Ducenii aggregate without discomfort to that company. Likewise the Arruntii.

The consulate of M. Arruntius (?Aquila) fell towards the end of 66, the year that witnessed the ruin of Thrasea Paetus. A son becoming consul eleven years later implies that he was more than mature in age. That son (*suff.* 77) began with fair prospects, being *triumvir monetalis* (a post generally reserved for the high aristocracy), and he was quaestor to Nero. His *cursus* (*ILS* 980) carries no occupation in the provinces. Which separates him from those who had to earn advancement in that fashion.

The rank of these Arruntii went back quite a long way (as men now reckoned ancestry). Cornutus Arruntius Aquila, governor of Galatia in 6 B.C., had a son called Marcus (*PIR*², A 1127), after whom intervenes a gap. The line appeared to resume, but not with a senator. In 50, M. Arruntius Aquila stood attested as imperial procurator in Pamphylia (*ILS* 215). The general assumption (cf. A 1138) is now blown away. His family is shown Lycian (see below). |

It remains to look for the missing generation. One of the most enigmatic consuls all through the first dynasty is M. Aquila C. f. Iulianus, the *ordinarius* of 38, in office for six months. His nomenclature has failed to stimulate a proper curiosity (cf. A 982). The *cognomen* functions in place of the *gentilicium*, as happens. Compare M. Vestinus Atticus (*cos.* 65), a magnate from Vienna in Narbonensis. In this case the absent *nomen* is patently 'Iulius'.[76] The man looks like an Atticus (perhaps indeed a Julius Atticus), adopted by M. Julius Vestinus: otherwise his mother was a Julia Attica.

On this parallel, the consul of 38 appears to be the son of a C. Julius adopted by M. Aquila. It does not pass belief that the missing *nomen* is 'Arruntius'.

Their next consul after 77 is L. Arruntius Stella (*suff.* 101). About the year 90 he married Violentilla, a rich widow resident at Naples. Statius furnished a lavish epithalamium (*Silvae* i 2). Martial styled her

---

[76] *PIR*², J 624, where he is assumed the son of L. Julius Vestinus, the Prefect of Egypt (622). Rather the son (by birth or by adoption) of a Marcus Julius Vestinus.

'Ianthis' (vi 21, 1), but her name has nothing floral in its nature. It derives from 'Violens', an ancient *cognomen* surviving among Volumnii at Perusia.[77] Otherwise, no clue to Violentilla's family or origin. She may not be Stella's first wife. In that event a happy pair benefited from recent deaths.

Both poets were emboldened to predict a speedy consulship for Arruntius Stella. Indeed, Statius acclaimed a son of the patriciate, 'quem patriciis maioribus ortum / Nobilitas gavisa tulit (i 2, 71 f.).

Stella or his father may have owed that status to Vespasian.[78] If so, they outstripped the other branch, since the *suffectus* of 77 was certainly plebeian. However, the term 'patricius' can be applied loosely, as several times in Juvenal, and perhaps once in Suetonius.[79]

A further item in Statius' laudation is of clear value. Stella was a *XVvir sacris faciundis* (i 2, 176 f.). To annex one of the four 'amplissima sacerdotia' before the praetorship denotes either high birth or conspicuous success. The latter is exemplified by Cornelius Tacitus who held that priesthood when praetor in 88: early laurels in oratory aided by influences not verifiable.

Like Pliny (who never names him), Stella was praetor in 93, a year hazardous for the eager and incautious. Pliny was not deterred from visiting in the suburbs a philosopher who had been banished from Rome (*Ep.* iii 11, 2). Stella assumed the charge of the games that celebrated Domitian's Sarmatian victory (Martial viii 78).

In a similar function in 55 an Arruntius Stella was put on record by the careful historian (*Ann.* xiii 22, 1): Stella's father—or better, the grandfather. Given the language of Statius (on the lowest count 'nobilitas'), at least one consul should be postulated in generations anterior to the socially eminent coeval of Pliny. |

On the *Fasti* Patavines supplant the line of L. Arruntius from Atina (*cos.* 6), which ended with Arruntius Camillus Scribonianus (*cos.* 32). In their turn they disappeared, giving way to Arruntii from Lycia, who derived the name from an Arruntius active in the eastern parts during the early imperial epoch.

This family produced M. Arruntius Claudianus from Xanthos, adlected to the Senate in the late years of Domitian, but perhaps not achieving a consulship.[80] Xanthos has recently disclosed the ancestor, namely L. Arruntius Hermacotas, defining him as the parent of the

---

[77] *ILS* 6618; 7833. See further *Some Arval Brethren* (1980), 23.

[78] Stella is assumed patrician, e.g. by Groag (A 1151); R. Syme, *Tacitus* (1058), 666. Beneficiaries of Claudius Caesar are not excluded. Some lacked high distinction, despite the language of Tacitus (xi 25, 2). Observe M. Helvius Geminus (*ILS* 975).

[79] Suetonius, *Titus* 9, 1. Though plausible for C. Silius (the paramour of Messallina), that status is not proved by Juvenal x 332.

[80] *ILS* 8821 (Xanthos), supplemented by *AE* 1972, 572 (Ephesus).

imperial procurator M. Arruntius Aquila.[81] Hermacotas is described as an 'educator of emperors'. That is to say, to princes of the dynasty, perhaps indeed the sons of Germanicus Caesar.

Once again, education and court influence, as earlier with Veranius, the guardian of Drusus, as later with Asconius Labeo.

So far eight certified consuls. In an experimental science nothing should be disdained that reinforces uncertainties in the method or limits of knowledge. For this reason a fragile hypothesis about Caecina Paetus was allowed cursory mention. More important, the Arruntii. The enigmatic M. Aquila Julianus (*cos.* 38) invited speculation; on the lowest count one more Arruntius Stella in the consulate is an expedient postulate; and it is not certain that M. Arruntius, the colleague of a L. Nonius, is identical with the *suffectus* of 66.[82]

So much having been said about the Asconii, it is desirable to put under inspection a polyonymous Asconius Sardus who may have acceded to the *fasces* early in the reign of Trajan. In any event he was a senator.

The fragmentary inscription (*CIL* v 2824) stands as follows, with supplementation as suggested by Groag (*PIR*[2], A 1207):

C. ASCONIO] C. F. FAB. SA[RDO
SECVN]DO. P. CESTI[O
VM]BRIO. DEXTRO
DVCENIO
PROCO]S. PROVINCIA[E

Of the aggregated names, 'P. Cestius' offers no clue, but the rare 'Ducenius' is Patavine. Instead of Groag's 'Um]brius Dexter' it is easy and expedient to introduce 'Su]brius Dexter', as has elsewhere been pointed out.[83] Subrius Dexter was a tribune in the Guard in January of 69; and he is discovered, with the *praenomen* | 'Sextus', as the procurator governing Sardinia in 74.[84] He is presumed a brother to Subrius Flavus, also a tribune, whose role and comportment in Piso's conspiracy earned generous acclaim from Tacitus (*Ann.* xv 49 f. etc.).

Their *nomen* happens to be portentously rare. Etruscan derivation

---

[81] A. Balland, *Fouilles de Xanthos* vii (1981), 157.

[82] That is to say, the pair revealed by *AE* 1947, 2 (Samothrace). If the pair were put early in the reign of Hadrian, a hypothesis emerges: M. Arruntius Claudianus from Xanthos as not only the first Lycian senator but the first consul, displacing Ti. Claudius Agrippinus (C 776).

[83] *JRS* lviii (1968), 139 = *RP* (1979), 701.

[84] *Hist.* i 31, 2; *CIL* x 8023 f.

has been surmised.[85] Yet it may also be northern and native, although *CIL* V offers only one specimen, namely C. Subrius Secundinus, a magnate of some status at Cemenelum in the Alpes Maritimae.[86]

So far nothing much emerges. Help arrives from an inscription registering another *polyonymus* (v 7447). It was found at Valentia, a distant town in the north-eastern corner of 'Regio IX'.[87]

At the lowest, resemblances in the nomenclature of this *Ignotus* will indicate a relative of Asconius Sardus. Rather the man himself: 'quod mihi probabilius videtur', so Groag stated (in *PIR*[2], A 1207).[88]

From a broad and handsome document four truncated lines survive:

> PONIANVS. SECVNDVS. P. CEST
> IVS. PRISCVS. DVCENIVS. PROC
> ES. NERVAE. TRAIANI. AVG. LEGION
> TVRM. VI. TRIBVN. MILIT. LEGION. XXI RA

First of all, the names that recur. 'Pom]ponianus Secundus' amplifies the 'Secun]dus' of the Patavine inscription. It might appear to echo back to the illustrious P. Pomponius Secundus, the consular dramatist (*suff.* 44). Hesitation is prescribed. Both *nomen* and *cognomen* are common and indistinctive.

'Ducenius Proc[ulus' is in a different case. It evokes C. Ducenius Proculus, consul suffect in 87, but 'P. Cestius' remains a total enigma. Cestii occur on only two inscriptions in *CIL* V.[89] Any connection with the three consular Cestii under the first dynasty is ruled out.[90] One might wonder about an obscure Cestius Proculus, proconsul of Crete and Cyrene (*Ann.* xiii 30, 1). Hence the faintest of faint chances that the *suffectus* of 87 was polyonymous: possibly C. Ducenius P. Cestius Proculus.

Inferences from the Latin *cognomina* of the most common type are strongly to be deprecated. One will recall the problems inherent in Plinian characters called 'Maximus' and 'Priscus'.[91] Along with

---

[85] In *LE* 237 Schulze adduced 'Supri' (*CIE* 53: Volaterrae); 'Zupre' (2251: Clusium). Also C. Subernius from Cales in Campania (*Ad fam.* ix 13, 1).

[86] *CIL* v 7917. He was *patronus* and *flamen provinciae*.

[87] Valentia (Valenza) was east of Hasta, north-west of Dertona. It has yielded only five other inscriptions. For the problems of Valentia in relation to Forum Fulvii see Chilver, op. cit. 66 f.

[88] Matching the two documents in *RE* v 1755 (1903), Groag said 'nicht unmöglich'. He there assumed that the senator was a son of Ducenius Proculus (*suff.* 87), taken in adoption by the magistrate C. Asconius Sardus (*ILS* 6692).

[89] *CIL* v 1228 (Aquileia); 7538 (near Aquae Statiellae, in 'Regio IX').

[90] C. Cestius Gallus (*cos.* 35), C. Cestius Gallus (*suff.* 42), N. Cestius (*suff.* 55). They might be from Praeneste, or Campanian.

[91] For some desperate cases, *JRS* lviii (1968), 143 = *RP* (1979), 707.

'Proculus', those two belong to the six on highest frequency. |

None the less, the luck of epigraphy may supervene.[92] A 'Priscus' occurs in line 2. Ephesus has recently disclosed a proconsul of Asia styled 'Sex. Subrius Dexter Cornelius Priscus'.[93] He was on previous attestation as Cornelius Priscus, a correspondent of Pliny (iii 21), as L. Cornelius Priscus (*suff.* ?104), proconsul in 120/1 (*PIR*[2], C 1420). The item 'Sex. Subrius Dexter' comes as a revelation, since name and *cognomen* stand on the Patavine inscription (v 2824).

That is not all. The local origin of the consular had in fact been detected.[94] Brixian fragments disclose the senator ']elius Q. f. Fab.[', and also his wife 'Secunda Prisci'.[95] Adventitious comfort now accrues. A Lycian city paid honour to an earlier member of the family, the senator Q. Cornelius Priscus.[96]

New information thus adds substance to both inscriptions: (Cornelius) Priscus on the second harmonizes with Subrius Dexter on the first. Corroboration if not proof ensues for a northern origin of the Subrii.

Next, the fragmentary career on the inscription at Valentia. It stands in descending order. First in time, the tribunate in XXI Rapax. That gives a *terminus ante quem*. The legion was destroyed by Sarmatians who invaded Pannonia in 92. Of the next post only 'turm. VI' is preserved. That is to say, the man was a *sevir equitum Romanorum*. The formula is not normally subject to drastic abbreviation.[97] Hence a valuable indication: the lines were very long. In confirmation of which, observe that space is requisite for the quaestorship (perhaps held in a province), for the posts of either aedile or tribune, for the praetorship—and perhaps for some other occupation before the command of a legion.

To that command is attached the nomenclature of the Emperor Trajan. It lacks the *cognomen* 'Germanicus' which he at once inherited from Nerva when adopted in October of 97.[98] Sporadic omission occurs, it is true.[99] On the inscription of a Roman senator it may without discomfort be taken to imply a quite early date, earlier perhaps than the end of the year.

---

[92] Thus the army commander Priscus (*Ep.* ii 13) can now be identified as L. Neratius Priscus (*suff.* 97), and legate of Germania Inferior: thanks to the revision of *ILS* 1034 (Saepinum) effected by G. Camodeca, *AAN* lxxxvii (1976), 19 ff. (whence *AE* 1976, 195).

[93] Cited by W. Eck, *Epigraphica* xli (1979), 82.   [94] *Tacitus* (1958), 805.

[95] *CIL* v 4364, cf. 4363. Further a 'Q. Cornel[' was a magistrate there (4412), but he might be identical with Q. Cornelius Q. f. Fronto (4413).

[96] A. Balland, *Fouilles de Xanthos* vii (1981), 121. For a Priscus legate of Galatia early in the reign of Tiberius see M. Grant, *NC* x (1950), 43.

[97] As shown by the details in Dessau, *ILS*, Vol. iii, p. 410 f.

[98] Pliny, *Pan.* 9, 2.

[99] For the statistics, P. Kneissl, *Die Siegestitulatur der römischen Kaiser* (1969), 70.

For legionary legates in office at that turn of events, bright prospects unfolded. Thus, for example, the *Ignotus* of Nemausus (*CIL* xii 3169). He had a legion under Nerva and Trajan, proceeded to a praetorian province, and later earned the military decorations of a consular legate: perhaps D. Terentius Scaurianus (*suff.* 102 or 104).[100] Conjectures about the promotion of some other early Trajanic consuls, such as L. Fabius Justus (*suff.* 102), could be admitted to the rubric. |

It is therefore not beyond belief that the *Ignotus* acceded to a consulship. Coincidences in nomenclature (now reinforced) had moved Groag to claim him identical with '[C. Asconius] C. f. Fab. Sa[rdus]'. If, despite some hesitations, that hypothesis be accepted for the convenience of the present exposition, various consequences ensue. The length of the lines postulated on the second inscription entails a vast and pretentious aggregation of names. Further, this man was perhaps the son of the magistrate C. Asconius Sardus (*ILS* 6692). And finally, he was the first senator of the Asconii, since Q. Asconius Gabinius Modestus is not beyond doubt an Asconius by paternity (as suggested above). And also their last senator, though perhaps ending as a consul.

The crop of consuls from 36 to 101 (eight, or perhaps close on a dozen) is a proper response to the solid renown of an opulent and conservative city. Ancient allies of Rome against the Gauls, the Veneti never faltered in allegiance, and their inner stability was disturbed once only, when in 174 B.C. Patavium had to request a consul to intervene.[101] Along with sound morality, social harmony prevailed in the sequel. It was manifested during the Civil Wars. Not only was Patavium held strong for the cause of the Republic.[102] When in 41/0 Asinius Pollio, governing Cisalpina, imposed exactions and the rich went into hiding, no slave betrayed his master.[103]

As has been shown, Patavines duly enjoyed prime favour with the first dynasty—and indeed close access to the 'domus regnatrix'. Apart from Thrasea Paetus, none of the consuls appears to play a marked role in political life. The urban prefecture of Ducenius Geminus may be something of an accident, the product of loyal aid to a usurper in a troubled season. Ducenius, legate of Dalmatia, stands out as their only governor of an armed province. Ducenius

---

[100] *Tacitus* (1958), 646, cf. *JRS* xlvii (1957), 134 = *Ten Studies in Tacitus* (1970), 115.

[101] For this incident, W. V. Harris, *ZPE* xxvii (1977), 283 ff.

[102] As asseverated by Cicero, *Phil.* xii 10.

[103] Macrobius i 11, 22. Harmony was later advertised by 'concordalis' in the title of municipal *seviri*. For example, 'L. Ducen./Atimeti/Patavi Aug. Conc./Pyrallidi lib.' (*ILS* 6693: between Patavium and Ateste).

ended as proconsul of Asia—if the Epidaurian inscription (*ILS* 963) is assigned to him. Otherwise, no proconsuls of either Asia or Africa, so far as known.

Their distinction is mainly social and conformist. That is implied by the priesthoods they held. No fewer than five of the eight were *quindecimviri sacris faciundis*, viz. Papinius Allenius, Thrasea Paetus, Ducenius Geminus, Arruntius Aquila (*suff.* 77), Arruntius Stella.

That college tended to annex senators of cultivated tastes. A catalogue of those who shared membership with Cornelius Tacitus during a period of about thirty years furnishes various instruction.[104] It includes Valerius Flaccus, whose decease (*c.*93) was a great loss to poetry, so Quintilian averred—and also to the *Fasti*, since *quindecimviri* can hardly miss consulships.[105] |

Education and polite letters were far from neglected in the *patria* of Titus Livius. He had encouraged the young Claudius to turn to history—and the erudite emperor may further have acknowledged 'pietas' towards a city which produced Asconius Pedianus. A scholiast alleges that Pedianus wrote a life of Sallust.[106] None of that tribe comes out with the more plausible notion that Pedianus dealt in like fashion with the other classic historian.

Livy frequented the schools of rhetoric, but no citizen of Patavium is inscribed among the Transpadane orators. Prudent men might conceive distaste for a profession which for full success entailed dubious operations or damage to repute, as witness Silius Italicus. Vibius Crispus on his first entrance in the *Historiae* of Tacitus carries the label 'inter claros magis quam inter bonos' (ii 10, 1).

Of poets there was a plethora in Transpadana, with sundry performers commended in the correspondence of Pliny. The earliest from Patavium is Largus, named by Ovid. Next a certain Flaccus, matched by Martial with Arruntius Stella on his first mention (i 61, 4), and to recur many times.[107] This Flaccus baffles any approach to identity. Finally, both Martial and Statius extol the talent of Stella their patron. No other Patavine writers can be recovered.[108]

Despite the fame of Patavium, the city finds mention only once in

---

[104] *Tacitus* (1958), 664. Add now M. Hirrius Fronto Neratius Pansa, consul suffect *c.*75 (*AE* 1968, 145).

[105] The *Ignotus* of *ILS* 1039, a governor of Galatia, was probably consul early in Hadrian's reign.

[106] Pseudo-Acro on Horace, *Sat.* i 2, 41.

[107] Down to ix 90, if not further. For the detail, F 170. Not identical with the author of the *Argonautica*, as held possible in *Tacitus* (1958), 609, n. 7. He may be provincial. Observe L. Julius Ursus Valerius Flaccus (*PIR*¹, J 418), who is probably L. Valerius Flaccus (*suff.* 128).

[108] Unless Sardus be conceded (*Ep.* ix 31).

the pages of Pliny. The austere grandmother of a Brixian derives 'e municipio Patavio. nosti loci mores: Serrana tamen Patavinis quoque severitatis exemplum est' (i 14, 6).

A ready explanation avails: separate regions in broad Transpadana and the distance from Comum. The 'Pliny country' admits a definition.[109] It is the kernel of 'Regio XI' in the Augustan scheme as described by Pliny's uncle: 'Transpadana appellatur ab eo regio undecima, tota in mediterraneo' (*NH* iii 123). But the ambit of Pliny's correspondents extends over the border into 'Regio X', to take in Brixia and Verona. It does not go much further eastwards. No citizen of Vicetia or of Ateste receives a letter. From Patavium one surmises only two persons patently obscure, a Sardus (ix 31) and a Mustius (ix 39), cf. above. The surprise is Arrianus Maturus, styled 'Altinatium princeps' (iii 2, 2 etc.). That town lies about 40 km. north-east from Patavium, on the road to Concordia and Aquileia.

As elsewhere, negative evidence can help. Transpadane senators occurring in the collection engross due attention. A strong word should be put in for absentees, of various categories. Pliny sent no missive to any senator belonging to Arruntii, Ducenii, Asconii. |

Enthusiastic both for regional loyalties and for the cult of eloquence, Pliny nowhere annexes Cornelius Tacitus for 'illa nostra Italia'; and they do not appear to have numerous northern friends in close community.[110] The quest for the historian's *patria* narrows to Narbonensis or Transpadana.[111] For the latter zone (and indeed for Patavium in particular) sundry arguments have recently been adduced, some of them by no means unattractive.[112] The theme is important. Briefly as follows.

First of all, sporadic items that converge (as likewise in the plea for Narbonensis). The method is legitimate—and not to be eschewed if a reticent author is put under scrutiny. A clear instance implying exact knowledge is the wife of the consul Papinius Allenius (vi 49). The historian knew her name, and left it out, and the *patria* likewise (cf. above). Furthermore, some might now discover significance in Asconius Labeo and Arruntius Stella, each on isolated report early in Nero's reign (xiii 10, 1; 20, 1); and, for that matter, the prominence accorded to Subrius Flavus in the account of the Pisonian conspiracy. He is presumed a brother of Subrius Dexter, and can be supposed northern by origin (cf. above).

[109] *JRS* lviii (1968), 136 = *RP* (1979), 696.   [110] *Tacitus* (1958), 801.
[111] M. L. Gordon, *JRS* xxvi (1936), 145 ff.
[112] E. Koestermann, *Athenaeum* xliii (1965), 167 ff.; *Archivio Veneto* lxxvii (1965), 5 ff. A generous exposition is furnished by S. Borzsák, *RE, Suppl.* xi 379–84.

However, Patavium and Thrasea Paetus engross prepollence in the argument. Tacitus was careful to name his priesthood (xvi 22, 1); and he specified the local pageant at which Thrasea performed: 'quia idem Thrasea Patavi, unde ortus erat, ludis cetastis a Troiano Antenore institutis habitu tragico cecinerat' (21, 1).

Caution imports hesitance and strong doubts.[113] The keen and exact interest of Tacitus carries its own reason, whatever his provenance.Thrasea's character inspired admiration, his firm stand for freedom, honour, and dignity was resonant at the time and in later history. Nor will the author's design and structure be left out of account. In the third hexad he chose to put emphasis on three persons: Seneca, Corbulo, Thrasea, diverse but united by a common fate as victims of the tyrant. Thrasea is presented in five spaced episodes from 58 onwards, before the catastrophe in 66.

Certain cities in Transpadana acknowledged a close affinity. Thus Verona's poet acclaims 'Brixia Veronae mater amata meae' (67, 34). The same person might hold magistracies in both.[114] Further, while the senatorial Nonii of the second century are patently Brixian, two of them are at home in Verona and carry the tribe | 'Publilia'.[115] Pliny's Brixian friend Minicius Macrinus (who preferred not to enter the Senate) had a mother from Patavium, it will be recalled (i 14, 6). He married an Acilia, from the home town.[116] Many families of that class were content with a local bride. Thus the father of Patavium's first consul married an Allenia: that uncommon name is borne by two equestrian officers at Patavium. Asconius Pedianus also took a local wife.

Rising families extend the ambit of their alliances. The praetor Q. Asconius Gabinius Modestus has been noted (*CIL* v 2820), with some uncertainty about his full nomenclature.The item 'Gabinius' might pertain to a consular family; and an Asconia married the father of Silius Italicus (from a different town of Transpadana).

Attention was drawn to the polyonymous senator '[C. Asconius] C. f. Fab. Sa[rdus]'. Some of the names on the two documents (v 2824; 7447) arouse curiosity, though they cannot be exploited to establish propinquity of blood or marriage. However 'Subrius

[113] Despite the conclusion of Borzsák, op.cit. 384: 'so kann doch Koestermanns umsichtige Schlussfolgerung (206) hingenommen werden.'

[114] Thus Q. Minicius Q. f. Pob. Macer (v 4443, cf. 4292: Brixia): presumably related to Pliny's Brixian friend Minicius Macrinus, parent of the senator Minicius Acilianus (i 14, 5).

[115] *RE* xvii 864 f.; 897 f. For the relations between the two cities, M. Frézouls-Fasciato, *Mél. Grenier* (1962), 689 ff.

[116] A sister of P. Acilius. At Brixia P. Acilius P. f. Fab. Florus set up a statue to Aequitas (*AE* 1954, 75).

Dexter' may be assumed northern, and 'Cornelius Priscus' evokes a consular house at Brixia.

Of the eight Patavine consuls under discussion, two are equipped with known wives (Thrasea Paetus and Arruntius Stella). Papinius' delinquent spouse is absent from the written record, and nothing can be ascertained about the marriages of three Ducenii and two Arruntii. As with Stella, the brides may well be extraneous.

An Asconia married Ummidius Quadratus from distant Casinum. Alliances of this type, transcending regions or provinces, might have portentous repercussions. Ulpius Traianus from Italica married Pompeia L. f. Plotina, a lady of Nemausus; and the husband of Hadrian's niece Julia was a Pedanius from Barcino.

Hazard and variation in the epigraphic testimony impedes enquiry all through. First, sheer numbers of inscriptions. Brixia and Verona each yield over 800, Patavium less than the half. Brixia includes populous Alpine valleys and attributed tribes (Trumplini, Sabini, Camunni). Its *territorium* surpasses any city of Italy, likewise its contribution of recruits for the legions; and a quarter of Verona's total of inscriptions comes from the Arusnates. By contrast, Cremona and Mantua, each with less than forty. Cremona's deficiency is in part explained by the catastrophe of the year 69. Mantua, although at a junction of roads, appears secluded. It fails to respond to the fame accruing from its poet. The first senator and the last is Vespronius Candidus (*suff. c.*176), a military man of low birth: attested not at Mantua but in a far country.[117] |

Second, the type and quality of the documentation. Brixia offers a mass of senatorial families, and so does Verona. Ateste has none, and not even an equestrian officer. That city has to serve another purpose—Venetic inscriptions and many veteran soldiers. Ateste was an Augustan military colony, founded soon after the Battle of Actium.[118]

The ethnic composition of Transpadane cities has not failed to stimulate curiosity. Immigration from the south has been surmised, and brought into relation with historical transactions or economic development. Its character and volume defies any estimate. Among the notables a few avow extraneous origin, such as the Arruntii from Atina or Pontius Paelignus, a Brixian senator (*ILS* 942).

For the rest, appeal can be made to name forms emanating from

---

[117] *CIL* viii 2754 (Lambaesis). It registers the tribe 'Sabatina'—and, exceptional in a person of rank, the city.

[118] It is absent from Strabo—for whom Tergeste was still only a fort or a village (v 215; vi 314). Cf. Chilver, op. cit. 54 (on the geographer's obsolescence).

regions of central Italy. Endings in '-idius' indicate the Abruzzi territories. Among the better sort at Patavium one may note the knight P. Opsidius Rufus (v 2791). Again, '-ienus' denotes the Etrusco–Umbrian zone. Aquileia supplies about twenty, but Aquileia is an old Latin colony.[119] Patavium is deficient.

Apart from statistics, Transpadane nomenclature conceals many traps. Natives shaped their names on Latin models. Thus 'Vergilius', 'Verginius', 'Atilius'.[120] The substratum was indigenous, by heavy preponderance. Evidence from Ateste is decisive. Natives lurk under Aemilii, Ennii, Rutilii, Titinii.[121]

Patavium avoided disturbance through long ages, and in the civil wars it was spared confiscation for the benefit of veteran colonists. The inscriptions duly parade a collection of rare or unique names. A single document would suffice, viz. 'Birrius / Voltiom. f. / Sumbica Ostiala / Birria Frem. / Birria Quarta' etc.[122] Other prime exhibits are to hand: the four ladies Vossinia, Poppiaca, Parcilia M. Oxoni f., Muttiaena.[123]

The Asconii are indigenous. No need to cite the 'fossa Asconis' from a late writer.[124] Theirs is a name of public note, but found only once in the Roman provinces.[125] Apart from consuls, 'Ducenius' is extremely rare: in the north once at Patavium, once at Verona.[126] It has a native look, yet it occurs on an Etruscan bilingual.[127] Nor is 'Allenius' found often outside Venetia.[128] |

Attention to uncommon names prevalent either in some town or region (and even there confined) can furnish valuable results. For example, in the foregoing pages, Allenii, Ducenii, Mustii, Sepullii.[129] And a Transpadane origin has been argued for Cingonius Varro. One should be alert for other senators.[130] Other names, familiar to

---

[119] A. Calderini, *Aquileia Romana* (1930), 574. The mixed population is amply documented in that book. The veteran colony Ateste has eight specimens of names ending in '-enus'.

[120] Chilver, op. cit. 82 ff., with other instances.

[121] M. Lejeune, *Ateste* (1978), 135.

[122] *CIL* v 2906. For the name 'Ostiala', compare ']ni/M. f. Ostialae Galleniae' on the early stele published in *Padova Preromana* (the Mostra of 1976), 48, cf. 304 with pl. 83.

For the Venetic name 'Frema' on v 2906, cf. 'Frema Rutilia P. f. Sociaca' (i² 2781: Ateste).

[123] *CIL* v 3071; 3019; 3003; 2899. And one might add M'. Laeponius (2972); Albarenius (2845).   [124] Jordanes, *Getica* 29.

[125] *CIL* xii 3426 (Nemausus: of late date). Apart from Patavium, Transpadana shows examples at Ateste, Altinum, Concordia (2607; 2243; 8676). None in *CIL* IX, X, XI.

[126] *CIL* v 2525 (= *ILS* 6693); 3609.

[127] *CIL* xi 3208 (Nepet): 'Ducenius tucuntal tucuntines' (cited by Schulze, *LE* 375).

[128] Where, apart from Patavium, it occurs at Ateste (2538) and Vicetia (3162). Add from Pais, *Supp. It.* (1883), Vicetia (613); Aquileia (206).

[129] Benefit can accrue on the side. Thus a *patria* for the Augustan *rhetor* Sepullius Bassus (*PIR*¹, S 360).

[130] For example, the senator C. Mocconius Verus (*CIL* vi 1463), the tribe 'Fabia' pointing to Brixia or Patavium (cf. n. 68 above). Again, L. Mestrius Florus (*suff. c.*75), the friend and

the reader from literature or history can offer a surprise. Transpadana offers no Papinii (except the consul), no Pedii despite Asconius Pedianus. At Patavium the eminent Arruntii are vouched for only by a consul (*ILS* 980) and by Arruntia T. f.[131] 'Gabinius' occurs along with 'Asconius' in the name of a senator: in *CIL* V no other specimen. Yet it might be native. There are also Gabii; and no fancier of nomenclature will neglect 'Gabo', the *gentilicium* borne by the Brixian senator L. Gabo Aurunculeius.[132]

Epilogue

Patavium in relation to neighbouring cities would open a broad and engaging theme. In one direction, the boundary is clear; only a dozen km. short of Ateste, and the station Ad Fines lies half-way on the road to Vicetia.[133] To the north and north-east, Patavine territory may have extended a long distance towards Acelum, Tarvisium, Altinum. On the south, Atria was the neighbour, situated between the mouths of Po and Atesis. Patavium thus occupied a central position in a large area of Venetia, comparable to Mediolanum in 'Regio X'.

Patavium prospered at the expense of those cities. On comparison of their senators, some instruction might emerge, albeit modest and imperfect. As concerns Vicetia, Tacitus, when alluding to the *patria* of the Vitellian general Caecina Alienus, stated 'modicae municipio vires' (*Hist.* iii 8, 1). It also produced Salonii and Matidii of the senatorial order, acquiring adventitious fame through Salonia Matidia, the niece of Trajan and mother of Vibia Sabina.[134]

On the known facts, no senators issued from ancient Atria, from Ateste, or from Altinum (where Arrianus Maturus declined Vespasian's offer of that status), while Acelum and Tarvisium are enveloped in an obscurity no doubt well deserved.[135] | Atria went into decay, perhaps long since. The *colonia* of Ateste was overshadowed by the

patron of Plutarch, to whom he bequeathed his *gentilicium*. That native name, also Illyrian and Balkan, has 22 specimens in *CIL* V. See further the remarks on Mestrius Florus in *MH* xxxvii (1980), 105 = *RP* iii (1984), 1252.

[131] *CIL* v 2996. The curious may notice a magistrate at Verona, '] M. f. Pob. Aquila' (Pais, *Supp. It.* 629).

[132] *CIL* v 4332. That volume has three Gabii: 1225 (Aquileia); 2631 (Ateste); 3672 (Verona). Rational doubt will therefore attend upon the extraction of Q. Asconius Gabinius Modestus—and even upon the origin of consular Gabinii (*suffecti* in 35 and 43).

[133] For the boundaries, *CIL* v, p. 268.

[134] Matidia is attested as 'Salonia Matidia' by *AE* 1954, 62. For the family, *Some Arval Brethren* (1980), 61 f.

[135] For Acelum (not in *RE* i), see Chilver, op. cit. 66. For the inscriptions, *CIL* v 2086–108; Pais, *Supp. It.* 448–65.

near vicinity of Patavium. In the opposite direction Altinum was not far distant, on the road to Aquileia. It had acquired some strategic importance, for a branch of the Via Claudia Augusta ran thence across the Alps into Raetia. For the poet Martial the beauty of its country mansions evoked comparison with the bay of Baiae.[136]

Patavium itself waned before the splendour of Verona.[137] That city went on being prolific in senators. After Arruntius Stella and Asconius Sardus, Patavium makes a poor showing. In the Antonine age it will not be easy to discover any senator except Q. Mustius Priscus, governor of Dacia and consul suffect in 144.[138]

Of the eight consuls under review, six belong to two families. All faded out quickly. It would be worth knowing who inherited the wealth of Arruntii and Ducenii. The name of Ducenius Proculus enjoyed a double perpetuation.[139] First, it occurs among the fourteen *gentilicia* paraded by Q. Pompeius Sosius Priscus, the consul of 169 (*ILS* 1104). Second, in an ostentatious person whose tribe indicates libertine extraction, namely ']Quintius C. f. / [Pa]latina / Cestianus Ducenius / Proculus'.[140]

Becoming senators, the municipal magnates departed to Rome, and some failed to maintain attachments to the *patria*, hence a lack of local inscriptions in the sequel to commemorate either their honours or any benefactions. Others again had never been thus documented. Thus the Aurelii Fulvi and Arrii Antonini of Nemausus. Their *patria* is established through extraneous evidence—or by rational conjecture. On this theme, as on others relevant to Patavium, much more could be said.

---

[136] Martial iv 25. Apart from Atestina Sabina and her husband Clemens (x 93), the sole sign that his journey to the North went across the Po.

[137] Chilver, op. cit. 54 f.

[138] G. Alföldy, *Konsulat u. Senatorenstand unter den Antoninen* (1977), 147; 244; 304.

[139] As duly registered by Groag in *RE* v 1755.

[140] *CIL* x 5821 (Ferentinum). 'Cestianus' is of interest because of 'P. Cestius' in the nomenclature of the senator C. Asconius C. f. Sardus (v 2824; 7447).

22

P. Calvisius Ruso, One Person or Two?

P. CALVISIUS RUSO came on register as consul suffect in 79, proconsul of Asia, legate governing the province Cappadocia–Galatia in the vicinity of the year 106.[1] Further testimony accrued. In 1913 Hermann Dessau published and discussed an inscription from Pisidian Antioch.[2] The document disclosed the *cursus* of Ruso and equipped him with a second member for his nomenclature, viz. 'Julius Frontinus'. That adjunct later emerged on a milestone at Philomelium, and on a dedication at a small town in Lycaonia.[3] Along with coin evidence, these items endow a handsome entry: *PIR*[2], C 350.

The career of this consular is noteworthy, carrying sundry problems and anomalies. Not less so the person. Ruso attaches to the nexus that produced rulers of Rome in the Antonine dynasty. His son Tullus Ruso (*cos.* 109), marrying Domitia Cn. f. Lucilla, became through a daughter the maternal grandfather of Marcus Aurelius. A renewed investigation was welcome. It takes the form of an ample exposition, fully documented.[4]

Meanwhile, however, disquiet had percolated, although nowhere made public. Ruso, consul in 79, and the Trajanic governor of Cappadocia: are they in truth identical? The universal persuasion encounters firm denial in a simultaneous paper from Eric Birley, now making explicit the doubts he conceived many years ago.[5]

The thesis need not provoke alarm. In the original entry Elimar Klebs, nowhere prone to excesses of scepticism, gave voice to hesitations. He concluded with 'plane incertum est, utrum legatus

---

[1] *PIR*[1], C 285.

[2] *JRS* iii (1913), 301 ff., with a drawing of the text (p. 302), whence *AE* 1914, 247.

[3] *MAMA* viii 193; vii 211.

[4] B. Rémy, 'La carrière de P. Calvisius Ruso Julius Frontinus, gouverneur de Cappadoce-Galatie', *MEFRA* xcv (1983), 163–82.

[5] E. Birley, 'The Enigma of Calvisius Ruso', *ZPE* li (1983), 263–9. His dubitations were in fact voiced over a quarter of a century ago. I shared them. For a trace, observe the entry in the Index to *Tacitus* (1958), viz. 'suff. ?79'.

Zeitschrift für Papyrologie und Epigraphik lvi (1984), 173–92.

idem atque proconsul an (quod magis crediderim) filius huius fuerit.'[6]

More significant perhaps the procedure adopted by Dessau. He omitted this splendid *cursus* from the 'Mantissa' to *ILS* (published in 1916). Perhaps it came too late.[7] Or else, devoted as ever to proper economy in citation, | Dessau was reluctant to encumber his footnotes with controversy and a whole sequence of uncertainties. He might even have changed his mind almost at once.

It will be convenient (and on several counts instructive) to present Dessau's text.

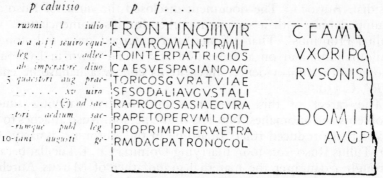

p caluisio   *p f . . . .*

rusoni	*l* *iulio*	FRONTINOIIIVIR CFAM
a a a f f scuiro equi-		VMROMANTRMIL
leg . . . . . . adlec-		TOINTERPATRICIOS VXORIP
ab imperatore diuo		CAESVESPASIANOAVG
5 quaestori aug prae-		TORICOSGVRATVIAE RVSONISL
. . . . . . xv uira		SFSODALIAVGVSTALI
. . . . . . (?) ad sac-		RAPROCOSASIAECVRA
-tori aedium sac-		RAPETOPERVMLOCO DOMIT
-rumque publ leg		PPOPRIMPNERVAETRA
10-iani augusti gr-		RMDACPATRONOCOL AVGP

FIG. 74.   INSCRIPTION FROM ANTIOCHIA (p. 301).

Surviving letters, copied by Sir W. M. Ramsay, are in capitals; restorations of lost parts in italics.
Owing to the position of the stone it was not possible to see the stops at the ends of words.

First of all, the shape of the document. The photograph published in 1925 furnishes guidance.[8] The lines on the right happen to end in regular order (except for l. 8). Hence indications of space for supplements. The tribe of Ruso should go at the beginning of the first line as extant, with '[P. Calvisio P. f.]' to stand in isolated emphasis at the head.[9] Further, in l. 4 the photograph reveals the letter 'p' preceding 'Caes.' in the titulature of Vespasian. Therefore 'im]p.'. That was known to Groag, who proposed 'a divo? im]p.'.[10] Not attractive as a formula, and it fails to fill out the line. Read therefore the innocuous 'per censuram ab im]p. Caes. Vespasiano Aug.'.[11]

[6] *PIR*[1], C 285.

[7] Dessau was able to include, from JRS ii (1912), 240, the inscription of Favonius, consul and proconsul of Asia (*ILS* 9483).

[8] *JRS* xv (1925), pl. xxxv. 3.   [9] Cf. *ILS* 1025; 1018; 1035; 1052.

[10] *PIR*[2], C 350. Reproduced by B. Rémy, op. cit. 164.

[11] That formula occurs on the inscription of Glitius Gallus (*ILS* 999): not there relating to an adlection.

Finally, ']ra' in l. 7, before 'procos. Asiae', the first letter was transmitted by Ramsay. Dessau suggested a third priesthood for Ruso: the tentative 'regi ad sac]ra'.[12] He refrained from printing 'regi'—and that item again was too short for the line. By good fortune, Ramsay's 'r' is not discernible on the photograph. The post remains so far a total enigma. As Groag avowed, 'quid fuerit nescio'.[13] |

Several reasons impelled Birley to reject identity between the known consul and the *polyonymus* who was legate of Cappadocia under Trajan. First, and of prime weight, the narrow interval from quaestorship to the consulate in 79. The Ruso of the inscription was adlected into the patriciate by Vespasian during his censorship in 73/4. After which, he became *quaestor Aug.*

Rigour and system will be deprecated, exceptions occur almost everywhere. As parallel and support for the rapid advancement of Ruso, P. Glitius Gallus has been adduced (*ILS* 999). He was adlected a patrician, became quaestor soon after; and his consulship cannot fall later than the first half of the year 79 since Vespasian is not styled 'divus', so it is argued.[14] Nothing of that can stand. Three reasons tell against and dismiss the alleged parallel.

First, admission to the patriciate is not registered on the inscription. Glitius began as *triumvir monetalis* and *salius Palatinus*. That priesthood declares him patrician from the outset. His father, it follows, had been adlected by Claudius Caesar: belonging to an illustrious company, namely descendants of Vistilia, the lady of the six husbands, he was sent into exile by Nero in 65.[15]

Second, the date of his quaestorship. On *ILS* 999 stands 'quaestor[i T. C]ae[s]aris'. Conceivably, Glitius was 'quaestor imp. Caesaris', the formulation masking one of the ephemeral emperors of 69. If the supplement is retained, a date quite early in the reign of Vespasian is not excluded, before his son was admitted to full partnership in the imperial authority. Titus as Caesar had the right to a quaestor of his own. Possessing proconsular *imperium*, he also took an imperatorial salutation at the siege of Jerusalem.[16]

Third, the absence of 'divus'. Not in fact valid for dating. As has been shown, the word 'divo' has to be banished from Ruso's inscription at Antioch. Observe further the careers of the Domitii,

---

[12] H. Dessau, op. cit. 307.   [13] *PIR*[2], C 350.

[14] *PIR*[2], G 185, citing Groag in *RE, Suppl.* iii 790.

[15] Tacitus, *Ann.* xv 71, 3. A Glitius Gallus, styled a 'clarissimus civis', was the earliest of Vistilia's husbands (Pliny, *NH* vii 39).

[16] Josephus, *BJ* vi 316.

Lucanus and Tullus. Inscribed after they had held proconsulates in Africa under Domitian, each shows Vespasian as 'imp. Vespasianus Aug'.[17]

To resume, Glitius might after all have become quaestor as late as 74. But not consul as little as five years thereafter. Other patrician careers illustrate and confirm (see below). In 84 an unidentified Gallus was consul suffect. The year is suitable. Glitius is on every count a better candidate than M. Raecius Gallus from Tarraco, who began as a young equestrian partisan of Galba.[18] |

Next, the Cappadocian government held by P. Calvisius Ruso Julius Frontinus. Not merely subsequent to a proconsulate in Asia but arriving when a quarter of a century had elapsed since the consulship of P. Calvisius Ruso. The post falls between the limits of 103 and 109. For present purposes, closer dating can be waived.[19]

On the double showing, the polyonymous governor honoured at Pisidian Antioch ought not to be identified as the Ruso who was consul suffect in the last year of Vespasian and in due course proconsul of Asia (for the tenure 92 to 93).[20] However, the author of the firm and explicit negation ran into difficulty. He assumed a son of the known consul and proconsul, but he was not able to discover a suitable year for the consulship of P. Calvisius Ruso Julius Frontinus, and, by corollary, a place among the proconsuls of Asia. As he confessed, he was 'left with an enigma unresolved'.[21]

None the less, a path lay open. Going by the inscription, the legate of Cappadocia, quaestor in 74 or 75, was born *c.* 50. How and why did he acquire the adjunct 'Julius Frontinus'? Various problems infest the investigation of polyonymous persons. First of all, the 'real name', that is, the paternal. Two ways offer.

First, adoption. The son of a Julius Frontinus was adopted by P. Calvisius Ruso, consul suffect in 79 and born about 40. That they were close in age, in itself no bar. In this epoch it is not easy to certify an adoption that is not testamentary. On that assumption, a Julius Frontinus acquired the prefix after the decease of Ruso (i.e. at some time between 93 and 103).

Second, maternal ascendance. In binary nomenclature (the simplest of the phenomena), adoption tends to get invoked, all too often. On the contrary, the second member will frequently denote the mother's

[17] *ILS* 990 f.
[18] *RIT* 145.
[19] For the evidence, R. K. Sherk, *ANRW* ii 7 (1980), 1017 f.; B. Rémy, op. cit. 164 ff.
[20] For 92/3, W. Eck, *ZPE* xlv (1982), 151; *Chiron* xii (1983), 320.
[21] E. Birley, op. cit. 267.

name, socially superior it may well be.[22] To take one instance:
M. Cornelius Nigrinus Curiatius Maternus (*suff.* 83), the remarkable
general from Liria in Tarraconensis.[23] On one view, a Cornelius
adopting a Curiatius.[24] Better, a Cornelius whose mother was
Curiatia. In short, sister to Curiatius Maternus, orator and poet and
the central character in the *Dialogus* of Tacitus.[25] On this analogy, the
father of the *polyonymus*, that is P. Calvisius Ruso (consul suffect in
53), | had married a Julia Frontina.[26] Hence his second son, probably
from a different mother, and a decade younger than the *suffectus* of
79. That brothers should bear the same *praenomen* is not an obstacle.
It is the *cognomen* that serves to distinguish.[27] When the name of the
younger Ruso was abridged, for example on consular lists or
consular dates, he might have been styled 'P. Calvisius Frontinus'.

Those formulations normally register a man's paternal name. For
example, M. Hirrius Fronto Neratius Pansa (*suff.* ?75) stands as
'M. Ner]atio Pansa cos.'[28] Evidence of a different kind confirms the
'real name' of the Cappadocian legate. On one of the coins he is
P. C(alvisius) Ruso.[29]

Either way, Ruso would be close kin to a Julius Frontinus: a son or
a nephew. For convenience of exposition, if for nothing else, the
second alternative will here be employed. Nor is the maternal
extraction far to seek.

So far as ascertained, the illustrious Sex. Julius Frontinus makes his
earliest entrance as urban praetor in 70.[30] He is already a consul in 73.
How explain the rapid advance? Frontinus cannot pass muster as a
patrician. Rather a former equestrian officer, of age towards forty,
adlected to the Senate by Galba.[31]

On the hypothesis here in process of evolution, P. Calvisius Ruso
(*suff.* 53) married a sister of Julius Frontinus. His son (his younger
son), born *c.*50, after adlection *inter patricios* entered the Senate as
quaestor in 74 or 75. He will be conjectured consul suffect in 84,
proconsul of Asia for the tenure 97/8—which happens to be
providentially vacant (see below).

---

[22] See *Some Arval Brethren* (1980), 47 f. Further, 'Clues to Testamentary Adoption', in
Epigrafia e ordine senatorio i (1982), 397 ff. = pp. 159 ff., above.

[23] *AE* 1973, 283.

[24] The reverse order was assumed by G. Alföldy and H. Halfmann, *Chiron* iii (1973), 340;
348.

[25] Cf. *ZPE* xli (1981), 137 = *RP* iii (1984), 1387; *Chiron* xiii (1983), 144 = p. 276, above.

[26] His consular year is now certain, cf. L. Vidman, *Fasti Ostienses* (ed. 2, 1982).

[27] Thus L. Neratius Marcellus (*suff.* 95), L. Neratius Priscus (97).

[28] *ILS* 4537.   [29] That of Sebastopolis (B. Rémy, op. cit. 166).

[30] Tacitus, *Hist.* iv 39, 1.

[31] This conjecture was proposed in *Tacitus* (1958), 780. Frontinus reported an anecdote about
Corbulo's capture of Tigranocerta, in 59 (*Strat.* ii 9, 5).

Brief reference to the promotion of patricians is expedient. They are exempt from the post between quaestor and praetor but they do not always accede to the *fasces* after an interval of only two years from the praetorship, thus becoming consuls at thirty-two or thirty-three. A pair of young patricians adlected by Vespasian furnishes various instruction, namely M. Ulpius Traianus (*cos.* 91) and L. Neratius Marcellus (*suff.* 95).

Traianus, born in 53, is quaestor perhaps in 78, praetor perhaps as late as 85.[32] When elected consul, he was aged thirty-seven. Marcellus saw the light of day in the vicinity of 59, and some twenty years later was military tribune in Cappadocia, serving under M. Hirrius Fronto Neratius Pansa | (*suff.* ?75), his uncle and adopting parent.[33] When consul he was about thirty-five, with no cause to suspect any retardation.[34]

In the light of these parallels, albeit imperfect (and in the case of Traianus one reckons with a liking for service abroad), no discomfort intrudes if the consulship of Ruso Frontinus is assigned to 84, nine or ten years subsequent to his quaestorship. By the same token Glitius Gallus, a subject of contention, becomes his close coeval if correctly identified as the Gallus who was consul suffect in 84.

It remains to see how far the new hypothesis concords with the data supplied by the inscription at Antioch. Some of the posts there registered are out of order, so it has been supposed.[35] The present enquiry operates on the contrary assumption.

Antioch yields four other careers of senators from the same period, all on inscriptions set up between 93 and 117.[36] One of them, that of L. Caesennius P. f. Sospes, betrays two errors of orthography—and probably an error of fact in the enumeration of the regions comprised in the complex of Cappadocia–Galatia.[37] In none can a faulty order

---

[32] As concerns Trajan's praetorship, one might read 'praetorem tunc' instead of 'praetorium tunc' in *HA Hadr.* 1, 4. That reading was in fact adopted without explanation by Stein in *PIR*[2], A 184.   [33] *ILS* 1031, cf. E. Groag, *RE* xvi 2543.

[34] For peculiarities in his career, E. Birley, op. cit. 265 ff. Marcellus' tribunate in XII Fulminata was put about four years earlier by A. R. Birley, *The Fasti of Roman Britain* (1981), 89. That is, he assigned it to the special command of Pansa disclosed by *AE* 1968, 145 (Saepinum).

[35] J. Devreker, *Epigraphica* xxviii (1976), 183; E. Birley, op. cit. 266.

[36] Viz. *AE* 1925, 126 (Antistius Rusticus); *ILS* 1017; 1038 f.

[37] In *ILS* 1017 the list of regions leads off with Galatia and ends with 'Arm.' That is, Armenia minor. The omission of Cappadocia (normally at the head) implies a temporary division of the complex (i.e. after the decease of Antistius Rusticus); and, on a rational partition, Armenia Minor belongs with Cappadocia.

For this hypothesis, *JRS* lxvii (1977), 40 = *RP* iii (1984), 1046 f.; *Historia* xxii (1983), 371 = p. 290, above. Not all are prepared to concede. Thus R. K. Sherk, *AJP* ci (1979), 167 f.

be established. Sospes received honour from his freedman Thiasus after he had left the province, and after the death of Domitian. By contrast, Ruso Frontinus earned recognition from the *colonia* itself, as its *patronus*—and he might even have vouchsafed the formulation. No error has been proved.

For brevity, the exposition will concentrate on the items that convey problems or invite conjecture.

(1) The initial stages. The young man became a *monetalis*, the post normally allocated to patricians, as witness Glitius Gallus and Neratius Marcellus. It can fall to others if enjoying favour, for example Caesennius Sospes, son of a consul and related to the Flavian dynasty.[38]

This Ruso, it is a fair surmise, benefited from the events of 68 and 69, passing in allegiance like some of his seniors from one ruler to the next, | and not without aid from Julius Frontinus. The legion and the province of his military tribunate might (or might not) be worth knowing. Antistius Rusticus from Corduba, a near coeval, derived signal honour and advancement from having been tribune in II Augusta, in the year 69. He was adlected *inter praetorios* and received the military decorations appropriate to a legate of praetorian rank.[39]

Finally, Ruso entered the Senate as quaestor. He was now patrician, and line 6 of the inscription is duly supplemented 'quaestori Aug. prae]tori'.

(2) From praetor to consul, no post of any kind. That is no surprise in a patrician but anomalous in a senator who goes on to hold one of the consular commands in the portion of Caesar. He normally has a legion and a praetorian province.[40] Attention has duly been drawn to the inscription of Neratius Marcellus, sadly deranged although set up in his native Saepinum.[41] Marcellus proceeded to be governor of Britain (?101–104). Curiosity has asked whether the command of a legion has not fallen out of the inscription.[42] For Ruso, governing Cappadocia two decades from his consulship, no conjecture is needed. He is an anomaly anyhow. Whatever the antecedents or beginnings, whether high promise or the lack of it, the career of a senator can take a paradoxical turn in the sequel, or in the termination.[43]

(3) The consulship. The early epoch of Domitian (82–5) witnessed lengthy lists. In 84 no fewer than eight suffects are assumed.[44] For

[38] *ILS* 1017. His father, the consul of 61, had for wife a Flavia Sabina (*ILS* 995).

[39] *AE* 1925, 126, cf. *Historia* xxxii (1983), 362 = p. 281, above. Note also E. Birley, *Britannia* ix (1978), 245 f.   [40] And he is normally a *novus homo*.

[41] *ILS* 132.   [42] E. Groag, *RE* xvi 2543; E. Birley, op. cit. 266.

[43] The notable instance is C. Bruttius Praesens (*suff.* ?118).

[44] W. Eck, *ZPE* xxxvii (1980), 55.

404   *P. Calvisius Ruso, One Person or Two?*   [*179*]

Ruso that year is indicated by the tenure that will be proposed for his proconsulate, viz. 97/8 (cf. below).

(4) The charge of a road, the name of which is missing. Not without parallel for a consular. Cornutus Tertullus (*suff.* 100) had the Aemilia.[45] Furthermore, the same road was administered by Funisulanus Vettonianus (*suff.* 78) just before the consulate to which he already stood in prospect, being *praefectus aerarii Saturni*.[46] The Aemilia fits the space available in line 6 of the inscription. Less attractive would be the Flaminia. As illustrating caprice in the evidence, the earliest curators of the Flaminia happen to occur between 137 and 148.[47] |

(5) The priesthoods, emblems of social rank or political success. The 'quattuor amplissima' retain their primacy, and so far no senator had held more than one of them.[48] Next in estimation stood the *sodales Augustales*.

A person of station or prospects would not be drawn towards *fetiales* or *sodales Titii*, save at an early stage in his career.[49] And in this epoch the Arval Brethren had forfeited their erstwhile prestige. None of the young patricians adlected by Vespasian is discovered in their company, apart from the unobtrusive Annius Verus (*suff.* 97).[50]

One of the five eminent 'sacerdotia' often accrued in the season of a man's consulship, and it tends to stand at the head, along with other distinctions. When occurring in the body of the inscription, it indicates the point of entry. Thus Valerius Festus, *sodalis Augustalis* after the praetorship and before his command in Numidia; and after a consular post he became *pontifex*.[51]

Valerius Festus (*suff.* 71) was a successful *novus homo*, related to Vitellius and found highly acceptable by Vespasian. That the patrician Ruso in a long life should acquire two priesthoods is not an occasion for surprise. However, *quindecimvir sacris faciundis* and *sodalis Augustalis* are registered together—and not until he has occupied as consular the charge of a road.

Hence a problem. Which of the two 'sacerdotia' came first, and when? They perhaps stand on order of rank, not of time. Parallels can be adduced.[52] Furthermore, Ruso may well have annexed one or

---

[45] *ILS* 1024. [46] *ILS* 1005.

[47] W. Eck, *Die staatliche Organisation Italiens in der hohen Kaiserzeit* (1979), 82 f.

[48] The earliest on attestation is P. Cluvius Maximus Paullinus, consul suffect *c.* 142 (*AE* 1940, 99).

[49] Thus Caesennius Sospes, with 'fetiali' following his name (*ILS* 1017).

[50] With a solitary entry on the protocol of 105, cf. *Some Arval Brethren* (1980), 114.

[51] *ILS* 989.

[52] Thus clearly C. Julius Proculus (*suff.* 109), with 'cos., XVvir. sacris faciundis, fetiali' (*ILS* 1040). And perhaps A. Ducenius Geminus (*suff.* 60 or 61), with 'cos., XVvir. sacris faciundis, sodali Augustali' (*ILS* 9484).

other of the two honours when quite young.[53] They are bunched together for convenience, at the point when the second arrived. On that explanation, the sole verifiable departure from strict chronological order in the inscription of Ruso.

(6) The next consular function. Only the letter 'a' survives in line 7, preceding 'procos. Asiae'. As has been stated, no solution offers. To renounce would be pardonable as well as prudent.

Nevertheless, the missing word may be the name of some province or other. Certain formulations are instructive.

(a) A legate of Caesar Augustus, 'i]n Gallia Comat[a' (*ILS* 916) |
(b) Crassus Frugi (*cos.* 27), legate of Claudius Caesar 'in M[aure-tani]a' (954)
(c) C. Ummidius Quadratus (*suff. c.*40), legate of Claudius 'in Illyrico', of Claudius and Nero 'in Syria' (972)
(d) L. Neratius Priscus (*suff.* 87), 'leg. pr. pr. in prov. Pannonia' (1033).

For guidance in supplementing the line, observe that in the first three instances 'pro pr.' is omitted, whereas 'Aug.' is omitted from the fourth. The inscription of Neratius Priscus (*suff.* 87), the father of the jurist (*suff.* 97), is truly remarkable, exhibiting long survival for the original style that designated Caesar's legate in a region of his 'provincia'.

To pursue a topic that defies precision. As 'comiti Aug.' in a named province, Ruso might have been with Domitian 'in Germania' at the beginning of 89, or 'in Pannonia' (either 89 or 92). Otherwise, several alternatives can be canvassed, carrying civilian rather than military functions.

(a) *Dalmatia*, with 'leg. Aug.', or even with 'leg. pro pr.' (cf. *ILS* 1033). Dalmatia lost its legion when the Dacian War broke out in 85. No governor is attested between 83 and 93, when a legate of praetorian rank emerges.[54]

(b) *Macedonia*. By exception an imperial legate might have been sent there in the sequel to a period of disturbances in the northern hinterland of the province, disturbances that originated in Dalmatia, Moesia, or Thrace. Compare, during the Danubian wars of Marcus Aurelius, the insurrection of brigands 'in confinio Macedon. et Thrac.'[55]

For that notion, support happens to be to hand. Tacitus in a curt

---

[53] As the younger Minicius Natalis (*suff.* 139), an augur between his quaestorship and tribunate of the plebs (*suff.* 1029).
[54] Viz. Q. Pomponius Rufus (*suff.* 95), cf. *IRT* 537; *CIL* xvi 38.
[55] *AE* 1956, 124 (the inscription of Valerius Maximianus).

summary thought it worth while to report, along with the Danubian wars, 'turbatum Illyricum, Galliae nutantes'.[56] He was referring to the interior, not to the frontier.[57]

(c) *Achaia*. Domitian, an emperor marked by interest in Hellas and by care for good government, may at some time have appointed an imperial legate. A suitable juncture occurred in 89, after a false Nero had made his advent in the East, with repercussions in Asia. To counter that portentous name and conciliate Greek sentiment, Domitian now chose senators from western Asia, namely Julius Celsus and Julius Quadratus, to govern the provinces Cilicia and Lycia–Pamphylia, so it has been surmised.[58] Those posts led straight to consulates—which Vespasian hardly contemplated when admitting Celsus and Quadratus to the Senate.

About the year 112, Trajan took over Achaia, with for governor a consular: C. Avidius Nigrinus (*suff.* 110), of a philhellenic family and a close friend of Hadrian. Nigrinus carries the title 'leg. Aug. pro pr.' at Delphi, and | also (in Greek) at Athens.[59] If Nigrinus, there is no call to debar Ruso some twenty years earlier. Therefore, taking into account the length of the previous two lines, '[leg. pro pr. in Achai]a' could be introduced.

Innovations arise earlier than their earliest report. The inscription of Caesennius Sospes is a salutary reminder. As legate of XIII Gemina in Pannonia, Sospes won decorations in Domitian's campaign against Suebi and Sarmatae. That was in 92. Previously he was 'curator coloniarum et municipiorum'. Not conceivable earlier than the reign of Trajan, so a number of scholars contended. Hence, aberrant datings for Sospes.[60]

The above alternatives are presented merely *exempli gratia*. They also serve to illustrate caprice and hazards in the extant records of history and draw attention to sporadic items in danger of being overlooked.[61]

A provincial occupation for Ruso in the vicinity of 89 can thus be conjured up. After 92 tranquillity ensued on the frontiers. To Pannonia, now with four legions the prime command, Domitian sent Neratius Priscus (*suff.* 87), not perhaps a military man. He

---

[56] *Hist.* i 2, 1.

[57] Thus G. E. F. Chilver in his *Commentary* (1979).   [58] *Tacitus* (1958), 510.

[59] *SIG*³ 827; *Hesperia* xxxii (1963), 24. Testimony which some have neglected, cf. *JRS* lviii (1968), 150 = *RP* (1979), 720.

[60] On which, *JRS* lxvii (1977), 48 f. = *RP* iii (1984), 1060 f.

[61] For parallel observe an ex-praetor sent to be Nero's legate in Syria (A. Balland, *Fouilles de Xanthos* vii (1981), no. 48). Probably to be explained by the fact that in 55 the consular Ummidius Quadratus had surrendered two of his four legions to Corbulo's command in Cappadocia.

acceded to the *fasces* after the charge of the *aerarium Saturni*; and he was fairly old, to judge by the short interval before his son's consulship.

(7) The proconsulate of Asia. Like Tiberius Caesar at first, Vespasian wished to keep Asia and Africa at about ten years from consulates. The interval gradually extended, to eleven with Frontinus in 84/5, and soon to thirteen in 90. In that year Agricola (*suff.* 77) was induced by friends of Caesar to forgo the sortition (for the benefit of persons high in favour).[62]

In 92 came the turn of P. Calvisius Ruso (*suff.* 79). As concerns Ruso Frontinus, his polyonymous brother (*suff.* ?84), the latest list exhibits the following names:[63]

96/7	Sex. Carminius Vetus (*suff.* 83)
97/8	
?98/9	Cn. Pedanius Fuscus Salinator (?84)
99/100	
100/1	Q. Julius Balbus (85)
101/2	(Q. Vibius?) Secundus (86)

Ruso, it becomes evident, suits the tenure 97/8. The alternative, viz. 99/100, would entail 86 for his consulship, one place being vacant in that | year, whereas 85 is now complete. Africa lends parallel and support for Ruso, since Marius Priscus (?84) went there in 97.

The sortition took place early in the year. It was a momentous season (about five months from the assassination of Domitian), with ambitions eager or frustrated, with rancour and revenge on open show, as was manifest before long when they debated the promotion of prefects of the *aerarium Saturni*.[64] Ruso clearly had to face sharp competition. Chance may have helped. The orator Salvius Liberalis (*suff.* 85), coming back from exile, got Asia but declined it.[65]

If the present hypothesis is accepted, Ruso in 97/8 is a welcome accession to the rubric. Thereafter, until the first year of Antoninus Pius, proconsuls of Asia run all but continuous, four gaps only subsisting: viz. 99/100, 102/3, 127/8, 133/4.[66]

(8) The post of *curator operum publicorum*. Registered subsequent to a proconsulate, it lacks parallel, totally. Hence perplexity—and worse. The inscription is out of order, so it has been supposed. An

[62] Tacitus, *Agr.* 42, 1.

[63] See now W. Eck, *Chiron* xii (1982), 326 ff.; xiii (1983), 214.

[64] Pliny, *Ep.* ix 13, 11, cf. 22 f.

[65] *ILS* 1011. For the year of his consulship, *Some Arval Brethren* (1980), 34; L. Vidman, *Fasti Ostienses* (ed. 2, 1982).

[66] Cf. now *ZPE* li (1983), 271 = p. 325 f., above.

assumption is current that the post had to follow close upon the consulate.[67]

That was premature. Between 70 and 117 eight *curatores* are known.[68] Only two of them permit a close dating. First, Neratius Pansa (*suff.* ?75). He held it, one presumes, after his governorship of Cappadocia (which probably lasted from 76 or 77 to 80).[69] Second, convergent reasons counsel putting the tenure of C. Catellius Celer (*suff.* 77) in the vicinity of 82.[70] Pansa and Celer look like successive occupants.

Regularity is not discoverable before the early years of Hadrian. Bruttius Praesens (*suff.* ?118) had the post before he went to Cappadocia;[71] and Metilius Secundus (*suff.* 123), before a governorship the name of which has fallen out.[72] Moreover, a collegiate pair soon emerges: so far on attestation for the first time in 128.[73] |

The use and value of sundry occupations in a senator's career, that is an engaging question. In most ages, office and title enjoy precedence over any work to be done or expected. As concerns the 'opera publica', a noteworthy phenomenon obtrudes. Between 135 and 161, seventeen *curatores* are on record. Of that total no fewer than twelve proceed at once to consular commands.[74] An explanation is not far to seek. For senators destined to hold those commands Caesar has amicably devised a privilege. They earn a spell of residence at the capital, especially desirable if they had come straight to the consulate after employment abroad; and they have leisure for serious pursuits such as society life, political intrigue, the care of a patrimony.[75]

The season of Ruso's occupancy, agreed, is a total anomaly. Perhaps in close sequel to his return from Asia in the summer of 98. Nerva had put Julius Frontinus in charge of the Roman aqueducts; and Frontinus entered on his second consulship early in 98, succeeding Cn. Domitius Tullus as colleague of the new emperor in a sequence of four *consules iterum*.

Influence from Frontinus might be invoked; and it is a pleasing

---

[67] J. Devreker, *Epigraphica* xxxviii (1976), 183. Assuming it the first post for 'de jeunes consulaires', he puts Ruso early in the reign of Domitian. By contrast, under Nerva for B. Rémy, since Ruso is an anomaly anyhow (op. cit. 179).

[68] Seven will be found in A. E. Gordon, 'Quintus Veranius Consul A.D. 49', *U. of Cal. Pub. in Class. Arch.* ii 5 (1952), 284 ff. Add Neratius Pansa (*AE* 1968, 145: Saepinum).

[69] In Cappadocia between Cn. Pompeius Collega and A. Caesennius Gallus.

[70] Cf. *Some Arval Brethren* (1980), 29 ff.

[71] *IRT* 545; *AE* 1950, 60.   [72] *ILS* 1053.

[73] *AE* 1973, 76. The consul was Q. Insteius Celer: probably to be identified as the 'Q.[' in the last pair of the year 128 on the *Fasti Ostienses*. Thus H. Halfmann, *Arh. Vestnik* xxviii (1977), 157 f.

[74] *Historia* xiv (1965), 358 = *Danubian Papers* (1971), 241 f.

[75] E. Birley, *PBA* xxxix (1953), 209. An annual tenure was assumed by G. Alföldy, *Konsulat und Senatorenstand unter den Antoninen* (1977), 26; 287. A *biennium* is preferable.

notion that his salubrious example furnished an incentive of devotion to duty not lost on his nephew. It may be recalled in this place that loyalty to the memory of Frontinus was evinced by the son of Ruso. Deprecating the praise lavished on the verse epitaph of Verginius Rufus, he extolled Frontinus who said 'impensa monumenti super-vacua est: memoria nostri durabit si vita meruimus.'[76]

(9) At last, Cappadocia–Galatia. The coin of Sebastopolis, long known, gives 106/7 (October to October); and recently Cybistra adds 104/5.[77] The two inscriptions should be waived, because of uncertainties about Trajan's titulature. Let it suffice to state that Ruso is securely lodged in the interval between the enigmatic Q. Orfitasius Aufidius Umber and Julius Quadratus Bassus (*suff.* 105), who came to Cappadocia after the command of an army corps in the conquest of Dacia.[78] A tenure of three or four years is available.

The second genuine problem now comes up, namely a military province at a portentous interval after a consulship. It is not much abated when 84 | takes the place of 79. Curiosity subsists. For what reason should Cappadocia, with two legions, receive as governor a consular of extreme seniority, lacking military experience—and a patrician at that? One explanation has been put forward: warfare on the Danube occupying more suitable legates.[79]

On a wider perspective, other considerations come into the count. Claudius Caesar (or rather his counsellors) put Ummidius Quadratus (*suff. c.*40) in charge of Syria, although he lacked experience with the armies.[80] When he died there a decade later he was about seventy. Again, Trajan's second legate of Syria from 100 to 104, was his close friend the Pergamene magnate, A. Julius Quadratus (*suff.* 94), who had been adlected *inter praetorios* by Vespasian. Likewise no previous military post of any kind.[81]

With little danger of active warfare, Syria demanded diplomatic talents. Similarly, although to a lesser degree, the Cappadocian command, with not only Armenia in its purview but Colchis, Iberia, Albania. Many of the Caesars had a preference for elderly legates; and influence or patronage took their customary course, not always excluding a man of high birth.

[76] Pliny, *Ep.* ix 19, 6. For the identity of the Ruso to whom the letter is addressed see *Tacitus* (1958), 99: plainly preferable to the Cremutius Ruso mentioned in vi 23, 2, cf. C. P. Jones, *Phoenix* xxii (1968), 116 f.

[77] For the coins, B. Rémy, op. cit. 165 f.

[78] R. K. Sherk, *ANRW* ii 7 (1980) 1016 ff. The item 'Q. Orfitasius' in the nomenclature of Aufidius Umber was revealed by *AE* 1979, 620 (Antioch).

[79] W. Eck, *ANRW* ii 1 (1974), 217.

[80] *ILS* 972.   [81] *ILS* 8819.

To Ruso in Cappadocia stands a parallel a few years later which some have overlooked. It is disclosed in a letter written by Pliny when he had been in Bithynia for about twelve months. He commends to the attention of Trajan a young equestrian officer (Nymphidius Lupus) with the words 'cum praefectus cohortis plenissimum testimonium meruerit Iuli Ferocis et Fusci Salinatoris, clarissimorum virorum.'[82]

Hence two legates probably exercising the same command, since the junior in rank is named first. Ti. Julius Ferox was consul suffect in 99. By contrast, Cn. Pedanius Fuscus (*suff.* ?84), proconsul of Asia (?98/9), and like Ruso a patrician. The province evades ascertainment. Moesia Inferior has been proposed, with due diffidence.[83]

A military command for Pedanius Fuscus *c.*110, that is a fact of some significance. In the year 106 he had betrothed his son to Julia, the daughter of Julius Servianus (*cos. II* 102).[84] She is none other than the niece of P. Aelius Hadrianus (*suff.* 108).[85] Servianus had married his sister, Domitia Paulina.

An obscure period intervenes between the conquest of Dacia and Trajan's | departure in 113 to wage war in the East. Social eminence intertwines with high politics in the entourage of Caesar. The command of Pedanius may be sharply relevant to the ambitions of rival factions. In 108 or not long after died the great Licinius Sura (*cos. III* 107), Trajan's most favoured ally—and a strangely isolated figure. His disappearance from the scene would gratify Julius Servianus and improve the prospects of Hadrian.[86]

Hadrian was the next of kin to Trajan, but he had not benefited by abnormal advancement. It was not at all clear that he would survive long enough to inherit the power, even were he congenial to the Imperator.

Hadrian was born in 76. Fate and the hazards of mortality might beckon towards some younger aristocrat. Fuscus, the husband of Hadrian's niece, was only about ten years his junior. He aggregates to the same age group as C. Ummidius Quadratus (*suff.* 118) and T. Aurelius Fulvus (*cos.* 120), the third consul of that name. Fulvus acquired for bride a daughter of Annius Verus, the tranquil master of matrimonial srategies.[87]

[82] Pliny, *Ep.* x 87, 3.
[83] *JRS* xlix (1959), 29 = *Danubian Papers* (1971), 127. For proper doubts about a governorship of that province, W. Eck, *Chiron* xiii (1983), 210.   [84] Pliny, *Ep.* vi 26.
[85] Absent from *PIR*², since she is nowhere on named record.
[86] How Hadrian stood with Sura, that is an engaging question. According to the *HA*, Hadrian when consul 'a Sura comperit adoptandum se a Traiano esse' (*Hadr.* 3, 10). The item may be apologia, deriving from the Autobiography.
[87] Another daughter may have been consigned to Ummidius Quadratus. For this hypothesis, *HSCPh* lxxxiii (1979), 307 f. = *RP* iii (1984), 1176 f.

In the event, young Fuscus was to share the *fasces* with the new ruler in 118, the destined successor to Hadrian—if he survived. Fuscus and Julia lapse at once from all record.[88]

The parent of young Fuscus belonged to a family from Barcino in Tarraconensis, endowed with wealth and high prestige. Early in the reign of Nero, in 56, Pedanius Secundus (*suff.* 43) came out as Prefect of the City.[89]

Not so conspicuous as Pedanius Fuscus, his coeval, P. Calvisius Ruso Julius Frontinus possessed advantages which time and design enhanced. Old Frontinus, consul for the third time in 100, passed away three or four years later. He left no son of the blood, and none by adoption discoverable.[90] His daughter married Q. Sosius Senecio (*cos.* 99), consul for the second time in 107 as colleague to Licinius Sura.

Along with inheritance, matrimony contributes 'decus ac robur'. The stone at Antioch subjoins the wife of Ruso Frontinus as 'Eggia] C. f. Amb[ibula'.[91] The family is that of C. Eggius Ambibulus, the consul of 126. Not among the notables previously, but Trajan had adlected this Eggius to the patriciate | in early youth.[92]

However, an earlier wife is looked for, to supply the mother of Ruso's son Tullus, the consul of 109, who was born *c.*75. She was found in a Dasumia, sister to L. Dasumius Hadrianus (*suff.* 93), a senator from Baetica with valuable connections.[93] The reason for this conjecture is at first sight extremely remote. Ruso's son had for wife Domitia Cn. f. Lucilla, maternal grandmother to Marcus Aurelius. Now Marcus had for ancestor Dasummus, a prince of the Messapians—according to a figment transmitted by Marius Maximus, the consular biographer.[94]

Tullus Ruso when consul was *consul ordinarius*, in this season a distinction of abnormal rarity. Hitherto since 98 the reign had exhibited only eight of them, Trajan and the numerous iterations having engrossed so many places. And the colleague of Tullus was a *consul iterum*, namely A. Cornelius Palma (*cos.* 99), one of the military men.

Ruso the legate of Cappadocia had contrived a splendid match for

[88] And from some modern narrations or imperial biographies.
[89] Succeeding the aged Volusius Saturninus (*suff.* 3)—and succumbing to assassination in 61. In that year a Cn. Pedanius Salinator was consul suffect.
[90] That is, unless the polyonymous Ruso was his son, taken in adoption by the *suffectus* of 79. Whether son or nephew, it makes little difference to the arguments developed in this paper.
[91] Cf. Groag in *PIR*², C 350. She lacks a separate entry.
[92] *ILS* 1054 (Aeclanum).   [93] As conjectured in *Tacitus* (1958), 793.
[94] *HA Marcus* 1, 6, cf. Eutropius viii 9, 1.

his son. Domitia Lucilla, daughter of Lucanus and adopted by his brother Tullus (consul for the second time in 98), inherited the vast fortune amassed by the orator Domitius Afer and since augmented.

An approximate date for the marriage is not beyond the reach of conjecture. It produced a daughter, Domitia P. f. Lucilla, who went to the elder son of Annius Verus: whence Marcus, born in 121. The match may have been contracted about 100, perhaps as late as 104 or 105.[95] The bride was perhaps born in the vicinity of 70, hence some years senior to Tullus Ruso: her father, Domitius Lucanus, was born *c*.40. She had been previously married, at least once.

Young Ruso in due gratitude took over 'Tullus' in his nomenclature, but not perhaps until the decease of Domitius Tullus. On which, much and varied enlightenment issues from a letter of Pliny. The testament aroused lively comment. Ample provision was made for the widow, described as 'mulier natalibus clara, moribus proba, aetate declivis, diu vidua, mater olim'.[96] The author, it is to be regretted, does not vouchsafe the identity of this elderly lady, who was not the first or only wife of Domitius Tullus.[97] |

Nor is the daughter named, to whom fell the bulk of the fortune. Lucilla had sons—and a granddaughter already.[98] Therefore she had been married to an *Ignotus* some time previously.

By his son's marriage the legate of Cappadocia became comparable to Pedanius Fuscus, and political reasons can be invoked to explain their late governorships of a military province. The fortunate Tullus Ruso should have had a second consulate, if he survived, in the early years of Hadrian. That is, in the company of Annius Verus (*cos. II* 121), Prefect of the City. That distinction in fact stands in the *Vita Marci* of the *Historia Augusta*.[99] Long accepted without disquiet, the text has to be modified and supplemented, transferring the second consulship to Cn. Domitius Tullus, in 98.[100]

Tullus Ruso, it will be recalled, had for mother a postulated Dasumia. That name is on the order of the day. It brings in the

---

[95] On the inscription at Antioch, below the governor's wife, stands in large letters the word 'Domit[' (*JRS* iii 302). In Groag's view, Domitia Lucilla was there registered as the wife of his son, serving as a praetorian legate in Cappadocia. Not all scholars concur, e.g. B. Rémy, op. cit. 108 f. No other explanation avails. The handsome monument honoured the whole family.

[96] Pliny, *Ep.* viii 18, 8.

[97] If it be conjectured that the widow was now annexed by L. Catilius Severus (*suff.* 110, *cos. II* 120), one sees how that person could be described as the 'proavus maternus' of Marcus Aurelius (*HA Marcus* 1, 4).

[98] Pliny, *Ep.* viii 18, 2. Hence several unidentifiable persons; and either a son or daughter of Domitia Cn. f. Lucilla can be parent of the girl. One may note that Pliny does not allude to Lucilla's present husband, P. Calvisius Tullus Ruso: already a stepfather.

[99] *HA Marcus* 1, 3.

[100] As shown in *JRS* xliii (1953), 156 = *RP* (1979), 246.

Testamentum Dasumii, that document of portentous amplitude in length as well as width, of which two continuous fragments were found beside the Via Appia.[101] The document names Julius Servianus more than once, and mentions a daughter of Servianus. A Da[sumia occurs, also the nurse Dasumia Syche; and provision is made for a monument to be set up at the city of Corduba.

Such, on the curtest of statements, is the testament indited in the summer of 108, precisely. Identity of the opulent and pretentious testator, who but L. Dasumius Hadrianus, consul suffect in 93, proconsul of Asia in 106?[102] The heir to whom he bequeathed his name is patently P. Dasumius Rusticus, who shared the *fasces* with Hadrian in 119; and Dasumii, rare name, are on show in Baetica.

No doubts impaired the identity of the testator. A new fragment imports manifold perturbations.[103] Slender and truncated, it is parallel on the right to the first nineteen lines of the inscription. Combined therewith, it reveals the four principal heirs, as follows:

(1) A daughter, registering her especial 'adfectus'; and lower down she is 'pientissima'
(2) The 'amicus rarissimus', who is enjoined to assume the name of the testator |
(3) A Domitia
(4) Dasumia Polla.

There follow seven heirs by default, one of whose names is supplemented, viz. 'Julia Paulina f]ilia Serviani'. Finally, Julia Paulina heads the long list of legatees.

Such is the conclusion of a sober and careful investigation.[104] Julia Paulina, it appears, is Julia, niece to Hadrian, the daughter of his sister Domitia Paulina; and Dasumia Polla (so the author argues) is the mother of the testator.

That is not all. The testator himself is not Dasumius the consular, but an *Ignotus*. Probably from Spain, but not (as many assumed) a citizen of Corduba. On the document another city was mentioned before Corduba.[105]

Hence intricate questions not here to be gone into concerning Julius Servianus, the Dasumii, the family of Hadrian.

An attractive response to the new fragment calls for urgent

---

[101] *CIL* vi 10229. See also Bruns, *Fontes*[7] (1909) and *FIRA* iii (1943), no. 48—where the document is styled 'Testamentum P. Dasumii Tusci Nobilis Viri'.
[102] *PIR*[2], D 13.
[103] Published by A. Ferrua, *RAC* lii (1976), 211 f., whence *AE* 1976, 77.
[104] W. Eck, *ZPE* xxx (1978), 277 ff.
[105] W. Eck, op. cit. 283.

attention.[106] It makes appeal to the testamentary dispositions of Cn. Domitius Tullus, expounded in the Plinian letter (viii 18), which was generally assigned to 107 or 108. With Dasumia Polla thus emerges the anonymous widow of Domitius Tullus. A further step follows without discomfort. That is to say, the 'amicus rarissimus', who is to take the testator's name, is P. Calvisius Tullus Ruso (*cos.* 109). On the *Fasti Ostienses* he stands as 'P. Calvisius Tullus'. He might also have been known as 'Cn. Domitius Tullus Calvisius Ruso' or 'Cn. Domitius P. f. Tullus Ruso'. However, despite all manner of complications to vex or delight an enquirer, it is high time to close this rubric.[107]

By resplendent matrimony, Tullus Ruso gained entrance to a potent nexus. Becoming strongly Narbonensian with Aurelius Fulvus from Nemausus (i.e. Antoninus Pius), the maternal grandson of Arrius Antoninus, the dynasty avows a blend of Narbonensis and Baetica in the person of Marcus, son of Domitia P. f. Lucilla, grandson of Annius Verus. It remains to cast about for the local origin of the maternal grandfather.

Calvisii might issue from any region of Italy except old Latium. Their earliest consul was C. Calvisius Sabinus (39 B.C.), from the Latin colony of Spoletium.[108] No clue to the Rusones. |

Various alternatives have been canvassed. For example, southern Etruria, because of a 'villa Calvisiana' among the properties of a Hadrianic consular.[109] Again, in no way valid. But there is Puteoli, which yields both a slave of P. Calvisius Tullus and the military tribune Calvisius P. f. Fal. Verus.[110]

Better perhaps for a senator, the Transpadane zone. Calvisii are fairly frequent (fifteen in *CIL* V), most of them no doubt indigenous, not immigrant. Observe C. Calvisius Rufus at Comum, in receipt of six missives from his fellow townsman, or C. Calvisius Statianus, of Verona, Prefect of Egypt in 175.[111] Yet they lead nowhere.

Spain might occur, the name being transmitted by clients of Calvisius Sabinus who governed the Peninsula in the season of Actium. The sole specimen in all the land is C. Calvisius Aionis f.

---

[106] Now proposed by Carmen Castillo García, *Actas del I Congreso Andaluz de Estudios Clásicos* (1982), 159 ff.: with stemma of the Domitii (163). On amicable enquiry from the author, I could not refrain from full endorsement.

[107] For an explicit statement and exposition see 'The Testamentum Dasumii. Some Novelties', *Chiron* xv (1985), 41 ff. = pp. 521 ff., below.

[108] *ILS* 925, cf. further *Historia* xiii (1984), 113 = *RP* (1979), 591.

[109] *ILS* 5771 (near Viterbo). The estate belonged to the consular Mummius Niger Valerius Vegetus. On whom, and his origin from Baetica, see now *Historia* xxxii (1983), 373 f. = pp. 292 f., above.

[110] *CIL* ix 2625; 1708. Adduced by E. Birley, op. cit. 268.

[111] *ILS* 1453.

Sabinus.[112] A predilection abides in favour of Narbonensis, although only one of its ten Calvisii is useful.[113]

A distinctive *cognomen* is sometimes enlisted to reinforce a chancy hypothesis. Extreme caution is enjoined. 'Ruso' has been supposed Celtic.[114] That is not much help. Only one of them in *CIL* XIII, two in *CIL* XII.[115] However, there is M. Licinius Ruso at Aquae Sextiae, held identical with, or related to, the consul suffect of 112.[116] On the other side, Etruria. Touching Cremutius Ruso, mentioned in Pliny, one notes that he bears a family name that is discovered only at Falerii.[117] Add the rare *nomen* 'Rusius' and the Etruscan city of Rusellae.[118]

From this excursus or divagation, valid consequences fail to issue. Had the tribe been extant on the inscription, it might have led to a decision. Short of renouncing the search, another device can be tried. Senators in the early process of their ascent often select a bride from the natal town or country. P. Calvisius Ruso (*suff.* 53) chose a Julia Frontina before her | family attained to senatorial status. Frontinus, it is a plausible assumption, came from Vienna.[119] About the time when the first Calvisius Ruso became consul, powerful influences were active in promoting Narbonensian senators.

Later alliances tend to form at the capital, from city to city, or soon uniting aristocracies from different provinces: as witness Ulpius Traianus from Italica, Pompeia Plotina from Nemausus. For enquiry into origins, the bride of the first Ruso is more significant than the fact that his grandson annexed Domitia, an heiress from Narbonensis, her *patria* and *ultima origo*.[120]

Epilogue

In assessing the public occupations of P. Calvisius Ruso Julius

---

[112] *CIL* ii 2822 (Uxama).

[113] Viz. P. Calvisius Trophimus at Dea Vocontiorum (*Inscr. lat. de Gaule* 236); six of the nine in *CIL* XII bear *praenomina*, but never 'Publius'.

[114] W. Schulze, *LE* 222.

[115] *CIL* xiii 7031 (= *ILS* 2500) names the commander of a cavalry regiment. On whom, E. Birley, op. cit. 268. He adds a centurion at Moguntiacum (*AE* 1939, 130).

[116] *CIL* xii 2433, cf. *PIR*[2], L 238.

[117] *CIL* xi 3155, cf. Schulze, *LE* 222. On the other hand, the senator Abudius Ruso (*Ann.* vi 30, 2) bears a name that looks Celtic, cf. *LE* 66 where Abudiacum in Raetia is invoked. Perhaps a Transpadane.

[118] Cicero offers the orator C. Rusius (*Brutus* 259).

[119] That city supplies the senator Q. Valerius Lupercus Julius Frontinus (*CIL* xii 1859 f.).

[120] Only Jerome discloses Nemausus as the *patria* of Domitius Afer (*Chron.* p. 179 H). The brothers he adopted (Lucanus and Tullus) were sons of the Narbonensian Sex. Curvius Tullus (*CIL* vi 16671, cf. *PIR*[2], C 1623). Add Sex. Curvius Silvinus, quaestor of Baetica (*AE* 1962, 287).

Frontinus an ample measure of conjecture could not be avoided. It extended to embrace his family and *patria*, a predilection in favour of Narbonensis not being dissembled. The science, or rather method, is experimental. As is evident, standard dates or identities are liable to be overthrown all the time, under the sudden impact of a single new fact.

The present discourse testifies, in abundance. Other examples are pertinent. A small piece discovered at Tomis reveals the full nomenclature of C. Ummidius Quadratus (*suff.* 118) and corroborates his conjectural governorship of Moesia Inferior.[121] Again, by reading 'Germania] inferiore' on an inscription of two Neratii at Saepinum (*ILS* 1034), a new consular governorship is established for L. Neratius Priscus the jurist (*suff.* 97)—and further, a homonymous son, previously assumed legate of Pannonia Inferior under Hadrian, is abolished.[122]

The purpose of the present indagation was to disjoin the Trajanic legate of Cappadocia from P. Calvisius Ruso, consul suffect in 79, proconsul of Asia in 92/3. In the process the order of posts on the inscription at Antioch was respected, anomalies were accepted; and a new Ruso emerges without effort, consul in 84, proconsul of Asia in 97/8. The test of a reconstruction is whether it coheres, even though it has to invoke the unascertained.[123]

[121] *AE* 1977, 745. Being the grandson of Ummidia Quadratilla, he was certainly a *polyonymus*; and he is now disclosed as 'C. Ummidius Quadratus Sertorius Severus'.

[122] G. Camodeca, *AAN* lxxxvii (1976), 19 ff., whence *AE* 1976, 195. The consequences are multiple, concerning in the first place the Priscus of Pliny, *Ep.* ii 13 and the career of Javolenus Priscus. See remarks in *ZPE* xli (1981), 141 f. = *RP* iii (1984), 1390 f.; *JRS* lxxii (1982), 68 = p. 199, above. For some hesitations about Germania Inferior see now W. Eck *Chiron* xiii (1983), 209.

[123] For a correction of errors and for notable improvements, I am happy to acknowledge a debt to T. D. Barnes.

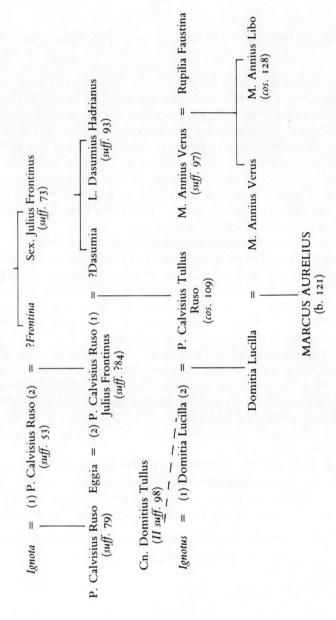

THE CALVISII RUSONES

23

Neglected Children on the *Ara Pacis**

WHEN Caesar Augustus returned from the western provinces in the summer of 13 B.C., the Senate decreed an 'ara pacis Augustae', to be the object of ceremonies conducted each year by magistrates, priests, and the Vestal Virgins. The altar was 'constituta' on July 4, dedicated in 9 on the thirtieth day of January.[1] The procession that parades on two of the enclosing walls corresponds with the first date. In the meantime, changes had supervened. Marcus Agrippa died in March of 12 B.C., and his widow Julia had been transferred to Claudius Nero, the stepson of the Princeps. How and where they should stand on the monument might be a question.

The *Ara Pacis* conveys manifold instruction and delight. It appeals in the first place to experts in the field of Roman art and to those who study governmental policy in its public advertisement. Next, the dynastic group on exhibit. Sundry identities provoked debate, since exact iconography was not to be expected, and some of the heads are partly restored. A certain measure of consensus has emerged, without much discussion in the recent time.

The present enquiry is limited in scope. It deals with a pair of children belonging to the 'domus Augusta'. A handsome and elaborate publication of the *Ara Pacis* is available.[2] For present purposes recourse will suffice in the main to the excellent and economical edition of Erika Simon.[3] Furthermore, only the first of the two processions comes into the count, namely the frieze on the right or southern wall.

For preface a brief statement concerning the principal figures is expedient. Caesar Augustus can be recognized, standing between two men (Simon pl. 10, cf. pl. 11). On one supposition, the consuls of 13, viz. Ti. Claudius Nero and P. Quinctilius Varus.[4] Next, four

* The author is happy to acknowledge aid and improvements from G. W. Bowersock and W. Eck.
    [1] *RG* 12; Ovid, *Fasti* i 709 ff., with the calendar items quoted by J. Gagé, *Res Gestae Divi Augusti* (1935), 167, 174.
    [2] G. Moretti, *Ara Pacis Augustae* (1948).
    [3] E. Simon, *Ara Pacis Augustae* (1967).
    [4] Dismissed by Simon, op. cit. 17, since neither appears to resemble Tiberius.

American Journal of Archaeology lxxxviii (1984), 583–9.

flamines, marked by their leather caps (Simon pls. 10 and 13). Then, after an attendant, a veiled man, who is identified as the deceased Agrippa; and there follows a stately matron, that is, Livia (Simon pl. 13, cf. pl. 14).[5] In consequence, the next person should be Tiberius, her elder son. Finally, next to Tiberius stands a younger man, in lesser prominence. Enigmatic, he has failed to arouse much curiosity.[6]

Approach can now be made to the problem at issue. It is introduced by a young matron (with a small boy), looking toward her left, toward her male companion (pl. I). Beyond doubt Antonia (the younger of Octavia's daughters) and her husband Claudius Drusus. Two signs confirm. First, Drusus wears a cloak and has military sandals. He was away from Rome at the time, having been left in charge of Gaul by the Princeps. Second, the small boy clasping the left hand of his mother. He looks about two years old. Quite so. The eldest child, later to be known as Germanicus, was born in 15 B.C., on May 24.[7]

This welcome certitude determines the next pair of | adults, none other than the elder Antonia and her husband, L. Domitius Ahenobarbus, the consul of 16. They are equipped with two children. The boy, podgy in face and of heavy build, is holding onto the cloak of Drusus with his right hand. The attachment is appropriate—to the husband of his aunt. This boy appears to be about six or seven. Next to him stands a slender girl, about ten, smiling in the direction of her brother.

The appended children serve a double function. They lend variety and animation to the scene, they differentiate the parental couples. The boy's attachment to Drusus is decisive. There would never have been any call to invoke Messalla Appianus (*cos.* 12) and Iullus Antonius (*cos.* 10), each now married to a Marcella: likewise nieces of Caesar Augustus.

Most scholars have been suitably alert to Drusus and his wife. The other pair, although identified long ago, has attracted little attention.[8]

---

[5] For a long time supposed to be Julia—who along with two children is now discovered on a much-damaged fragment of the other procession (Simon pl. 16.1: the piece in the Louvre); cf. Simon op. cit. 21, not, however, offering names for either the boy or the girl. See further below, *Epilogue.*

[6] See below, *Epilogue.*   [7] *PIR*[2], J 221.

[8] Identified by A. v. Domaszewski, *JÖAI* vii (1903), 64. Denied by H. Riemann in *RE* xviii 2100, s.v. Pacis Ara Augustae. He made peculiar asseverations: the son of Ahenobarbus (i.e. the consul of A.D. 32) was of about the same age as Gaius Caesar, or better, Germanicus Caesar; and further, he had a younger sister called Livilla.

THE AHENOBARBI

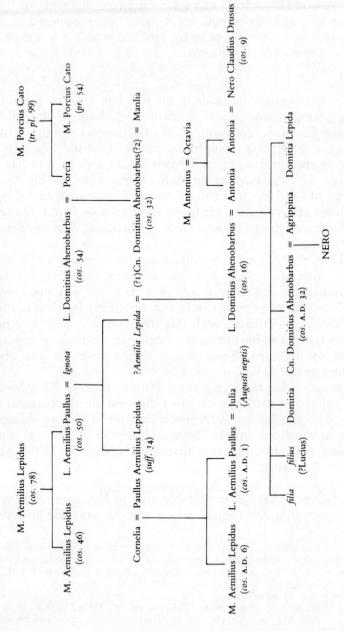

Some discussions of the *Ara Pacis* omit Ahenobarbus and Antonia altogether.[9] Nor is an estimate often supplied of the apparent ages of their two children.[10]

On the standard view those children are Gnaeus (the consul of A.D. 32) and Domitia, the elder of his two sisters. Exponents seem oblivious to certain pieces of extraneous evidence.[11]

First, Domitia. The girl on the *Ara Pacis* was born in the vicinity of 23 B.C. Observe, therefore, the subsequent vicissitudes of the historical Domitia, a formidable lady—and notably her quarrels with Agrippina (Nero's mother), who was born in A.D. 15. When Domitia died in 59 she was 'grandis natu'.[12] But hardly over eighty. No damage or deception ensues if Domitia's birth be conjectured to fall about 4 B.C. Few of the princesses on record in the *Annales* of Tacitus could hope to reach the sixty-third year, the grand climacteric in human life.

Next, the boy, by his size to be assumed close coeval to Gaius, the eldest child of Agrippa and Julia, born in 20 In A.D. 28 young Cn. Domitius Ahenobarbus acquired for bride Agrippina, then just nubile. Four years later he became consul.

That is, if identical with Antonia's son on the *Ara Pacis*, not consul until he had passed the age of fifty. Retardation of that order is not credible in one of the high aristocrats, apart from his being close kin to the dynasty.

Tiberius Caesar had no cause to cherish the Ahenobarbi. While he abode in exile at Rhodes, the father (*cos.* 16 B.C.) had been entrusted with the great commands in Illyricum and on the Rhine. Both father and son earn from Velleius Paterculus the label of 'nobilissima simplicitas'.[13] Suetonius when expounding Nero's ancestry supplies the necessary corrective: scandalous detail about the one, the other defined as 'omni parte vitae detestabilis'.[14]

No matter. Caesar cannot deny to a *nobilis* prompt access to the *fasces*, at thirty-two, or not much later. Some abatement might accrue to the husband of a princess, it is true. But not very likely from Ti. Caesar, hostile to privilege and averse from court life. Ahenobarbus, it follows, saw the light of day in the vicinity of 2 B.C.

[9] Thus I. S. Ryberg, *MAAR* xix (1949), 79–101: U. Kähler, *JDAI* lxix (1954), 66–100; K. Hanell, *ORom* ii (1960), 33–120; A. H. Borbein, *JDAI* xc (1975), 242.
[10] None in Moretti, op. cit. 231; Simon, op. cit. 19; D. E. E. Kleiner, *MEFR* xc (1978), 759.
[11] Some vague doubts were expressed by Moretti, op. cit. 321. However, in a summary list of the personages (250) he registered 'Antonia Maggiore e i figli Cn. Domizio Ahenobarbo, Domizia, Domizia Lepida (?)'.
[12] Suetonius, *Nero* 34, 5, cf. Dio li 17, 1 f.
[13] Velleius ii 10, 3; 72, 3.
[14] *Nero* 5, 1.

Among his coevals were Sulpicius Galba (*cos.* 33), born in 3 B.C., and Fabius Persicus (*cos.* 34), born in 2 or 1.

An answer to the problem has already been shaping. In short, two children who perished untimely. No surprise, given what is known or postulated about mortality in the city of Rome, adults as well as infants, without any call to deplore the absence of statistics.

Born in 39 B.C., Antonia was betrothed in 37 to Lucius, the son of Cn. Domitius Ahenobarbus, Republican admiral and ally of Marcus Antonius.[15] About the year 25 came the season for matrimony. Also for two other girls, her precise coevals. Julia was consigned to Claudius Marcellus, the nephew of the Princeps. About Marcella (the younger) there is no direct attestation: either Messalla Appianus (*cos.* 12 B.C.) or some other aristocrat.

The surviving progeny of Ahenobarbus and Antonia did not arrive before a long efflux of years since their marriage. That phenomenon is common enough in the *nobilitas*. Late-born children evoke the rational conjecture of previous deaths—or of a previous marriage that has left no traces.

Paullus Fabius Maximus (*cos.* 11 B.C.) is illustrative, in more ways than one. In or about the year 16 he took a wife. Ovid wrote the epithalamium, and Ho|race in an ode came out with the barely disguised equivalent.[16] In view of his age and rank, that was not perhaps Fabius' first experiment in matrimony—or else he had been waiting for an heiress to become nubile. The bride was Marcia, daughter of L. Marcius Philippus (*cos. suff.* 38 B.C.) and a lady styled 'matertera Caesaris': that is, Atia. Unlike Antonia and Marcella, Marcia benefits from multiple authentication, being named by Ovid and by Tacitus and honoured on an inscription as cousin to Caesar Augustus.[17] Not but that she has suffered some obscuration in the recent time.[18]

From this significant and dynastic match, no son is known before Persicus (*cos.* A.D. 34). In the summer of A.D. 15 he was co-opted by the Arval Brethen, to take the place of his deceased parent.[19] That is, on assuming the *toga virilis*, about the time of his fifteenth birthday.

---

[15] Plutarch, *Antonius* 33; Dio lviii 54, 4.

[16] Ovid, *Ex Ponto* i 2, 131 f.; Horace, *Odes* iv 1.

[17] Ovid, *Fasti* vi 802; *Ex Ponto* i 2, 138; iii 1, 78; Tacitus, *Ann.* i 5, 2; *ILS* 8811 (Paphos).

[18] No hint of Marcia (or of marriage) in the long exposition of E. Fraenkel, *Horace* (1957), 410–14. Even her name is absent from the annotation of F. R. D. Goodyear on *Ann.* i 5, 2 (1972). Missing also from L. Richardson, *AJA* lxxxi (1977), 355–61. That article in fact quoted the passage about Marcia and her parents (*Fasti* vi 797–812). The article was consecrated to the edifice 'Hercules et Musarum'—which it went on to assign to Marcia's grandfather (*cos.* 56).

[19] *AE* 1947, 52.

So far, no impediment—and nothing to disturb a student of Roman society. Chance now takes a hand. The existence can be certified of the boy who stands visible and blatant on the *Ara Pacis*.

Enlarging on the detestable character of Nero's father, the biographer states that when a young man he was a *comes* of Gaius Caesar on the expedition in the Orient. He then killed one of his freedmen 'quod potare quantum iubebatur recusarat.' Expelled from the 'cohors amicorum', in the sequel 'nihilo modestius vixit'. In fact, driving along the Appia in his chariot, he wilfully ran down a small boy.[20]

None who had care or curiosity for the age of Cn. Domitius Ahenobarbus (*cos.* A.D. 32) could fail to discern error and confusion. He must have been a *comes* of Germanicus Caesar, nearly twenty years later. That was the easy and obvious remedy.[21] It found general acquiescence.[22] Only a faint demur is perceptible, hinting at an elder brother otherwise unknown.[23] No heed was accorded.

Close in age to C. Caesar, the boy on the *Ara Pacis* now supplies an explanation, painlessly; and he concords with the unamiable character of the Ahenobarbi. In the verdict of the orator L. Crassus, the consul of 96 B.C. was authentic metal: 'os ferreum, cor plumbeum'.[24] His son, the enemy of Pompeius and of Caesar, was arrogant and violent; and some called him stupid.

Several families in the *nobilitas* ran true to type, from choice and mimesis, from a kind of 'pietas'. Thus, 'ferocia' in one branch of the Pisones. Generations may also have transmitted a resemblance in face or form. A coin struck by Ahenobarbus the admiral shows on the obverse a heavy jowled head: clearly his father at the age of fifty, when he fought and died for the Republic at the battle in Thessaly.[25] The boy on the *Ara Pacis* looks like a genuine 'stolidus' already (although the head is restored).

Suetonius made an error. By no means isolated in his copious account of Nero's ancestry. He amalgamated the consuls of 122 and 96. Also impercipient, he failed to notice that the praiseworthy Ahenobarbus (the Antonian partisan) was a nephew of Cato. And

---

[20] *Nero*, 5, 1.

[21] H. Dessau, *PIR*[1], D 109; *RE* v 1331, s.v. Cn. Domitius Ahenobarbus (E. Groag). The dissident was Domaszewski, op. cit. 64. He accepted Suetonius and regarded Gnaeus (*cos.* A.D. 32) as a coeval of Gaius Caesar—with some portentous consequences. He had overlooked Velleius ii 10, 3 and 72, 3 (that consul a 'iuvenis' in A.D. 30).

[22] Thus K. R. Bradley in his *Commentary* on the *Nero* (1978), 42, cf. 43.

[23] The consul was perhaps confused with 'fratre maiore eius sane aliunde ignoto' (*PIR*[2], D 127). The articles on the Domitii carried no allusion to the *Ara Pacis*.

[24] *Nero* 5, 2; 6, 3; 7, 1.

[25] J. M. C. Toynbee, *Roman Historical Portraits* (1978), 160, no. 83.

finally, not only careless in research but incompetent in exposition, Suetonius named three times Domitia Lepida as an aunt of Nero.[26] Then, in a later place he mentioned an unnamed elderly aunt whose decease Nero accelerated.[27] Incautious readers have been taken in.[28]

Suetonius proffered a statement about the different ways in which the Ahenobarbi used 'Gnaeus' and 'Lucius', their only *praenomina*. He would have had to modify it, had he known about an elder son of Lucius and Antonia (probably called 'Lucius'). The | family had never been prolific. Writing in the year 30, Velleius noted their 'artata numero felicitas', seven consuls with son succeeding father before 'hunc nobilissimae simplicitatis iuvenem, Cn. Domitium'.[29] Having served on the staff of C. Caesar in the eastern lands, Velleius would be aware of 'Lucius'.

If delinquencies of Suetonius are adduced, equity demands that an oversight on the part of Tacitus be not omitted. The consular historian was at great pains with names and identities in the aristocracy. For example, defining Haterius Agrippa, praetor in A.D. 17, as 'propinquum Germanici', he enables one to infer what is nowhere recorded: Q. Haterius (*cos. suff.* 5 B.C.), the elderly orator and *novus homo*, had married a daughter of Marcus Agrippa.[30] Nevertheless, for Tacitus the younger Antonia is the wife of Ahenobarbus and mother to Domitia Lepida.[31] The author had made the easy and even natural assumption, namely that the elder Antonia went to the stepson of the Princeps.

The nomenclature of Domitia Lepida has not enlisted much attention. It indicates that either Ahenobarbus or his father had married an Aemilia Lepida. Now Antonia has left no signs of her existence, apart from marriage and children.[32] A suspicion arises that she might have died soon after giving birth to Gnaeus. Hence a Lepida as second wife for Ahenobarbus, as mother to Domitia Lepida.

A casual anecdote dispels the notion. The elder Seneca discloses 'Domitium, nobilissimum virum'. He constructed a bathhouse during his consulship and then took to frequenting the schools of

---

[26] *Nero* 5, 2; 6, 3; 7, 1.   [27] *Nero* 34, 5.

[28] The two aunts are amalgamated in the index to the Loeb edition (1914). Also by J. H. D'Arms, *Romans on the Bay of Naples* (1970), 211–12; *Commerce and Social Standing at Rome* (1981), 76.

[29] Velleius ii 10, 2. For 'elegance of argument', the item 'iuvenis' was not brought up when a quinquagenarian consul was ushered out.

[30] Tacitus, *Ann.* ii 51, 1, cf. *PIR*[2], H 24: 'fortasse filia M. Agrippa et Marcellae maioris.'

[31] *Ann.* iv 44, 2; xii 64, 2.

[32] Observe her sparse entry, *PIR*[2], A 884. In marked contrast to the long-lived widow of Claudius Drusus.

rhetoric. That was predictable, said Asilius Sabinus, in comment to his mother who complained about sloth in her son.[33]

That is, Gnaeus—and a long survival is thereby attested for Antonia. In consequence, the postulated Aemilia Lepida goes to the father of Ahenobarbus. Further, his first wife. An inscription happens to reveal a Manlia, married to a Cn. Domitius Ahenobarbus.[34] He is taken to be the admiral.[35] With no discomfort. There was ample time for him to acquire a second wife between the birth of his son (presumed in 49) and his own decease on the eve of Actium.

The alternative has less appeal. A wife for Gnaeus (*cos.* A.D. 32), preceding Agrippina, is not excluded. But not a Manlia. That patrician house, of ancient splendour, had now lapsed.[36]

The age of Domitia Lepida is requisite to round off the rubric. Her first husband was Barbatus, the son of Messalla Appianus (the consul who died early in 12), on solitary attestation.[37] His birth cannot fall later than 12 B.C., and he would have become consul by A.D. 23 had he survived. That is one indication. Next, Sulla Felix, her son by her second marriage.[38] Sulla Felix became consul in A.D. 52. Therefore her daughter Valeria Messallina cannot have been born later than A.D. 20.[39] Domitia Lepida herself, it follows, was born in the vicinity of A.D. 2.

Tacitus matched Lepida with Agrippina, 'utraque impudica infamis violenta'. Of about the same age, so he states.[40] A dozen years separate them.

Thanks to the *Ara Pacis*, two children of Ahenobarbus and Antonia, recuperated from erudite negligence, illustrate and reinforce the general themes of marriage and progeny, of duration and mortality. The girl, born about 23 B.C. and probably destined for some illustrious youth, may have been cut off short of matrimony. Perhaps very soon. In 12 died a consul and a consul suffect (Messalla Appianus and Caninius Rebilus), permitting a surmise of a plague or some noxious infection.

---

[33] Seneca, *Controv.* ix 4, 18. Registered in *PIR*², D 127, but not in A 884. In the index to the Loeb text (1974) Domitius is an 'unidentified nobleman', perhaps identical with the consul of 32 B.C.

[34] *CIL* vi 31735.

[35] With a query, on the stemma of the Domitii, *PIR*², Pars iii, p. 30.

[36] None known after Torquatus, the friend of Horace.

[37] Suetonius, *Divus Claudius* 26, 2: 'Valeriam Messalinam, Barbati Messalae consobrini sui filiam.'

[38] *PIR*², D 180, cf. C 1464.

[39] C. Ehrhardt, *Antichthon* xii (1978), 55. Observe by contrast *RE* viiiA 246 (R. Hanslik): 'das Geburtsjahr der M. muß also um 25 angesetzt werden.' [40] *Ann.* xii 64, 3.

The son, coeval with C. Caesar and his *comes* in the Orient, might expect a wife soon after, and a consulship toward the year A.D. 14. Sex. Appuleius and Sex. Pompeius then held the *fasces*, kinsmen both to Caesar Augustus.[41]

Between 22 B.C. and A.D. 65 Roman annals happen to acknowledge one pestilence only. A casual no|tice dicsloses it, in the vicinity of A.D. 6, in a season of warfare and famine.[42] Young Ahenobarbus perhaps succumbed then, in his middle twenties. Surviving, he might have benefited like others from opportune deaths—or, regarded as a nuisance, have ended, like others again, on a penal island. The unsatisfactory Agrippa Postumus was 'robore corporis stolide ferox'.[43]

Epilogue

On the above showing, the 'domus Augusta' is augmented by two children. Other members, of rank and consequence, tend to attract little curiosity when the history of the period is composed with concentration on the policy and actions of the ruler. Notably the Appuleii. One of the four *flamines* on the *Ara Pacis* is an elderly man with worn features (Simon pl. 12). He finds identity as Sextus Appuleius, whom an inscription certifies as *flamen Iulialis*.[44] Which is appropriate, since he had married the elder Octavia, the half-sister of the Princeps.[45]

It will do no harm to register in one place a dozen members of the dynastic group relevant to the ceremony of 4 July, 13 B.C.[46]

(1) Sex. Appuleius (*cos.* 29) and Marcus (*cos.* 20), to be presumed his brother. Nephews of Caesar Augustus.

(2) Iullus Antonius (*pr.* 13, *cos.* 10). He married the elder Marcella when Agrippa discarded her in 21. Eager attempts were made to detect Iullus.[47] Attention is now directed to a fragmentary portion of the other frieze (Simon pl. 16.1). The figure on the right is taken to be Julia. She is followed by a boy. Then a matron (? Octavia), and a *togatus*, with his right hand lightly poised on the head of a small girl. Perhaps Iullus himself, and the children are children of Agrippa and

---

[41] Dio lvi 29, 5.

[42] Pliny, *NH* vii 149: 'pestilentia urbis, fames Italiae'. [43] *Ann.* i 3, 4.

[44] *ILS* 8963 (Carthage), cf. Simon, op. cit. 17. For Moretti, op. cit. 226, the homonymous son.

[45] *ILS* 8783 (Pergamum).

[46] Nor should it be dissembled that information, controversy, and conjecture will be found in *The Augustan Aristocracy* (1986), especially in the chapters entitled 'Two Nieces of Augustus' and 'Nero's Aunts'.

[47] Thus F. Poulsen, *AArch* (1946), 4–5. He claimed for Julia and Iullus the figures now recognized as Livia and Tiberius (pl. 13).

Julia.[48] One might hazard identities. The boy resembles Gaius (cf. the enlargement, Simon pl. 23).[49] If he is Gaius, the girl should be Julia, born either in 19 or in 18. In 5 or 4 she was given in marriage to L. Aemilius Paullus (*cos.* A.D. 1), the son of Paullus Aemilius Lepidus (*cos. suff.* 34 B.C.).[50]

(3) M. Valerius Messalla Appianus (*cos.* 12 B.C.). He annexed the younger Marcella, whence Barbatus and Claudia Pulchra. Not perhaps a first marriage either for Messalla or for Marcella (born in 39 B.C.).

(4) Paullus Aemilius Lepidus (*cos. suff.* 34). Three years previously he lost his wife Cornelia, half-sister to Julia, the daughter of Caesar Augustus. He took over Marcella when Messalla Appianus died early in 12, so it can be conjectured.[51]

(5) Paullus Fabius Maximus (*cos.* 11). Married to Marcia, the daughter of L. Philippus and Atia.

(6) P. Quinctilius Varus (*cos.* 13). Husband of a Vipsania. The papyrus fragment of Augustus' funeral oration on Agrippa declares him brother-in-law to Claudius Nero.[52] Further, one of his sisters had married Sex. Appuleius (*cos.* 29).[53]

(7) Q. Haterius (*cos. suff.* 5). Husband of a Vipsania.

(8) L. Calpurnius Piso (*cos.* 15). Son of Caesoninus (*cos.* 58), hence the little brother of 'Calpurnia C. Caesaris'. Wife (or wives) not ascertained.[54]

(9) M. Livius Drusus Libo (*cos.* 15). Step-brother to Livia. No known wife.[55]

(10) L. Volusius Saturninus (*cos. suff.* 12). First cousin to Claudius Nero, so it appears.[56]

The present enquiry, devoted to Ahenobarbus and his family, eschewed certain aspects or themes adherent to the historic monument.

---

[48] Simon, op. cit. 23.

[49] Compare the head from Moguntiacum: in fact, published and discussed by E. Simon, *MZ* lviii (1963), 1–18. The author, then taking the processions to represent the persons as they were in 9 B.C., identified the children as Lucius and Agrippina: Simon 10.

[50] The younger son, so it can be argued, cf. *History in Ovid* (1978), 140; 208.

[51] If Regillus (*ILS* 949: Saguntum) be regarded as his son. Regillus, quaestor to the Emperor Tiberius, cannot have been born earlier than 11 B.C. For problems about the marriages of the younger Marcella, *PIR*[2], C 1103.

[52] *Kölner Pap.* 1 (1976), no. 10. Whether Varus' wife was a daughter of Caecilia Attica or of the elder Marcella, that is a question.

[53] *AE* 1966, 442 (Cyme).

[54] A strikingly individual head behind one of the consuls (Simon pl. 10.2) was claimed for Piso by Poulsen, op. cit. 6–7.

[55] This character, often lost to view, was thoroughly investigated by E. J. Weinrib, *HSCPh* lxxii (1968), 247–78.

[56] His father had married an aunt of Tiberius, as can be deduced from Cicero, *Ad Att.* v 21, 6. Cf. *Historia* xiii (1964), 156 = *RP* (1979), 605.

By way of preface, cursory mention was accorded to what may be regarded as the principal figures on the southern frieze. Three of minor prominence were withheld, so as not to encumber the argument.

They now call for comment, diffident no less than | summary. Sundry identities previously thrown up were hazardous or even illicit. Let that serve as an admonition.

First, after Livia and Tiberius, and partly eclipsed, a male figure (Simon pl. 13). His head is smaller than that of Tiberius, he appears slighter in build and younger. Tiberius at this time was twenty-eight. The illustrious Messalla Corvinus, consul in 31 B.C., has been proposed.[57] Yet Corvinus avows no link with the dynasty—and he was fifty-one.

One should cast about for a younger man. In A.D. 56 died L. Volusius Saturninus (*cos. suff.* A.D. 3), the *praefectus urbi*, at the age of ninety-three.[58] Hence four years younger than Tiberius, the cousin of his father. Otherwise a thought might go to a young son (none is on record) of L. Marcius Philippus (*cos. suff.* 38).

Second, the lady standing next to Claudius Drusus and a little to the rear (pl. I). Perhaps a Vipsania.[59] At least three daughters of Agrippa come into the reckoning.[60] Perhaps the younger Marcella, soon to be bereaved of Messalla Appianus.

Third, the head of an old man with distinctive features, bowed and inclined to his right: most of his body is occluded by the girl and by her father Ahenobarbus (Simon pl. 15). Speculation has fastened on Maecenas.[61] Or even on Horace.[62] Neither deserved a place in a family party and procession on a public monument.

A proper identity imposes, none other than Paullus Aemilius Lepidus (*cos. suff.* 34), the censor of 22. In his own right, and no call to evoke the fact that his son Marcus could be styled 'vir nomini ac fortunae Caesarum proximus'.[63]

This disquisition assumes that the father of Ahenobarbus had for wife an Aemilia Lepida. Therefore old Paullus found suitable lodgement in the procession, behind his nephew and behind the girl.

On this showing the dynastic nexus becomes manifest earlier than

---

[57] Moretti, op. cit. 230.

[58] Tacitus, *Ann.* xiii 30, 2, cf. Pliny, *NH* xi 223.   [59] Moretti, op. cit. 231.

[60] It would be cruelty to add Agrippa's sister Polla, who survived him. Named only in Dio lv 8, 4.

[61] Moretti, op. cit. 231, cf. 256.

[62] Simon, *Ara Pacis Augustae*, 19: 'doch der Vorschlag auf Maecenas entbehrt leider einer Grundlage. Vielleicht darf man auch an Horaz denken.'

[63] Velleius ii 114, 5.

credited—and much tighter. In the sequel, sundry ambitions and prospects took shape during the decade when Claudius Nero was in eclipse. Ahenobarbus, Caesar's legate in Illyricum and Germany, was cousin to the young Aemilii, the sons of Paullus, one of them being married to Julia, the granddaughter of the Princeps. Concord or rivalry, who can tell?

Ara Pacis, south wall, Augustan children (after E. Simon, *Ara Pacis Augustae*, pl. 15)